No. 554
$12.95

Computer Technician's Handbook

By Brice Ward

TAB BOOKS
Blue Ridge Summit, Pa. 17214

FIRST EDITION

FIRST PRINTING—MARCH 1971
SECOND PRINTING—NOVEMBER 1972
THIRD PRINTING—MAY 1974

Printed in the United States
of America

Hardbound Edition: International Standard Book No. 0-8306-1554-7

Paperbound Edition: International Standard Book No. 0-8306-0554-1

Library of Congress Card Number: 74-147384

Preface

If you are interested in the very lucrative area of computer maintenance, here is a book that will get you there almost as quickly as a 1000-hour course on the subject. Computer technicians are in short supply and commanding excellent salaries, so here in a single volume is the way to take advantage of your present electronics training and become a capable computer technician.

Written for the working technician with some background in semiconductor circuitry, the **Computer Technician's Handbook** starts you out with a brief introduction to computer systems and explains briefly the similarities in concept and implementation of all computers from the small $10,000 machine to multimillion dollar systems. Also, in Part One you will find chapters on number systems, coding, computer circuits and logic diagrams. Finally, binary Boolean Algebra and system block diagrams are covered in enough detail to make them part of your everyday work.

Part Two details a small representative computer. Hardware topics cover registers, memory, arithmetic, control, and input-output equipment with enough information to give you an understanding of all machines. Part Three finishes the groundwork by covering some specific examples of computer maintenance, including instruction sets and diagnostic routines.

Many people have helped make this book possible, not the least of which is my family who are convinced frequently that they live with a bear and not a man. Next would have to be Mr. Dave Armstrong of Computer Automation Inc., who, along with CAI, was instrumental in helping me obtain a computer and the necessary information to supply in book form for perhaps the first time complete information and logic on a small central processor. Without that information this book would have little meaning.

Hewlett-Packard supplied a Model 180 oscilloscope which served beautifully as a medium for photographing waveforms and Polaroid supplied the necessary film. To these and others go my sincere thanks for making this book what I hope will be a route to the status of computer technician for many people.

Brice Ward

Contents

Part 1: Techniques & Circuitry

Chapter 1

Introduction To Computers

It probably will be hundreds of years before anyone will really be able to assess the impact the modern digital computer has had on our society. And it probably will take the same length of time to determine the true effect that computer science has had on modern electronic technology. In the relatively short span of 24 years we have moved from ENIAC which used 18,000 vacuum tubes and took several rooms of equipment, several kilowatts of power and excellent air conditioning to the ability to put the same 18,000 active elements (FETs) on a .01-inch thick chip 1 inch long by 0.1 inch wide! Not only that, but this same chip uses less than 10 watts of power! We could presently build ENIAC's computational power into a unit the size of a pack of cigarettes.

ENIAC required 200 microseconds to perform an addition. The CDC 7600 does 36 additions per microsecond. That works out to 7200 additions in the time it took ENIAC to do 1 addition! In fact, the technological plunge that has marked this industry has been enough to leave even the most avid science fiction fan in a state of wonder. Actually, it really makes any effort to write a history of the computer industry sound a little silly. What I write today is likely to be in some respects history tomorrow, although it is not entirely inconceivable that the industry will slow down to take a breath; but even if it does the need for trained people will continue to grow for the next several years.

The large-scale computer was conceived many years ago as a device that would make time-consuming and tedious mathematical problems solvable in much less time than it would take a man or men to solve them. Without this capability we would not have gone to the moon in the last decade. It has now reached the point where solving for the value of pi to several dozen decimal places can be done in seconds where it took years originally, and most beginning programmers can write the program that will develop pi to this many places. This was the original intent behind these machines and it is doubtful that anyone really foresaw that within two decades these machines would have taken up some tasks as "robots."

IBM moved the computer into the business data processing field and Digital Equipment Corp. moved the computer into the process control, communication, and other fields. ENIAC, then, had the solution of advanced mathematical problems as its chief aim. IBM put the computer into the accounting business which is more involved in handling large amounts of data than with mathematical calculations, and from that time computers have moved out into just about every field of endeavor imaginable.

It runs in my mind that as of some recent reckoning there were in the neighborhood of 50,000 computers currently in operation in some capacity or other. They run machine tools, control and monitor petroleum cracking plants, keep track of baggage and passengers on airlines, route trucks and trains, concentrate messages for delivery at the best rates, and so on.

The big machines (over $100,000) are normally maintained by a well trained staff of computer technicians. The smaller machines, however, have service facilities available to them but are not necessarily maintained by "on-site" customer engineers. So the field is wide open. You can read a hundred books on the history of computers, so I will leave that subject largely to the history experts. Let's go on to learning what is essential to enter the computer industry!

THE BIG PICTURE

These three words are forever cropping up in computer technology. They imply an overview of a broad range of information that will ultimately be broken down into smaller "bite-size" pieces for easier "digestion." The real problem occurs when this attempted "big picture" presentation is made. It invariably starts with the good old "5-block block diagram," a lot like early (and some recent) transistor books that start out with one third of the book devoted to semiconductor physics.

You can pick up practically any computer book and find, neatly nestled in the pages, the "5-block" block diagram and I present it here in Fig. 1-1 so that you will recognize it!

Output what? Input what? Control what? And a computer does not have a memory. Computers have electrical or magnetic media in which, or on which, they can permanently, semipermanently or temporarily store information in the form of binary digits but they do not have a memory! This book is a storage medium, and whether you accept this or not is irrelevant at this point. Just be sure that it is correct.

Finally, and perhaps oddly, computers do very little arithmetic! They are concerned with processing electrical information and spend the greatest share of operational time actually collecting data from an input device, reconstructing it for some output device, such as a page printer, and doing encoding and decoding of data or data transfers within the machine itself. The truth of this will become apparent as this book progresses.

When they do arithmetic, they add, subtract, multiply and divide—nothing exotic like algebra or calculus. These operations and any other higher math operations must be synthesized by the programmer using the arithmetic functions listed.

Let's develop a block diagram for a modern piece of digital data processing equipment that is a better model of equipment currently being used. Standardization has not come along too well in this area because of the very swift advance of technology and the rather secretive attitude taken

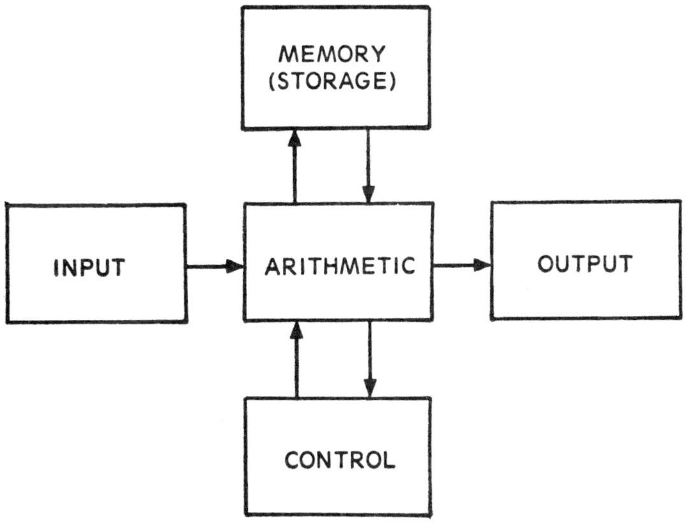

Fig. 1-1. Basic "5-block" block diagram.

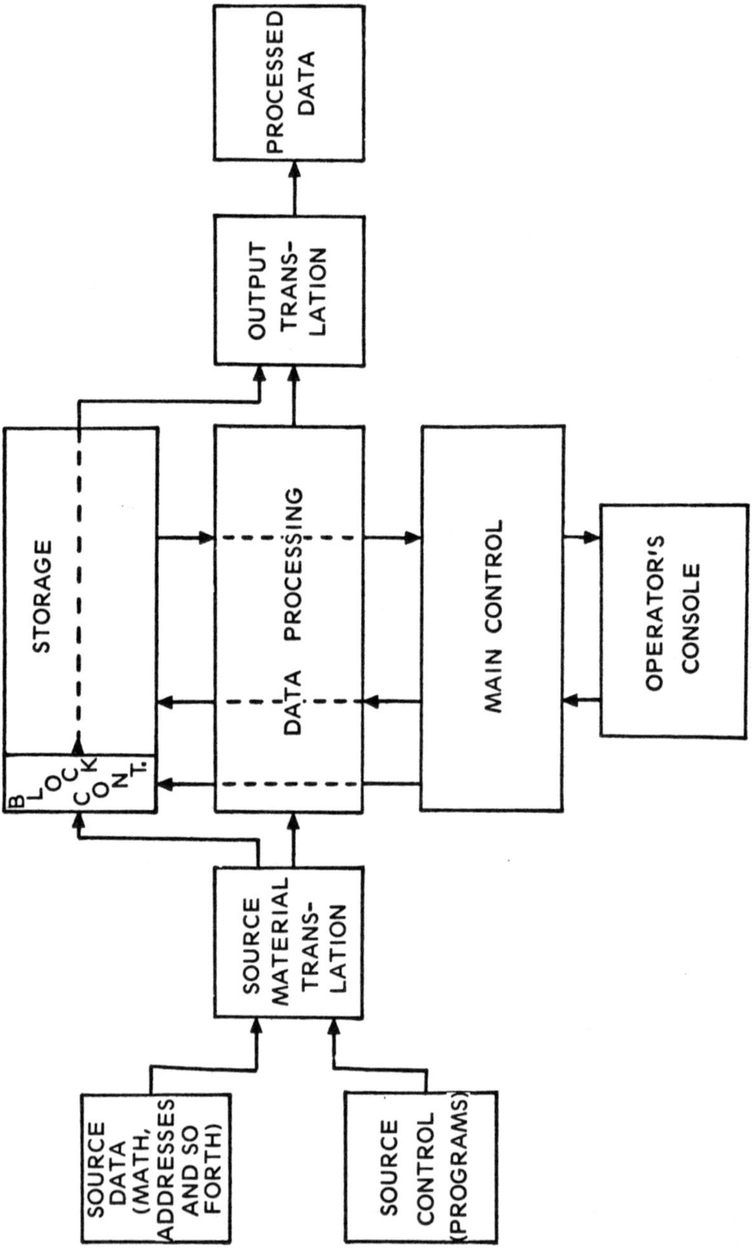

Fig. 1-2. A block diagram such as this is more descriptive of current digital data processing equipment.

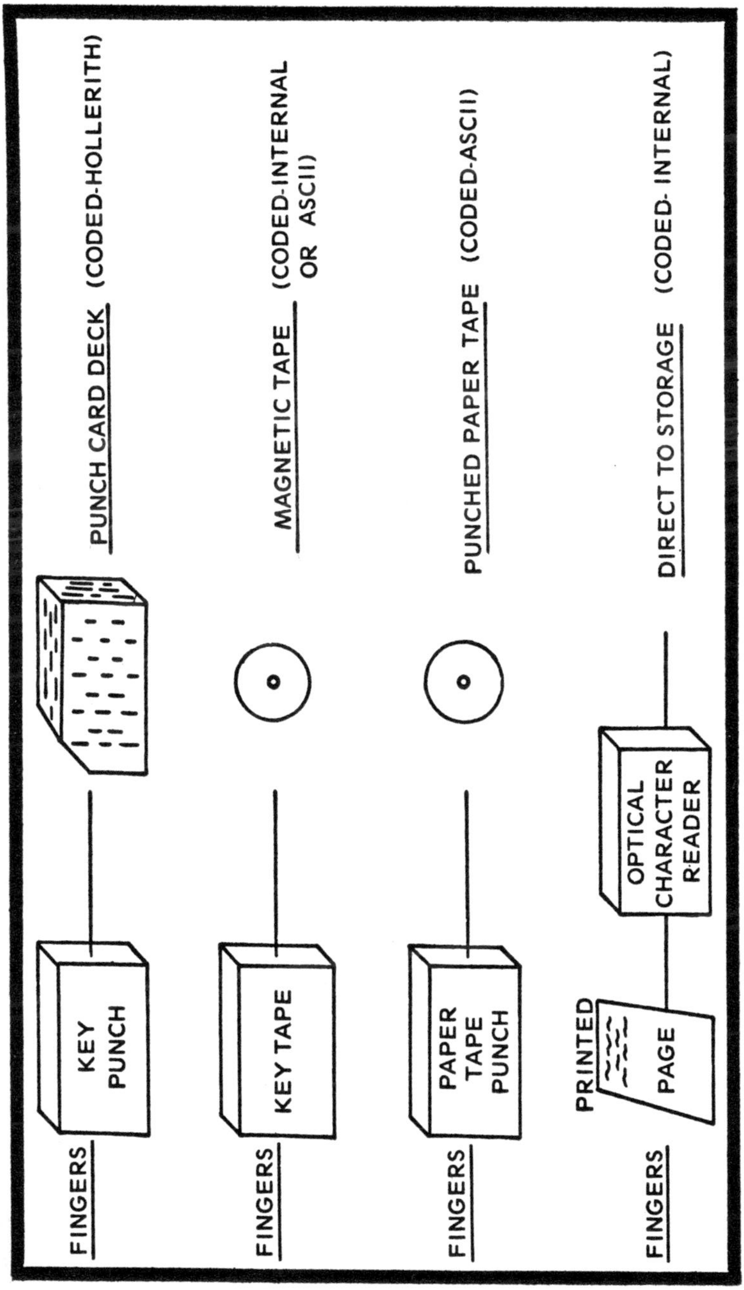

Fig. 1-3. Four data sources are currently used to feed data into a computer.

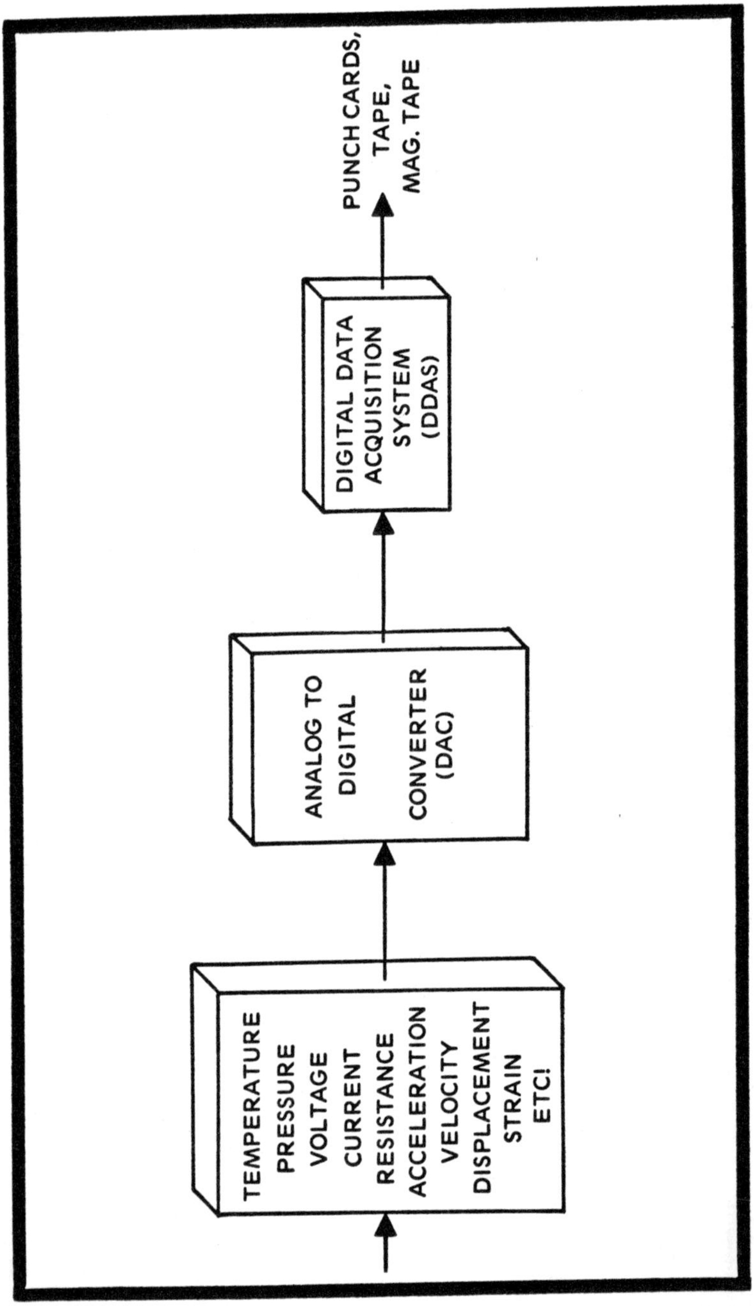

Fig. 1-4. Block diagram representing an analog data system.

by developers, but a number of somewhat standardized approaches have been taken.

The block diagram of Fig. 1-2 is a fair starting point. There are basically two sources of input information to any computer. They may go in via the same input device (cards, paper tape, or magnetic tape) but they are two distinctly different types of information.

1. The **data** is information that will be processed. It could be figures denoting the value of pi, the diameter of the earth, the distance to the moon, or the acceleration of a spacecraft. In the same category would be pay account information, lists of names to be alphabetized, and so forth. These are all data.

2. The **program** is a sequential (because the computer is designed to read the instructions sequentially) list of instructions telling the computer to take in data in some way, process it in some way and put it out to some device in a form that a human being can understand. The program may also store the information, in coded form, on magnetic tape or a magnetic drum or disc for future use in calculations. As one example, an employee's name would be fed to the machine once and would remain as a coded record in the machine until he terminated his employment. All of his cumulative records would also be stored in coded form and retained.

In the block diagram shown, the first type of information is called **source data**, the second type **source control**! Notice that both types of information feed through a **source material translation** device. All information going into a computer must be encoded in a language the computer uses.

Notice in Fig. 1-3 that all **data** and **programs** that are fed to a computer must be entered by a typist, keypunch operator or a paper tape punch operator before the computer can begin to use it. This may be self evident after stating it but think back to it occassionally as we progress. **Source data and programs must be put into one of the forms in Fig. 1-3 before anything else can be done.**

REAL TIME OPERATIONS

Real time operation means that the computer is taking in, processing, and putting out **data** as something is occurring. An example might be found in a steel rolling mill. The programs required are already in storage and the programmer has determined, for example, that he wants to check the Station 10 temperature every 10 seconds and make adjustments if required.

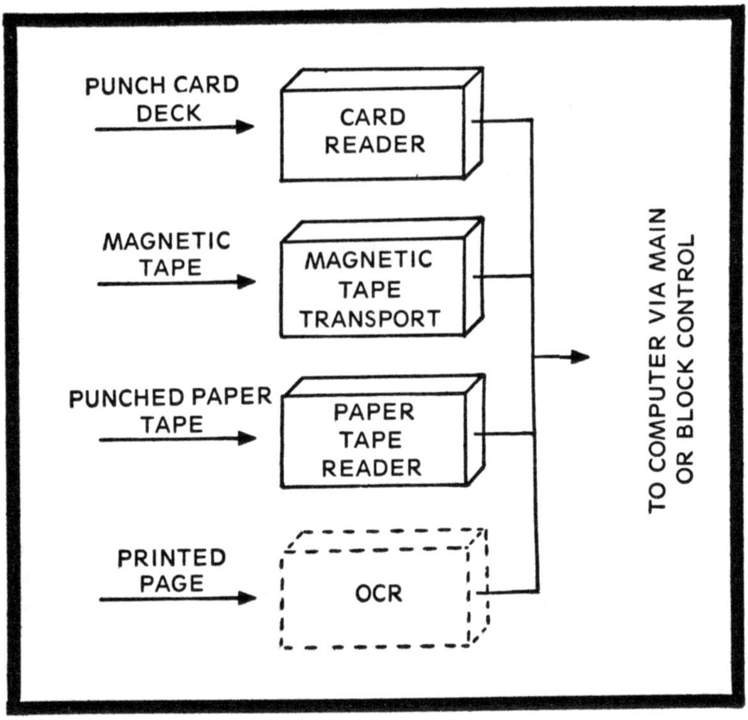

Fig. 1-5. Source material translators are not a part of the actual computer system and are supplied separately. The translator selected must, of course, "speak" the computer's language.

This means that every 10 seconds the program executes an instruction that reads the "digital data acquisition system" and takes temperature data from Station 10. The question then is asked (program) is the temperature too high or too low. The appropriate action is taken in either case. This is true real time-on line operation and requires the type of equipment shown in Fig. 1-4 to acqure the necessary information.

SOURCE MATERIAL TRANSLATORS

Most computers of the medium- or large-scale variety are not supplied with devices for making punched cards or punched paper tape. This equipment must be purchased or rented separately. It is also the equipment that will first encode the information into some machine usable form. In each case Fig. 1-3 shows the coded form on the cards, paper tape, or magnetic tape as the case may be.

Source material translators are usually supplied by the computer manufacturer and each usually has provisions for reading the code indicated (Fig. 1-5) and translating it, either internally or under program control, to the proper machine language code.

At this point, let's take a look at the modern computer as it is delivered to the customer. When delivered, the computer will not run. To make the machine operational, several steps are required.

1. A short program called a **bootstrap loader** will be entered into the machine via the operator's console. This short program is normally used only to load a larger **loader** program into storage.

2. From this point, other programs and data can be entered into the machine and this information normally is applied via the source material translators and goes either through the arithmetic unit (accumulator) or directly into the proper area of storage through **direct memory access** (DMA) or **block control** which controls the handling of blocks of data.

Most of the material that follows will be involved with what transpires in and past the source material translators. The input device we will be most concerned with in this book is the ASR33 teletypewriter. This machine incorporates in one package a page printer, keyboard, paper tape punch, and paper tape reader, and for small computers it is used as the major method of information input and output.

Chapter 2

Number Systems

Before we proceed further with computer systems or equipment, it is necessary to develop an acquaintanceship with computer number systems.

My daughter can count to 4 and sometimes a little further. She cannot as yet write the symbols that represent the number of years she has been around, but she will **memorize** those when she starts school, or possibly earlier. Notice that I said memorize, just as you memorized the various symbols when you were learning to count in the decimal system with its nine symbols and zero to represent any number.

The first and most important point to get here is that there is nothing magic about these symbols. They are symbols used to describe certain things. The symbol 0 for example says empty ...no apples, no oranges, no beef, and so forth. My daughter holds up 4 fingers and says "I'm this many!" She could communicate the number of years she's been in the world to anyone that understood English, whether they understood number systems or not.

So we have a unique set of counting symbols that represent quantities of things. The symbols are:

0	3	7
1	4	8
2	5	9
	6	

If I were to say, "Give me six cents," you would take pennies out of your pocket and count out loud or mentally and give me the number of pennies represented by the symbol I spoke.

Again, nothing magic. Nor is there anything magic about the mathematical functions we perform with numbers. Addition, subtraction, multiplication, and division were all learned using tables or rules, which were memorized.

With our new number systems, we are going to develop rules for the use of these systems, then we are going to learn how to convert from one number system to the other. The most important conversions are from **decimal** to **octal** and back, and the ability to read binary and convert it directly to octal on sight, which is not really difficult.

Counting may seem an odd way to start but take a look at the systems:

Decimal: 1, 2, 3, 4, 5, 6, 7, 8, 9, 10, 11, 12, 13, 14, 15

Octal: 1, 2, 3, 4, 5, 6, 7, 10, 11, 12, 13, 14, 15, 16, 17, 20

Notice that the octal system has only eight symbols including 0. The decimal system has 10, and we are using the decimal again to indicate the number of symbols in each system.

Now, to get you off to a good start, Table 2-1 lists the decimal, octal, and binary count from decimal 0_{10} to 255_{10}. When we start counting and using these new number systems it is desirable when doubt may exist that the base be indicated by a subscript as shown.

Notice that in the binary counting table the only digits that show up are 0 and 1. Also notice that each number is unique. Follow the counting sequence through or, even better, take a separate sheet of paper and try to duplicate the first 100_{10} numbers in the table.

TABLE 2-1. DECIMAL-OCTAL-BINARY EQUIVALENTS.

Decimal	Octal	Binary
0	0	0
1	1	1
2	2	10
3	3	11
4	4	100
5	5	101
6	6	110
7	7	111
8	10	1000
9	11	1001
10	12	1010
11	13	1011
12	14	1100
13	15	1101
14	16	1110
15	17	1111
16	20	10000
17	21	10001

Decimal	Octal	Binary
18	22	10010
19	23	10011
20	24	10100
21	25	10101
22	26	10110
23	27	10111
24	30	11000
25	31	11001
26	32	11010
27	33	11011
28	34	11100
29	35	11101
30	36	11110
31	37	11111
32	40	100000
33	41	100001
34	42	100010
35	43	100011
36	44	100100
37	45	100101
38	46	100110
39	47	100111
40	50	101000
41	51	101001
42	52	101010
43	53	101011
44	54	101100
45	55	101101
46	56	101110
47	57	101111
48	60	110000
49	61	110001
50	62	110010
51	63	110011
52	64	110100
53	65	110101
54	66	110110
55	67	110111
56	70	111000
57	71	111001
58	72	111010
59	73	111011
60	74	111100
61	75	111101
62	76	111110

Decimal	Octal	Binary
63	77	111111
64	100	1000000
65	101	1000001
66	102	1000010
67	103	1000011
68	104	1000100
69	105	1000101
70	106	1000110
71	107	1000111
72	110	1001000
73	111	1001001
74	112	1001010
75	113	1001011
76	114	1001100
77	115	1001101
78	116	1001110
79	117	1001111
80	120	1010000
81	121	1010001
82	122	1010010
83	123	1010011
84	124	1010100
85	125	1010101
86	126	1010110
87	127	1010111
88	130	1011000
89	131	1011001
90	132	1011010
91	133	1011011
92	134	1011100
93	135	1011101
94	136	1011110
95	137	1011111
96	140	1100000
97	141	1100001
98	142	1100010
99	143	1100011
100	144	1100100
101	145	1100101
102	146	1100110
103	147	1100111
104	150	1101000
105	151	1101001
106	152	1101010
107	153	1101011

Decimal	Octal	Binary
108	154	1101100
109	155	1101101
110	156	1101110
111	157	1101111
112	160	1110000
113	161	1110001
114	162	1110010
115	163	1110011
116	164	1110100
117	165	1110101
118	166	1110110
119	167	1110111
120	170	1111000
121	171	1111001
122	172	1111010
123	173	1111011
124	174	1111100
125	175	1111101
126	176	1111110
127	177	1111111
128	200	10000000
129	201	10000001
130	202	10000010
131	203	10000011
132	204	10000100
133	205	10000101
134	206	10000110
135	207	10000111
136	210	10001000
137	211	10001001
138	212	10001010
139	213	10001011
140	214	10001100
141	215	10001101
142	216	10001110
143	217	10001111
144	220	10010000
145	221	10010001
146	222	10010010
147	223	10010011
148	224	10010100
149	225	10010101
150	226	10010110
151	227	10010111
152	230	10011000

Decimal	Octal	Binary
153	231	10011001
154	232	10011010
155	233	10011011
156	234	10011100
157	235	10011101
158	236	10011110
159	237	10011111
160	240	10100000
161	241	10100001
162	242	10100010
163	243	10100011
164	244	10100100
165	245	10100101
166	246	10100110
167	247	10100111
168	250	10101000
169	251	10101001
170	252	10101010
171	253	10101011
172	254	10101100
173	255	10101101
174	256	10101110
175	257	10101111
176	260	10110000
177	261	10110001
178	262	10110010
179	263	10110011
180	264	10110100
181	265	10110101
182	266	10110110
183	267	10110111
184	270	10111000
185	271	10111001
186	272	10111010
187	273	10111011
188	274	10111100
189	275	10111101
190	276	10111110
191	277	10111111
192	300	11000000
193	301	11000001
194	302	11000010
195	303	11000011
196	304	11000100
197	305	11000101

Decimal	Octal	Binary
198	306	11000110
199	307	11000111
200	310	11001000
201	311	11001001
202	312	11001010
203	313	11001011
204	314	11001100
205	315	11001101
206	316	11001110
207	317	11001111
208	320	11010000
209	321	11010001
210	322	11010010
211	323	11010011
212	324	11010100
213	325	11010101
214	326	11010110
215	327	11010111
216	330	11011000
217	331	11011001
218	332	11011010
219	333	11011011
220	334	11011100
221	335	11011101
222	336	11011110
223	337	11011111
224	340	11100000
225	341	11100001
226	342	11100010
227	343	11100011
228	344	11100100
229	345	11100101
230	346	11100110
231	347	11100111
232	350	11101000
233	351	11101001
234	352	11101010
235	353	11101011
236	354	11101100
237	355	11101101
238	356	11101110
239	357	11101111
240	360	11110000
241	361	11110001
242	362	11110010

Decimal	Octal	Binary
243	363	11110011
244	364	11110100
245	365	11110101
246	366	11110110
247	367	11110111
248	370	11111000
249	371	11111001
250	372	11111010
251	373	11111011
252	374	11111100
253	375	11111101
254	376	11111110
255	377	11111111

After better than a year teaching number systems in this way to classes, I have noticed that the first mistake made, as a rule, is the transition from: 78_8 to 100_8. Notice that we have run out of counting symbols in the units position and we have also run out of counting symbols in the 8s(10) position. Did that hang you up? If it did not, you are off to a fine start. If it did, let's take a look at "positional notation" and a thing that goes

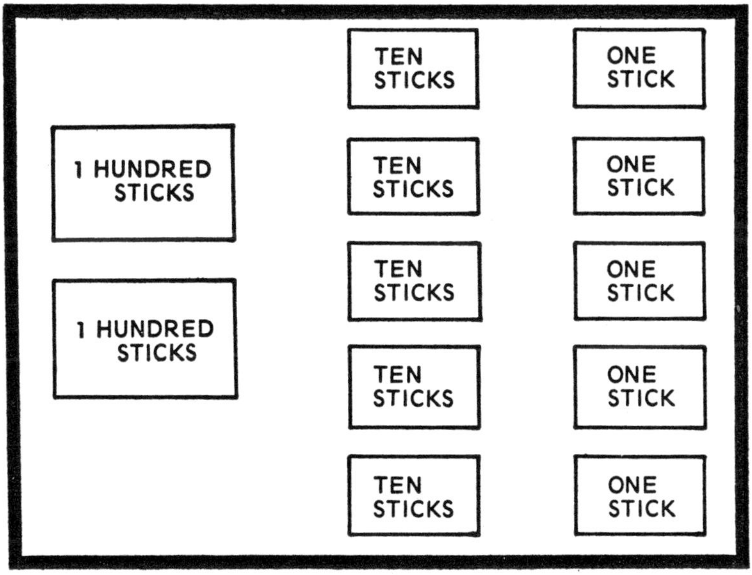

Fig. 2-1. Simple illustration of the decimal weighting technique.

by the big name of "polynomial expansion." But to save worries over big words that mean little, let's call it "weighting." We are going to give each position a decimal weight and see if we can explain a little reason into this thing called number systems, which is probably one of the most important subjects you will study.

First, let's take a look at the decimal number 255 as some of our second graders are studying it now (Fig. 2-1). Here's a little reassurance: This is not meant to insult your intelligence but rather is designed to make you think back over how you learned things when you were in grammar school. Did you always know that 2 times 2 equals 4 in the decimal system? I can guarantee that you did not. You **memorized a multiplication table based on certain rules.**

In the little stick algorithm you could count out two groups of one hundred sticks and you would have something less than a full hundred left. You could record that as: 200. Notice that the tens position and the units position contain nothing so far. You could count out five groups of ten sticks and still have some left over. You would record the five groups of ten sticks as: 50.

Notice that the hundreds position is ignored (even though it still exists!); we could have recorded the five groups of ten sticks as 050 equally well, but we normally resort to a thing called "suppressing leading zeros" automatically. Now the IIIII remaining sticks have a one-to-one relationship with the symbol 5 so we will record the last digit as: 5. Or we could say: 005.

Now let's reassemble what we have. We discovered:

005 units
050 tens
200 hundreds

Combined they make: 255

Let's look at it one more way: 5 x 1 equals 5; 5 x 10 equals 50, and 2 x 100 equals 200, or a total of 255. How about that?

And still one other way: Remember your powers of ten? 1 equals 10^0. By definition 10 equals 10^1 and 100 equals 10^2. So:

$$5 \times 10^0 = 5 \times 1 = 5$$

$$5 \times 10^1 = 5 \times 10 = 50$$

$$2 \times 10^2 = 2 \times 100 = 200$$

and again we arrive at the sum of 255.

Now let's try something else using this information, and don't try to jump ahead of me: We are going to take the octal equivalent of decimal 255 and see if we can determine its decimal value in some manner or other.

The octal equivalent of decimal 255 is 377. In the powers of ten we weight the decimal positions with some power of the base or radix of the number system. The base of the decimal system is 10 while the base of the octal number system (expressed in decimal terms...please notice) is 8_{10} or 8 decimal. Therefore, we should be able to give each position in the octal system a decimal weight, perform the necessary math, and come up with the decimal equivalent:

$$\begin{array}{lcrcrcr} 7 \times 8^0 & = & 7 & \times & 1 & = & 7 \\ 7 \times 8^1 & = & 7 & \times & 8 & = & 56 \\ 3 \times 8^2 & = & 3 & \times & 64 & = & \underline{192} \\ & & & & & & 255_{10} \end{array}$$

As practice you might try some others and go slowly because I made two goofs on the first try in the above problem! Which are now corrected, but the point is, in all your early work with computer arithmetic and computer programming and computer maintenance, work **slowly** and methodically and great rewards will be yours. IBM's standing admonition is **THINK** and that requirement hasn't changed.

Now that you have done a few conversions of octal numbers to decimal numbers we will proceed to discover several ways to do all types of conversions, but while we have "weighting" in mind let's take a look at the simplest conversion technique of them all and get that out of the way.

We've discovered a sad fact, for the computer industry, about the decimal system. It does not have a direct relationship to the binary number system and as a consequence the conversion methods get a little bit involved in converting from binary and octal to decimal and back. Therefore, we use a system of decimal to octal and octal to decimal conversions. Simple proof: 2 x 2 x 2 equals 8, the base of the octal system, so that three positions of binary should be directly convertible to an octal number and we will show this to be the case in a minute. 2 x 2 x 2 x 2 equals 16 (not ten which falls somewhere in between). 16 incidentally is the base of the hexidecimal number system which we will touch on briefly for

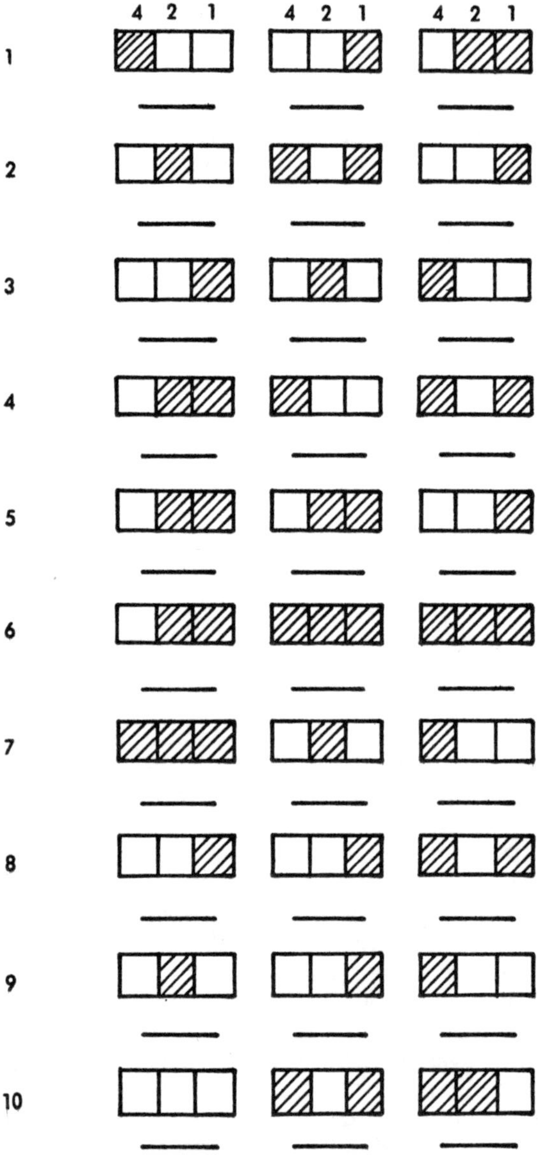

1 413
2 251
3 124
4 345
5 331
6 377
7 724
8 115
9 214
10 056

Fig. 2-2. A binary-to-octal conversion example. The black squares indicate a lamp lit, the white a lamp not lit.

conversion purposes after you have binary-octal-decimal under your belt. Let's make a table:

Binary	Octal		
000	0	2^0	= 1
001	1		
010	2	2^1	= 2
011	3		
100	4	2^2	= 4
101	5		
110	6		
111	7		
001 000	1 0		

Notice that for every nonrepeating group of three binary digits there is a corresponding octal digit, so we have the one-to-one relationship required to make the conversion from octal to binary and from binary to octal very simple. Of course, there are a million additional things that you could be told about this but you can pick those little niceties up in any book on number systems. Your goal with this book should be to develop the knowledge necessary to maintain small central processors and that is what we are going to put the stress on.

The next few illustrations represent computer registers which are frequently blocked off in groups of three to facilitate the reading of binary information in octal to save time. Instructions (computer instruction in machine language) are frequently written in octal as well as are addresses in memory so you are going to be working extensively with the octal number system, which reminds me to suggest that you turn your checkbook over to your wife because the bank frowns on calculations in octal in a checkbook!

In Figs. 2-2, 2-3, 2-4, a shaded square indicates a lamp **lit** and an open square indicates a lamp **not lit**. A lamp lit equals binary 1 and not lit, binary 0, so read the following displays, record your answers in octal then check the inverted answers and work the next set.

Now shall I let you in on a little secret? You just entered the **bootstrap load routine** for the computer we will be using as a model later. Since this computer uses an 8-bit register, the

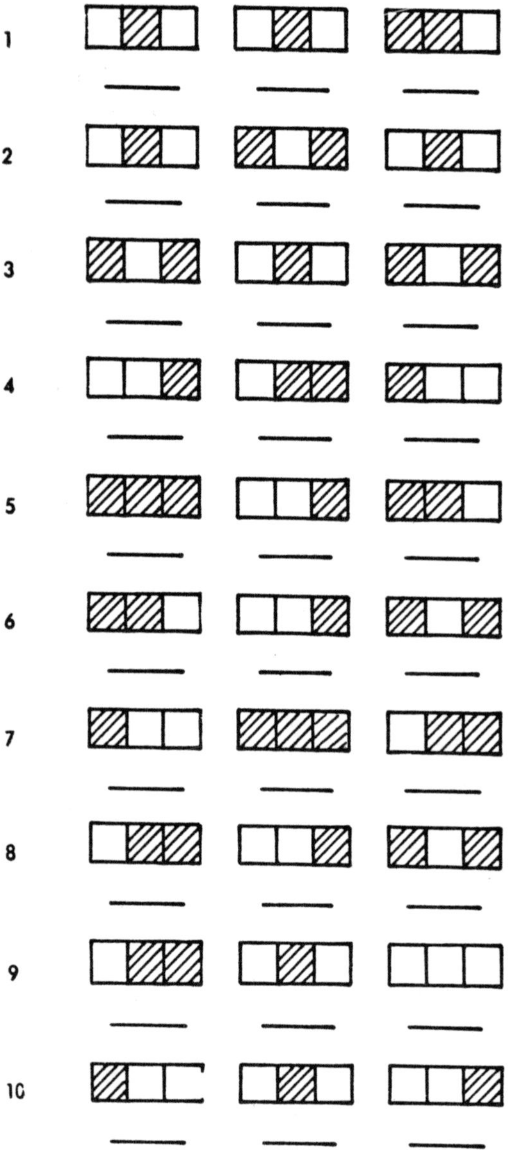

1 226
2 252
3 525
4 134
5 716
6 615
7 473
8 315
9 320
10 421

Fig. 2-3. Another conversion example, following the procedure in Fig. 2-2.

instructions are each two computer words long. The first instruction is:

100 072—Initialize the teletype reader

131 071—Input from the teletype to the A register

345 002—This sends the computer back to the previous instruction to wait on the teletype.

331 347—Store the contents of the A register at location 347.

371 007—Increase the address (347) in the above instruction by 1.

345 000—Go back to the beginning and repeat

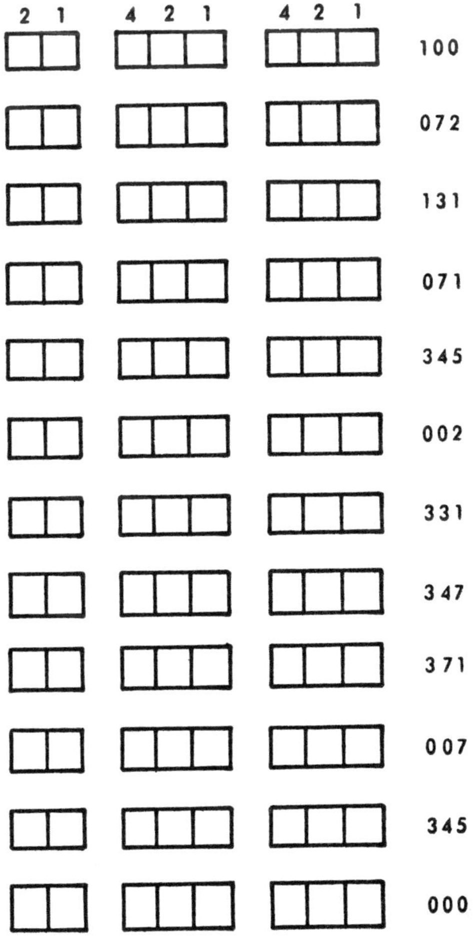

Fig. 2-4. Now you can do the operation in reverse translate octal to binary. Enter the octal numbers at the right into the proper block to indicate an on state.

The entire effect is that the computer reads each successive character from the tape in the teletype reader and stores the information at successive addresses in storage! So who says you can't learn computer technology?

CONVERSIONS

Here is a list of the conversion techniques you should be familiar with to understand most machines available today:

1. Binary to:
   - A. Octal
   - B. Decimal
2. Octal to:
   - A. Binary
   - B. Decimal
3. Decimal to:
   - A. Binary
   - B. Octal

						8^4	8^3	8^2	8^1	8^0	Power
						4096	512	64	8	1	Equals

Taking our original decimal number again: 255, we first subtract the highest power of 8 that we can find. The number is smaller than 512 but larger than 64, so the first digit of the new octal number must be some multiple of 64. Multiplying 64 by 3 gives 192. Multiplying by 4 gives 256 which is one more that the original number, so from that we can say that the first digit is 3 and:

3 x 64 equals 192 subtracted from 255 gives a remainder of 63.

7 x 8 equals 56 subtracted from 63 gives a remainder of 7.

7 x 1 equals 7 subtracted from 7 gives a remainder of 0.

So the octal number is 377_8. Decimal-to-binary would work the same way with powers of 2 substituted for the powers of 8 and would be equally cumbersome.

Fig. 2-5. Subtraction of powers conversion procedure.

The best way to study these conversion systems is to take them in groups. We have already gone through the binary-to-octal and octal-to-binary. This leaves decimal-to-binary, binary-to-decimal, decimal-to-octal and octal-to-decimal. Either low-base-to-high-base conversions or high-base-to-low-base could be taken first but let's consider the methods of going from high-base (decimal) to low-base (octal and binary) first.

The methods could be gone over for the next 50 pages but the best way to learn conversion techniques is by doing problems. Convert the following numbers from decimal to octal and binary:

Decimal	Octal	Binary
1. 14		
2. 15		
3. 44		
4. 97		
5. 235		
6. 1		
7. 294		
8. 117		
9. 86		
10. 4090		
11. 4095		
12. 1502		
13. 377		
14. 501		
15. 828		
16. 907		
17. 4000		
18. 3456		
19. 2278		
20. 1967		

Answers to previous problems

Decimal	Octal	Binary
1. 14	16	001 110
2. 15	17	001 111
3. 44	54	101 100
4. 97	141	001 100 001
5. 235	353	011 101 011

Divide the number by the radix of the system that the number is to be converted to and save the remainders. The remainders will be the digits of the new number with the first remainder being the least significant digit and progressing up from there. 255_{10} converted to octal (base 8):

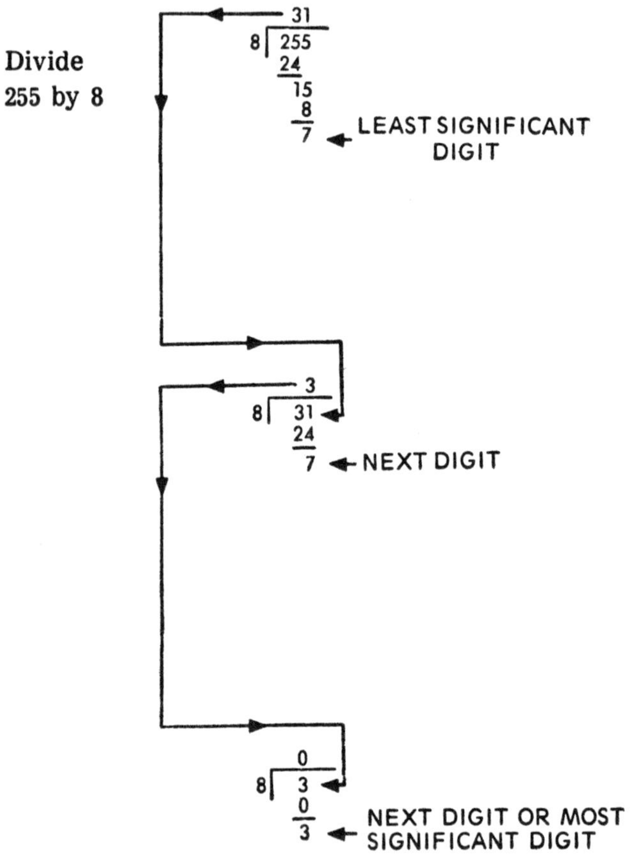

The result is 377_8 and this is probably the simplest system for high-base to low-base conversion. Just be sure to convert until the quotient is 0!

Laying the problem out a little differently may help. Convert 36_{10} to binary:

		QUOTIENT	REMAINDER
36 divided by 2	=	18	0
18 divided by 2	=	9	0
9 divided by 2	=	4	1
4 divided by 2	=	2	0
2 divided by 2	=	1	0
1 divided by 2	=	0	1

1 0 0 1 0 0

Notice that in each case the division was continued until the quotient equalled 0. This is one of the most common errors in conversions, so insure that this step is not missed. Also remember that the remainder from the first division is the least significant digit.

Fig. 2-6. Division method for converting high base to low base.

6. 1	1	001
7. 294	446	100 100 110
8. 117	165	001 110 101
9. 86	126	001 010 110
10. 4090	7772	111 111 111 010
11. 4095	7777	111 111 111 111
12. 1502	2736	010 111 011 110
13. 377	571	101 111 001
14. 501	765	111 110 101
15. 828	1474	001 100 111 100
16. 907	1613	001 110 001 011
17. 4000	7640	111 110 100 000
18. 3456	6600	110 110 000 000
19. 2278	4346	100 011 100 110
20. 1967	3657	011 110 101 111

Octal-to-decimal or decimal-to-octal conversion is easiest using the tables. A section of these tables is reproduced in Table 2-2. The number 2021_8, for example, would be found by looking down the left side for 2020. Then looking across the top for the final 1, you will find 1041_{10} as the decimal equivalent of 2021_8.

Converting decimal-to-octal requires locating the decimal number within the large block of numbers. Notice that the count is one at a time. Looking down the left column (under 0) and looking for the number 1054_{10}, 1048 is too small, 1056 is too large so the number has to be in the preceding line. Under 6 on the preceding line you find 1054_{10}. Looking back to the left you find 2030 and since the number is located under 6, the conversion becomes 2036_8.

TABLE 2-2. OCTAL-DECIMAL CONVERSION TABLE.

	0	1	2	3	4	5	6	7
2000	1024	1025	1026	1027	1028	1029	1030	1031
2010	1032	1033	1034	1035	1036	1037	1038	1039
2020	1040	1041	1042	1043	1044	1045	1046	1047
2030	1048	1049	1050	1051	1052	1053	1054	1055
2040	1056	1057	1058	1059	1060	1061	1062	1063

Convert the following numbers from binary to octal and decimal:

	Binary	Octal	Decimal
1.	110	**6**	**6**
2.	101	**5**	**5**
3.	1 110 110	**166**	**118**
4.	1 011 110	**136**	**94**
5.	0 110 110	**066**	**54**
6.	001 111	**37**	**31**
7.	001 010	**12**	**10**
8.	110 111	**67**	**55**
9.	011 011 011 101	**3335**	**1757**
10.	111 000 111 001	**7071**	**3641**
11.	111 010 110 100	**7264**	**3764**
12.	111 111 110 111	**7767**	**4087**
13.	101 011 010 101	**5325**	**2773**
14.	111 111	**77**	**63**
15.	000 101 001	**051**	**41**
16.	111 111 111 111	**7777**	**4095**
17.	010 101 010 101	**2525**	**1365**
18.	101 010 101 010	**5252**	**2730**
19.	110 101 011 001	**6531**	**3417**
20.	000 000 000 101	**0001**	**1**

(Answers bold face)

Here is a general summary of conversion methods with the most desirable listed first for each type of conversion.

1. Decimal to octal:
   A. Tables
   B. Division by 8, saving remainders
   C. Subtraction of powers

2. Decimal to binary:
   A. Use tables to convert to octal then convert to binary by inspection
   B. Division by 2, saving remainders
   C. Subtraction of powers

3. Octal to binary:
    A. Convert by inspection

4. Octal to decimal:
    A. Tables
    B. Synthetic division
    C. Addition of powers (weighting)
5. Binary to octal:
    A. Convert by inspection

6. Binary to decimal:
    A. Convert to octal by inspection, then use the tables to convert octal to decimal.
    B. Synthetic division
    C. Addition of powers (weighting)

First, don't ask why it's called **synthetic division.** A lot of experts have been unable to give a good reason. But let's take our old favorite 377_8 and convert it to decimal:

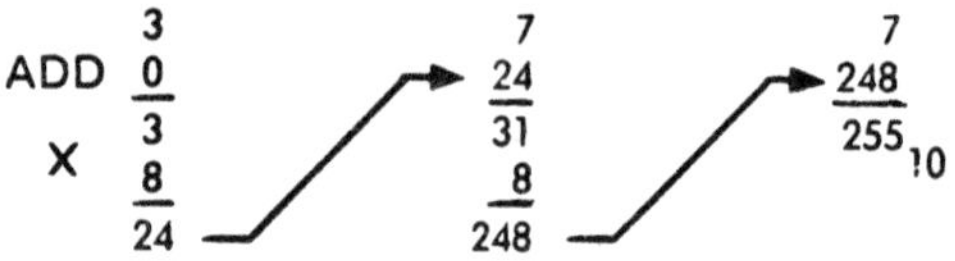

The steps are:

1. Add 0 to the most significant digit position (for structuring the problem).

2. Multiply the result by the base of the number system from which the conversion is being made (8 for octal and 2 for binary).

3. Add the result to the next most significant digit position and again multiply.

4. Continue this procedure for all digits except the least significant digit which is simply added to the previous result.

5. **With long numbers, leave yourself plenty of room!**

Fig. 2-7. Octal-to-decimal conversion, synthetic division method.

Hexidecimal (Base 16) Conversions

Although your requirement for a knowledge of the hexidecimal number system will be quite limited, some knowledge of the system is desirable. At this point it is recommended that all arithmetic operations be done by converting hexidecimal to decimal, octal, or binary, and then back to hexidecimal. There is a one-to-one correspondence between hexidecimal digits and binary. Here it is:

Hexidecimal	Binary
0	0000
1	0001
2	0010
3	0011
4	0100
5	0101
6	0110
7	0111
8	1000
9	1001
A	1010
B	1011
C	1100
D	1101
E	1110
F	1111
10	0001 0000
1F	0001 1111

Since there is a one-to-one correspondence between hexidecimal and binary, it makes conversion to binary quite simple. Just write the hexidecimal number as groups of four binary digits:

$$1F_{16} = 0001 \quad 1111$$

To convert the binary number to octal, simply regroup the binary in groups of three:

$$00 \quad 011 \quad 111 = 037_{8}$$

The tables will now give the decimal value as 31_{10}. So that hexidecimal 1F equals decimal 31.

To go back the other way, simply convert the decimal number to octal, convert the octal number to binary by inspection and regroup the binary number in groups of four and convert to hexidecimal.

Let's do one more: 2CE4 (looks funny I agree but it is a legitimate hexidecimal notation):

```
 2        C                   E         4

0010     1100                1110      0100
              010    110     011   100   100

               2      6       3     4     4
```

Since the resulting number goes over the capability of our table, another method will have to be used. Looking along the edge of the chart you will find some smaller tables near the top. They give octal 20,000 a decimal value of 8192. The conversion tables themselves give octal 6344 a decimal value of 3300. Adding these two values:

$$\begin{array}{r} 8192 \\ \underline{3300} \\ 11492_{10} \end{array}$$

Then: $2CE4_{16} = 11{,}492_{10}$

Reversing the process would give the opposite result. This may seem a little involved but it gets the job done and should be adequate for any hexidecimal operations you may be involved with. Should you find yourself working on hexidecimal machines, you will find extensive information available from the companies that manufacture these machines.

Finally, tables are included for the conversion of fractions but most CEs will find that they do practically no work with fractional conversions, so any information you need can be found in books devoted to number systems.

BINARY ARITHMETIC

If you think back, you may remember that in grammar school somewhere you learned to add by memorizing a set of addition tables. Even now if you take time to add two decimal numbers you may discover some unusual things about the manner in which you do calculations. The important point is that you did use a table.

The table for binary addition is a study in simplicity:

0	+	0	=	0
0	+	1	=	1
1	+	1	=	10

That's it!

Now see if you can't add the following binary numbers. Just be sure to use the rules above and do your carrying in the usual manner:

0111	=	7	decimal
+ 1000	+	8	decimal
1111	=	15	decimal

It would be a good idea to use the leading zeros for a while since we will be going into a system that requires the existence of the leading zeros.

1.	10 110		22	3.	111 011	59
	+ 00 111	+	7		+ 110 011	+ 51
	11 101	=	29		1 101 110	110
2.	1111		15	4.	1 110 110	118
	+ 1001	+	9		+ 1 001	+ 11
	11000	=	24		10 000 001	129

These problems should give you a fair capability with binary addition. Try making your own problems from the counting list; do the arithmetic in both binary and decimal and double check your procedures. Once you are satisfied that you can handle binary addition, move on to the section on subtraction.

COMPUTER ARITHMETIC

For the next few pages we are going to be involved with a subject that is probably entirely new to you. Though not difficult, there are new terms to be learned and a number of new thoughts to be considered. The addition of binary numbers should and does lead into the subtraction of binary numbers. These numbers can be subtracted directly with the binary addition table serving as a guide and the rules of borrowing applied, but there is an easier and much simpler way to do it!

The new way is called **complement arithmetic**, the arithmetic the computer uses in performing calculations. To handle it properly a knowledge of word length restrictions is required. All the arithmetic you have used up to the present time has allowed you to go to millions, billions, trillions, or beyond, because the length of the number you used was restricted only by the size of the sheet of paper you had.

With the computer, the length of number you can have is restricted by the word length of the machine, and as a starter we are going to consider the small computer we are using as a model. This machine has an 8-bit word. It can be programmed to do multiple precision arithmetic where several words are used to represent one number but we are going to concern ourselves with what it does with a single word.

The largest number that we can put in an 8-bit register, expressed in binary is:

$$11\ 111\ 111 = 377_8 = 255_{10}$$

That's not very big, but it will serve well for the purposes we are going to study.

If, in the example above, we were to try to add 1 to the existing number it would go to:

$$100\ 000\ 000$$

but the 1 on the left would go off the end and be lost. For this reason there is an additional part of the machine that accepts this digit and, through logic, signal that the computer has **overflowed.**

We can also say that the **modulus** of the register has been exceeded. The modulus of a register is the maximum number of values it can represent. The register above can represent all numbers from 1 to 255 or 255 values. But to this we must add all zeros as one of the values it can represent, so we say that the modulus is actually 256_{10}.

If this still bothers you, consider a 1-digit odometer on a car! The odometer starts with:

0, 1, 2, 3, 4, 5, 6, 7, 8, 9

which says it can count to 9 but counting the number of symbols including 0 gives a total of 10 symbols or 10 values the odometer can represent.

That is modulus, a restriction placed on the size number you can work with. We are now going to use this restricted number size to evaluate some new things, but first let's take a look at complement. The dictionary definition says that complement has something to do with "that which fills or completes." All right, what are we going to fill?

In computer arithmetic, it would be nice to perform all mathematical operations using one type of circuit. But who ever heard of subtracting by adding? Watch!

We will discuss the 9s complement for decimal, the 7s complement for octal and the 1s complement for binary. The 9s complement of:

0 is 9:	6 is 3:	0 + 9 = 9
1 is 8:	7 is 2:	1 + 8 = 9
2 is 7:	8 is 1:	2 + 7 = 9
3 is 6:	9 is 0:	3 + 6 = 9
4 is 5:		4 + 5 = 9
5 is 4:		

So to obtain the 9s complement of a number, it is only necessary to determine, by inspection, what number when added to the number would equal 9. This can be extended to any number of digits:

145 627 385 462 895

854 372 614 537 105

Each of the above numbers is the 9s complement of the other since when added together they total 9 at each digit position. OK, so how does that help?

```
  27
- 13
----
  14
```

In other words, subtracting 13 from 27 gives a difference of 14. Not such a big deal. Let's add the 9s complement of 13 to 27 and see what results:

```
  27
+ 86          the 9s complement of 13.
----
 113
```

Doesn't look to promising at this point, does it? But we said that in this system we have a restricted register length. So the 1 on the left exceeds the two digit positions we have and we're going to use it for what is called an "end-around-carry."

```
  13
   1
----
  14
```

How about that! The answer is correct!

It would appear that we have a successful system and that we can, in fact, subtract by adding, in this case, the complement of the number. But let's try one more:

```
  627        627
- 145      + 854     (9s complement of 145)
-----      -----
  482       1481
               1     (end-around-carry)
           -----
             482
```

You can make up a group of additional problems if you like and try the system with other numbers.

TABLE 2-3. OCTAL ADDITION TABLE.

	1	2	3	4	5	6	7
1	2	3	4	5	6	7	10
2	3	4	5	6	7	10	11
3	4	5	6	7	10	11	12
4	5	6	7	10	11	12	13
5	6	7	10	11	12	13	14
6	7	10	11	12	13	14	15
7	10	11	12	13	14	15	16

Up to this point, nothing much has been said about octal arithmetic. It requires a completely new set of rules and an octal addition table is reproduced in Table 2-3. Using the table, make a few problems and try adding. A check of your results can be made by converting to decimal and performing the addition in decimal to see if the results are the same. Several problems like this might help bring the following into solid focus.

If you find yourself without an octal addition table you can make one, but there is another way. Use the following rules:

1. In adding a position, add as you would in decimal, and if the result is not larger than 7, put that number down.

2. If the result is 8 or above, add 2 using decimal arithmetic and put down the resulting digit and carry. (See Fig. 2-8.)

I could continue to explain this in far greater detail, but the only way it will come is with practice. Computer arithmetic takes practice and nothing will substitute for practice.

Octal subtraction is best performed using the 7s complement form. The 7s complement is used in the same way as the 9s complement but to form the 7s complement, each digit position must total 7. End-around-carry is performed in the same way as for 9s complement arithmetic.

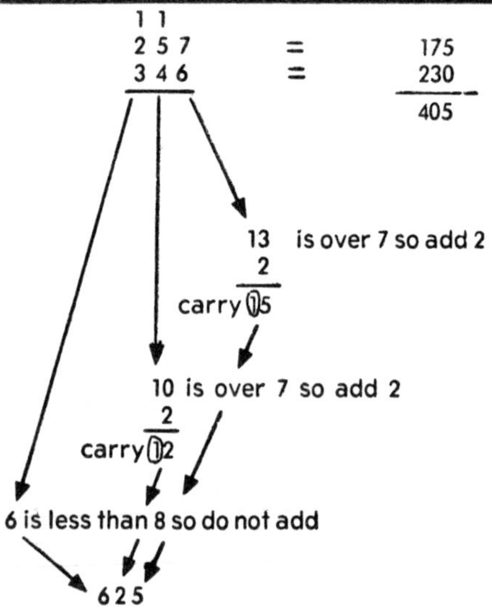

Try a number of additional problems by selecting numbers from the counting list. Check your results by converting to decimal and then back to octal. This is excellent practice and there is little need of giving you the answers when they are easily checked for accuracy.

Fig. 2-8. Simplified octal division procedure.

Binary subtraction can be performed using the 1s complement. The nice part about complementing a binary number is that each 0 is changed to 1 and each 1 to a 0! End-around-carry is used with binary numbers also.

Multiplication and division of binary and octal numbers are best achieved by converting the numbers to decimal, performing the operations and converting back to the original base.

There are a fairly large number of books available on more advanced computer arithmetic, which would be worth studying if an in-depth knowledge of number systems is desired. The information that has been presented here is specifically designed to give you what you will need for 99 percent of all problems encountered. The remaining one percent can be taken care of by doing conversions to decimal and working problems out that way, then converting back to the original base.

Chapter 3

Coding Systems

The point was made in the introduction that information must be coded (encoded) for use in a computer system, and now, with a fair understanding of number systems, we can prepare to go a little deeper into coding and coding systems.

At the present time there are two major entry methods for any computer. The first is the ASR33 teletype, which is used as an input-output device for practically every small computer on the market. The second is the keypunch-card reader system used on most medium- and large-scale machines.

The paper tape punch of the ASR33 encodes information as a row of eight punched or unpunched positions for each character and function to be encoded. This code is called the ASCII code as mentioned in the introduction; it is discussed in detail in the next chapter. The keypunch machine punches cards in Hollerith code. This code also is discussed in detail in Chapter 4. These are the data source codes and as such are worth studying in detail because there will be times when you will want to read them directly.

Input-output devices, for example, normally are more prone to failure than other equipment. You may want to step the reading operation of a tape and watch the accumulator register to insure that the correct data is getting that far correctly. To do this, it would be desirable for you to be able to read the codes or at least know where to find them.

We have a listing of the various codes in the last part of this chapter. These codes are listed in octal so let's take a quick look at their binary counterparts:

ASCII	Octal	Binary
0	260	10 110 000
5	265	10 110 101
A	301	11 000 001
J	312	11 001 010

Channels in paper tape are numbered from 1 to 8 from right to left. With this in mind, for 0, Channels 5, 6 and 8 would be punched.

In reading the tape, the holes allow a reading finger to pass through which in turn allows a contact in the reader to close, transmitting a 1. These holes could also be sampled using a light beam and a photocell for high-speed reading operations.

Hollerith code is broken up in columns with the normal card having 80 characters. Each of these characters is represented by one or more punches in a vertical column on the card.

Part of this diversity of codes can be attributed to the fact that there has been very little effort to standardize anything in the computer industry until quite recently. Companies are still quite jealous of anything they do and hold on closely to proprietary rights, which would be laudible if it did not tend to create mass confusion.

USASCII is one of the newer and as yet not widely adopted codes that includes lower case letters as well as a number of other characters, and EBCIDIC is a special IBM code.

Internal and external machine codes are found in individual manufacturer's literature. Especially with medium- and large-scale machines using card readers, the card reader itself contains logic circuitry which immediately converts the Hollerith code contained on the punched card to a coded form more easily used and stored by the computer.

BINARY CODED DECIMAL AND OTHER WEIGHTED CODES

Binary coded decimal or BCD is exactly what the acronym states, a binary code used to represent numbers in the base 10 system. There is also binary coded octal which we have touched on already where each group of three binary digits can be used to represent some specific octal digit. We could also say we have touched on binary coded hexidecimal.

Binary coded octal uses three binary digits to represent all octal digits. Binary coded hexidecimal uses four binary digits. In the binary coded octal, the decimal weights given to each position are 4-2-1. In the BCH system the weights are 8-4-2-1 and these are the same weights used in the binary coded decimal system' most of the time.

The most important thing to notice here is that the BCO column in Table 3-1 would next count 000 in the positions shown with a 1 carried into the next digit position. The BCH would count 0000 after F with a 1 carried to the next position but the

BCD would have to be forced into an unnatural counting sequence to return to zero and in the electronic circuitry used to perform a BCD count that is exactly what is done. Notice also that totaling the decimal weights for a particular group gives the decimal number on the left:

BCD: 0010 for example, the weight assigned to the digit position containing a 1 is decimal 2.

BCD: 0110 has a 1 in weight positions 2 and 4 which totals 6 and so forth.

These are some of the most important numerical codes but it would be interesting to explore a few more.

One of the very earliest codes had a weighting system of 2-4-2-1. The count for this system would progress as shown in Table 3-2. At the time this code was conceived it was cheaper to disrupt the normal counting progression at 5 and leave out 0110, 0111, 1000, 1001, 1010 and 1011 with the next count being picked up as 1100 and making 9 equal to 1111 allowing the system to roll back to zero normally.

TABLE 3-1. BINARY CODED OCTAL WITH 4-2-1 WEIGHTS AND BINARY CODED HEXIDECIMAL WITH 8-4-2-1 WEIGHTS.

	BCO	BCD	BCH
0	000	0000	0000
1	001	0001	0001
2	010	0010	0010
3	011	0011	0011
4	100	0100	0100
5	101	0101	0101
6	110	0110	0110
7	111	0111	0111
8		1000	1000
9		1001	1001
A			1010
B			1011
C			1100
D			1101
E			1110
F			1111

TABLE 3-2. EARLY CODE WEIGHTED 2-4-21.

0	0000	1	0001	2	0010
3	0011	4	0100	5	0101
6	1100	7	1101	8	1110
9	1111				

The code in Table 3-2 is still used by sôme instrument manufacturers and, if I recall history correctly, was the code used in a device called the Potter Timer-Counter which was used for counting nuclear reactions. In any event, this code and several others will come up in various places and you should be able to dissect and understand them.

Going back to 8-4-2-1 coded BCD, the following would be examples of decimal numbers written in this code:

22	0010 0010
35	0011 0101
671	0110 0111 0001
2579	0010 0101 0111 1001

AN INTERMEDIATE REVIEW

ASCII, USASCII, Hollerith, and similar codes are numeral and character codes. They also include codes for space, line feed, carriage return, and similar functions. These are codes that are used for initial information entry and to communicate with the outside world by operating hard copy machines, punches, and other devices. Such codes enter the original device via a typist's fingers and are returned via machines that electronically or electromechanically copy these actions. Inside the computer, the material is represented and handled as binary numbers which are in turn represented by switch closures, lamps, and voltage levels.

Taking a look at the situation at this point might clear up a tremendous amount of misunderstanding later. Suppose we want to add 2 + 2 within the computer, and let's say it has a register that is 8 bits long. Some way is going to have to be found to get the 2s into the machine. Using the teletype, if I type 2 the code 262 (10 110 010) is punched on the tape. Another 2 would give the same results. If I now read that tape into the computer it is going to read and store 10 110 010.

To make a number the computer can understand or a number that is usable by the computer I must get rid of the 26 and leave the 2. What happens here is rather simple. The upper two octal digits, or in this case the upper five binary digits, are masked out by a code as soon as the number is input to the computer and the resulting 2 is stored.

There is a little more to this procedure when larger numbers are involved but this should give you a feeling for some of the minor technical complications involved in simply handling data in and out of the computer.

ASCII, USASCII and Hollerith among others, then, handle all types of information including numbers, the alphabet, and functions in and out of the computer. Internally, the information is handled as strictly binary in some form or other. BCD, BCO and BCH are "weighted" codes that may be used for some internal applications. Binary coded octal is one of the codes of principle interest to us because it is easy to read binary grouped in threes and octal numbers and saves writing down long binary numbers.

There are several other more or less popular "unweighted" codes that are worth looking at. Possibly one of the oldest of these is the "biquinary" meaning essentially 2 + 5 code. It is the code that was used in the abacus (still is for that matter) and there might be some argument about whether it is a weighted or unweighted code. See what you think:

	5 0	4 3 2 1 0
0	0 1	0 0 0 0 1
1	0 1	0 0 0 1 0
2	0 1	0 0 1 0 0
3	0 1	0 1 0 0 0
4	0 1	1 0 0 0 0
5	1 0	0 0 0 0 1
6	1 0	0 0 0 1 0
7	1 0	0 0 1 0 0
8	1 0	0 1 0 0 0
9	1 0	1 0 0 0 0

The basic problem with the code from modern concepts is that it requires seven flip-flops at $4 each instead of four which is the number required for BCD.

Two other unweighted coding systems are of interest for a couple of reasons. First, you are going to hear of them, even though they are not widely used and, secondly, it is worth looking at some of the broad aspects of codes so that you will be somewhat prepared for others that show up.

The first one is the excess 3 code. In this code, 0011 binary is added to each conventional BCD code to obtain a new code. Since there are a number of machines that do BCD arithmetic, this code would be very desirable in such a machine. The excess 3 code will yield the 9s complement of the original number simply by complementing the excess 3 binary number.

TABLE 3-3. EXCESS 3 CODE COMPARED TO BCD.

	BCD	Excess 3
0	0000	0011
1	0001	0100
2	0010	0101
3	0011	0110
4	0100	0111
5	0101	1000
6	0110	1001
7	0111	1010
8	1000	1011
9	1001	1100

Notice in Table 3-3 that the 9s complement of 2 is 7; 2 is BCD 0010 and the complement is 1101 which is certainly not BCD 7. With excess 3, 2 is 0101 complemented equals 1010 which is the excess 3 code for 7.

Finally, the gray code, which was designed for electromechanical and electronic shaft encoders. These are commutators and brushes or slip rings and brushes or optical systems that encode the position of a shaft in degrees. For reasons of size and tolerance they can be designed to allow one bit to change at a time. If more than one bit is allowed to change, the mechanical inaccuracies can cause large errors in the digital output. Without going into mechanical details, it would be difficult to say more, and if you are involved with this

TABLE 3-4. GRAY CODE WITH BINARY EQUIVALENTS.

Decimal	Binary	Gray
0	0000	0000
1	0001	0001
2	0010	0011
3	0011	0010
4	0100	0110
5	0101	0111
6	0110	0101
7	0111	0100
8	1000	1100
9	1001	1101
10	1010	1111
11	1011	1110
12	1100	1010

type of equipment the manufacturer can give you much more concise information. Table 3-4 is a gray code and the binary equivalent to 12 places.

As you proceed through the balance of the material in this book, it would be worth while to come back and review number systems and codes occasionally since something new will occur to you each time you work through these sections.

Following is a listing in octal of the various codes used in computers.

Symbol	ASCII	Printer	Mag Tape	Hollerith	FORTRAN
@	300	00	32	0-2-8	77
A	301	01	61	12-1	13
B	302	02	62	12-2	14
C	303	03	63	12-3	15
D	304	04	64	12-4	16
E	305	05	65	12-5	17
F	306	06	66	12-6	20
G	307	07	67	12-7	21
H	310	10	70	12-8	22
I	311	11	71	12-9	23
J	312	12	41	11-1	24
K	313	13	42	11-2	25
L	314	14	43	11-3	26
M	315	15	44	11-4	27
N	316	16	45	11-5	30
O	317	17	46	11-6	31
P	320	20	47	11-7	32
Q	321	21	50	11-8	33
R	322	22	51	11-9	34
S	323	23	22	0-2	35
T	324	24	23	0-3	36
U	325	25	24	0-4	37
V	326	26	25	0-5	40
W	327	27	26	0-6	41
X	330	30	27	0-7	42
Y	331	31	30	0-8	43

Symbol	ASCII	Printer	Mag Tape	Hollerith	FORTRAN
Z	332	32	31	0-9	44
[	333	33	75	12-5-8	76 *
\	334	34	36	0-6-8	76 *
]	335	35	55	11-5-8	76 *
↑	336	36	17 **	7-8	76 *
←	337	37	20	2-8	76 [1]
blank	240	40	20	no punch	00
!	241	41	52	11-2-8	51
"	242	42	35	0-5-8	62
#	243	43	37	0-7-8	63
$	244	44	53	11-3-8	60
%	245	45	57	11-7-8	64
&	246	46	77	12-7-8	65
'	247	47	14	4-8	66
(	250	50	34	0-4-8	52
)	251	51	74	12-4-8	53
*	252	52	54	11-4-8	47
+	253	53	60	12	45
,	254	54	33	0-3-8	54
−	255	55	40	11	46
.	256	56	73	12-3-8	51
/	257	57	21	0-1	50
0	260	60	12	0	01
1	261	61	01	1	02
2	262	62	02	2	03

Symbol	ASCII	Printer	Mag Tape	Hollerith	FORTRAN
3	263	63	03	3	04
4	264	64	04	4	05
5	265	65	05	5	06
6	266	66	06	6	07
7	267	67	07	7	10
8	270	70	10	8	11
9	271	71	11	9	12
:	272	72	15	5-8	67
;	273	73	56	11-6-8	70
<	274	74	76	12-6-8	76 *
=	275	75	13	3-8	55
>	276	76	16	6-8	76
?	277	77	72	12-2-8	76

Delete	377	DCO	220
NUL	200	X-ON	221
SOM	201	TAPE ON	222
EOA	202	X-OFF	223
EOM	203	TAPE OFF	224
EOT	204	ERROR	225
WRU	205	SYNC	226
RU	206	LEM	227
bell	207	S0	230
FE	210	S1	231
H TAB	211	S2	232
Line feed	212	S3	233
V TAB	213	S4	234
FORM	214	S5	235
RETURN	215	S6	236
SO	216	S7	237
SI	217		

* Undefined form control
** End of file

Chapter 4

The Teletype

The ASR 33 teletype machine manufactured by Teletype Corp. is the basic input-output device for most small computers. The reason is quite simple. The machine runs approximately $800 complete and includes a keyboard, page printer, paper tape punch, and paper tape reader. It is relatively easy to interface to a computer and, although its life is limited, it will run for a long time in most installations because it is not used a great deal once the processor is put in operation.

The teletype can be operated by itself, disconnected from the computer, or it can be operated on line with the computer. This means that if necessary tapes can be generated while the computer is being used for other purposes.

TELETYPE COMPONENTS

A teletype machine is shown in Fig. 4-1 mounted on the pedestal supplied by the manufacturer. Figs. 4-2 and 4-3 are top views showing most of the remaining controls.

The four (middle left) paper punch controls are:

REL—A mechanical release used for threading tape into the punch.

B.SP.—A mechanical backspace that allows the tape to be backed up one space for obliterating unwanted characters.

OFF—A mechanical control that disengages the paper tape punch.

ON—A mechanical control that engages the paper tape punch and allows what is typed on the keyboard to be punched on the tape.

One note of caution here: Any time the teletype is being used the punch should be turned off when the line-off-local switch is being operated or when any other condition exists that might generate a transient signal and cause the punch to operate.

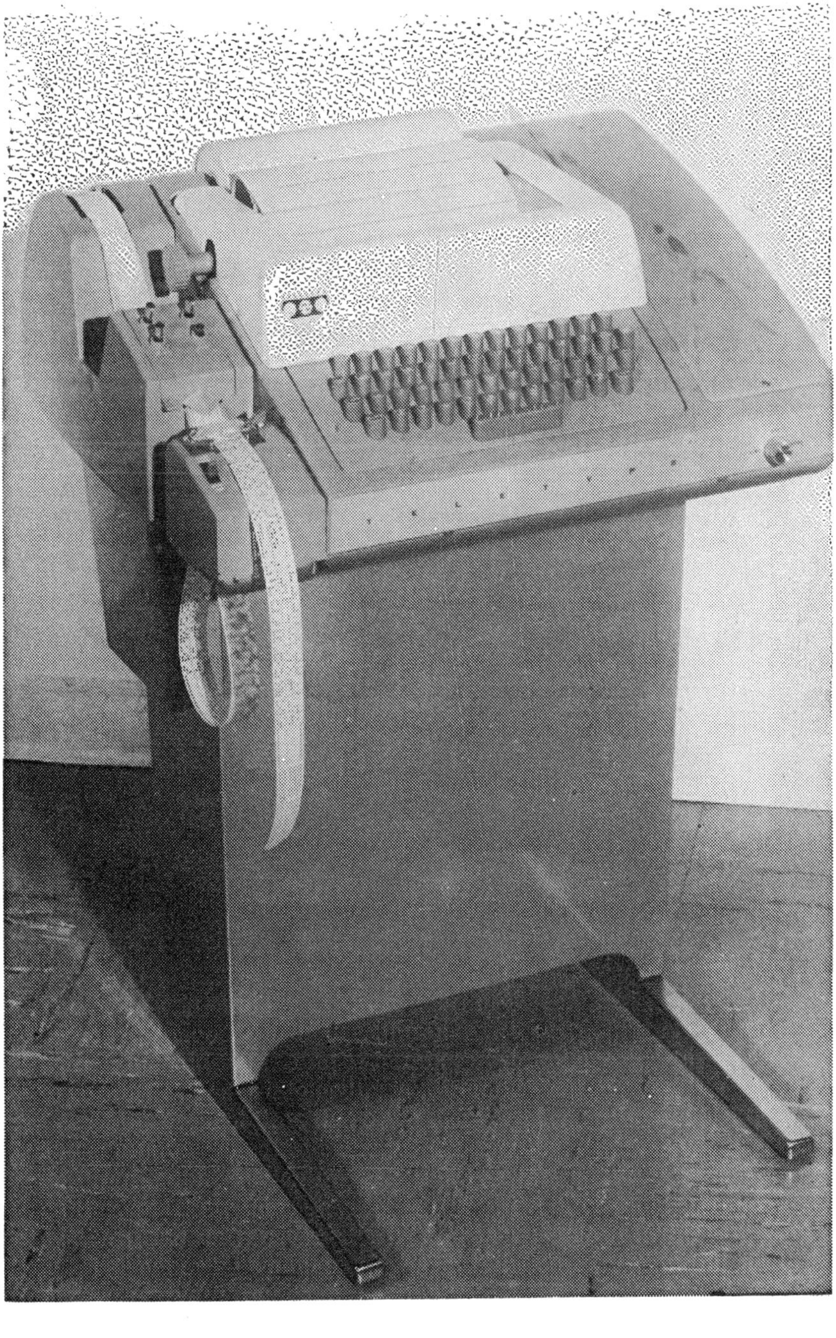

Fig. 4-1. ASR33 teletype machine.

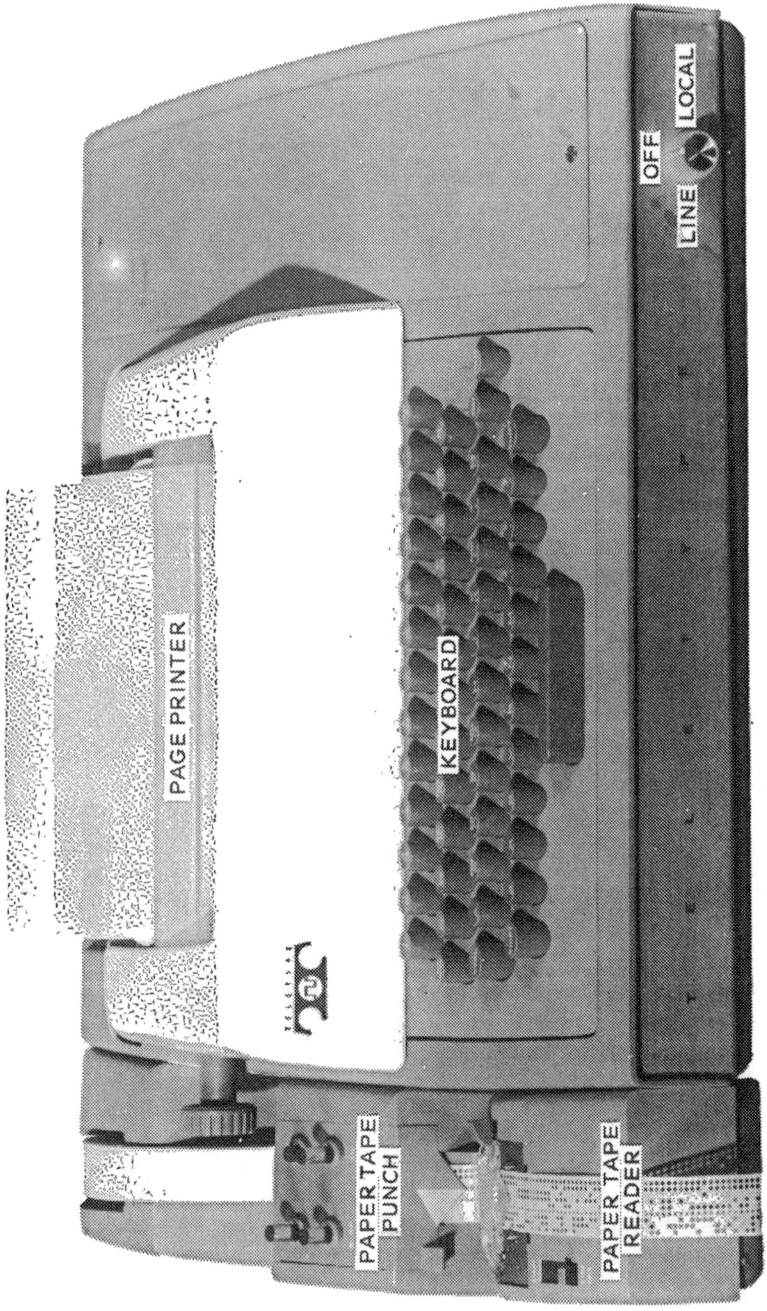

Fig. 4-2. Top view of the ASR33 teletype machine.

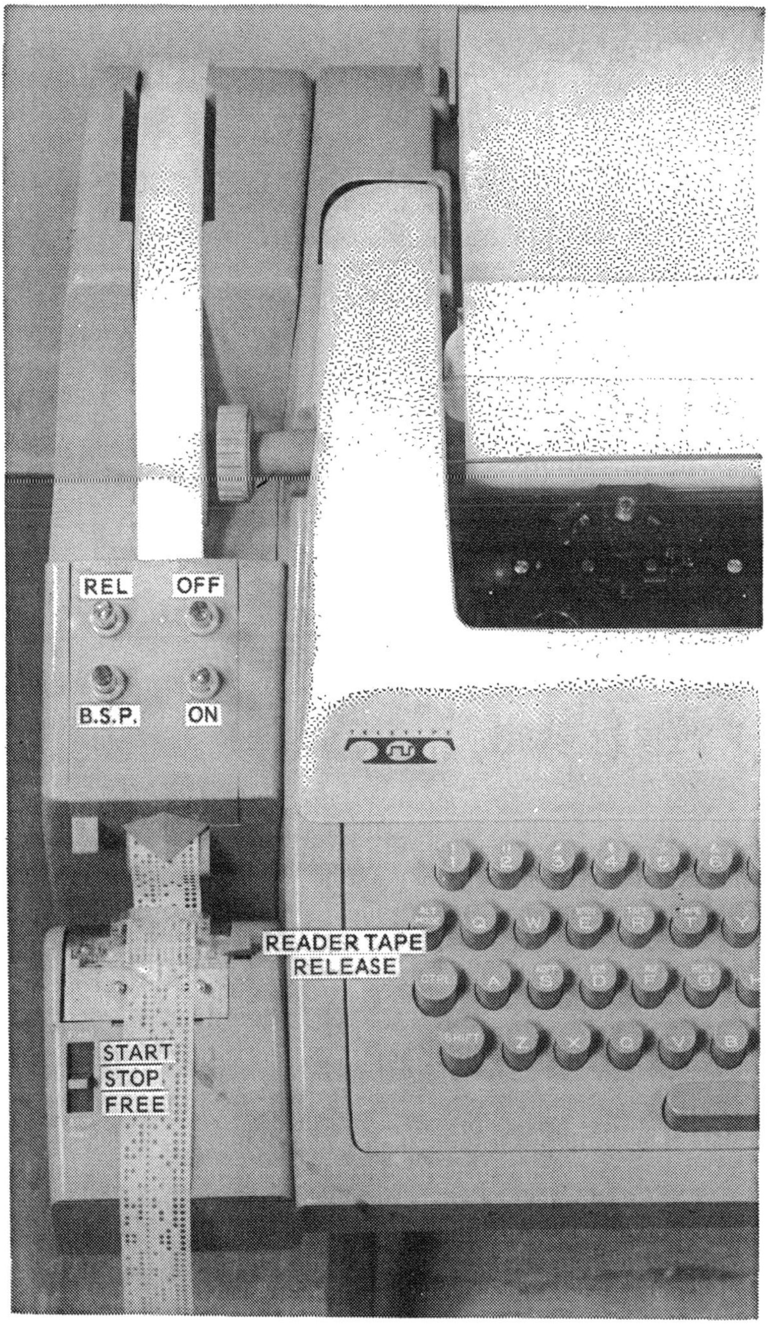

Fig. 4-3. Partial top view showing punch and reader controls.

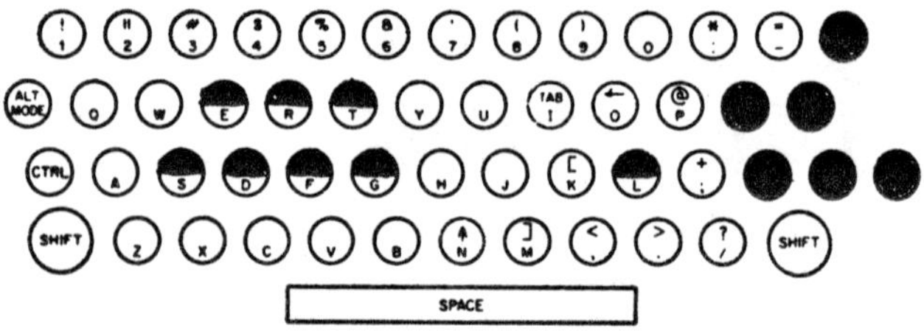

Fig. 4-4. Teletype keyboard.

A B C D E F G H I J K L M N O P Q R S T U V W X Y Z

1 2 3 4 5 6 7 8 9 0 ! " # $ % & ' ( ) * - = @ ← [ ]

\ + ? > < ↑

Fig. 4-5. Type font used in the ASR33 teletype.

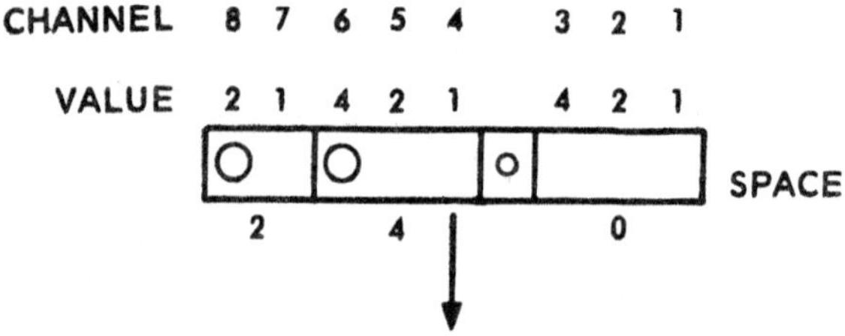

Fig. 4-6. Sketch showing the eight tape channels with space code punched.

The 3-position lever on the paper tape reader controls operation of the reader. In the local position, turning this switch to "start" causes the reader to read a tape. "Stop" causes the reader to stop and "free" allows the tape to be positioned over the reader pins. In the "line" position, the computer is connected to the teletype and, depending on the arrangement, the reader will not function until the computer energizes the proper circuitry.

The reader "tape release" button releases one end of the transparent plastic cover and allows it to be hinged away for tape insertion or removal.

KEYBOARD

The teletype keyboard is somewhat similar to a typewriter keyboard (Fig. 4-4). The main difference lies in the fact that "functions" must be encoded in order to be transmitted to the computer. With a typewriter, the carriage return, line feed and similar things do not have to be sent to a computer or to other equipment, nor do they have to be encoded into electrical signals. The teletype and other computer peripherals, on the other hand, must receive this function information in the form of electrical signals.

With both the "shift" and CTRL keys released, the teletype will print alphabetic characters, numerals, colon, semicolon, minus sign, period, comma, and slash. All other characters are printed with the shift key depressed (Fig. 4-5).

HERE IS—This key operates a drum in the rear of the teletype that is set up in computer operations to do nothing more than generate tape leaders since nothing is punched on the tape while this drum goes through a cycle and generates 20 spaces.

LINE FEED—Normally abbreviated LF, does a line feed operation in the page printer and at the same time generates the electrical code for line feed.

CARRIAGE RETURN—Normally abbreviated CR and combined with line feed CRLF causes the teletype page printer to perform a carriage return and at the same time generates the electrical code for carriage return.

RUB OUT—Will cause no printer action but punches holes in all eight locations across the tape.

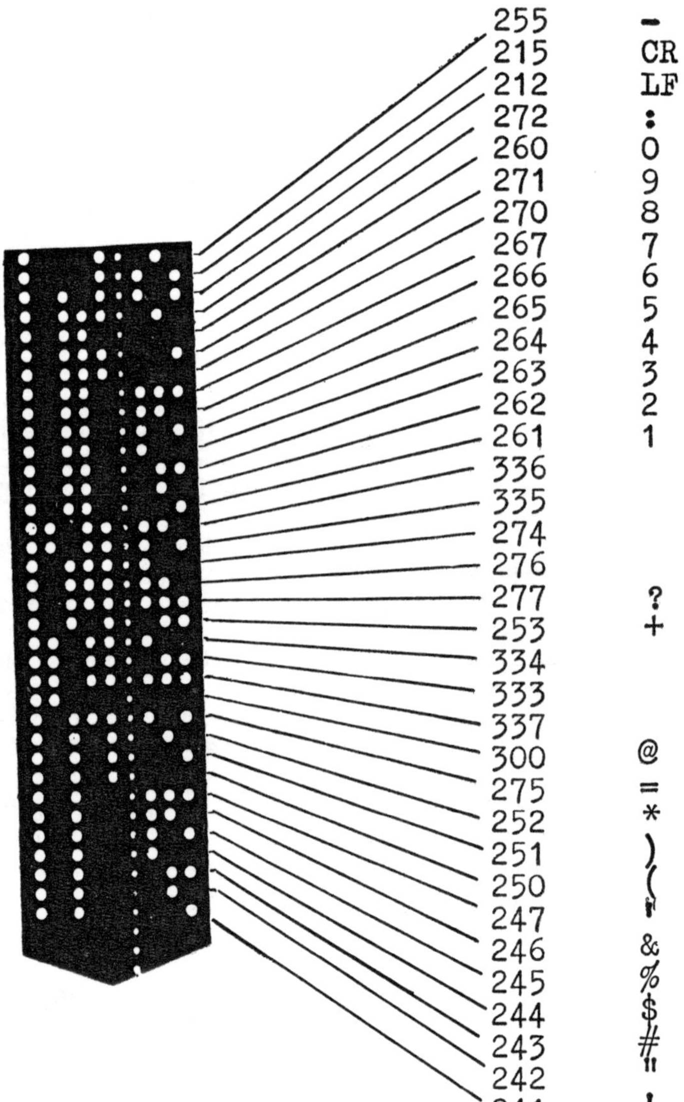

Fig. 4-7. Tape code used with the shift key.

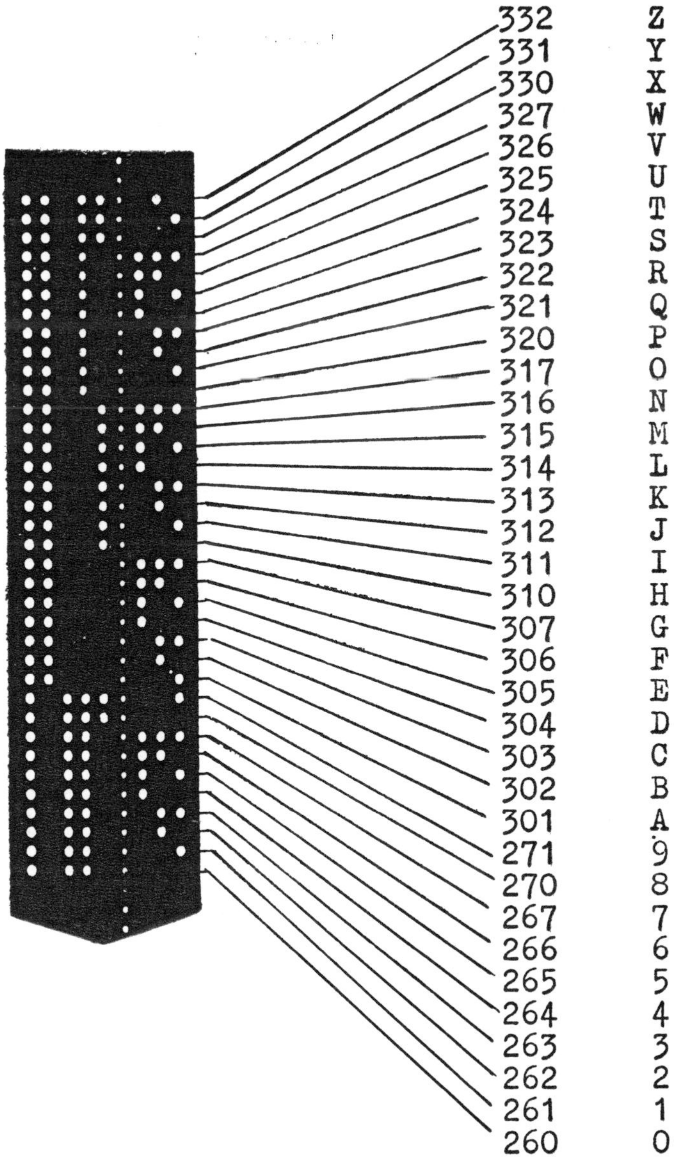

Fig. 4-8. Alpha-numerical codes.

REPT—When pressed before another key will cause the character or function of the second key to be repeated indefinitely as long as both keys are held down.

BREAK—This key breaks the signal line to allow interruption of another teletype.

The keys that are half shaded in Fig. 4-4 generate various control functions when used in conjunction with the CTRL key (and don't confuse this with CRLF which is the combined abbreviation for carriage return, line feed).

SPACE—The space bar is easy to neglect. It causes the page printer to generate a space between words and generates the electrical code for space.

PRINTER

The page printer is used to obtain a printed (hard) copy of anything desired. With the teletype in "local" (off-line operation) every key struck generates copy or the required function and simultaneously punches the character on tape if the tape punch is on. With the teletype in "line" (on-line operation) the teletype is connected to the computer and the computer will control what is printed or punched.

In the next several illustrations, the method of reading punched paper tape is illustrated. To read tape,

1. Determine the direction of motion and insure that the first end that would normally go through the reader is toward you. For the tapes shown you read the bottom character first, then the next one up and so forth.

2. Turn the tape upside down (face down). This should put Channel 1 on your right and leave three channel positions before the sprocket hole.

3. Channels 1, 2, and 3 are treated and read as an octal group; Channels 4, 5 and 6 are read the same way, and Channels 7 and 8 are treated as the first two bits of an octal group. With all of this in mind, the character shown in Fig. 4-6 would be a space function.

Figs. 4-7 through 4-11 show punched tapes and cards with identification of the characters.

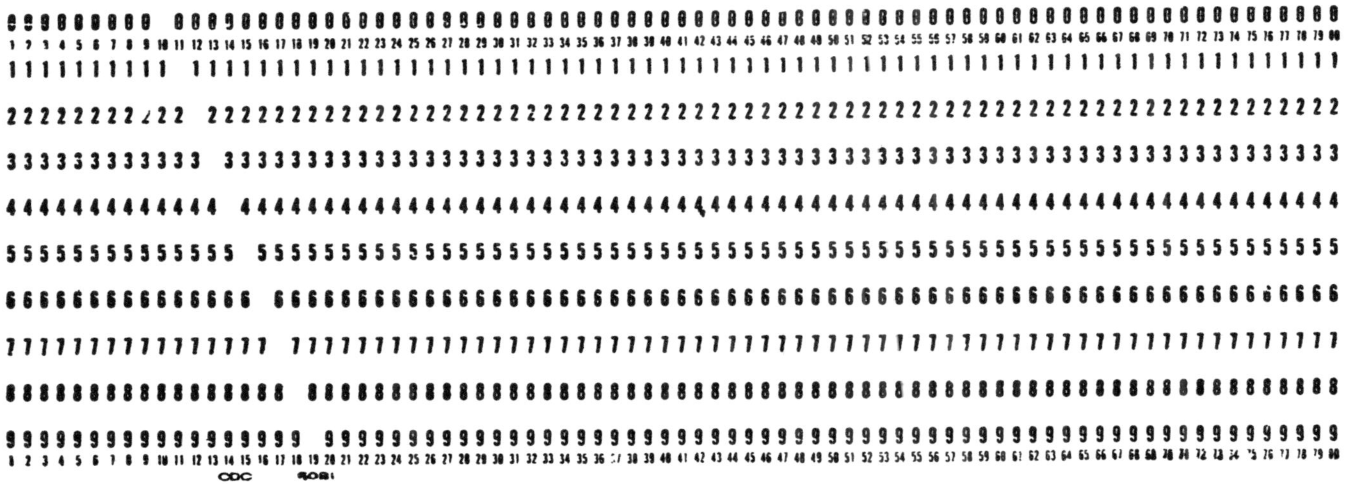

Fig. 4-9. Number codes punched on a card.

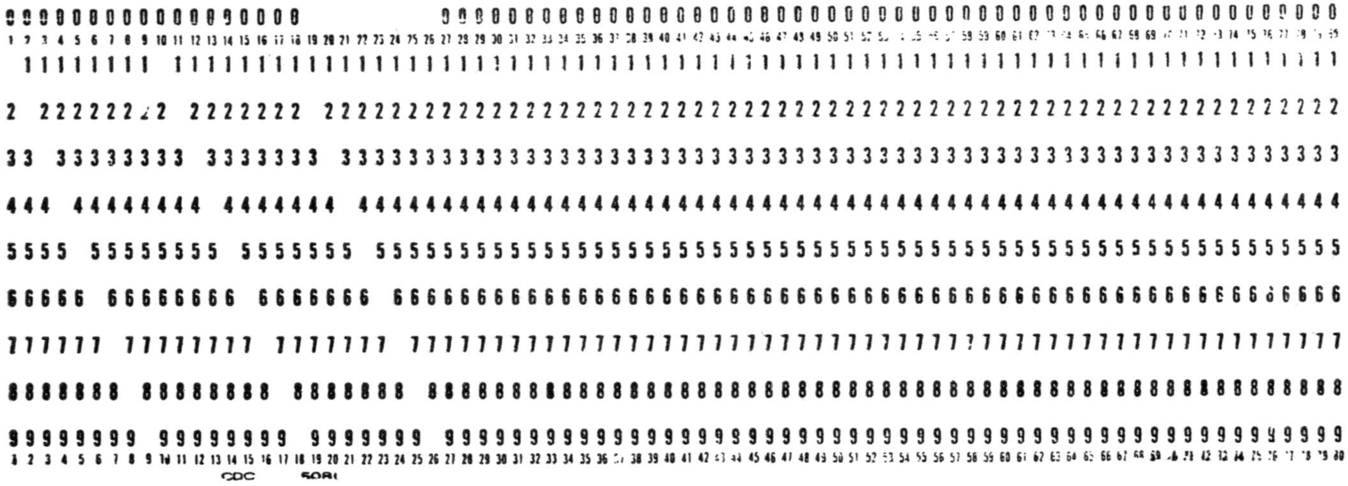

Fig. 4-10. Alphabet code punched on a card.

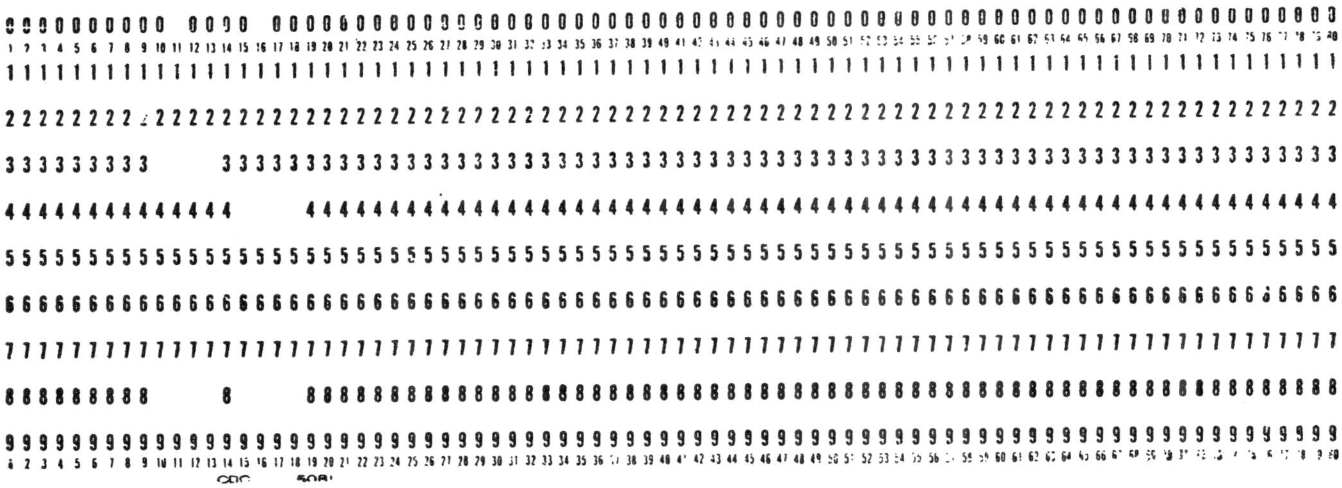

Fig. 4-11. Punched card with random shift key characters.

Chapter 5

Boolean Algebra

For the technician with a reasonably good background in semiconductor circuits and general electronics, the first requirement for an understanding of computer technology is a knowledge of the number and coding systems. With this material covered, the next step is logic. And the requirements in the area of logic are not nearly as involved as a person might expect.

The title of this chapter—Boolean algebra—covers a number of things. Boolean algebra in itself is a 2-state algebra with rules similar to, but not exactly like, regular algebra. Boolean algebra allows the logic designer to state in a very closely structured system the problems associated with computer circuitry. Having stated the problem, he can use the rules of Boolean algebra to manipulate and simplify the circuitry involved to achieve the lowest cost, best operating system with a minimum of effort.

A technician, of course, is not concerned with design; however it is important that he is able to read Boolean algebra statements which are frequently included as part of the computer maintenance manual. It is quite possible to get by without Boolean algebra and still maintain computers, but the attention given to it here makes it a little easier to understand some of the material that follows. If a better understanding of Boolean algebra is required or desired, there are several good books available on the subject.

One of your most important needs is the use of **truth tables**, a means of describing the function of various components in a computer circuit in terms of the output or **function** as a function of the input.

AND, OR AND NOT

Every computer circuit can be reduced to three basic functions: **AND**, **OR** and **NOT**. And two rules will give you almost instant access to any computer diagram as far as determining what the circuits do.

1. AND

A. All inputs to an AND gate must equal 1 for the output or function to equal 1.

B. Any 0 input to an AND gate will result in a 0 output.

2. OR

A. Any 1 input to an OR gate will result in a 1 output.

B. All inputs to an OR gate must be 0 in order to get a 0 output.

3. NOT

A. A 1 input to an inverter (NOT) will give a 0 output.

B. A 0 input to an inverter (NOT) will give a 1 output.

With these six facts under your belt it is possible to analyze practically any computer circuitry. Let's take that a step further and see if we can analyze a NAND gate and a NOR gate with the information just given.

A NAND gate is an AND gate followed by an inverter. Going back to the AND statement, the first parts of it still hold true. The output will be inverted; therefore, where the output is stated as 1 we will change it to 0 and where it is stated as 0 we will change it to 1. The statements for a NAND gate then, would be:

4. NAND

A. All inputs to a NAND gate must equal 1 for the output to equal 0.

B. Any 0 input to a NAND gate will result in a 1 output.

And for the NOR gate (OR with an output inverter)

5. NOR

A. Any 1 input to a NOR gate will result in a 0 output.

B. All inputs to a NOR gate must be 0 in order to get a 1 output.

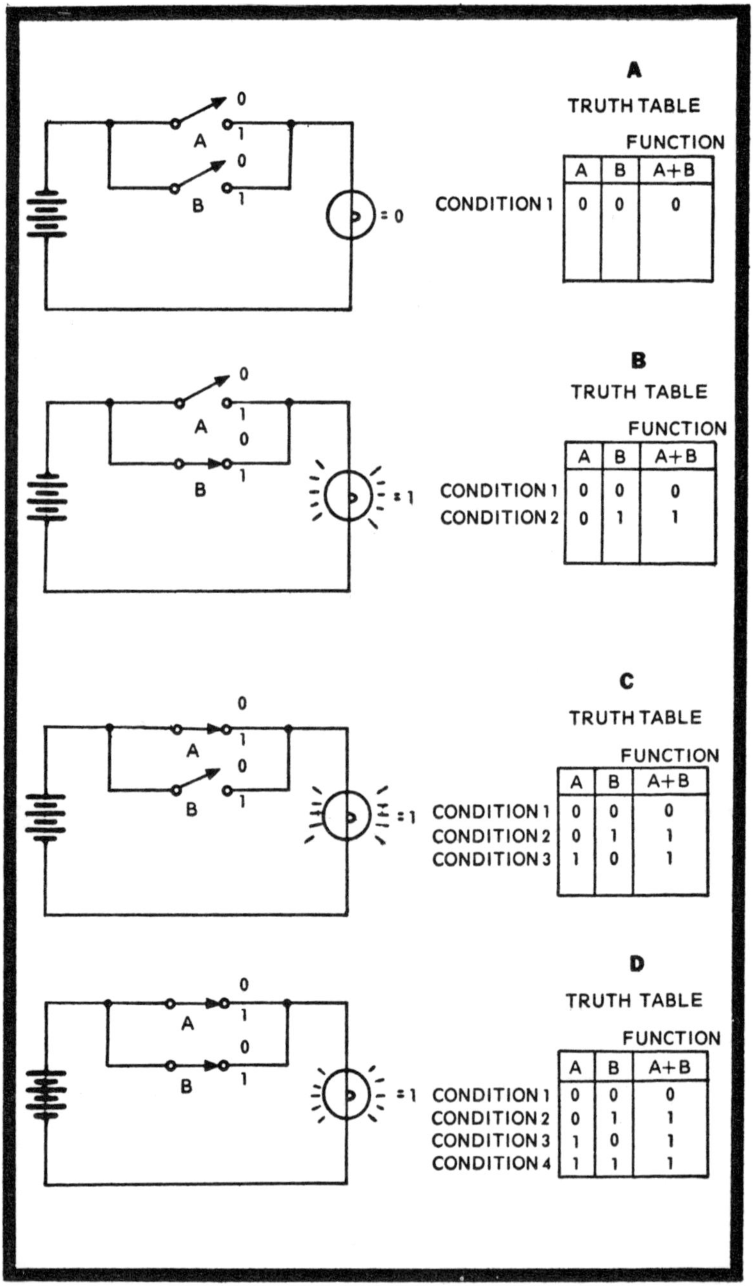

Fig. 5-1. Development of a truth table for an OR function.

From those 10 statements almost any condition in a circuit can be analyzed, so you are on your way.

TRUTH TABLES

Truth tables have been refined over several years time to make them more useful in the study of digital logic equations. They serve as a proof of various functions in Boolean algebra and switching logic. Let's start by predefining conditions:

1. Any switch with an open contact represents a binary 0.

2. Any switch with a closed contact represents a binary 1.

3. A lamp not lit represents a binary 0.

4. A lamp lit represents a binary 1.

With these predefined conditions, we can start examining some situations. We will assign variable names to the switches and attempt to discover under which switch conditions, open or closed, the lamp is lit or not lit.

Fig. 5-1 will be used to demonstrate the condititions and develop the truth table for an OR function. First, Fig. 5-1A shows a battery, two switches labeled A and B, and a lamp. From your knowledge of electronics it is obvious that the lamp will not be lit. We said that an open switch would represent a 0, so we have plotted a zero under the corresponding variable in the truth table, and since the lamp will not be lit we have plotted a zero in the function column. The function A+B is read A OR B. Since both A and B are 0 in Fig. 5-1A we have plotted 0s in both columns A and B.

Now, referring to Fig. 5-1B, we have a closed switch, B (equal to 1), and an open switch, A (binary 0). Again, from your knowledge of electronics, you know that the lamp will now be lit or equal to 1. Again we plot (under condition 2) a 0 in column A, a 1 in column B, and the function is now 1.

Fig. 5-1C shows the third condition. Switch A is closed (binary 1), switch B is open (binary 0) and the lamp will be lit. Condition 4 (Fig. 5-1D) shows the final combination and the output function.

From the forgoing, we can learn several things. First, truth tables can be developed for any logic function and they are extremely useful for determining the conditions of logic systems. The output function for two different logic equations can be developed and the two output functions compared to see if they correspond or are equal.

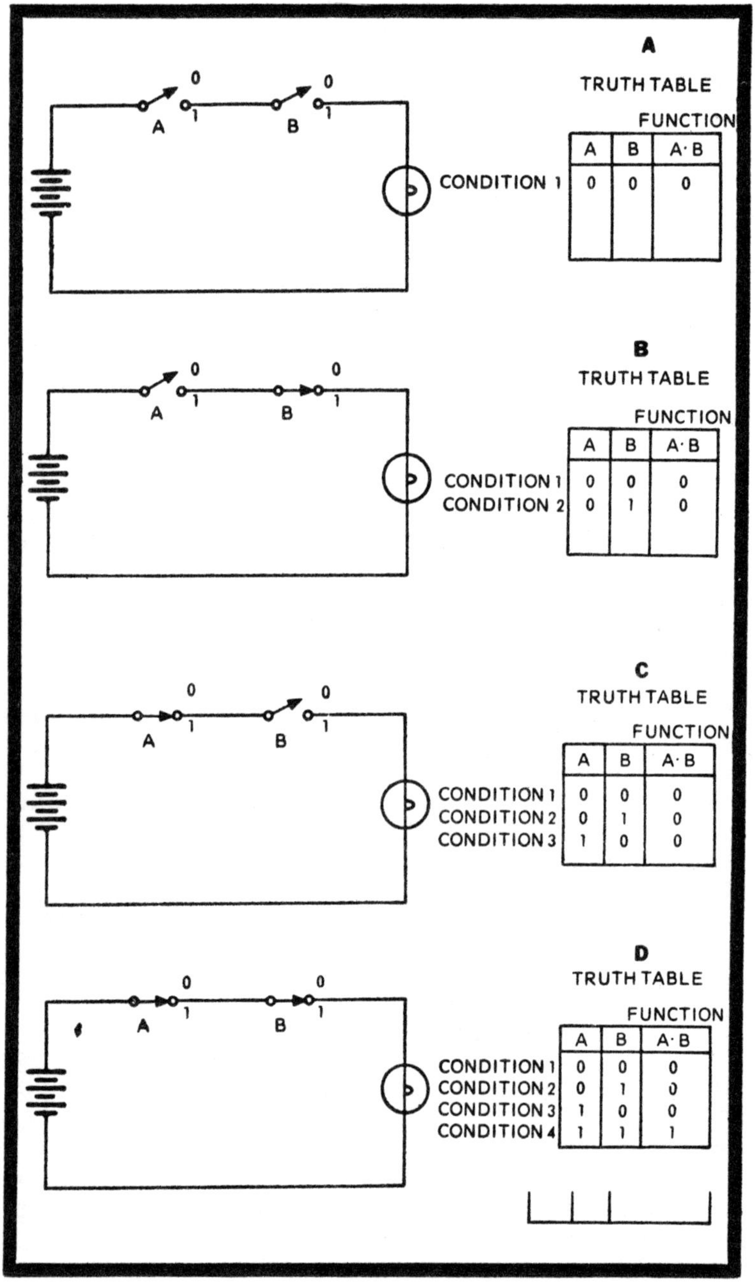

Fig. 5-2. Development of a truth table for an AND function.

One thing should be apparent at this point. The various combinations of conditions could be listed in any order, but the most advantageous is a listing in binary counting sequence. In this way, all combinations are covered and none omitted.

Figs. 5-2A through 2D show the various conditions for an AND gate circuit. Although actual gating circuitry involves diodes, transistors, and common-emitter amplifiers, the voltage levels are defined as 1 or 0 (there are only two) and the gates follow the same rules.

The remaining element mentioned was the NOT or negation or inverter. The truth table for the NOT function is simply stated: a 0 in equals a 1 out and a 1 in equals an 0 out.

For two variables (A and B), there are 2 squared (2x2) combinations or four combinations that must be evaluated (see Table 5-1). Three variables require cubed (2x2x2) or eight combinations and the progression continues from there; 2 to the fourth power for four variables, 2 to the fifth power for five variables, etc.

POSITIVE & NEGATIVE LOGIC

In every instance, one of the first things that a logic designer must do is define circuit conditions. We will start by saying we are using positive logic definitions.

In positive logic, we define the most positive voltage level as a binary 1 and the least positive as a binary 0. The waveforms in Fig. 5-3 illustrate this a little better. Negative logic is the reverse of positive logic. We define the most negative level as a binary 1 and the least negative level as a binary 0.

TABLE 5-1. LOGIC COMBINATION WITH AND THREE VARIABLES.

A	B		A	B	C	
0	0		0	0	0	
0	1	4 Combinations	0	0	1	
1	0		0	1	0	
1	1		0	1	1	8 Combinations
			1	0	0	
			1	0	1	
			1	1	0	
			1	1	1	

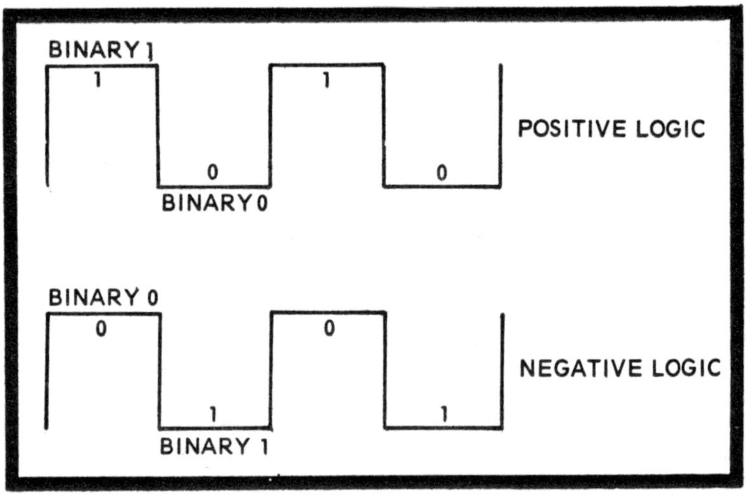

Fig. 5-3. Logic circuits use either positive or negative 1 and 0 conditions.

Notice that we have said nothing about either the absolute voltage levels (i.e., 5 volts, 3 volts, 20 volts, -10 volts) nor have we mentioned the ground reference level. For the definition of positive and negative logic, these two items make no difference. If two types of logic circuits, using different voltage levels and-or different ground references are to be used, then it becomes necessary to consider these items to insure that the circuits will work with each other without one destroying the other.

For our purposes let's say that 5 volts positive equals a binary 1 and 0 volts equals a binary 0. We would not have to mention the voltage levels to determine that the high level was a binary 1 (positive logic) and the low level was a binary 0.

The AND circuit shown in Fig. 5-4A is drawn in Standard MIL806B form. It shows the input variables and says, for logic purposes, that the conditions shown in Fig. 5-4B will prevail. If 0 volts (binary 0) is applied to both inputs, the output will be a binary 0 or 0 volts for condition 1. Conditions 2, 3, and 4 are shown in the truth table as well as in Fig. 5-4B. Fig. 5-5 shows the conditions for a logic OR gate and Fig. 5-6 the conditions for an inverter.

BOOLEAN LAWS

Boolean algebra is based on a set of laws in the same way that conventional algebra is based on laws. But there are some

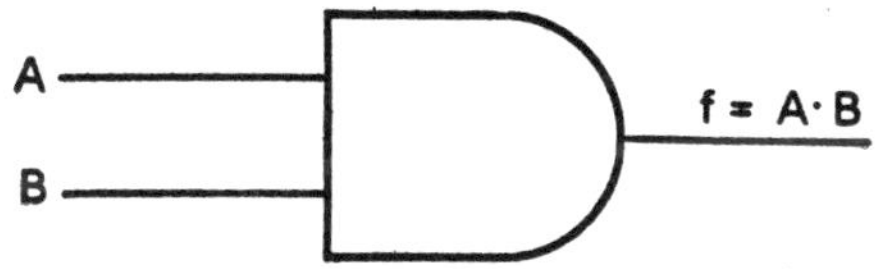

A

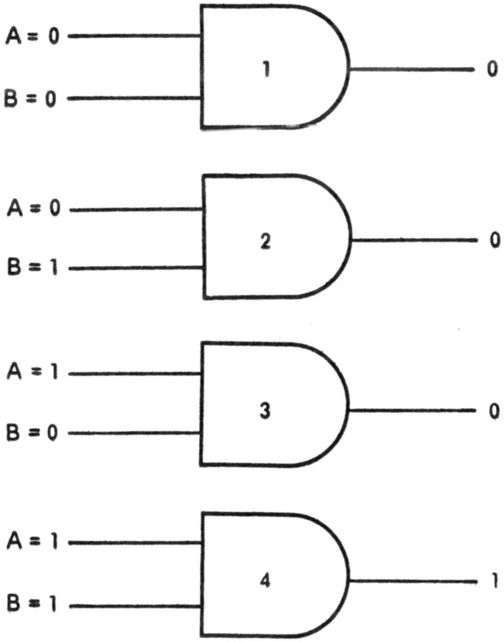

B

	A	B	A·B
1	0	0	0
2	0	1	0
3	1	0	0
4	1	1	1

C

Fig. 5-4. AND gate conditions and truth table.

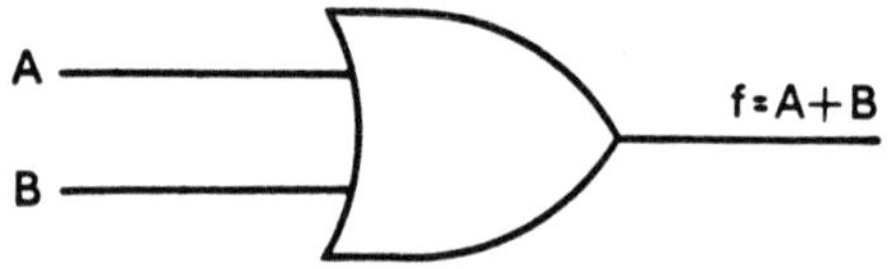

A

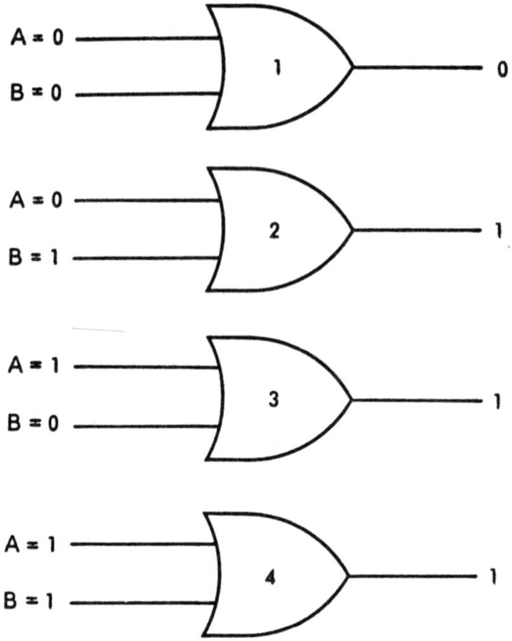

B

	A	B	A+B
1	0	0	0
2	0	1	1
3	1	0	1
4	1	1	1

C

Fig. 5-5. OR gate conditions and truth table.

differences. Probably the first and most important is that Boolean deals with only two variables, 0 and 1, where algebra can have an infinite number of positive and negative numbers. The second difference is that Boolean algebra laws do not apply to ordinary algebra and vice versa.

The uses of Boolean algebra in the computer industry are many and varied, but most are involved in the design area and this book is written to make you a competent technician. This being the case we cover Boolean algebra in a simplified form. When you are finished with this chapter you should be able to write simple expressions from diagrams, turn simple expressions into diagrams, simplify and manipulate uncomplicated logic expressions and have a fair knowledge of Veitch diagrams. This should give you enough information to understand the remainder of the material.

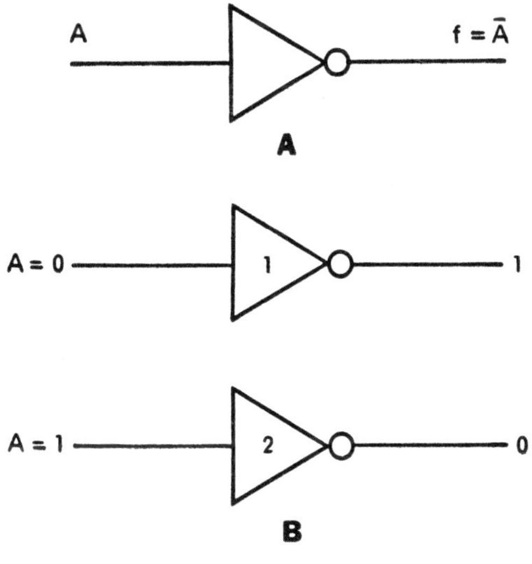

	A	$\bar{A}$
1	0	1
2	1	0

C

Fig. 5-6. Inverter conditions and truth table.

CONVENTIONS

1. A OR B is written A + B.

2. A AND B is written A·B or simply AB. Here we use the form AB.

3. A OR B is sometimes referred to as a **logical sum.**

4. A AND B is sometimes referred to as a **logical product.**

5. Logical equations or logical statements may take two general or basic forms:

   A. The sum of products form: AB + BC

   B. The product of sums form: (A+B)(B+C)

6. In the sum of products form, AB and BC are considered natural groups requiring no sign of grouping.

7. In the product of sums form, the parentheses are considered signs of grouping.

8. The complement or negation or NOT of A is written $\overline{A}$, and is called NOT· A.

9. A vinculum or NOT sign over more than one variable is considered a sign of grouping and must be removed for certain purposes in procedures that will be described later. $\overline{A+B+C}$ is grouped by the vinculum which covers all three variables and the OR operators connecting them.

In the following material, cover the page with a card, move the card down to the first asterisk and read the statement, then fill in the blank or answer as appropriately as possible.

1. In the logical statement A + B + C, the logical operator(s) is or are____________. (AND; OR)

*

OR

2. The following statement is a__________________ (product of sums or sum of products). ABC + BCD.

*
Sum of products

3. The vinculum is considered a sign of ________________ when it extends over more than one variable.

*
Grouping

4. Parentheses are considered ________________.

*
Signs of grouping

A	B	C	AB	BC	AB+BC		
0	0	0	0	0	0		= $\bar{A}\bar{B}\bar{C}$
0	0	1	0	0	0		$\bar{A}\bar{B}C$
0	1	0	0	0	0		$\bar{A}B\bar{C}$
0	1	1	0	1	1		$\bar{A}BC$
1	0	0	0	0	0		$A\bar{B}\bar{C}$
1	0	1	0	0	0		$A\bar{B}C$
1	1	0	1	0	1		$AB\bar{C}$
1	1	1	1	1	1		ABC
			4	5	6		

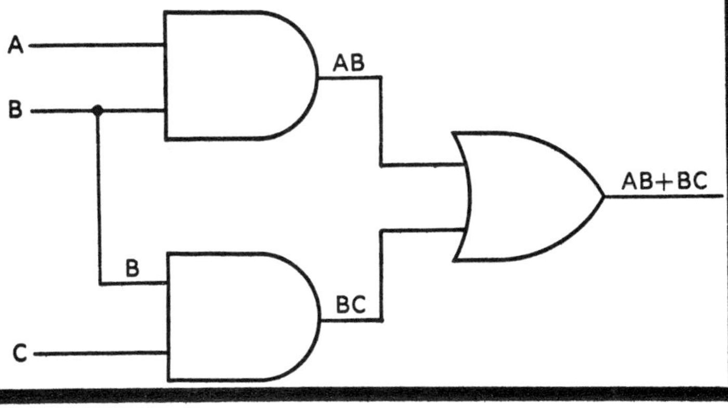

Fig. 5-7. Logic diagram and truth table for a sum of products.

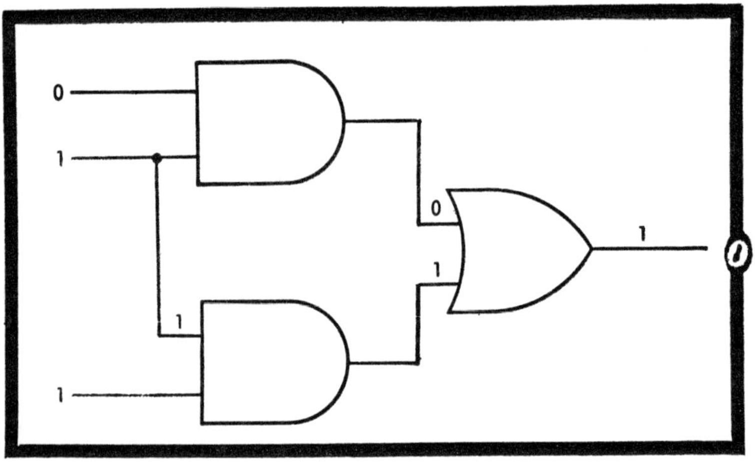

Fig. 5-8. ABC input into this sum of products logic circuit gives a 1 output.

The logic for a sum of products statement could be drawn as shown in Fig. 5-7. Notice that the output gate is an OR gate since the final operation to be performed is the OR operation or logical sum. The AND gates form the logical products which are then logically summed by the OR gate. The truth table in Fig. 5-7 depicts the entire operation.

Notice that to start, we place A, B and C across the top left columns in the truth table to indicate the inputs. We then determine that for three inputs there are eight possible combinations and we write in these possibilities. In the first column we determine what A ANDed with B gives as an output. Remember that both of these inputs must be 1 to get a 1 out and the only two combinations which have A and B a 1 at the same time are 110 and 111. In the next column we evaluate the AND function of B and C. In the last column we evaluate the entire expression by ORing columns 4 and 5 and arrive at column 6 which tells us that the only time AB + BC would give a 1 output would be when A is 0, B is 1 and C is 1; when A is 1, B is 1 and C is 0, or when all three equal a 1.

Later, in Veitch diagrams we are going to assign individual terms to each of these sets of variable conditions. The initial assumption is made that A normally equals 1, B normally equals 1, and C normally equals 1. Then, where A equals 0, we use $\overline{A}$; where B equals 0 we substitute $\overline{B}$; and where C is 0 we substitute $\overline{C}$. Now back to the evaluation we were making. With the truth table complete it is easy to see which inputs will result in a 1 output.

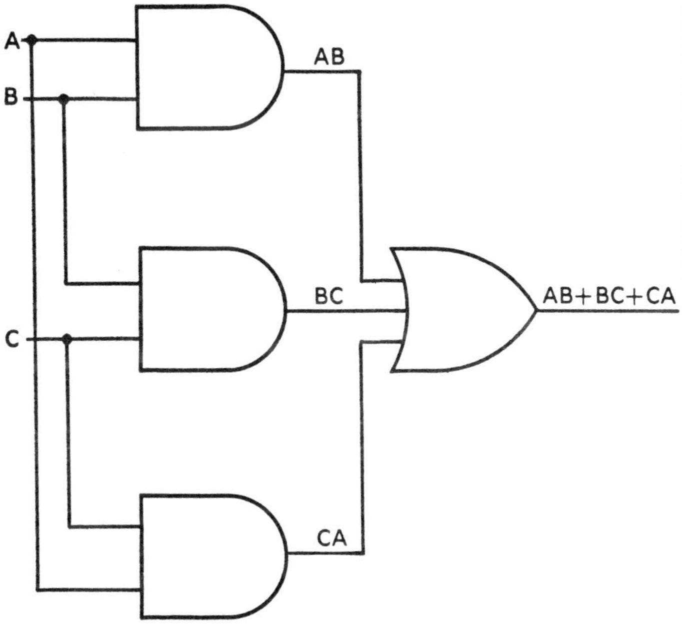

A	B	C	AB	BC	CA	AB+BC+CA
0	0	0	0	0	0	0
0	0	1	0	0	0	0
0	1	0	0	0	0	0
0	1	1	0	1	0	1
1	0	0	0	0	0	0
1	0	1	0	0	1	1
1	1	0	1	0	0	1
1	1	1	1	1	1	1

Fig. 5-9. Sum of products gating circuit with three AND gates ORed.

TABLE 5-2. BASIC LAWS AND COMMON IDENTITIES OF BOOLEAN ALGEBRA

Identity:	A equals A	$\bar{A}$ equals $\bar{A}$
Commutative:	AB equals BA	A+B equals B+A
Associative:	A(BC) equals ABC	A+(B+C) equals A+B+C
Idempotent:	AA equals A	A+A equals A
Double Negative:	$\bar{\bar{A}}$ equals A	
Complementary:	$A\bar{A}$ equals 0	$A+\bar{A}$ equals 1
Intersection:	A·1 equals A	A·0 equals 0
Union:	A+1 equals 1	A+0 equals A
DeMorgan:	$\overline{AB}$ equals $\bar{A}+\bar{B}$	$\overline{A+B}$ equals $\bar{A}\bar{B}$
Distributive:	A(B+C) equals AB+AC	A+BC equals (A+B)(A+C)
Absorption:	A(A+B) equals A	A+AB equals A
Common Identities:	$A(\bar{A}+B)$ equals AB	$A+\bar{A}B$ equals A+B

Proof that $\bar{A}BC$ will give a 1 output is shown in Fig. 5-8. Remember that any 0 into an AND gate results in a 0 out. The upper AND gate has a 0 input, so will give a 0 out. The lower AND gate has two 1s in and therefore gives a 1 out. Any 1 into an OR gate will result in a 1 output and that is what we have. It would be good practice to do the same analysis with the other conditions and prove that where the truth table says a 0 would be the output, assigning these values actually results in a 0 output and where a 1 output is indicated, a 1 is the output.

In Fig. 5-9 we have drawn a gating circuit for the expression: AB + BC + CA. In this case the sum of products form is used, but there are three products ORed together, which requires a 3-input OR gate with three AND gates.

There are a number of basic laws and some "common identities" associated with Boolean algebra. Studying these can give a little better understanding of computer logic. It is not imperative that a computer technician have an in-depth knowledge of the methods of Boolean expression simplification and manipulation, but a basic understanding is very useful. The Basic Laws and Common Identities are listed in Table 5-2.

The Laws of Identity say nothing more complicated than that all variables with the same name must have the same value. If A is a 1, any other A in the system will be 1 at the same time. In the computer you will be studying, for example, one of the much used variables is MSCX. This is a 1-microsecond pulse occurring once every 8 microseconds and it is wired directly to every point in the computer that uses it.

The Commutative and Associative Laws simply indicate that the arrangement of variables is not important and can be changed or grouped differently as long as they are either ANDed or ORed. Some additional rules apply for sum of products and product of sums arrangements.

Finally, before proceeding to examine the remaining laws with truth tables and switches, the Double Negative Law says simply that if an expression or variable is inverted twice it will be the original.

The Idempotent Law is an extension of the basic law of identity. If As must all be equal, then they must be ganged as shown in Fig. 5-10 to properly illustrate the Idempotent Law. The first truth table in Fig. 5-10 shows that A+A is equal to either A alone.

For the Complementary Laws, two things must be remembered: 1. Any 1 into an OR circuit gives a 1 output; and 2. The complement of a variable always has a value opposite the variable. In Fig. 5-11, if A equals 0, $\bar{A}$ must equal 1, if A

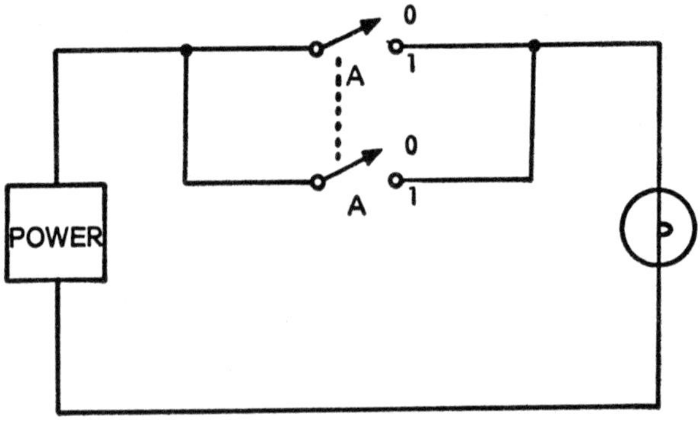

A	A	A+A
0	0	0
1	1	1

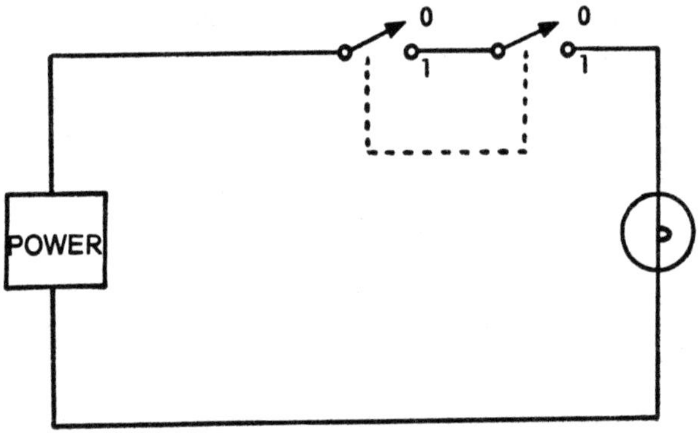

A	A	A·A
0	0	0
1	1	1

Fig. 5-10. Circuits and truth tables illustrating the Idempotent Law.

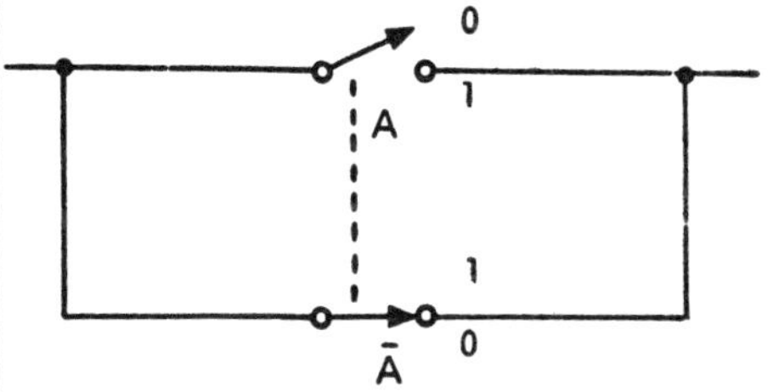

A	Ā	A+Ā
0	1	1
1	0	1

Fig. 5-11. Circuit and truth table illustrating the Complementary Laws.

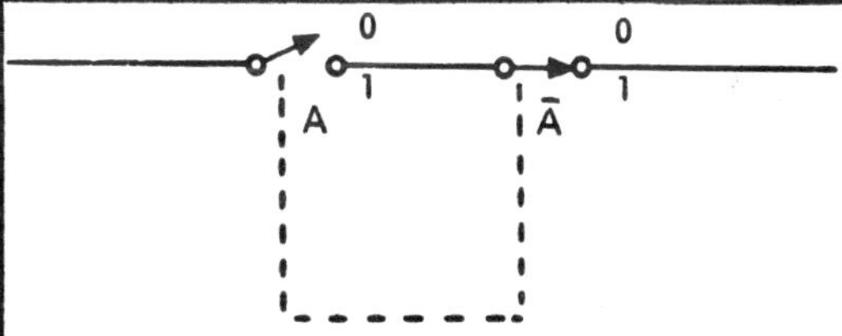

A	Ā	A·Ā
0	1	0
1	0	0

Fig. 5-12. Circuit and truth table illustrating the second Complementary Law.

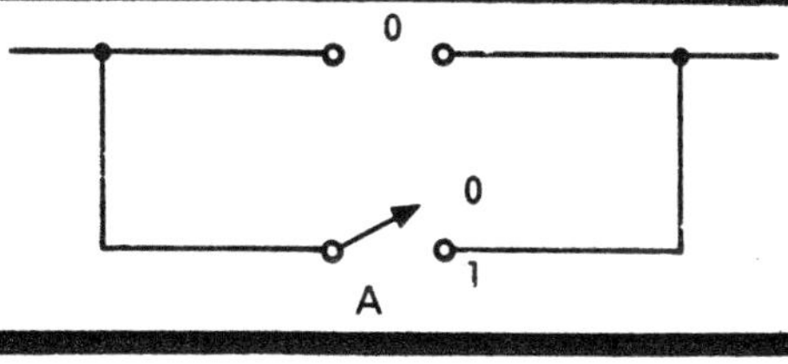

A	0	A+0
0	0	0
1	0	1

Fig. 5-13. Circuit and truth table illustrating the first Law of Union.

A	0	A·0
0	0	0
1	0	0

Fig. 5-14. Circuit and truth table illustrating the first Law of Intersection.

equals 1, then Ā must equal 0. If this is the case there will always be a 1 into an OR circuit with A and Ā as inputs and the output will always be 1.

For the second part of the Complementary Law, since any 0 into an AND circuit results in a 0 output, the diagram and truth table in Fig. 5-12 illustrate that the output would always be 0.

The first Law of Union (OR) says A + 0 equals A. The truth table and diagram in Fig. 5-13 show why.

The first Law of Intersection (AND) says A • A equals 0. Again, the diagram and truth table in Fig. 5-14 show why. The second Law of Union is illustrated in Fig. 5-15 and the second Law of Intersection in Fig. 5-16.

The truth tables and gate structures in Fig. 5-17 show the fundamental ideas behind DeMorgan's Theorem. In each case all three variables are for a 3-variable expression and their complements are shown as inputs. Finally, both the inverted input and inverted output functions are shown along with the gates that illustrate the functions. Gate structures available in modern ICs are the NOR and NAND.

The first part of the Distributive Law says A(B + C) equals AB + AC. The truth table proof of this is shown in Fig. 5-18. Truth tables, used carefully and with thought, are

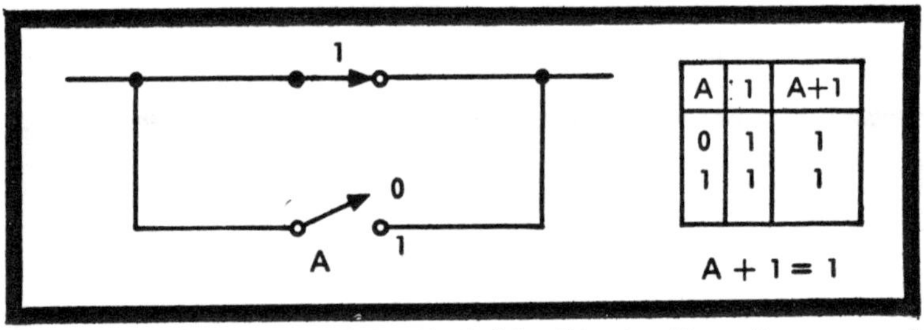

Fig. 5-15. Circuit and truth table illustrating the second Law of Union.

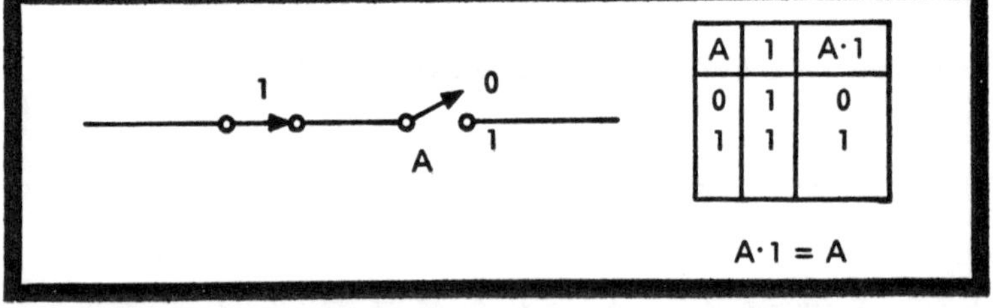

Fig. 5-16. Circuit and truth table illustrating the second Law of Intersection.

A	B	C	$\bar{A}$	$\bar{B}$	$\bar{C}$	A+B+C	$\overline{A+B+C}$	$\bar{A}\cdot\bar{B}\cdot\bar{C}$
0	0	0	1	1	1	0	1	1
0	0	1	1	1	0	1	0	0
0	1	0	1	0	1	1	0	0
0	1	1	1	0	0	1	0	0
1	0	0	0	1	1	1	0	0
1	0	1	0	1	0	1	0	0
1	1	0	0	0	1	1	0	0
1	1	1	0	0	0	1	0	0

A	B	C	$\bar{A}$	$\bar{B}$	$\bar{C}$	A·B·C	$\overline{A\cdot B\cdot C}$	$\bar{A}+\bar{B}+\bar{C}$
0	0	0	1	1	1	0	1	1
0	0	1	1	1	0	0	1	1
0	1	0	1	0	1	0	1	1
0	1	1	1	0	0	0	1	1
1	0	0	0	1	1	0	1	1
1	0	1	0	1	0	0	1	1
1	1	0	0	0	1	0	1	1
1	1	1	0	0	0	1	0	0

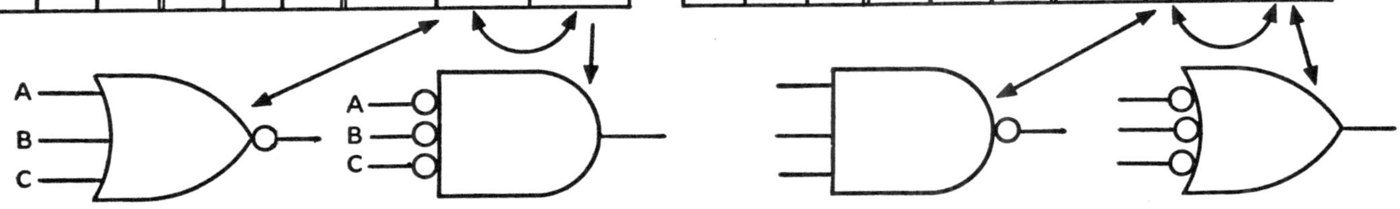

Fig. 5-17. Principles of DeMorgan's Theorem.

A	B	C
0	0	0
0	0	1
0	1	0
0	1	1
1	0	0
1	0	1
1	1	0
1	1	1
1	2	3

B+C	A·(B+C)	A·B	A·C	A·B+A·C
0	0	0	0	0
1	0	0	0	0
1	0	0	0	0
1	0	0	0	0
0	0	0	0	0
1	1	0	1	1
1	1	1	0	1
1	1	1	1	1
2 and 3 ORed	ANDed with 1	1 and 2 ANDed	1 and 3 ANDed	Last 2 ORed

Fig. 5-18. Truth table proof of the Distributive Law.

A	B	C	BC	A+BC	A+B	A+C	(A+B)(A+C)
0	0	0	0	0	0	0	0
0	0	1	0	0	0	1	0
0	1	0	0	0	1	0	0
0	1	1	1	1	1	1	1
1	0	0	0	1	1	1	1
1	0	1	0	1	1	1	1
1	1	0	0	1	1	1	1
1	1	1	1	1	1	1	1

Fig. 5-19. Truth table showing the equivalence of A + BC and (A+B)(A+C).

powerful tools for the evaluation of logical expressions. Use them frequently as you study this book. Get familiar with them.

The truth table in Fig. 5-19 illustrates the equivalence of A + BC and (A + B)(A + C). Notice again that many things can be learned from a truth table. Also notice that the equations are worked (again) from inside the brackets out. Also notice two very important uses of the OR and AND operators:

1. Anytime the OR function is being performed, simply look for a 1 in either (or any) of the variables. If any of them is a 1, the output will be a 1.

2. Anytime the AND function is being performed, any 0 in any variable or expression will yield a 0 as an output.

Some simple practice in the use of truth tables should be worth while. Attempt to prove the following relationships using truth tables:

1. $A(A+B)$ equals A

2. $A + AB$ equals A

3. $(A + B)(\bar{A} + B)$ equals B

4. $AB + \bar{A}B$ equals B

5. $(A + B)(B + C)(C + \bar{A})$ equals $(A + B)(C + \bar{A})$

6. $AB + BC + C\bar{A}$ equals $AB + C\bar{A}$

7. $A + \bar{A}B$ equals $A + B$

8. $A(\bar{A} + B)$ equals AB

VEITCH DIAGRAMS

Veitch diagrams can be used to advantage in a number of areas in the computer field. In particular, it is sometimes desirable to decode time segments from counters. Since this is done quite extensively in computers, it is sometimes nice to be able to pinpoint the source of unwanted signals which can creep in for one reason or another in computer circuitry and cause more that the required time segment to be generated or remove a desired part.

For these reasons and for the reason that encoders and decoders of other types can be studied to advantage using Veitch Diagrams, we present them here in an abbreviated form but with sufficient detail to promote a sound understanding without spending days.

One of the most desirable ways to begin a discussion of Veitch Diagrams is to start with the truth table again since it is from this that the diagrams are derived. The Veitch diagram, in addition to being a good tool, is nothing more than an extension of truth tables, allowing the user to see the various relationships a little better.

If the assumption is made that all variables are 1 (A equals 1, B equals 1 and C equals 1) and that all complements of variables are 0 ($\bar{A}$ equals 0, $\bar{B}$ equals 0 and $\bar{C}$) then each of the counts represented in the truth table can be represented in terms of variables as shown in Fig. 5-20. Notice the effect in Fig. 5-21:

$$f_0 = \bar{A}\ \bar{B}\ \bar{C}.$$

If this were plotted in a truth table, when A is 0, B is 0 and C is 0, then $\bar{A}$ is 1, $\bar{B}$ is 1, $\bar{C}$ is 1, and f0 will equal 1. These functions, f0, f1, f2, and so forth are the basis for the Veitch diagram.

Some additional interesting and helpful relationships are worth mentioning before getting into the actual use of Veitch

A	B	C	FUNCTION	
0	0	0	$\bar{A}\ \bar{B}\ \bar{C}$	f_0
0	0	1	$\bar{A}\ \bar{B}\ C$	f_1
0	1	0	$\bar{A}\ B\ \bar{C}$	f_2
0	1	1	$\bar{A}\ B\ C$	f_3
1	0	0	$A\ \bar{B}\ \bar{C}$	f_4
1	0	1	$A\ \bar{B}\ C$	f_5
1	1	0	$A\ B\ \bar{C}$	f_6
1	1	1	$A\ B\ C$	f_7

Fig. 5-20. Truth table based on the assumption that all variables are 1 and all complements are 0.

						f0=1	f2=1		
A	B	C	$\bar{A}$	$\bar{B}$	$\bar{C}$	$\bar{A}\cdot\bar{B}\cdot\bar{C}$	$\bar{A}$	B	$\bar{C}$
0	0	0	1	1	1	1		0	
0	0	1	1	1	0	0		0	
0	1	0	1	0	1	0		1	
0	1	1	1	0	0	0		0	
1	0	0	0	1	1	0		0	
1	0	1	0	1	0	0		0	
1	1	0	0	0	1	0		0	
1	1	1	0	0	0	0		0	

Fig. 5-21. Truth table establishing the basis for a Veitch diagram.

diagrams. Notice in the truth table in Fig. 5-22 that the C column alternates once each count, that the B column alternates every second count and that the A column alternates once every fourth count.

There are a total of 26 possible combinations of three variables that can occur. The A, B and C could be any letter or letter combination that could have a value of either 1 or 0 at any given time. In Fig. 5-23 these combinations are plotted as they would appear in a Veitch diagram for simplification.

Although many problems could be used to illustrate the utility of Veitch diagrams, two are presented here and these will give you a pretty fair idea of the utility of the diagrams. In Fig. 5-24A, since the terms AB, AC and $A\bar{B}\bar{C}$ plot in the areas shown and since this 4-square pattern is described by the single variable A, the expression reduces to A. Prove this with a truth table if you like. In Fig. 5-24B there are no 4-square patterns that correspond to any single variable and as a result, no simpler expression. There is, however, an equivalent expression:

$$AB + AC + \overline{AB}$$

This could also be proven using truth tables.

Although not an intensive coverage of Boolean algebra, the information presented is designed to give you the necessary information to troubleshoot digital computers. If the following five rules are remembered, it will be all that is really required in most instances to assess the condition of gating circuitry within most processors.

1. AND

   A. All inputs to an AND gate must equal 1 for the output to equal 1.

   B. Any 0 input to an AND gate will cause the output to be 0.

2. OR

   A. All inputs to an OR gate must equal 0 for the output to equal 0.

   B. Any 1 input to an OR gate will cause the output to be 1.

3. INVERTER

   A. A 1 input to an inverter will give a 0 out.

   B. A 0 input to an inverter will give a 1 out.

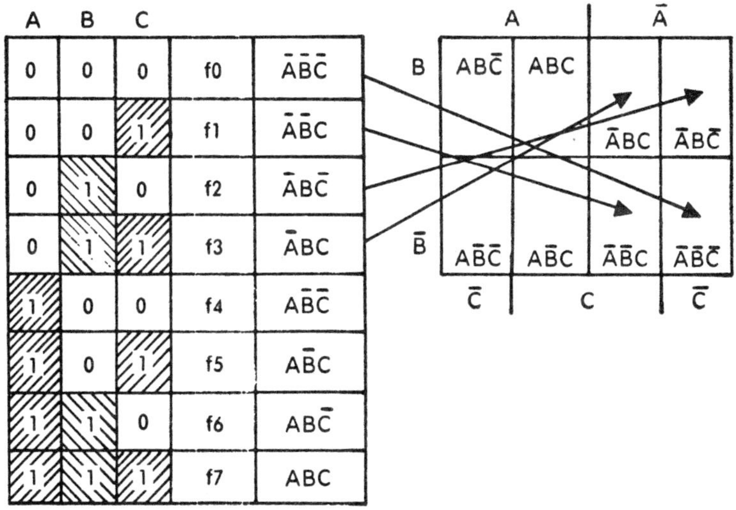

Fig. 5-22. The squares on the right illustrate the alternations of columns A, B, and C in the truth table.

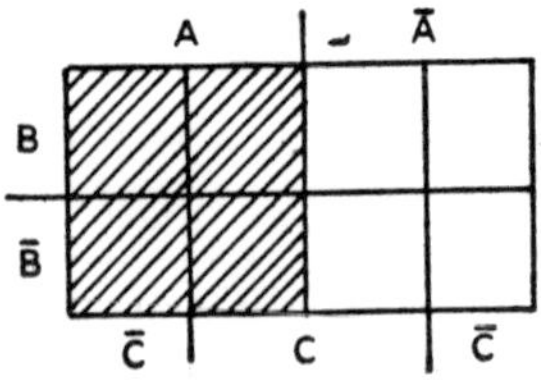

A

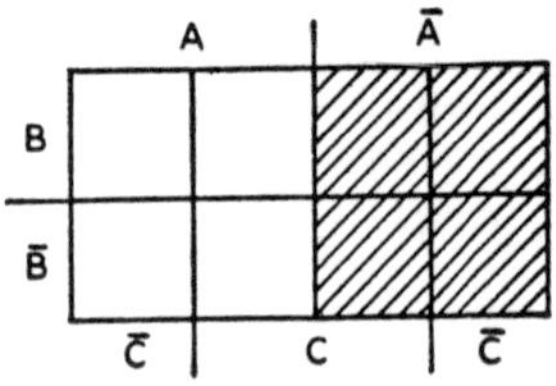

$\bar{A}$

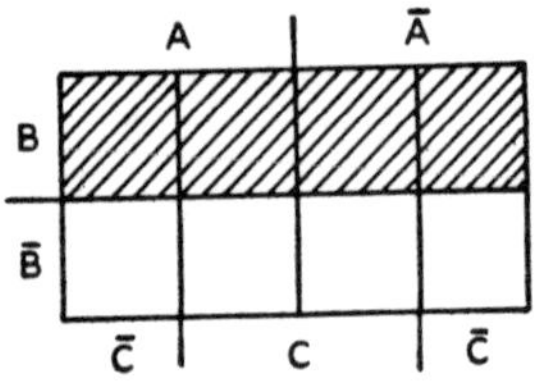

B

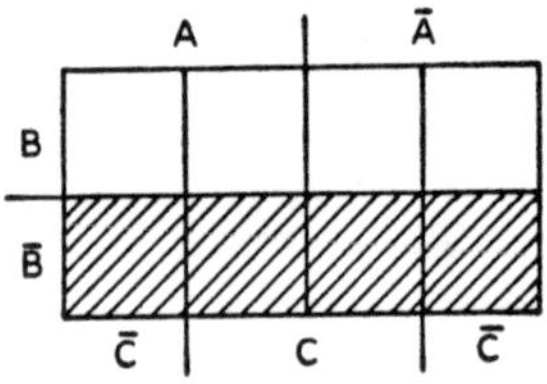

$\bar{B}$

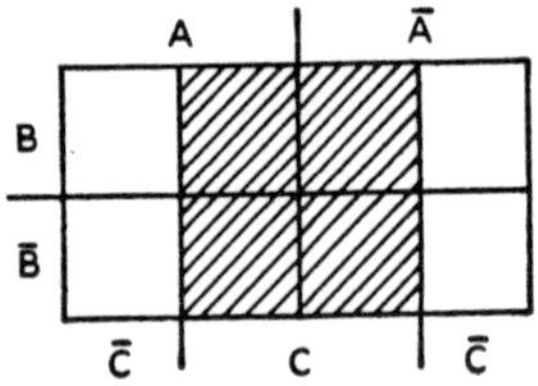

C

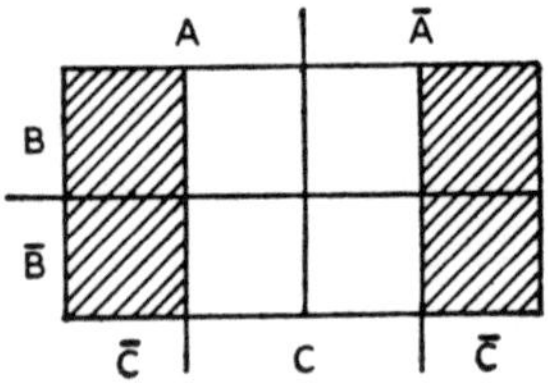

$\bar{C}$

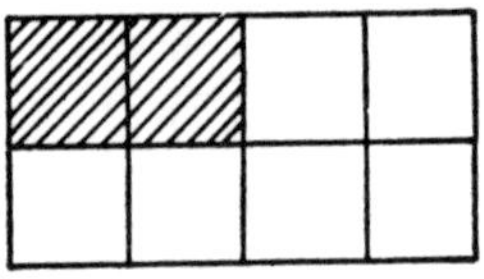

A B

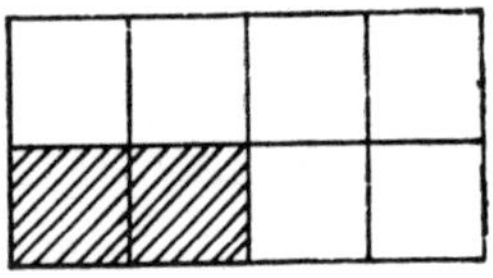

A $\bar{B}$

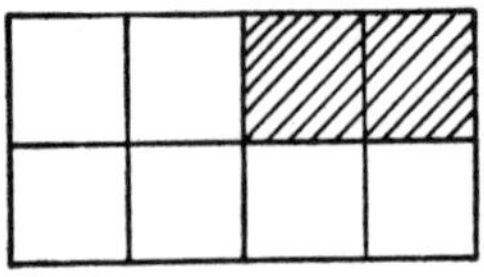

$\bar{A}$ B

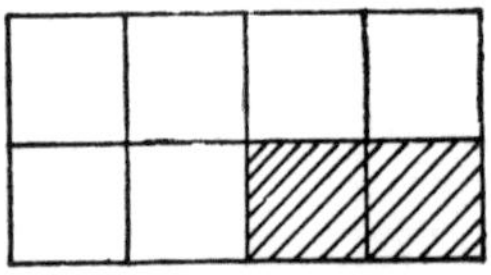

$\bar{A}$ $\bar{B}$

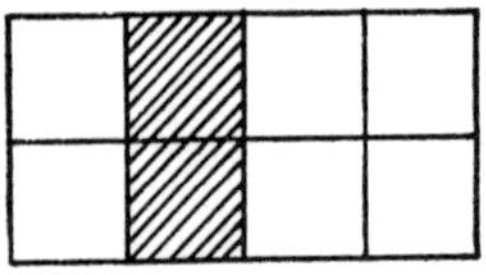

A C

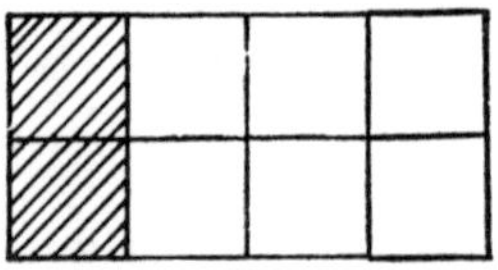

A $\bar{C}$

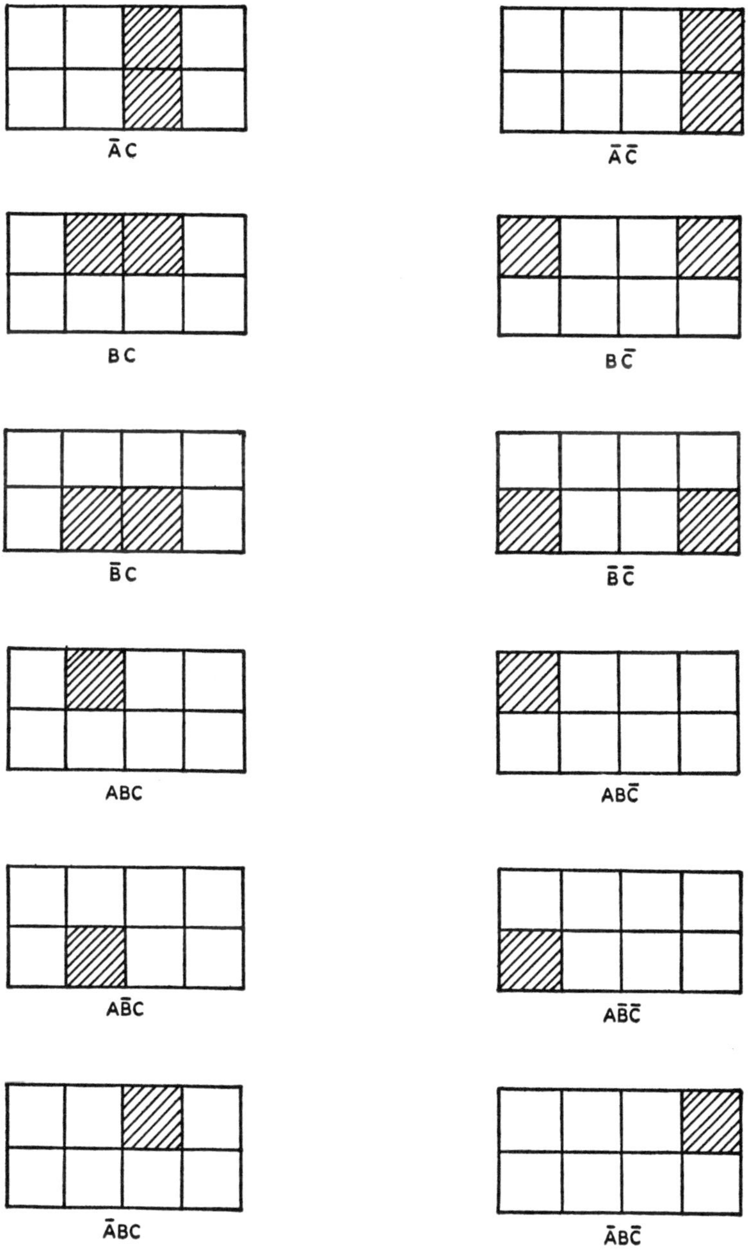

Fig. 5-23. Veitch diagrams illustrating the 26 possible combinations of three variables.

4. NAND

A. All inputs to a NAND gate must equal 1 for the output to equal 0.

B. Any 0 input to a NAND gate will cause the output to be 1.

5. NOR

A. All inputs to a NOR gate must equal 0 for the output to equal 1.

B. Any 1 input to a NOR gate will cause the output to be 0.

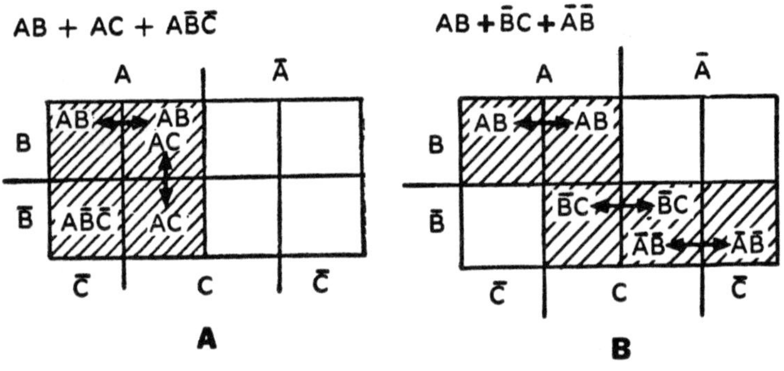

Fig. 5-24. Two basic Veitch diagram solutions.

TABLE 5-3. TWENTY-SIX POSSIBLE COMBINATIONS OF THREE VARIABLES (SEE FIG. 5-23).

A	AB	$\bar{A}C$	ABC	$\bar{A}\bar{B}C$
$\bar{A}$	$A\bar{B}$	$\bar{A}\bar{C}$	$AB\bar{C}$	$\bar{A}\bar{B}\bar{C}$
B	$\bar{A}B$	BC	$A\bar{B}C$	
$\bar{B}$	$\bar{A}\bar{B}$	$B\bar{C}$	$A\bar{B}\bar{C}$	
C	AC	$\bar{B}C$	$\bar{A}BC$	
$\bar{C}$	$A\bar{C}$	$\bar{B}\bar{C}$	$AB\bar{C}$	

Chapter 6

Basic Computer Circuits

Computer technology has made great strides in many areas during the past 10 years. One of these areas is in circuitry. Many if not most presently available mini computers and many medium- and large-scale machines use integrated circuits. For this reason, not too much will be said about discrete component circuits.

The one circuit worth looking at from the standpoint of relative simplicity and modern design technology is Control Data Corporation's basic 1604 logic switching card or inverter circuit (Fig. 6-1). Control Data uses negative logic definitions, a fact not really germain to the discussion but worth mentioning for information's sake.

In this basic circuit the transistor collector has several diodes connected to it which serve to implement the AND function. Some cards have two or three identical inputs with a 6.8K resistor to -20 volts and a diode which implements the OR function.

With more than one input, looking from the input to the collector output, this basic inverter circuit is an OR input with an inverted output, making it a NOR circuit. A diode cross coupled from each of the two inverter outputs back to an ORed input of the opposite inverter forms a NOR latch type flip-flop.

The circuit is nonsaturated and the current from 1 to 0 output changes only 1.2 milliamps. A -0.5 volt at the test point (TP) is a negative logic 0 and a -3.0 volts is a negative logic 1. The propagation delay, referring to the length of time that it takes a signal change on the input to appear at the output is on the order of 20 to 80 nanoseconds, which is fast by any standard.

The voltages used are +20 and -20 volts. These supply voltages come from extremely simple power supplies, making the overall reliability of the equipment something not achieved by many manufacturers. This reliability and up time is one of the things that has prompted one of the largest computer manufacturers in the country to stay with discrete components in much of their logic. The circuit and voltages in both the 0 and 1 state are shown in Fig. 6-1.

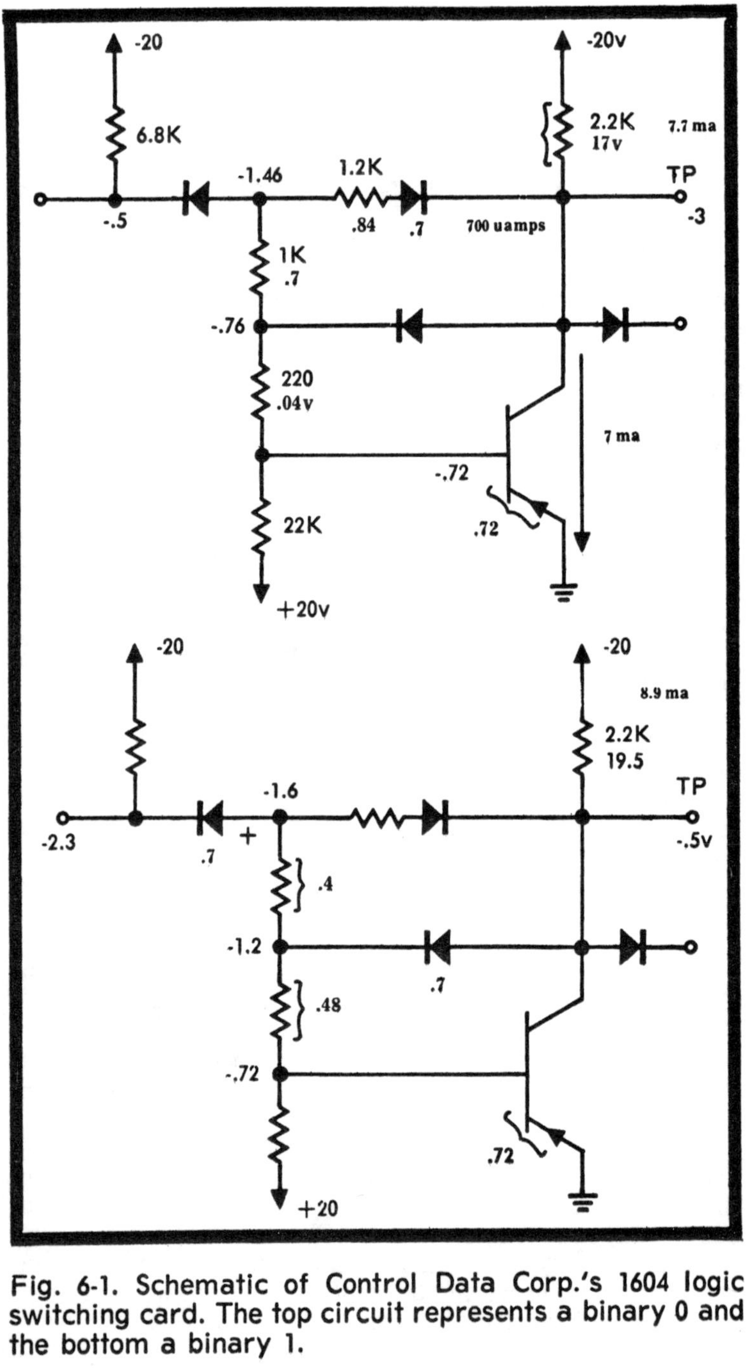

Fig. 6-1. Schematic of Control Data Corp.'s 1604 logic switching card. The top circuit represents a binary 0 and the bottom a binary 1.

The top diode with its cathode connected to the collector of the transistor begins to conduct as the collector voltage reaches about -3 volts and supplies the necessary feedback to prevent the collector voltage from going much above 3 volts. When the collector voltage goes to -0.5 volts, this diode cuts off and the lower diode takes over to maintain conduction in the transistor, thus preventing saturation and speeding up the switching time of the circuit. As is the case with all computer gating circuitry, the circuits are designed to go to and remain at some predefined voltage levels.

As was the case with the switches discussed earlier, it is always necessary to predefine conditions. Throughout the industry, a lamp off normally indicates a binary 0 and a lamp on normally indicates a binary 1. To achieve these conditions we have been opening and closing switches. The closure represents a 1 in almost all of the industry and an open switch normally represents a 0. These conditions are used for all of the discussions that follow.

Where Control Data logic is mentioned or used, and if it is necessary to know, a binary 0 will be represented by a voltage level of -0.5 volts and a binary 1 by a voltage level of -3.0 volts. All other discussions of logic including the small central processor covered later, use positive logic definitions associated with integrated circuits with a voltage between 2.4 and 5 volts positive representing a binary 1 and 0.8 volts or less representing a binary 0.

DIODE GATING CIRCUITS

Diode gating circuits are among the most used gates in the industry. Integrated circuit diode transistor logic circuits (DTL) use diode input gates with transistor inverters following them to implement the NAND function.

Fig. 6-2 shows the development of the possible output combinations from a 2-input AND gate. The AND gate in this form is seldom used alone. Since the diodes and resistors consume power, and since there are normally numerous circuits that must be driven with the output, some type of amplifier normally follows the gating circuit.

In analyzing the conditions, the supply voltage is shown as an ideal +5 volts and the input batteries are considered +5 volts, all with respect to the common line. Ideal diodes (no forward voltage drop and infinite reverse impedance) are also considered. A 0-volt level is defined as a binary 0 and a +5-volt level as a binary 1.

In Fig. 6-2, illustrating the AND function, the first case shows both inputs tied directly back to the common line.

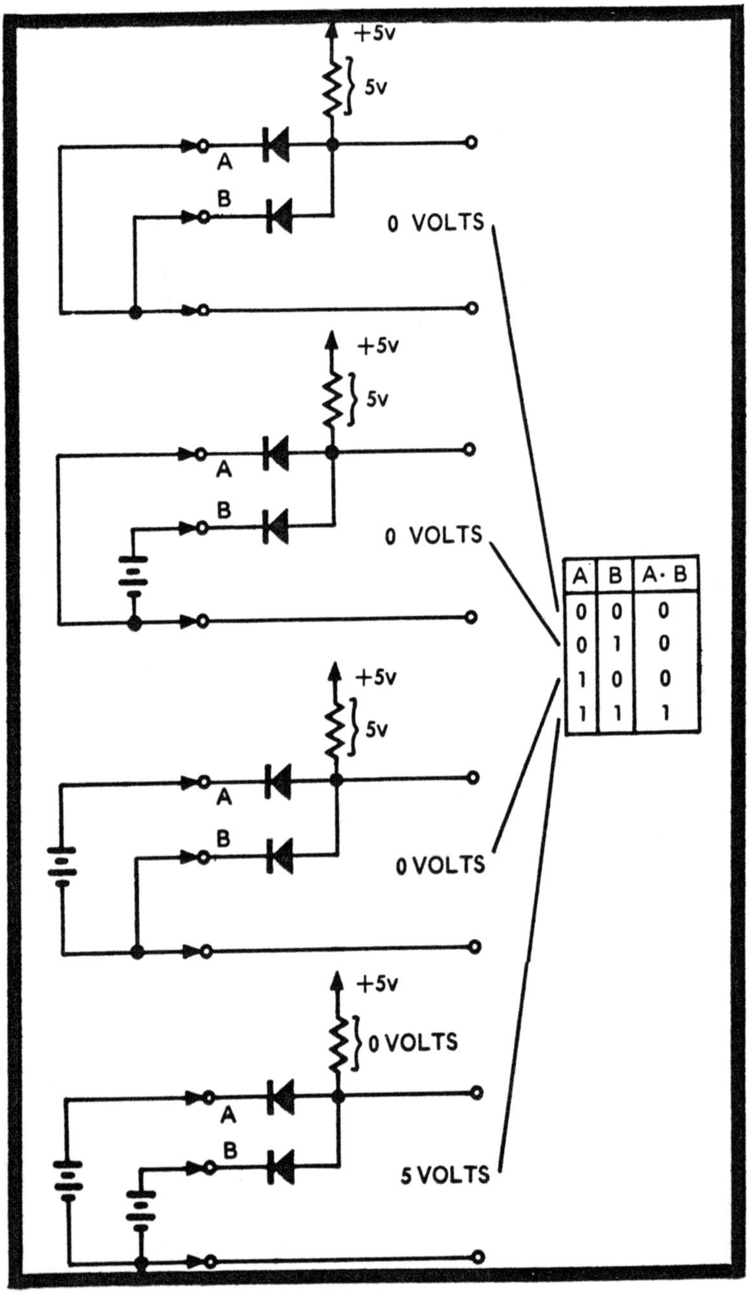

Fig. 6-2. Diode gating circuits illustrating the AND function.

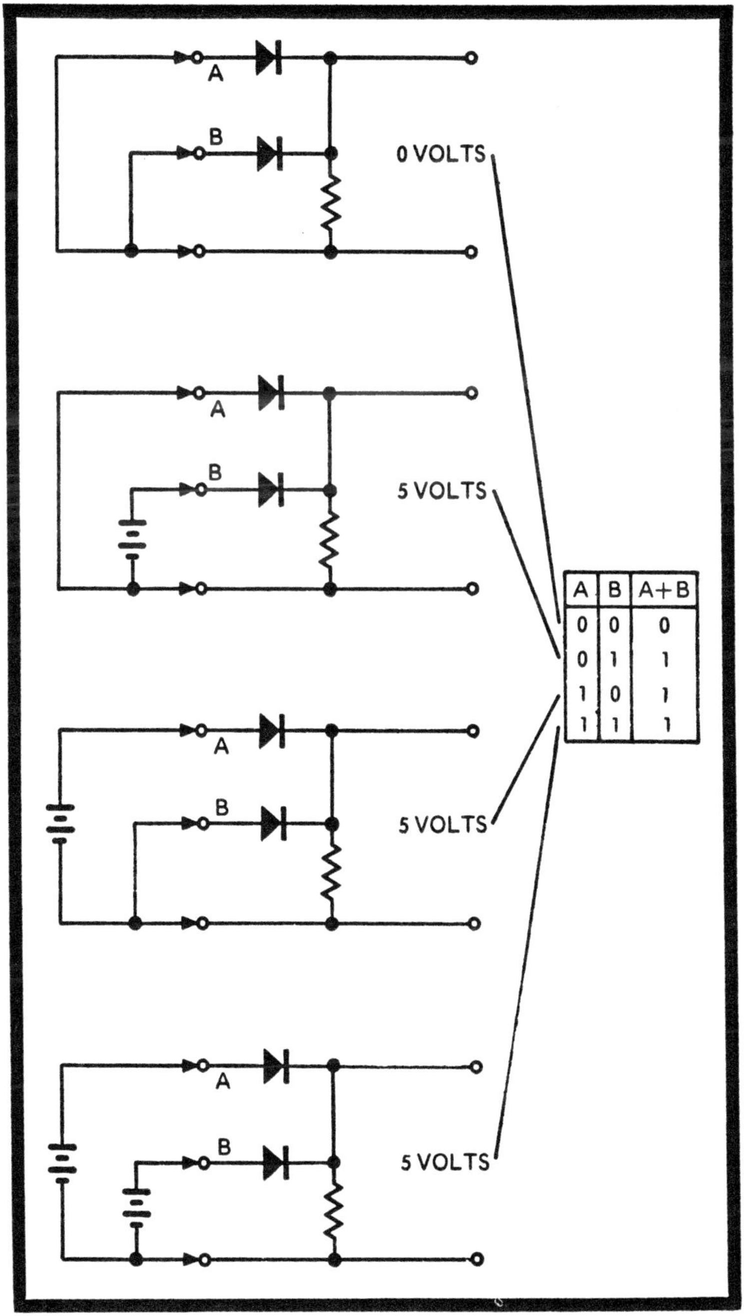

A	B	A+B
0	0	0
0	1	1
1	0	1
1	1	1

Fig. 6-3. Diode gating circuits illustrating the OR function.

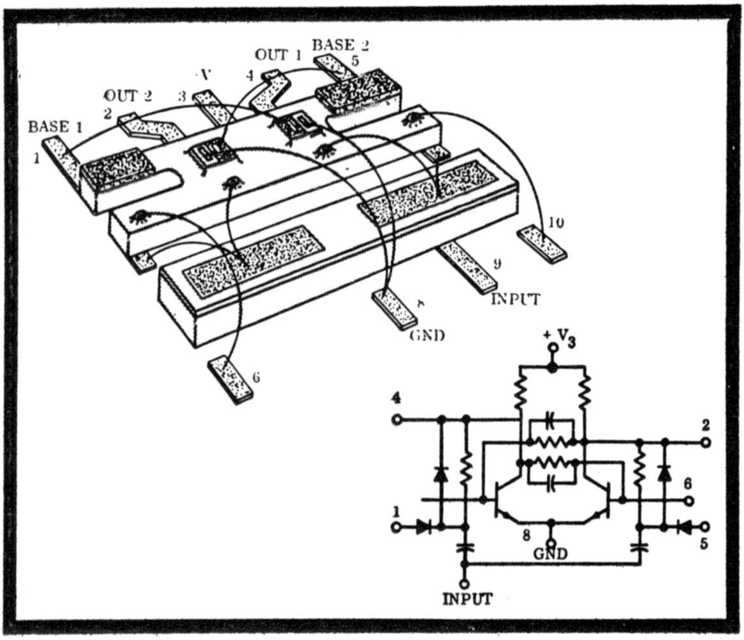

Fig. 6-4. Construction details and circuit of an early Texas Instruments IC.

Under normal circumstances this connection would be accomplished through the collector-to-emitter junction of a conducting transistor or transistors as input sources.

With both A and B tied to common, the diodes are forward biased and, since we are assuming that they are perfect diodes, the voltage drop from the output to common would be 0, giving a binary 0 output. In both of the next two cases, at least one diode is conducting, which causes the output to be 0 volts or a binary 0. Finally, in the last condition, both inputs are at 5 volts and, although both diodes are conducting, this 5 volts is coupled to the output and gives a binary 1.

In the OR configuration (Fig. 6-3) the diodes are installed in such a way that any input voltage (positive in this case) causes one or both of the diodes to conduct and develop a voltage across the output resistor. If the circuit reminds you of a full-wave rectifier, it is not surprising since a full-wave rectifier is an OR circuit to the input sine wave with the A and B inputs connected to alternate half cycles of the input waveform! The only time a 0 output is obtained is with both inputs 0. At any other time, as the truth table illustrates, the output will be 1 with any 1 input.

INTEGRATED CIRCUITS

Some of the first integrated circuits were produced by Texas Instruments in 1960 using mesa construction. Mesa construction has since been superseded by Planar techniques, but the "ball bonding" system used then is still applied in many integrated circuit applications. Fig. 6-4 shows both construction details and the circuit for this early integrated circuit.

Resistor Transistor Logic

One of the earliest applications of ICs was in connection with RTL circuitry. The circuitry is basically NOR logic and is currently manufactured by several IC houses. When developed, engineers were still thinking in terms of discrete components. The logic, for this reason, is not designed to make best use of integrated circuit technology, nor is it the most economical approach to circuitry.

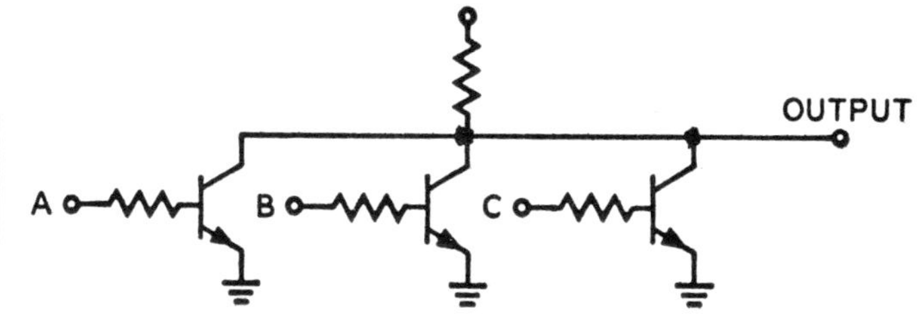

A	B	C	$\overline{A+B+C}$
0	0	0	1
0	0	1	0
0	1	0	0
0	1	1	0
1	0	0	0
1	0	1	0
1	1	0	0
1	1	1	0

Fig. 6-5. This RTL configuration has also been called direct-coupled transistor logic (DCTL) to differentiate it from a very old logic system that used the division of voltages across input resistors to develop the various functions.

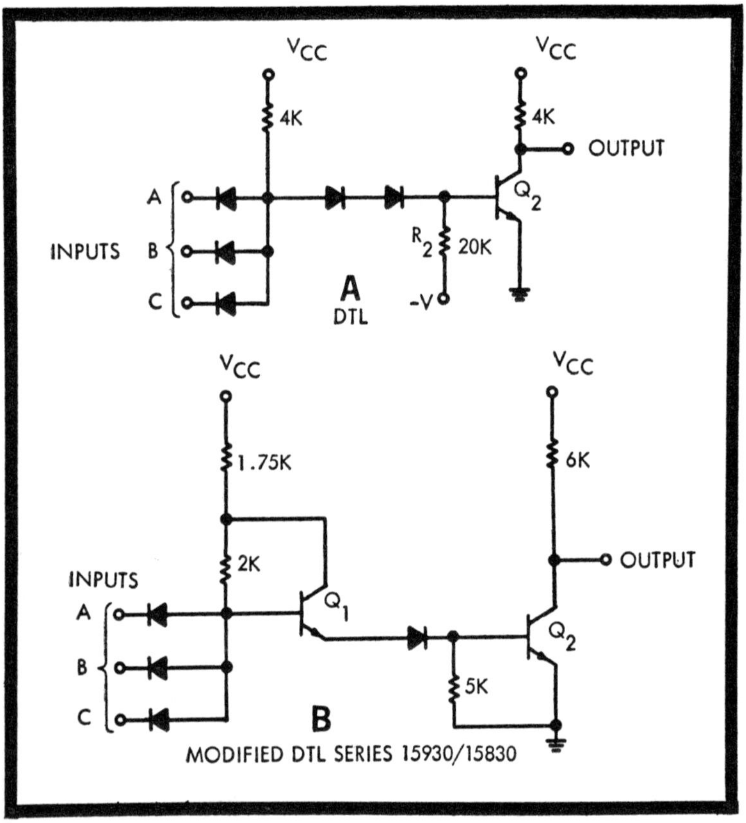

Fig. 6-6. Circuits of the DTL and Series 15930-15830 integrated circuits.

The basic circuit configuration is shown in Fig. 6-5. With all inputs at or near 0 volts (binary 0) the output will be high since all transistors are cut off, resulting in a binary 1 out. Applying a voltage (binary 1) to any input will turn the appropriate transistor on, dropping the output to 0. The NOR truth table shown with the gate proves the above statement.

Diode Transistor Logic

The next series of integrated circuits to be developed used diode transistor logic. Again, the implementation was achieved by designing the circuits with discrete components and then transferring the design to ICs.

The basic gating structure performs the NAND function with diode AND gates and a transistor inverter. As a statement, if all inputs are logical or binary 1, the output will go to logical 0. If any input is a logical 0, the output will be a logical 1.

In the circuit of Fig. 6-6A, if all or any one of the diodes has a logical 0 (ground) on the cathode, current flows through the diode and the 4K resistor to Vcc, resulting in one diode drop, or approximately 0.7 volts at the junction of the input diode and the 4K resistor. This voltage is insufficient to forward bias the series diodes in the base-emitter circuit and the transistor is cut off, resulting in a high level or logical 1 at the output.

With all inputs at a logical 1 or approximately at the 3- to 5-volt level, the voltage at the junction of the input diodes and the 4K resistor is high enough to cause base-emitter current to flow, turning Q2 on. The output voltage drops to approximately the saturation voltage of Q2 or 0.4 volts. The biggest disadvantage of this circuit is the requirement for two power supplies.

Since transistors are almost as easy to make (and as economical) the circuit in Fig. 6-6B is the method used to make the majority of presently available DTL circuitry. Here, one of the first deviations has been made from discrete circuit philosophy. A transistor would normally be more expensive to use than a diode, but with transistors practically as easy to make as a diode, one of the first advantages of integrated circuits becomes available.

For the user, a power supply requirement has been eliminated with little or no increase in the device cost. The transistor also serves to improve switching speed (Q1) and thus makes the device more valuable still.

DTL circuitry is still one of the most used types of logic. And with the design relatively stable, manufacturing processes set and so forth, the price has continued to drop, making it one of the more desirable logic forms for today's computers.

Transistor-Transistor Logic

TTL or just transistor-transistor logic has become one of the most popular and most widely used integrated circuit gating structures. Until integrated circuit technology had achieved a fair foothold, there was no such thing as a multiple-emitter transistor. Somewhere it became obvious that components could be saved if the requirement for diodes was eliminated in the available ICs. The multiple-emitter transistor was easy to make; a large collector was first diffused, then a large base region, and finally multiple-emitters. It

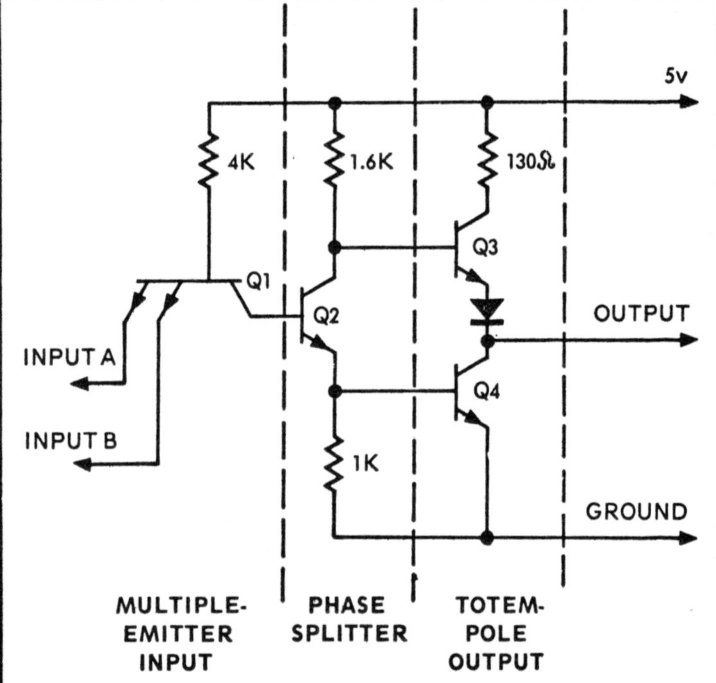

A	B	C	$\overline{A\cdot B\cdot C}$
0	0	0	1
0	0	1	1
0	1	0	1
0	1	1	1
1	0	0	1
1	0	1	1
1	1	0	1
1	1	1	0

Fig. 6-7. The truth table for the TTL NAND gate illustrates the fact that with any 0 input the output will be a 1. All inputs must be a 1 for the output to be a 0.

takes up less space, makes for manufacturing economy and has the advantage of being about twice as fast as DTL (12 nanoseconds switching time as compared to 25 nanoseconds in DTL). Many designers worried in the early years of TTL that it would be more noise succeptible than DTL, but the fact is that the system has better noise immunity.

The basic gating structure presently used in TIs 74 series logic (second sourced by a large number of manufacturers) is shown in Fig. 6-7. The TTL system implements the NAND function and is broken up for description purposes into three basic parts:

1. A multiple-emitter input transistor

2. A phase splitter

3. A "totem pole" output circuit

With less than 0.8 volts on any of the input emitter leads (logical 0), Q1 is biased into conduction. With Q1 conducting, the voltage present on the base of Q2 is not sufficient to turn Q2 on so the voltage on the collector of Q2 is high, which turns Q3 on. The voltage on the emitter of Q2 is low and will not turn Q4 on so the phase splitter holds Q4 cut off and Q3 turned on. The resultant output is high or logical 1.

If all of the input transistor emitters are brought above 1.4 volts, the transistor turns off or, should we say, the collector voltage rises. When the collector voltage of Q1 rises, the base of Q2 becomes forward biased and Q2 is turned on. Turning Q2 on also turns Q4 on, and since the collector of Q2 goes low, Q3 is cut off, allowing a voltage of about 0.4 volts (the saturation drop of the collector-emitter circuit).

The SN7480 is a complete full adder in a single package. It can perform with one package the full add function and it allows some logic to be performed at the input. The logic diagram is shown in Fig. 6-8. Equivalent circuitry would require three to four packages of regular logic and a handfull of discrete components. There are devices available now that can do so much more than this on a single chip that it is difficult to comprehend without further extensive reading in IC technology, but you will learn it from a number of other sources if you remain in the computer industry.

Should you want further information on any of these integrated circuits, manufacturers are as a rule happy to supply data sheets and application information that goes into considerable detail about testing, circuitry, and similar items involving integrated circuits.

INTEGRATED CIRCUIT CONSTRUCTION

The TTL circuits built by Texas Instruments and others are diffused planar, double-layer epitaxial structures. Such

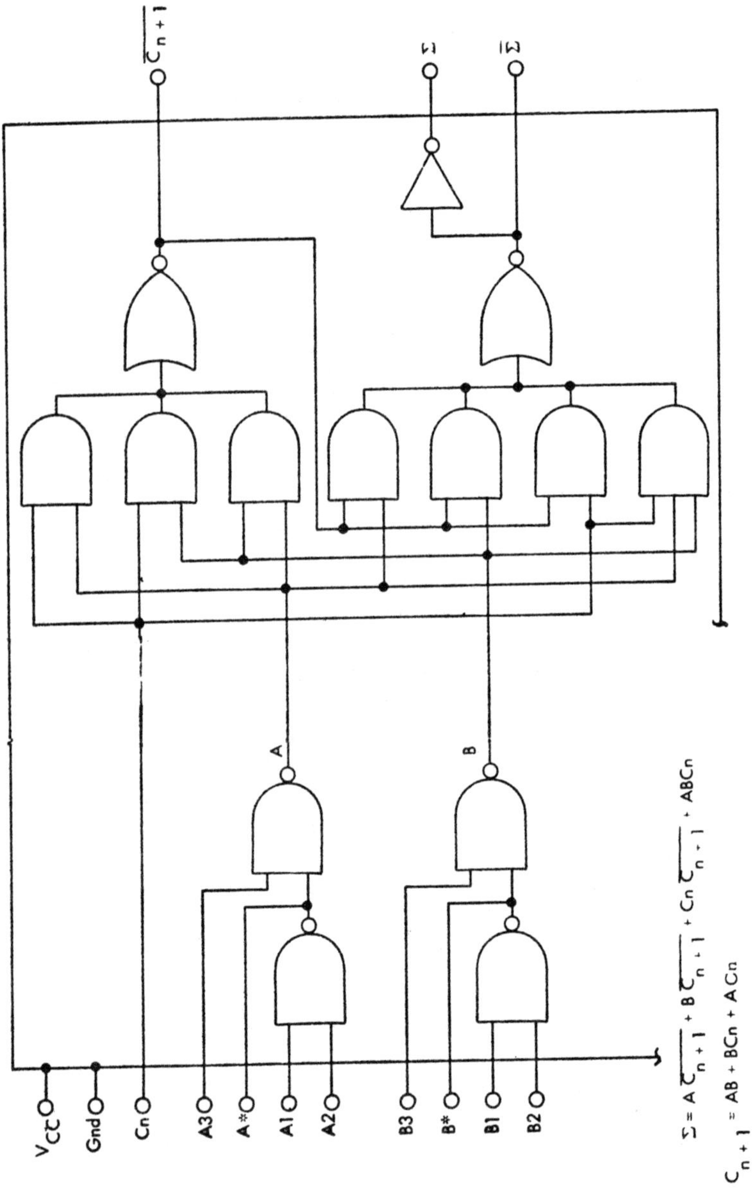

Fig. 6-8. Schematic of the SN5480-7480 complete full adder with single-stage carry.

devices are the result of years of work and are backed up by many patents, but the mouthful above can be broken down to a bit simpler language. Diffused means simply that various materials are vaporized in a proper atmosphere and allowed to seep into the surface of a device. Planar simply means on a flat surface. Double-layer is self explanatory and epitaxial means to grow upward on a surface. So the description says that these are devices grown on the surface of a material and doped by allowing gaseous materials to diffuse into the surface.

There are a number of detailed books on the actual construction of ICs but let's look at the basic procedure. First, a P-type silicon slice is polished to a very fine finish. This device is then heated in an oxygen atmosphere in a special furnace to form a layer of silicon oxide which is very resistant to most chemicals and materials. Masks are made for the various parts that are to be put on the surface and the wafers are coated with a photo-sensitive resist. This resist is nothing more than a material that hardens when exposed to ultraviolet light. The resulting "sandwich" is silicon-silicon oxide-resist. The resist is then exposed to light and hardened in the areas that must remain silicon oxide.

After hardening, the resist-covered wafer is placed in a solvent that dissolves the unhardened resist and exposes the silicon oxide. The silicon oxide layer is etched (dissolved) by a mixture of hydrochloric-hydrofluoric acid to expose the bare silicon beneath. The wafer is then stripped of the remaining resist to leave a silicon wafer with silicon oxide on the surface except for the windows that have been etched through.

An N-type impurity is now vaporized in a furnace and the hot silicon wafers are passed through the furnace and allowed to absorb N-type impurities through the etched windows. This process is repeated once more to form diodes and another time to form NPN transistors.

There are other steps involved in the total process, which is quite involved, but as many as 100 IC chips may be made on a single wafer and many wafers can be handled at a time so the process becomes quite economical for a manufacturer with the equipment.

Basic Circuit Layout

The circuit construction or layout of a TTL device is essentially the same as that for a DTL device. The basic difference is that the input diode gate of the DTL circuitry is replaced with a multiple-emitter transistor as shown in Fig. 6-9.

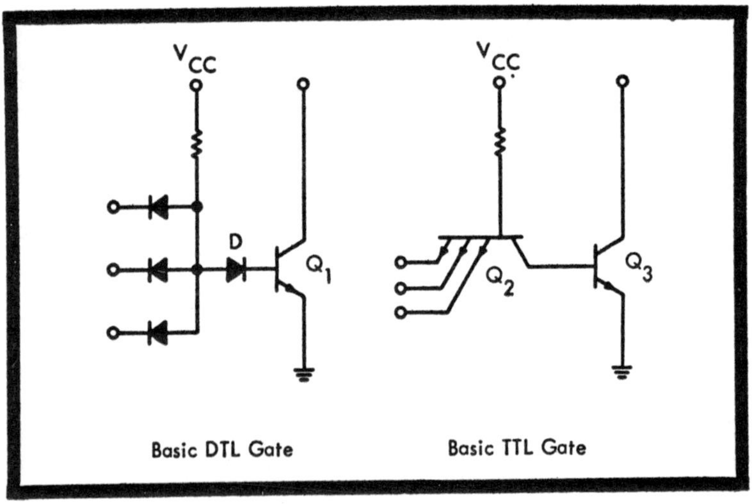

Fig. 6-9. Comparison of the basic DTL and TTL circuit layout.

A major fault of the DTL circuit is that in turning off the output transistor, which is driven by heavy base current to ensure saturation, the coupling diode D may cut off too soon and block the removal of the stored charges in the base of the output transistor, which would result in an excessively long turnoff time. To remedy this undesirable condition, a bypass resistor from the base of the output transistor to ground or to a negative bias may be inserted to insure an adequate turnoff time.

Another technique is to construct diode D in a way that results in a stored-charge diode which will remain on longer than the transistor. The problem is that it is difficult to construct fast switching input diodes and stored-charge diodes on the same IC wafer.

These disadvantages—difficult construction, extra resistors, and possibly extra power supplies, are all eliminated by using the multiple-emitter transistor, Q2. The transistor performs the same logic function as the diode gate and has a faster recovery time since the transistor is never turned off.

Input Transistor Layout

The layout of several devices is shown in Fig. 6-10. In Fig. 6-10A the single-emitter transistor is shown and the area given. In Fig. 6-10B the multiple-emitter transistor is shown as

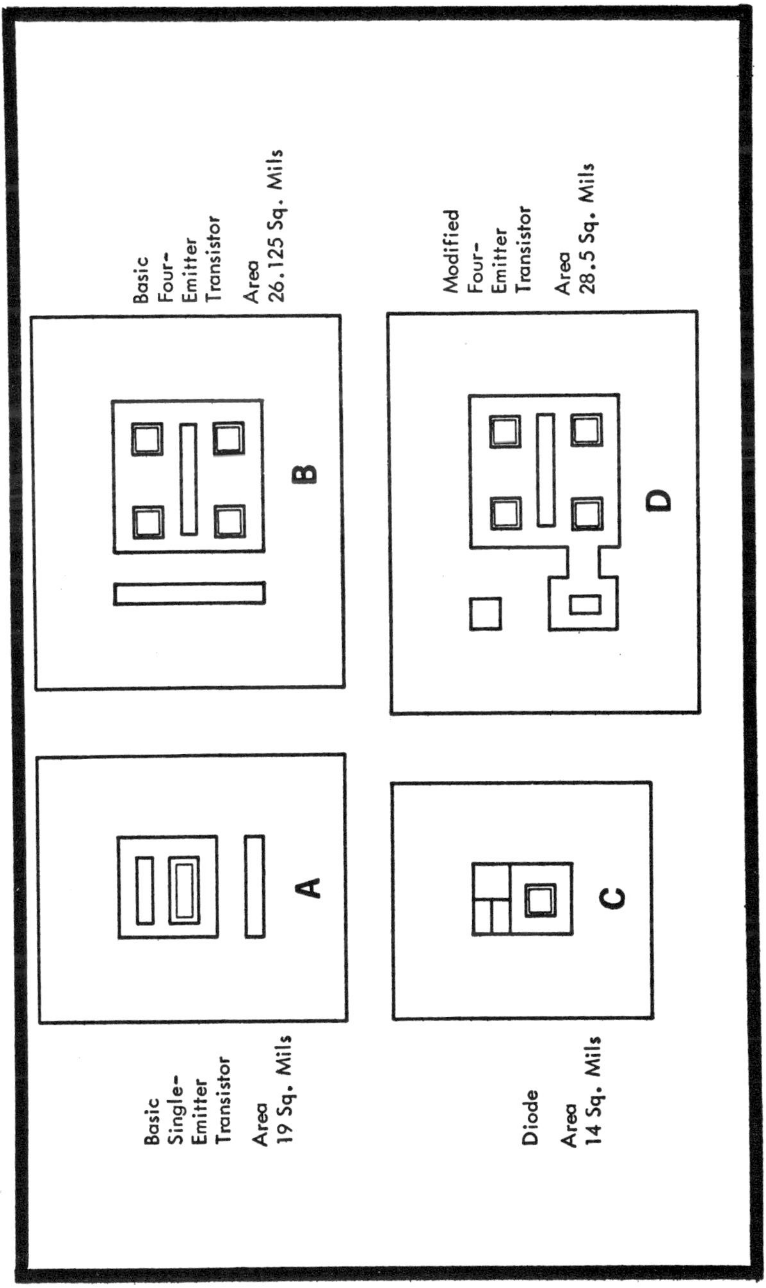

Fig. 6-10. Physical layout of the input transistor and diode.

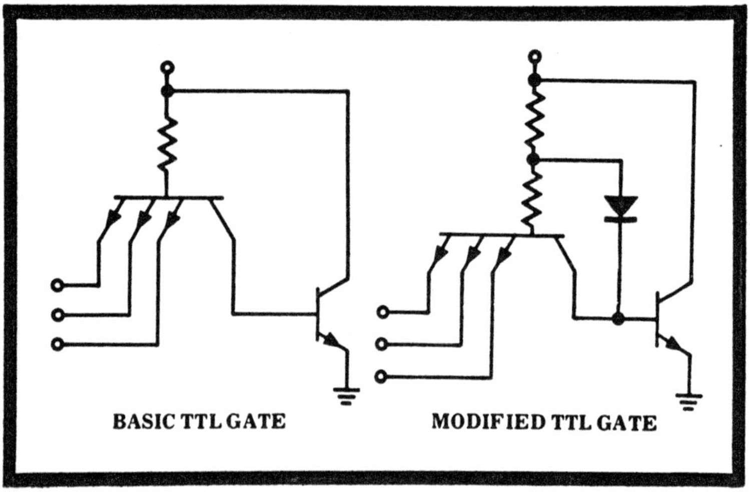

Fig. 6-11. Basic TTL gate and a modified TTL gate circuit.

nothing more than a diffused transistor with several (four) emitters in this case. As many as eight emitters can be made with little trouble, and the area used is not appreciably increased! Another thing that Fig. 6-10 shows is that the multiple-emitter transistor does not require as much area as four diodes and even less space than four diodes constructed as a common anode device as would be the case with DTL logic.

Notice the different configuration of the multiple-emitter transistor shown in Fig. 6-10D. This special configuration is shown from a circuit standpoint in Fig. 6-11B. It eliminates one of the problems that can occur with multiple-emitter transistors.

Isolation is not as good between the inputs of multiple-emitter transistors as it is between the diode inputs. When one of the emitters is at a high or logic 1 level, it may draw excessive input current by inverse transistor action or transistor action between two emitters and the base.

The combination of the resistor, connected directly to the base of the multiple-emitter transistor, and the diode reduces the input leakage current by a factor of five or more. The input current may also be reduced by making the inverse current gain of the transistor very low. This is accomplished by making the base-emitter ratio smaller, by doping the base with gold to reduce the carrier lifetime and by reducing the carrier concentration of the collector to make it a poor emitter.

Still further modifications can be made to the basic gate circuitry of either DTL or TTL to improve noise immunity by an amount equal to the forward drop of the base-emitter junction of a transistor.

Output Circuits

Fig. 6-13 shows some of the output circuits that can be used in conjunction with the improved gate structure of Fig. 6-12D.

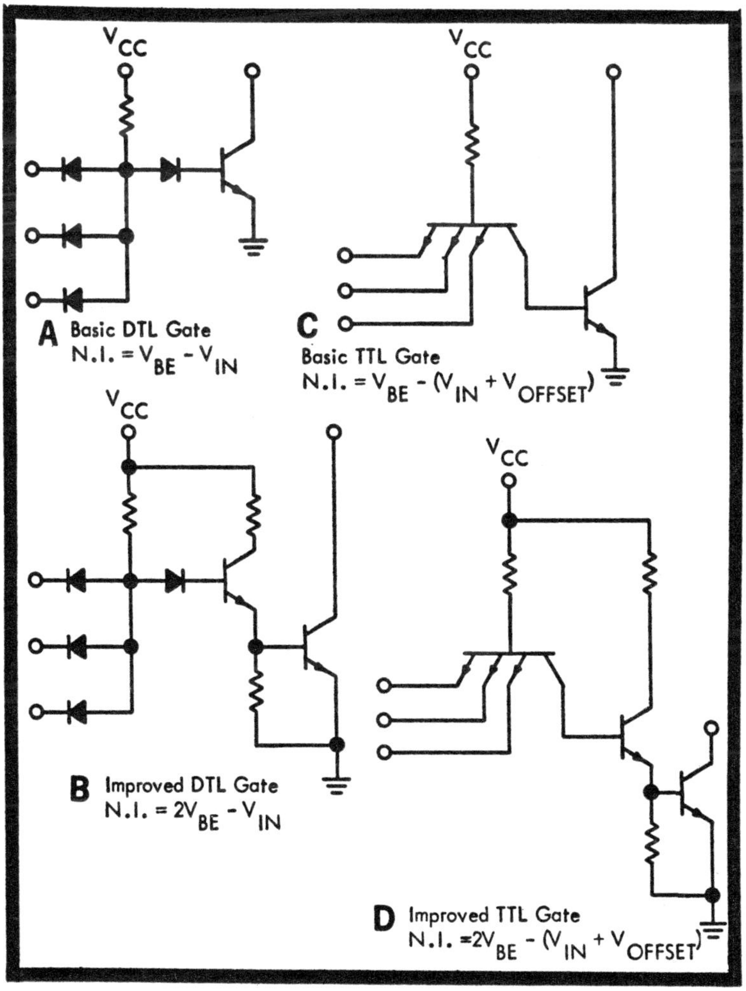

Fig. 6-12. Schematics showing circuit changes to increase noise immunity.

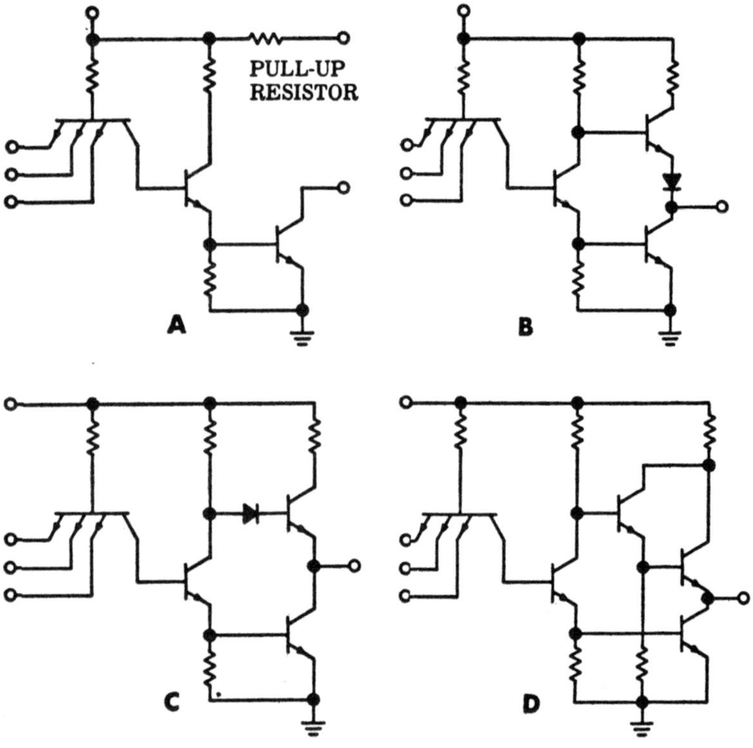

Fig. 6-13. Four output circuits designed to meet a variety of requirements.

The particular output circuit chosen depends on the requirements of the system in which the device will be used.

The circuit of Fig. 6-13A consists simply of a pull-up resistor which may or may not be connected to the output switching transistor. This configuration is also indicated in specification sheets as having an uncommitted output transistor collector. The pull-up resistor, if used, is connected as shown by the dotted line.

The advantage of the uncommitted collector configuration is that several collectors can be tied together to perform an OR function. The disadvantages of this type of circuit depend on the size of the pull-up resistor. If the resistance is low, the power drain on the gate is greatly increased. If it is a high resistance, the output impedance of the gate (with a logical 1 output) is high and very little capacitive drive capability is achieved and the susceptibility to noise is high.

The circuits of Fig. 6-13B, C, and D are all similar in that each presents a low output impedance in both the logical 1 and logical 0 conditions. This low-impedance type of drive provides a good capability for driving capacitive loads with good noise immunity, but the "wired OR" configuration cannot be achieved.

The diodes shown in B and C insure proper operation of the "totem-pole" output. They insure that the top transistor is off when the bottom transistor is on. Putting the diode in the

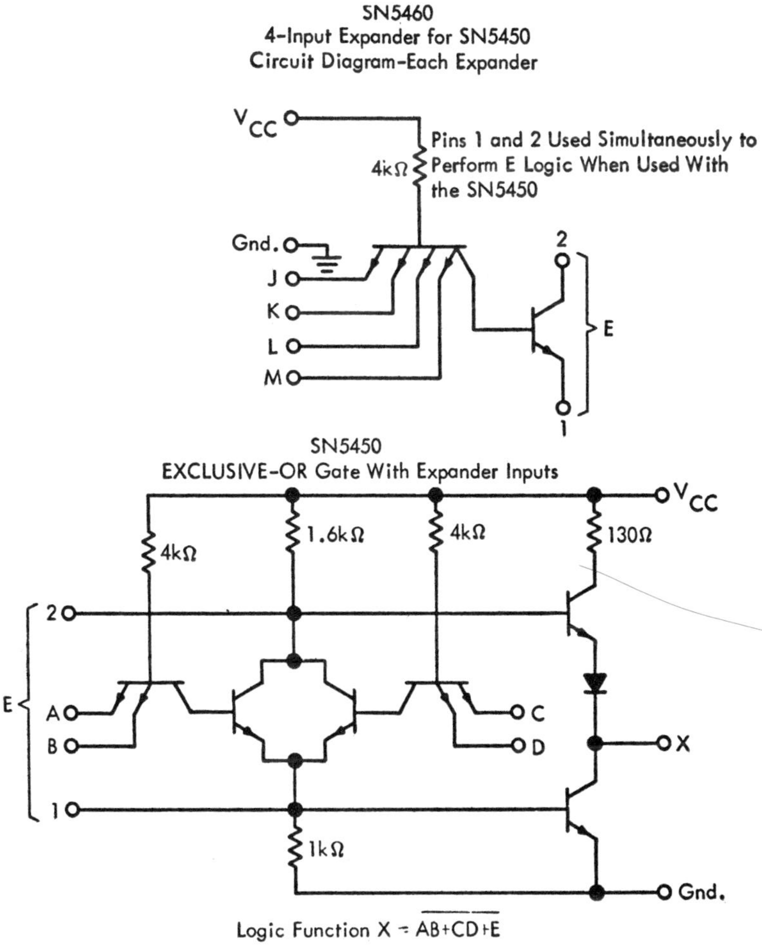

Fig. 6-14. Schematic of an exclusive OR gate and expander.

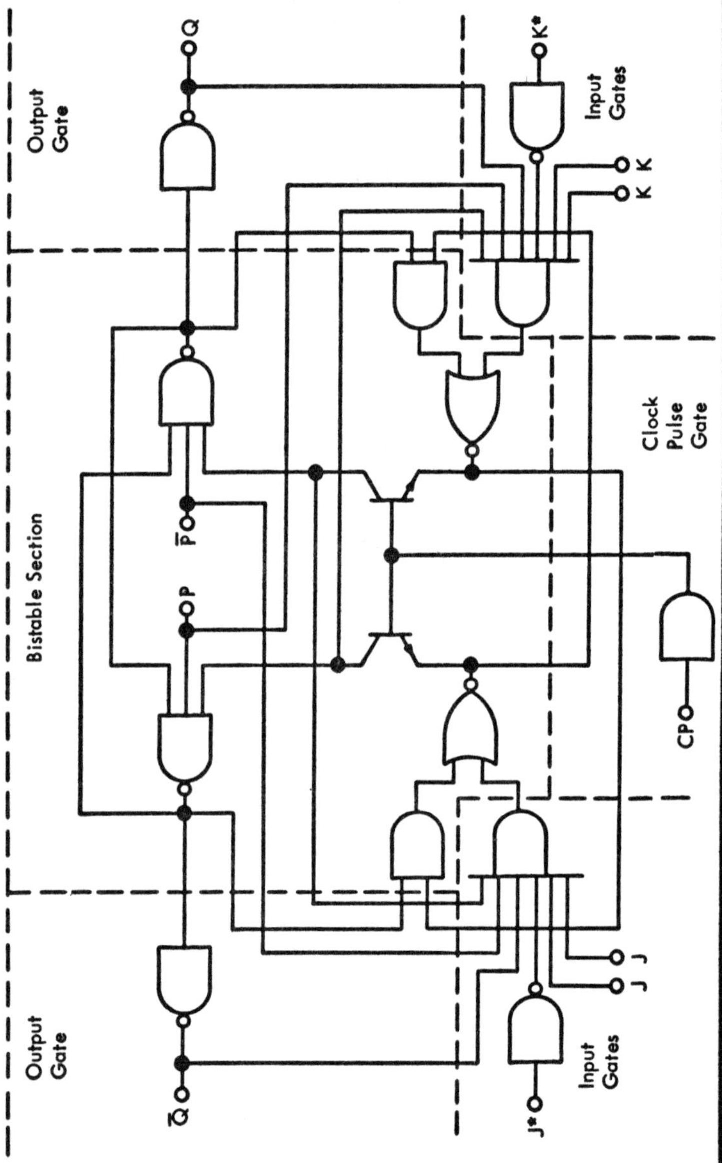

Fig. 6-15. Block diagram of an SN5470 J-K flip-flop.

emitter circuit instead of the base circuit also tends to eliminate stored charge problems. The emitter diode also reduces the amplitude of the current that exists during gate turnoff.

Finally, the Darlington configuration in D provides slightly greater speed because of transistor action and considerably lower steady-state output impedance, but it has the disadvantage of using more power in the off condition.

FLIP-FLOPS

Flip-flops, probably one of the most descriptive terms in the industry and also one of the most used and least sophisticated, describe a circuit that dates back at least to World War II and possibly before. Flip-flops are probably the second most used device in a computer. They have come a long way since the early Eccles-Jordan multivibrator and bear little resemblance to that circuit.

Better words for them might be a bistable latch or simply a latch because that is their basic purpose. As long as the power is on, flip flops retain the last information presented to their inputs. They can and are used to store information on a temporary basis and to count and to shift data in a serial manner through external circuitry. For the very reason of their utility, they are presented in some detail to allow you to become as completely familiar with them as possible.

NAND Gate Latch

The NAND gate latch or simply latch is the device used in the PDC 808 for all registers. It is probably one of the neatest arrangements in the business for storing data on a temporary basis. This type of "bistable" or "binary" element is used for

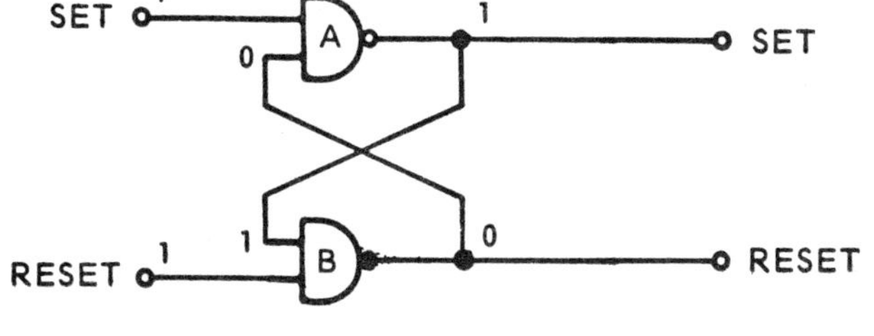

Fig. 6-16. NAND gate latch diagram.

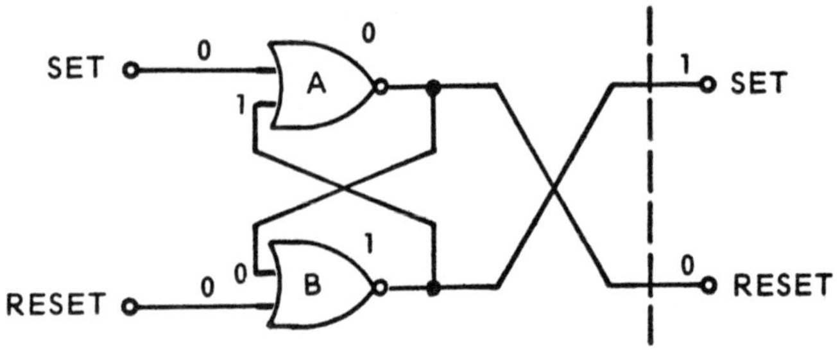

Fig. 6-17. Diagram of the CDC flip-flop.

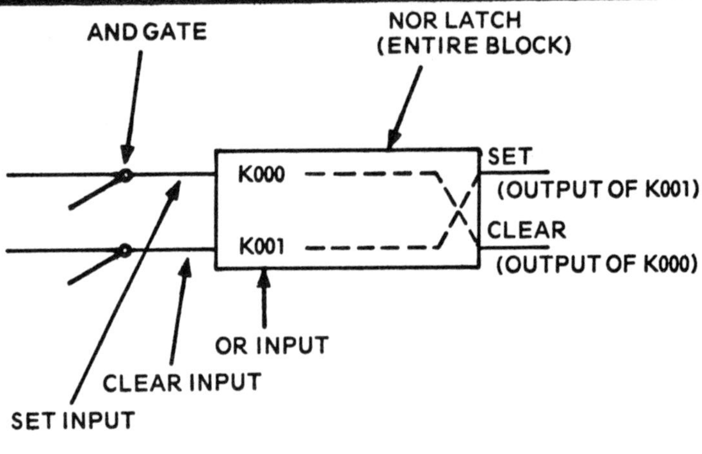

Fig. 6-18. Drawing illustrating other symbols used in logic diagrams.

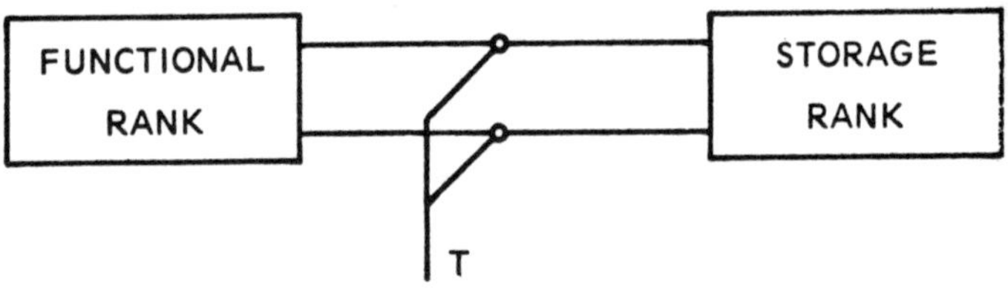

Fig. 6-19. Diagram of a forced transfer system.

storage functions only. Alone, it cannot be used as a counter or shift register. Notice in Fig. 6-16 that the inputs are held high (binary 1) and driven low since the inital function is an AND function. In this arrangement the outputs need not be crossed since the output of NAND gate A is the set output and the output of NAND gate B is the reset (clear) output.

Using standard MIL 806B logic symbols, the CDC flip-flop is as shown in Fig. 6-17. And to aquaint you with at least one other type of logical representation, the symbols Fig. 6-18 are used in CDC logic.

If a binary 1 is applied to the reset line, the NOR gate input will be driven high and the output of B will go to D. ORing zeros at the input to A will result in a 1 output, latching the flip-flop in a reset condition.

Nearly every operation in a CPU is performed synchronously or in step with some master time source, in this instance the computer clock oscillator. In many instances, data is received at various places, and delayed by different amounts of time depending on how far and through how many gates it has traveled. To insure proper operation, this data must be retimed or synchronized to the master clock. For this reason it is necessary to obtain triggered, clocked or synchronous operation of a flip-flop with respect to the incoming data.

The flip-flops we have looked at so far can operate any time data appears at the input. This is known as asynchronous

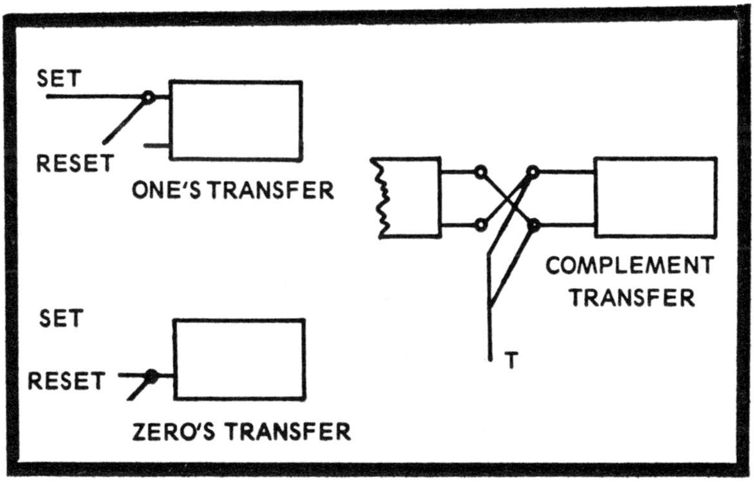

Fig. 6-20. Diagrams representing 1s, 0s, and complement transfer systems.

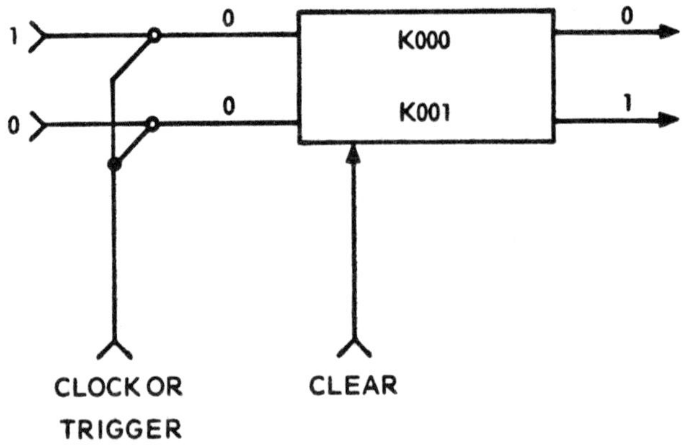

Fig. 6-21. Diagram of a simple clocked flip-flop.

operation. We could apply a reset pulse to a set flip-flop and have it change state. In the next second we could then reset it and one microsecond later set it again. In other words, the state of the flip-flop can be changed at any time without reference to any master time source.

This type of binary or flip-flop is known as a **single rank register** stage in CDC systems and it is always preceded by AND gates connected to one or both inputs. It is used strictly for data storage. The functional rank or master rank (Fig. 6-19) actually does the counting or shifting operation while the storage rank holds the information. The **transfer or T line** is driven high (binary 1) to transfer the contents of the functional rank to the storage rank. This is a dual or double rank configuration and is the system used in CDC counters and shift registers.

The transfer method shown in Fig. 6-19 is called a **forced transfer**. Other transfer systems are shown in Fig. 6-20. In this type of register operation, clocking is performed by a timed application of the transfer pulse.

We jumped into two subjects in the previous discussion: (1) clocked or synchronous operation and (2) gated inputs. Taking these one at a time, let's look at a simple clocked flip-flop.

In Fig. 6-21 we will assume that a binary 1 has been applied (pulse) to the ORed clear input line. This clears the flip-flop and prepares it to accept new data. At some later time, we apply data to the set and reset input AND gates. Since the clock or trigger line is at a binary 0 level, the data does not appear directly on the flip-flop input lines.

We know that the flip-flop is going to change state swiftly once an input is applied to the set input so all we need to do is pulse the transfer line high and the flip-flop will set. We can say that the DATA, as it was applied, **enabled** the set input AND gate on the input to K000 and when the clock or transfer line went high the data was transferred to set the binary.

Since this is still an RS configuration with a gated clock capability added, if we apply a binary 0 to both input AND gates and then apply the clock pulse, neither gate is enabled and there is no information transferred or the output remains what it was before the application of the clock or transfer pulse.

If we apply a binary 1 to both inputs, both input AND gates are enabled and the output will be indeterminate since there is no way to know, except by physically measuring the output, which output took precedence and overrode the other. The output will definitely assume some output state but we cannot predict it. Fig. 6-22 is the truth table for the flip-flop in Fig. 6-21. The S and R in Fig. 6-22 refer to the input conditions at the input to the set (S) and reset (R) AND gates. N or n refers to

Fig. 6-22. Truth table for the flip-flop diagrammed in Fig. 6-21.

SN	RN	Qn+1	
0	0	Qn	
0	1	0	
1	0	1	
1	1	NOT ALLOWED	OR ?

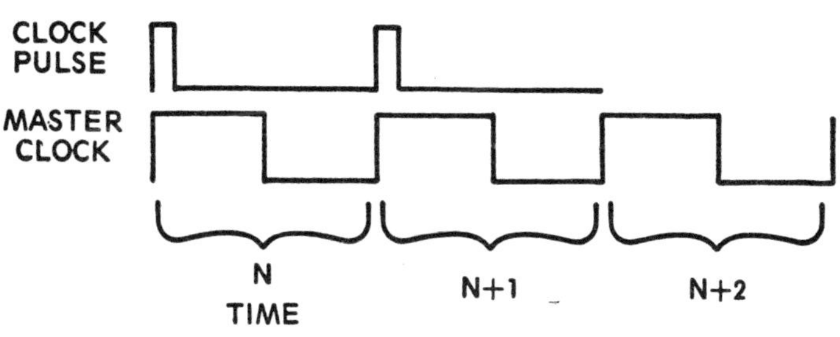

Fig. 6-23. Diagram showing the relationship of clock pulses and N time periods.

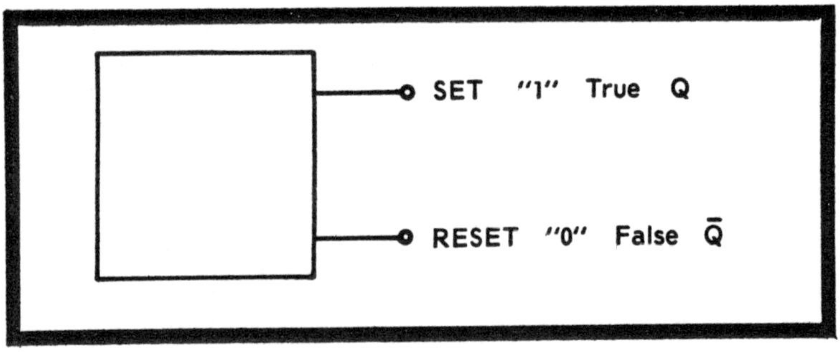

Fig. 6-24. If the set output of a flip-flop is a 1, the reset will be a 0.

some particular time period of the clock. Qn+1 refers to the condition after the clock pulse just following the N time period (Fig. 6-23) and so forth. The Q always refers to the set output side.

Either side may be either a binary 1 or a binary 0 and we may use either side to drive lamps or gates or other circuitry. If the set is a binary 1, we say the flip-flop is in a set condition and the reset side has a binary 0 output or the complement of the set side output. If the reset is a binary 1 we say the flip-flop is in a reset or clear condition and the set side has a binary 0 output or the complement of the reset output.

We can state all of this another way: The set, 1, true or Q output of a flip-flop can be either a 1 or a 0 and the output of the reset, 0, false or $\bar{Q}$ side will be its complement (Fig. 6-24).

So, returning to the truth table in Fig. 6-22, when Sn equals 0 and Rn equals 0, the output of the flip-flop after the application of the clock pulse (Qn+1) equals Qn or the condition of the flip-flop just before the application of the clock pulse or, in other words, the flip-flop **did not change state**.

When Sn equals 0 and Rn equals 1 the flip-flop will be reset or the Q side output will equal 0 at Qn+1. When Sn equals 1 and Rn equals 0 the flip-flop will be set or the Q (set) side will equal a binary 1 at Qn+1. When Sn equals 1 and Rn equals 1 there is no way to predict what the output will become at Qn+1 and the output cannot be determined, so this condition is not allowed.

A similar circuit in IC logic appears in Fig. 6-25. Without the heavier lines the circuit uses a cross-coupled inverter which responds to a positive-going signal or binary 1 by positive logic definition. With a binary 1 on the set input and a binary 1 on the clock line, the output of gate A becomes a 0 and the output of C goes to a binary 1. This output is cross-coupled back to the input of D which already has a 1 on it from the output of gate B. The 1s ANDed together are 1 which is inverted through the gate to become a binary 0 at the output of D. This 0 is cross-coupled back to the input of C to latch the binary in a set condition. The heavier lines in Fig. 6-25, coupled back to the input set and reset lines, are used to demonstrate the operation of a counter. It will be seen shortly that it is not a good counter but let's look.

Let's assume that the flip-flop is set (Q equals 1). This 1 output is wired back to the reset side of the flip-flop. Also the $\bar{Q}$ output (binary 0) is wired back to the set input. Look at the following binary count:

000
001
010
011

100
101

110
111

If this flip-flop is in the least significant digit position, we can easily see that it will change state (from 0 to 1 or from 1 to 0) with each incoming pulse to be counted. Therefore we might conclude that the wiring indicated by the heavier lines is used to force the flip-flop to change state with each incoming pulse on the clock line, and that is a correct assumption.

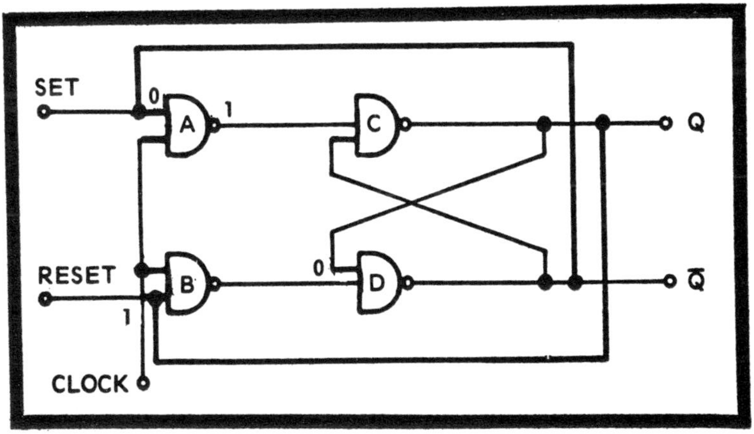

Fig. 6-25. Flip-flop using cross coupling to demonstrate the operation of a counter.

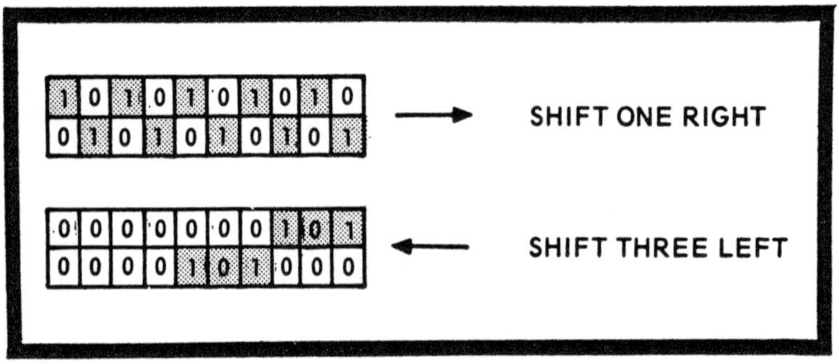

Fig. 6-26. Shift register diagram showing how data is moved serially through a register.

With a 1 on the reset line, when a clock pulse (or count pulse) comes along, both inputs on the B gate go to 1 and the output goes to 0. Previous to this, a 1 from the Q output and a 1 from the B output held the $\overline{Q}$ output at 0. Now the $\overline{Q}$ output goes to binary 1 and is coupled back to the input of C which, along with the 1 output from A, drives the Q output to binary 0 and the flip-flop is reset (Q equals 0 and $\overline{Q}$ equals 1).

Now we come to the problem mentioned earlier. If the clock line is still at binary 1 after the flip-flop changes state, it will couple the new signal conditions back to the input and the flip-flop will set, then reset again, and so forth, until the clock input is removed. This is known as a race condition and there are ways to cure it. One little used method is to insure that the clock pulse is shorter in duration than the propagation time of the circuit. With TTL logic, for example, the propagation time per gate (meaning the time it takes the signal to move from input to output) is 10 to 20 nanoseconds. If we assume the fastest operation, the signal would get through two gates from input to output in 20 nanoseconds; the clock pulse would have to be, for safe operation, on the order of 10 to 15 nanoseconds wide to insure that the clock pulse would go to 0 by the time the output changed state. This would be an extremely short pulse and it would be difficult to generate, so we will normally use other techniques.

The RS flip-flop is the lowest cost device to implement and it is used for storage purposes only. In the integrated circuit industry it is called a bistable latch or simply a latch. Texas Instruments puts four of them in a 14-pin package and calls it a Quad-latch. The circuit is normally fed directly by the outputs (Q and $\overline{Q}$) of a flip-flop stage.

To this point we have developed a simple storage element. We need storage capabilities, of course, but far more than this we need counters and shift registers. We have discussed counters briefly. They are used to count pulses either from some outside source or from the computer clock. They may count synchronously or asynchronously. They may count up or down or both. They may count sequentially in a binary up or down count or they may count in some forced format (non-sequentially) such as BCD or gray code, but they each have the characteristic of counting pulses.

We also use shift registers. These are used to move data serially through the register (Fig. 6-26). If we want to put data into a piece of equipment on a single wire, we run it into a shift register (Fig. 6-27).

Data comes in (is shifted in) from left to right in Fig. 6-27. Each block represents a flip-flop stage. Once data is in the register, it can be removed in parallel on eight wires (an 8-bit bus). Thus the information (data) comes in on a single wire (serially) and is taken out on eight wires (in parallel). It could be loaded into the register in parallel and shifted out serially just as easily so we could say that a shift register performs serial-parallel, parallel-serial conversion.

The above should give you some idea of the uses to which flip-flops are put. To review, they are used for:

1. Storage

2. Counters

3. Shift registers

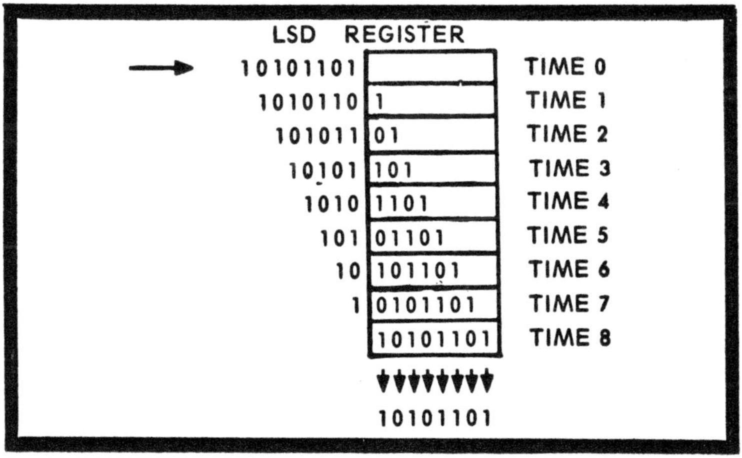

Fig. 6-27. Diagram showing data coming into a register serially and going out in parallel.

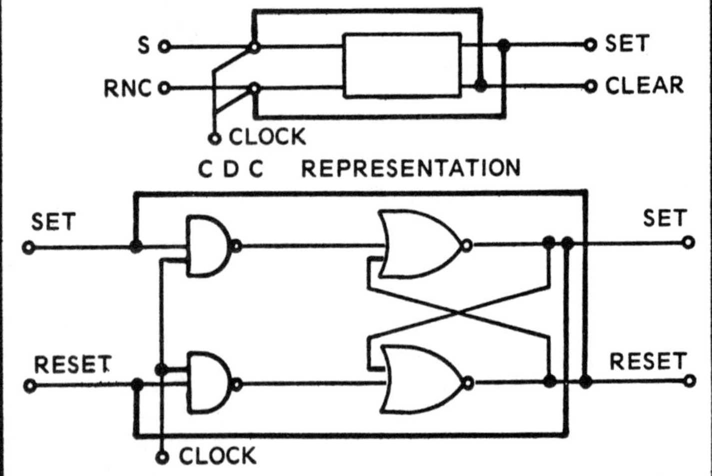

Fig. 6-28. CDC single rank gated input register stage.

Now, let's develop flip-flop types that do something besides store information. We decided that our basic CDC single rank gated input register stage could be illustrated with two cross-coupled NOR gates and a pair of input AND gates, as shown in Fig. 6-28. Each of these circuits can do precisely the same thing; therefore, the application of the wiring indicated by the heavy lines would make a one-bit counter. Since it can do everything the IC counter can do, it will also race unless the input clock pulses are kept extremely short.

Let's see if we can cure our race problem. Then we will discuss additional flip-flop types and finally, cover a number of circuit applications. In the circuit in Fig. 6-29 use the "advance count" line to apply the counting information which appears at the output of flip-flop A immediately. Since the feedback information is coming from flip-flop B and it has not changed state yet, we do not have to worry about the width of the advance count pulse as long as we do not apply the transfer pulse until the advance count input has gone to 0. The fact is that we use two control delay circuits, one following the other, to insure that the advance count line has gone low before the count is transferred to the B flip-flop.

The entire system (two flip-flops and four gates) is known as a two, dual, or double rank flip-flop or register stage, and there will be this amount of circuitry for each counter or shift register stage. For example, a counter that will count to octal

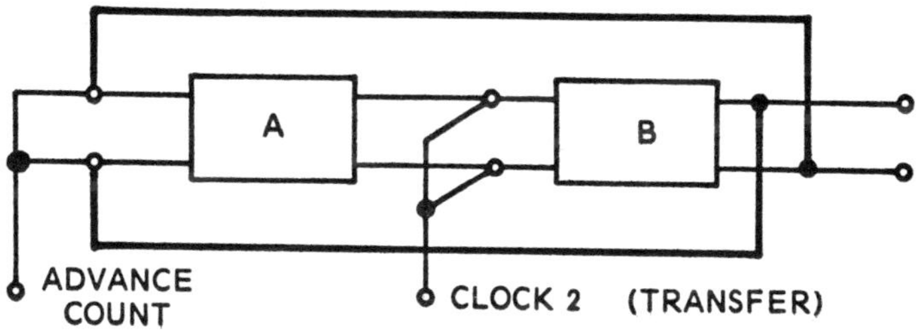

Fig. 6-29. Advance count is used to overcome racing.

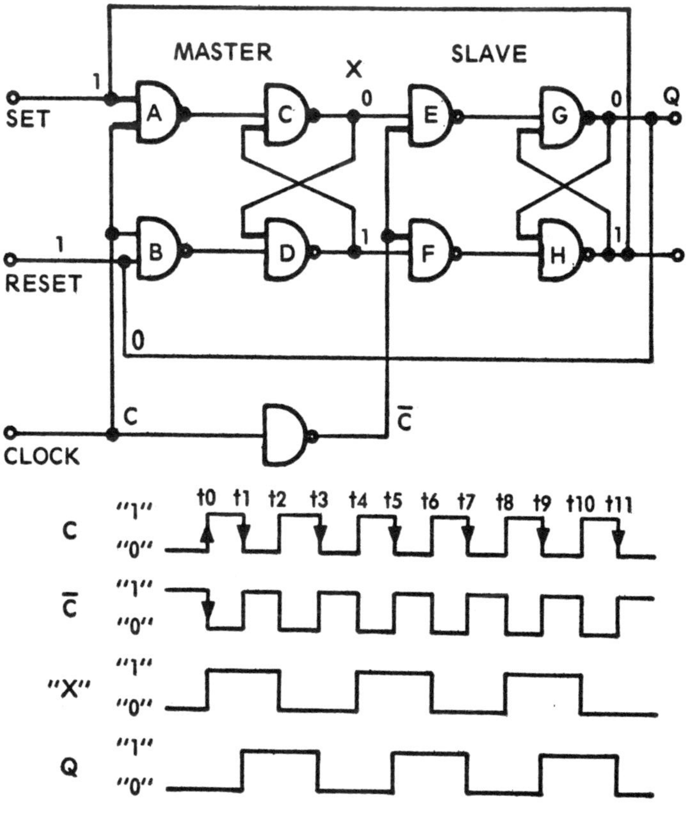

Fig. 6-30. Double rank register stage.

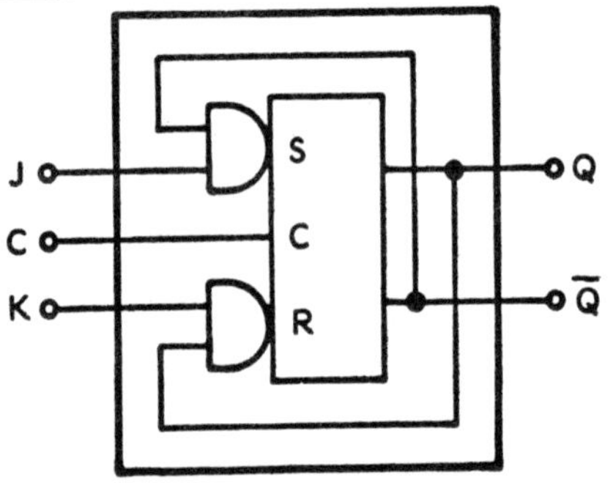

J	K	Qn+1
0	0	Qn
0	1	1
1	0	0
1	1	$\overline{Qn}$

Fig. 6-31. J-K flip-flop diagram and truth table.

7 (Binary 111) requires three double rank register stages or one for each bit position.

The double rank principle is used with integrated circuits as follows: We can start by assuming the conditions shown in Fig. 6-30. With the binary reset (clear) the reset input (gate B) has a binary 0 and the set input (gate A) a binary 1. The clock input is at a binary 0 level and any 0 on the input to a NAND gate forces the output to binary 1 so the output of both A and B are a logical 1. With 0 coupled from the output of C to the input of D, D's output is a 1 coupled back to the input of C to form the master latch. At this point, E and F are enabled by a 1 on the $\overline{\text{CLOCK}}$ line and the master output is applied to the slave.

At t0 the input clock goes high. At this same time gates E and F are disabled by the inverted clock ($\overline{C}$) going to 0. With a binary 1 on the set input and a binary 1 on the clock line, the output of A goes to a logical 0 (the output of B remains a logical 1). This drives the output of C to a logical 1 and couples a logical 1 back to the input of D which, NANDed with the output of B, drives the output of D to 0. At t1 the input clock C goes back to 0, locking out input gates A and B and the output of the master is transferred to the slave as gates E and F are enabled by the rise of $\overline{C}$.

The overall effect is that Q changes state on each "clock fall" (look at times t1, 3, 5, 7, 9, and 11 and Q's output). The other waveforms are shown for comparison purposes. This flip-flop configuration is known as an RST master-slave binary or simply an RST flip-flop.

So far we have discussed the simple RS and RST flip-flop configurations. These two have the same simple problem which says, in effect, that when we apply an activating input level to both the R and S lines at the same time, the output is indeterminate. We also showed a pair of cross-coupling connections from output to input that allow us to easily use the configuration as a counter.

The next configuration makes use of a similar hookup. The J-K flip-flop (binary) is shown schematically in Fig. 6-31. The RST flip-flop is shown in the small box while the outer box contains the complete J-K flip-flop circuit. We have simply added two input AND gates and coupled one input of each back to the opposite output, similar to the technique employed with the RST counter stage. This makes the flip-flop much easier to use and wire.

The new state (where we had a question mark for the RS and RST) simply says that should both inputs be high the output will simply change state or be complemented. This means that if we tie J and K to a high-level (logical 1) we can apply a count pulse to the C input and have an operating counter. J-K binaries may have multiple inputs and even complement input connections for wiring simplicity.

Two other flip-flop types are the "T" and "D" types. The T or toggle type (Fig. 6-32) simply ties the J and K inputs together internally and brings them out as a T input. In this manner we can make counters that are very simple to wire and control. A high level on the T input allows the flip-flop to count. A low input on the T line disables the counter.

The "T" stands for toggle and is another term you will hear used frequently in connection with flip-flops. The rate at which the binary will count is referred to as its toggle rate and it is one of the operating parameters for flip-flops. The T truth table in Fig. 6-32 simply says that if the input is low, the output condition does not change. If the T input is high, the flip-flop complements (or changes state) with each input clock pulse.

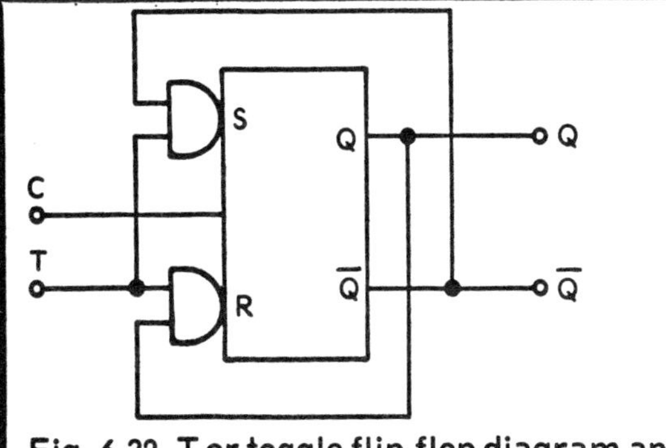

	T	Qn+1
	0	Qn
	1	$\overline{Qn}$

Fig. 6-32. T or toggle flip-flop diagram and truth table.

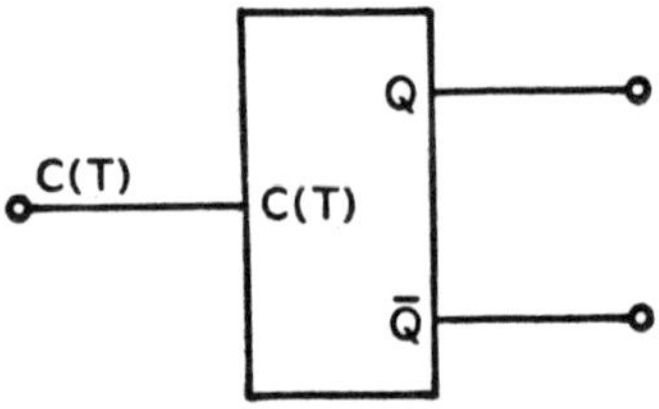

Fig. 6-33. T type binary diagram showing the T input tied high.

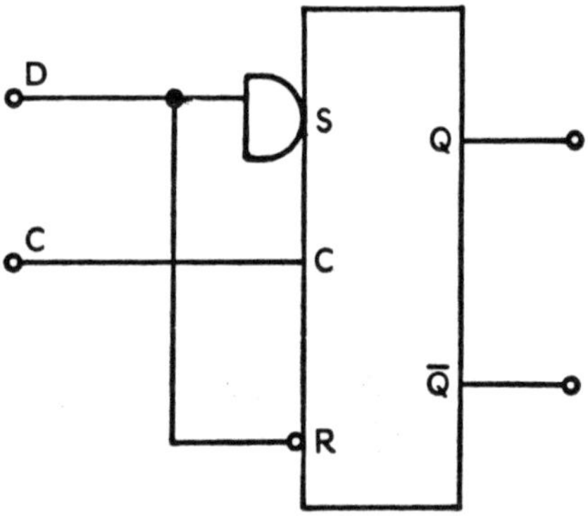

D	Qn+1
0	0
1	1

Fig. 6-34. D flip-flop diagram and truth table.

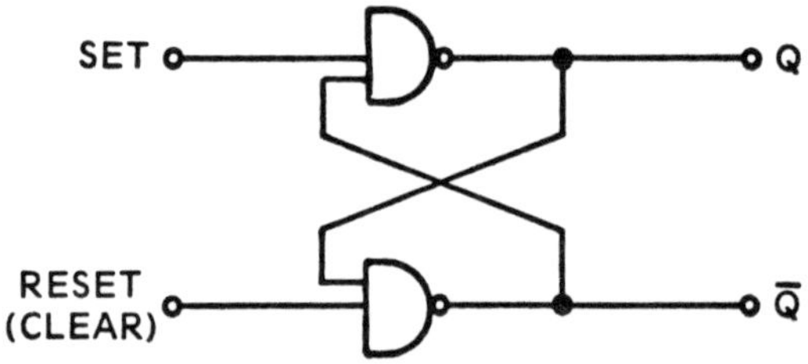

Fig. 6-35. RS latch circuit using NAND gates.

Some T type binaries allow no control over the T input. It is permanently tied high internally and the input connection is just the clock input terminal (Fig. 6-33).

The "D" flip-flop (Fig. 6-34) is basically a delay or retiming flip-flop. The input condition (1 or 0) appears at the output after the clock goes low. For this flip-flop the truth table is even simpler. Remember again that for each of these truth tables using the n designation (Qn+1 for example), we are describing the output conditions of the flip-flop after the clock transition (rise or fall) that controls the transfer of information to the slave or output.

At this point we might review the basic flip-flop types and get a general idea of where we stand. The simply RS latch should be considered first. For integrated circuit work, it is normally inplemented with NAND gates (Fig. 6-35). The latch is the simplest flip-flop type and is normally used for memory or storage. One excellent example is a switch-bounce eliminator (Fig. 6-36). In this circuit, even though the switch might move away from the contact point (bounce), the latch will not return to its original state until the opposite contact is made. Before trying to analyze this circuit, two things are important. With IC logic, an open input is considered high or a binary 1. Also, the input switch must have Form C contacts, frequently called single pole, double throw or SPDT.

CDC's basic RS latch or single rank flip-flop stage uses a cross-coupled NOR gate configuration (Fig. 6-37) to obtain essentially the same type of operation. This accounts for the statement that the basic single rank stage is used for storage only. The RS latch is an asynchronous device, meaning that it is not and cannot be operated under clock pulse control.

CLOCKED OR SYNCHRONOUS OPERATION

For clocked, or synchronous operation, and to perform many of the chores required by flip-flops, it becomes

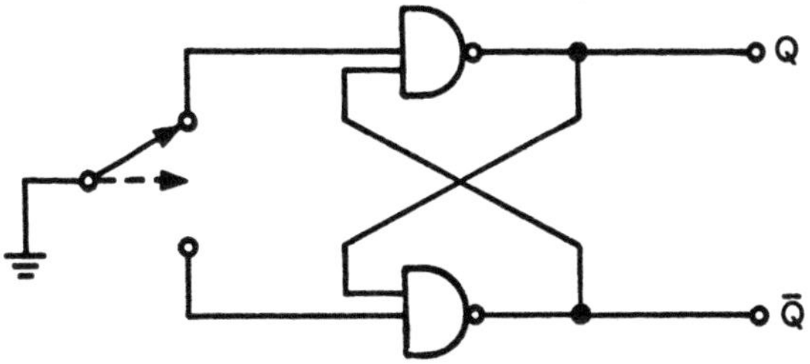

Fig. 6-36. Switch-bounce eliminator.

necessary to have them operate under the control of a system clock. There are a number of ways that this can be done but the normal method is through a master-slave principle in that two latches under gate control are used. The information is allowed to enter the master flip-flop at one part of the clock time and at a later time it is transferred to the slave latch. With CDC logic, this becomes a dual or double rank flip-flop stage and the transfer of information into the first latch is controlled by one control delay that operates on one half cycle of the clock, while transfer of the information to the storage rank is controlled by a transfer input that comes from a second control delay operating on an alternate half cycle of the clock.

RS-T AND RST BINARIES

So far we have touched on two types of operation and one use for binaries. The two types are clocked and unclocked or synchronous and asynchronous. The single use is storage. And the switch-bounce protector is a storage function. It stores the switch position information, even though the switch may come momentarily off the made contact.

A second use for binaries is in counting binary pulses. I may have a string of pulses coming from some source and I want to know how many. For this type of operation, the flip-flop used is frequently called a T or toggle flip-flop and it is precisely like any toggle switch in your home. You flip the switch once and the light goes on, flip it again and the light goes off.

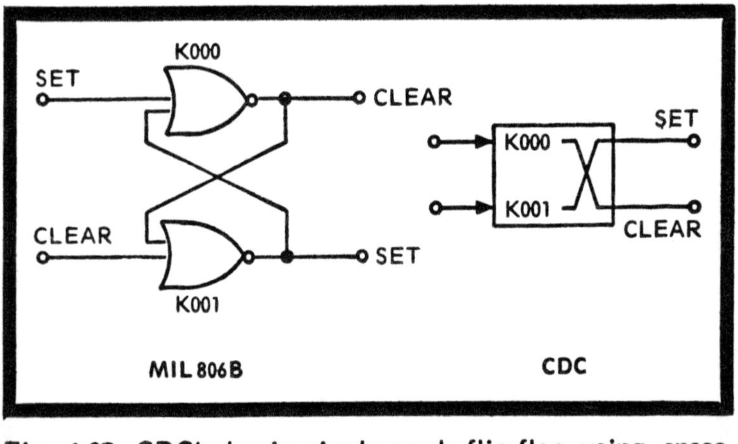

Fig. 6-37. CDC's basic single rank flip-flop using cross-coupled NOR gates.

Now if you and two of your neighbors manned toggle switches and you threw yours once each time a good looking girl walked by, and each time your light went off, your neighbor threw his switch (just moved it to the next position), his light would go on half as often as yours, and the next neighbor, watching the first neighbor's light, would move his switch to the opposite position each time he saw your neightbor's light go off, you could count a total of eight girls and at any time you could read the octal number from the lit lamps and determine how many girls had walked by. But if you put out a photocell (sensitive to pretty girls) and three T type binaries with the set outputs attached to lamps you could do the same job with much greater ease (though not as much fun).

This, then, is the function of the T type binary and it is implemented by coupling the set output back to the clear input and the clear (reset) output back to the set input. With the RS-T, this must be wired in by the user. With the RST it is already wired in. The RS-T and RST types normally have clock connections and a means for setting or resetting them with a steady DC input from some external source such as a master clear button or a switch input.

J-K BINARIES

We determined earlier that with both inputs at an enabled level in the RS, RS-T or RST binary, the output state is indeterminate or a big question mark. The J-K binary does away with this problem by gating the inputs to the flip-flop with the cross-coupled outputs of the flip-flop. In this way, should both inputs be enabled the flip-flop simply complements the output state.

We also determined that this would be a good way to implement a toggle because it is simply necessary to connect the J and K inputs to a level that keeps them enabled. However, there is another desirable thing. Suppose we wanted to count pretty girls for only a few minutes each morning, we could tie the J and K inputs together and enable them only during the morning minutes that we wanted to do our counting. In this way, we can count selectively.

T TYPE BINARIES

We have rather thoroughly described the T type binary already so little more detail is required. The diagram and truth table in Fig. 6-32 tell the story.

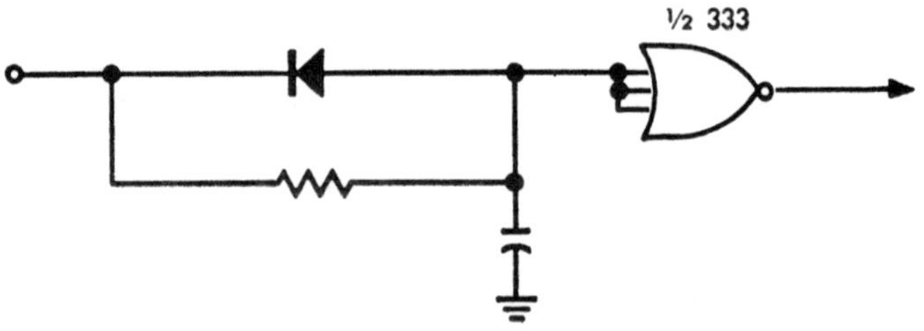

Fig. 6-38. Pulse width discriminator.

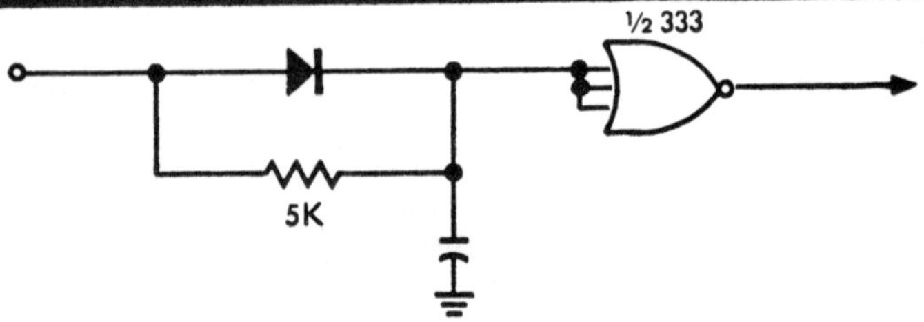

Fig. 6-39. Pulse stretcher diagram.

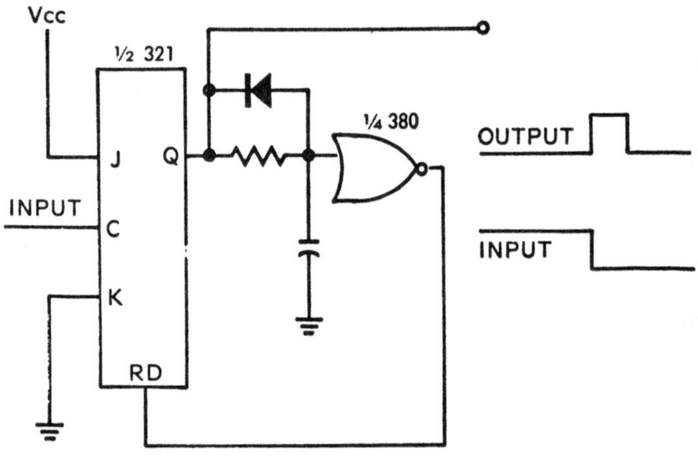

Fig. 6-40. Diagram of a one-shot or monostable multivibrator.

D TYPE BINARIES

This is probably the simplest flip-flop of the group. If an input appears on the D line, whether it is high or low, the output will not change until a clock pulse occurs on the clock line. There are many configurations, AC coupling, many input designations, and so forth, for the various systems of logic available. We have covered the basic ground rules and from here you should have little trouble recognizing the various types of circuits and the various nomenclature and designations involved.

If you are involved with a new type of logic (new manufacturer) get data sheets on the various devices used. Learn the ground rules for the system. Do they call it reset or clear. Do they label the output Q and $\overline{Q}$ or 1 and 0? Do they transfer data in the flip-flops on the clock rise or clock fall? Once you have learned the ground rules for the new logic system, you will have no trouble applying Boolean algebra and chasing 1s and 0s through it.

MISCELLANEOUS CIRCUITS

There are many miscellaneous circuits possible with both discrete components and integrated circuits. The circuits in Figs. 6-38 through 6-42 make use of some discrete components and various Signetics Utilogic integrated circuits.

The first circuit shown is a pulse width discriminator (Fig. 6-38). When the input is zero, the circuit is stable and the

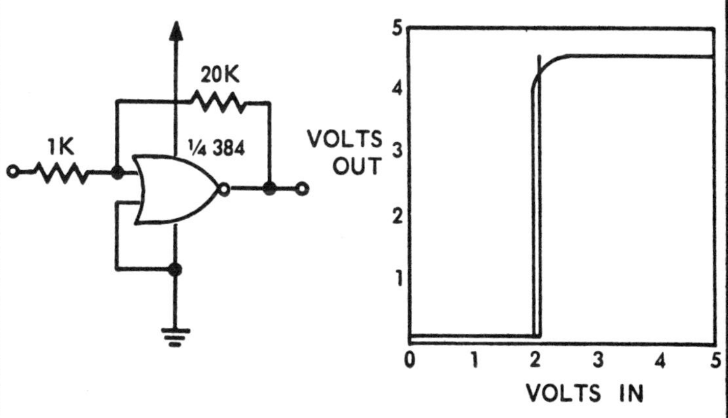

Fig. 6-41. Schmitt trigger circuit.

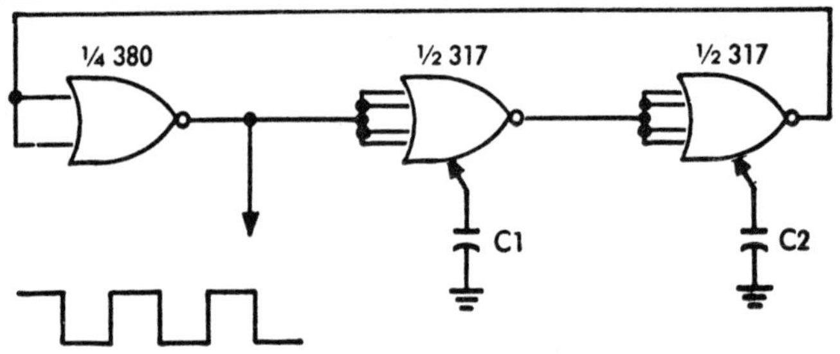

Fig. 6-42. Oscillator circuit using NOR gates.

capacitor discharges swiftly through the diode to effect no delay in a transition to zero. When the input goes high, the capacitor must charge through the 5K resistor before the one appears on the input to the gate. This gives an effective delay determined by the value of the capacitor and resistor.

In the second circuit (Fig. 6-39), a 1 input causes the capacitor to charge rapidly through the diode and the 1 is applied almost instantaneously to the gate input. When the input goes to zero, the capacitor must discharge through the 5K resistor and the pulse is lengthened by an amount determined by the capacitor and resistor.

The one shot or monostable multivibrator (Fig. 6-40) is a little more complex. When the pulse applied to the C input of the J-K flip-flop goes negative, the permanent 1 (Vcc) on the J input causes the flip-flop to set and the Q side (output) goes to 1. Prior to the fall of the input clock (C), the set output was zero and the output of the NOR gate was high, maintaining a high level on the R_D input as required. At some time after the Q goes to 1, determined by the value of R and C, the input to the NOR gate goes to 1, driving the output to 0 and resetting the flip-flop. That drives the input to the NOR gate to zero quickly (through the diode) and the output of the NOR gate returns to 1, ready for the next input pulse to the flip-flop. The net result is the generation of a pulse whose width is determined by the value of R and C.

No effort will be made to go into detail on the last two circuits. The Schmitt trigger (Fig. 6-41) is a circuit that goes to 1 on the output with a tiny bit in excess of 2 volts input (in the case of this circuit) and to zero at just under 2 volts.

The oscillator (Fig. 6-42) used makes use of gates for feedback (an odd number causing positive feedback) and thus gives an oscillator that operates from 250 kHz and up, depending on the capacitor values.

Chapter 7

Computer Blocks

All computers are made up of recognizable circuit blocks. These blocks may vary some in structure and size but they perform the same general functions.

Shift registers are used to convert data from serial to parallel, from parallel to serial, and for other general data handling operations. For example, teletype information comes in on a single line and must be converted to parallel form to move through the computer. Data is shifted into a shift register in serial form, then transferred out on six or eight parallel lines to the accumulator for storage.

Counting circuits of many different types are used to control computer operations. They count word lengths, serve as a program sequence counter, and count the number of bits moved into a shift register in order to control the operation of that shift register.

Encoders and decoders are used to convert data from one form to another form. The computer normally works in pure binary as far as the internal function is concerned. The information coming in and going out is perhaps ASCII or BCD and encoders and decoders are used to convert binary to the proper form.

Finally, every machine has adder and subtractor circuitry with the subtractor frequently nothing more than a 1s complement addition operation.

The circuits that follow are simplified to make them a little easier to understand. In most instances the actual circuitry in a computer is quite different and somewhat more complex but the circuits presented here serve to illustrate the principles in sufficient detail to allow you to understand the more complicated circuits.

SHIFT REGISTER

The basic shift register in Fig. 7-1 is used to handle four bits of data presented in a serial fashion to the input. The data being shifted in is 0101 or decimal 5. The least significant bit

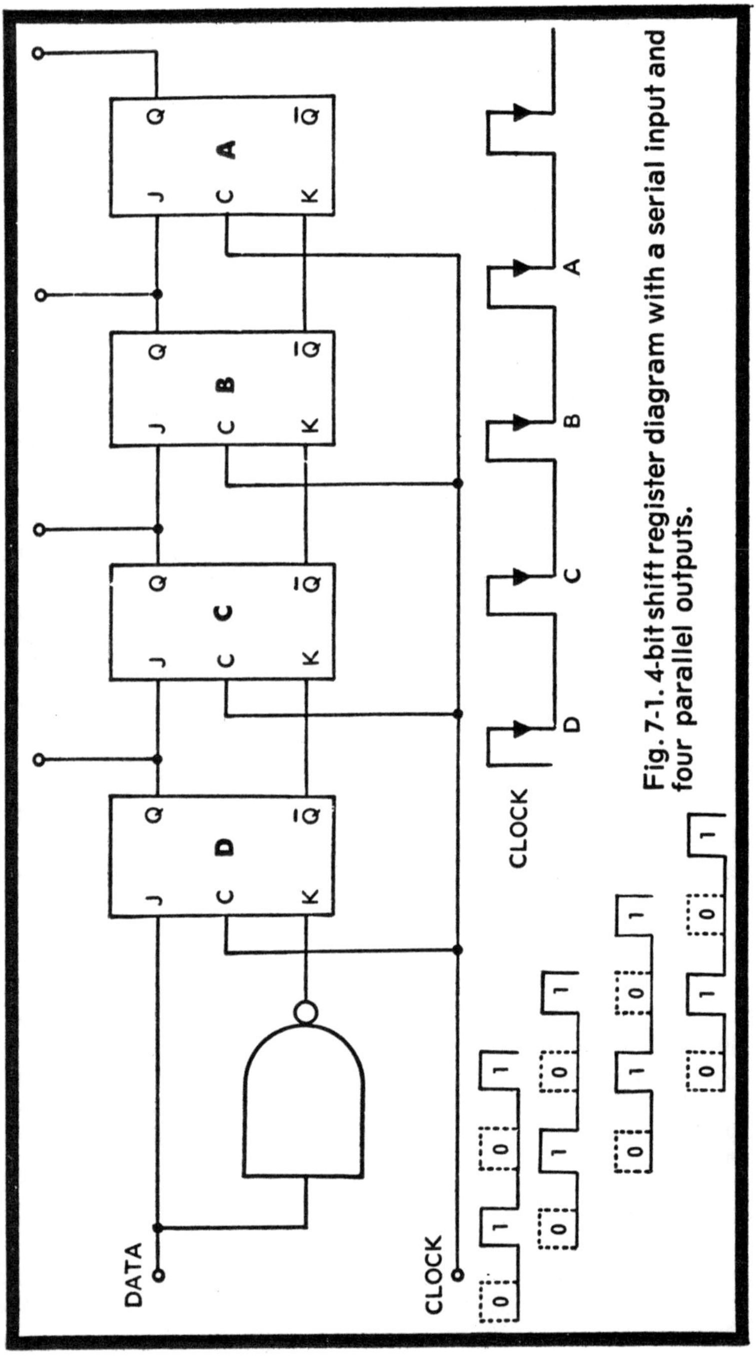

Fig. 7-1. 4-bit shift register diagram with a serial input and four parallel outputs.

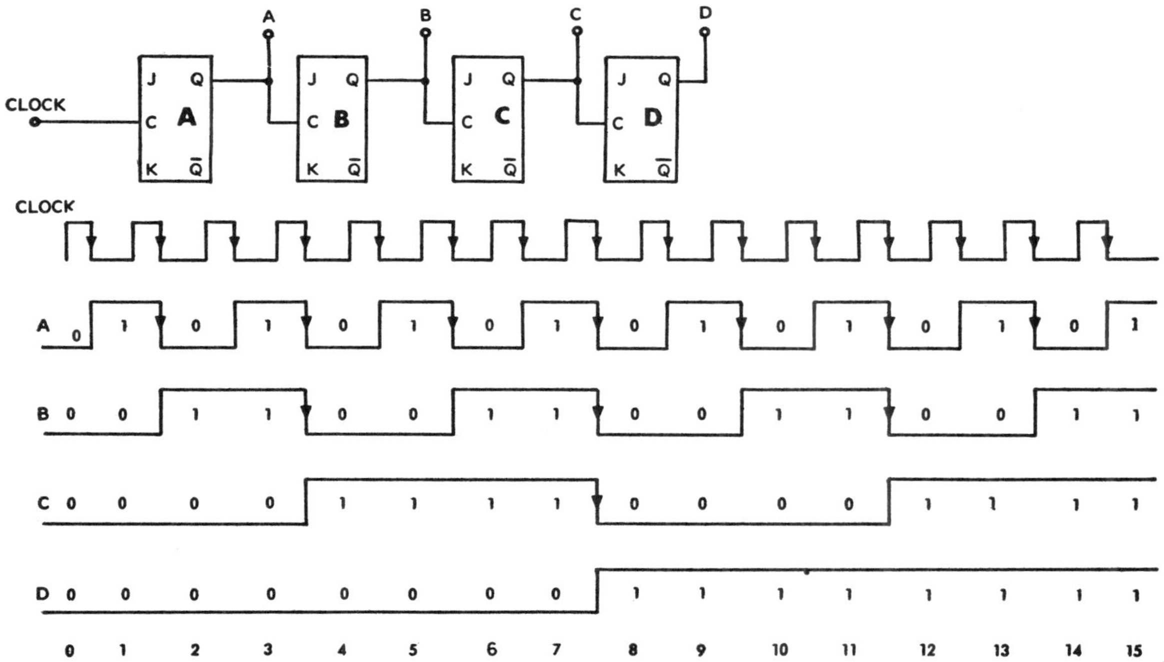

Fig. 7-2. 4-bit binary ripple up counter diagram.

(1) is the first bit presented to the input and it should be realized that there is additional external circuitry controlling the shifting of the data into this register.

Since many modern IC flip-flops are activated by a clock fall, all of the circuits presented here use the clock fall as the precise time of data transfer. Notice that the incoming data, according to the timing diagrams, becomes available to the input ½ bit time before the clock falls. This is a fairly normal procedure and again this data would be under the control of some external circuitry.

On the first clock fall, flip-flop D goes to a 1. The input data is 1 and the inverter gate at the input then forces the K input to a 0 while J is 1. On the next clock fall, the Q output of flip-flop D is a 1 while the new information being presented to D is a 0. Under these conditions, a 1 will be entered in C and D will go to a 0. This procedure is continued until all four bits of information or data have been entered into the shift register.

COUNTERS

The counter in Fig. 7-2 is an asynchronous 4-bit up counter. The input clock pulses shown in the timing diagram are all occurring in an even time sequence but they could occur at odd intervals and the counter would still function. In other words, the counter is not dependent on an outside time source.

The assumption is made in the timing diagram that the counter is reset, meaning that all Q outputs are 0. The fall of each preceding stage (Q) is used to clock the next flip-flop and this is where the system gets the name "ripple counter" or "ripple-through counter." In the timing diagram both the clock and the idealized waveforms for the Q output of each stage are shown.

Fig. 7-3 illustrates a down counter. The only difference between the two counters is that the clock for the next stage is taken from $\overline{Q}$. Again the idealized waveforms for the Q outputs are shown in the diagram and the counter is considered to be preset (set) with all Q outputs equal to 1 prior to the first clock pulse.

Fig. 7-4 is the logic diagram for a synchronous binary up counter. Notice that in this counter the clock is applied to all stages simultaneously. Since this is the case, succeeding stages must be controlled in some other way and they are controlled in this case by gates. Input gates 2 and 3 (numbered 1 and 2) actually perform the AND function with the inverter going to the J and K inputs.

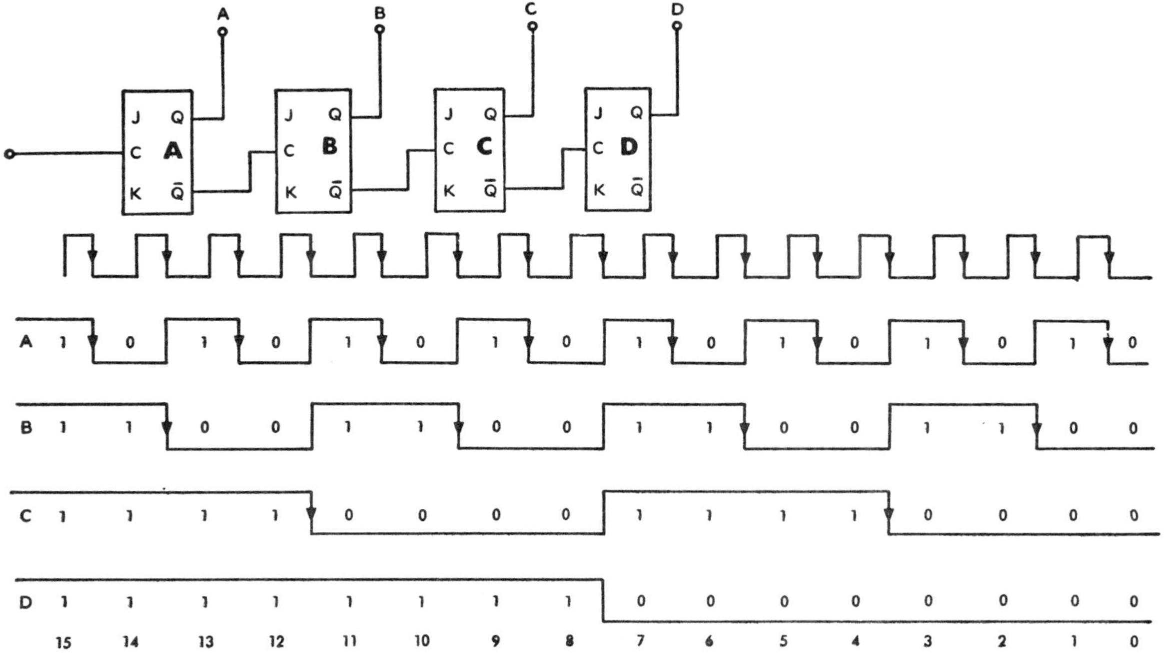

Fig. 7-3. 4-bit binary ripple down counter.

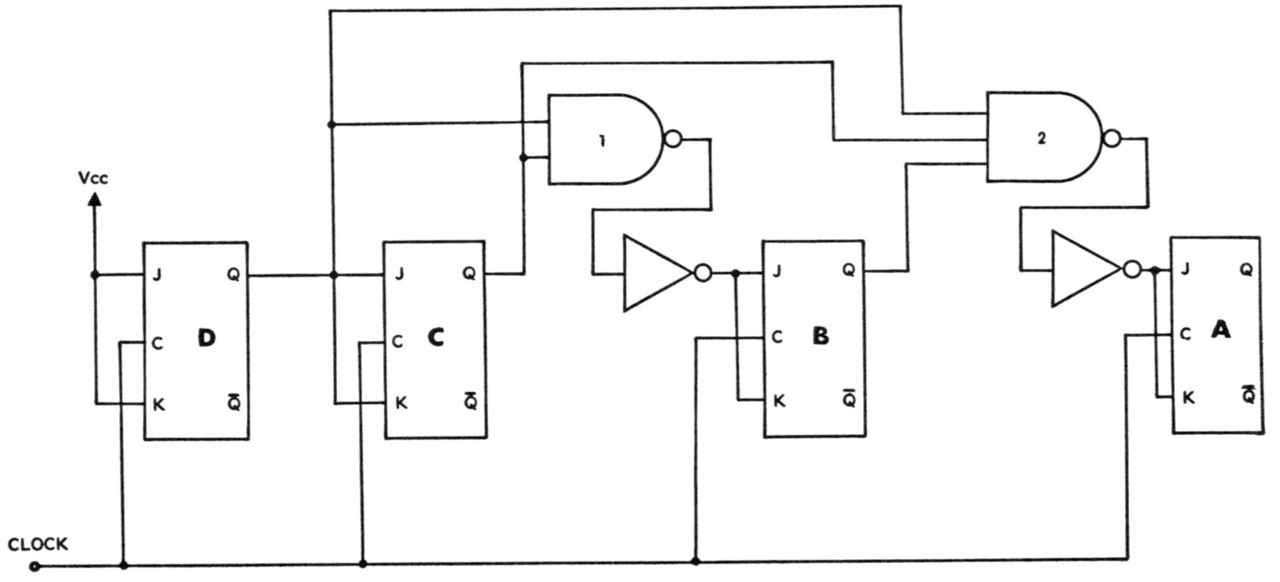

Fig. 7-4. Synchronous binary up counter. Notice that with this counter, all stages change at the same time under gate control.

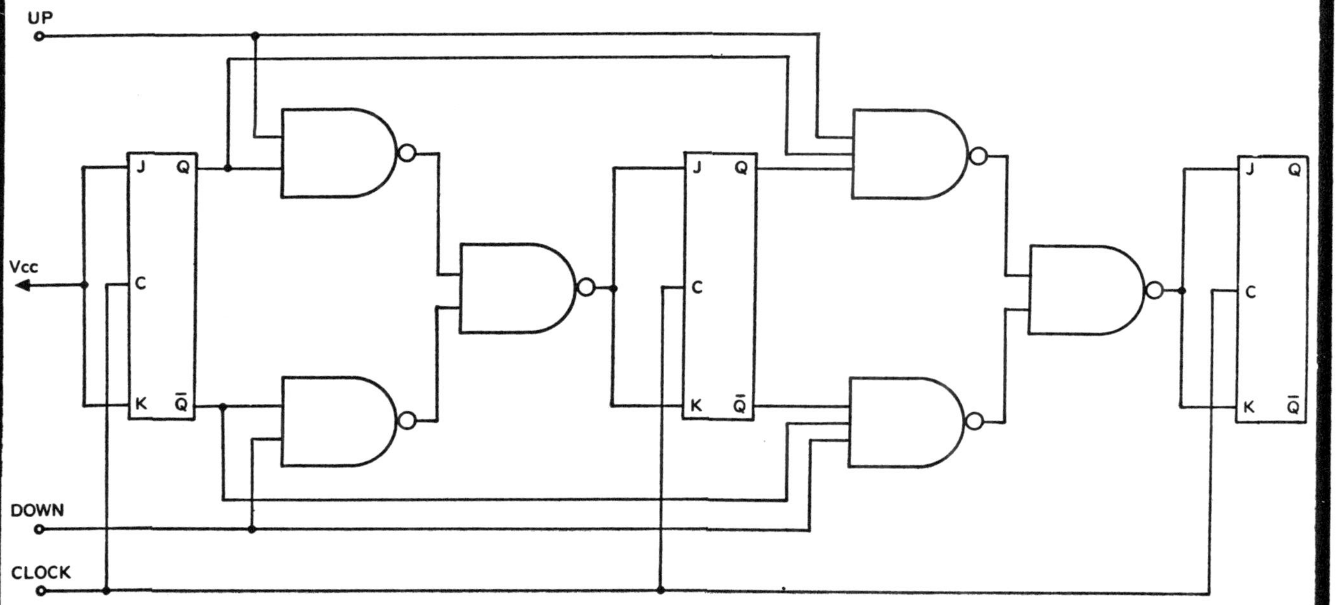

Fig. 7-5. Diagram of a synchronous binary up counter.

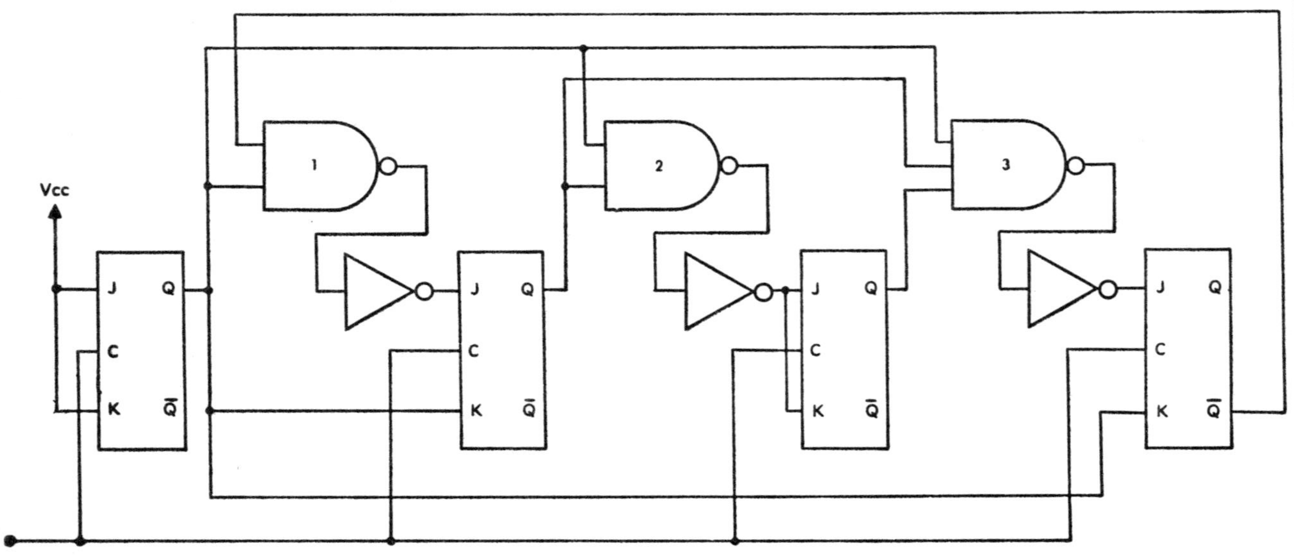

Fig. 7-6. Synchronous 8-2-4-1 BCD counter.

	D	C	B	A
0	0	0	0	0
1	0	0	0	1
2	0	0	1	0
3	0	0	1	1
4	0	1	0	0
5	0	1	0	1
6	0	1	1	0
7	0	1	1	1
8	1	0	0	0
9	1	0	0	1

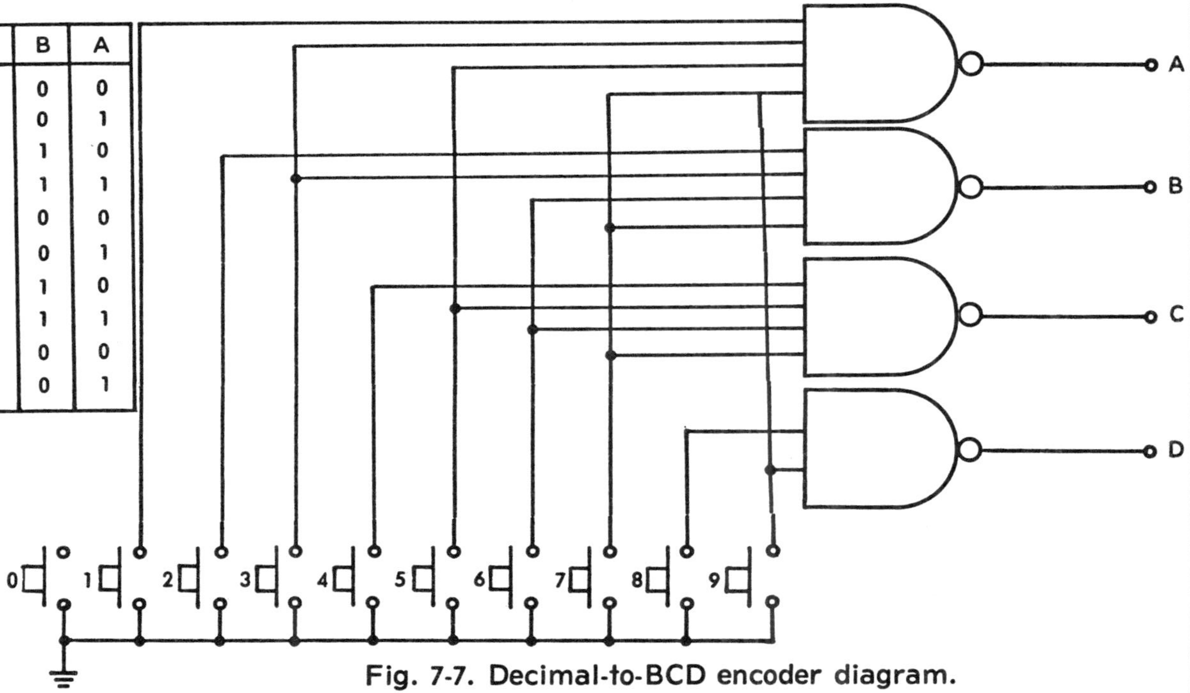

Fig. 7-7. Decimal-to-BCD encoder diagram.

On the first clock pulse, again assuming the counter to be reset before starting the count, all Q outputs will be 0. In order for the flip-flops to change state, remember that the J and K inputs must both be 1.

The inputs to J and K on the D flip-flop are held at 1 by tying them to Vcc. The first clock pulse, then, will cause D to toggle and Q will become 1. This applies a 1 to one of the inputs to gate 1 but this is not enough to cause the output of the inverter connected to J and K of B to go to a 1. On the next clock pulse the Q output of D goes back to 0 and the Q output of C goes to 1.

On the third clock pulse, the Q output of both D and C go to a 1, enabling the inputs to B so that on the fourth clock pulse the Q output of B goes to a 1 and D and C are both returned to 0. The cycle for D and C repeats and on the seventh clock pulse all inputs to gate 2 will be 1, allowing A to be set while all three preceding flip-flops return to 0.

The problem with this type of counter is that as the length of the counter increases, the number of inputs to the control gates goes up. There are other ways to control the system that will not be developed here, but these counters are usually built up in blocks with one block controlling the next block to keep the number of gate inputs to a reasonable level.

The 3-bit counter in Fig. 7-5 can be used to count either **up** or **down**. The method is simple. The gates shown are controlled by inputs to the **up** or **down** line and will allow the counter to use either the Q or the $\overline{Q}$ side of the preceding stage to clock the succeeding stages. Beyond that the operation is identical to the asynchronous counters studied earlier.

The BCD counter in Fig. 7-6 is similar to all of the other counters except that at count 1001 the counter is forced back to all zeros (0000). With this in mind, and realizing that this is a synchronous counter, a good exercise would be to trace the count through and see why the counter is forced to 0000 after 1001. Remember that the gates perform the AND function with the inverters.

ENCODERS

The decimal-to-BCD encoder in Fig. 7-7 depends on the fact that an open input to a NAND gate looks like a binary 1. Thus the outputs of all the gates are 0 with no switches depressed. Pressing the 0 button does not cause the situation to change so that the output of A, B, C and D is 0000. Normally switch 0 is also connected to a transfer gate that allows the 0000 to be transferred to a register.

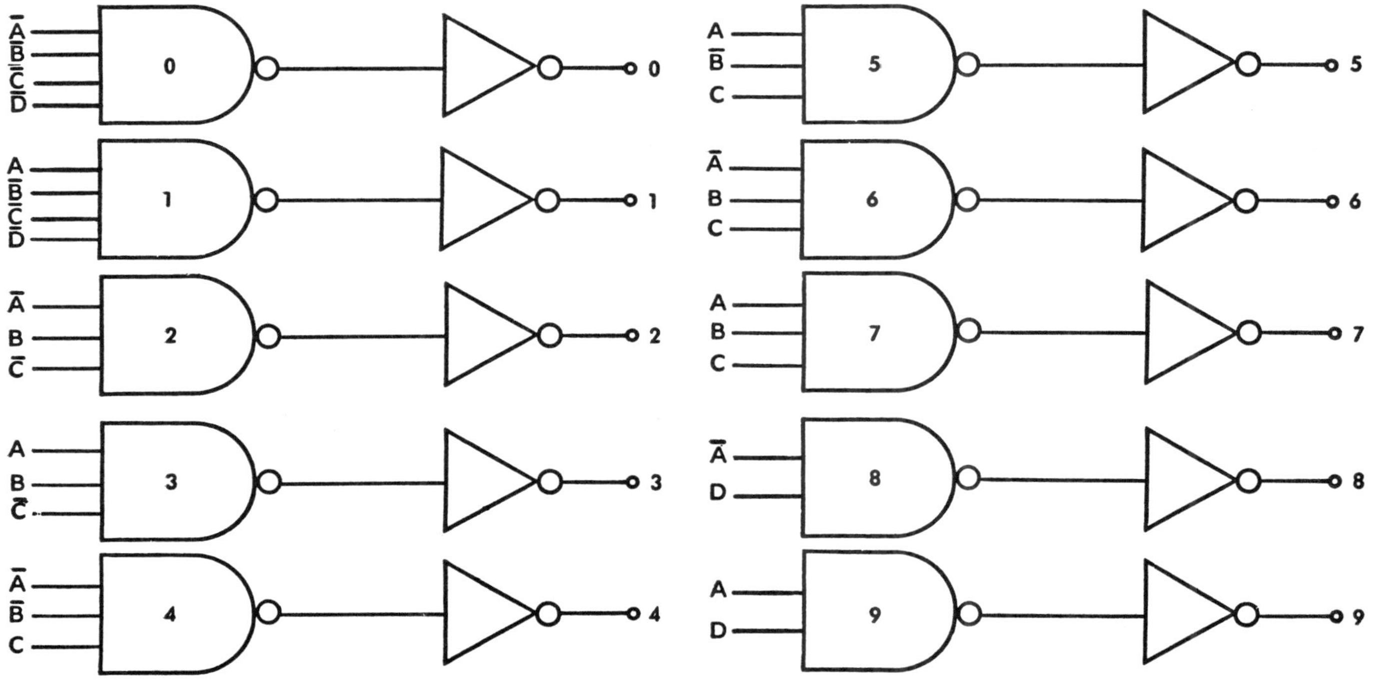

Fig. 7-8. Diagram of a BCD-to-decimal decoder.

A	B	$\bar{A}$	$\bar{B}$	$A\bar{B}$	$\bar{A}B$	$A\bar{B}+\bar{A}B$
0	0	1	1	0	0	0
0	1	1	0	0	1	1
1	0	0	1	1	0	1
1	1	0	0	0	0	0

Fig. 7-9. Truth table for the half add sum function.

Pressing the 1 button causes one input to A to drop to 0. The output then goes to 1, giving an output of 0001 (DCBA). Pressing 5 causes the outputs of A and C to go to 1 giving 0101 or BCD 5! The rest you should be able to trace.

DECODERS

Fig. 7-8 illustrates a BCD-to-decimal decoder. When the inputs to the gates are taken from flip-flops, $\bar{A}$ indicates the $\bar{Q}$ output of flip-flop A and so forth. With a count of 0000 in the register, the output of $\bar{A}$, $\bar{B}$, $\bar{C}$ and $\bar{D}$ is 1. This gives all 1s into the 0 gate. The output goes to 0 and the inverter makes it a 1 out of the gate-inverter combination which could be used to light a lamp behind the numeral 0. None of the other gate-inverter combinations would output a 1 under these circumstances. The other gate-inverter combinations can be analyzed in the same way.

ADDERS

There are probably almost as many adder circuits as there are computers, but they all implement the same set of equations. The sum equation for any adder is Sum equals $A\bar{B}$ + $\bar{A}B$ and Carry equals AB.

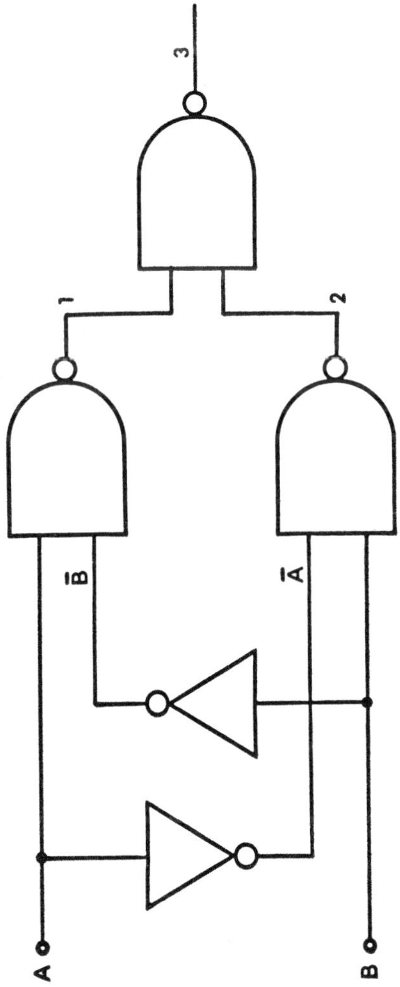

A	B	Ā	B̄	$A\bar{B}$	1 $\overline{A\bar{B}}$	$\bar{A}B$	2 $\overline{\bar{A}B}$	$\overline{A\bar{B}}\cdot\overline{\bar{A}B}$	3 $\overline{\overline{A\bar{B}}\cdot\overline{\bar{A}B}}$
0	0	1	1	0	1	0	1	1	0
0	1	1	0	0	1	1	0	0	1
1	0	0	1	1	0	0	1	0	1
1	1	0	0	0	1	0	1	1	0

Fig. 7-10. A NAND gate half adder with truth table.

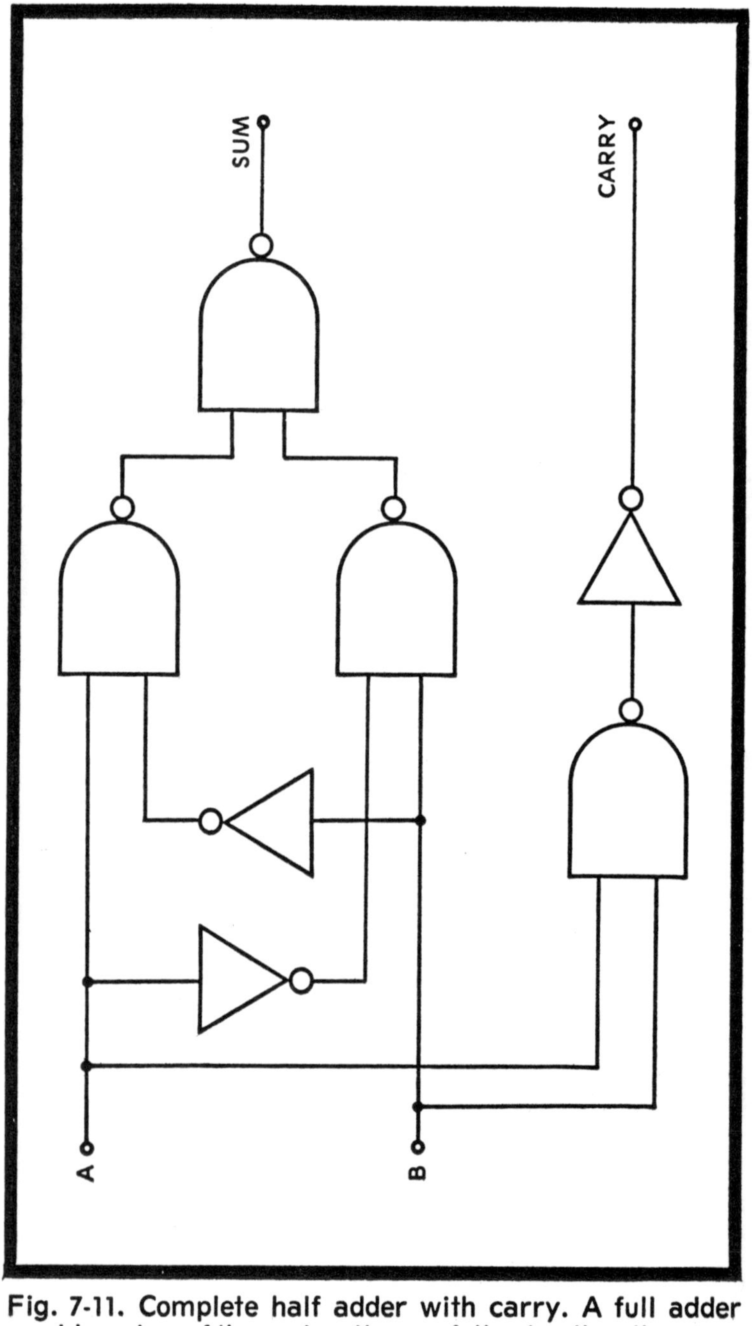

Fig. 7-11. Complete half adder with carry. A full adder would use two of these circuits, one following the other.

This simple set of equations becomes involved due to the high speeds involved in modern computers, because of the necessity to generate a previous carry before it can be included in the next sum, and for many other reasons. The truth table in Fig. 7-9 illustrates the sum part of the equation. Fig. 7-10 shows one of many **half adders.** These are called half adders because they do not recognize a carry. Again, the truth table for the NAND gate implementation is shown to prove that the output is identical to the simple truth table shown earlier.

Fig. 7-11 illustrates a half adder and a **carry gate.** To make a **full adder,** the sum and carry outputs are applied to the A and B inputs of another half adder identical to the first and the output of the full adder is the actual and complete sum and carry for one stage of addition.

SERIAL ADDER

Serial addition is normally performed using a single full adder and a pair of shift registers. The entire operation would be controlled by an external counter and gating circuits that would start, stop, and control the entire operation.

The upper shift register in Fig. 7-12 is the **accumulator** register and it stores the final sum of the add operation. One

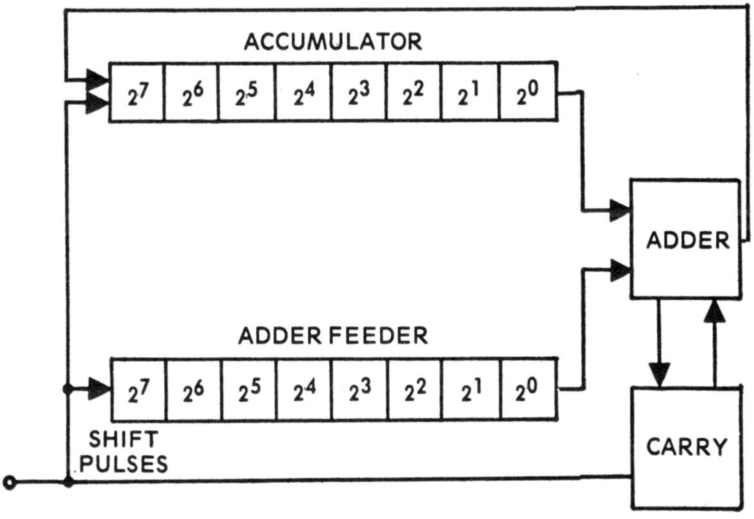

Fig. 7-12. Serial adder used in slow machines.

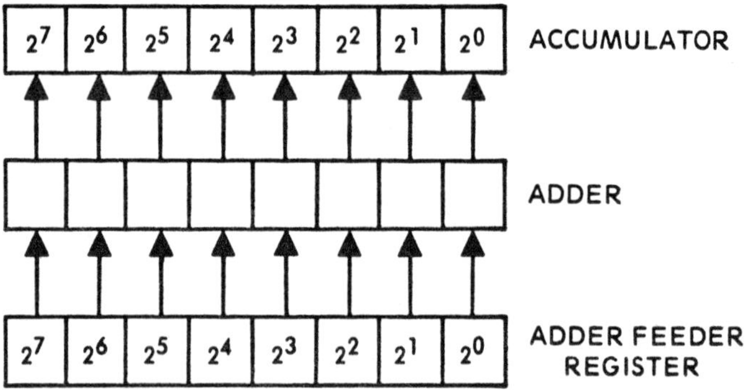

Fig. 7-13. Parallel adder block diagram.

operand is stored in the accumulator, the other is stored in an adder feeder register (in this case the lower register). Both registers present their least significant digit to the adder on the first shift and a sum and carry are generated. The carry is stored in a carry flip-flop which is used to sum the next least significant digit and so on until a complete sum is formed.

The output of the adder is returned to the accumulator and as the original information is shifted out and added the new sum is shifted in behind it. A new number could be entered in the adder feeder and the process continued for as many additions as desired.

In Fig. 7-13 a parallel adder is illustrated; the only difference is that all positions are added simultaneously. The cost of such circuitry goes up but so does the speed. Most modern high-speed computers use parallel adders.

Chapter 8

Decoding, Gating & Steering Arrays

In Chapter 7 we began to develop a general familiarity with computer circuit blocks. This chapter and the two following go into more detail on specific circuits developed by Signetics Corp. Most of the illustrative and text material in Chapters 8, 9, and 10 was supplied by Signetics.

8-INPUT DIGITAL MULTIPLEXERS—8230, 8231, 8232

The 8230, 8231 and 8232 are 8-bit digital multiplexers having internal select decoding and an output inhibit control line. These devices are designed using standard TTL input and output structures (the 8231 is an open collector version); thus, they are compatible with DTL as well as TTL. Pin for pin the 8230 is interchangeable with the 9312. The 8231 has the same pins and logic configuration as the 8230, but with open collector output transistors.

The 8230 is available in 16-pin flat and dual-in-line packages in both 0 degrees to +75 degrees C and -55 degrees to +125 degrees C temperature ranges. Eight multiplex input pins, three select decoding inputs, an output inhibit, f and $\bar{f}$ outputs and Vcc and ground are provided. The output inhibit control performs the function described in Fig. 8-1. As can be seen, the difference between the 8230, 31 and 8232 is that the 8230, 31 "inhibit" forces f equals 0 and $\bar{f}$ equals 1, while on the 8232 "inhibit" forces f and $\bar{f}$ equal 0. The device accepts eight different inputs and gates one of the eight to the output, depending on the three binary bits that form the input code.

Expansion Of The 8230, 8231, 8232

Sixteen-line to one-line multiplexers are shown in Fig. 8-2A and 8-2B (data inputs to the multiplexers are not shown). The basic idea is to simultaneously address the same input code line in both multiplexers and enable the output of only one. The 2^3 and $2^{\bar{3}}$ inputs act as the enable-inhibit control so that only one of the multiplexers is allowed to transmit information at a time. Remember, if the inhibit input is a 1, then

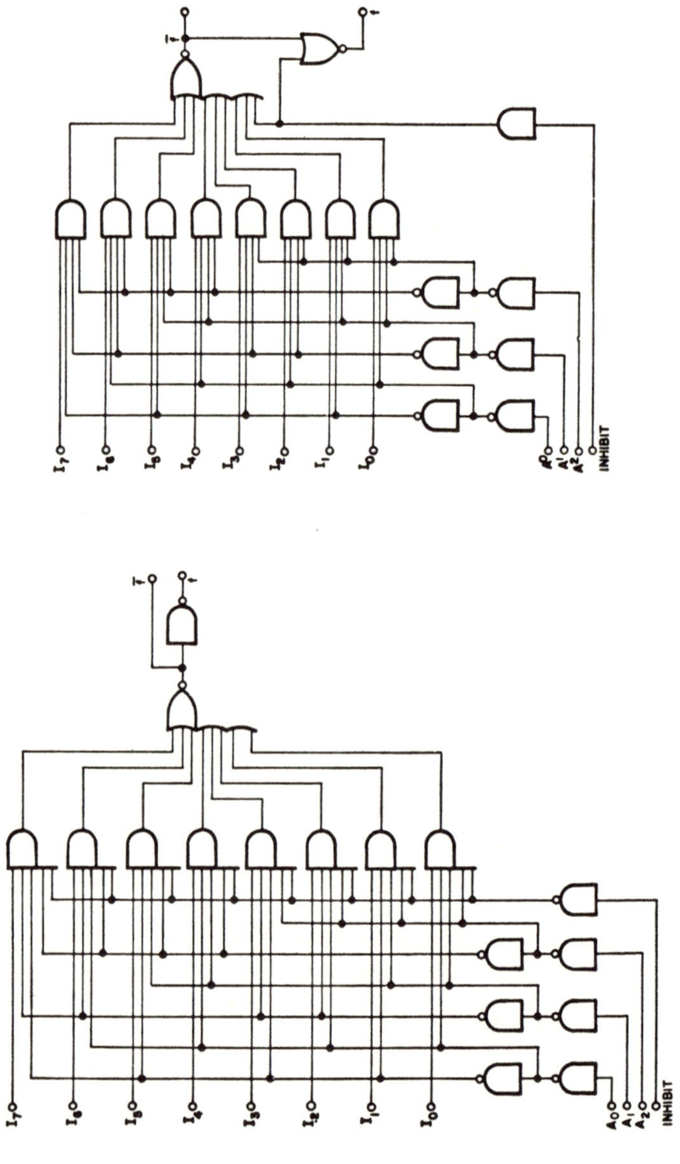

Fig. 8-1. Signetics 8230 8-input multiplexer.

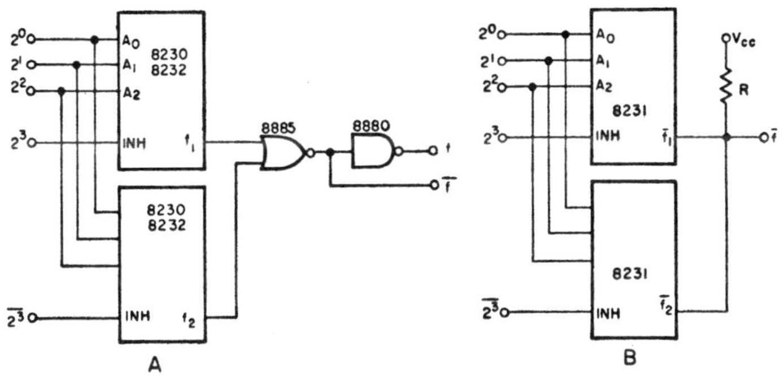

Fig. 8-2. Sixteen-line to one-line multiplexers.

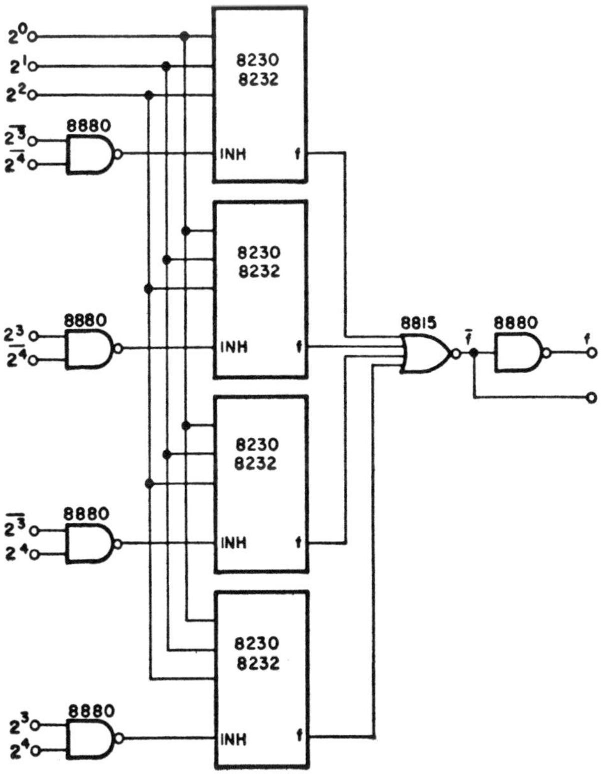

Fig. 8-3. Circuit using four 8230 or 8232 multiplexers.

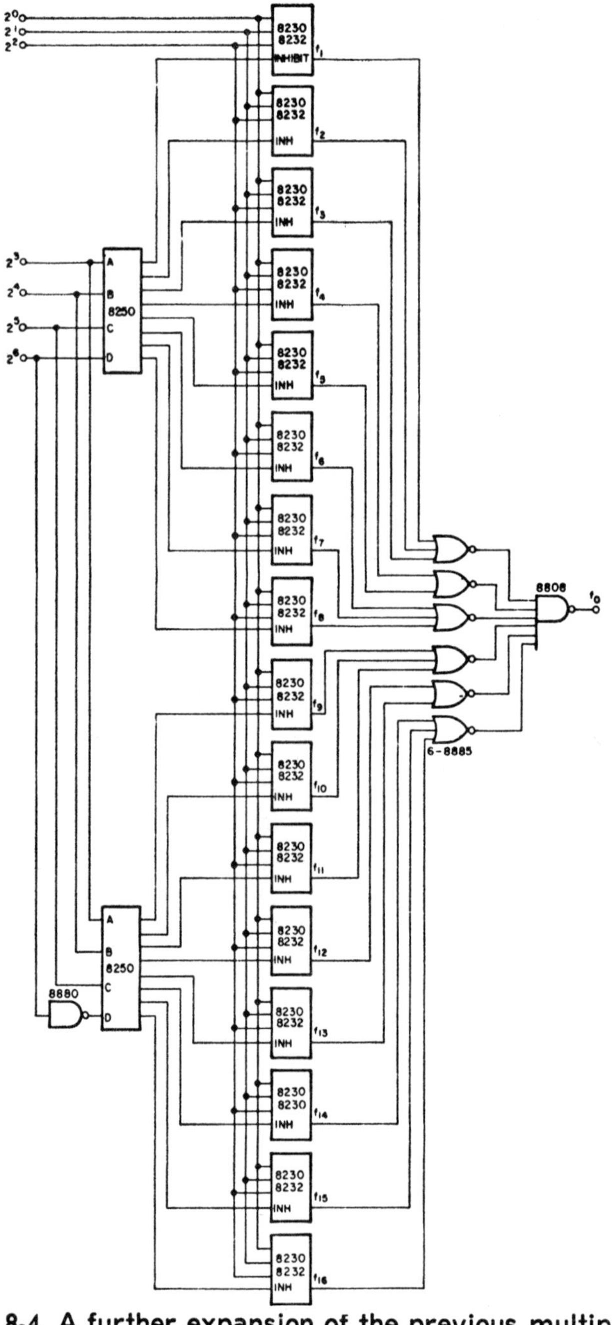

Fig. 8-4. A further expansion of the previous multiplexer circuits using 16 8230 or 8232s.

the f output of the 8230, 31, 32 is forced to a 0. Therefore, in Fig. 8-2A, one input to the 8885 (NOR gate) is always a logic 0, allowing the other multiplexer to be selected. An advantage of the 8231 (open collector) is that the outputs may be tied common and only an external pull-up resistor is necessary. (The $\bar{f}$ outputs are used, as illustrated in Fig. 8-2B, since the enable-inhibit line forces $\bar{f}$ to logic 1.)

Figs. 8-3 and 8-4 show further expansion using the same technique as in the example of Fig. 8-2. The same address coding techniques may be used to expand the number of data inputs of the 8231. The $\bar{f}$ outputs are tied in common and an external pull-up resistor replaces the NOR and NAND output gating.

Fig. 8-5 is an example of a scratch pad memory of 64 words, each 16 bits in length. The memory is implemented using the 8221 (scratch pad 8 words, 4 bits per word) and the 8230. Only the addressing and readout functions are shown, for clarity.

The addressing technique is to allow four 8221s to be addressed simultaneously and have the information transmitted to the bit lines numbered 1 through 16. Address selection is performed as follows:

1. Address all 8221s simultaneously, thereby attempting to read 4 bits from each memory.

2. Address all 8230s simultaneously, thereby selecting the same input in all 16 multiplexers.

3. Referring to Fig. 8-5B, the result is that 4 bits are read out from each of four individual memories, thus generating a 16-bit word.

Fig. 8-6 represents a simple frequency selector. Two 8281s (divide-by-16 binary counters) are connected in series. All eight outputs are fed to the multiplexer. By selective addressing, as shown in the truth table in Fig. 8-6, the various quantitized frequencies are selected.

Boolean Function Generator

The 8230, 32 may be used as a Boolean function generator that will produce any four variable Boolean functions. Fig. 8-7 illustrates how to implement the function generator using an 8271 4-bit shift register and the 8230 or 8232.

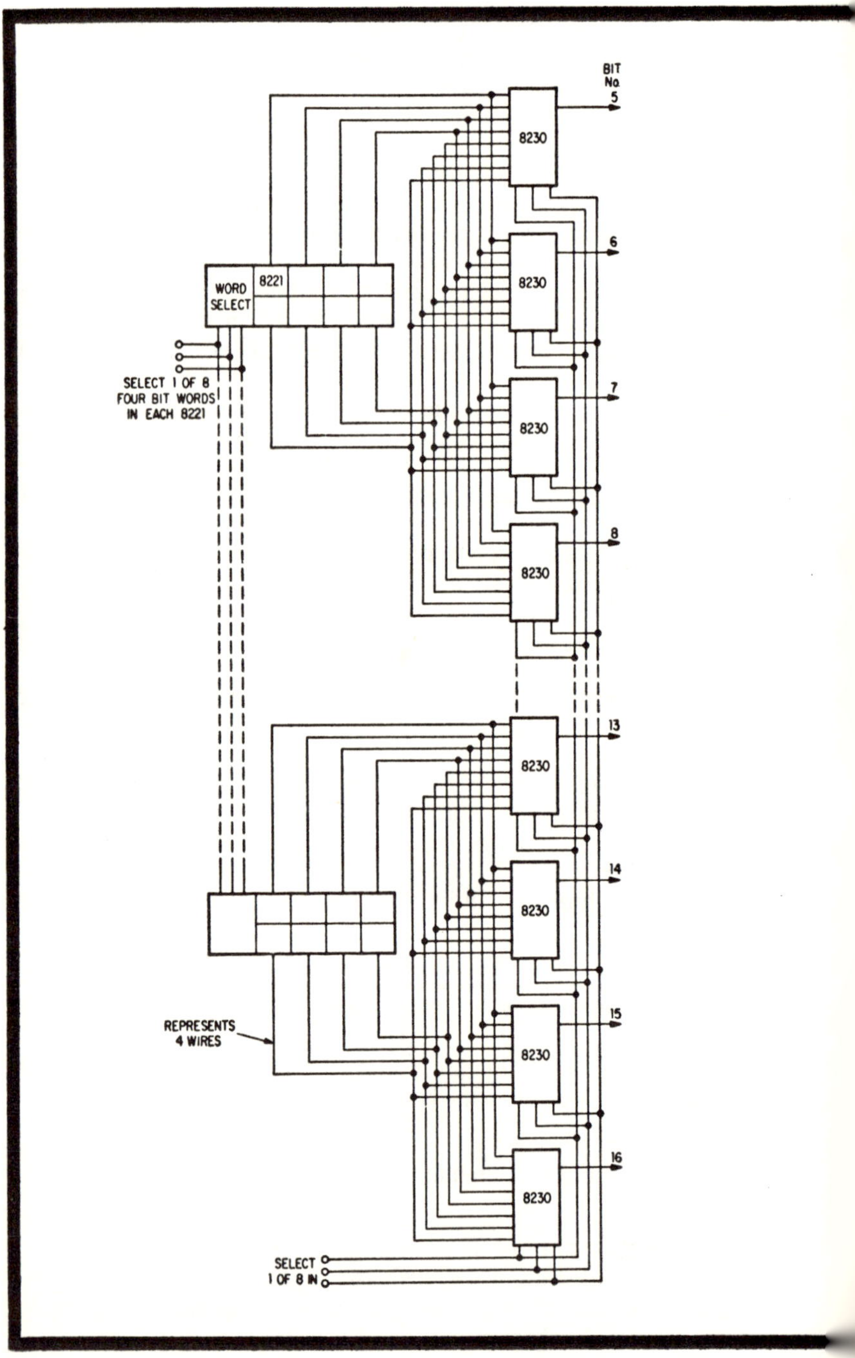
BIT
No.
5
8230
6
8230
7
8230
8
8230
13
8230
14
8230
15
8230
16
8230
WORD
SELECT
8221
SELECT 1 OF 8
FOUR BIT WORDS
IN EACH 8221
REPRESENTS
4 WIRES
SELECT
1 OF 8 IN

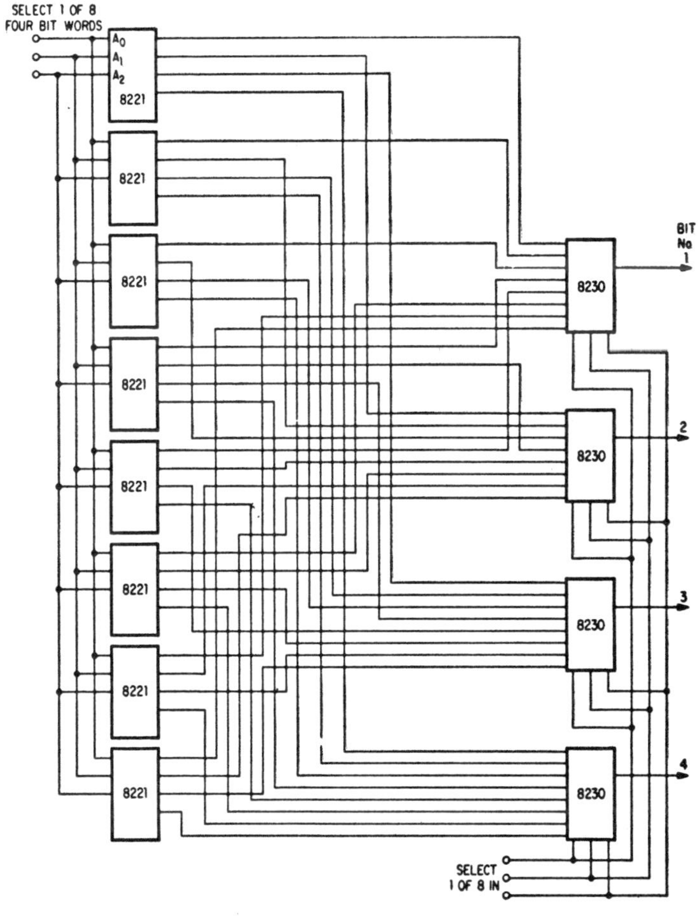

Fig. 8-5. 64-word scratch pad memory.

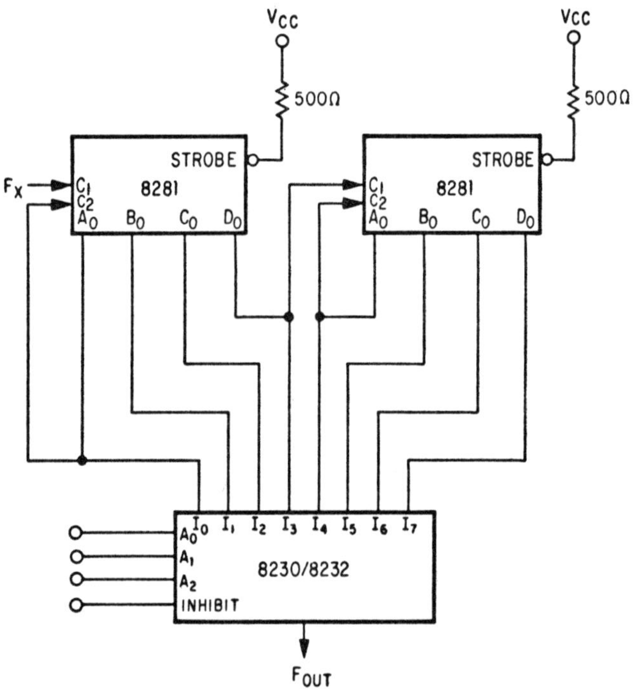

INHIBIT	A_2	A_1	A_0	F_{OUT}
0	0	0	0	$F_X/2$
0	0	0	1	$F_X/4$
0	0	1	0	$F_X/8$
0	0	1	1	$F_X/16$
0	1	0	0	$F_X/32$
0	1	0	1	$F_X/64$
0	1	1	0	$F_X/128$
0	1	1	1	$F_X/256$
1	X	X	X	0

Fig. 8-6. Diagram and truth table of a simple frequency selector.

Example: the function that was chosen is:

$$f_{out} = \bar{A}\bar{B}\bar{C}\bar{D} + AB\bar{C}\bar{D} + \bar{A}B\bar{C}D + \bar{A}\bar{B}CD + A\bar{B}\bar{C}D + A\bar{B}C\bar{D} + \bar{A}BC\bar{D} \qquad \text{(Eq.1)}$$

This function was arbitrarily chosen and is nonreducible. To implement Eq. 1, Karnough maps are used to tell what logic states should be provided to the data inputs and input code lines. Three of the variables are always applied to the code select pins (A0, A1, A2). The fourth variable is connected to the appropriate data inputs (I0 through I7), depending on the Karnough maps. Karnough Map No. 1 (Fig. 8-8) is the 4-variable Boolean function that is implemented. Karnough Map No. 2 (Fig. 8-8) describes the logic requirements at the data inputs.

Procedure

From Maps 1 and 2, the I0 through I7 connections can be determined. The content of the two squares (in Karnough Map No. 1) associated with an input on Karnough Map No. 2 determines which connection is made to that data input.

1. If both squares (Map No. 1) contain 0, ground the input.

2. If both squares (Map No. 1) contain 1s, connect the input to Vcc.

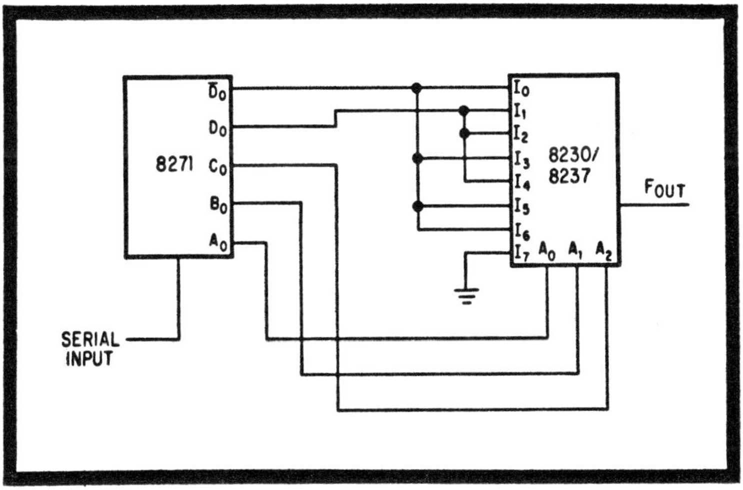

Fig. 8-7. Diagram showing how to use an 8271 4-bit shift register and an 8230 or 8232.

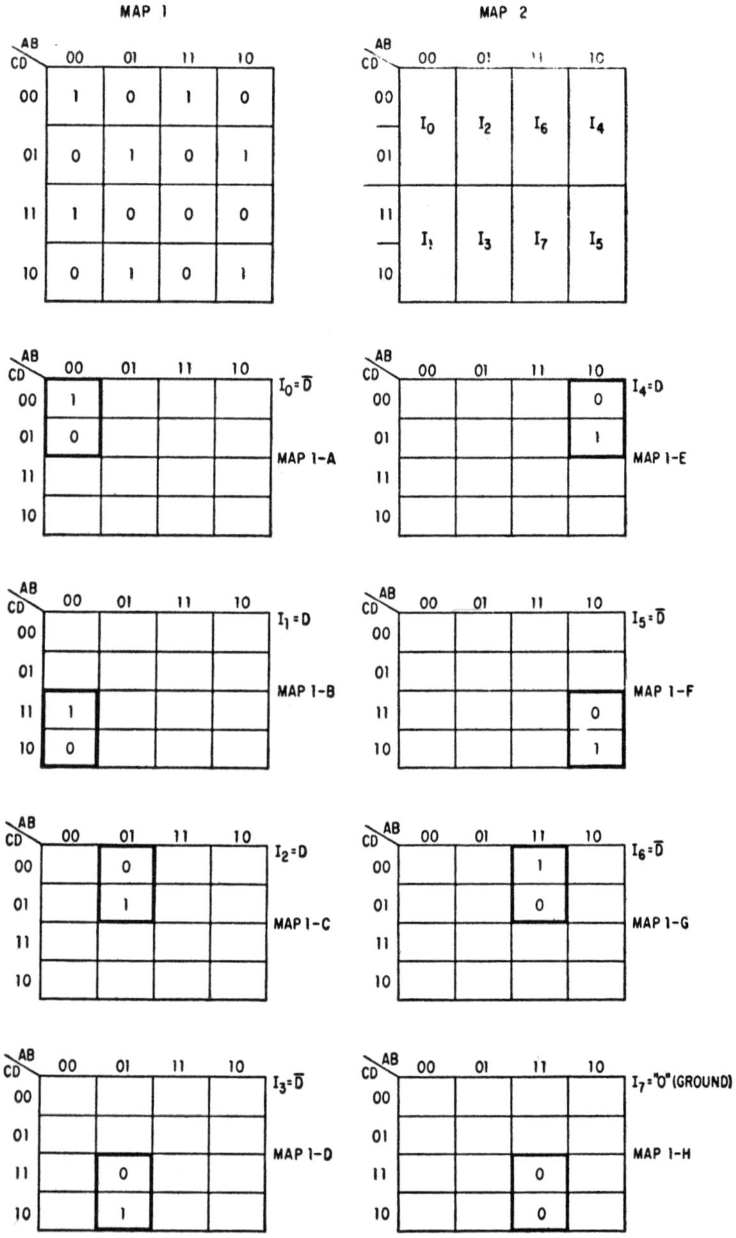

Fig. 8-8. Karnough maps used to determine the logic states for Fig. 8-7.

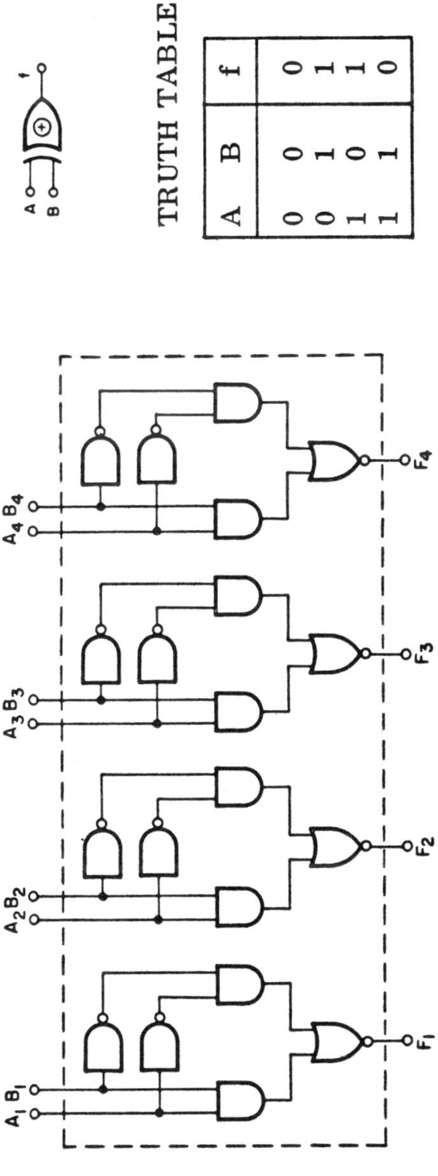

TRUTH TABLE

A	B	f
0	0	0
0	1	1
1	0	1
1	1	0

Fig. 8-9. 8241 quad exclusive OR logic diagram.

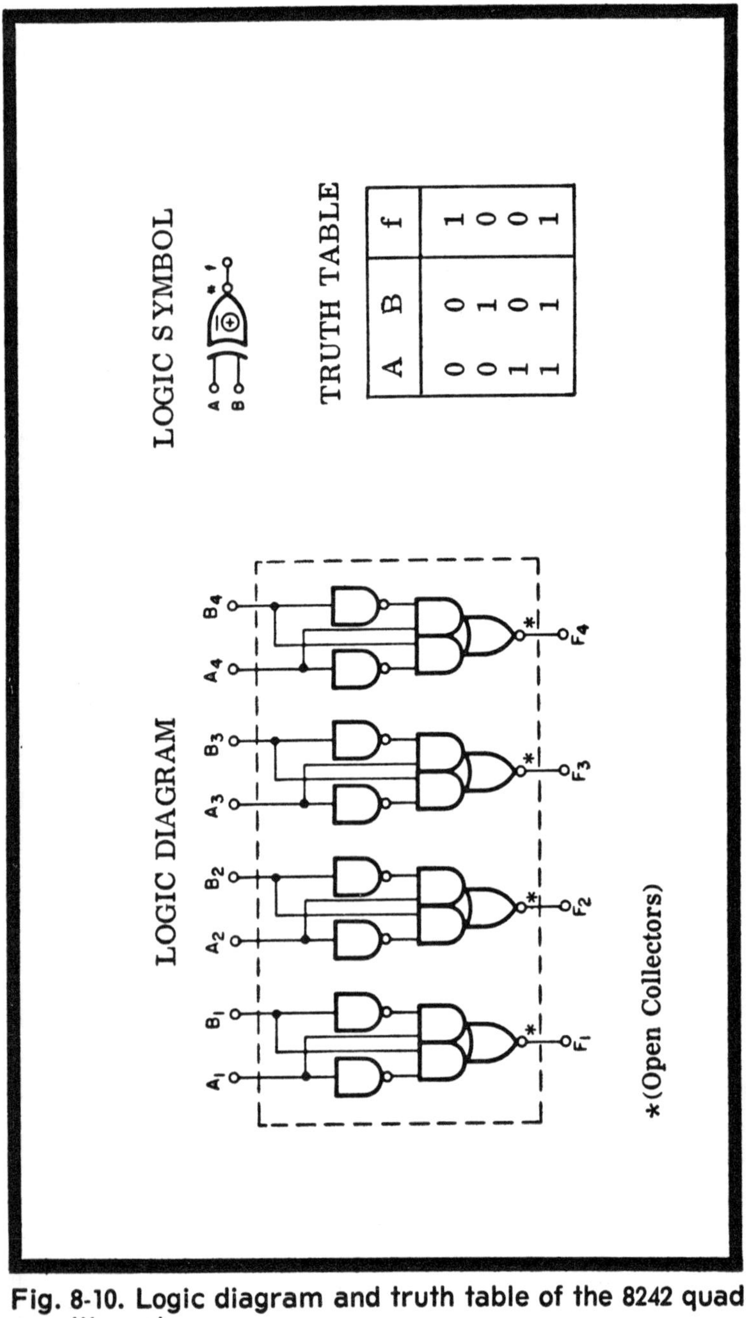

Fig. 8-10. Logic diagram and truth table of the 8242 quad equality gate.

3. If the squares contain 1 and 0 (Map No. 1), and the "1" occurs in the square associated with the true form of the fourth variable, then connect the true output to the input specified by Map No. 2.

4. If the squares contain 1 and 0 (Map No. 1), and the 1 occurs in the square associated with the complement form of the fourth variable, connect the complement to the input specified by Map No. 2.

MS1 GATING ARRAYS

Device Description: 8241

The 8241 is a quad exclusive-OR gate used in a variety of digital comparator and adder systems. The logic diagram is shown in Fig. 8-9 along with its logic symbol and truth table. Both Military (-55 degrees C to +125 degrees C) and Industrial (0 degrees C to +75 degrees C) temperature range devices are available in 14-pin dual-in-line and flat package configurations. Conservative design practices require that the user decouple the 8241 by placing a .01-mfd capacitor between the Vcc and ground terminals of the device. Decoupling capacitors should be noninductive.

Device Description: 8242

The 8242 is a quad equality comparator or coincidence gate. Input bits AnBn are compared for equality. If An equals Bn, the corresponding output Fn will be a logical 1. If An + Bn, output Fn will be a logical 0. The logic diagram, symbol and truth table for the 8242 are shown in Fig. 8-10.

Although TTL circuit design techniques are used in the 8242, the outputs feature open collector switching transistors.

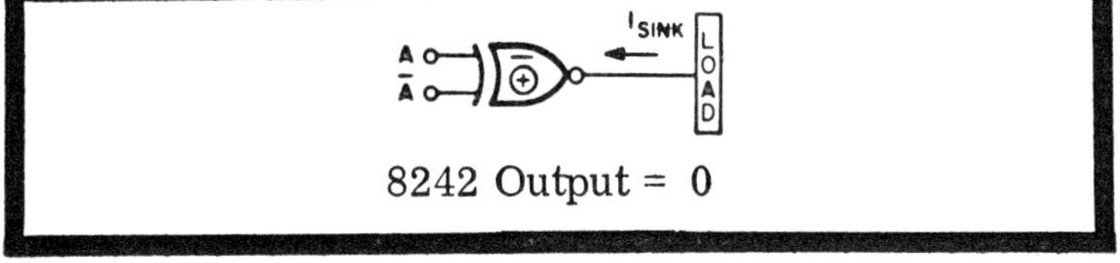

Fig. 8-11. Pull-up resistor value calculations are begun with a determination of the maximum current the 8242 must sink from the load when the device is the 0 output state.

$$I_R + I_{SINK} \leq 16.0\text{mA}$$

$$\text{max. } I_R \leq 16.0\text{mA} - I_{SINK}$$

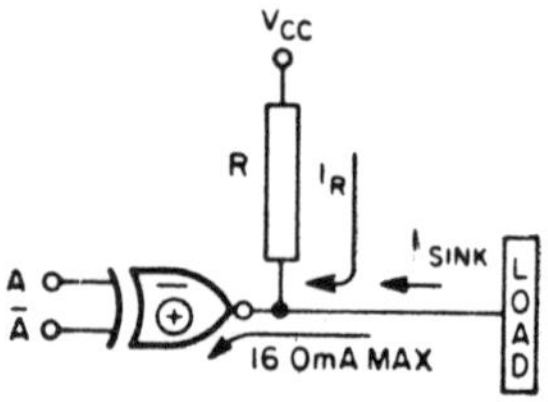

8242 output = 0

Fig. 8-12. The sink current is subtracted from the total sink capability of the 8242 to determine the amount of sink current that may be allowed to flow through the pull-up resistor.

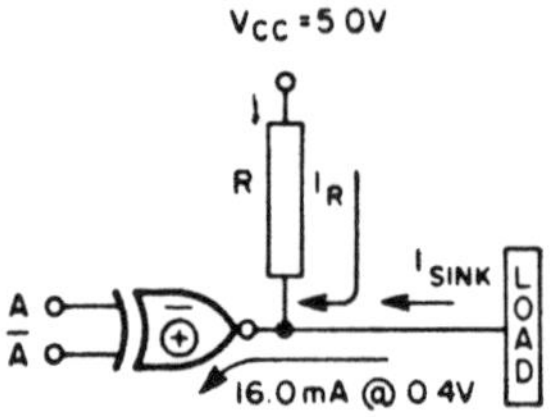

8242 Output = "0"

$$\text{min. } R \geq \frac{V_{cc} - V_{out}\ \text{"0"}}{16.0\text{mA} - I_{SINK}}$$

$$\geq \frac{V_{cc} - V_{out}\ \text{"0"}}{I_R}$$

$$\geq \frac{5.0\text{V} - 0.4\text{V}}{I_R}$$

$$\text{min. } R \geq \frac{4.6\text{V}}{I_R}$$

Fig. 8-13. Calculation to determine the minimum value of the pull-up resistor.

This feature allows the designer to select a variety of comparator lengths by tying the outputs F1, F2,..Fn together and selecting an external pull-up resistor in accordance with his specific requirements.

When selecting a pull-up resistor the following guidelines are suggested:

1. Determine the maximum current that the 8242 must sink from the load when the 8242 is in the 0 output state (Fig. 8-11).

2. Subtract the required sink current from 16.0 ma, the total sink capability of the 8242. This determines the amount of

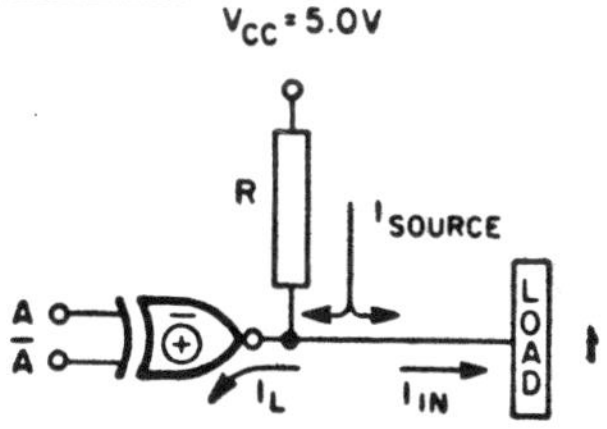

$$\text{8242 Output} = \text{"1"}$$

$$I_L = 50\mu A \text{ max.}$$

$$I_{SOURCE} = I_L + I_{in}$$

$$\text{"1" Output Voltage} = V_{cc} - (I_{SOURCE} \times R)$$

$$\text{max. } I_{SOURCE} \times R = V_{cc} - \text{"1" Output Voltage}$$

$$= 5.0V - 2.8V$$

$$\text{max. } I_{SOURCE} \times R \leq 2.2V$$

$$\text{max. } R \leq \frac{2.2V}{I_{SOURCE}}$$

Fig. 8-14. Calculations to determine whether or not the pull-up resistor value selected is consistent with the output voltage and current in the 1 state.

$$\tau = R_{EQ}C$$

$$R_{EQ} = \frac{R \times R_L}{R + R_L}$$

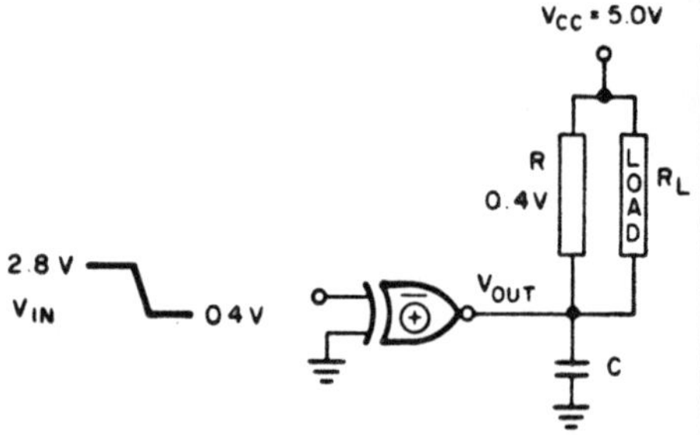

Fig. 8-15. Calculations used to determine the relationship between the rise time into a capacitance load and the pull-up resistor value.

current which may be allowed to flow through the external pull-up resistor (Fig. 8-12).

3. Assume Vcc is 5.0v and output 0 level is 0.4v maximum, then calculate (Fig. 8-13) the minimum value of the pull-up resistor required to satisfy:

$$I_R + I_{SINK} \leq 16.0 \text{ ma}$$

4. Check to ensure that the pull-up resistor selected is consistent with the 1 output voltage and 1 output current required (Fig. 8-14).

To ensure that normal 1 level noise margins are maintained, the 1 output voltage should be maintained at 2.8v or above for Vcc equals 5.0v.

Under light fan-out conditions, a relatively large resistor (4K to 10K) may be considered by the designer. Two considerations must be weighed in selecting a large value pull-up resistor. First, rise time into a capacitance load at the output will be directly related to the value of the pull-up resistor used (Fig. 8-15). An approximation of the time required for the rising output voltage to reach a defined 1 level (2.0v) is:

$$\tau/2, \text{ or } 1/2R_{EQ}C$$

The voltage level attained in time:

$$\tau \approx 0.63 \times V_{CC} = 3.15V,$$

well above minimum 1 logic input threshold voltage (Fig. 8-16).

The second consideration which should be given to the use of a large value pull-up resistor is the resulting susceptibility to capacitively coupled noise along printed-circuit runs or wire interconnects. Since the magnitude of coupled noise is related to the equivalent impedance between the output of the 8242 and its load, care should be taken in the physical layout to isolate the output of an 8242 where a large value pull-up resistor has been chosen. In general, a pull-up resistor of 1K or less is recommended where 0 DC fan-out is less than 10.0 ma and power supply drain current is not critical. There is no current spike associated with the output transition in the 8242 since the active pull-up of classic TTL designs has been removed. It is not necessary to capacitively decouple the 8242.

Device Description: 8266

The 8266 is a 2-input, 4-bit multiplexer which finds extensive applications in selecting which data from two different sources is to be processed. This mode of operation is the multiplex mode.

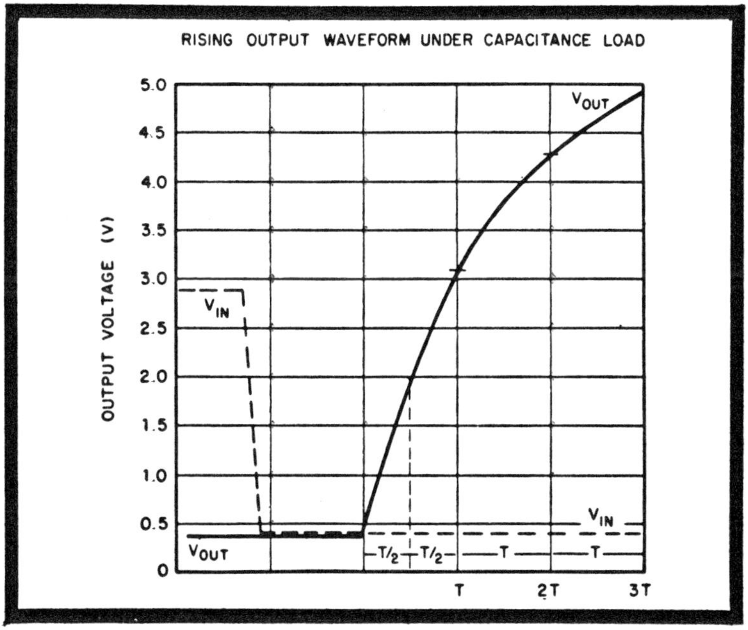

Fig. 8-16. Curve expressing the output voltage-time relationship.

LOGIC DIAGRAM

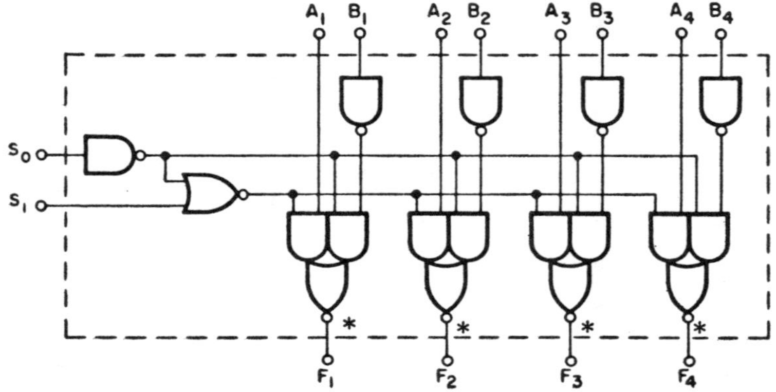

*8267 has open collectors.

TRUTH TABLE

S_1	S_0	F_n
0	0	B_n
0	1	$\overline{A}_n$
1	0	B_n
1	1	1

Fig. 8-17. 8266 2-input 4-bit multiplexer.

The second area of application for the 8266 is in central processors. When the two inputs for each bit position (Ai Bi) are connected together, the 8266 performs as a conditional complementor required in conjunction with adders to provide addition-subtraction subsystems. Also while operating in this mode, the 8266 is ideal for parallel data transfer within an arithmetic section. The logic diagram and truth table are shown in Fig. 8-17. Both Military (-55 degrees C to +125 degrees C) and Industrial (0 degrees C to +75 degrees C) devices are available in 16-pin dual-in-line and flat packages. Conservative design practices require that the user decouple the 8266 by placing a .01-mfd capacitor between Vcc and ground. Decoupling capacitors should be noninductive.

Device Description: 8267

The 8267 has the same logic configuration and truth table as the 8266 (Fig. 8-17). The 8267 features open collector output switching transistors to facilitate expansion of the number of input terms per bit when used in multiplex applications.

Since there is no active pull-up, it is not necessary for the user to capacitively decouple this device. However, an external pull-up resistor must be selected by the user. Guidelines for selecting pull-up resistors are the same as those described earlier for the 8242. The 8267 is available in both Military (-55 degrees C +125 degrees C) and Industrial (0 degrees C to +75

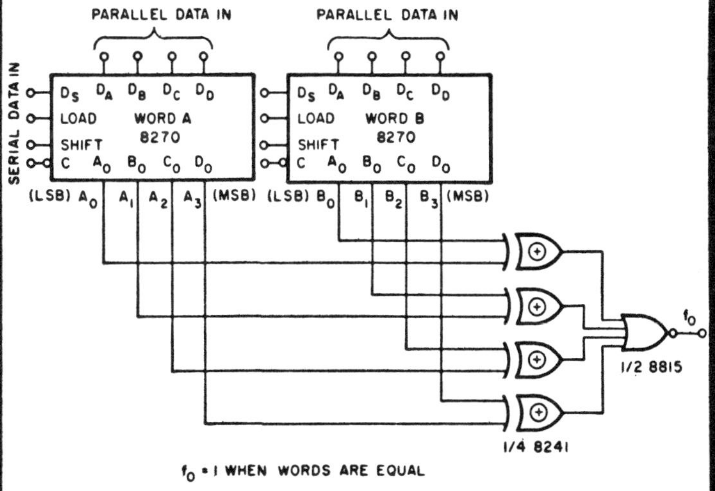

Fig. 8-18. Equality comparator for two 4-bit words.

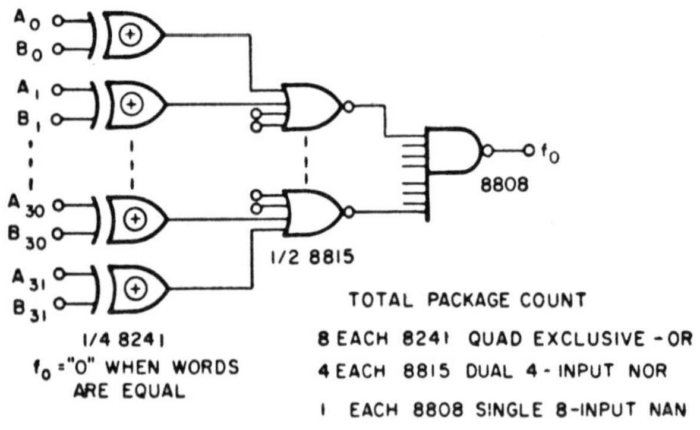

Fig. 8-19. High-speed 32-bit word equality comparator.

degrees C) temperature ranges and in 16-pin dual-in-line and flat package configurations.

HIGH-SPEED EQUALITY COMPARATORS

The exclusive-OR may be used to check the equality of two binary coded words. From the truth table (Fig. 8-9), the output of the exclusive-OR is 1 when the inputs are not equal and 0 when the inputs are equal. By connecting the output of the exclusive-OR to one input of a NOR gate (Fig. 8-18), the output (fo) will be 1 if and only if all bits of the two words are equal. Fig. 8-18 shows a high-speed equality comparator capable of comparing two 4-bit words.

Fig. 8-19 demonstrates a method of designing a high-speed equality comparator for a maximum word length of 32 bits using TTL elements. This method may also be used to design high-speed equality comparators for other word lengths between 4-bits and 32-bits. The addition of the single 8-input NAND (8808) provides fo equals 0 when words A (A0, A1, A2...An-1, An) and B (B0, B1, B2...Bn-1, Bn) are equal and fo equals 1 when words A and B are unequal.

MAXIMUM LENGTH EQUALITY COMPARATORS

The 8242 is specifically designed for use in equality comparison of word lengths in excess of 4 bits, while providing minimum can-counts. From the truth table (Fig. 8-10) the 8242 will provide a 1 output when the inputs are equal and 0 when the inputs are unequal. The open collector output of the 8242 can be connected together to perform a logical AND of the output terms when returned to Vcc through an external resistor. Guidelines for selecting the pull-up resistor value are given under Device Description: 8242. The can-count reduction for the 32-bit word length equality comparator shown in Fig. 8-19 is demonstrated in Fig. 8-20. The maximum word length equality comparator which can be implemented under worst case specifications is shown in Fig. 8-21. In this implementation, two words of 128 bits each can be compared for equality.

PARITY TESTER-GENERATOR

The exclusive-OR and equality comparator may be used in parity testing or generating applications. Parity generators

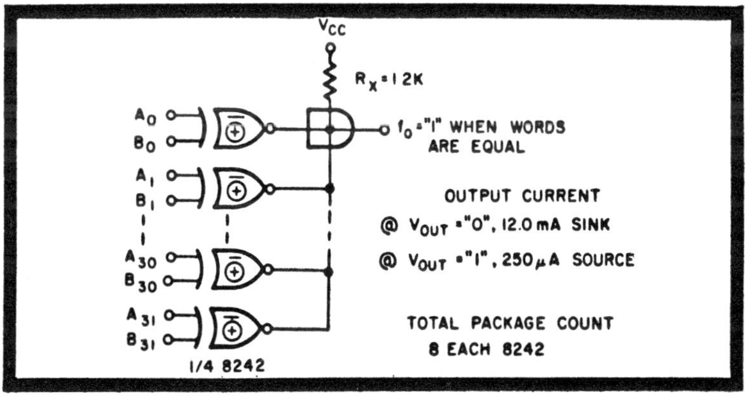

Fig. 8-20. Implementation of the 32-bit word comparator.

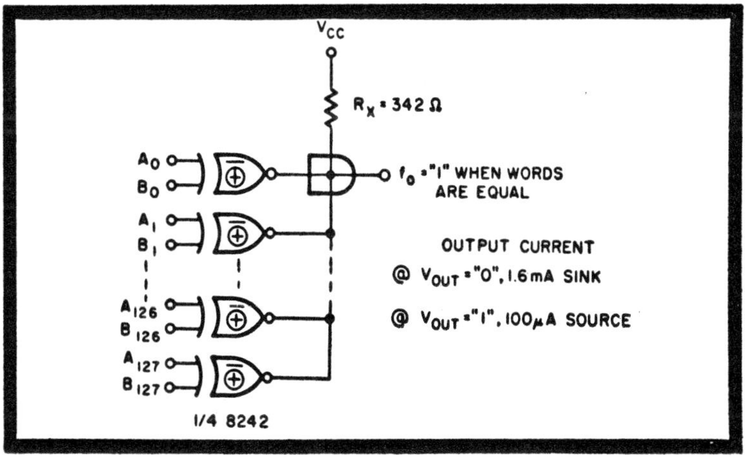

Fig. 8-21. Maximum length (128-bit words) equality comparator.

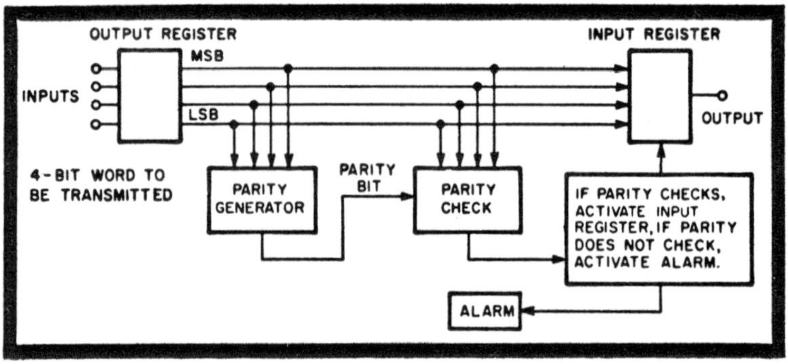

Fig. 8-22. General case parity generator and parity check.

find wide application in output equipment which records or transmits data. A parity bit is generated to ensure that the total number of logical ones in the word being recorded or transmitted is either even or odd. On the reading or receiving end of the data transmission a parity check is performed on the transmitted data (including the parity bit) to ensure that no word bit has been "dropped" (i.e., no 1 has been lost). Fig. 8-22 shows a general case implementation of parity generation and parity check in the recording or transmission of a 4-bit word. Notice that there are five bits of transmitted data, the 4-bit word plus the parity bit.

In data transmissions which include a parity bit, the designer chooses between the even parity system and the odd parity system. In the even parity system, an even number of logical ones is always transmitted (data plus parity bit). Therefore, the even parity generator examines the data to be transmitted and produces an additional 1 if the data contains an odd number of logical ones. If the data to be transmitted already contains an even number of logical ones, the even parity generator produces a parity bit equal to 0. In either case an even number of logical ones (data plus parity bit) will be transmitted. The 8241 may be used to design an even parity generator, as shown in Fig. 8-23.

Conversely, the odd parity generator examines the terms in the data to be transmittted and produces a 0 when the data already contains an odd number of logical ones. If, however, the data contains an even number of logical ones, the odd parity generator produces an additional 1. In either case the total number of logical ones (data and parity bit) transmitted is odd. An advantage of odd parity is that transmission of 0 data is not mistaken for no-information (always have one 1 bit). The odd parity generator is shown in Fig. 8-24. It differs

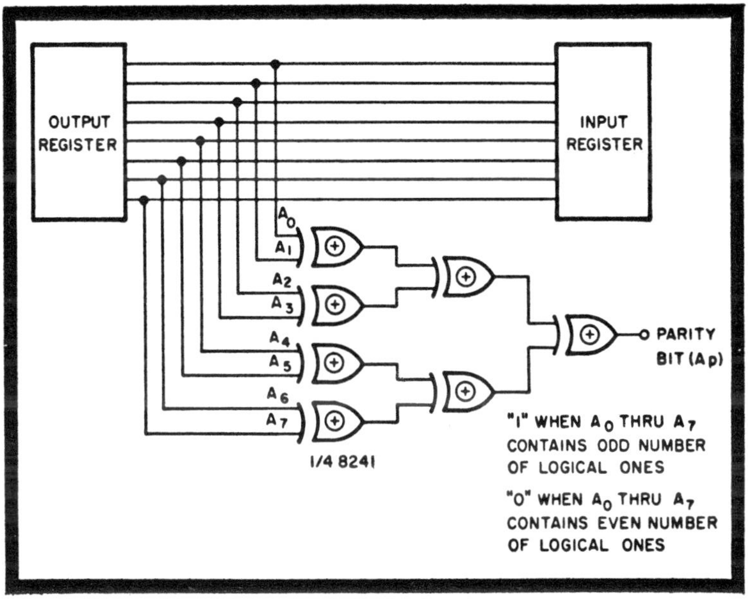

Fig. 8-23. Even parity generator used with an 8-bit word.

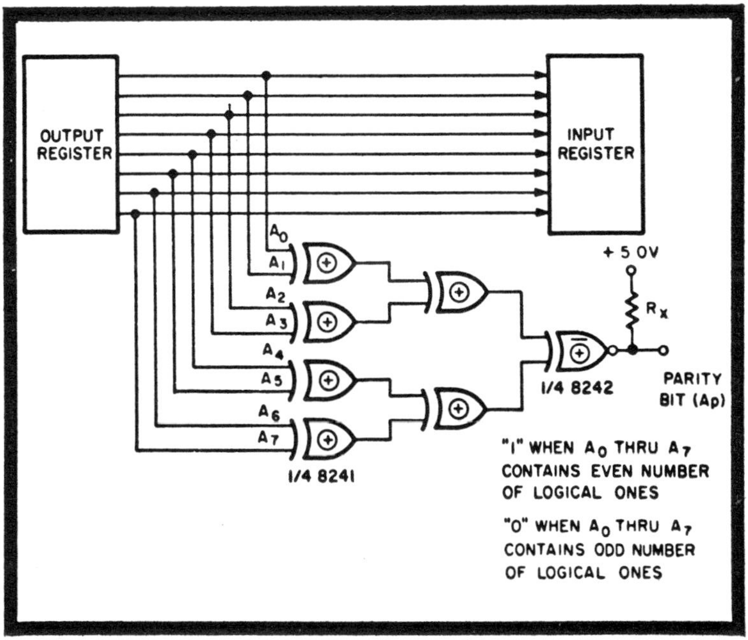

Fig. 8-24. Odd parity generator used with an 8-bit word.

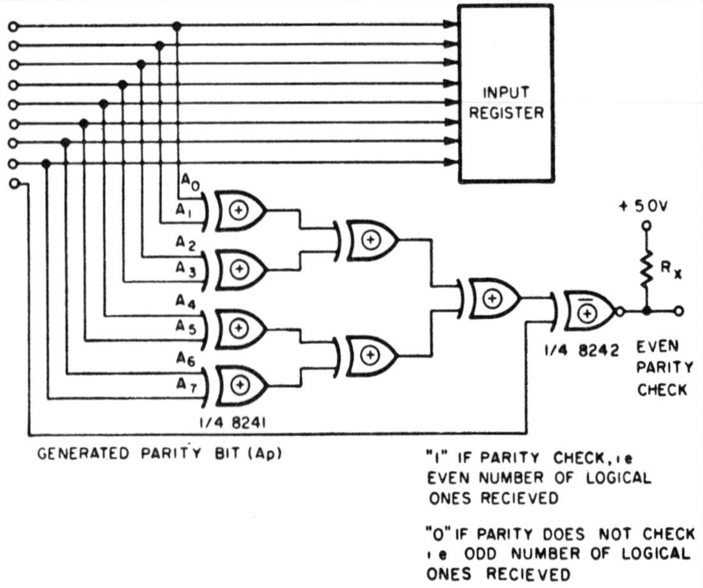

Fig. 8-25. Even parity checker used with an 8-bit word.

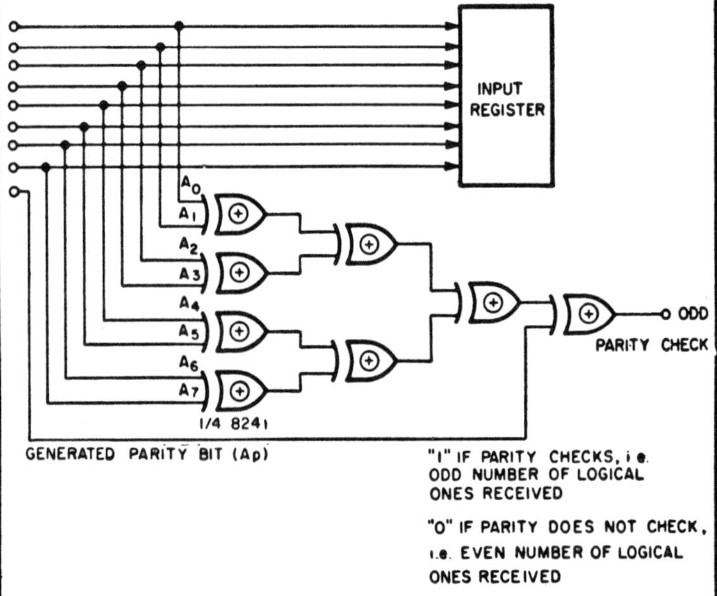

Fig. 8-26. Odd parity checker used with an 8-bit word.

from the even parity generator only in the output stage which incorporates ¼ of an 8242. As described in Fig. 8-22, the receiving equipment must check all incoming lines to ensure that no bits have been dropped in data recording or transmission.

In the even parity system, an even parity checker examines all incoming terms (data plus parity bit) and provides a 1 output if there is still an even number of logical ones contained in the data received. If a bit has been dropped and an odd number of logical ones is received, the output of the even parity checker will be 0. An example of an even parity checker is shown in Fig. 8-25.

The odd parity checker provides a 1 output when the total number of logical ones received (data plus parity bit) is odd and produces a 0 when the total number of logical ones received is even. Fig. 8-26 shows an example of an odd parity checker.

ADDERS

The exclusive-OR is the heart of an adder system. Fig. 8-27 shows 4-bits of a binary adder with ripple carry. Each 2-wide 2-input AND-OR-INVERT gate shown in Fig. 8-27 may be ½ an 8440 and each inverter one-sixth of an 8490 if power consumption is of prime concern. If speed is of prime concern, the 8440 may be replaced by 8840 and the 8490 by 8H90.

The binary adder shown in Fig. 8-27 may be expanded to arbitrary length by simply continuing the pattern of interconnection shown. The carry-in term of the least significant bit (LSB) is grounded in actual implementation.

Fig. 8-28 shows the construction of a BCD adder. A second decade of addition would be constructed exactly as shown in Fig. 8-28. The carry-in term of the least significant decade is grounded in actual implementation. Each 2-wide, 2-input AND-OR-INVERT gate shown in Fig. 8-28 may be ½ an 8440 (low power) or ½ an 8840 (high speed). Each inverter shown may be one-sixth an 8490 (low power) or one-sixth an 8H90 (very high speed). Each 2-input NAND may be ¼ an 8480 (low power), ¼ an 8880 (high speed) or ¼ an 8H80 (very high speed). The 3-input NAND may be one-third an 8470 (low power), one-third an 8870 (high speed) or one-third an 8H70 (very high speed).

CONDITIONAL COMPLEMENTORS

Add-subtract subsystems require the ability to present information to the inputs of the adder in its true form for ad-

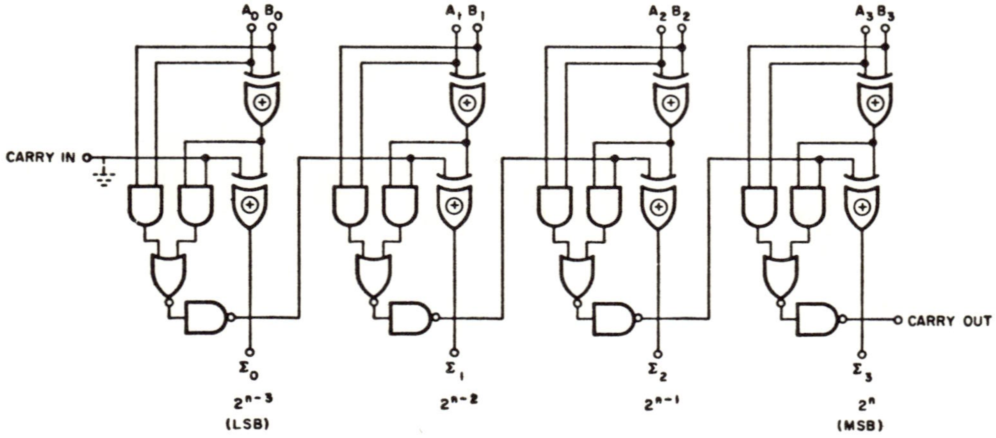

Fig. 8-27. Binary adder with ripple carry (4 bits).

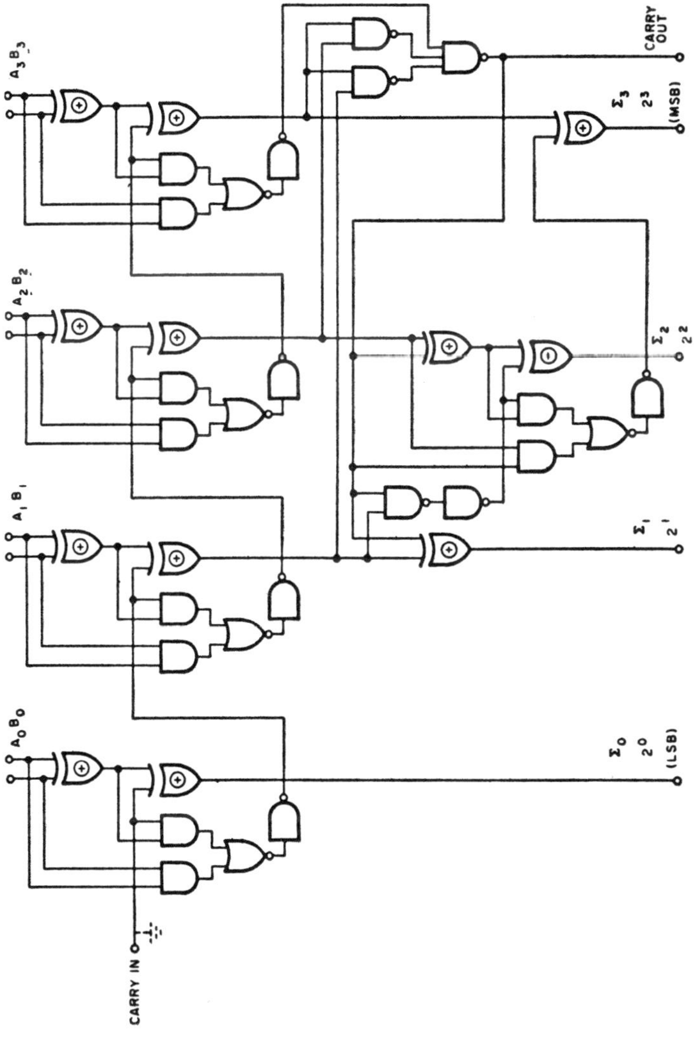

Fig. 8-28. BCD adder with ripple carry (one decade).

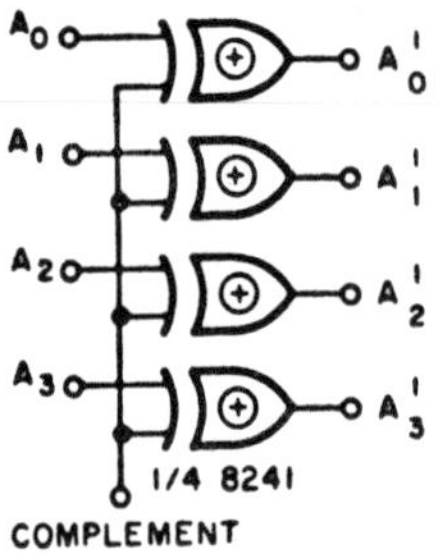

INPUTS		OUTPUT
Complement	A_i	A_i
0	0	A_i
0	1	A_i
1	0	$\overline{A}_i$
1	1	$\overline{A}_i$

Fig. 8-29. 4-bit conditional complementor.

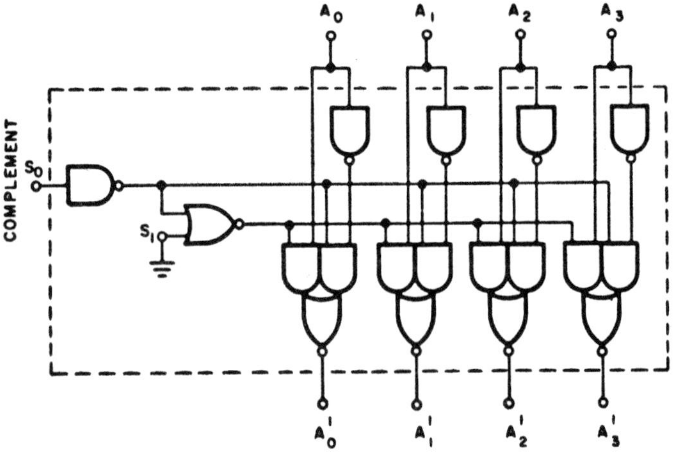

TRUTH TABLE

INPUTS		OUTPUT
Complement	A_i	A_i
0	0	A_i
0	1	A_i
1	0	$\overline{A}_i$
1	1	$\overline{A}_i$

Fig. 8-30. 4-bit conditional complementor using the 8266.

dition and in its complement form for subtraction. The exclusive-OR may be used to implement a 4-bit conditional complementor as shown in Fig. 8-29.

The conditional complementor may be expanded by connecting the complement inputs together. The designer should consider the additional fan-out required to drive the complement input on expanded conditional complementors designed with 8241s. The gate driving the complement input of Fig. 8-29 must sink 12.8 ma at Vo equals 0 and source 200 microamp at V0 equals 1.

The 8266 and 8267 are devices specifically applicable in performing the conditional complement function for long word lengths. Because the select line inputs are buffered, the 8266 and 8267 can be expanded without particular concern about the fan-out to the complement input which delivers 1.6 ma in the 0 state and requires 25 microamp in the 1 state for each four bits. Fig. 8-30 shows an example of a 4-bit conditional complementor using the 8266.

ADDER-SUBTRACTOR

The 8266 is intended specifically for use in conjunction with the 8260 (4-bit full adder with look-ahead carry) to form an extremely high-speed parallel adder-subtractor. The subsystem shown in Fig. 8-31 is an 8-bit adder-subtractor for use with a 2s complement addition.

The subsystem shown in Fig. 8-30 assumes that in the subtract mode (X-Y), Y(Y0, Y1...Y6, Y7) is always the smaller of the two binary numbers. If Y is not the smaller of the two numbers, correction may be made by detecting the presence of a carry term at the most significant bit (MSB), then initiating the appropriate correction procedure.

MULTIPLEXERS

The 8266 and 8267 also find application in multiplex circuits. The 8266 is specifically intended for application as a 2-input 4-bit multiplexer. Examples of 4-bit multiplexers using the 8266 are shown in Figs. 8-32 and 8-33. These examples assume the designer wishes to multiplex true data inputs only. Notice that the $\overline{Q}$ (not true) outputs of the A register were used to accomplish multiplex of the true terms. When the not true outputs are unavailable, the A0, A1, A2 and A3 input terms to the 8266 must be inverted to provide the multiplex of the true terms only, as shown in Fig. 8-33.

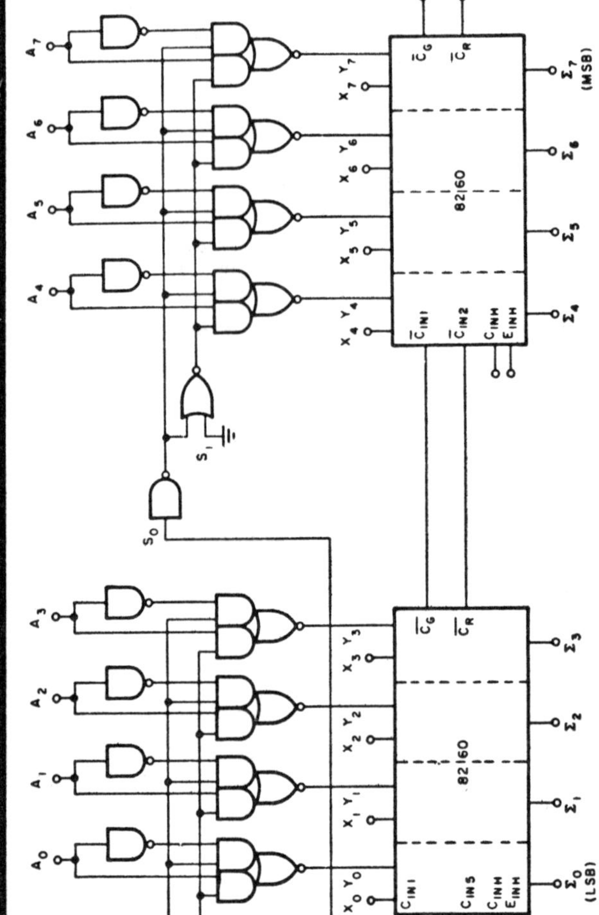

Fig. 8-31. High-speed 8-bit binary adder-subtractor.

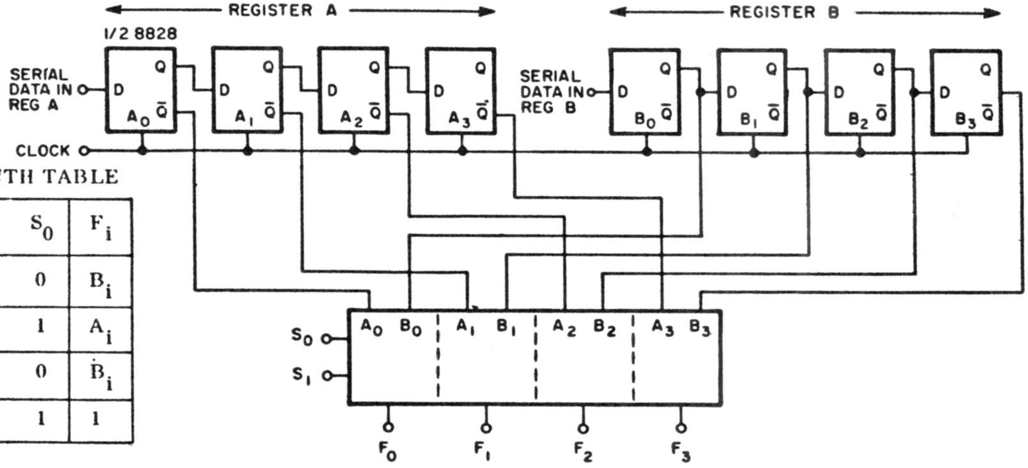

TRUTH TABLE

S_1	S_0	F_i
0	0	B_i
0	1	A_i
1	0	$\dot{B}_i$
1	1	1

Fig. 8-32. 2-input 4-bit multiplexer.

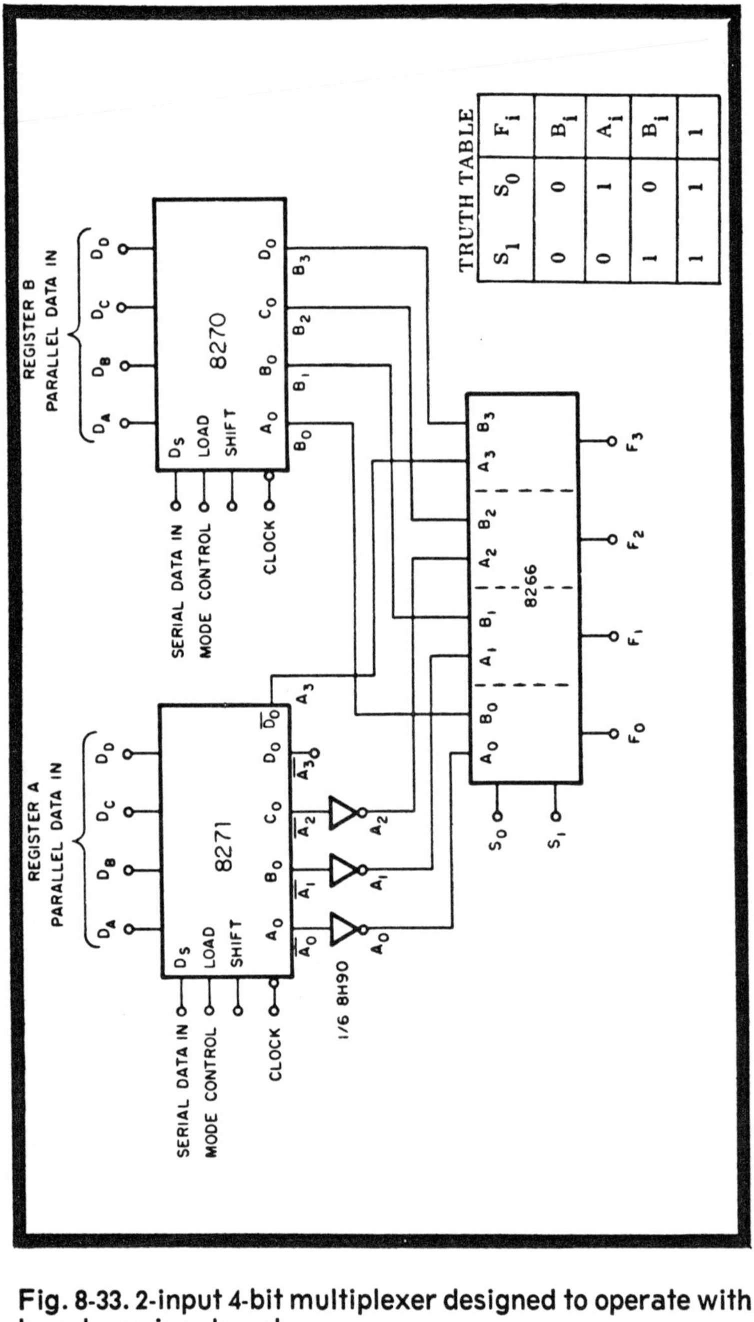

TRUTH TABLE

S_1	S_0	F_i
0	0	B_i
0	1	A_i
1	0	B_i
1	1	1

Fig. 8-33. 2-input 4-bit multiplexer designed to operate with true term inputs only.

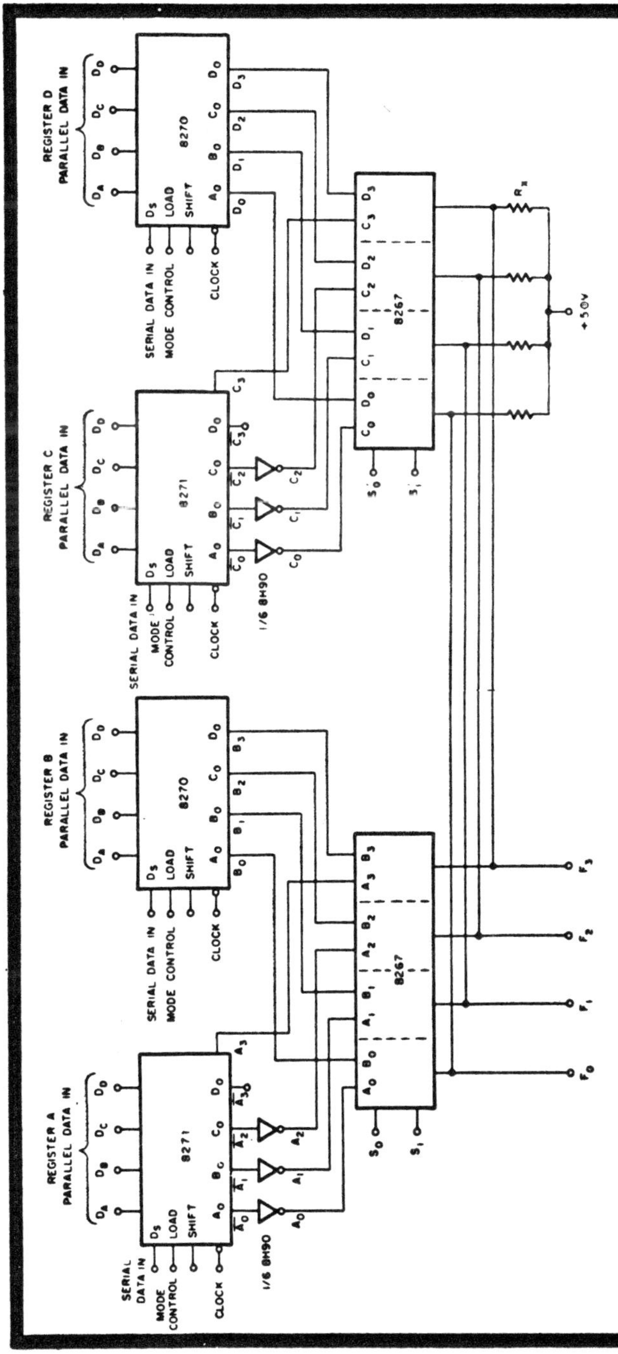

$$F_i = \left[S_0' S_1' (A_i \bar{S}_1 S_0 + B_i S_1 \bar{S}_0)\right] + \left[S_0 S_1 (C_i \bar{S}_1' S_0' + D_i S_1' \bar{S}_0')\right]$$

Fig. 8-34. 4-input 4-bit multiplexer.

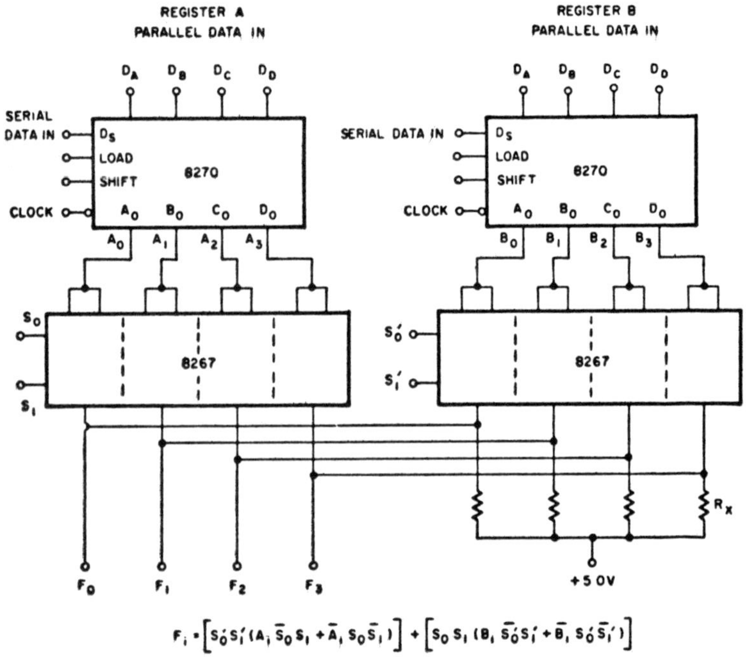

Fig. 8-35. 2-input 4-bit conditional complementor-multiplexer.

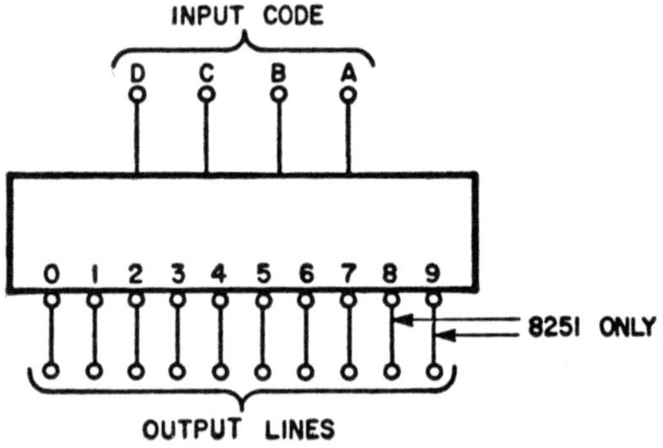

Fig. 8-36. Input and output connections, octal-decade decoders.

The 8267 was specifically designed for use in the multiplexing of conditional complement terms and general multiplex applications requiring expansion of input terms. The 8267 features open collector output switching transistors which may be used to perform the collector AND function, thus increasing the number of input terms to be multiplexed per bit. The maximum expansion requires an external pull-up resistor of 342 ohms and provides a 128-input, 4-bit multiplexer. Selection of input terms is accomplished by applying the desired code on the S0, S1 lines of the appropriate 8267 while S0 equals S1 equals 1 is applied to the unselected 8267s as shown in Fig. 8-34.

The 8267 is well suited for multiplex applications of conditional complement terms in add-subtract subsystems as shown in Fig. 8-35.

OCTAL-DECADE DECODERS—8250, 8251

The decade decoder, 8251, accepts a 4-bit input code and activates one of the ten mutually exclusive outputs. The octal decoder, 8250, decodes an octal number (3-bit) applied to the input pins and one of the eight outputs will be activated, representing the decoded number. The 8250-8251 are available in different configurations (Figs. 8-36 and 8-37).

Decade Decoder (8251)

Let us assume that ten different, sequential operations must be controlled. In this case, ten control lines must be available and one of the ten lines is activated for each state. Assuming the ten different states are characterized by its binary number, the truth table in Fig. 8-38 results. The 8251 decade decoder provides this function. As can be seen from the truth table, all non-activated outputs are high and the output number corresponding to the binary input number is low.

The decade decoder may be used conveniently in conjunction with the decade counter (8280). The change of the different states is controlled by the clock-signal (Fig. 8-39).

Octal Decoder (8250)

The octal decoder decodes the binary numbers 0 to 7 which are applied to the pins (CBA). The D-input provides gating of the input. When D is high, decoding is inhibited; when D is low, decoding occurs. The truth table of an octal decoder appears in Fig. 8-40. The octal decoder can be extended to 64 control

PIN CONFIGURATIONS

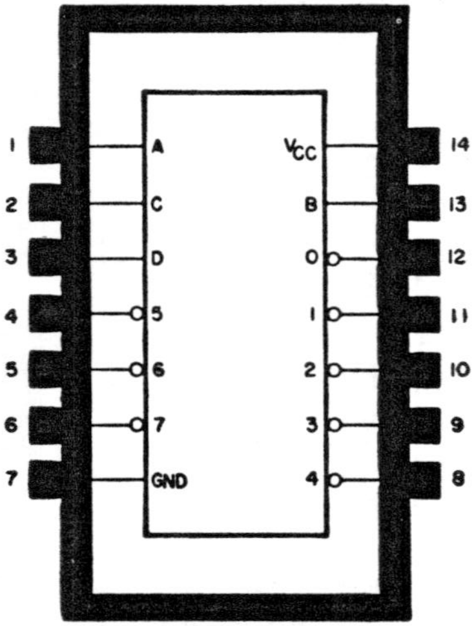

S8250A
N8250A

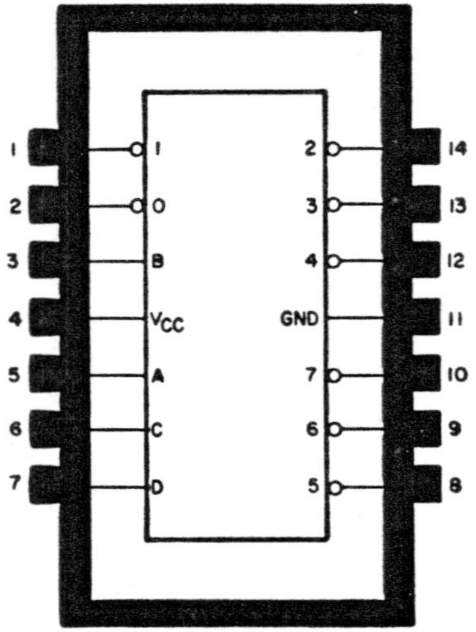

S8250J
N8250J

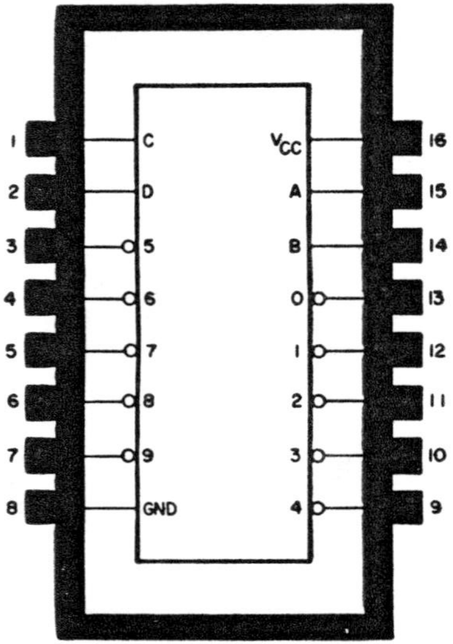

S8251B
N8251B

LOGIC DIAGRAM

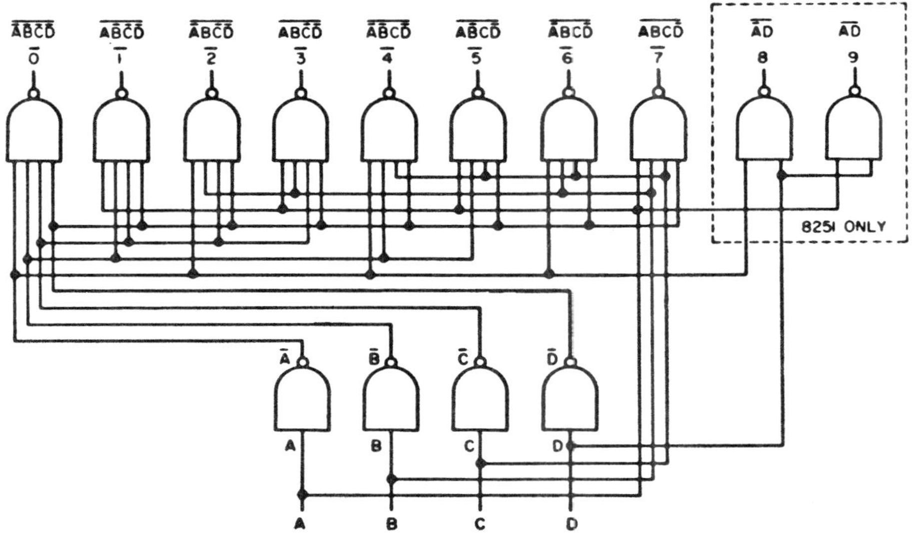

Fig. 8-37. Pin configurations and logic diagrams, octal-decade decoders.

STATE	INPUTS D C B A	OUTPUTS $\overline{0}\,\overline{1}\,\overline{2}\,\overline{3}\,\overline{4}\,\overline{5}\,\overline{6}\,\overline{7}\,\overline{8}\,\overline{9}$
0	0 0 0 0	0 1 1 1 1 1 1 1 1 1
1	0 0 0 1	1 0 1 1 1 1 1 1 1 1
2	0 0 1 0	1 1 0 1 1 1 1 1 1 1
3	0 0 1 1	1 1 1 0 1 1 1 1 1 1
4	0 1 0 0	1 1 1 1 0 1 1 1 1 1
5	0 1 0 1	1 1 1 1 1 0 1 1 1 1
6	0 1 1 0	1 1 1 1 1 1 0 1 1 1
7	0 1 1 1	1 1 1 1 1 1 1 0 1 1
8	1 0 0 0	1 1 1 1 1 1 1 1 0 1
9	1 0 0 1	1 1 1 1 1 1 1 1 1 0

Fig. 8-38. Truth table depicting operation of the 8251 decade decoder.

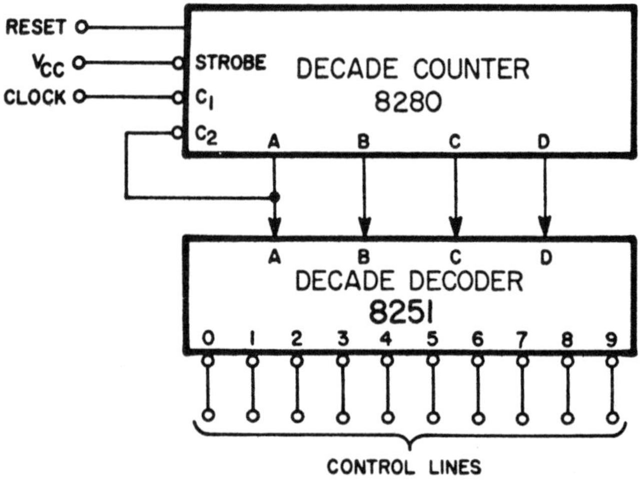

Fig. 8-39. Diagram showing the decade decoder connected to a decade counter.

lines. Fig. 8-41 shows a "One-of-64 Decoding" example. Fig. 8-42 is a load chart.

Notice that the decoder device with inputs Din, Ein, Fin controls the other eight octal decoders by the D-inputs. The decoding process may be stopped by the inhibit line.

Arbitrary 4-Bit Decoding

Using two decoders, every 4-bit code may be decoded. As an example we apply the excess-3 code to the pins (X3, X2, X1, X0) and examine the generated outputs (Fig. 8-43). The well-defined outputs are listed at the right most column in the chart in Fig. 8-43. In the table in Fig. 8-44 other codes are shown with their corresponding outputs.

Code Conversion

The decade decoders are also useful in code conversion applications. As an example let us convert the gray code into the BCD Code. First we apply the gray code to the pins of two decade decoders. The activated outputs are listed in Fig. 8-45.

STATE	D INPUT	INPUT C B A	OUTPUTS $\overline{0}\ \overline{1}\ \overline{2}\ \overline{3}\ \overline{4}\ \overline{5}\ \overline{6}\ \overline{7}$
0	0	0 0 0	0 1 1 1 1 1 1 1
1	0	0 0 1	1 0 1 1 1 1 1 1
2	0	0 1 0	1 1 0 1 1 1 1 1
3	0	0 1 1	1 1 1 0 1 1 1 1
4	0	1 0 0	1 1 1 1 0 1 1 1
5	0	1 0 1	1 1 1 1 1 0 1 1
6	0	1 1 0	1 1 1 1 1 1 0 1
7	0	1 1 1	1 1 1 1 1 1 1 0
8	1	0 0 0	1 1 1 1 1 1 1 1
9	1	0 0 1	1 1 1 1 1 1 1 1
10	1	0 1 0	1 1 1 1 1 1 1 1
11	1	0 1 1	1 1 1 1 1 1 1 1
12	1	1 0 0	1 1 1 1 1 1 1 1
13	1	1 0 1	1 1 1 1 1 1 1 1
14	1	1 1 0	1 1 1 1 1 1 1 1
15	1	1 1 1	1 1 1 1 1 1 1 1

Fig. 8-40. Octal decoder truth table.

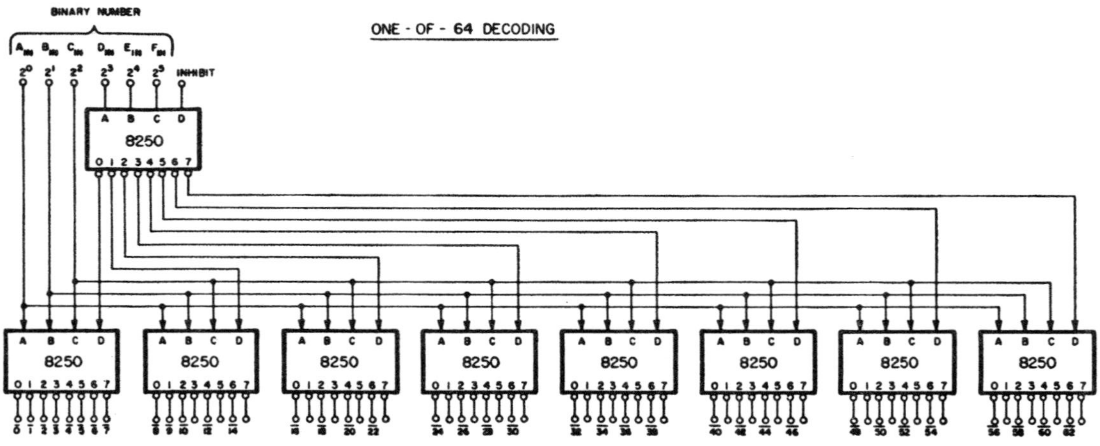

Fig. 8-41. Diagram showing the octal decoder expanded to 64 control line

N	A_{in}	B_{in}	C_{in}	D_{in}	E_{in}	F_{in}
16	5.25	5.25	5.25	4	-	-
24	6.50	6.50	6.50	4	4	-
32	7.75	7.75	7.75	4	4	-
40	9.00	9.00	9.00	4	4	4
48	10.25	10.25	10.25	4	4	4
56	11.50	11.50	11.50	4	4	4
64	12.75	12.75	12.75	4	4	4

Fig. 8-42. Load chart for one-of-N decoding.

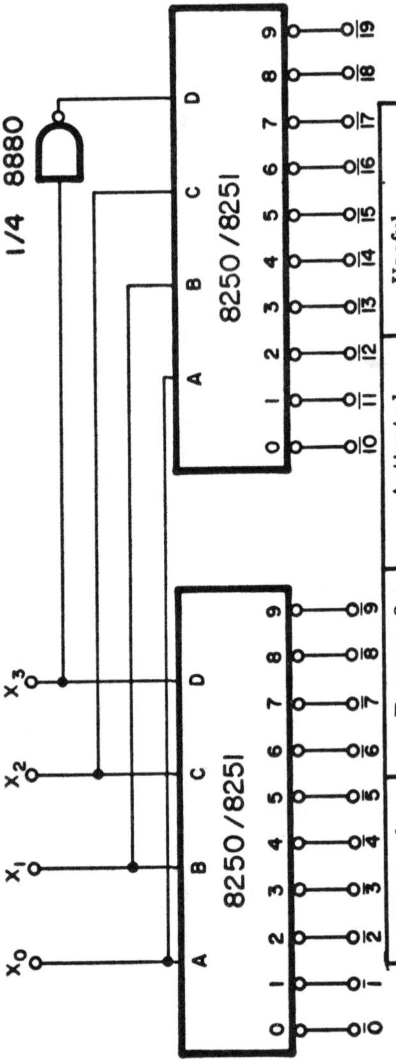

Decimal Quantity	Excess -3 Code X_3 X_2 X_1 X_0	Activated Outputs (Not true levels)	Useful Outputs (Not true levels)
0	0 0 1 1	3 19	3 -
1	0 1 0 0	4 18	4 -
2	0 1 0 1	5 19	5 -
3	0 1 1 0	6 18	6 -
4	0 1 1 1	7 19	7 -
5	1 0 0 0	8 10	- 10
6	1 0 0 1	9 11	- 11
7	1 0 1 0	8 12	- 12
8	1 0 1 1	9 13	- 13
9	1 1 0 0	8 14	- 14

Fig. 8-43. Diagram showing two decoders for arbitrary 4-bit decoding and a table of generated outputs.

Decimal Quantity	Gray Reflected Code X_3	X_2	X_1	X_0	Decoder Outputs	Binary Coded Decimal Z_5	Z_4	Z_3	Z_2	Z_1
0	0	0	0	0	$\overline{0}$	0 0 0 0	0	0	0	0
1	0	0	0	1	$\overline{1}$	0 0 0 0	0	0	0	1
2	0	0	1	1	$\overline{3}$	0 0 0 0	0	0	1	0
3	0	0	1	0	$\overline{2}$	0 0 0 0	0	0	1	1
4	0	1	1	0	$\overline{6}$	0 0 0 0	0	1	0	0
5	0	1	1	1	$\overline{7}$	0 0 0 0	0	1	0	1
6	0	1	0	1	$\overline{5}$	0 0 0 0	0	1	1	0
7	0	1	0	0	$\overline{4}$	0 0 0 0	0	1	1	1
8	1	1	0	0	$\overline{14}$	0 0 0 0	1	0	0	0
9	1	1	0	1	$\overline{15}$	0 0 0 0	1	0	0	1
10	1	1	1	1	$\overline{17}$	0 0 0 1	0	0	0	0
11	1	1	1	0	$\overline{16}$	0 0 0 1	0	0	0	1
12	1	0	1	0	$\overline{12}$	0 0 0 1	0	0	1	0
13	1	0	1	1	$\overline{13}$	0 0 0 1	0	0	1	1
14	1	0	0	1	$\overline{11}$	0 0 0 1	0	1	0	0
15	1	0	0	0	$\overline{10}$	0 0 0 1	0	1	0	1

Fig. 8-45. Table of activated outputs gray to BCD code conversion.

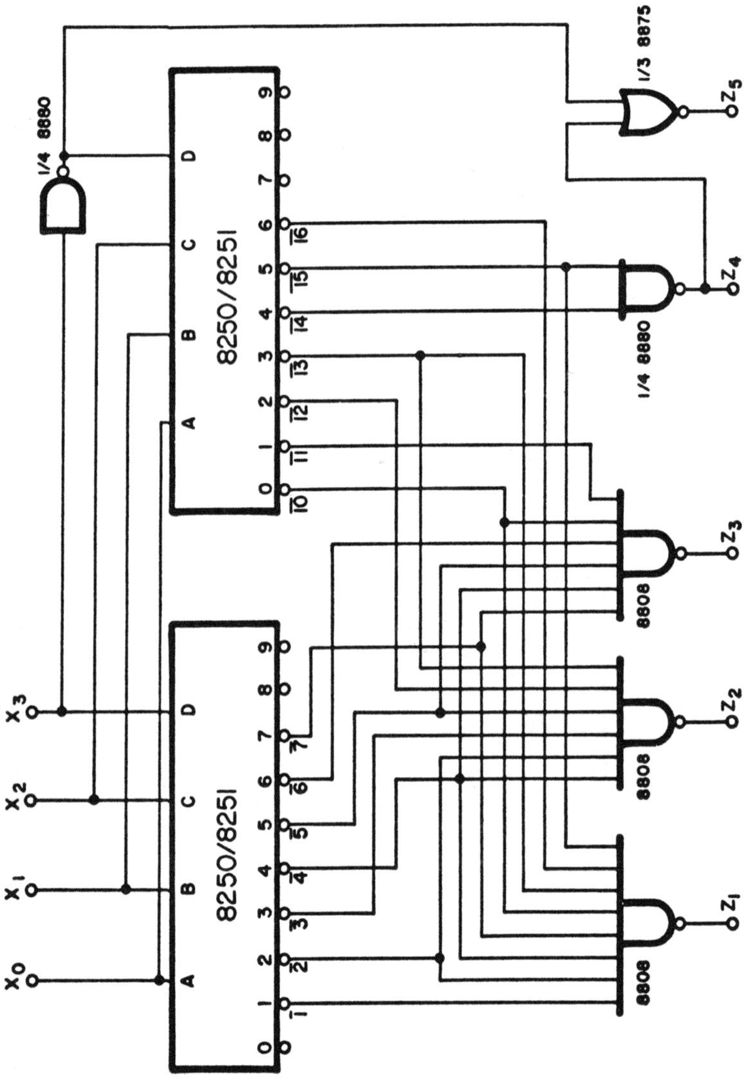

Fig. 8-46. Diagram of a gray to BCD decoder.

Now the decoder outputs will be used to form the BCD code (Fig. 8-46).

Z4 equals 14 + 15

Z3 equals 6 + 7 + 5 + 4 + 11 + 10

Z2 equals 3 + 2 + 5 + 4 + 12 + 13

Z1 equals 1 + 2 + 7 + 4 + 15 + 16 + 13 + 10

Z5 equals $\overline{X}3$ + Z4

Decimal Quantity	Well-Defined Outputs (Not true levels)		
	Binary Coded Decimal	Aiken Code 2*4 2 1	4 2* 2 1
0	0	0	0
1	1	1	1
2	2	2	2
3	3	3	5
4	4	4	6
5	5	13	11
6	6	14	12
7	7	15	15
8	8 10	16	16
9	9 11	17	17

Fig. 8-44. Table of other codes useful with the decoder in Fig. 8-43.

Chapter 9
Counters, Shift Registers & Memories

In this chapter we continue to examine Signetics computer components and circuit blocks, with emphasis on counters, shift registers, and memories.

4-BIT SYNCHRONOUS SHIFT REGISTER—8270, 8271

The 8270 has serial and parallel entry, serial and parallel output. Further there are two control inputs, **load** and **shift**, which have the effect listed in Fig. 9-1. Therefore, depending on the control states 0 . . . 3, the shift register operates in the different modes. Thus a free-running clock signal can be applied. The buffered clock stage triggers the shift register with the falling edge. In addition to the 8270 features, the 8271 provides the not-true output of the fourth stage ($\overline{D}$out) and a reset input ($\overline{R}_D$), which is common for all four flip-flops. If the $\overline{R}_D$ input is low, all stages are cleared independent of the clock or the logic input state. The clock transition dominates over the reset. Thus, a positive-going spike may be expected at the output, although the reset input is low. Fig. 9-2 shows the input connections; Fig. 9-3 is a logic diagram and pin configuration sketches.

SHIFT REGISTER APPLICATIONS

Simple 8-Bit Right Shift Register

Looking at Fig. 9-4, let us assume first that the shift register flip-flops are reset to zero, applying a logic low to the $\overline{R}_D$ input. Now the first bit X1 (X1 equals 1 or 0), using the

State	LOAD	SHIFT	Effect (If CLOCK-Input Level Falls)
0	0	0	Store - No entry
1	0	1	Shift Right (D_s data)
2	1	0	Parallel Load (D_p data)
3	1	1	Shift Right (D_s data)

Fig. 9-1. Table of the load and shift effect, 8270.

series data input is shifted in the first flip-flop A10 by the first falling transition of the clock signal. The second trigger pulse of the clock shifts the first bit X1 to the second flip-flop B10 and at the same time the second bit X2 is loaded in the first flip-flop A10. To make it more clear, let us study an example with the series data (X1 X2 X3 0 0 0 . . . 0) in Fig. 9-5.

Ring Circuit

To demonstrate the parallel loading and serial shift operations we intend to preload the shift register with the data (D_A, D_B, D_C, D_D) equals (1, 0, 0, 0). Therefore, we apply a logic 1 to the pin D_A (Fig. 9-6) and a logic 0 to the pins D_B, D_C, D_D. A logic 0 at the control input shift enables the falling clock signal to transfer the data (D_A, D_B, D_C, D_D) equals (1, 0, 0, 0) to the shift register. To shift right now the shift input must stay on a logic 1 level permanently. The diagram in Fig. 9-7 results.

A ring circuit is applied successfully if gating problems should be solved. A modified version of a ring circuit with self-correcting feature is shown in Fig. 9-8. We start with an arbitrary state (A, B, C, D) and after maximum three shift pulses we reach the state (0, 0, 0, D); for this state the shift input is low. Thus the word (1, 0, 0, 0) is preloaded by the next negative-going transition of the clock signal. The truth table for the ring circuit is given below:

1	0	0	0	preloaded data
0	1	0	0	
0	0	1	0	
0	0	0	1	'feedback logic detects this state
1	0	0	0	preloaded data

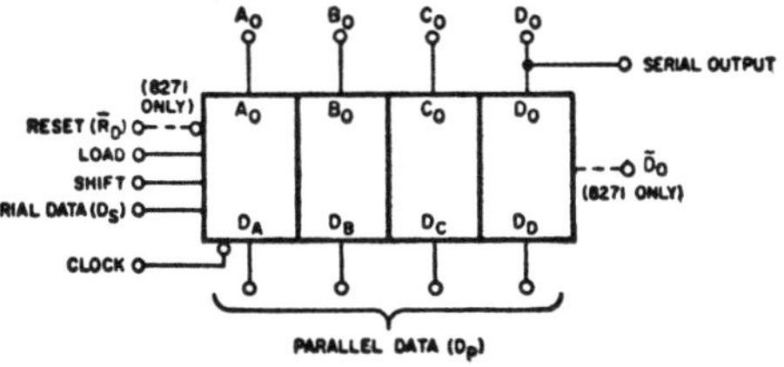

Fig. 9-2. Input connections, 8270.

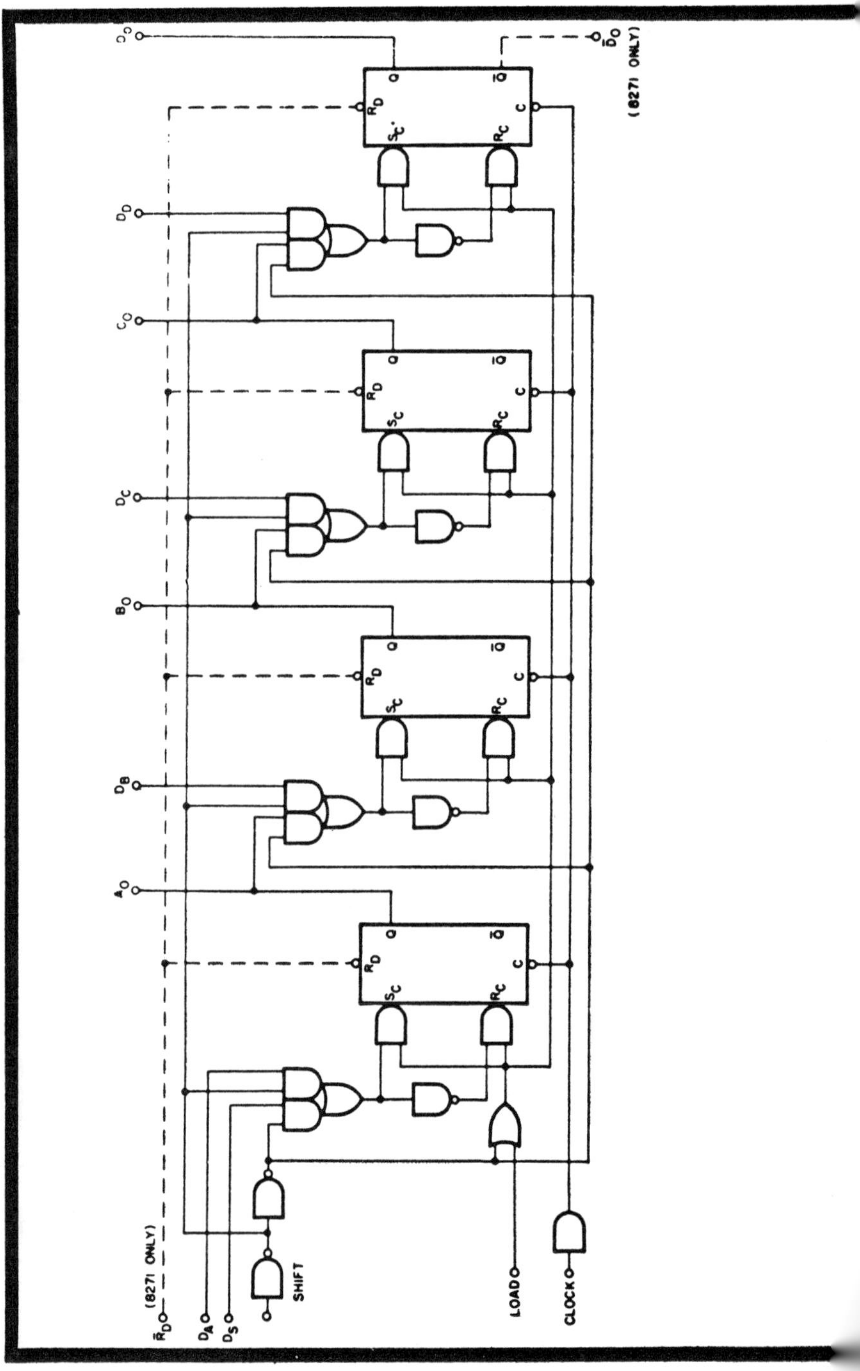
Q_D
D_D
C_Q
D_C
B_Q
D_B
A_Q
R_D
S_C
R_C
Q
Q̄
C
D̄_Q
(8271 ONLY)
R̄_D
(8271 ONLY)
D_A
D_S
SHIFT
LOAD
CLOCK

PIN CONFIGURATIONS

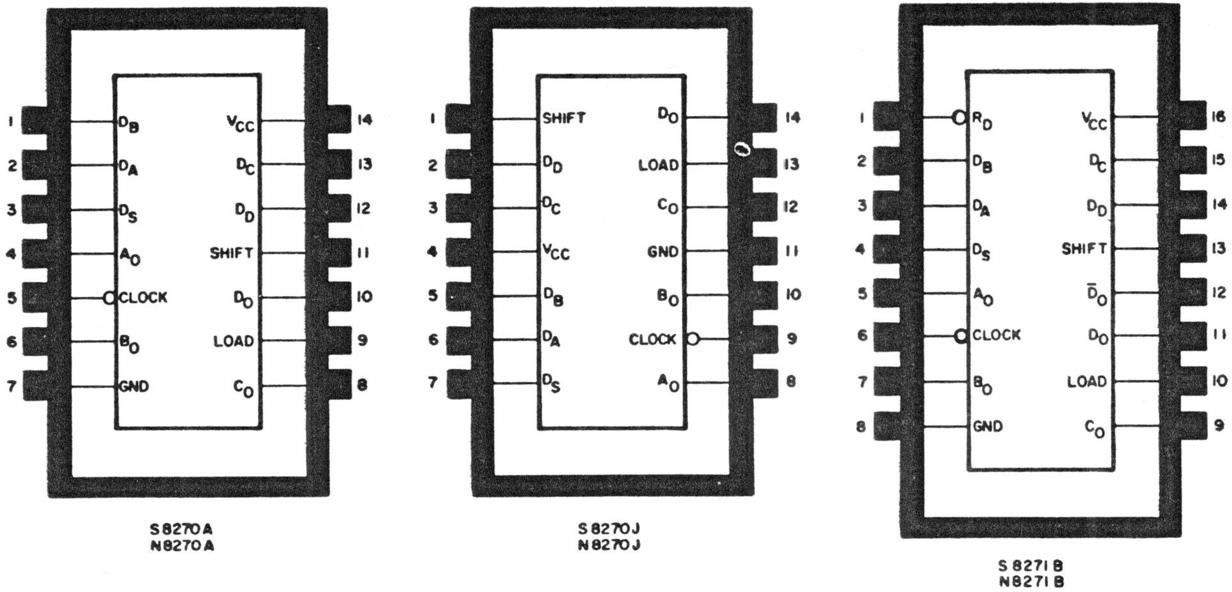

Fig. 9-3. Logic diagram and available pin configurations, 8270.

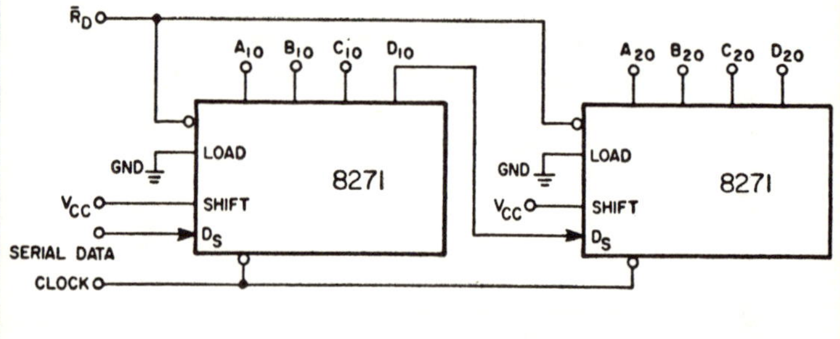

Fig. 9-4. Simple 8-bit right shift register.

CLOCK PULSE	STATE	SERIAL DATA (X_1 X_2 X_3 00...0)	FLIP-FLOP A_{10}	B_{10}	C_{10}	D_{10}	A_{20}	B_{20}	C_{20}	D_{20}
		RESET								
	0	X_1	0	0	0	0	0	0	0	0
	1	X_2	X_1	0	0	0	0	0	0	0
	2	X_3	X_2	X_1	0	0	0	0	0	0
	3	0	X_3	X_2	X_1	0	0	0	0	0
	4	0	0	X_3	X_2	X_1	0	0	0	0
	5	0	0	0	X_3	X_2	X_1	0	0	0
	6	0	0	0	0	X_3	X_2	X_1	0	0
	7	0	0	0	0	0	X_3	X_2	X_1	0
	8	0	0	0	0	0	0	X_3	X_2	X_1
	9	0	0	0	0	0	0	0	X_3	X_2
	10	0	0	0	0	0	0	0	0	X_3
	11	0	0	0	0	0	0	0	0	0

Fig. 9-5. Table of series data for Fig. 9-4.

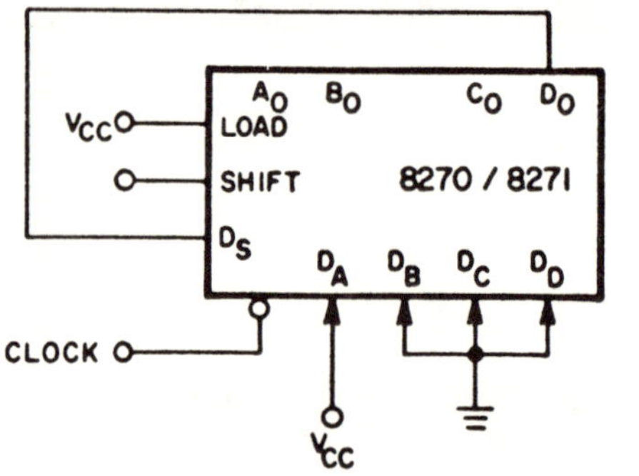

Fig. 9-6. Ring circuit connections.

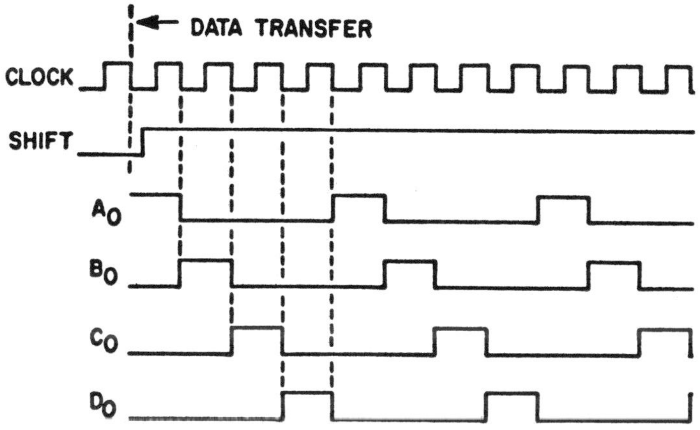

Fig. 9-7. Data timing diagrams for Fig. 9-6.

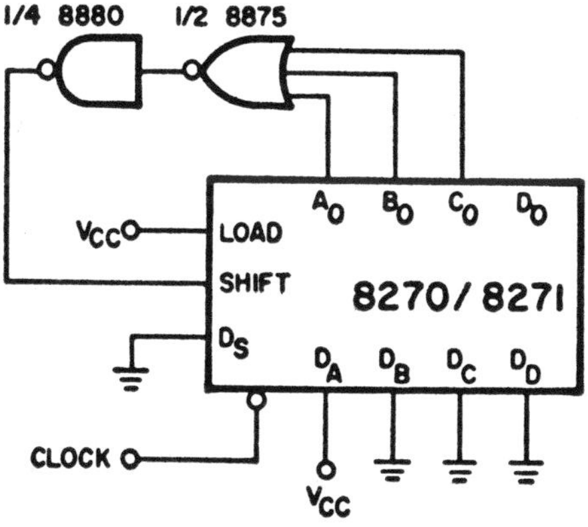

Fig. 9-8. Modified version of the ring circuit in Fig. 9-7.

STATE	A B C D	BCD	REMARK
1	1 1 1 1	15	FEEDBACK LOGIC DETECTS THIS STATE
2	0 1 1 1	7	PARALLEL LOADED DATA
3	0 0 1 1	3	
4	0 0 0 1	1	
5	0 0 0 0	0	
6	1 0 0 0	8	
7	1 1 0 0	12	
8	1 1 1 0	14	END OF PERIOD
1	1 1 1 1	15	

Fig. 9-9. Tabulation of the eight states of a ring counter with an n-stage shift register.

STATE	A B C D	BCD	REMARK
1	1 0 1 1	11	FEEDBACK LOGIC DETECTS THIS STATE
2	0 1 0 1	5	AND (0111) IS PRELOADED
3	0 0 1 0	2	
4	1 0 0 1	9	
5	0 1 0 0	4	
6	1 0 1 0	10	
7	1 1 0 1	13	
8	0 1 1 0	6	END OF PERIOD
1	1 0 1 1	11	

Fig. 9-10. In the remaining unused states another stable loop exists, as tabulated here.

Ring Counter

A ring counter built with an n-stage shift register counts through 2n states. For n equals 4 the eight states are listed in Fig. 9-9. Notice that another stable loop exists (Fig. 9-10) with the remaining unused states. With an additional feedback loop the ring counter corrects itself from stable loop conditions which exist in the unused states (Fig. 9-11).

Left-Right Shift Registers (8270 or 8271)

Fig. 9-12 shows an 8-bit serial entry, left-right shift application. Notice that a free-running clock can be applied. A left-right shift register with parallel entry is shown in Fig. 9-13.

Variable 4-bit Modulo N Counter ($2 \leq N \leq 15$)

It is well known that an n-stage binary shift register, when provided with suitably designed feedback paths, can count through 2^n-1 distinct states without any external input. For n equals 4 there are two linear recurrences for a maximum period p equals 2^4-1 equals 15:

$$X_1 = A_0\overline{D}_0 + \overline{A}_0D_0 \qquad (\overline{X}_1 = \overline{A}_0\overline{D}_0 + A_0D_0)$$

or

$$X_1 = C_0\overline{D}_0 + \overline{C}_0D_0 \qquad (\overline{X}_1 = \overline{C}_0\overline{D}_0 + C_0D_0)$$

X1 is a generated bit which is fedback to the first flip-flop.
As an example, we notice the different states (Fig. 9-14) for the recurrence:

$$\overline{X}_1 = \overline{C}_0\overline{D}_0 + C_0D_0$$

starting with:

$$A_0B_0C_0D_0 = (0\ 1\ 1\ 1)$$

We notice only the state 1 1 1 1 is not generated. Starting with 1 1 1 1 and applying the rule:

$$X_1 = \overline{C}_0\overline{D}_0 + C_0D_0$$

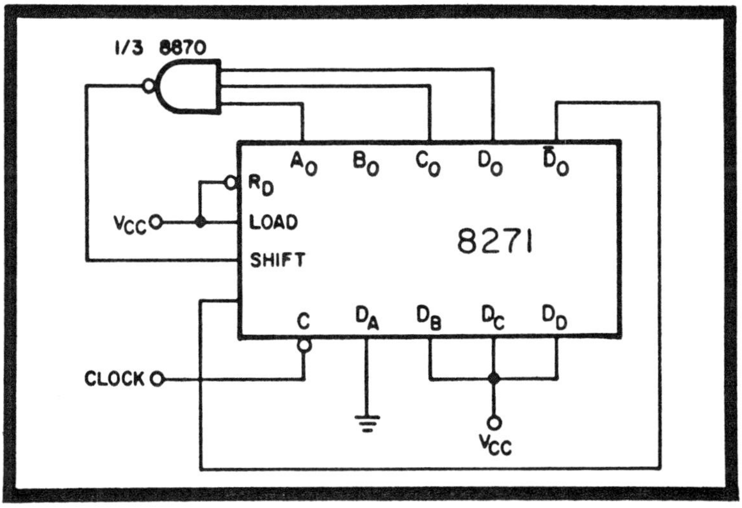

Fig. 9-11. With another feedback loop the ring counter corrects itself in the unused states.

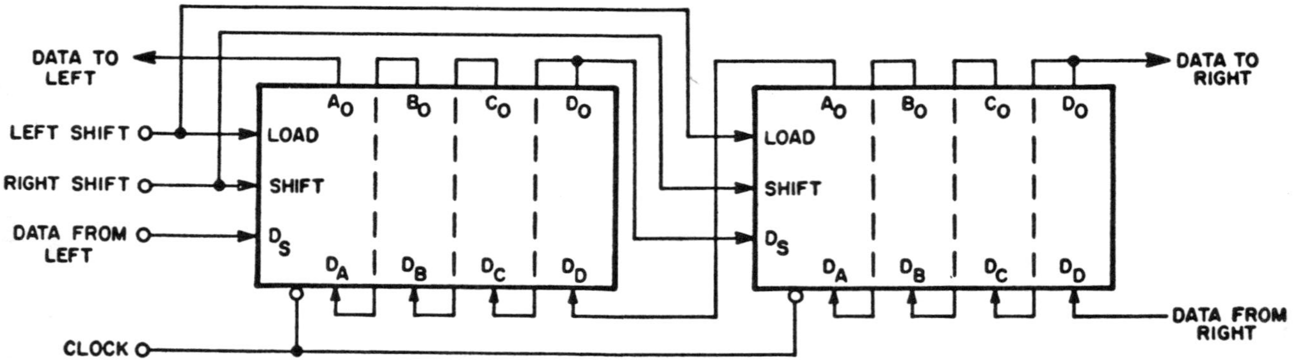

THE DIFFERENT MODES ARE:

LOAD	SHIFT	REMARK
0	0	DATA STORED
0	1	DATA SHIFTED RIGHT
1	0	DATA SHIFTED LEFT

Fig. 9-12. Diagram and truth table for an 8-bit serial entry left-right shift register.

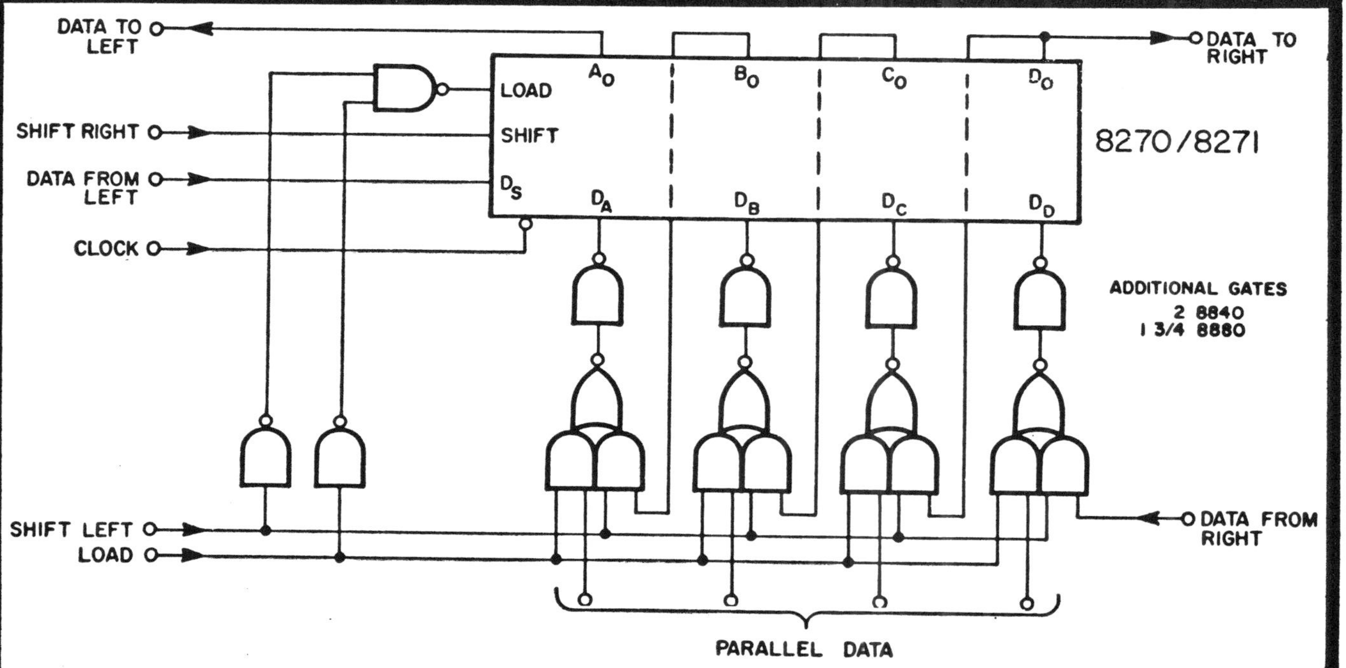

Fig. 9-13. Left-right shift register with parallel entry.

STATE	$\bar{X}_1 \equiv A_0$	B_0	C_0	D_0	N
1	0	1	1	1	15
2	1	0	1	1	14
3	1	1	0	1	13
4	0	1	1	0	12
5	0	0	1	1	11
6	1	0	0	1	10
7	0	1	0	0	9
8	1	0	1	0	8
9	0	1	0	1	7
10	0	0	1	0	6
11	0	0	0	1	5
12	0	0	0	0	4
13	1	0	0	0	3
14	1	1	0	0	2
15	1	1	1	0	-
16≡1	0	1	1	1	

$\rightarrow \bar{C}_0 \bar{D}_0 + C_0 D_0 = 1 = \bar{X}_1$ FOR STATE 2

Fig. 9-14. Tabulation of the recurring states in an n-stage shift register.

the combination 1 1 1 1 will be generated once again. Therefore, it is obvious that the long period (p equals 15) cannot include this state.

To implement a variable modulo N counter, we preload the shift register with the logic configuration:

$$N = (A_0 B_0 C_0 D_0)$$

whenever the end of the period (1 1 1 0) is reached. (For N see the truth table in Fig. 9-14.) The counter can be locked at the end of each period with the control input load. Further the counter has a self-correcting feature for all N, because every possible state leads back to the original period (truncated period for $2 \leq N \leq 14$). Notice, that the special state (1 1 1 1) influences the shift input as well as the state (1 1 1 0).

Error-Correcting Code Generator

A 4-bit shift register with a feedback loop is preloaded with an arbitrary 4-bit number. The shift register feedback path is given by the equation:

$$X_1 = A_0 \oplus B_0 \oplus D_0 = Y \oplus D_0 = Y\bar{D}_0 + \bar{Y}D_0$$

and

$$Y = A_0 \oplus B_0 = A_0\bar{B}_0 + \bar{A}_0 B_0$$

The preloaded numbers are shifted seven times, generating the output sequences tabulated in Fig. 9-16. The value of this procedure is that the set of 16 code words thus generated has the property that any two of them differ in at least three of their seven bits. Further the additional bits b1 b2 b3 enable the device to correct the code, if one but only one error occurs. To check and correct (if necessary) the received message, we form the sums S1, S2, S3:

S1 equals b2 + b5 + b6 + b7

S2 equals b1 + b4 + b5 + b6

S3 equals b3 + b4 + b5 + b7

If each sum is even no correction is necessary. If, as an example, S1 is odd, one of the bits b2, b5, b6, b7 is not correct. Assuming further the sum S2 is also odd, only one of the bits b5, b6 being contained in S1 as well as in S2 can be incorrect. If the sum S3 is even, bit b5 has the correct binary value, implying that b6 is the erroneous bit. Assigning now the logic value Z equals 1, if the corresponding sum is odd and Z equals 0 whenever the sum is even, we are able to construct a truth table for the erroneous bit, as seen in Fig. 9-18.

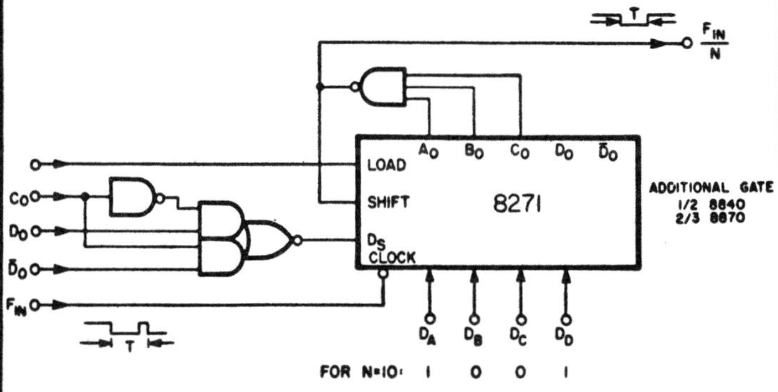

Fig. 9-15. Diagram of a variable modulo N counter.

	INPUT INFORMATION				OUTPUT CODEWORDS						
	A_0	B_0	C_0	D_0	b_1	b_2	b_3	b_4	b_5	b_6	b_7
0	0	0	0	0	0	0	0	0	0	0	0
1	0	0	0	1	0	1	1	0	0	0	1
2	0	0	1	0	1	1	0	0	0	1	0
3	0	0	1	1	1	0	1	0	0	1	1
4	0	1	0	0	1	1	1	0	1	0	0
5	0	1	0	1	1	0	0	0	1	0	1
6	0	1	1	0	0	0	1	0	1	1	0
7	0	1	1	1	0	1	0	0	1	1	1
8	1	0	0	0	1	0	1	1	0	0	0
9	1	0	0	1	1	1	0	1	0	0	1
10	1	0	1	0	0	1	1	1	0	1	0
11	1	0	1	1	0	0	0	1	0	1	1
12	1	1	0	0	0	1	0	1	1	0	0
13	1	1	0	1	0	0	1	1	1	0	1
14	1	1	1	0	1	0	0	1	1	1	0
15	1	1	1	1	1	1	1	1	1	1	1

THE RELATIONS ARE

$b_1 = A_0 \oplus B_0 \oplus C_0$

$b_2 = B_0 \oplus C_0 \oplus D_0$

$b_3 = A_0 \oplus B_0 \oplus D_0$

$b_4 = A_0$

$b_5 = B_0$

$b_6 = C_0$

$b_7 = D_0$

Fig. 9-16. Error-correcting code generator output sequences.

SYNCHRONOUS UP-DOWN COUNTERS

The 8284 hexadecimal (4-bit binary) synchronous up-down counter has 16 unique 4-bit output codes which occur synchronously. The 8285 is a BCD decade synchronous up-down counter and has ten unique binary-coded-decimal (8421) synchronous output states. The input-output functions of the 8284 and 8285 permit cascading of ten stages at the guaranteed operating frequency of 20 MHz. One of the major advantages of synchronous counters over ripple or asynchronous counters is that all outputs change at the same time, eliminating false output transition codes.

Operation

The 8284 and 8285 are synchronous up-down counters with reset to 0 and set to 15 (8284) or 9 (8285) asynchronous entry clock override (refer to Fig. 9-19). Carry-out and propagation of data occur synchronously with the falling edge of the clock input. The Q outputs of all four binaries are available, together with $\overline{Q}4$ and carry-out.

The count-enable input (see Fig. 9-20 also) goes to an AND gate which is tied to the toggle enable input of each binary element. This toggle enable AND gate also has the carry-in, set and reset inputs connected to it. As shown in Fig. 9-19, if one of these inputs is 0, the counter is disabled and will not count.

Additional gates 3/4 8880
1 8840
SHIFT = 0 Preload the input information
SHIFT = 1 Shift Right

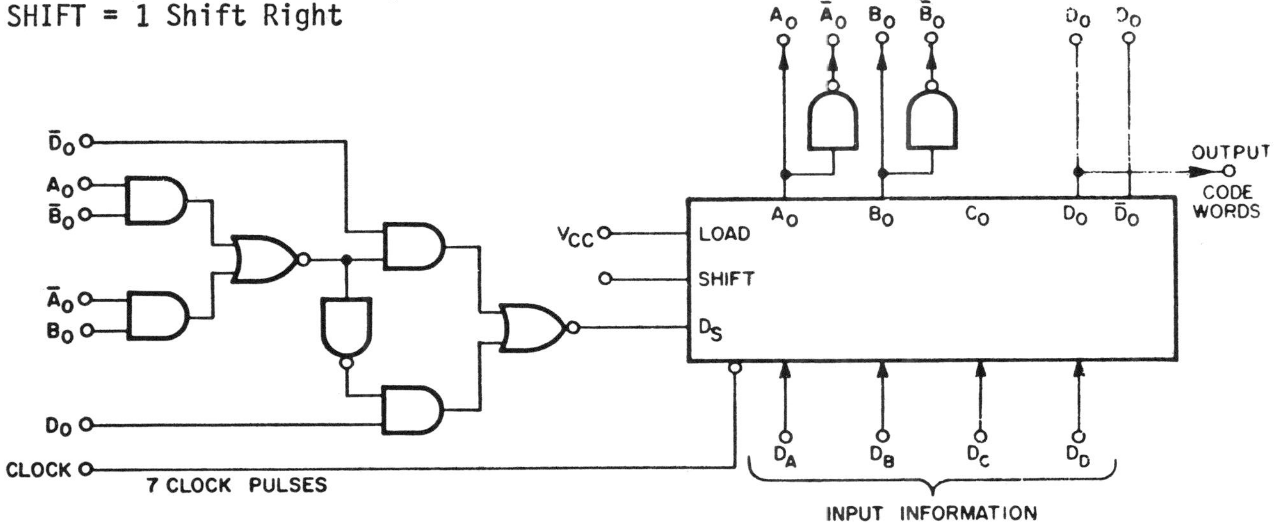

Fig. 9-17. Diagram of the error-correcting code generator.

Z_3 Z_2 Z_1	ERRONEOUS BIT
0 0 1	b_2
0 1 0	b_1
1 0 0	b_3
0 1 1	b_6
1 0 1	b_7
1 1 0	b_4
1 1 1	b_5

INFORMATION

$$Z_1 = b_2 \oplus b_5 \oplus b_6 \oplus b_7$$

$$Z_2 = b_1 \oplus b_4 \oplus b_5 \oplus b_6$$

$$Z_3 = b_3 \oplus b_4 \oplus b_5 \oplus b_7$$

Fig. 9-18. Erroneous bit truth table.

The carry-in input, besides being tied to the toggle enable AND gate, also enables the carry-out output. The count-enable input has no effect on the carry-out. Therefore, the carry term can propagate through the counter while counting is inhibited by the count-enable (0). This input-output configuration makes it possible to cascade up to 11 stages of 8284s or 8285s with completely synchronous operation at 20 MHz.

For the 8284 hexadecimal counter, a binary coded 15 (Q1 equals Q2 equals Q3 equals Q4 equals 1) in the count up mode (up/$\overline{\text{down}}$ equals 1 level) will generate a carry-out (Co equals 1 level) when carry-in goes high. The 8285 BCD decade counter in the count up mode generates a carry-out for a binary coded nine (Q1 equals Q4 equals 1, Q2 equals Q3 equals 0) when the carry-in input goes to a 1 logic level. In the count down mode (up/$\overline{\text{down}}$ equals 0 level), both counters generate a carry-out when the carry-in is a logic 1 level and a binary coded zero (Q1 equals Q2 equals Q3 equals Q4 equals 0) is detected. The propagation delay from carry-in going to a logic 1 to carry-out going to a logic 1 level is typically 15 nsec. The propagation delay from clock to carry-out is typically 30 nsec. (All propagation delay measurements are taken at the 1.5v level.)

The stored-charge clocking mechanism is buffered to reduce the clock line loading to a single TTL load. The rise and fall times should be less than 200 nsec into the internal clock buffer. This rise and fall time limitation will prevent possible oscillations due to poor Vcc to ground bypassing. With proper bypassing, fall times in excess of 1 microsec have been used to clock the 8284 and 8285 counters. The clock input pulse width

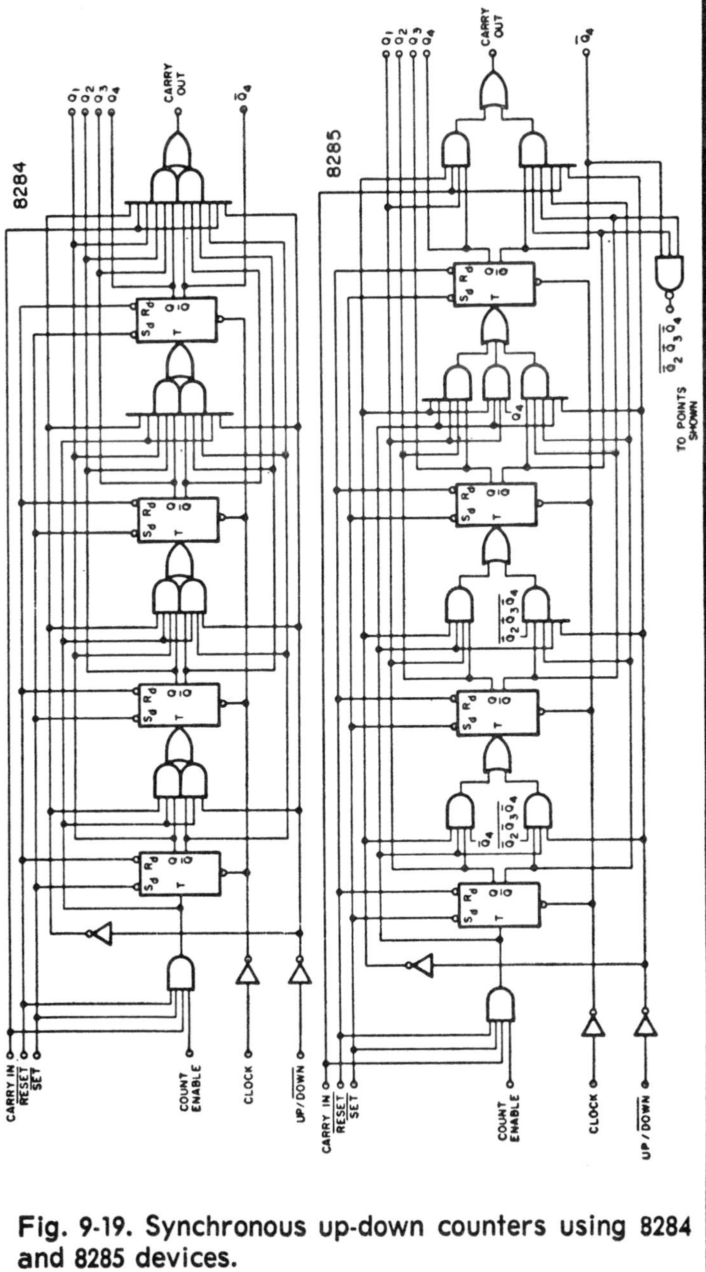

Fig. 9-19. Synchronous up-down counters using 8284 and 8285 devices.

	Set	Reset	Carry In	Count Enable	Up/$\overline{\text{Down}}$	Function
A. Asynchronous						
	1	0	X	X	X	"0" (0 0 0 0)
8284 Only	0	1	X	X	X	"15" (1 1 1 1)
8285 Only	0	1	X	X	X	"9" (1 0 0 1)
B. Synchronous						
	1	1	0	X	X	Hold *
	1	1	X	0	X	Hold *
	1	1	1	1	0	"Down" Count *
	1	1	1	1	1	"Up" Count *

*Function is synchronous with NEGATIVE going transition of the Clock pin.
X = don't care.

CARRY OUT

$$\text{Carry Out}_{8285} = \text{Carry In } (Q_1Q_4\ \text{UP} \cdot \overline{Q}_1\overline{Q}_2\overline{Q}_3\overline{Q}_4\ \overline{\text{UP}})$$

$$\text{Carry Out}_{8284} = \text{Carry In } (Q_1Q_2Q_3Q_4\ \text{UP} \cdot \overline{Q}_1\overline{Q}_2\overline{Q}_3\overline{Q}_4\ \overline{\text{UP}})$$

Fig. 9-20. Table showing mode of up-down counter operation.

must be greater than 20 nsec at the 1.5v points of the rising and falling edges with an amplitude of 2.6v or greater.

The manner in which the first two 8284s or 8285s are connected is the key to cascading ten stages at the maximum guaranteed toggle rate of 20 MHz (Fig. 9-22). The least significant counter (1) has the count-enable and the carry-in inputs tied together to optimize speed. These paralleled inputs are used to enable (1 level) or inhibit (0 level) the counter. The carry-out is connected to the count-enable inputs of all succeeding stages. The carry-in input of the second stage (2) is tied to Vcc which generates an anticipated carry-in 16 counts (8284) or 10 counts (8285) before the count-enable is activated (1 level) by the carry-out of the first stage (1). The set and reset inputs provide complete clock lock-out when activated (0 level). Reset and set are accomplished in typically 20 nsec. The 2s complement is generated for all negative binary counts of the 8284. The 2s complement $2(\overline{A})$ of a binary word is found in Fig. 9-21.

Design Precautions

Certain precautions must be taken to ensure optimum system performance of MSI circuit designs using TTL techniques. High-frequency distribution techniques should be used for Vcc and ground. These techniques should include large ground planes to minimize DC offsets and provide an extremely low-impedance path to reduce transient noise on the printed-circuit boards. The Vcc power supply should be +5v, within 5 percent with RF (1 GHz) bypassing.

The current spike produced by the totem-pole output structures during 0 to 1 switching transitions can cause MSI elements to malfunction if Vcc is not properly decoupled to ground. A ceramic disc capacitance of 2000 pf or more for each totem-pole structure should be connected between Vcc and ground in close proximity to the MSI device to provide proper bypassing. The six output and two internal totem-pole structures of the 8284 and 8285 require a 0.02-mfd ceramic disc capacitor Vcc bypass.

Electrically open inputs degrade the AC and DC noise immunity as well as the switching speed of an MSI circuit. All inputs must be connected to low-impedance sources for optimum noise immunity and switching speed. Unused inputs should be tied to a driving source, Vcc or ground. Unused inputs may be tied directly to Vcc if the power supply voltage never exceeds 6.0v; otherwise, the input should be tied to Vcc through a resistor (1K). More than one unused input may be tied to Vcc through the same resistor.

For the 8284 and 8285, reset and set should be connected to Vcc when unused. Count-enable when unused should be connected to the carry-in input or to Vcc. The carry-in input for a single counter or the first in a series of cascaded counters can be used to inhibit counting (0 logic level) by a gate or, when

2's Complement of A $^{2}(\bar{A}) = {}^{1}(\bar{A}) + 2^{0}$ where: $^{2}(\bar{A})$ = 2's Complement of A

$^{1}(\bar{A})$ = 1's Complement of A

EXAMPLE:

$$^{2}(\overline{0\,1\,1\,0}) = {}^{1}(\overline{0\,1\,1\,0}) + 0\,0\,0\,1 = 1\,0\,0\,1 + 0\,0\,0\,1 = 1\,0\,1\,0$$

Count Sequence - UP/$\overline{\text{DOWN}}$ = "0"

0 0 1 1	+3
0 0 1 0	+2
0 0 0 1	+1
0 0 0 0	0
1 1 1 1	-1
1 1 1 0	-2
1 1 0 1	-3

The 1's complement of a word is found by inverting all bits:

$^{1}(\overline{1\,0\,1\,0}) = 0\,1\,0\,1.$

Fig. 9-21. Definition of the 2s complement.

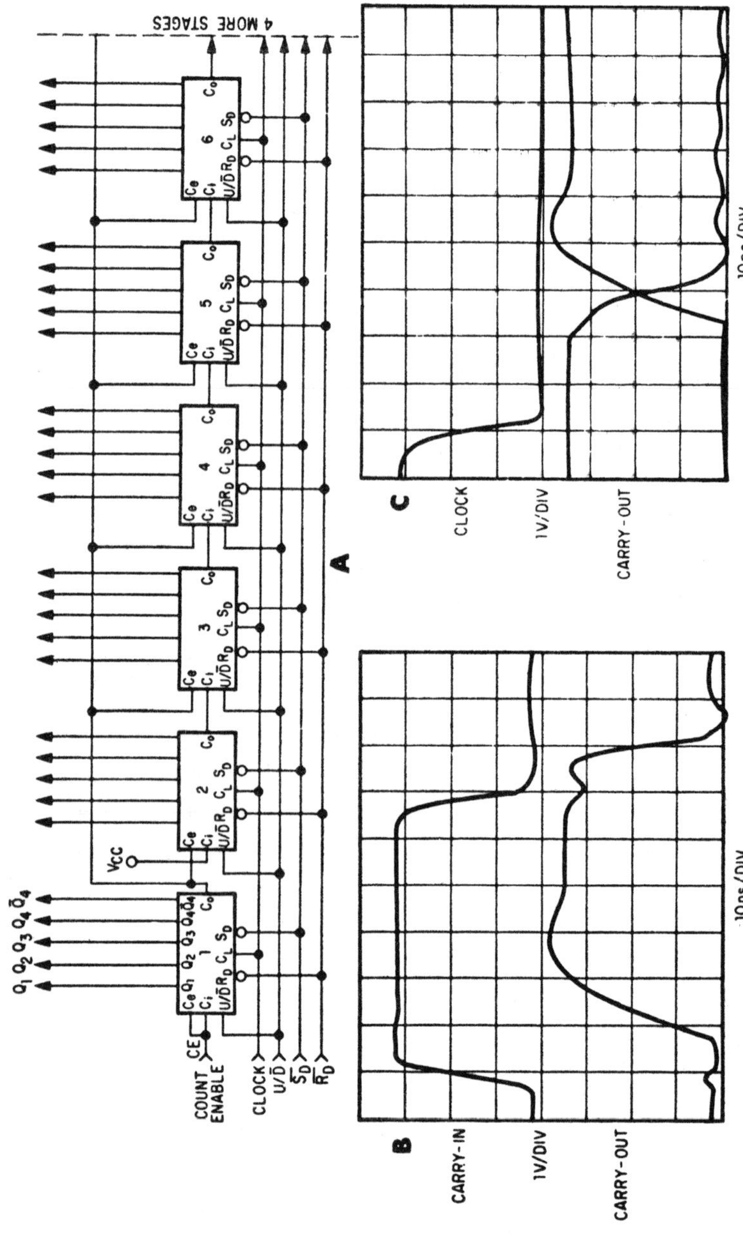

Fig. 9-22. Diagram showing the counter cascading technique. The curves depict propagation delay.

unused, should be tied to Vcc. All rise and fall times (10 percent to 90 percent) should be less than 200 nsec for a pulse amplitude of 2.6v or greater (not to exceed 6.0v).

If interconnections between devices are longer than eight inches, precautions should be taken to minimize line reflections and ringing. All inputs to the 8284 and 8285 counters are protected with diffused diode clamps. These diodes limit negative excursions to -1v or less.

Cascading Counters

Their unique input and output functions make possible the cascading of up to ten 8284 hexadecimal and 8285 BCD decade counters while operating at their guaranteed maximum frequency of 20 MHz. Being able to cascade ten stages permits the designer to count to 2^{40} or 1,099,511,627,776 counts for the 8284 and to 10^{10} or 10,000,000,000 counts for the 8285. These total counts can be achieved in both the up and down count modes with completely synchronous output code transitions at 20 MHz. Further cascading past the 11th stage is possible if necessary but the carry-out of the first stage (Co1) would have to be buffered.

Fig. 9-22 is intended to clarify the interconnection scheme, showing the cascading of ten 8285 BCD decade counters. The counters are connected to take full advantage of the "anticipated-carry" capability to achieve 20 MHz synchronous up-down counter operation. Fig. 9-21 shows only the count up mode:

Decade No.1 has the carry-in and count-enable inputs tied together. This input is used as the count-enable (CE) for the entire 10-stage counter. The carry-in (Ci) to carry-out (Co) propagation delay is typically 15 nsec (as shown in Fig. 9-22B) and the typical propagation delay from the falling edge of the clock (C_L) to Co is 30 nsec (as shown in Fig. 9-22C for the ninth and tenth clocking transition).

The second decade (2) has the Ci2 tied to Vcc. The Co2 is, therefore, always enabled. The Co1 of the first decade which is connected to the Ce of the other nine decades enables the second decade to count one count for every ten counts in the first decade. Co2 is allowed to ripple through all successive decades. The propagation delays are as follows. For the:

9999999989 to 9999999990 transition

C_L to C_{02} = 30 nsec x 1 decade = 30 nsec

$$C_{i3} \text{ to } C_{o3} = 15 \text{ nsec} \times 8 \text{ decades} = \underline{120 \text{ nsec}}$$
$$-150 \text{ nsec}$$

10 more counts in the first decade	-150 nsec
at 20 MHz = 500 nsec	+500 nsec
	+350 nsec

The 500 nsec between count-enables for the second through tenth decades allows three times the delay required for the carry term to propagate through nine decades. If the designer has a requirement for more than ten stages (either BCD decade or hexadecimal) of synchronous up-down counters, it is possible to buffer the Co of the first stage and drive the Ce inputs of 24 stages at the maximum operating frequency of 20 MHz. A 25-stage hexadecimal counter is able to store 2^{100} counts. It would take approximately 2×10^{15} years at 20 MHz to overflow this counter. A 10-stage hexadecimal will take over 15 hours to overflow at 20 MHz. Therefore, few requirements ever exceed ten stages.

1s Complement Generator

In the count down mode, the 8284 (hexadecimal) generates the 2s complement (Fig. 9-21) of any negative count. The 2s complement permits addition of positive and negative binary numbers without code conversion of the negative number. However, if the 1s complement or the reciprocal of the positive binary number is desired, 2^0 (LSB) must be subtracted from the 2s complement number:

$$-6 \text{ in 2s complement} = 1010$$
$$-2^0 \qquad -0001$$

then: -6 in 1s complement = 1001

where: $^2(\overline{A}) - 2^0 = {}^1(\overline{A})$

To generate the 1s complement automatically in the normal counting sequence of a system using 8284s requires the addition of a single 8H70 (Triple 3-input NAND gate). As shown in Fig. 9-23, the combined carry-out (Ce and Ci) detects all zero crossings. The 1s complement has two states for zero, all 0s and all 1s. All outputs are set ($\overline{S}_D$ equals 0) to 1s when all 0s

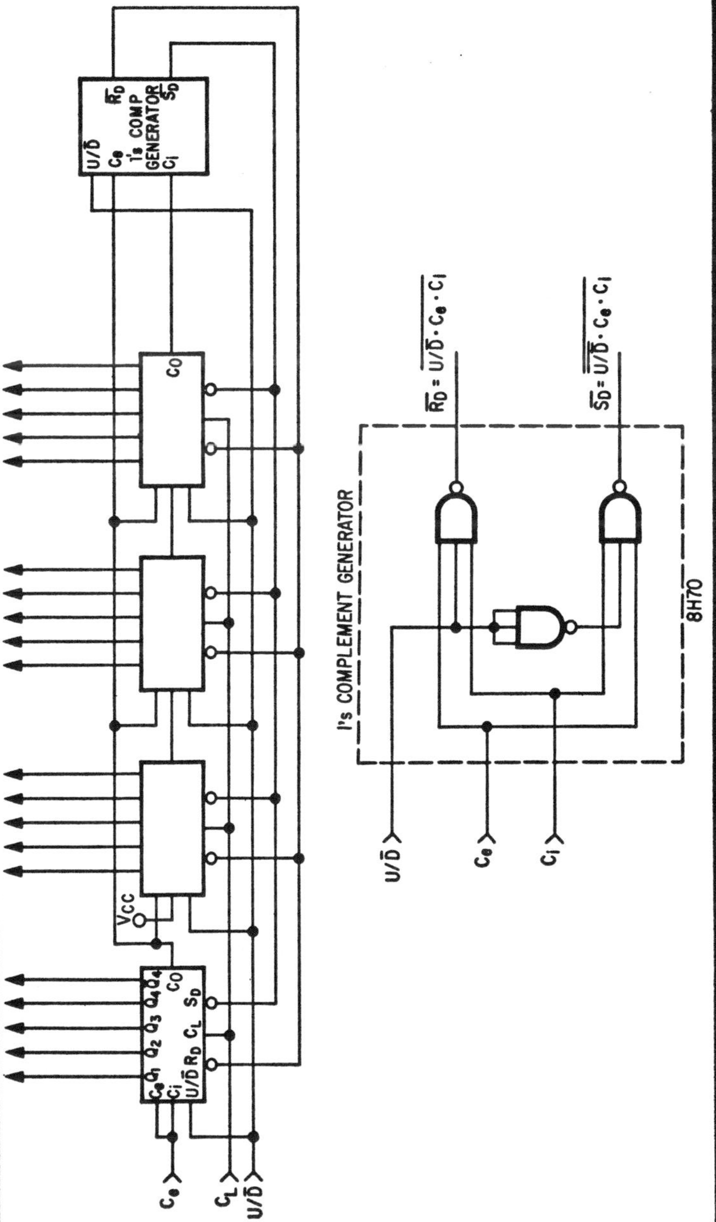

Fig. 9-23. 1s complement generator diagram.

Clock	Decimal	Binary		$C_e \cdot C_i$	$U/\overline{D}$	S_D	R_D
0	+3	0 0 1 1	1's Comp.	0	0	1	1
1	+2	0 0 1 0	←	0	0	1	1
2	+1	0 0 0 1		0	0	1	1
3	0	0 0 0 0		1	0	0	1
	0	1 1 1 1		0	0	1	1
4	-1	1 1 1 0		0	0	1	1
5	-2	1 1 0 1	←	0	0	1	1
6	-1	1 1 1 0		0	1	1	1
7	0	1 1 1 1		1	1	1	0
	0	0 0 0 0		0	1	1	1
8	+1	0 0 0 1		0	1	1	1

Fig. 9-24. 1s complement counting sequence.

are detected in the count down ($U/\overline{D}$ equals 0) mode. Conversely, all outputs are reset ($\overline{R}_D$ equals 0) to 0s when all 1s are detected in the count up ($U/\overline{D}$ equals 1) mode. An example of the generated 1s complement counting sequence is shown in Fig. 9-24.

Magnitude and Sign Generator

The 1s and the 2s complement representations of negative numbers are insufficient for some applications. When decoding the outputs of 8285s for numeric readouts, it is desirable to produce the absolute value of a number and its sign. A decoding system with these features eliminates any further decoding to display negative numbers. The magnitude and sign capability of the configuration shown in Fig. 9-25 simplifies the decoding of negative numbers for both the 8284 and the 8285.

As shown in Fig. 9-25, gates 1, 2, 3 and 4 form a D-type latch. The $U/\overline{D}$ input is transferred to Point P (gate 3) when the combined carry-out (Ce and Ci) goes to a 1 level. The function generated at the output ($U/\overline{D}$ is:

$$U/\overline{D}_0 = S \cdot P + \overline{S} \cdot \overline{P}$$

where:

$$P = 1 \ (\overline{P} = 0) \text{ then } N \geq 0$$

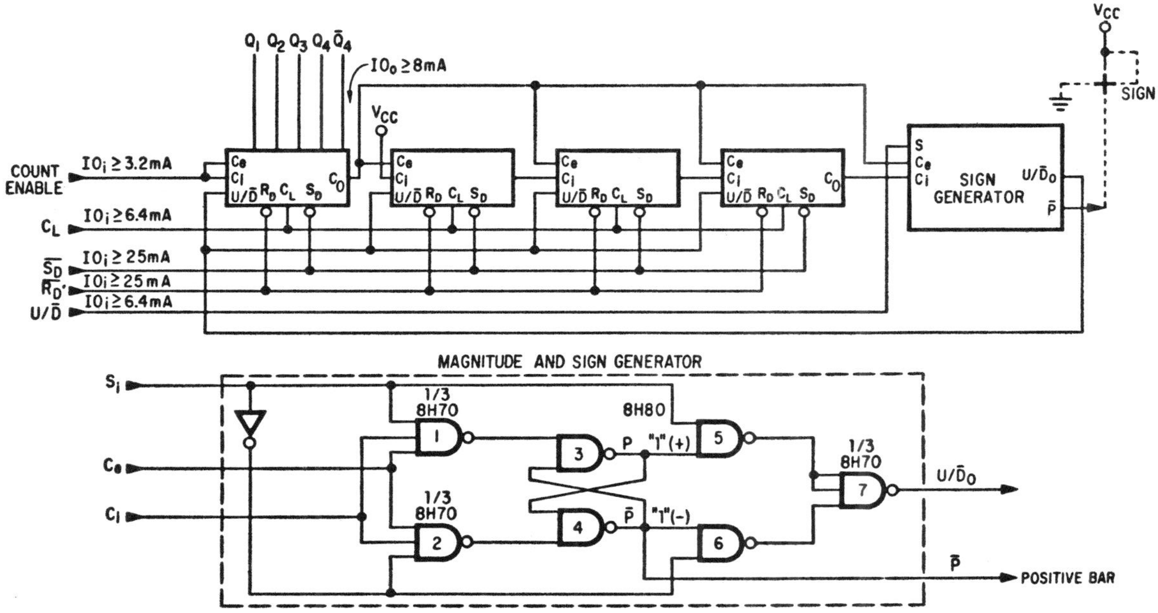

Fig. 9-25. Magnitude and sign generators diagram.

S*	Carry-Out $C_e \cdot C_i$	P	U/$\overline{D}$	N Clock	Binary	Decimal
0	0	1	0	0	0 0 1 1	+3
0	0	1	0	1	0 0 1 0	+2
0	0	1	0	2	0 0 0 1	+1
0	0	1	0	3	0 0 0 0	-0
0	1/0	0	1	4	0 0 0 1	-1
0	0	0	1	5	0 0 1 0	-2
0	0	0	1	6	0 0 1 1	-3
1	0	0	0	7	0 0 1 0	-2
1	0	0	0	8	0 0 0 1	-1
1	0	0	0	9	0 0 0 0	+0
1	1/0	1	1	10	0 0 0 1	+1
1	0	1	1	11	0 0 1 0	+2
0	0	1	0	12	0 0 0 1	+1
0	0	1	0	13	0 0 0 0	-0
0	1/0	0	1	14	0 0 0 1	-1

*S = "1" - Count Up S = "0" - Count Down

Fig. 9-26. Count sequence using the magnitude and sign generator.

$P = 0$ ($\overline{P} = 1$) then $N \leq 0$
N = Number of counts
S = 1, count positive
S = 0, count negative

The latch (P) is enabled when the carry-in (Ce and Ci) goes to 1 which occurs at all zero crossings.

Fig. 9-26 shows the count sequences generated for a single 8285 BCD decade counter with the magnitude and sign generator connected.

Synchronous Counter Decoding

Synchronous counters such as the 8284 and 8285 have an advantage over ripple or asynchronous counters (8280 and 8281) in high-speed decoding applications. The decoding of addressable memories and general high-speed multiplexer applications requiring precise code transitions should be driven by synchronous code changes. The outputs of an asynchronous counter change in a rippling sequence, as seen in Fig. 9-27A. To achieve synchronous code transitions, an 8275 quad D-type latch must be used to strobe the outputs of an asynchronous counter after the ripple interval (see Fig. 9-

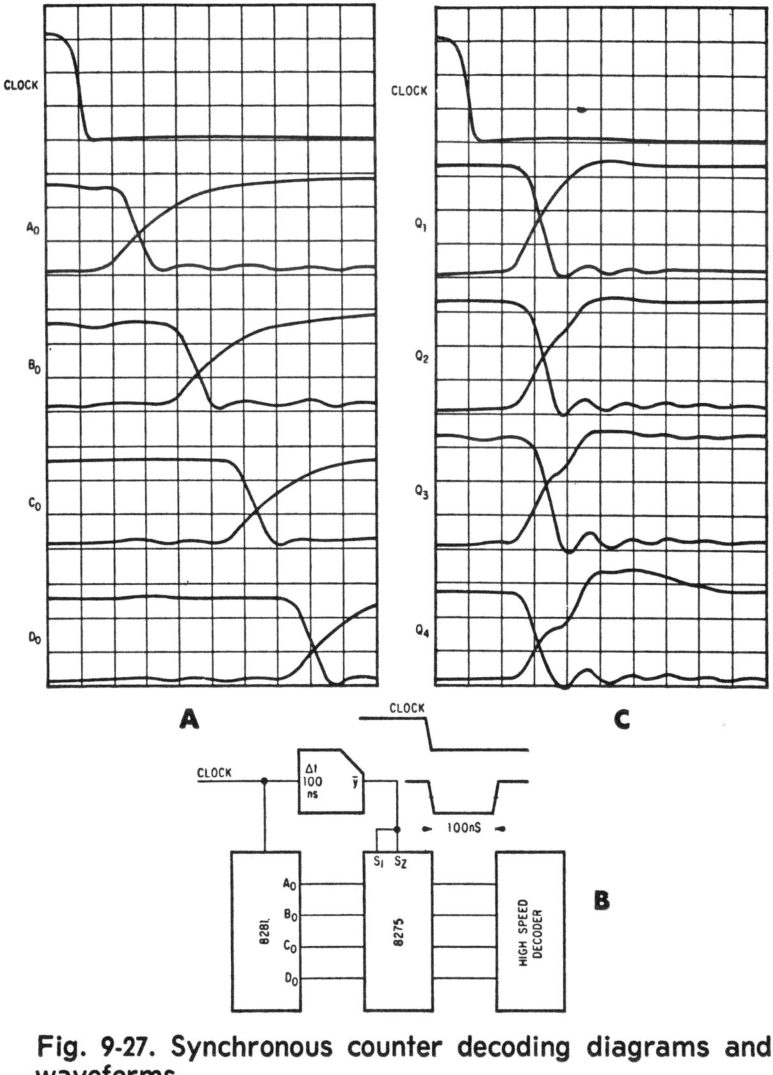

Fig. 9-27. Synchronous counter decoding diagrams and waveforms.

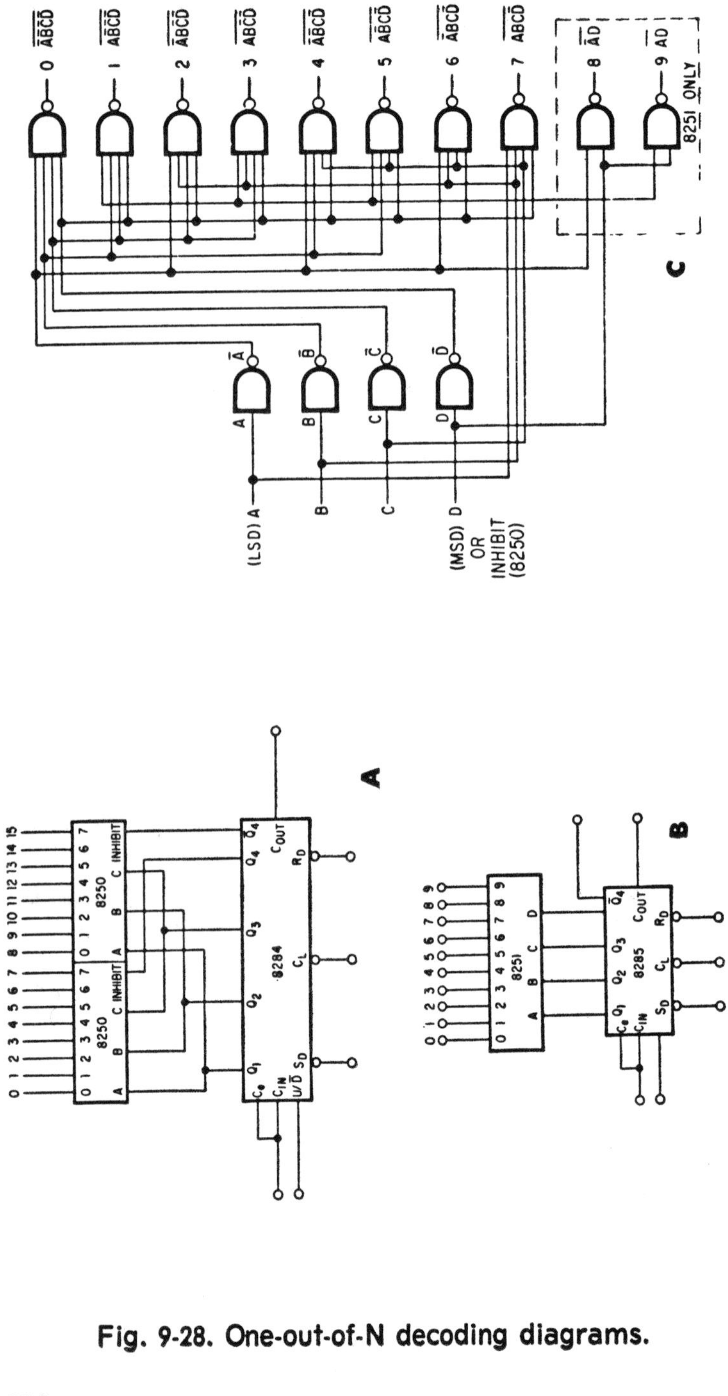

Fig. 9-28. One-out-of-N decoding diagrams.

27B). The 8281 requires a ripple interval of at least 100 nsec before the outputs can be strobed. Due to their low relative power consumption and low cost, the 8280 and 8281 ripple counters are excellent for all applications not requiring high-speed synchronous output code transitions or up-down counting capabilities.

All the outputs of an 8284 or 8285 synchronous counter change simultaneously, eliminating the generation of false transition codes. Fig. 9-27C shows the outputs of the 8284 changing 22 nsec (propagation delays are measured from the 1.5v points) after the falling edge of the input clock. However, as seen in Fig. 9-27A, the 8281 requires typically 80 nsec before the correct code is achieved.

1-Out-of-N Decoding

A 1-in-16 decoder (4 lines to 16 lines) using an 8284 (hexadecimal counter) and two 8250s (binary-to-octal decoders) is shown in Fig. 9-28A. The necessity of having the $\overline{Q}4$ output is apparent in this application. If $\overline{Q}4$ was not available, an inverter would have to be connected to the Q4 output to generate $\overline{Q}4$ at some finite delay time after Q4. This delay could cause possible decoding errors. Fig. 9-28B shows the use of an 8285 BCD decade counter in conjunction with an 8251 BCD-to-decimal decoder (Fig. 9-28C). The typical propagation delay for both counter decoder systems from clock input to decoded output is 30 nsec.

Frequency Multiplexer

The frequency multiplexer shown in Fig. 9-29A uses two 8284s and one 8232 8-input digital multiplexer (Fig. 9-29B). This circuit permits any one of the eight outputs of the 8-bit synchronous binary counter (two 8284s) to be decoded. The decoded output frequency is determined by the inputs N0, N1, N2 and inhibit as shown in the truth table in Fig. 9-29. The propagation delay from the falling edge of the clock to the outputs of the multiplexer (8232) is the same for all decoded frequencies. This propagation delay is typically 37 nsec for true output (fo) and 30 nsec for the inverted output ($\overline{fo}$).

Variable Modulus Counter

Fig. 9-30 shows a variable modulus counter or programmable frequency divider using synchronous counters (8284s or 8285s) and 4-bit digital comparators (8242s). The 8242 (see truth table) has open-collector outputs. As shown in Fig.

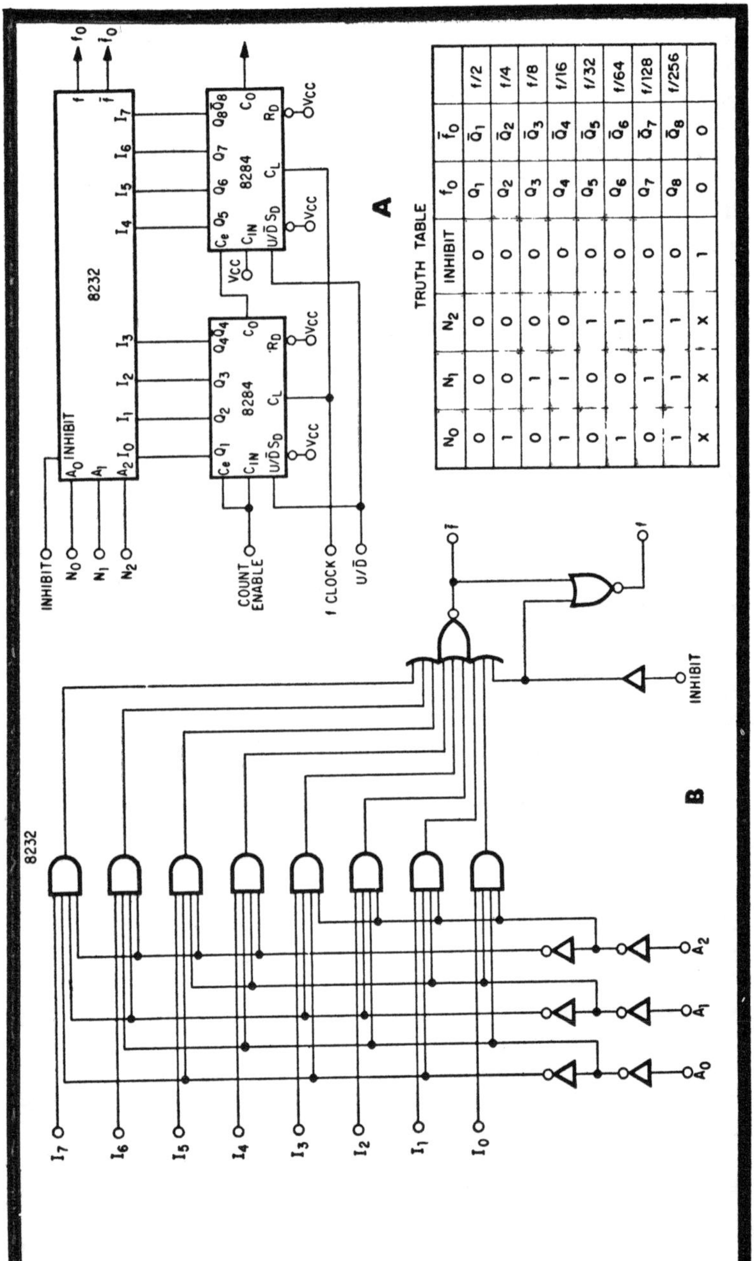

N_0	N_1	N_2	INHIBIT	f_0	$\bar{f}_0$	
0	0	0	0	Q_1	$\bar{Q}_1$	f/2
1	0	0	0	Q_2	$\bar{Q}_2$	f/4
0	1	0	0	Q_3	$\bar{Q}_3$	f/8
1	1	0	0	Q_4	$\bar{Q}_4$	f/16
0	0	1	0	Q_5	$\bar{Q}_5$	f/32
1	0	1	0	Q_6	$\bar{Q}_6$	f/64
0	1	1	0	Q_7	$\bar{Q}_7$	f/128
1	1	1	0	Q_8	$\bar{Q}_8$	f/256
X	X	X	1	0	0	

Fig. 9-29. Frequency multiplexer diagrams.

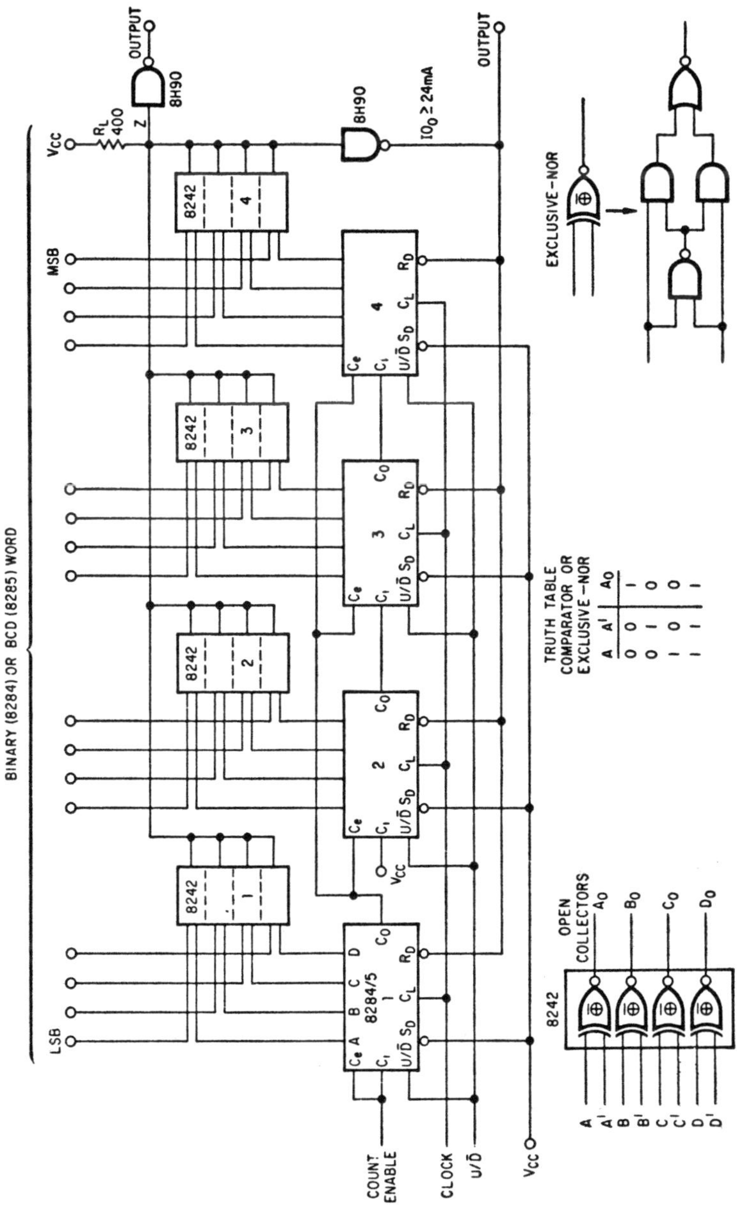

Fig. 9-30. Variable modulus counter or programmable frequency divider.

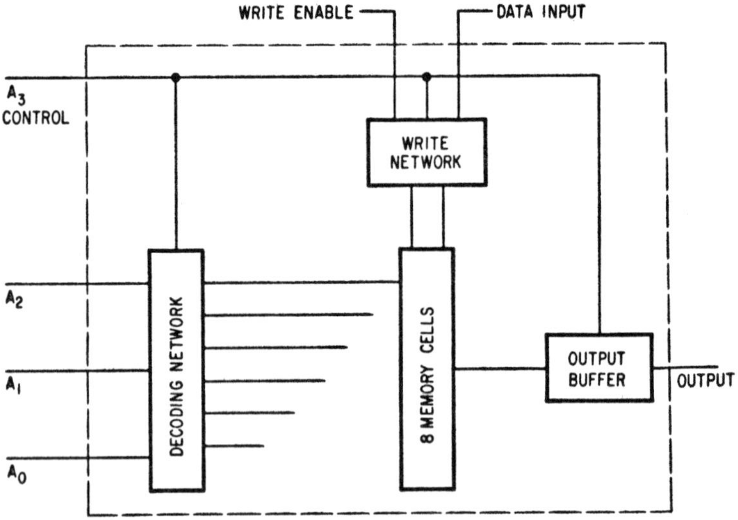

Fig. 9-31. Block diagram of the 1283 8-bit memory.

9-30 for four 8284s or 8285s, a 1 logic level is generated at Point Z when the counters' outputs digitally compare with the input binary (8284) or BCD (8285) 16-bit word. The counter must be connected in the count UP ($U/\overline{D}$ equals 1) mode. R_L was calculated for minimum propagation delay. The reset (0) pulse will be greater than 40 nsec. The reset driver, such as an 8H90 inverter, must be able to sink at least 24 ma (I0o is equal to or greater than 24 ma).

8-BIT SCRATCH PAD MEMORY ELEMENT

Logic arrays are a natural development in the improvement of integrated circuits. The advantages offered by the integrated circuit are provided by the integrated logic array to an even higher degree: greater density, fewer external connections, greater reliability, and lower cost per logic element. There is also a problem inherent in the concept of the logic array: how to configure a network of logic elements with a small number of terminals (10 to a TO-5 pack) to be sufficiently flexible to serve a broad class of uses in digital design. The Signetics 1283 8-bit memory element was designed to answer this problem.

Fig. 9-31 is a block diagram and Fig. 9-32 is a schematic of the 1283. It consists of eight flip-flops with address decoding

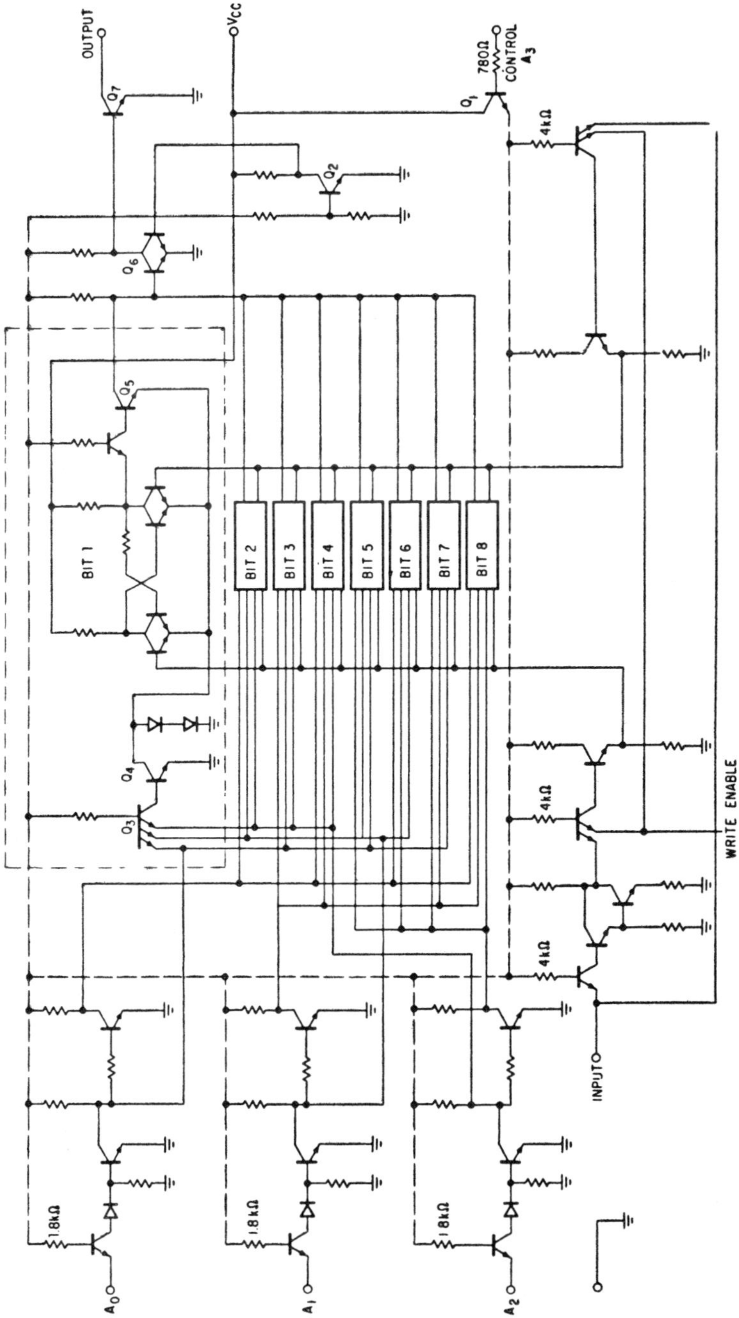

Fig. 9-32. Schematic of the 1283.

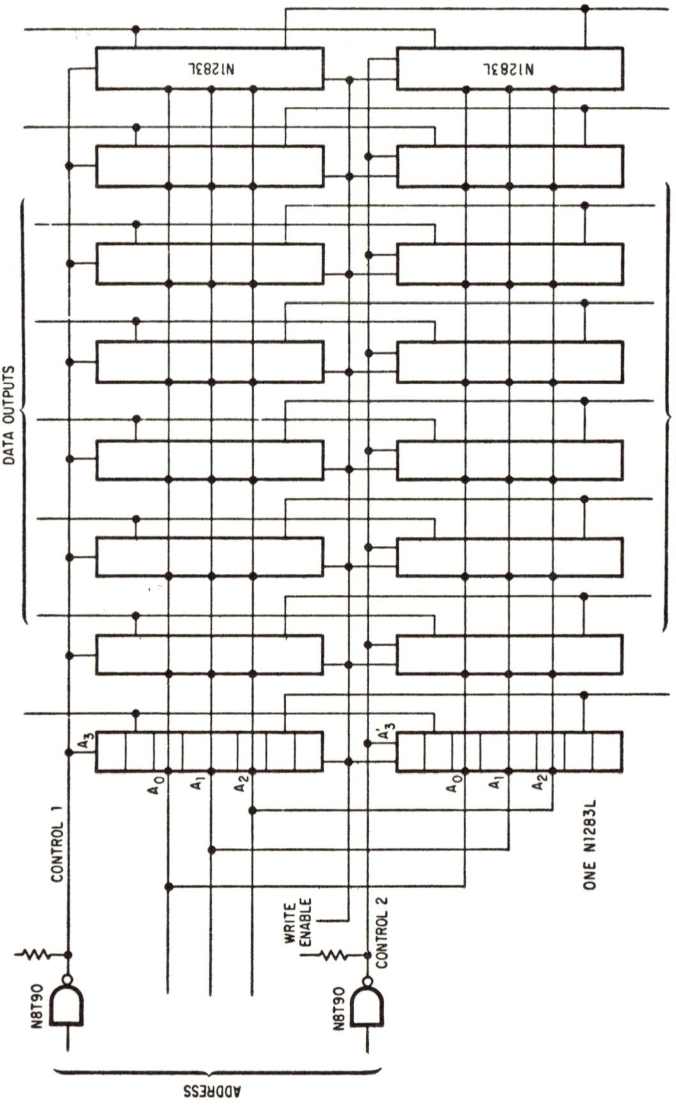

Fig. 9-33. Scratch pad memory, 16 words at 8 bits each.

logic and an output buffer packaged in a TO-5 can. A 3-bit address on leads 2, 3, and 4 selects one of the eight flip-flops for reading or writing as determined by the status of the write-enable input, lead 8. Input data is provided to the selected flip-flop on lead 7; output data appears on lead 6. Lead 1 is an additional selection control lead which serves several functions. When this lead is true, high-level, it switches the supply voltage to the input and output circuits, permitting writing or reading. When the input is false, low-level, these functions are inhibited and power is provided only to the flip-flop memory elements themselves. This permits reduction of the unit's power dissipation to 45 percent of that expended when the control is always true. The control is also an extension of the address selection logic which permits selection of one out of many 8-bit elements for reading-writing. For reading, the outputs of several 8-bit elements may be tied together, provided only one will be selected (lead 1 equals T) at any one time.

The flexible addressing scheme, nondestructive readout, buffered output and high speed (90 nsec for writing and 60 nsec for reading) permit the use of the 8-bit memory elements in a variety of applications. These include: scratch pad memory, buffers, pushdown stacks, ripple counters, shift registers, associative memories, character translators, and others. Following is a discussion of some of the applications.

Scratch Pad Memory

In many areas of computer design and elsewhere, it is desirable to have a high-speed random access memory. Fig. 9-33 illustrates a typical scratch pad memory organization. Each 1283 unit provides one bit for each of eight words. The number of bits in a word is determined by the number of elements in a row of Fig. 9-33. Therefore, word length is completely flexible. The number of words can be increased by multiples of eight through the addition of rows. A0-A3 are used to address a given word. A0-A2 select a given word of each row; A3, driven by an n-term AND gate for a 2^{n+3} word memory, selects the appropriate row. The data input and output lines would normally connect to a common external data register. Notice that his arrangement of the elements permits word transfer in bit parallel form.

High-Speed Buffer

An elaboration of the scratch pad configuration is the first-in-first-out memory, which can be used as a high-speed buffer.

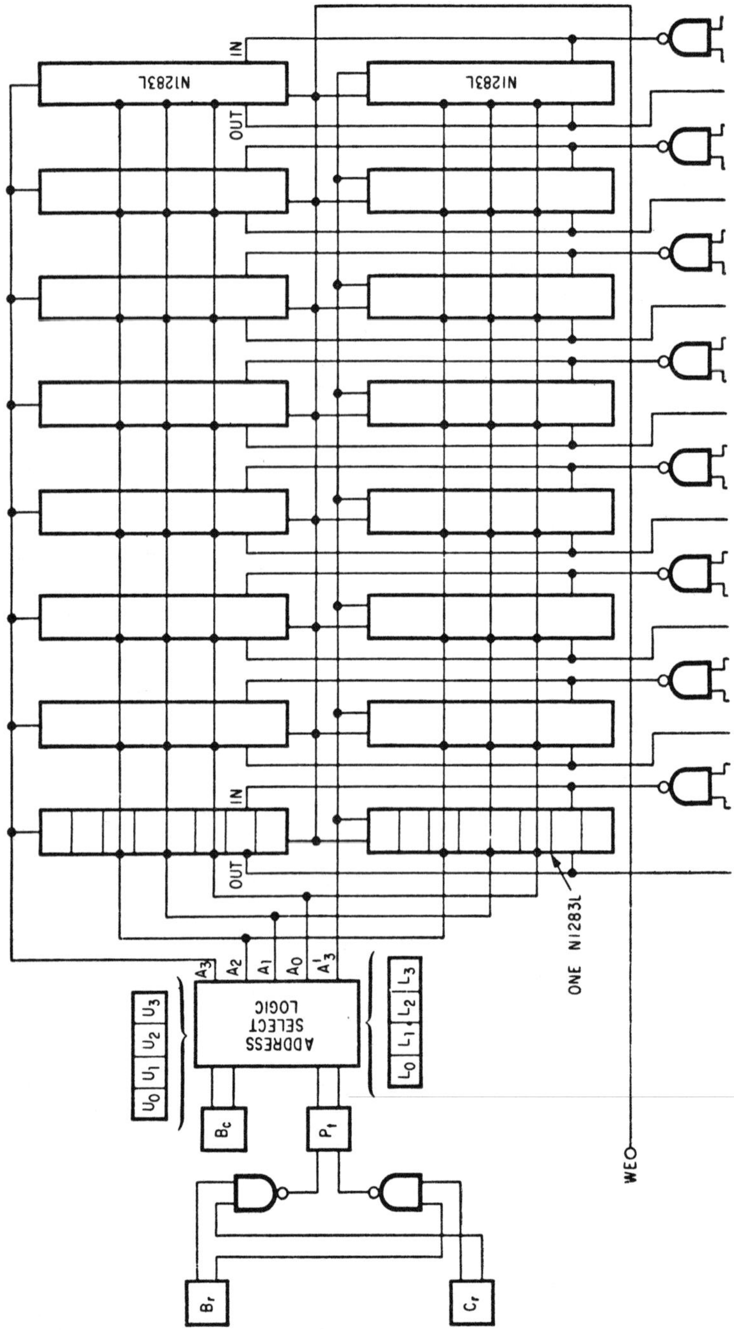
N1283L
N1283L
IN
OUT
IN
OUT
ONE N1283L
A_3
A2
A_1
A_0
A'_3
ADDRESS SELECT LOGIC
U_0 U_1 U_2 U_3
L_0 L_1 L_2 L_3
B_c
P_f
B_r
C_r
WE

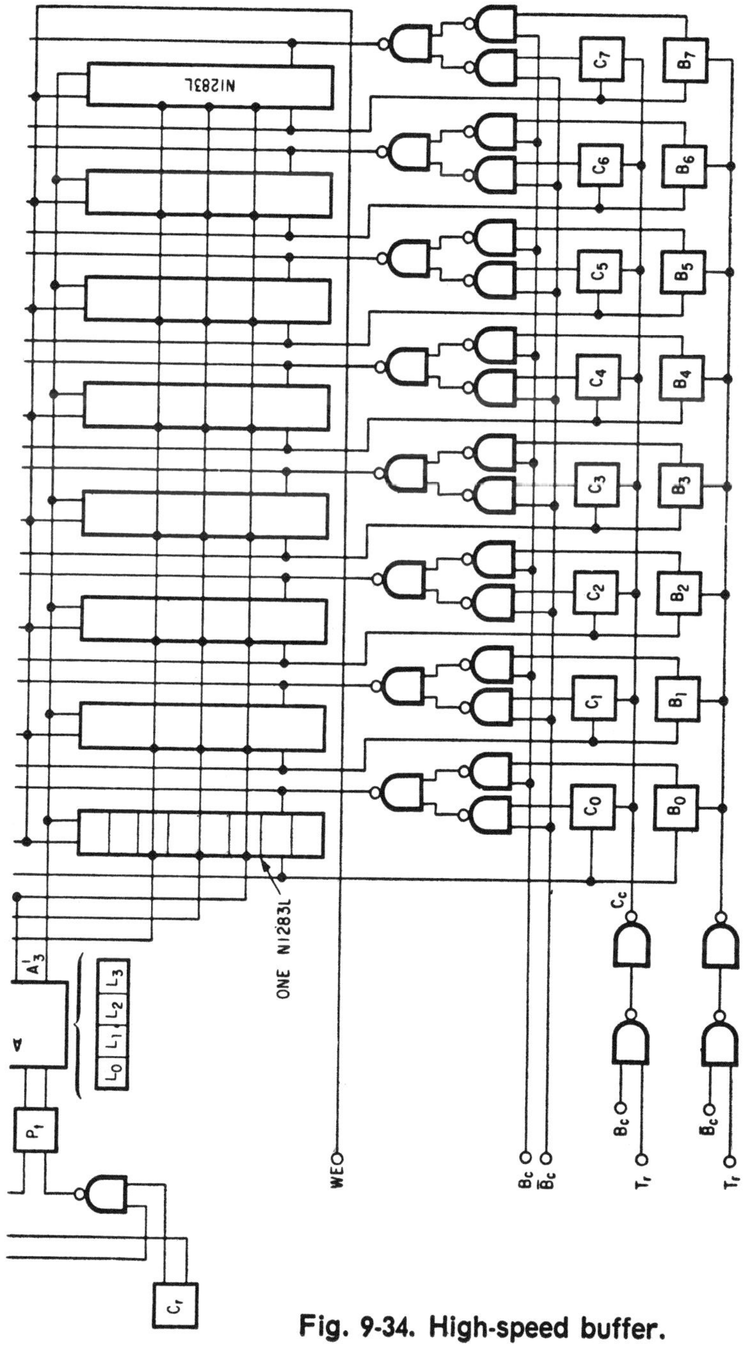

Fig. 9-34. High-speed buffer.

The buffer can transfer data asynchronously between high-speed devices such as core memories, discs, and magnetic tapes. Fig. 9-34 illustrates the configuration.

The arrangement shown permits data to be transferred in either direction between two devices, B and C; e.g., a magnetic core memory and a disc. B0-B7 is a one-byte (8-bit) flip-flop register associated with a device B. C0-C7 is a one-byte register associated with device C. The buffer itself, consisting of 16 8-bit memory elements arranged as shown, can store zero to 16 bytes of data. Of course, the buffer dimensions shown are arbitrary.

L0-L3 and U0-U3 are 16-state binary counters which at any time designate the byte in the buffer which is to be loaded and the byte which is to be unloaded. L0-L3 is incremented by 1 after each byte is loaded into the buffer. U0-U3 is incremented by 1 after each byte is unloaded. The difference between the contents of the two counters indicates the number of bytes in the buffer. An extra flip-flop can distinguish between the empty buffer and full buffer states.

Flip-flop Bc tells whether the transfer is to be from B to C or C to B. Flip-flop Br tells when the B0-B7 register is ready either to transmit a byte of data to the buffer or to receive a byte from the buffer. Cr performs a similar function for C0-C7. Pt is a priority toggle (cross-coupled NAND gates) which determines whether B0-B7 or C0-C7 is to be processed next. Pt is set by Br and $\overline{\text{Cr}}$ and reset by Br and $\overline{\text{Cr}}$; hence $\overline{\text{Pt}}$ means that B0-B7 should be processed (loaded or unloaded), and Pt means that C0-C7 should be. The purpose in using a toggle is to resolve races between Br and Cr turning on.

Consider the case of transferring data from B to C. At the outset, L0-L3 and U0-U3 are both zero, indicating the buffer is empty and that address zero will be first to be loaded. Bc gates the B0-B7 outputs onto the data input lines. As soon as device B places a byte of data into B0-B7, Br turns on. Br and $\overline{\text{Cr}}$ turns on toggle Pt; Pt and Bc causes the address line, A0-A3, A3' to be determined by L0-L3. A0-A2 follow L0-L2. A3 and A3', which determine the appropriate half of the buffer, follow L3 and $\overline{\text{L3}}$' respectively at write time, Tw. The turning on of Br initiates a timing sequence (controlled by circuitry not shown) which develops the writing pulse, Tw. Tw is gated with L3 to produce A3. It is gated with $\overline{\text{L3}}$ to produce A3'. Thus, the byte in B0-B7 is written into the addressed byte of the buffer at the Tw time. L0-L3 is then incremented and Br turned off.

Transfer of data out of the buffer to device C follows a similar sequence. When C is ready to accept the byte, Cr is turned on. Cr and $\overline{\text{Br}}$ turns off the toggle causing A0-A3, A3' to be determined by U0-U3. The timing sequence is also initiated; however, instead of producing a write pulse, it produces a read pulse, Tr, which is gated with Bc to produce a pulse on Cc. This clock pulse strobes the data output into C0-C7. Finally U0-U2 is incremented and Cr turned off. Devices B and C can be completely asynchronous, provided the buffer cycle time is less than half the shorter byte period of the two devices, B and C.

Push Down Stack

The buffer described previously is a first-in-first-out memory. It is sometimes useful to have a last-in-first-out memory or pushdown stack. It finds uses in list processing, processing of expressions in Polish notation, and reversal of data order. The configuration is like that of the scratch pad memory except that there is a single address register which is an up-down counter. This counter is incremented by 1 after each word is written; it is decremented by 1 before each word is read.

Binary Ripple Counters

The 8-bit memory elements (1283) implement multiplexed binary counters with the aid of a few additional components as

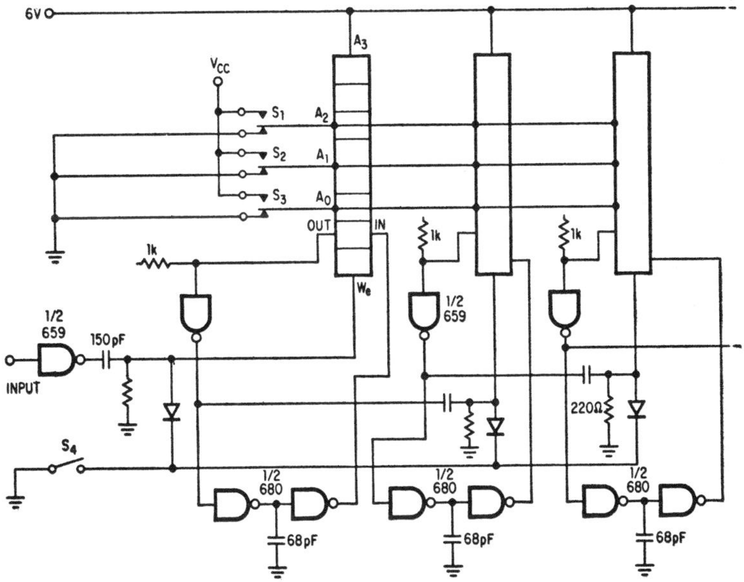

Fig. 9-35. Multiplexer ripple counter.

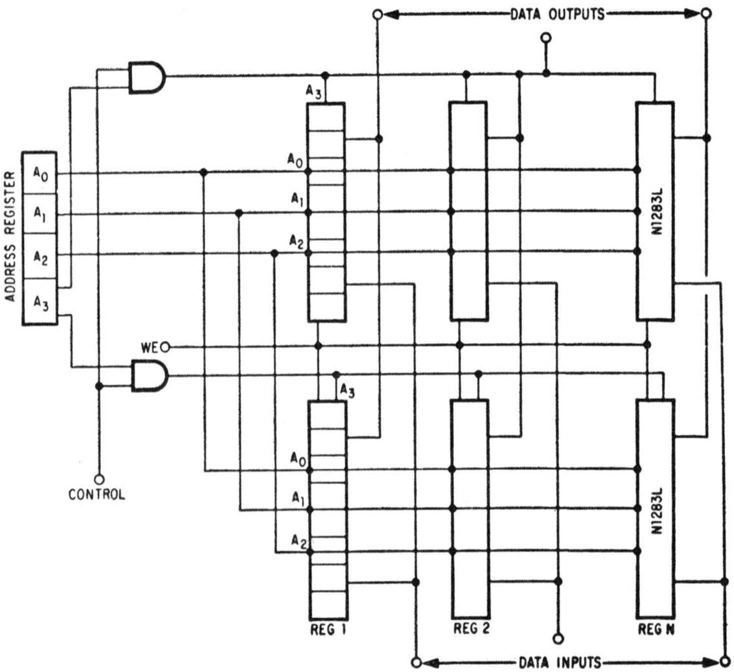

Fig. 9-36. Shift register configuration.

shown in Fig. 9-35. Each memory element provides one binary digit position for eight binary counters, hence the length of the counters is determined by the number of memory elements used. Switches S1, S2, and S3 select the desired counter (1 of 8), and S4 is a guard switch that prevents false counts during counter select switching. S4 must be in the ground position during counter select switching and in the Vcc position when counting. Switches S1 through S4 may be replaced with gates or flip-flops for fully electronic operation. Counting rates of several MHz have been obtained.

Shift Registers

The 8-bit memory elements can be organized to operate in a way resembling a set of circulating registers, Fig. 9-36. Actually, the registers do not shift but are scanned. As the address registers count up, corresponding bits of all registers are selected in sequence. The selected bits can be read and changed. The registers are conveniently mechanized in 8-bit multiples; however, other lengths can be achieved by sacrificing some of the bits in a unit. The number of registers is arbitrary, depending only upon the number of units used.

The Associative Memory

An interesting organization can be achieved by combining a set of shift registers, as described previously with a scratch pad memory. Fig. 9-37 shows an associative memory formed in this way.

The associative memory, or content addressable memory (CAM), does not use addresses or an addressing mechanism to locate a word. Instead, part of the contents of each stored word, the key, is used to identify a desired record. An external key is transmitted to all word locations; there, comparisons are made simultaneously between the stored and transmitted keys. Assuming that only one word stores a matching key, that word is tagged for writing or reading. There are many variations and elaborations of this technique.

The left half of Fig. 9-37 shows a set of n-shift registers. Each register contains one or more keys which can serve as the basis of a search. The D register is an external shift register which holds the search key. It is compared simultaneously with the corresponding field of all the other shift registers. This is accomplished bit serially but in all words at once by the comparison networks, C1-Cn, associated with the n words of memory. If the comparison is satisfied, in word i, then a flip-flop in Ci is turned on.

The address register counts through a specified range, selecting the appropriate field of all registers for comparison against the search key in D. Arbitrary fields of the key register can be chosen to represent the key by causing the address register to count through an appropriate sequence. The key can even consist of noncontiguous fields. This is useful in certain information retrieval applications. For instance suppose each stored key consists of a number of separate attribute indicators; e.g., part number, serial number, price, size, color, and weight. Then any combination of these indicators could be used to identify an item.

The right half of Fig. 9-37 shows the data section consisting of n words of scratch pad memory, each associated with a key register on the left. When one of the n-select flip-flops has been turned on by the comparison networks, that select flip-flop is used to designate the scratch pad word for reading or writing. Addressing a word in the scratch pad section is accomplished by the addressing networks, N1-Nk. Each N1 network has eight

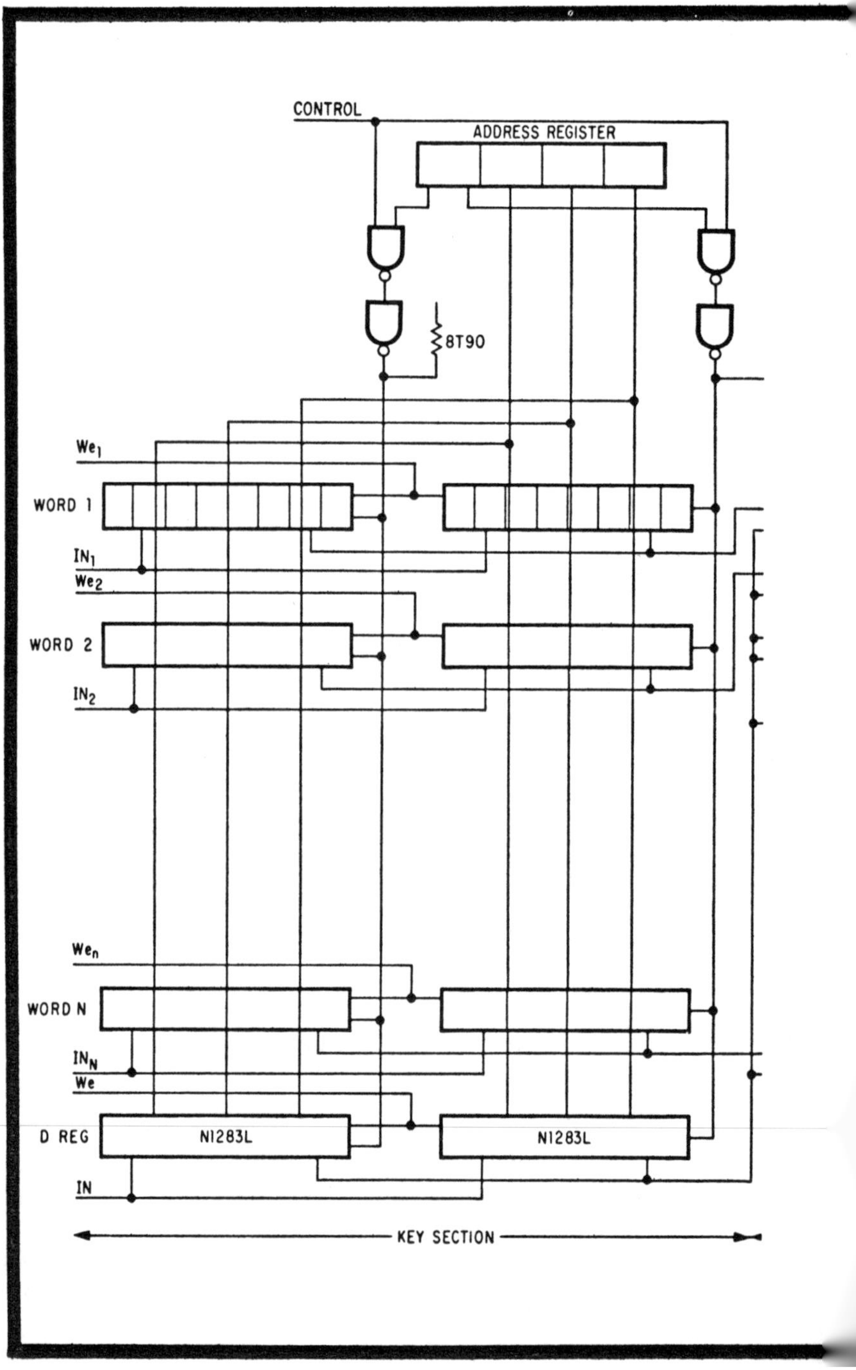
CONTROL
ADDRESS REGISTER
8T90
We1
WORD 1
IN1
We2
WORD 2
IN2
Wen
WORD N
INN
We
D REG
N1283L
N1283L
IN
KEY SECTION

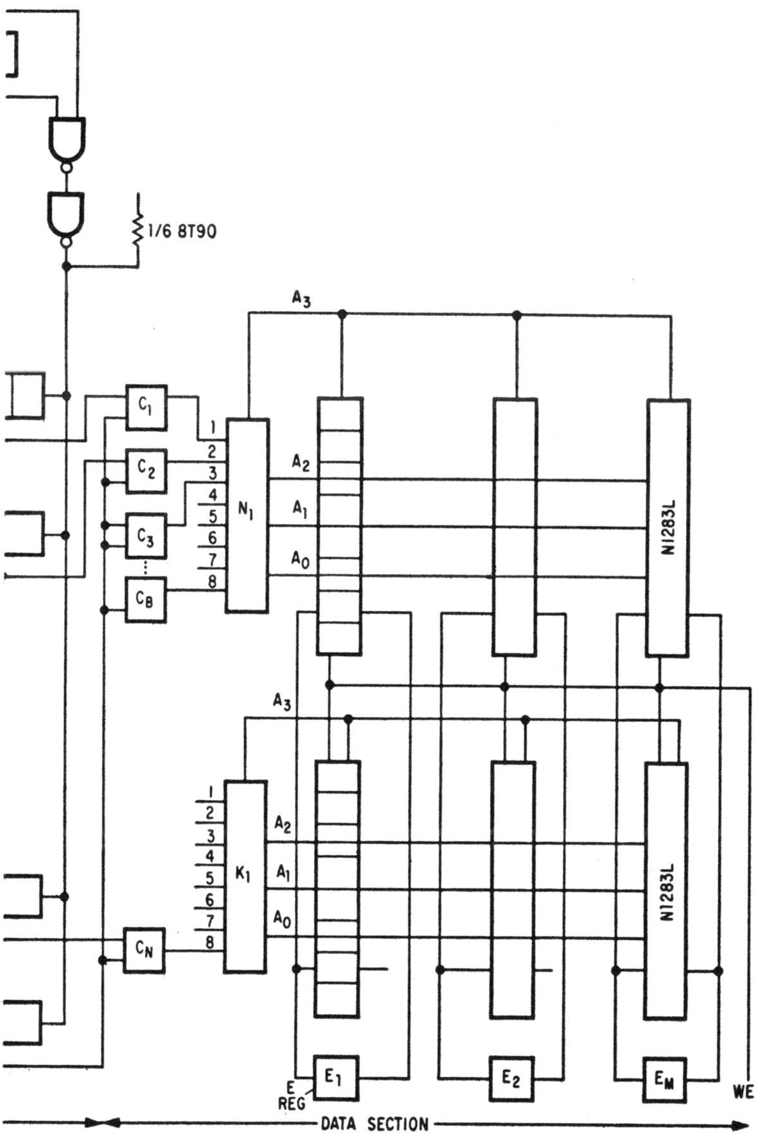

Fig. 9-37. Associative memory diagram.

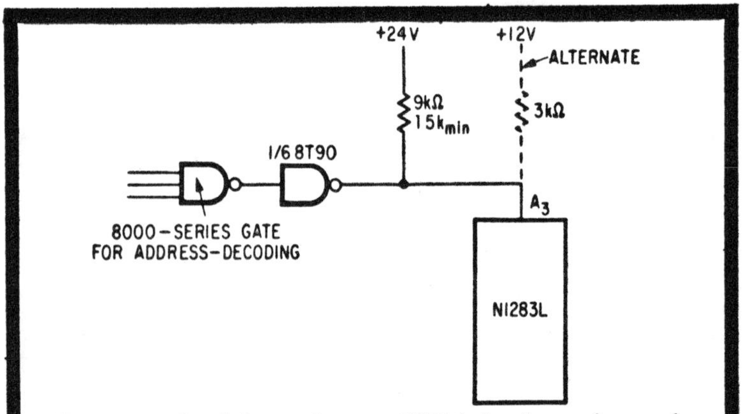

Fig. 9-38. A3 drive using an 8T90 interface element.

inputs from comparison networks and four output address lines, A0-A3. The equations for the N1 network are:

$$A_0 = C2 + C4 + C6 + C8$$

$$A_1 = C3 + C4 + C7 + C8$$

$$A_2 = C5 + C6 + C7 + C8$$

$$A_3 = A0 + A1 + A2 + C1$$

Once a word has been selected, it can be read or written by means of the write-enable signal, Wed. Information is written into and read from the data section by means of the external flip-flop data register, E1-Em. Notice that unlike comparison transfer with the key section, the data transfers with the data section are done in bit parallel.

Usage Rules

Supply voltage: The 1283 is designed for use with a 4-volt power supply. When used in systems which operate from a higher supply level, it is recommended that a separate power supply be utilized.

A3 control: The circuit shown in Fig. 9-38 is recommended for driving the A3 input. It utilizes the 8T90 interface unit and will ensure adequate drive while maintaining low power consumption levels.

Timing requirements: During writing operations, the address should be selected at least 45 nsec prior to raising the write-enable input to 1 to preclude any possibility of writing into the wrong memory location. The address selection should be retained for 20 nsec after write-enable has gone to 0. Data should precede write-enable by at least 25 ns and must be held for at least 5 ns after the removal of write-enable. The write-enable pulse should be at least 30 nsec wide (2.3 volts).

Output load resistor: The output load resistor should be chosen to maintain an adequate 1 margin at the input of any driven gate; e.g., 2.6-volt level in 8000 Series systems; 3.3-volt level in Utilogic systems. The current through the load resistor is the sum of all of 1 output currents of the 1283s connected together and the 1 input current of all driven gates. The resistor may be returned to +5 in 8000 Series systems. The minimum resistor value which may be connected to 5 volts is 300 ohms.

Loading rules: The inputs of the 1283 are three 8000 Series loads, 1.4 100 Series loads, four 400 Series loads, or 1.2 Utilogic sink loads. In all cases, the supply voltage for the 1283 is 4.0 volts. Fanout is 50 8000 Series loads, 22 100 Series loads, 66 400 Series loads, or 20 Utilogic loads.

Chapter 10

Adders

During the last two chapters we have been dealing with specific computer sections or circuit blocks. In this last of the 3-chapter series on such components we consider adders developed by Signetics Corp.

ARITHMETIC LOGIC ELEMENT—8260

The S-N 8260 consists of a high-speed 4-bit full adder with anticipated carry. This is a medium scale integration (MSI) product with 24 pins.

The arithmetic logic element is available in three different configurations.

A. S8260P: 24-pin flat pack, -55 degrees C to +125 degrees C

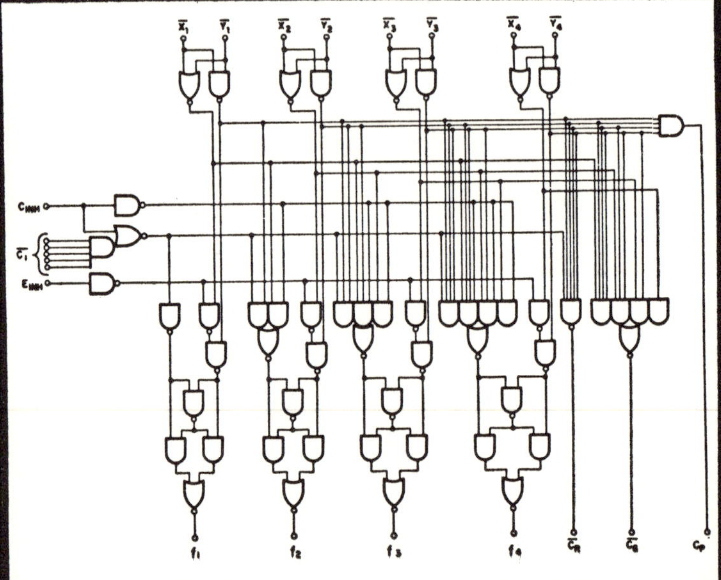

Fig. 10-1. Diagram of the 8260 full adder.

INPUTS	Least Significant C_{in} Inputs to be:	CONTROLS		f_i	FUNCTION
		C_{inh}	E_{inh}		
X_i, Y_i	1	0	0	Σ_i	Add
	1	0	1	--	not used
	1	1	0	$\overline{X}_i\overline{Y}_i + X_iY_i$	Coincidence
	1	1	1	$\overline{X}_i\overline{Y}_i$	AND
X_i, Y_i	0	0	0	Σ_i	Add
	0	0	1	--	not used
	0	1	0	$X_iY_i + \overline{X}_i\overline{Y}_i$	Coincidence
	0	1	1	X_iY_i	AND

Fig. 10-2. Table of the 8260 functions.

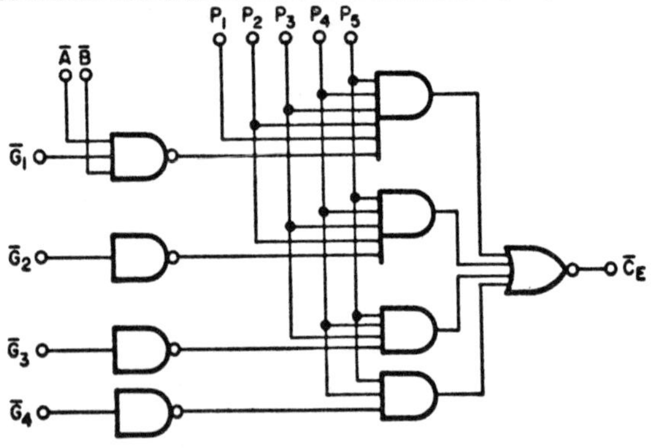

Fig. 10-3. Diagram of the fast-carry extender, 8261.

B. N8260P: 24-pin flat pack, 0 degrees C to +75 degrees C

C. N8260N: 24-pin dual-in-line, 0 degrees C to +75 degrees C

The inputs are $\overline{X}$ equals ($\overline{X}1$, $\overline{X}2$, $\overline{X}3$, $\overline{X}4$); $\overline{Y}$ equals ($\overline{Y}1$, $\overline{Y}2$, $\overline{Y}3$, $\overline{Y}4$), which represent the two 4-bit words to be added (Fig. 10-1). The carry input Ci is split in five carry terms, which will form the carry-in. The outputs are labeled as f equals (f1, f2, f3, f4) whereas the functions fi are listed in Fig. 10-2.

The carry outputs are split in the following manner:

$\overline{C}_G$: NOT-TRUE GENERATED CARRY

The generated carry indicates that a carry originated within the two 4-bit words (characters) to be added and is propagated to the next higher order character. It is not a function of $\overline{C}_I$.

$$\overline{C}_G \text{ equals } (X4Y4) + (X3Y3)(X4+Y4) + (X2Y2)(X3+Y3)(X4+Y4) + (X1Y1)(X2+Y2)(X3+Y3)(X4+Y4)$$

C_P: PROPAGATED CARRY

The propagated carry indicates that a carry generated within the lower order character is propagated to the next higher order character, but does not consider the state of C_I.

C_P equals (X1+Y1)(X2+Y2)(X3+Y3)(X4+Y4)

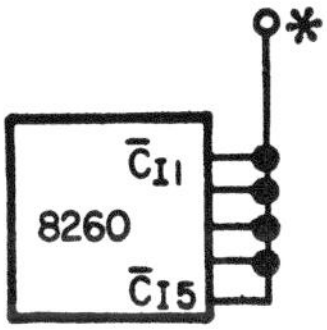

4 Bit, T_A = 28ns, typ. T_A: Total Addition Time

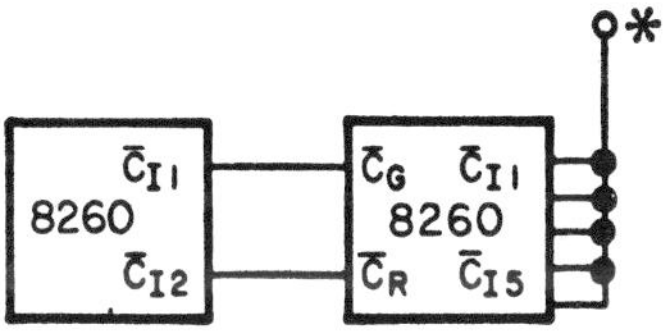

8 Bit, T_A = 42ns, typ. (Ripple Adder)

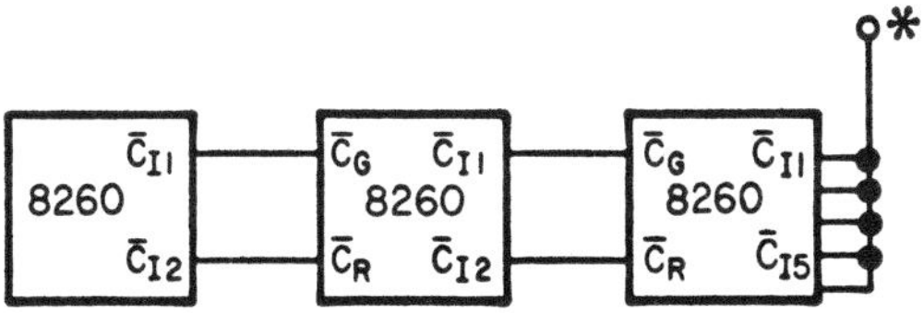

12 Bit, T_A = 56ns, typ. (Ripple Adder)

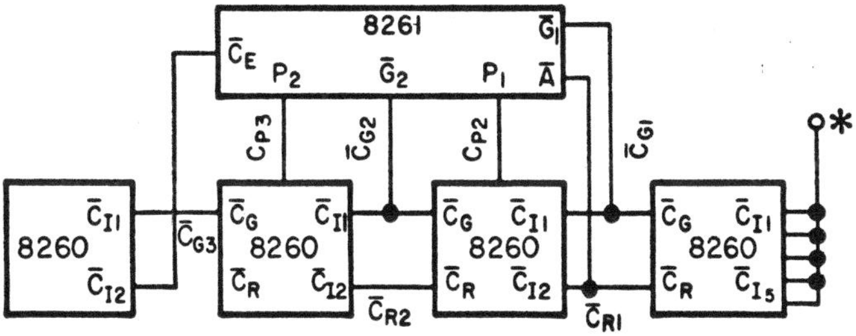

16 Bit, T_A = 56ns, typ. Fast Adder System (5 packages)

* Tied to V_{cc} if not-true inputs are used, otherwise to ground. Unused 8261 pins should be tied to V_{cc}.

Fig. 10-4. 8-, 12-, and 16-bit fast adder systems.

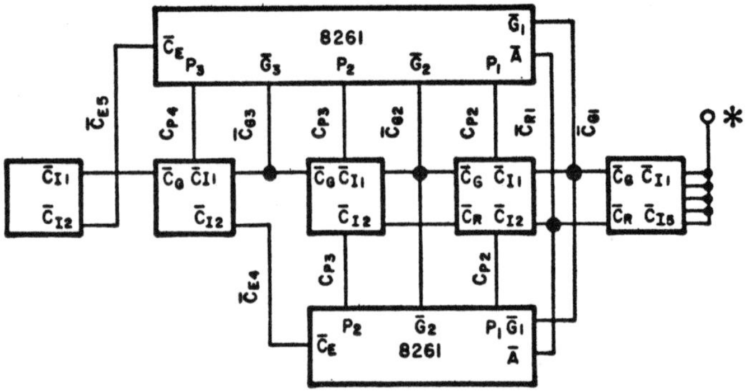

20 Bit, T_A = 56ns, typ. Fast Adder System

(7 packages)

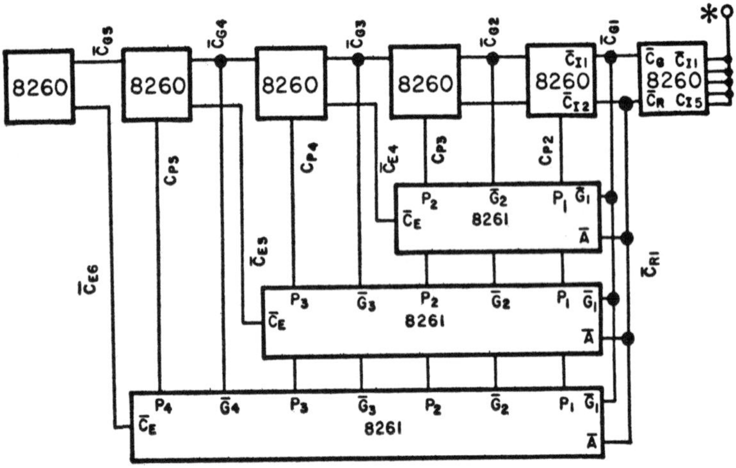

24 Bit, T_A = 56ns, typ. Fast Adder System

(9 packages)

*Tied to V_{CC} if not-true inputs are used, otherwise to ground.

Fig. 10-5. Diagrams of 20- and 24-bit fast adders.

C_R: NOT-TRUE RIPPLE CARRY

In certain adder configurations the full carry look-ahead capabilities of the 8260 are not utilized. For these cases the ripple carry output combined with the generated carry output form the carry-in for the next following package.

C_R equals C_P and C_I

Besides the normal adder applications, the 8260 acts as multi-purpose logic element. The control input carry inhibit (C_{INH}) provides the capability of inhibiting the bit-to-bit carries. In this case the device will operate as four independent exclusive-OR gates. The device also has an exclusive-OR inhibit (E_{INH}) to permit a single logical combination of the input bit pairs (Xi, Yi) and i equals 1, ... , 4.

We assume that we apply not true values to the inputs. Depending on the values of C_{INH} and E_{INH}, the resultant functions of the pin fi are listed in Fig. 10-2. On the other hand, we may assume that we apply true values to the inputs. In this case, the pins fi have the values shown in the lower half of the table.

Ripple Adder System

If we do not extend the look-ahead technique beyond one package, the ripple carry signal will ripple through between the different adder packages. The ripple adder system is the simplest but also the slowest application with the S-N 8260. The typical total addition time (input to sum output) for a ripple adder system is listed below:

Bit	Total Addition Time
4	28ns
8	42ns
12	56ns
16	70ns
20	84ns
24	98ns
28	112ns
32	126ns
36	140ns
40	154ns

The size of a ripple adder system is not limited.

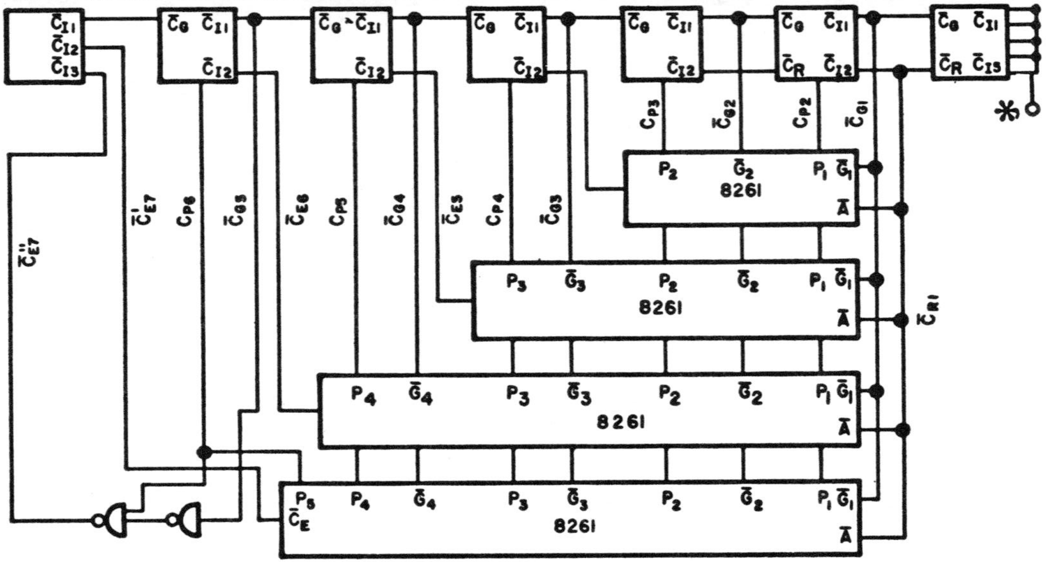

28 Bit, T_A = 56ns, typ. Fast Adder System

(11-1/2 packages)

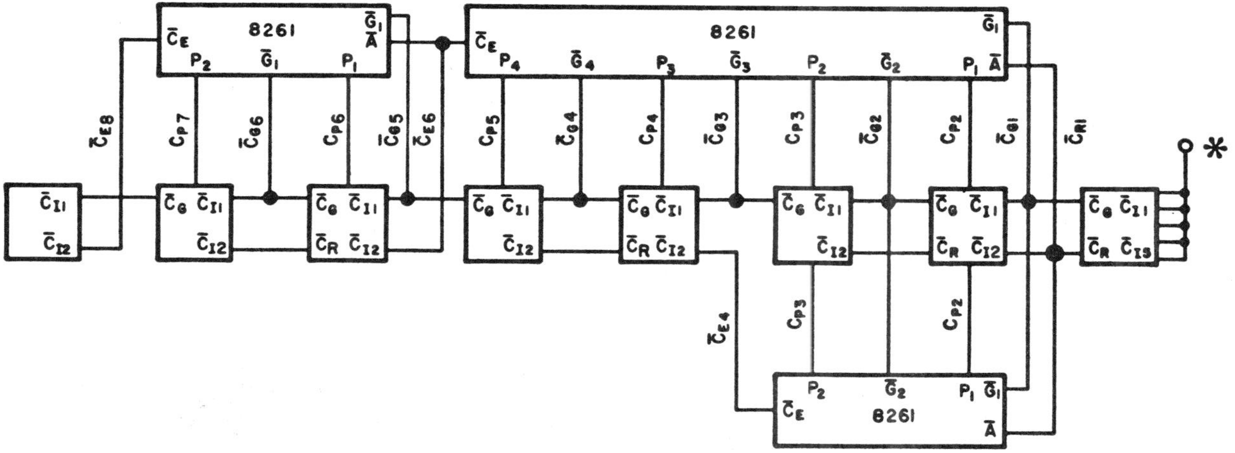

32 Bit, T_A = 70ns, typ.

(11 packages)

*Tied to V_{cc} if not-true inputs are used, otherwise to ground.

Fig. 10-6. 28- and 32-bit fast adders.

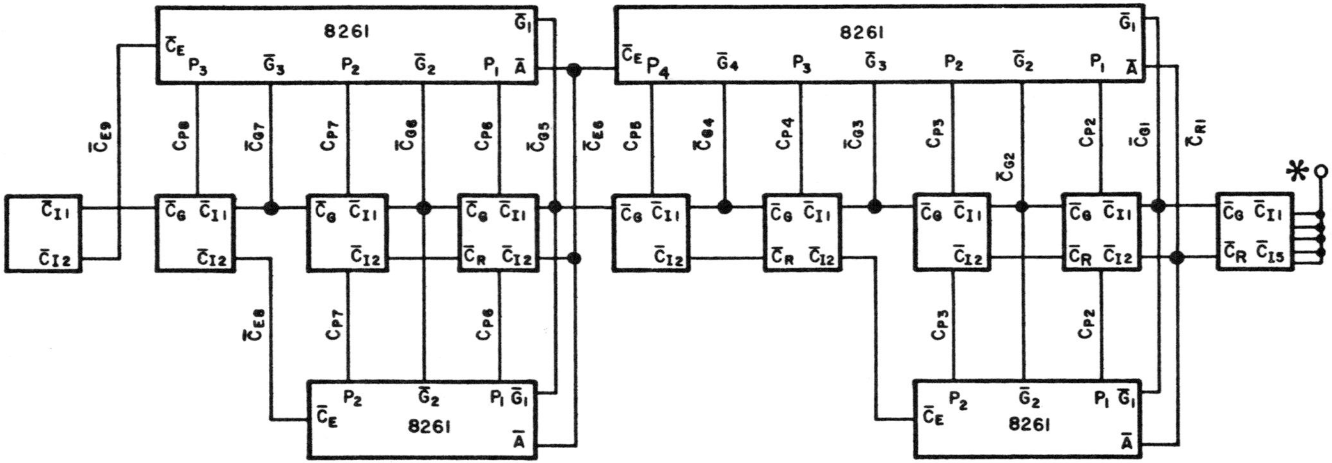

36 bit, T_A = 70 ns, typ. (13 packages)

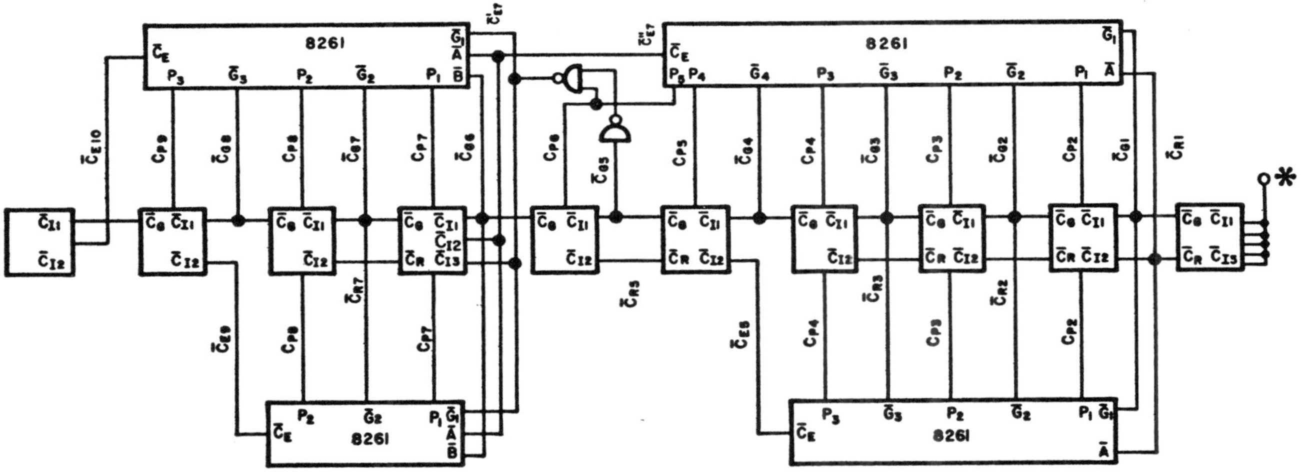

40 bit, T_A = 70 ns, typ. Optimum Adder with 2-Bridge Structure (14-1/2 packages)

*Tied to V_{cc} if not-true inputs are used, otherwise to ground.

Fig. 10-7. Diagrams of a 36-bit and a 40-bit fast adder.

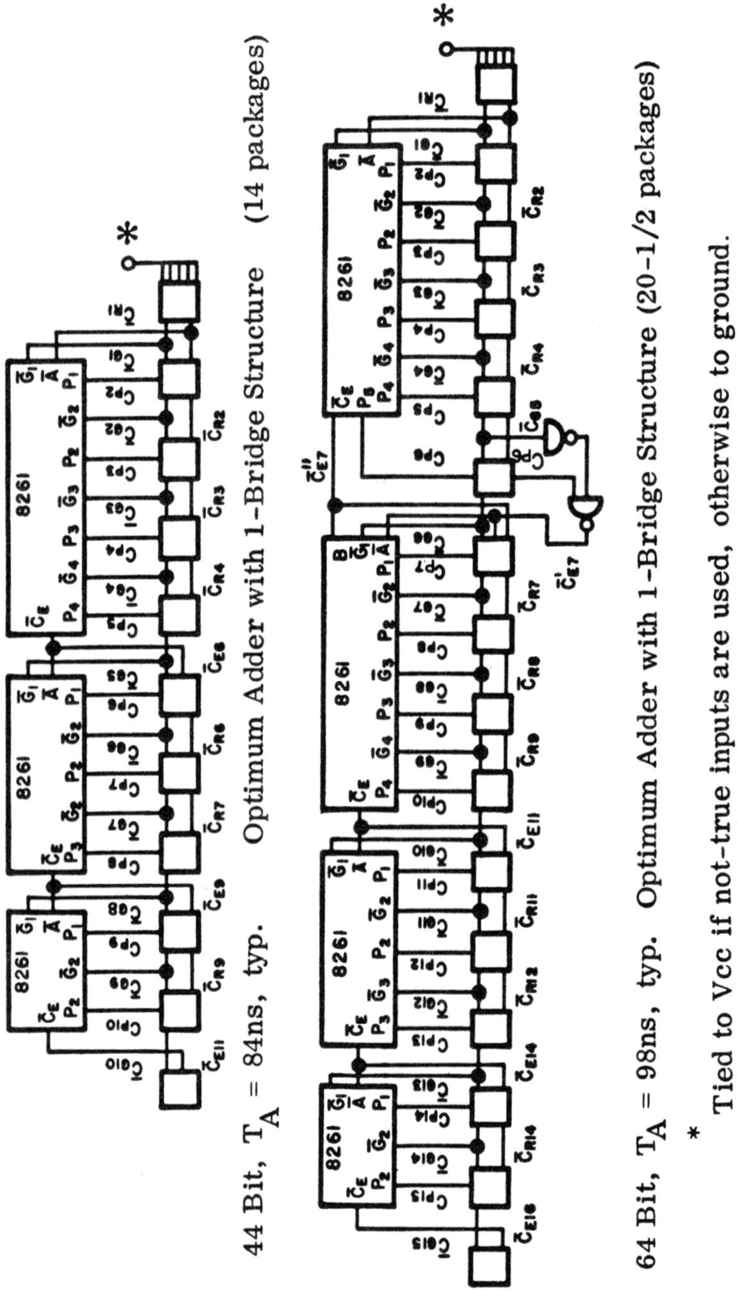

Fig. 10-8. 44- and 60-bit adders.

To avoid the ripple carry addition time, we replace C_R by the logically equivalent carry extender term C_E. Every term C_{Ei} is generated for the i-th package simultaneously and replaces the slower ripple carry signal. The fast-carry extender, 8261, will form the C_{Ei}-terms. The 8261 (Fig. 10-3) is available as a 14-pin dual-in-line and as a 14-pin flat pack with the normal temperature ranges of -55 degrees C to +125 degrees C and 0 degrees C to +75 degrees C.

The fast adder system is the fastest application of the 8260 and 61 units. The fast adder system provides complete carry look-ahead addition for words to 28 bits in length. For longer efficient adders, a combination of anticipated carry techniques (fast adder system) and ripple carry techniques are used, whereas optimum adder systems represent the most economical solutions among them.

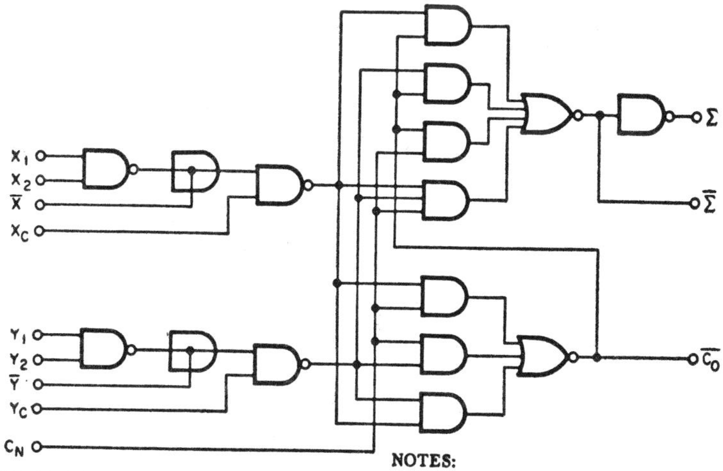

TRUTH TABLE (SEE NOTES 1,2 AND 3)					
C_N	Y	X	$\overline{C_0}$	$\overline{\Sigma}$	Σ
0	0	0	1	1	0
0	0	1	1	0	1
0	1	0	1	0	1
0	1	1	0	1	0
1	0	0	1	0	1
1	0	1	0	1	0
1	1	0	0	1	0
1	1	1	0	0	1

NOTES:

1. $X = \overline{\overline{X} \cdot X_c}$; $Y = \overline{\overline{Y} \cdot Y_c}$

   where $\overline{X} = \overline{X_1 \cdot X_2}$; $\overline{Y} = \overline{Y_1 \cdot Y_2}$
2. When $\overline{X}$ or $\overline{Y}$ are used as inputs, X_1 and X_2 or Y_1 and Y_2 respectively must be tied to GND.
3. When X_1 and X_2 or Y_1 and Y_2 are used as inputs, $\overline{X}$ or $\overline{Y}$ respectively must be left open or used to perform the dot-AND function.

Fig. 10-9. Logic diagram and truth table for the 8268.

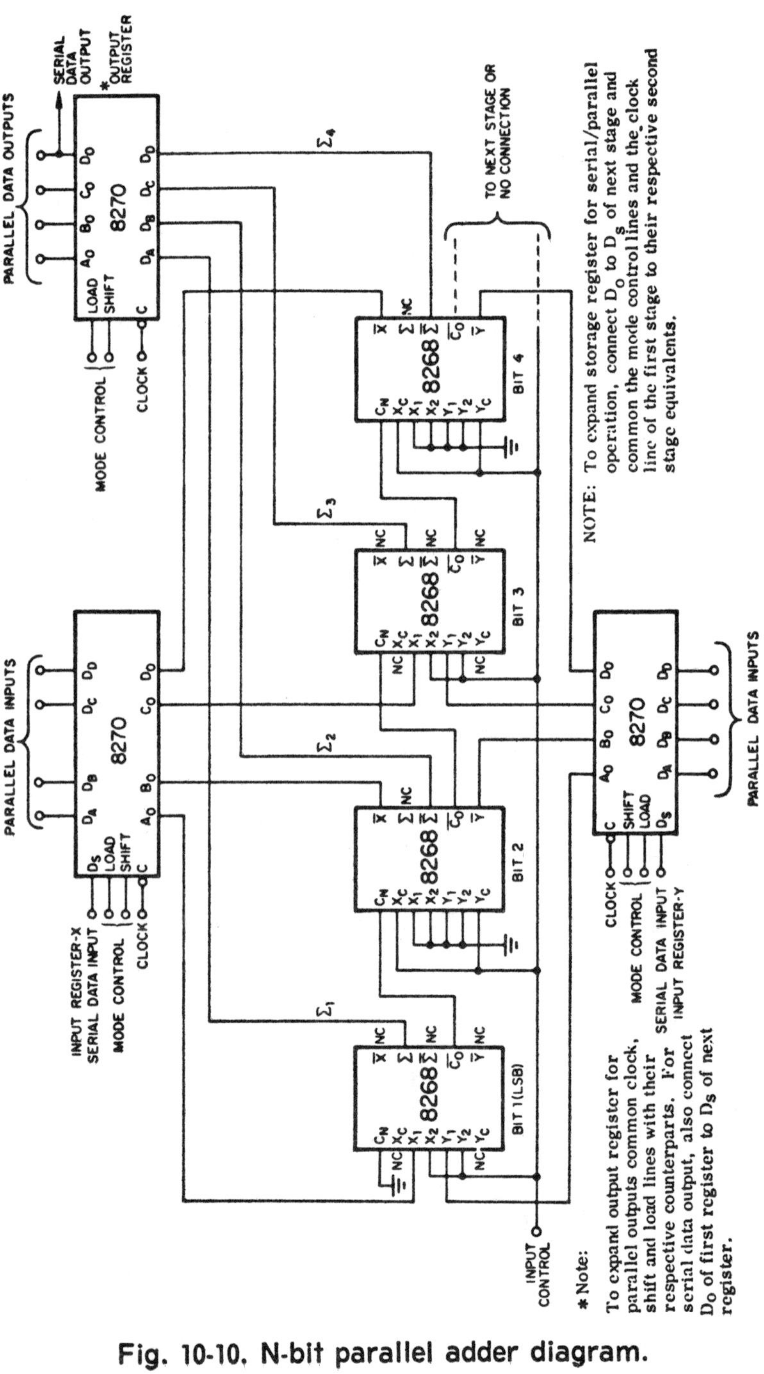

Fig. 10-10. N-bit parallel adder diagram.

GATED FULL ADDER—8268

The 8286 is a binary full adder with gated complementary inputs, sum and $\overline{\text{sum}}$ output, and inverted carry-out ($\overline{\text{carry-out}}$). The MSI circuit is designed with diode-transistor inputs and TTL output, completely compatible with DTL and TTL devices.

The full adder is designed especially for serial and ripple carry parallel add-sub arithmetic units. This array has single-ended inputs and outputs, so that only the true or complement information is necessary. The logic diagram and truth table for the 8268 are shown in Fig. 10-9. The 8268 is available in both Military (-55 degrees C to +125 degrees C) and Industrial (0 degrees C to +75 degrees C) temperature ranges in 14-pin dual-in-line and flat packages.

The factor which determines the maximum operating frequency for an N-bit parallel adder with ripple carry is the total propagation of the ripple carry term, or N x carry delay. To avoid the delay of an additional inversion required to provide carry out (Co), the 8268 provides $\overline{\text{carry out}}$ ($\overline{Co}$). When the $\overline{Co}$ term is used with the appropriate gated inputs ($\overline{X}$ and $\overline{Y}$) at the next significant bit, the desired result is available at the sum (Σ) output. This arrangement is used in every even-numbered bit in an N-bit parallel adder as shown in bit 2 and bit 4 of Fig. 10-10. For each even-numbered bit, input control is accomplished through gated inputs Xc and Yc. With input control (Xc and Yc) equals 0, the adder bit is disabled and all output terms are 0. This use of input control is twofold.

First, with the adder disabled, data in the input registers may be shifted without activating the adder subsystem. Second, with all output terms at 0 the output can be used to clear the output storage register by parallel loading the output register with all 0s. Notice that the $\overline{Co}$ of the second, fourth, etc. (all even-numbered bits) constitutes a true carry output. Therefore, to arrive at the true sum at the output of all odd-numbered bits $\overline{Co}$ is used in conjunction with the true data inputs X1 and Y1. The desired output result for all odd-numbered bits is available at the Σ terminal.

Input control is accomplished in the odd-number bits of an N-bit adder by inhibiting or enabling the gated inputs X2 and Y2. From the logic diagram of Fig. 10-9, it is apparent that a 0 at X2 and Y2 will inhibit the transfer of the bits to be added (X1 and Y1). When input control is 1, the information at X1 and Y1 is enabled and addition occurs. Since the data inputs used are the true inputs, the desired result is available at the sum

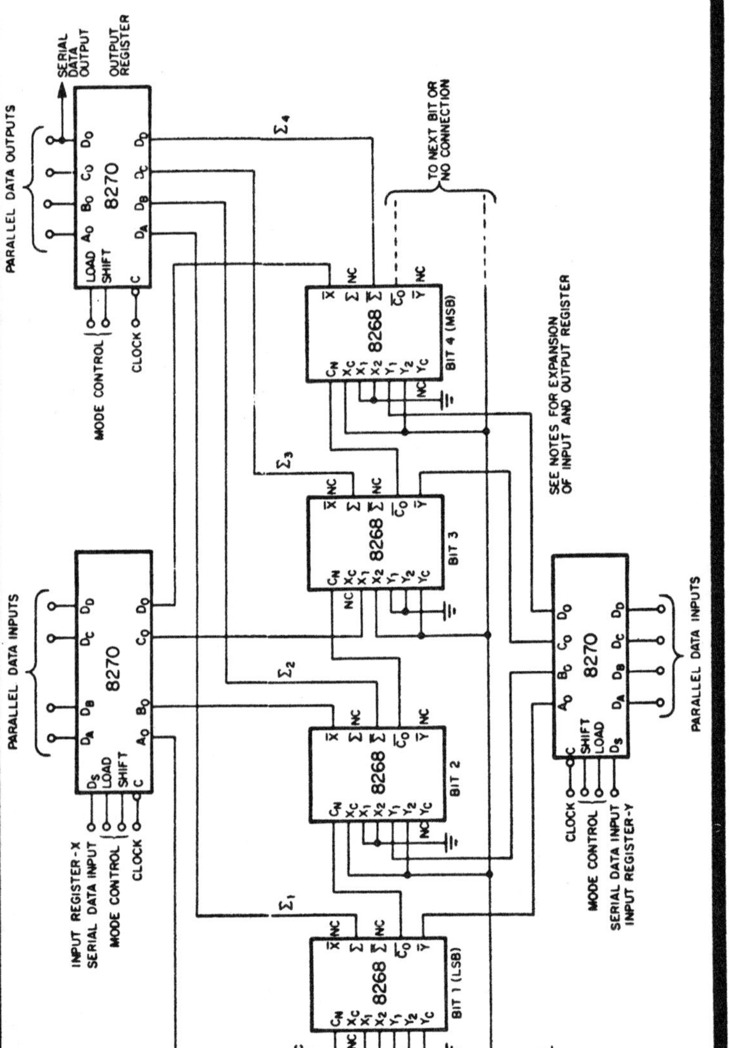

Fig. 10-11. N-bit parallel subtractor.

output (Σi). This operating mode is shown in bit 1 and bit 3 of Fig. 10-10. Notice that the carry in (Cn) term of the least significant bit of the binary adder in Fig. 10-10 is tied to ground, since Cn is a true term (activates on 1) and there is no carry term into the least significant bit.

To construct an N-bit binary subtractor (Fig. 10-11), the logic input of the subtrahend (register Y) is inverted on a by bit basis from the input arrangement for the binary adder. In addition, the input used for the Y register input control is effectively inverted (compared to the adder). Thus, for all odd-numbered bits (1, 3, etc.), input control equals X2 and Yc. For all even-numbered bits (2, 4, etc.), input control equals Xc and Y2. The input control connection pattern results from the inversion of the Y-register logic inputs. Notice that to provide the subtract function, the Cn input of the least significant bit must be connected to a logical 1 level.

Part 2: Analysis of a Typical Small Computer

Chapter 11

General Description of the PDC 808

The Computer Automation PDC 808 is one of the easiest small machines to understand. Therefore, it serves as an admirable vehicle for acquiring an understanding of the fundamental concepts behind all computers. The PDC 808 was chosen for several reasons, not the least of which was CAI's willingness to divulge what is normally held as closely guarded proprietary information. The material that follows is doubly valuable since the logic diagrams are practically impossible to come by without actually going to work for a computer company. This also holds true for the reference and maintenance data which applies in whole or in part to all general purpose computers.

BLOCK DIAGRAM

Terminology used in the PDC 808 requires some amplification. Earlier the various necessary computer registers were discussed in some detail. It was also mentioned that few if any machines use the same names for these registers and the PDC 808 is no exception to this.

One of the first and most important registers named was the accumulator which holds the results of all arithmetic operations. In the PDC 808, the accumulator register is called the **A** register. It is fed by the **A bus** and it feeds the **S bus**. The next register of importance is the instruction register and in the PDC 808 it is called the **I register**.

The program counter or instruction location counter is made up of two parts in the 808. Since the word length is only eight bits, the addresses that can be referenced by one word are 000 to 377 octal or 000 to 255 decimal. For this reason, the storage in the 808 is broken up into pages. With a 4K memory module, there are 16 decimal or 20 octal pages. For this reason, the **L counter** specifies a word in a page and the **P** counter specifies the page currently being referenced.

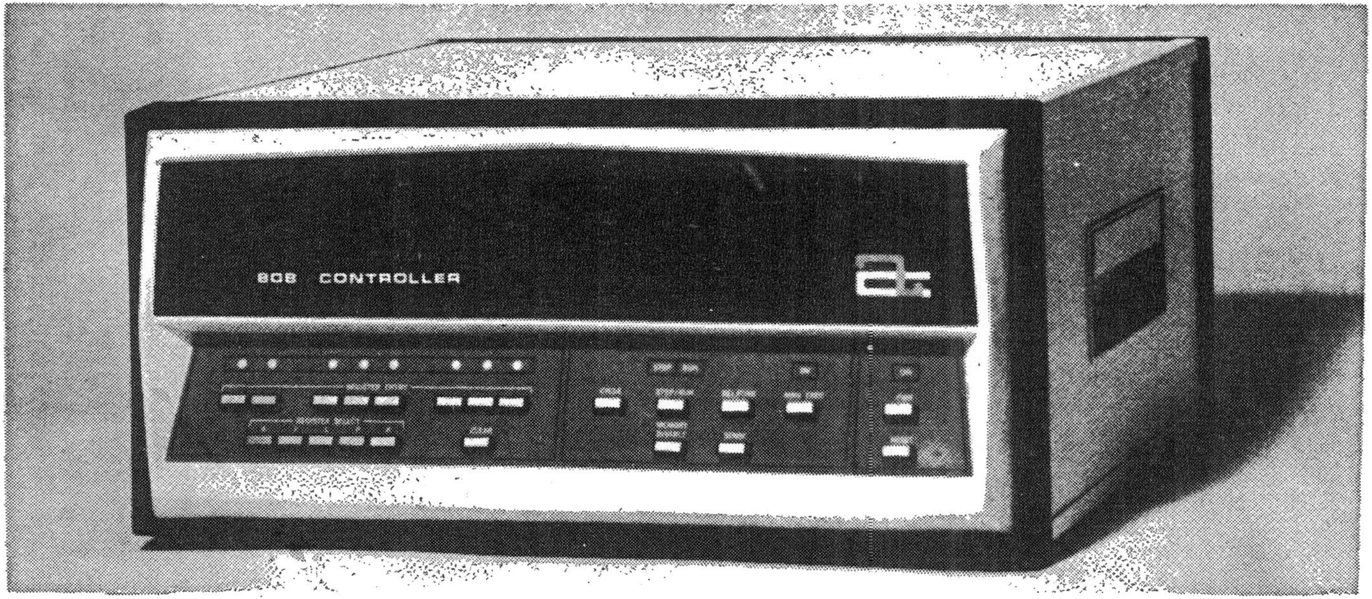

Fig. 11-1. Front view of the PDC 808.

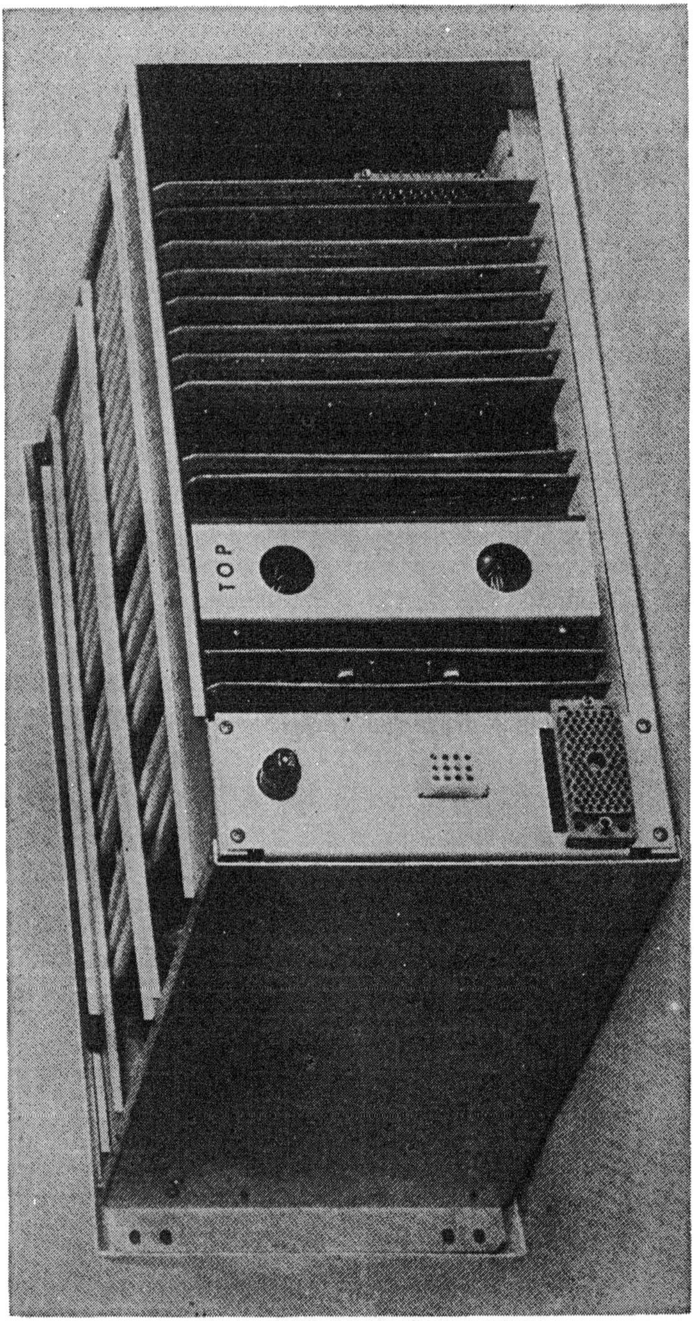

Fig. 11-2. Rear view of the typical PDC 208 and 808.

The M register in the 808 corresponds to the address register or memory address register and is used to store the location within a page during a memory reference instruction. The ME register holds the page information. Finally, the W register in the PDC 808 corresponds to the memory data register in our original discussion.

The PDC 808 and 208 computers (see Figs. 11-1 and 11-2) are digital stored-program units that utilize integrated circuits and a 3D core memory for simplicity and reliability. Parallel organization and over 70 instructions provide general-purpose computer power and flexibility.

The 208 and 808 computers contain eight hardware registers, the adder unit and the control section. Refer to Fig. 11-3. The adder is an 8-bit, parallel-add, serial-carry unit utilizing complex function TTL integrated circuits. Two 8-bit words are presented to the adder unit via the S and U buses. The sum appears on the A bus, which distributes it to the W, M, L, P and A registers. The sum is then strobed into the desired register by a set or load pulse. Control of the adder can be shifted left or right one place by selection gates between the adder and the A bus.

There are seven 8-bit registers and one 6-bit register in the basic processor. Information is transmitted within the controller to and from registers via several 8-bit transmission buses. One bit of a typical bus structure is shown in Fig. 11-4. The information on the buses is under the control of the processor control logic. By placing the contents of one register on a bus, it may be transferred to another bus by routing it through the various buses and-or adder unit until it appears as an input to one or more registers and then strobing it into the desired register.

The W register is an 8-bit register that interfaces the processor to the data circuits in memory. Data read from or stored in memory is held in the W register during the memory cycle. The W register is always cleared at the beginning of a memory cycle. If data is to be stored in memory, it is strobed into W halfway through the cycle. If data is being read from memory, it is placed in W approximately one fourth of the way through the memory cycle and held there during the restore portion (last half) of the cycle.

The M register is an 8-bit register that interfaces the processor to the lower eight bits of the memory address circuits. Address information is stored in the M register at the beginning of the memory cycle where it is held throughout the cycle.

The ME register is an extension to the M register which provides 16K addressing capability. The timing of the ME

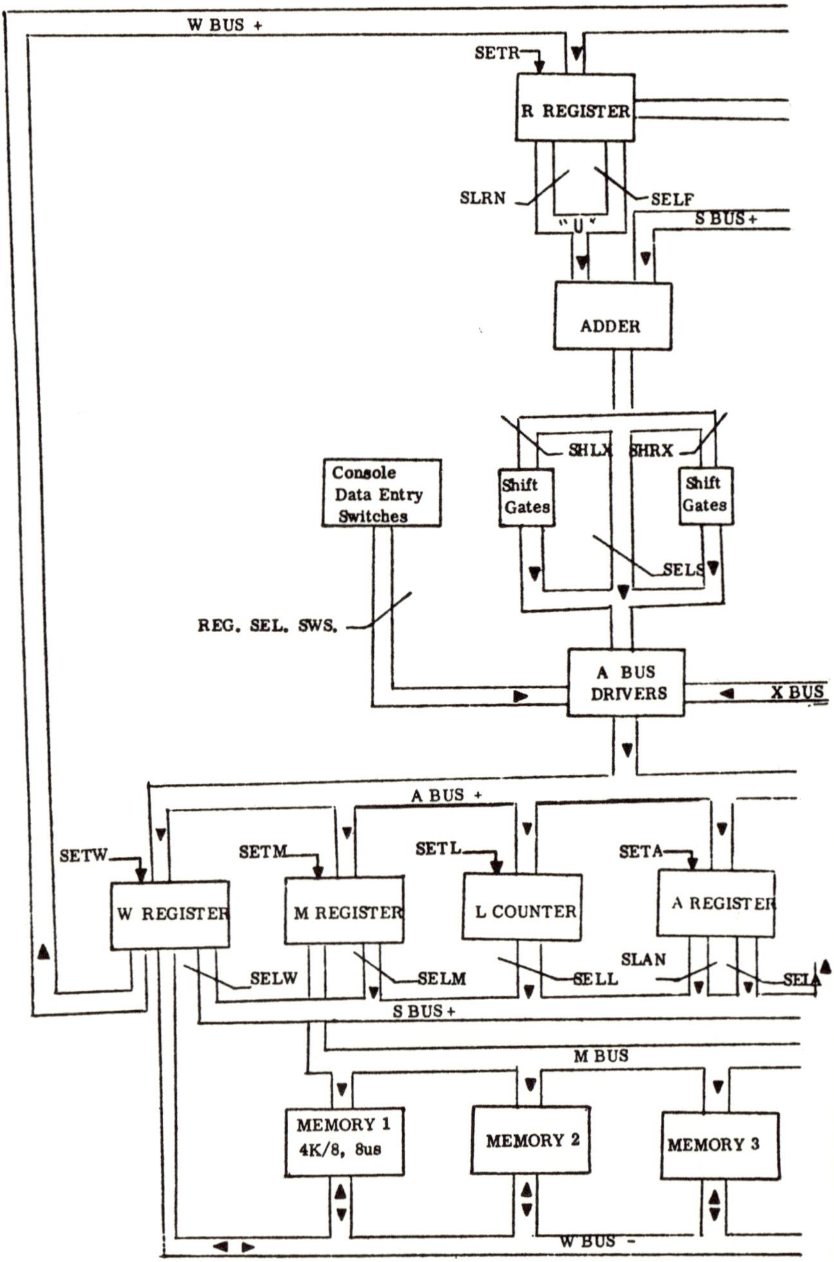

W BUS +
SETR
R REGISTER
SLRN
SELF
"U"
S BUS +
ADDER
SHLX
SHRX
Console Data Entry Switches
Shift Gates
Shift Gates
SELS
REG. SEL. SWS.
A BUS DRIVERS
X BUS
A BUS +
SETW
SETM
SETL
SETA
W REGISTER
M REGISTER
L COUNTER
A REGISTER
SELW
SELM
SELL
SLAN
SELA
S BUS +
M BUS
MEMORY 1 4K/8, 8us
MEMORY 2
MEMORY 3
W BUS -

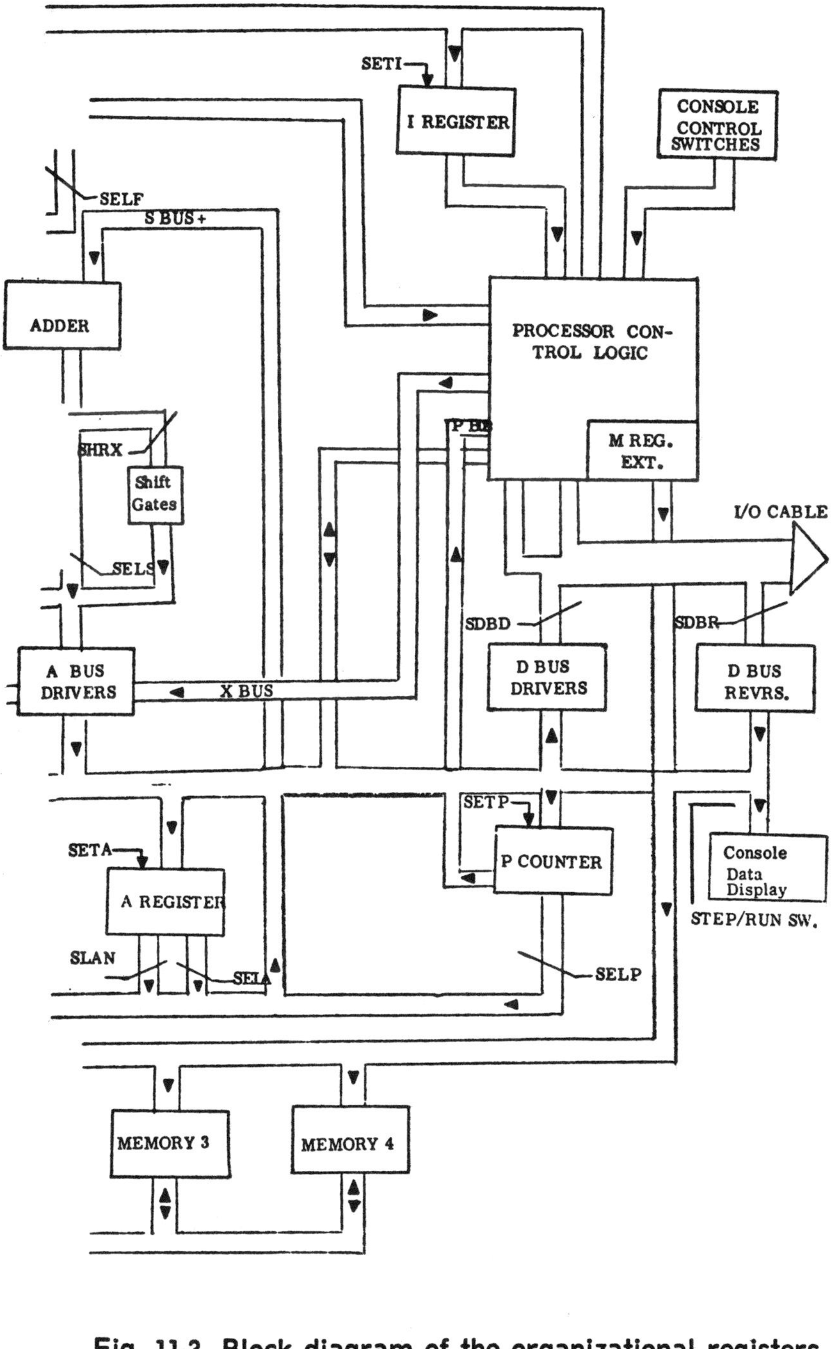

Fig. 11-3. Block diagram of the organizational registers.

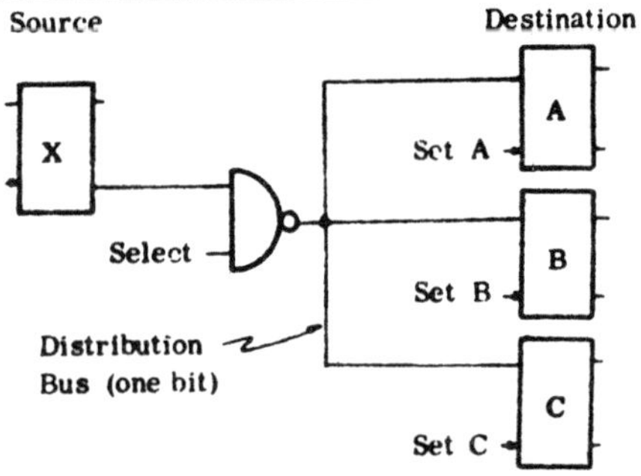

Fig. 11-4. Drawing off 1 bit of a typical bus structure.

register is identical with that of the M register. The ME register contains the page number of the memory page being accessed.

The L counter is an 8-bit register that is used as the lower portion of a 16-bit program counter. It is used to hold the word location of the next instruction word in the program.

The P counter in the 808 is an 8-bit register that is used as the upper portion of a 16-bit program counter. It is used to hold the page number of the next instruction; that is, the P counter defines the page and the L counter the word within that page where the next instruction word in the program is to be obtained. The two counters serve as a program sequencer. Notice that the upper two bits of the P counter are never used in a 16K-word machine. Thus, only 14 bits, eight of L and six of P, are used and loaded into the M and ME registers. In the 208, the P counter is a ripple counter that serves the same function.

The A register is an 8-bit hardware accumulator for arithmetic operations and serves as a word buffer register for programmed data transfers to or from I-O devices.

The I register is an 8-bit register that holds the first word of an instruction.

The R register is an 8-bit register that holds the second word of a double-word instruction or the operand for memory reference instructions. It is a time-shared register. For instance, during the execution of add, the second instruction word is held in R until the operand is obtained from memory. The operand then replaces the A field of the instruction during the actual add operation.

The basic computer memory is a conventional 4-wire, 3-D core memory described earlier. The basic configuration is 4096 words of eight bits and expansion is in 4096-word blocks up to 16K words. A power fail-safe option is available to prevent loss of memory as power collapses due to a primary power failure or a power turn-off. If low power is detected, an interrupt occurs which allows entry into a subroutine to effect an orderly halt to operations.

MEMORY ADDRESSING

The memory is a random access type requiring 14 bits of address (for 16K). The 14-bit address is supplied to the memory from two registers in the processor—the 8-bit M register and the 6-bit ME (M extension) register. Both registers hold the address for the duration of the memory cycle.

The memory is divided into pages of 256 words each. The L counter is used to specify one of the 256 words within a page, and the P counter specifies the page. The L and P counters together constitute the program counter, or sequencer, and specify the memory address of the next instruction in the program.

In addition to obtaining instructions from memory, operands (data) can be retrieved or stored in memory by the memory reference instructions and the block I-O instructions. The memory address of the operands must be specified by the instruction (direct addressing) or by referring to the contents of another pair of locations in memory (indirect addressing) or by a combination of both methods (block transfer uses a pointer in memory and part of the instruction word).

Direct addressing allows direct access to 512 words of memory: 256 in "page zero" (the first 256 memory words) and 256 in the "current page" (the page in which the instruction is located). Thus if the operating program is in page 4, all the words in page 0 and page 4 may be accessed directly.

To reach operands outside the current page or page 0, indirect addressing is used. The operand address is stored in two words located in page 0 or the current page. The instruction then specifies the first of these locations and also specifies indirect addressing. The contents of the two locations are then used to recall or store the operand. The first location specifies the address within the page and the second location specifies the page.

Multi-level indirect addressing is accomplished by setting the most significant bit of the indirect page address. The computer, after retrieving both indirect pointers (for L and P), examines MSB of the second pointer and uses the contents as a new pointer of an address if the MSB is a 1. If the MSB is a 0, the contents are used as the address of the operand.

The block I-O instructions can access a 2K-word block of memory (the second 2K of the first 4K memory). A combination of direct and indirect addressing is employed. Two pointers (one for input and one for output) are located in page 0. The contents of one of the pointers and three bits of the instruction word are used to form an 11-bit effective address, which is used to retrieve or store data with a block transfer instruction. (A 12th bit is added to the address to force the address into the upper 2K of the first 4K memory.)

When studying the instruction SET for any processor it is well to remember a few things. Each instruction is nothing more than a binary number stored in memory that will be called to the instruction register and decoded to cause the computer to perform some specified operation.

Looking at an instruction format, then (such as the one that follows), is nothing more than looking at the contents of the I register. In the case of memory reference instructions (instructions that have an address associated with them), there is an associated A or address field contained in the R register. In the condensed instruction list, on the other hand, these instructions are listed in octal! For this reason the following material contains both the binary format as it would appear in the I register and the octal listing as well.

Taking as an example, the add instruction; if the instruction is a direct page 0 instruction bit, position 0 would have a 0 in it and bit position 1 (A) would have a 0 so the octal notation would be 300. If bit position 0 (P) contained a 1, indicating the current page, the instruction would become 301; page 0, indirect, 302, and current page, indirect, 303.

Chapter 12

Processor Instructions

There are four classes or groupings of instructions defined by the first two bits of each instruction. Two classes are double-word instructions: memory reference and I-O instructions, and two memory cycles are required to establish the complete instruction. Skips, register change, and control instructions (register change and control instructions are in the same class) are all single-word instructions.

MEMORY REFERENCE

The format of the memory reference instructions is shown in Fig. 12-1. The first instruction word contains the class, op code, addressing mode, and page information. The second word contains an 8-bit address—the A field—which defines a location within a page.

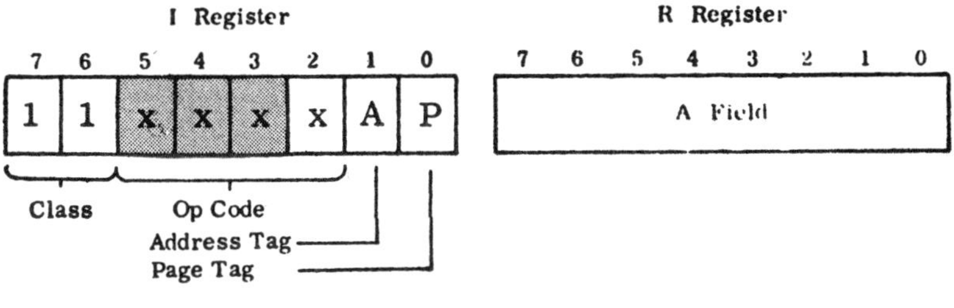

Fig. 12-1. Memory reference instruction format.

ADD

The instruction in Fig. 12-2 adds the contents of the effective memory location to the contents of the A register.

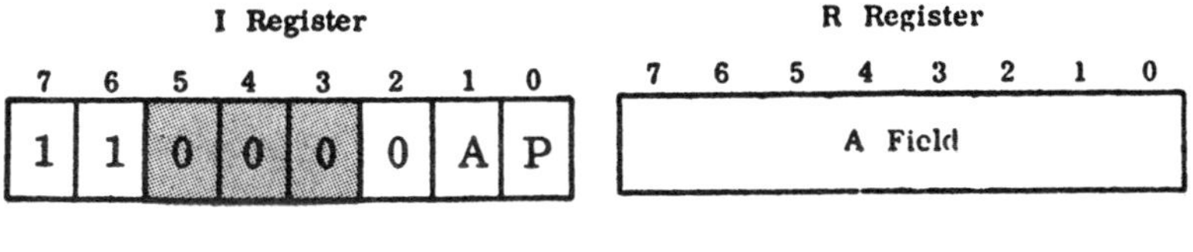

Fig. 12-2. Memory add instructions.

IOR: Inclusive OR

The instruction in Fig. 12-3 inclusively ORs the contents of the effective memory location to the contents of the A register.

I Register

7	6	5	4	3	2	1	0
1	1	0	0	0	1	A	P

R Register

7	6	5	4	3	2	1	0
A Field							

Fig. 12-3. Memory inclusive OR instructions.

SUB: Subtract

Fig. 12-4's instruction subtracts the contents of the effective memory location from the contents of the A register.

I Register

7	6	5	4	3	2	1	0
1	1	0	0	1	0	A	P

R Register

7	6	5	4	3	2	1	0
A Field							

Fig. 12-4. Memory subtract instructions.

LDA: Load A

The instruction in Fig. 12-5 loads the contents of the effective memory location into the A register.

I Register

7	6	5	4	3	2	1	0
1	1	0	0	1	1	A	P

R Register

7	6	5	4	3	2	1	0
A Field							

Fig. 12-5. Load A memory instructions.

STA: Store A

The contents of the A register is stored in the effective memory location with the instruction in Fig. 12-6.

I Register

7	6	5	4	3	2	1	0
1	1	0	1	1	0	A	P

R Register

7	6	5	4	3	2	1	0
A Field							

Fig. 12-6. Store A memory instructions.

ANA: AND to A

The instruction in Fig. 12-7 logically ANDs the contents of the effective memory location and the contents of the A register. Result appears in the A register.

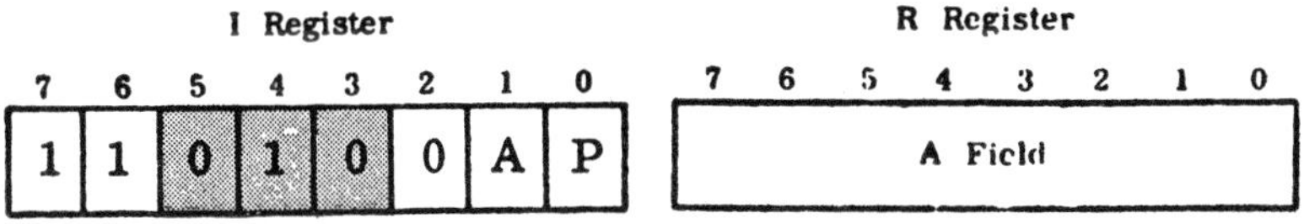

Fig. 12-7. AND to A memory instructions.

IMA: Interchange A with Memory

Fig. 12-8's instruction stores the contents of the A register in the effective memory location and loads the contents of the effective memory location into the A register.

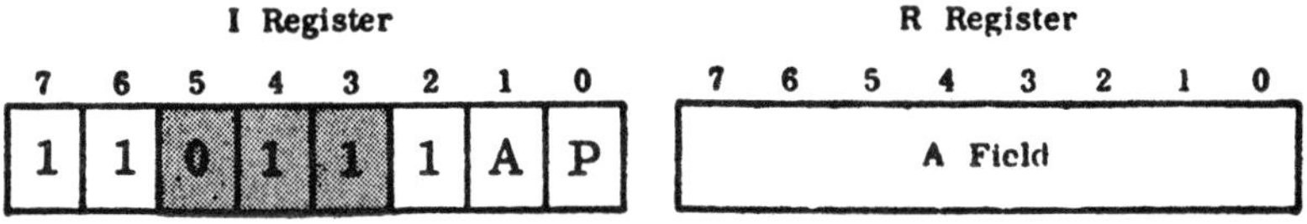

Fig. 12-8. Interchange with A memory instructions.

JMP: Jump

The instruction in Fig. 12-9 places the jump address in the program counters for a direct jump to page zero, the P counter is reset and the A field transferred to L. A jump in the current page leaves P unchanged. An indirect jump causes the two indirect address words to be placed in the L and P counters.

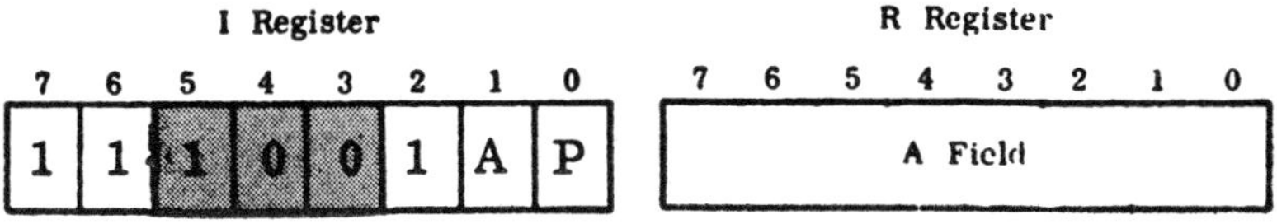

Fig. 12-9. Jump memory instructions.

IMS: Increment Memory & Skip-On-Zero Result

The contents of the effective memory location is incremented by one count and replaced with Fig. 12-10's instruction. If incrementing causes the result to become zero, a skip occurs. Overflow is set if the result of the incrementation is 200_8. Note: Neither skip nor OV occurs if IMS is executed as an interrupt instruction.

I Register

7	6	5	4	3	2	1	0
1	1	1	1	1	0	A	P

R Register

7	6	5	4	3	2	1	0
A Field							

Fig. 12-10. Increment memory and skip instructions.

JST: Jump & Store, L & P Counters

With the instruction in Fig. 12-11 the contents of the L and P counters are stored in memory at the effective jump address and jump address plus one, and the counters are altered to contain jump address plus two.

I Register

7	6	5	4	3	2	1	0
1	1	1	1	1	1	A	P

R Register

7	6	5	4	3	2	1	0
A Field							

Fig. 12-11. "Jump and store, L and P counters," memory instructions.

EOR: Exclusive OR

The instruction appearing in Fig. 12-12 exclusively ORs the contents of the effective memory location to the contents of the A register in the 208.

7	6	5	4	3	2	1	0
1	1	0	1	0	0	A	P

Fig. 12-12. "Exclusive OR" memory instructions, PDC208.

ADM: Add Magnitude

In the 208, Fig. 12-13's instruction adds the contents of the effective memory location to the contents of the A register, treating each value as an 8-bit unsigned integer.

7	6	5	4	3	2	1	0
1	1	1	0	1	0	A	P

Fig. 12-13. "Add magnitude" memory instructions, PD-C208.

CMS: Compare Memory and Skip If Not Equal

The instruction in Fig. 12-14 (in the 208) compares the contents of the effective memory location to the contents of the A register and skips if they are not equal. Otherwise, the next instruction is executed.

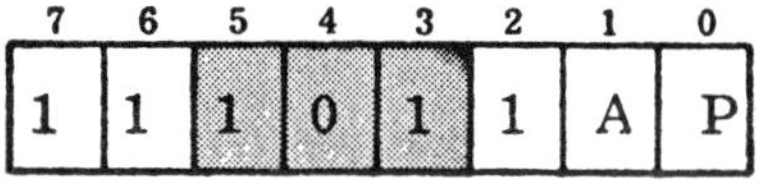

Fig. 12-14. "Compare memory and skip if not equal" memory instructions, PDC208.

SKIP INSTRUCTIONS

Instructions that test conditions within the computer and take action depending upon the results of the test fall in the skip instruction class. The term skip is derived from the action taken if a test condition is satisfied; the computer skips over the next two words in the program.

Skip is a single-word, micro-programmed instruction. The first two bits specify the skip class and the six remaining bits are used to specify the test conditions. Notice that only five of the six available bits are used, allowing 30 usable combinations for skip conditions, 15 in each of two groups.

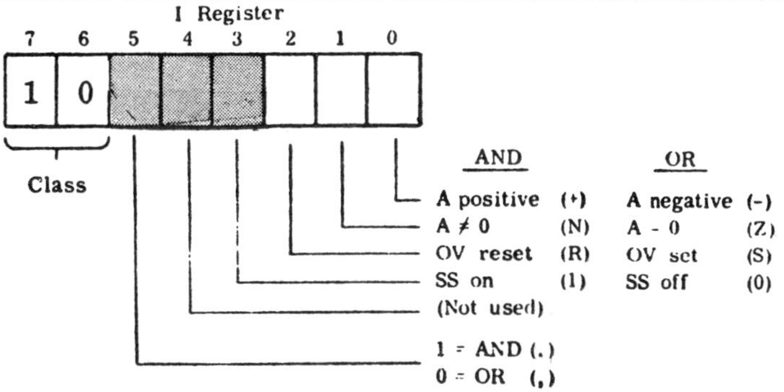

Fig. 12-15. Skip instruction format.

AND SKIP GROUP

The 15 instructions in this group are combinations of the four conditions in Fig. 12-16. If more than one condition is specified (by placing a 1 in the condition bit) the AND of all specified conditions must be met to cause a skip. Only a few of the combinations in this group will be presented here.

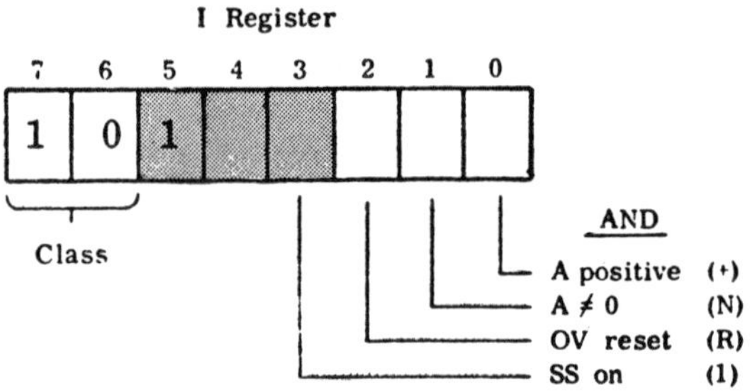

Fig. 12-16. AND skip instruction format.

IFT +: Skip If A Positive

With the conditions specified in Fig. 12-17 a skip occurs if the contents of the A register is equal to or greater than zero Otherwise, the next instruction in sequence is executed.

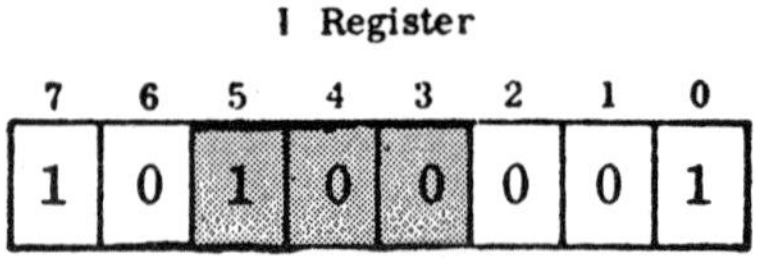

Fig. 12-17. "Skip if a positive" instruction.

IFT N: Skip If A Non-Zero

With the instructions in Fig. 12-18 a skip occurs if the contents of the A register is not zero. Otherwise, the next instruction in sequence is executed.

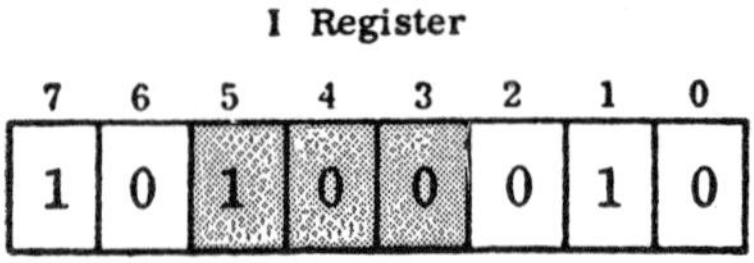

Fig. 12-18. "Skip if a non-zero" instruction.

IFT R: Skip If OV Reset

With the instruction in Fig. 12-19 a skip occurs if OV is not on. Otherwise, the next instruction sequence is executed. OV is reset.

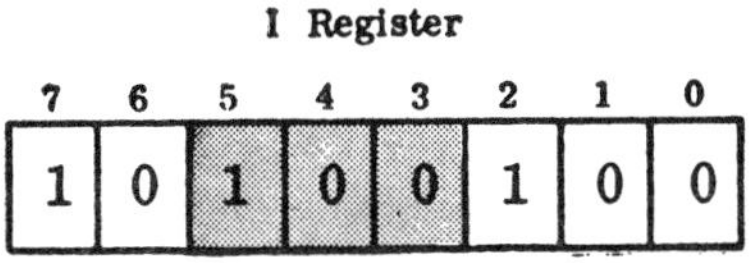

Fig. 12-19. "Skip if OV reset" instruction.

IFT 1: Skip If Sense Switch Is On

With the instruction appearing in Fig. 12-20 a skip occurs if the console sense switch is on. Otherwise, the next instruction in sequence is executed.

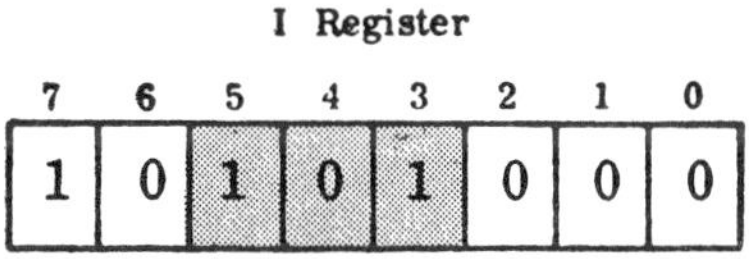

Fig. 12-20. "Skip if sense switch is on" instruction.

IFT + N: Skip If A Greater Than Zero

With Fig. 12-21's instruction a skip occurs if the contents of A register is greater than zero. Otherwise, the next instruction in sequence is executed.

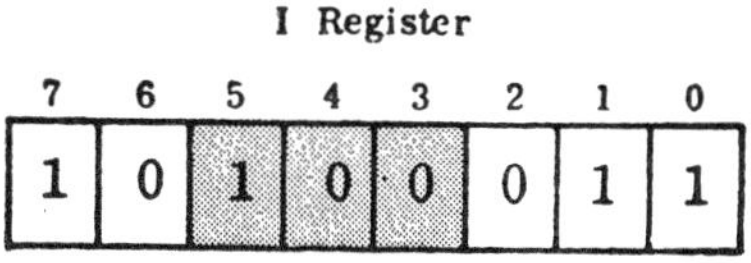

Fig. 12-21. "Skip if a greater than zero" instruction.

OR SKIP GROUP

The 15 instructions in this group are combinations of the four conditions in Fig. 12-22. If more than one condition is specified, a skip will occur if any of the specified contitions are met.

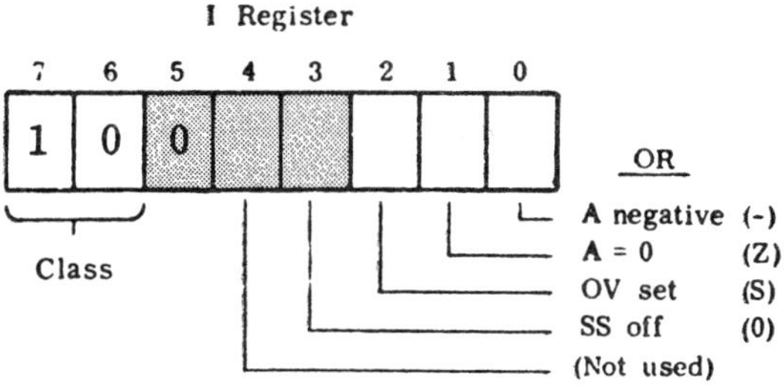

Fig. 12-22. OR skip group instruction format.

IFT: Skip If A Negative

The instruction in Fig. 12-23 causes a skip to occur if the contents of the A register is less than zero. Otherwise, the next instruction in sequence is executed.

I Register

7	6	5	4	3	2	1	0
1	0	0	0	0	0	0	1

Fig. 12-23. "Skip if a negative" instruction.

IFT Z: Skip If A Zero

With Fig. 12-24's instruction a skip occurs if the contents of the A register is zero. Otherwise, the next instruction in sequence is executed.

I Register

7	6	5	4	3	2	1	0
1	0	0	0	0	0	1	0

Fig. 12-24. "Skip if a zero" instruction.

IFT S: Skip If OV Set

If the instruction in Fig. 12-25 is applied a skip occurs if OV is set. (The OV will be reset at the end of the instruction). Otherwise, the next instruction in sequence is executed.

I Register

7	6	5	4	3	2	1	0
1	0	0	0	0	1	0	0

Fig. 12-25. "Skip if OV set" instruction.

IFT O: Skip If Sense Switch Off

The instruction in Fig. 12-26 tells the computer to skip if the console sense switch is off (not depressed). Otherwise, the next instruction in sequence is executed.

I Register

7	6	5	4	3	2	1	0
1	0	0	0	1	0	0	0

Fig. 12-26. "Skip if sense switch off"instruction.

IFT-, Z: Skip If A Equal To Or Less Than Zero

With the instruction in Fig. 12-27 skip occurs if the content of A is zero or negative. Otherwise, the next instruction sequence is executed.

I Register

7	6	5	4	3	2	1	0
1	0	0	0	0	0	1	1

Fig. 12-27. "Skip if A equal to or less than zero" instruction.

REGISTER CHANGE

The register change class contains the control, shift, and register change instructions. All are single-word instructions.

A Register Change (ARC)

ARC Z: Clear A Register

Fig. 12-28's instruction clears the A register.

I Register

7	6	5	4	3	2	1	0
0	0	0	0	0	1	0	1

Fig. 12-28. "Clear A register" instruction.

ARC I: Increment A Register

The combination in Fig. 12-29 adds one (least significant bit) to the contents of A. OV is set if the contents go from 0, 1111111 to 1, 0000000.

I Register

7	6	5	4	3	2	1	0
0	0	0	0	0	1	1	1

Fig. 12-29. "Increment A register" instruction.

ARC D: Decrement A Register

The combination in Fig. 12-30 subtracts one (least significant bit) from the contents of A. OV is set if the contents go from 1,0000000 to 0, 1111111.

I Register

7	6	5	4	3	2	1	0
0	0	0	0	0	0	1	1

Fig. 12-30. "Decrement A register" instruction.

ARC C: 1s Complement A Register

With the instruction in Fig. 12-31 the computer performs the 1s complement (bit-by-bit inversion) of the contents of the A register.

I Register

7	6	5	4	3	2	1	0
0	0	0	0	1	0	0	1

Fig. 12-31. "1s complement A register" instruction.

ARC N: 2s Complement A Register

With the instruction in Fig. 12-32 the computer performs the 2s complement of (negation of) the contents of the A register.

I Register

7	6	5	4	3	2	1	0
0	0	0	0	1	1	0	1

Fig. 12-32. "2s complement A register" instruction.

ARC -1: Transfer -1 To A

The instruction in Fig. 12-33 replaces the contents of the A register with 1, 1111111.

I Register

7	6	5	4	3	2	1	0
0	0	0	0	0	0	0	1

Fig. 12-33. "Transfer -1 to A" instruction.

ARC 1: Transfer +1 To A

The instruction in Fig. 12-34 replaces the contents of the A register with 0,0000001.

I Register

7	6	5	4	3	2	1	0
0	0	0	0	0	1	1	1

Fig. 12-34. "Transfer +1 to A" instruction.

Overflow Register Change (ORC)

ORC S: Set Overflow

Fig. 12-35's instruction sets the overflow flip-flop. If already set, there is no change.

I Register

7	6	5	4	3	2	1	0
0	0	1	1	0	0	0	0

Fig. 12-35. "Set overflow" instruction.

ORC R: Reset Overflow

The instruction in Fig. 12-36 resets the overflow flip-flop.

I Register

7	6	5	4	3	2	1	0
0	0	1	0	1	0	0	0

Fig. 12-36. "Reset overflow" instruction.

ORC C: Complement Overflow

The combination in Fig. 12-37 complements the content of the overflow flip-flop.

I Register

7	6	5	4	3	2	1	0
0	0	1	1	1	0	0	0

Fig. 12-37. "Complement overflow" instruction.

SHIFT INSTRUCTIONS SHF

There are three types of shift instructions: logical, rotate, and arithmetic. Each type affects only the A register and in some cases the overflow flip-flop.

Logical Shift

The logical shift instruction causes the contents of the A register to be shifted one place to the left or right. Zeros are shifted into one end of the register and the contents are shifted out and lost. Thus, if eight consecutive, logical shift left instructions were executed, the A register would contain all zeros. Note: The overflow flip-flop is reset on a logical shift instruction at the beginning of the operation and may be set at the end of the instruction.

Rotate

The rotate instruction, sometimes referred to as logical rotate, preserves the contents of the A register as it is shifted. This is accomplished by an "end around shift," but with the overflow flip-flop in the loop as shown in Fig. 12-38.

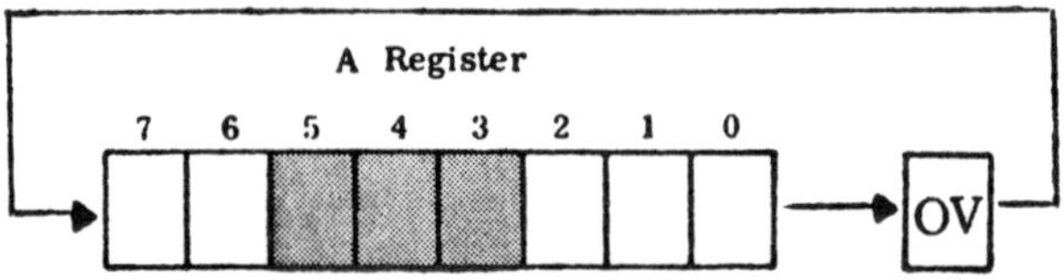

Fig. 12-38. "Rotate" or "end around shift" instruction.

For a rotate right (left), the content of the overflow flip-flop is shifted into bit 7 (bit 0) of the A register and bit 0 (bit 7) of the A register is shifted into OV. This essentially creates a 9-bit register. Thus, 9 consecutive rotate right (left) instructions leave the A register and the overflow flip-flop unchanged. Shifting A through the overflow flip-flop facilitates testing bits of A. For instance, rotate right and then skip on overflow reset tests bit 0 of the A register.

Arithmetic Shift

The arithmetic shift differs from the logical or rotate shifts in that the A register is assumed to contain a signed number. The sign bit is A7. Since shifting left multiplies by 2 and shifting right divides by 2, the sign of a number must not change. Thus an arithmetic shift canaffect only the magnitude position of the number and cannot change the sign bit. The 208-808 uses 2s complement arithmetic. If two numbers of equal magnitude but opposite signs are added together, the result is zero. Not surprising. Consider two binary numbers of the same magnitude but opposite sign:

$$+14_{10} = +\ 001\ 110$$

$$-14_{10} = -\ ?$$

Using 2s complement representation and substituting 0 for + and 1 for -

$$+14_{10} = 0,001\ 110$$

$$-14_{10} = 1,110\ 010$$

Where the sign bit has been separated from the magnitude with a comma. Notice that if the two numbers are added together, the result is all zeros with a carry.

Now if +14 is divided by 2, by performing an arithmetic shift right, the result is

$$+7_{10} = 0,\ 000\ 111$$

Dividing -14 by 2 produces

$$-7_{10} = 1,\ 111\ 001$$

Which is obtained by shifting -14_{10} right one place, propagating the sign bit and not changing the sign bit. Thus arithmetic shift right causes the sign bit to be shifted while remaining unchanged. An arithmetic shift left performs a logical shift left except the sign bit is unchanged. All shifts require 1 cycle.

SHF R: Logical Shift Right

The instruction in Fig. 12-39 resets OV, shifts the contents of the A register right one place. Zero is shifted into the sign bit, and the LSB of A is shifted into OV.

I Register

7	6	5	4	3	2	1	0
0	0	1	0	1	1	1	1

Fig. 12-39. "Logical shift right" instruction.

SHF L: Logical Shift Left

The Fig. 12-40 instruction resets OV and shifts the contents of the A register left one place. Zero is shifted into the LSB of A and the sign bit of A is shifted into OV.

I Register

7	6	5	4	3	2	1	0
0	0	1	0	1	1	0	1

Fig. 12-40. "Logical shift left" instruction.

SHF): Rotate Right

Fig. 12-41's instruction shifts the contents of the A register right one place through OV. The LSB of A is shifted into OV and the previous contents of OV is shifted into A7.

I Register

7	6	5	4	3	2	1	0
0	0	1	0	0	1	1	1

Fig. 12-41. "Rotate right" instruction.

SHF (: Rotate Left

The combination in Fig. 12-42 shifts the contents of the A register left one place through OV. The sign bit is shifted into OV. The previous contents of OV is shifted into the LSB of A.

I Register

7	6	5	4	3	2	1	0
0	0	1	0	0	1	0	1

Fig. 12-42. "Rotate left" instruction.

SHF >: Arithmetic Shift Right

Fig. 12-43's combination shifts the lower seven bits of the A register right one place. The sign bit remains unchanged and is also shifted into A6. The LSB of A is lost.

I Register

7	6	5	4	3	2	1	0
0	0	1	0	0	0	1	1

Fig. 12-43. "Arithmetic shift right" instruction.

SHF <: Arithmetic Shift Left

The instruction in Fig. 12-44 shifts the lower seven bits of the A register left one place. The sign bit remains unchanged. A6 is lost and zero is shifted into the LSB of A.

I Register

7	6	5	4	3	2	1	0
0	0	1	0	0	0	0	1

Fig. 12-44. "Arithmetic shift left" instruction.

Control

NOP: No Operation

The instruction in Fig. 12-45 causes an 8-microsecond pause in program for the 808 and a 2.67-microsecond pause for the 208

I Register

7	6	5	4	3	2	1	0
0	0	0	0	0	0	0	0

Fig. 12-45. "No operation" instruction.

HLT: Halt

The combination in 12-46 halts the computer.

I Register

7	6	5	4	3	2	1	0
0	0	1	0	0	0	0	0

Fig. 12-46. "Halt" instruction.

EIN: Enable Interrupts

Fig. 12-47's combination enables the computer to respond to a request for interrupt.

I Register

7	6	5	4	3	2	1	0
0	0	0	1	0	0	1	0

Fig. 12-47. "Enable interrupts" instruction.

DIN: Disable Interrupts

The instruction in Fig. 12-48 inhibits the computer from accepting a request for interrupt.

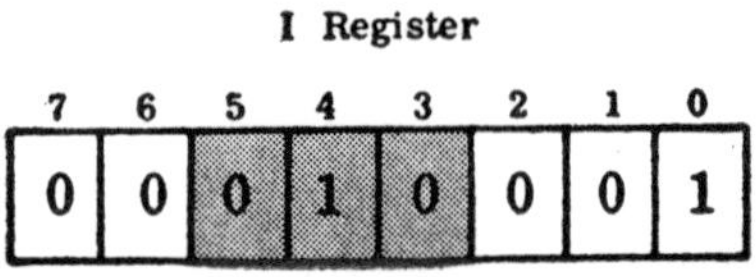

Fig. 12-48. "Disable interrupts" instruction.

Chapter 13

Input-Output Section

The 208 and 808 computers are designed for communications, control and monitoring applications. Thus, the I-O sections of the unit have capabilities usually found only in larger computers. The 13 I-O instructions provide the power and flexibility to allow the 208 and 808 to handle tasks other machines in their class cannot. Data transfers to and from the unit are 8-bits parallel. The I-O bus utilizes the party-line technique to simplify the interface system. For real time applications, the 208 and 808 have two fully implemented priority interrupt lines plus a third interrupt request line that can be used to implement additional priority interrupts.

INPUT—OUTPUT (I-O) INSTRUCTIONS

The I-O instructions allow the 208 and 808 to communicate with the "outside world"— peripheral device controllers such as the teletype controller and special logic generated by Computer Automation or the user Communication is in the form of commands which can trigger flip-flops or relays, sense signals which test the state of a flip-flop, relay, or incoming line, and data transfer operations which transfer parallel 8-bit words into or out of the computer.

All peripheral logic is connected in parallel on the I-O cable which contains the data bus, control lines, and the device address bus. Selection of the device (peripheral logic group) with which communication is desired is accomplished by assigning each device a number or address and applying this number to the device address bus in the I-O instruction. There are up to 32 device addresses available.

INSTRUCTION FORMAT

I-O instructions are double-word instructions. The first word specifies the class (I-O in this case), the operation code, and special conditions available by micro-coding. The second word specifies the device address (5 bits) of the device with which communication is to take place and a 3-bit function code. The 3-bit function code allows up to eight functions to be created within the same device address for a given op code. For instance, at device 4, eight different flip-flops may be tested (sensed) by executing the "sense device 4" instruction eight times with the eight different function codes.

The I-O instruction involves micro-coding. The 3-bit op code defines the type of instruction — sense, external control, or transfer. The next three bits are used to place conditions on the op code (see Fig. 13-1).

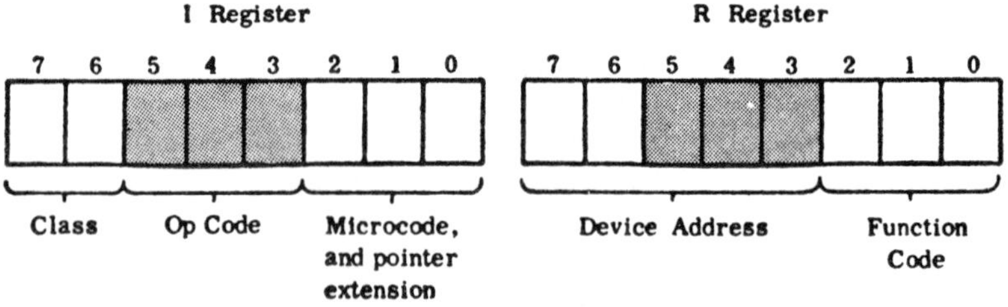

Fig. 13-1. I-O instruction format.

SENSE INSTRUCTIONS

The sense and skip instruction allows the 208 and 808 to test the state of a specified function in an I-O device. Up to eight different conditions may be tested in each device. The second word of the instruction specifies the device address and function code. The micro-code in the first word of the instruction is used to specify whether the skip is to occur on a sense response from the device being tested or on no response.

SSR: Sense and Skip on Response

The function specified in Fig. 13-2 is tested in the device specified and a skip will occur if a response is obtained. If no response occurs, the next instruction in sequence is executed.

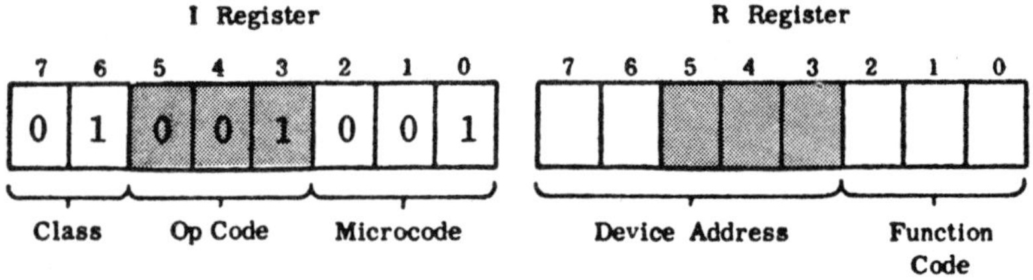

Fig. 13-2. "Sense and skip on response" instruction.

SSN: Sense and Skip on No Response

The function specified in Fig. 13-3 is tested in the device specified and a skip will occur if a response is not obtained. If a response occurs, the next instruction in sequence is executed.

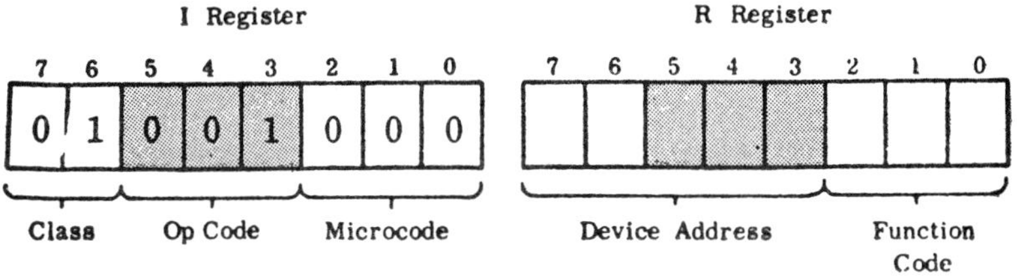

Fig. 13-3. "Sense and skip on no response" instruction.

EXTERNAL CONTROL INSTRUCTION

The external control (EXT) instruction allows the 208 and 808 to pulse a specified flip-flop, relay, or external line in a device controller or special logic connected to the I-O bus. Instructions such as start tape, rewind, clear, stop reader, are examples of uses of EXC instructions. Up to eight control functions may be implemented for each device.

EXC: External Control

The control function specified in Fig. 13-4 by the function code is executed.

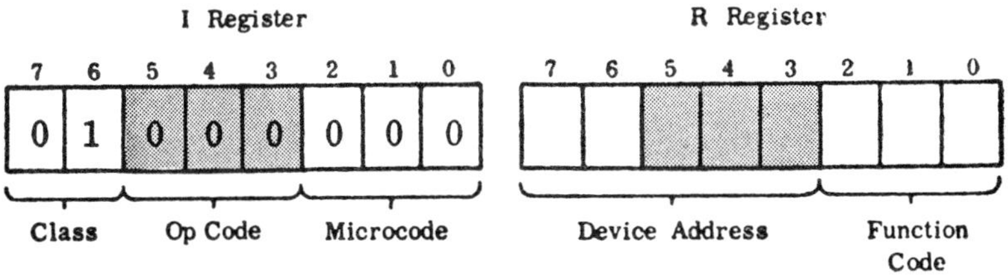

Fig. 13-4. "External control" instruction.

INPUT TO A INSTRUCTIONS

There are four I-O instructions that can cause data to be transferred from I-O devices to the A register. Two are unconditional transfers and two are transfers that are conditioned on a sense response. The latter two instructions are actually combinations of the sense and skip instruction with the input to A instruction. All transfers are 8-bit parallel.

INA: Input To A Register (Unconditionally)

With the code in Fig. 13-5 a data word is transferred from the device specified to the A register. The function code can be used to designate the source of data within the device if multiple sources exist, as in the case of a 16-bit converter output. Up to eight sources may be specified by the function code, allowing a 64-bit input data word to be handled in eight successive inputs, greatingly simplifying the device logic.

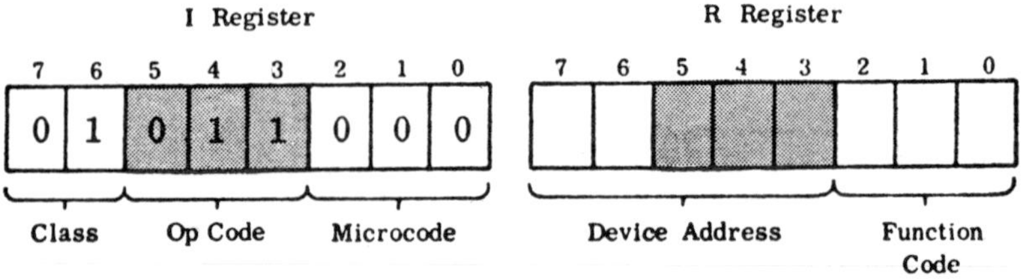

Fig. 13-5. "Input to A register (unconditionally)" instruction.

MIA: Masked Input To A Register (Unconditionally)

The masked input instruction in Fig. 13-6 causes the input data word from the specified device to be ANDed with the previous contents of the A register and the results placed in the A register. The source of the data word within the device may be specified by the function code if multiple sources exist.

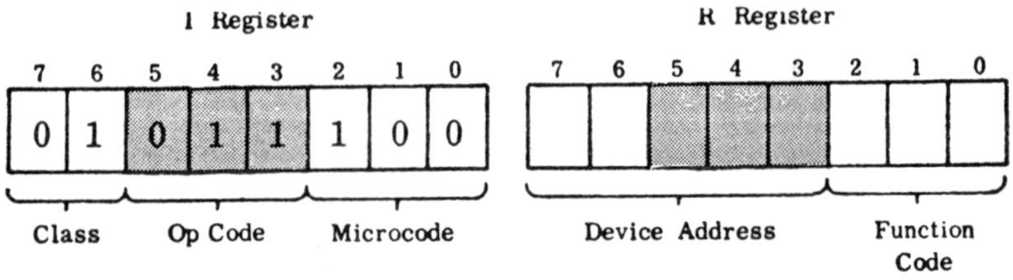

Fig. 13-6. "Masked input to A register (unconditionally)" instruction.

IAS: Input To A And Skip On Response

The IAS instruction in Fig. 13-7 first senses the function specified by the function code within the device specified. If a response is obtained, the data word is transferred to the A register and a skip occurs. If no response is obtained, the data word is not transferred, the A register is unchanged, and the next instruction in sequence is executed.

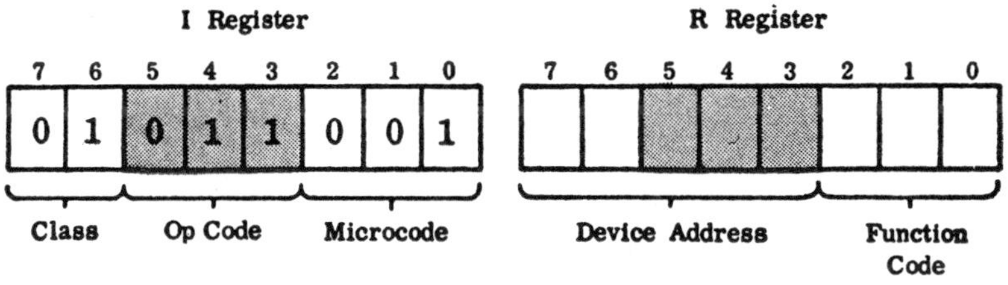

Fig. 13-7. "Input to A and skip on response" instruction.

MIS: Masked Input To A And Skip On Response

Fig. 13-8's instruction is a combination of the sense and the masked input to A. The instruction first senses the condition specified by the function code within the device specified. If a sense response is obtained, a masked input to A register and a skip occur. If no sense response is obtained, the A register is left unaltered and the next instruction in sequence is executed.

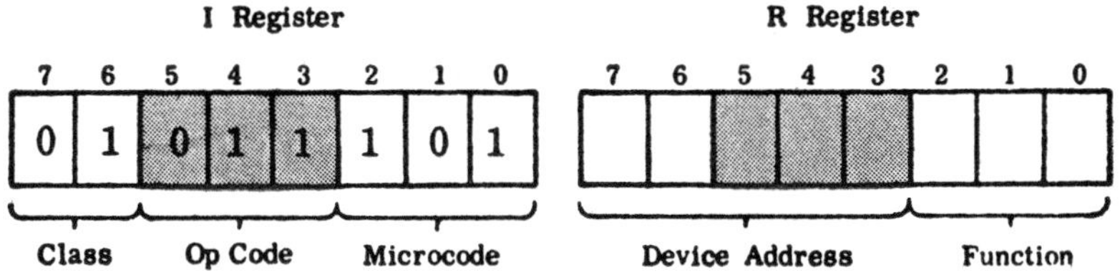

Fig. 13-8. "Masked input to A and skip on response" instruction.

OUTPUT FROM A INSTRUCTIONS

There are four I-O instructions that can cause data to be transferred from the A register to a device on the I-O bus. Two of the instructions are unconditional transfers and two are conditioned on a sense response. The latter two are actually combinations of the sense instructions with the output A instruction.

OTA: Output A Register (Unconditionally)

The OTA instruction in Fig. 13-9 transfers the contents of the A register to the device specified. The A register is not altered. The function code can be used to steer the data into multiple registers if required. For instance, if a 32-bit register is to be loaded by OTAs, the register can have four segments and each segment can be specified by the function code.

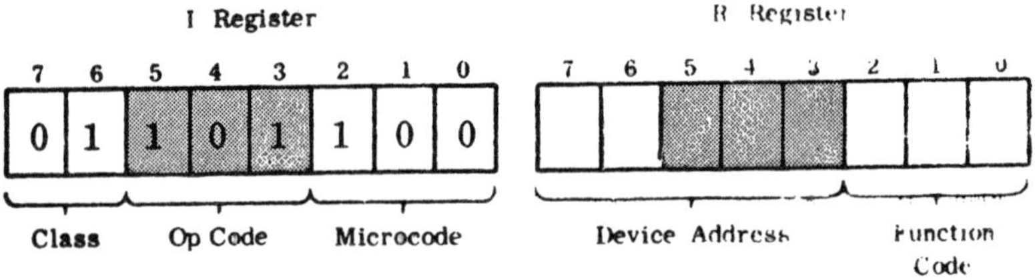

Fig. 13-9. "Output A register" instruction.

OTZ: Output Zero (Unconditionally)

The OTZ instruction in Fig. 13-10 is similar to the OTA except the contents of the A register is not selected onto the I-O bus, resulting in a transfer of all zeros in the data word. The contents of A is not altered.

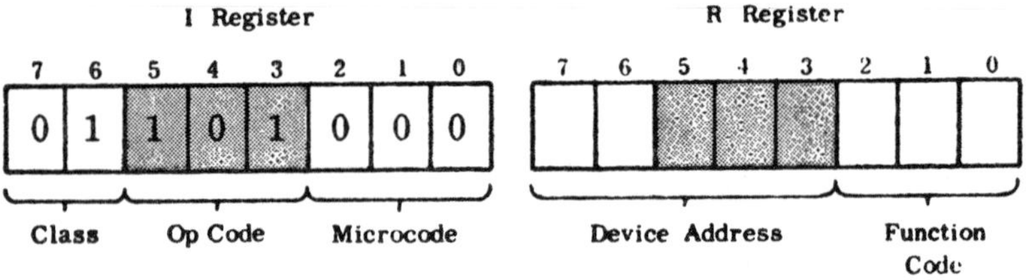

Fig. 13-10. "Output zero (unconditionally)" instruction.

OAS: Output A And Skip On Response

The OAS instruction in Fig. 13-11 is a combination of the OTA and the sense and skip instructions. The condition specified by the function code is first sensed and if a response is obtained, the contents of A is transferred to the I-O device and a skip occurs. If no sense response occurs, the transfer is not made and the next instruction in sequence is executed.

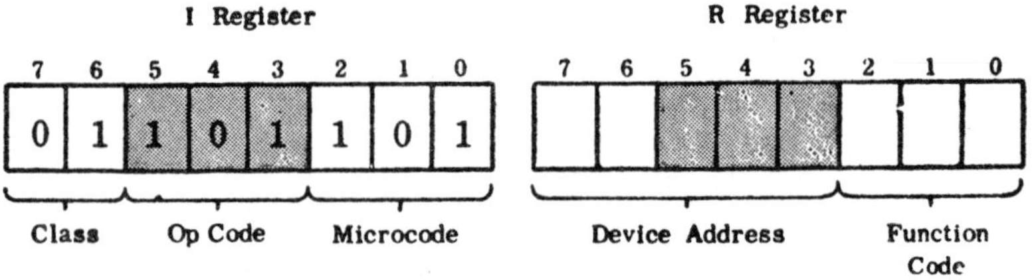

Fig. 13-11. "Output A and skip on response" instruction.

OZS: Output Zero And Skip On Response

The OZS instruction in Fig. 13-12 is a combination of the OTZ and the sense and skip instructions. The function code specifies the condition to be sensed. If no sense response is obtained, the A register is unaffected and the next instruction in sequence is executed.

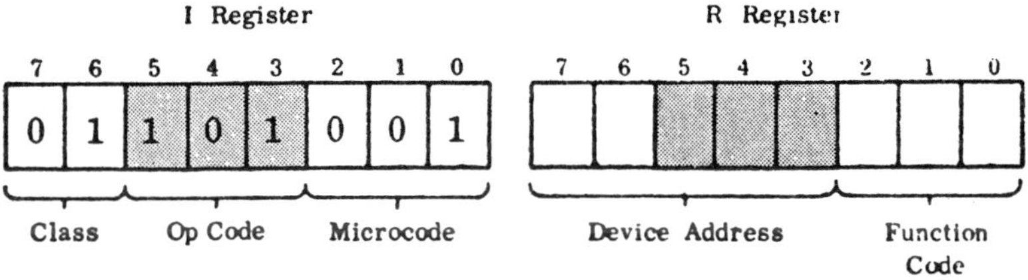

Fig. 13-12. "Output zero and skip on response" instruction.

BLOCK TRANSFER INSTRUCTIONS

The block input-output instructions (Fig. 13-13) are powerful I-O instructions that allow access to memory by peripheral devices without going through the A register. Automatic indexing of an address pointer reduces overhead time and allows the block I-O instruction to be used as single-execute interrupt instructions. Four memory cycles are required for each transfer: two cycles to retrieve the double-word instruction, one cycle to index the pointer and form the operand address, and one cycle to affect the transfer between memory and the I-O device.

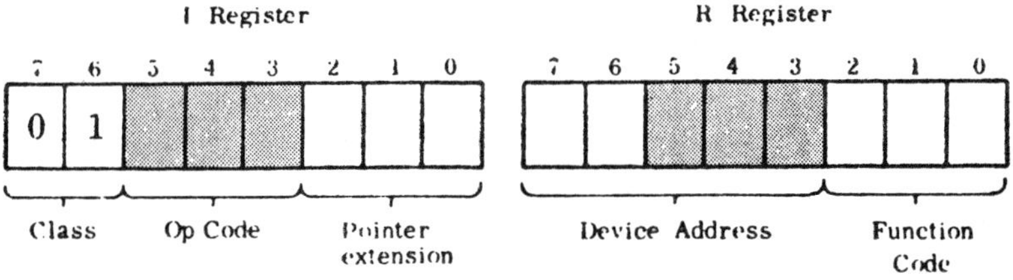

Fig. 13-13. Block I-O instruction format.

The A register is not altered by the block I-O instructions. The second 2K of memory provides the working area for the block transfers. Each block can be up to 256 words and up to eight blocks can be handled by the block instruction.

The second word of the instruction defines the peripheral and specifies a function code if needed. The first word of the instruction contains three bits that are used as an extension to the input pointer to provide 11 variable address bits. A 12th bit is a hardwired to force the block buffer areas to be in the second 2K of memory, preventing accidental storage in page 0.

The pointer (Fig. 13-14) is first indexed (incremented) and replaced and the indexed value is then used in the effective address. Thus, the pointer must be preset to one less than the starting address. For example, if the first word in the block is to be stored in page 12, location zero, the extension in the instruction word is 2, and the pointer is preset to 377. After the 256th word has been transferred, the pointer will again contain 377. The extension may now be incremented to 3 and the process restarted to transfer the second block in page 13 starting with word 000. The input pointer is stored at location 6, page 0, and the output pointer is stored at location 10, page 0.

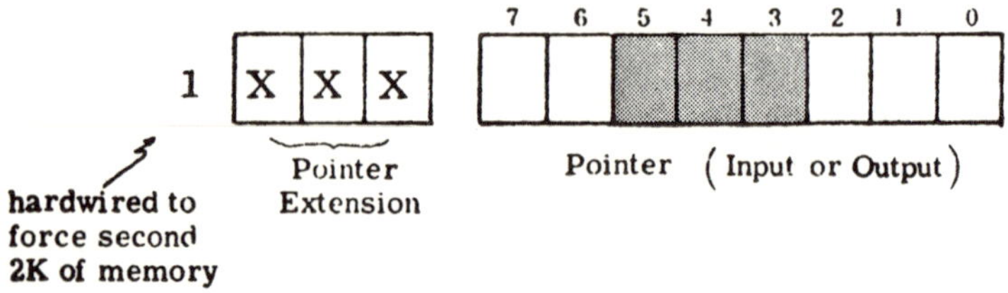

Fig. 13-14. Block pointer format.

The use of the block I-O instructions as interrupt instructions provide an extremely flexible and powerful data handling capability. By using two standard priority interrupt lines in the 208 and 808, blocks may be chained together to provide up to 2K-word records to be transferred to or from memory automatically without intervention of the main operating program.

Using block input (or output) as an interrupt instruction, a word may be transferred under interrupt control without disturbing the operating program except to cause the program to be delayed four cycles while the block input instruction is being executed. This requires one interrupt line. The second interrupt line is used for end-of-block as indicated by an echo pulse formed when the pointer goes to 377 after being indexed. The echo pulse is used to set a flag in the peripheral controller which causes the end-of-block interrupt. A subroutine is entered via the jump and save instruction to update the pointer extension and re-enable the first interrupt line (which is disabled by the echo pulse) and the next block transfer begins.

INB: Input Block To Memory

The instruction in Fig. 13-15 transfers a word from the specified device to the memory at the location specified by the input pointers +1 and the pointer extension. Up to 256 words may be transferred as a block (the INB instruction is executed 256 times). The input pointer is location 6, page zero.

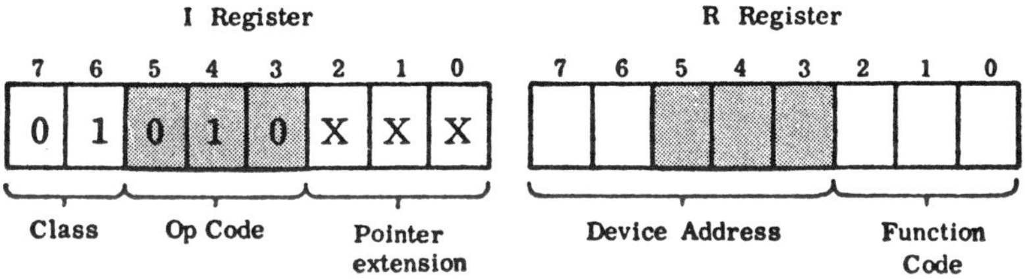

Fig. 13-15. "Input block to memory" instruction.

OTB: Output Block From Memory

The instruction in Fig. 13-16 transfers a word from memory at the address specified by the output pointer +1 and the pointer extension to the specified device. Up to 256 words may be transferred as a block. The output pointer is location 10_8, page zero.

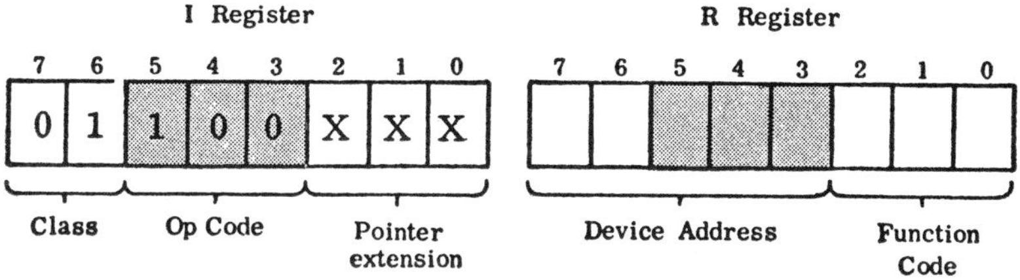

Fig. 13-16. "Output block from memory" instruction.

PRIORITY INTERRUPT SYSTEM

The 208 and 808 priority interrupt system makes the computer an extremely flexible and powerful real time systems component. The interrupt system provides the ability to obtain fast response to external stimuli, to transfer blocks of data without attention of the operating program, to generate timing intervals and-or time-of-day clock (with real time clock option), and to react to low power line conditions (using power fail-restart option).

When an interrupt request is received by the computer, the computer responds to the interrupt at the end of the current instruction being processed (provided interrupts are enabled). Control is transferred to the memory location associated with the particular interrupt line requesting the interrupt. There are two reserved memory locations in page 0 for each interrupt line in the system. These two memory locations contain the instruction to be executed by the interrupt. For single-instruction interrupts, the interrupt instruction is one of the 208 and 808 instructions that does not change the program counter or the A register. A single-instruction interrupt can be serviced without altering the operating program except to delay it for the amount of time it takes to execute the interrupt instruction. The normal interrupt instruction is "jump and save" which transfers control to a subroutine designated by the jump and save instruction. The contents of the L and the P counters are stored in the first two memory locations of the subroutine and are used later for a return jump back to the operating program.

Control

The PDC 208 and 808 can be inhibited from responding to any interrupt request by an interrupt mask. Two control instructions allow the interrupts to be disabled or enabled under program control. In addition, if a jump and save instruction is used as an interrupt instruction, the interrupt system is automatically disabled.

Single-instruction interrupts do not require control of the interrupt mask by the program; for example, if teletype buffer ready flip-flop is the stimuli causing an interrupt and the interrupt instruction is block output instruction. This removes the interrupt condition by the time the interrupt instruction is over. If the interrupt instruction had been a jump and save, the interrupt request would remain and would cause another interrupt before the transfer to teletype had occurred, with the result that the return address is within the interrupt subroutine and the computer cannot recover from the loop. Thus, it is necessary to disarm the interrupt system until one of two things occurs, either (a) the line in the teletype is disarmed or (b) the transfer to the teletype occurs, which satisfies the interrupt condition.

CONTROL CONSOLE

The computer console consists of an 8-bit register display, eight data switches, five register select switches, and miscellaneous control switches and indicators (Fig. 11-1).

Register display: An 8-bit register display is provided to allow viewing the contents of a selected register. Contents of the A, I, L, P, and R may be displayed while the computer is halted. In the run mode the contents of the A bus is displayed.

Data entry switches: Eight data entry switches are provided for entering data into a selected register. The switches are momentary-action types. Data is entered immediately upon depression if the computer is halted and in the step mode. In the run mode, the switches are disabled.

Register select switches: Five interlocked, alternate action switches are provided for selection of the register to be connected to the display and the data switches. The switches are wired on a priority basis so that if two switches are depressed at one time, the switch on the left takes priority, disabling the one on the right. This prevents the contents of the two registers from being ORed together and placed in both registers.

Clear switch: A momentary-action switch is provided for clearing a selected register. The switch is disabled in the run mode.

Cycle switch: A momentary action switch is provided for cycling the computer in the step mode (depressed position), and for initiating the run mode if the step-run switch is in the run (released) position.

Step-run switch: An alternate action switch is provided for controlling the two operating modes of the computer. When the switch is released, the computer enters the run mode when the cycle switch is depressed. If the computer is in the run mode, depressing the step-run switch causes the computer to enter the step mode; i.e., the computer will halt at the end of the next instruction.

Step indicator: An indicator is provided to indicate that the computer is in the run mode. The step and run indicators are driven from opposite sides of the run flip-flop in the computer.

Overflow (OV) indicator: An indicator is provided to indicate the state of the overflow flip-flop. The indicator lights when the OV flip-flop is set.

Relative switch: An alternate action switch is provided to allow addressing relative to the program counter when manually storing or examining a program in the core memory. The relative switch is for use with the load A and store A instructions in the step mode only. When it is depressed, the instruction in the instruction register is not allowed to change, and the A field in the R register is ignored. Instead, the lower eight bits of the operand address are obtained from the P counter if the current address is specified; otherwise, the operand address is in page zero.

Manual execute: An alternate action switch is provided to allow the operator to insert an instruction into the I and R registers and manually execute it by depressing the cycle switch. Normal operation of the computer requires retrieving an instruction when the cycle switch is depressed, since the instruction in the instruction register has already been executed before the computer halts. The manual execute switch forces the computer to execute the instruction in the instruction register. The program counter is not updated, which means the manual execute switch allows instructions to be executed manually without disturbing program location.

Sense switch: An alternate action switch is provided to allow the operator to interface to an operating program. The state of the sense can be sensed under program control, allowing branching conditions to be executed, conditioned on the state of the sense switch. The sense switch may be changed in the run mode.

Memory disable: An alternate action switch is provided to allow the operator to disable memory. When the memory disable is depressed, the current generators in the memory core stack drive circuitry are disabled, inhibiting the memory from operating. This allows the contents of the memory to be protected from transients when power on the controller is turned on or off manually. If the controller is equipped with the optional power fail restart option, the memory disable switch need not be used except in instances where the power fail subroutine is not in memory.

Reset switch: A momentary action switch is provided to allow the computer system to be initialized when power is turned on. The reset switch initializes the computer processor flip-flops, placing the computer in the stop mode, and provides a pulse on the I-O cable which is used by peripheral logic for initialization. The reset switch may also be used as a panic button to break a runaway loop.

Power switch: An alternate switch is provided for controlling AC power to the computer power supply. Power is on when the power switch is depressed.

Power indicator: An indicator is provided to show when the power switch is depressed. Power for the indicator lamp is obtained through the circuitbreaker on the back of the computer.

PERIPHERAL EQUIPMENT DESCRIPTION

Described in this section are some of the I-O devices that are available with the PDC-208 and 808.

33 Teletype Option

The 33 teletype option provides the PDC-208 and 808 system with four I-O features in one package: keyboard input, page printer, paper tape reader, and paper tape punch. The peripheral device is a Model 33TC send-receive set (manufactured by Teletype Corp.) operated in the duplex mode. A peripheral interface to connect the computer to the teletype is contained in one option logic board and is mounted in the basic PDC-208 and 808 chassis. The interface contains a buffer-shift register that performs parallel-to-serial conversion when feeding from the computer to the teletype and serial-to-parallel conversion when feeding from the teletype to the computer.

High-Speed Reader Option

The high-speed paper tape reader option (PTR) consists of a 300 character per second optical reader and the interface logic between the reader and the PDC-208 and 808. The reader is an undirectional, 8-level unit that reads continuously or steps one character at a time under control of the interface. Each word (8-bit character) is read in parallel and transferred to a buffer register in the interface where it is held until it is transferred to the computer. The reader mounts in a standard 19-inch equipment rack, requiring 7 inches of rack height. The interface is contained on one logic board and is mounted within the basic PDC-208 or 808 chassis.

High-Speed Punch Option

The high-speed paper tape punch option (PTP) consists of a 60 character per second punch and the interface logic between the punch and the PDC-208 or 808. The punch is an 8-level unit that can punch paper or mylar tapes. The punch interface contains an 8-bit buffer register to hold information being punched and the control and interface logic required to control the punch and communicate with the computer. The punch mounts in a standard 19-inch equipment rack and requires 10½ inches of rack height. The interface is contained in a logic board which mounts in the basic PDC 208 or 808 chassis.

MAINFRAME OPTIONS

This section describes some of the options available with the PDC-208 and 808 processor.

Power Fail-Restart Option

The power fail-restart (PFR) option allows the computer to be operated from an unreliable AC source. A low-power condition or a temporary power outage is detected in time to allow the operating program to prepare for the power loss. When power returns to normal the computer is automatically restarted. Unattended operation is possible at remote sites.

The PFR option consists of a voltage detector, interrupt register, and priority interrupt logic on an option module in the PDC-208 or 808 chassis. Two interrupts are provided with the option. One interrupt flags the low-power condition, and the other interrupt restarts the computer one second after power resumes.

Operation

The PFR option monitors the 115v AC line voltage and closes a switch when the voltage drops below a preset value (typically 100v). The switch closing sets a flip-flop which requests an interrupt. The interrupt location should contain a jump and save to the power fail subroutine. Approximately two milliseconds after low power is detected, inhibiting memory start pulses shunt the current sources in the memory drive electronics preventing spurious memory cycles as the power collapses. When power returns, the detector output (indicating power is normal) is delayed one second and then used to create the restart interrupt. During the one second interval between power up and the restart of the computer, the computer system is initialized. After the one second delay, the computer is forced to location zero in page 0 to obtain the restart interrupt instruction (jump to restart subroutine).

Real Time Clock Option

The real time clock (RTC) is a PDC-208 or 808 processor option that provides a means of determining elapsed time and-

or creating a time-of-day clock with software. The RTC derives time pulses from the 60 Hz primary input (120 PDS) to the PDC-208 or 808. These time pulses are then used to generate an interrupt (clock interrupt) every 8.33 milliseconds to increment a counter in memory.

A second interrupt (sync interrupt) is generated by the RTC when the counter in memory reaches a count of zero (overflow) while being incremented by the clock interrupt instruction. The sync interrupt is used to enter a time-keeping subroutine. The two interrupts required by the clock and sync pulses are contained within the RTC. Interrupt addresses for each line are also generated by the RTC logic, providing a complete stand alone option.

Operation

The instruction set of the basic PDC-208 or 808 system is increased by the RTC. The number of interrupts is also increased by two. Each instruction, including the suggested interrupt instructions, are described in Chapter 18.

Priority

Priority of the RTC interrupts, relative to other interrupts in a PDC-208 or 808 system, is determined by the wiring of the PROT line. Priority in the 808 is IL1X, IL2X, PF, RTC then others. In the 208 it is PF, IL1X, IL2X, RTC then others.

RESERVED MEMORY LOCATIONS

Since each interrupt line has two memory locations associated with it, these locations must not be used for other purposes. As an aid to the programmer, all reserved locations in the basic PDC-208 and 808 system plus mainframe options are listed. In larger systems additional locations may be required. Programming codes for I-O devices appear in Chapter 18.

Chapter 14

I-O Interface Reference

The PDC-208 and 808 use a minimum amount of interface logic. Standard DTL circuits are used throughout the I-O, providing savings in parts cost and power.

PARTY LINE I-O BUS

The PDC-208 and 808 incorporate a "party-line" I-O bus to communicate with peripheral logic. Each peripheral logic group or "device" is given an address which is used in all communications between the processor and that device. A block diagram of a PDC-208 or 808 system with three devices is shown in Fig. 14-1. Notice that while the I-O cable is physically connected in a serial fashion; the devices are electrically connected in parallel.

A termination "shoe" containing line-terminating resistors is connected to the end of the I-O cable at the last device. The resistor is required to maintain the integrity of the transmission line by terminating the line in its characteristic impedance (or approximation thereof) at the receiving end to minimize reflections. Since the data lines are bilateral; i.e., they can be driven from either end, a termination is required at each end. The unilateral lines require a terminating resistor only on the receiving end. Fig. 14-2 shows the circuit schematics of the two types of lines. All lines are twisted pairs.

The length of the I-O cable should be kept as short as possible to minimize cross talk between lines. When possible peripheral logic should be located adjacent to the computer. The maximum length allowable varies with the application, but in general it should be kept under ten feet.

The I-O cable consists of a number of lines grouped according to functions. Each functional grouping is called a bus.

Data bus—eight bidirectional lines that transmit data between devices and the computer. Each of the eight lines is terminated on each end.

Peripheral address bus—five lines that transmit the device address to devices during the execution of an I-O instruction.

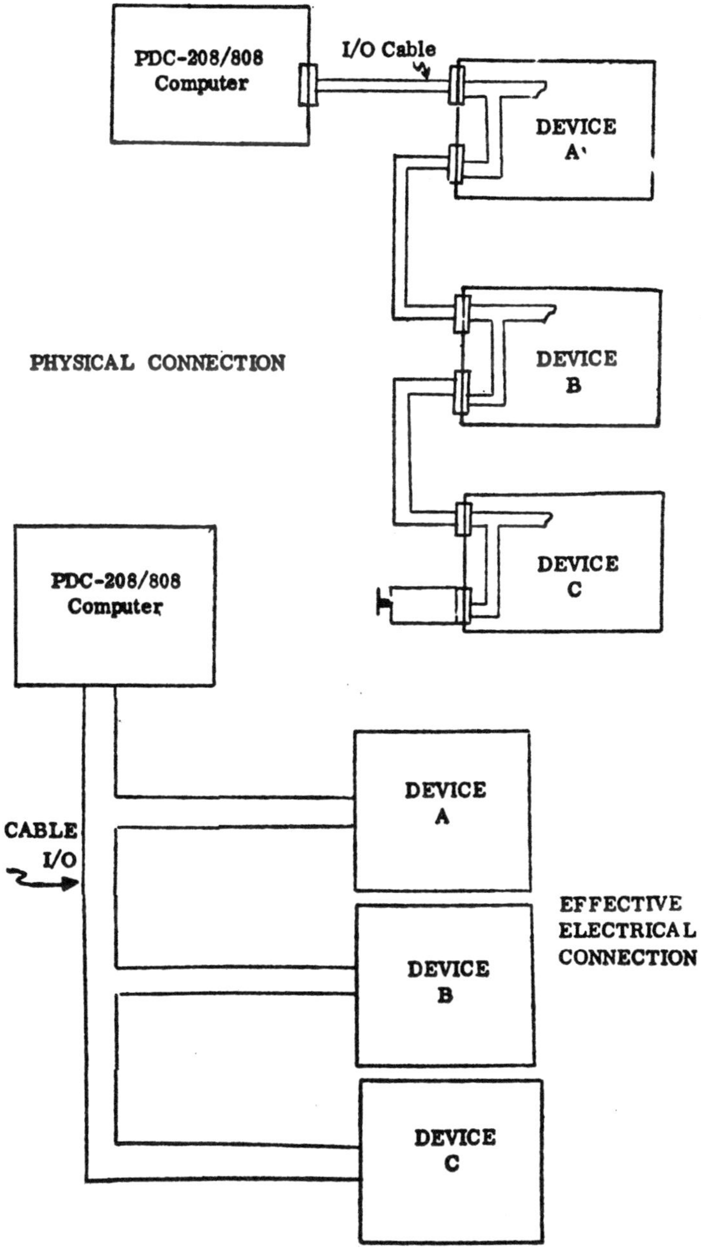

Fig. 14-1. Block diagram of a PDC 208 or 808 system.

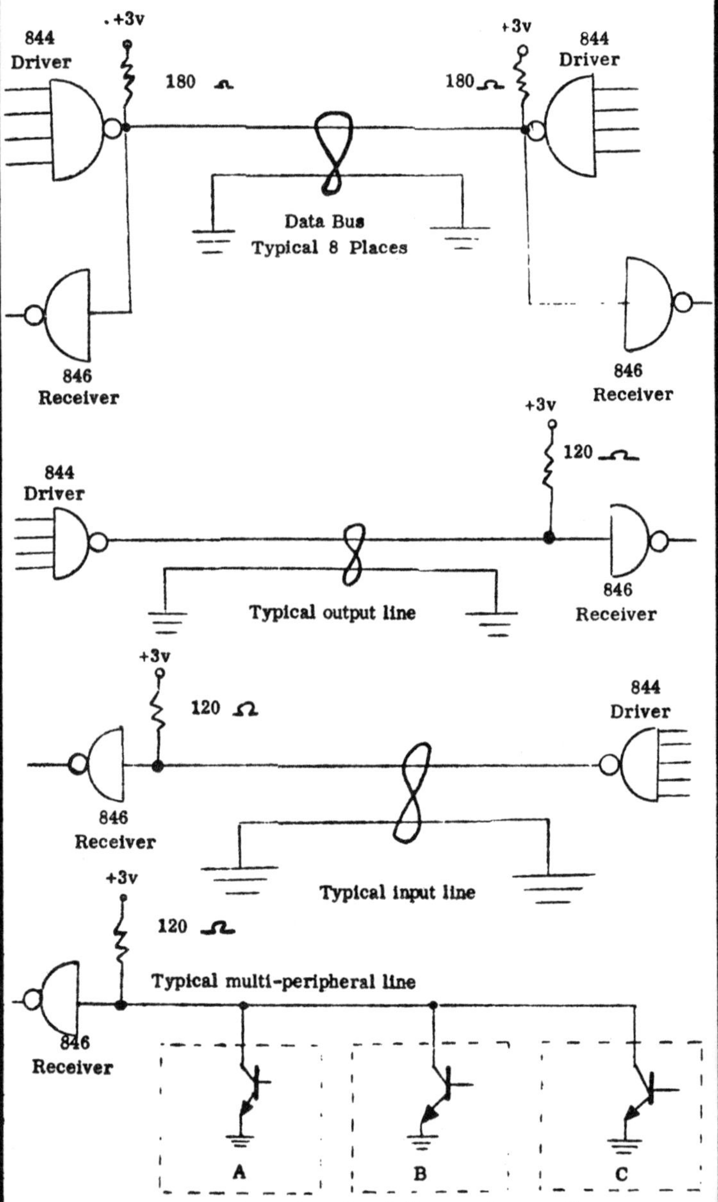

Fig. 14-2. Input-output line schematic.

Function bus—three lines that transmit the function code to the devices during an I-O instruction.

Control bus—fourteen lines that transmit control signals between the computer and I-O devices. Each signal is described in the function index in Chapter 15.

Miscellaneous lines—the power lines for the termination resistors and several spare lines that are not used for PROT wiring and other systems requirements. **Note:** The signals appearing on the I-O cable are "ground true" logic; i.e., the false level is the high level. This permits the parallel connection of devices using the "wired OR" technique and also conserves power since the line terminations do not dissipate power except when the true (ground) signal exists.

The PDC-208 and 808 employ a 2 to 2.75 ms I-O period. Consequently, considerable time is available in implementing the signals necessary to interface with peripheral logic, eliminating the need for fast or special circuits. The shortest pulse width used is the 500 ns PLSE signal which is used as a strobe. All other signals are at least two microseconds in duration, providing plenty of time for decoding and gating.

OUTPUT COMMAND

The output instructions—OTA, OTZ, OAS, OTB—all employ the same peripheral logic and timing. Data is placed on the data bus for two microseconds and at the same time the device address and function code is placed on the peripheral address bus and function bus, respectively. The OUTX control line is true for the two microseconds that data is present, indicating an output instruction is being executed.

At the end of the 2-microsecond OUTX signal, the PLSE signal occurs if the output transfer is to be made. In the case of a sense and output combination, the PLSE signal will not

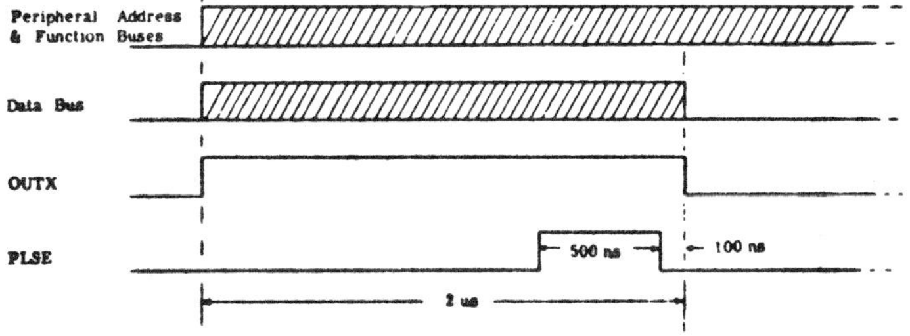

Fig. 14-3. Output timing diagram.

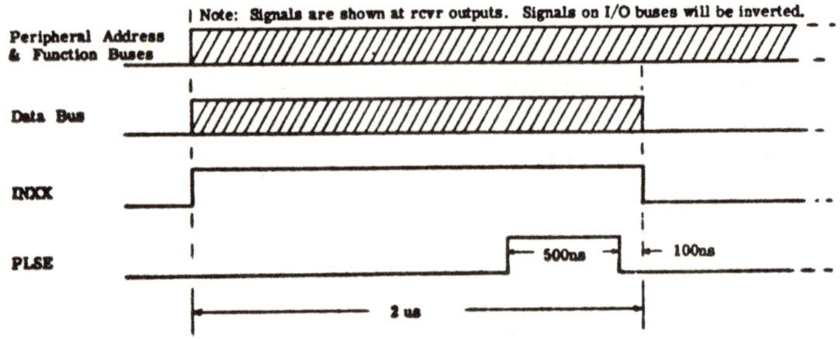

Fig. 14-4. Input timing diagram.

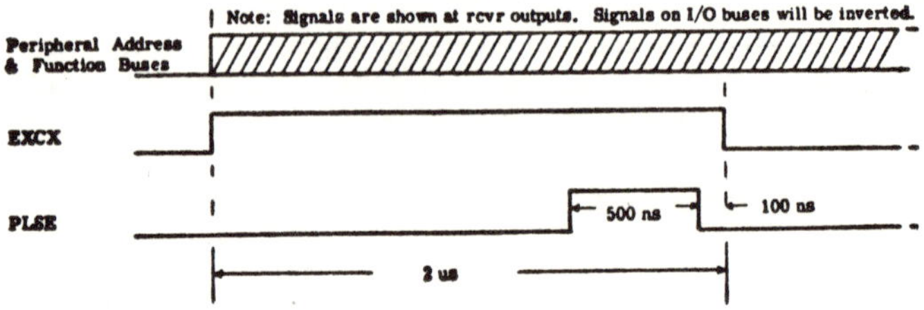

Fig. 14-5. External control timing diagram.

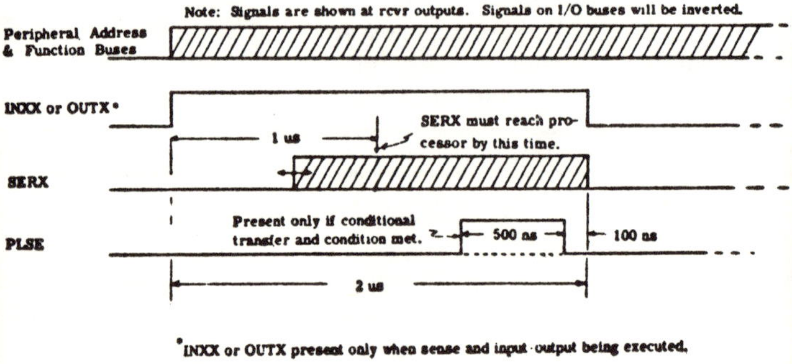

Fig. 14-6. Sense timing diagram.

occur unless a sense response is obtained by the processor. The composite timing of an output command is shown in Fig. 14-3.

INPUT COMMAND

The input instructions—INA, MIA, IAS, MIS—employ the same peripheral logic and timing. Data is placed on the data bus by the device which is addressed during the two microseconds the INXX signal is true. At the end of this time, the PLSE signal occurs if the input transfer is to be made. In the case of the sense and input instructions, the PLSE will not occur if a sense response is not obtained by the processor. The absence of the PLSE signal indicates the transfer was not made. The composite timing of an input command is shown in Fig. 14-4.

EXTERNAL CONTROL COMMAND

The EXC instruction timing is similar to the transfer instructions except the data bus is not active. The EXCX control signal is true for two microseconds. The PLSE signal occurs at the end of the EXCX signal and is used to generate set pulses which are gated by the function codes generated by decoding the function bus. Fig. 14-5 shows the timing of the EXC command.

SENSE COMMAND

The sense instructions do not use a sense control line, since the final gating for sense is done inside the processor. This allows the sense instruction to be combined with the input and output instructions, creating powerful I-O instructions that conserve memory and shorten program execution times.

When a peripheral device is addressed by the processor, the function code is used to gate the condition of a specified function onto the sense response line, SERX. If a true response exists, the SERX line in the control bus is driven to ground. Thus the sensing is accomplished during all I-O instructions, but using the results of the sense is determined by the instruction being executed. The processor must receive the sense response one microsecond after the beginning of the instruction to allow time for decision making within the processor. Fig. 14-6 shows the time for sense.

INTERRUPT TIMING

The use of the standard interrupts in the basic PDC-208 or 808 enables the computer to perform as a real time systems component responding to external stimuli and to allow considerable time savings in executing I-O programs that transfer data to or from peripheral devices. A typical interrupt sequence using one of the two fully implemented interrupt lines is as follows:

A. The buffer ready status flip-flop in a device turns on, indicating that the device desires data to be transferred from the computer and drives the IL1X line in the control bus to the ground (true) state, requesting an interrupt.

B. The processor finishes the current instruction and if interrupts are enabled; i.e., the processor is allowed to respond to interrupts, the request for interrupt is acknowledged and the instruction located in the two reserved memory locations associated with IL1X is executed. The IUAX signal becomes true as soon as the request is acknowledged and stays on for the time required to execute the interrupt instruction, typically two to four cycles.

C. If the interrupt instruction is a JST, the interrupt enable flip-flop in the processor is turned off, preventing further interrupts from being acknowledged until the enable flip-flop is again turned on by the program.

D. A subroutine is entered (if JST is used) which transfers the desired data to the interrupting device, satisfying the request and resetting the buffer ready flip-flop which removes the interrupt request. Interrupts can now be enabled and a return jump back to the operating program executed.

E. If the interrupt is a single-execute instruction such as block output, the request for data is satisfied by the execution of the interrupt instruction and the program continues as soon as IUAX goes off, creating only a 4-cycle pause in the program.

The use of the IURX line is different from that of the IL1X and IL2X lines in that the interrupt address must be specified by the device requesting the interrupt, whereas the IL1X and IL2X lines have associated address generators within the computer. To obtain the interrupt address from the device, the processor sends an interrupt address request signal IARX to the devices and the device requesting sends back the address the processor is to use to find the interrupt instruction. The IARX signal is two microseconds long. The PLSE signal occurs at the end of the IARX signal to notify the device that the processor has received the address. The timing of the interrupt sequence using the IURX line in this fashion is shown in Fig. 14-7.

Another method of using the IURX line is the scanning technique. Several devices are allowed to generate an interrupt request at will and a subroutine is entered which polls each device capable of having generated a request. The polling is done by executing sense instructions until the requesting device is located. In this manner, priorities may be changed at will by the programmer by simply changing the order in which the devices are sensed. The technique is slower, however, than a fully automatic interrupt sequence but is considerably less expensive. If a device requests an interrupt using IURX and does not respond with an address during IARX, the processor accesses memory locations 20 and 21 for the interrupt instruction (which in almost all cases must be a JST).

All PDC-208 and 808 standard peripheral interfaces have two interrupt line drives implemented. One driver is normally connected to IL1X and is used to generate an interrupt on buffer ready. The other driver is normally connected to IL2X and is used to generate an interrupt on end-of-block when performing block transfers under interrupt control. Each driver has a mask associated with it which may be controlled by the operating program.

Several peripheral devices may be connected to the IL1X and IL2X lines, provided only one device is allowed to be operating under interrupt control at a given time. Since the IL1X and IL2X lines are fully implemented and, therefore,

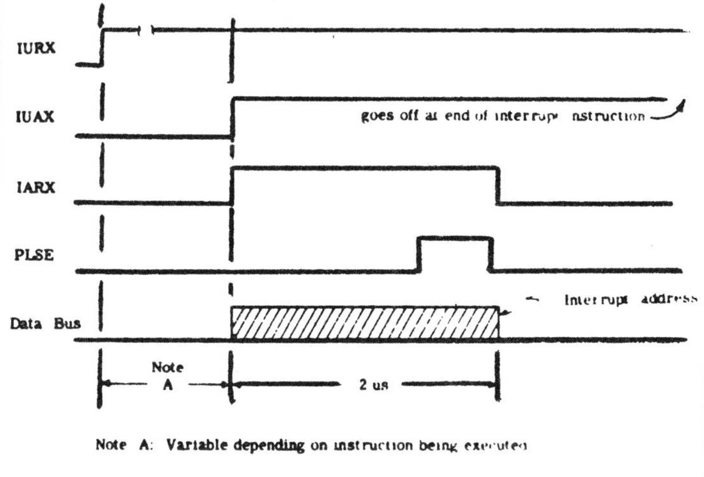

Fig. 14-7. Interrupt timing diagram.

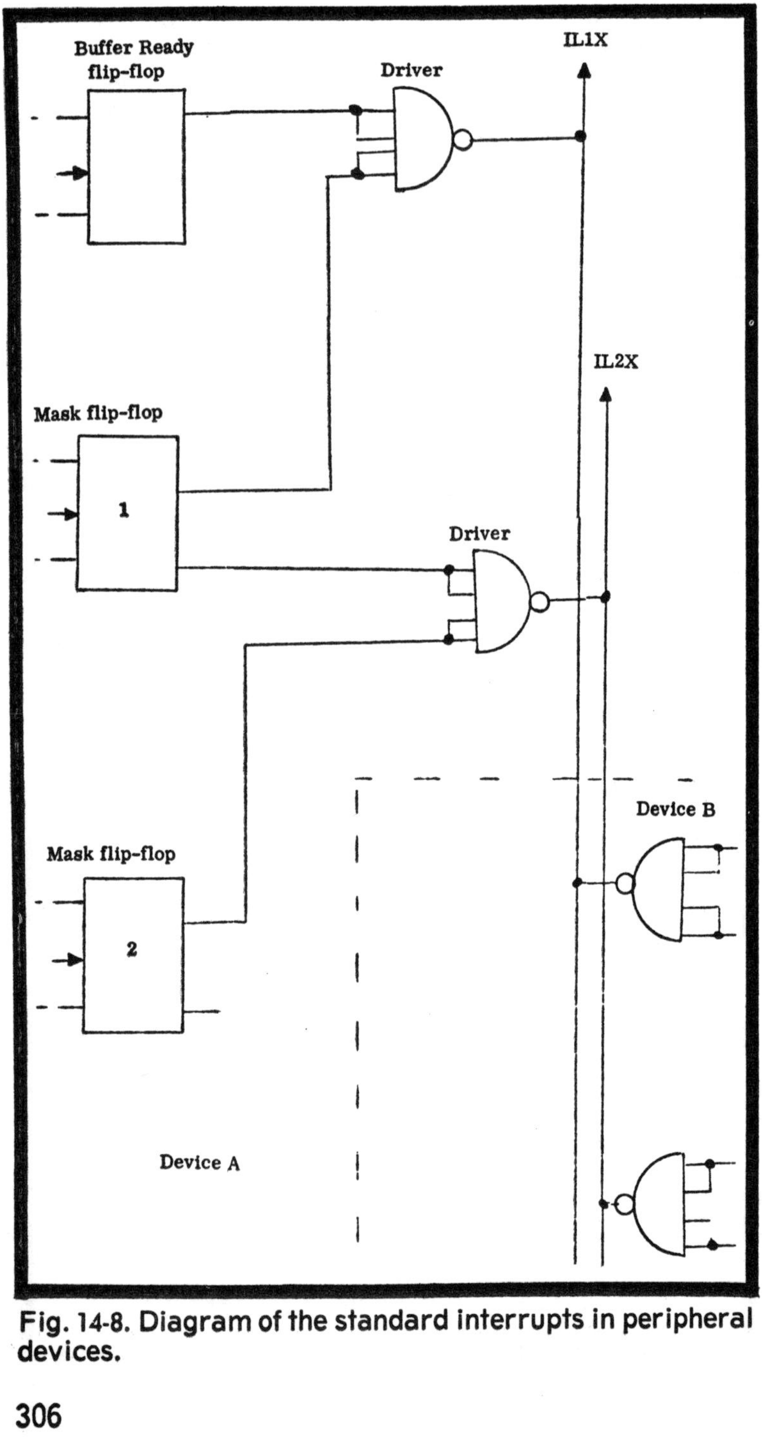

Fig. 14-8. Diagram of the standard interrupts in peripheral devices.

general purpose, they may also be used by customer interface logic without the need to generate priority and address logic outside the PDC-208 or 808.

Fig. 14-8 shows the logic in a standard PDC-208 or 808 peripheral computer that transfers data to or from the process or (TTY, high-speed reader, etc.). The buffer ready flip-flop is set when the device is ready to send or receive data. If the Mask FF 1 is on, an interrupt is generated on IL1X which is used to cause data to be transferred. If the block transfer instructions are used, an end-of-block echo pulse occurs when the pointer overflows which resets mask FF 1. This creates an interrupt on IL2X (if mask FF 2 has been previously set) which is used to signal the end of the block being transferred. Notice that each interrupt line driver can be disabled by the mask flip-flops, allowing complete system flexibility in the use of the interrupts.

Part 3: Maintenance

Chapter 15
Introduction To Maintenance

The logic diagrams in this section quite frequently, especially in the case of MSI devices, list only the pin numbers associated with a simple block. The diagrams included here (Figs. 15-1 through 15-12) allow the association of these inputs with specific circuit functions.

The logic diagrams are followed by a complete **Function Index List.** Every computer has a similar list which simply names the various signals used in the system. For a synchronous computer, such as the PDC 808, the logical place to start is with the clock signals since they, ultimately, control all internal operations.

Wherever possible, waveforms have been photographed to show the deviations that might be expected from the "idealized" waveforms presented in the text. In many instances the waveforms are practically unrecognizable when compared to the "idealized" waveforms.

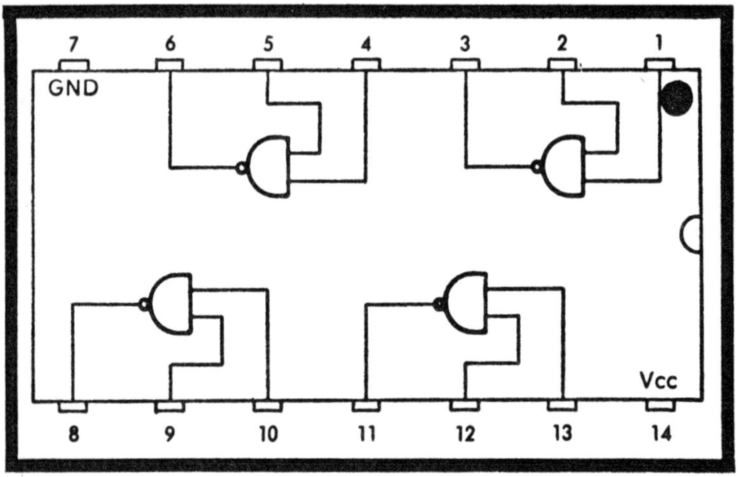

Fig. 15-1. Diagram of the MC846 and SN15846 quad 2-input NAND gate.

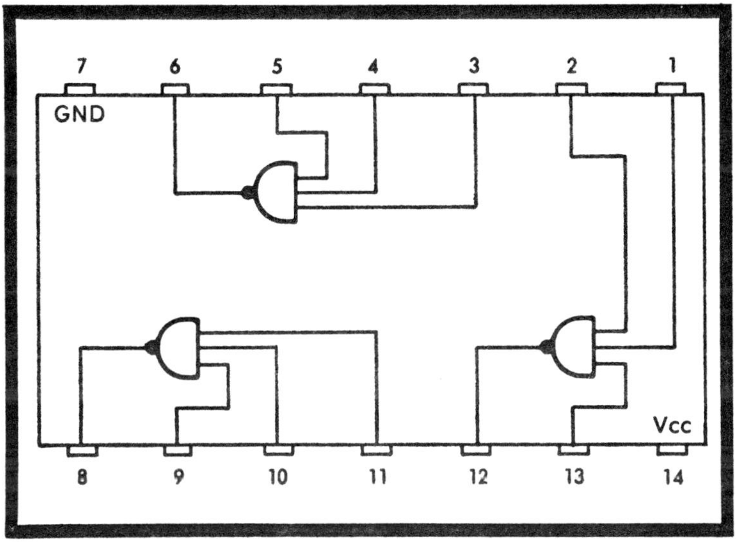

Fig. 15-2. Diagram of the MC862 and SN15862 triple 3-input NAND gate.

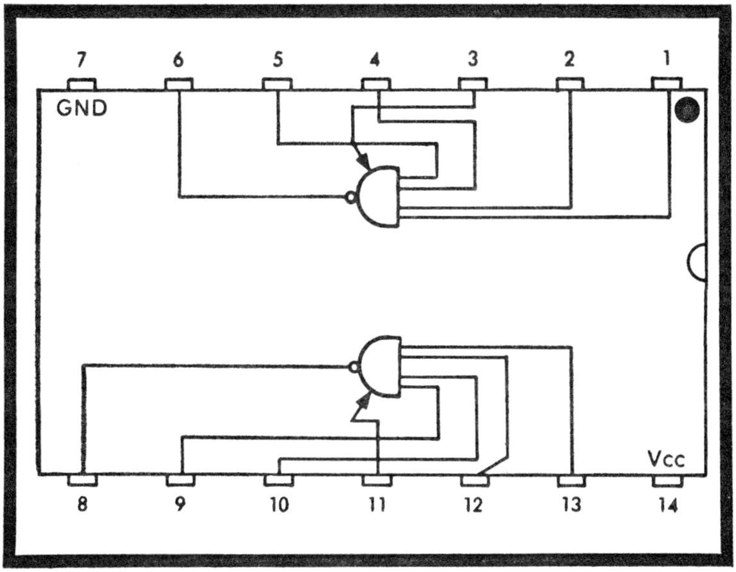

Fig. 15-3. Diagram of the MC830 and SN15830 expandable dual 4-input gate; the MC832 and SN15832 expandable dual 4-input buffer, and the MC844 expandable dual 4-input power gate (line, relay, or lamp driver).

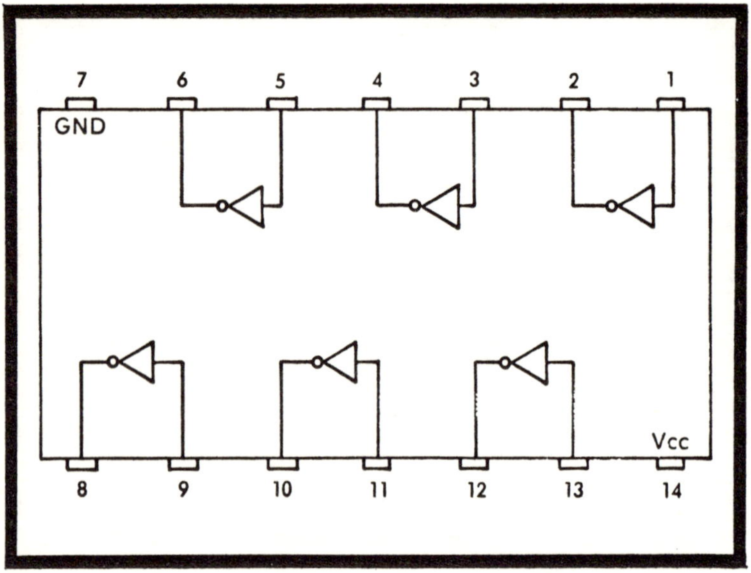

Fig. 15-4. Diagram of the MC836 and SN15836 hex inverter.

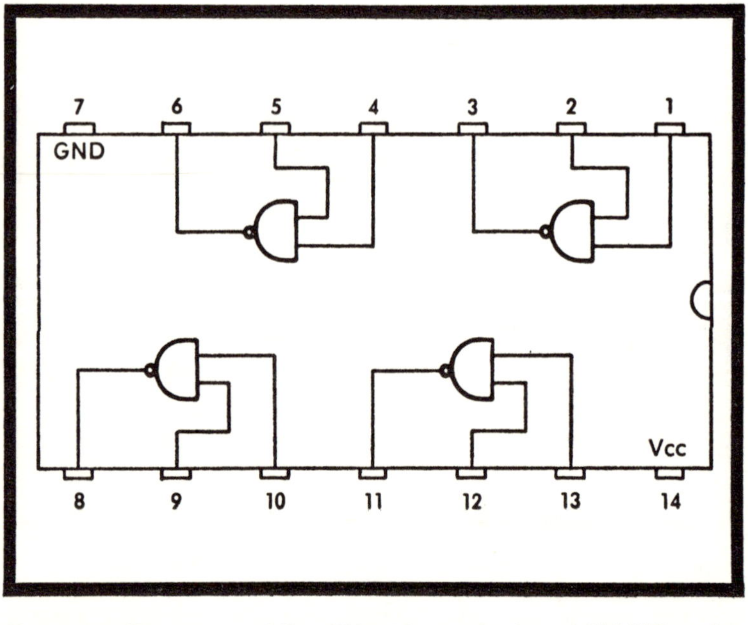

Fig. 15-5. Diagram of the SN7400 quad 2-input NAND gate.

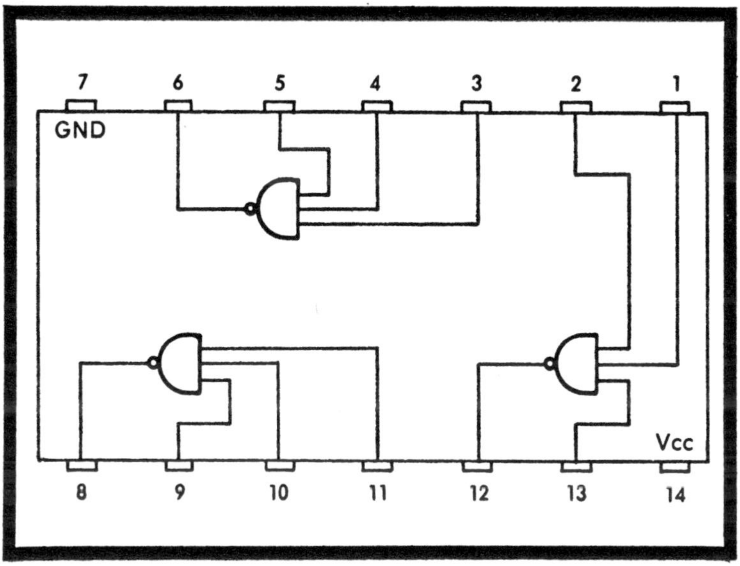

Fig. 15-6. Diagram of the SN7410 triple 3-input NAND gate.

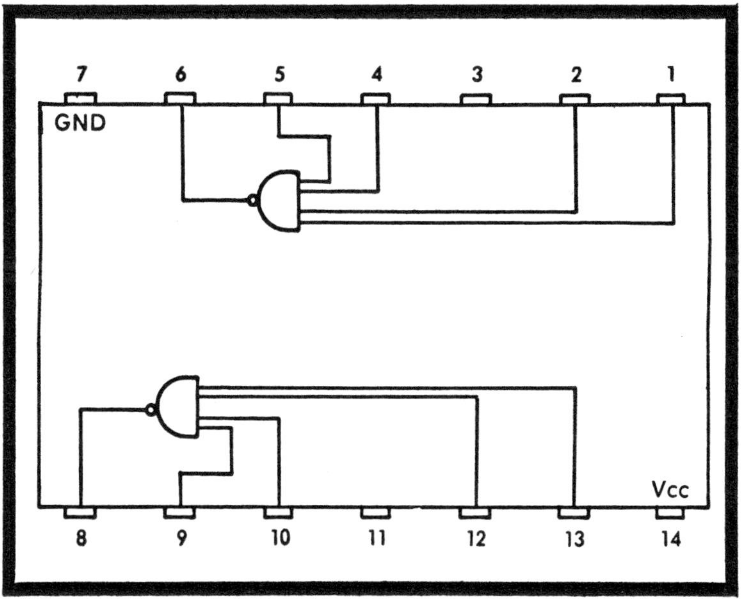

Fig. 15-7. Diagram of the SN7420 dual 4-input NAND gate and the SN7440 dual 4-input NAND buffer.

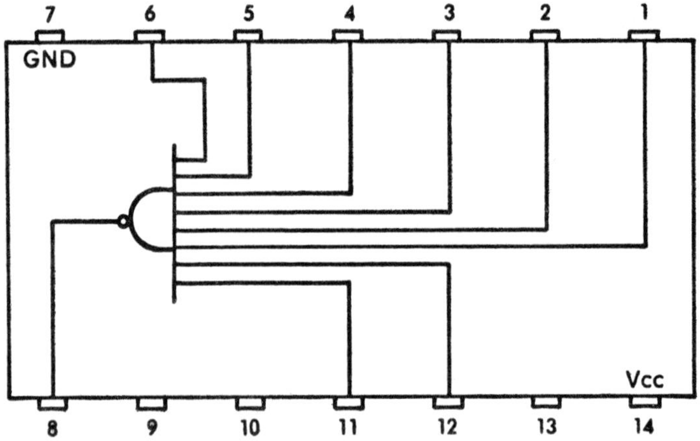

Fig. 15-8. Diagram of the SN7430 single 8-input NAND gate.

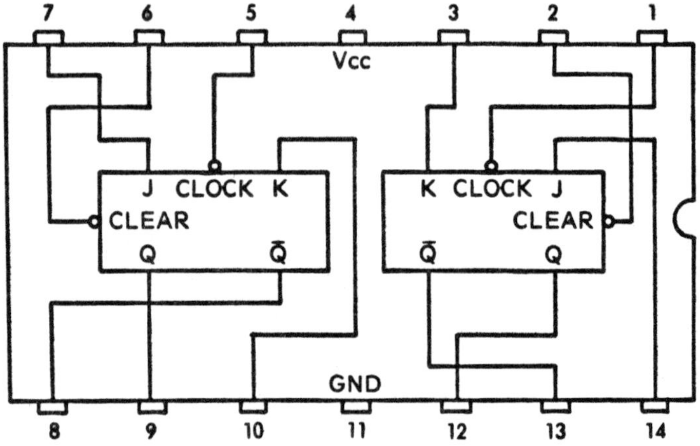

Fig. 15-9. Diagram of the SN7473 dual J-K flip-flop.

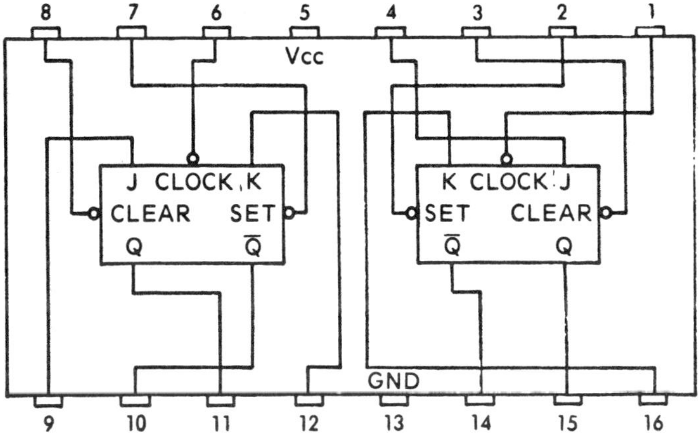

Fig. 15-10. Diagram of the SN7476 dual J-K flip-flop with direct set capability.

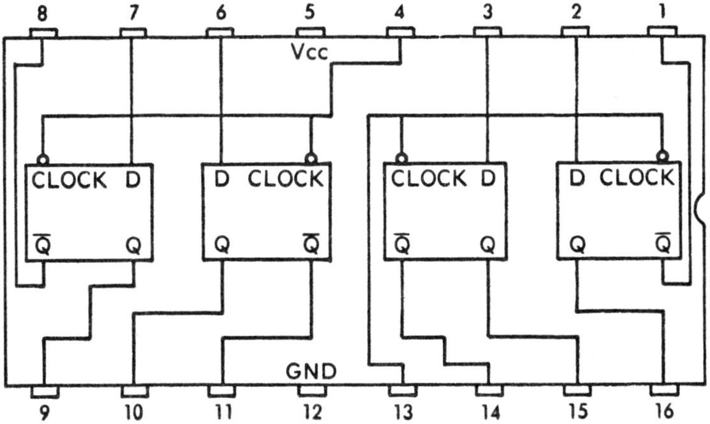

Fig. 15-11. Diagram of the SN7475 4-bit bistable latch.

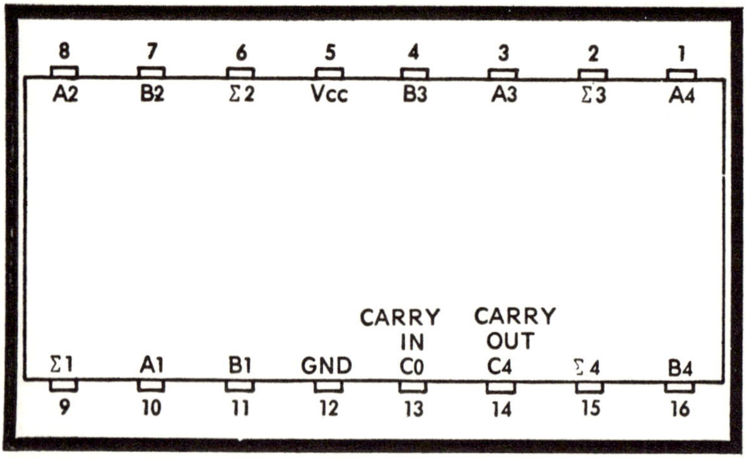

Fig. 15-12. Diagram of the SN 7483 4-bit binary full adder. Since each bit requires nine gates to illustrate it, the gate symbols have been omitted (Σ is the Greek sigma for sum.)

FUNCTION INDEX LIST

AAXX—1-MHz square wave.
AB00 to **AB07**—A bus. Distributes output of the adder to A, P, L, M, and W registers, console display, and D bus drivers.
ACY1—Address cycle 1. Signal time when the word being read from the memory is the least significant eight bits of an indirect address or is the pointer for a block I-O instruction.
ACY2—Address cycle 2. Signal true when the word being read from the memory is the most significant portion (page number) of an indirect address.
ACYE—Address cycle enable. Enables the ACY1 flip-flop when the next memory cycle is to be an address cycle.
AR00 to **AR07**—A register outputs.
ASHX—Arithmetic shift.
AXXX—500-kHz square wave.
BXXX—250-kHz square wave interrupted when the computer is in the step mode.
CARY—Carry from the adder.
CINP—Carry in pulse. Inputs a carry to the least significant bit of the adder.
CLRW—Clear W register. Occurs at the beginning of each memory cycle.
CLRX—Clear. Signal generated in the step mode when the clear switch on the console is depressed.

CXXX—125-kHz square wave interrupted when the computer is in the step mode.
CYCX—Cycle. Pulse of about 100 ns duration generated when the cycle switch on the console is depressed.
DB00 to DB07—D bus. Bilateral data bus in the I-O cable used for parallel transfer of data between the computer and I-O devices.
DJ2X—Direct jump. Signal true during ICY2 of a direct jump instruction.
DS00 to DS07— Data switch inputs to the A bus drivers.
DSSL—Data switch select. Signal is true in the step mode if any data entry switch is depressed.
ECHO—A pulse that occurs during execution of block I-O if the pointer overflows. Used to reset the interrupt enable flip-flop on the IL1X line in a peripheral.
EXCX—External control. Signal in the I-O cable that is true during execution of an external control instruction. 2-microsecond pulse width.
FEIX—"Fetch" instruction. Signal that indicates the next memory cycle is to be an ICY1 instruction cycle.
FJIX—"Fetch" jump instruction. Signal indicates that an indirect jump is in progress and the next memory cycle is to be an ICY1 cycle.
G0XX—Signal that is true for register change instructions, shift instructions and operate instructions. G0XX equals (IR06-)(IR07-)
G1XX—Signal that is true for I-O instructions. G1XX equals (IR06)(IR07-)
G2XX—Signal that is true for skip instructions. G2XX equals (IR06-)(IR07)
G3XX—Signal that is true for memory reference instructions. G3XX equals (IR06)(IR07)
H0XX to H7XX—Signals generated from decoding IR03 to IR04.
IARX—Interrupt address request. Signal on the I-O bus that requests interrupt address from the interrupting device if the device is using the IURX request line. 2 microseconds duration.
ICY1—Instruction cycle 1. True when the word being read from the memory is the first word (or only word) of an instruction and is to be placed in the I register. True for one memory cycle.
ICY2—Instruction cycle 2. True when the word being read from memory is the second word of a 2-word instruction, and is to be placed in the R register.
ICYX—Instruction cycle. True for either an ICY1 or ICY2 memory cycle.

+INH—Inhibit voltage supply to inhibit drivers in memory.
IMXX—Interrupt mask. Flip-flop that enables or disables interrupt requests to the IUAX flip-flop.
INXX—Input. Control signal on the I-O bus that indicates an input instruction is being executed.
IOCL—I-O clock. 1-MHz pulse train from the processor. Used in interrupt generation and for other clocking functions in peripheral logic. IOCL is interrupted when IUAX is on.
IORX—Inclusive OR. Signal that indicates that an inclusive OR instruction is being executed.
IR00 to IR07—I register stages.
IUAX—Interrupt acknowledge. Signal goes true at the end of the current instruction if an interrupt request is present and enabled. Stays true until interrupt instruction is executed.
JMPS—Jump and save. Signal that is true when a jump and save instruction is in the I register.
JMPX—Jump. Signal that is true when a jump instruction is in the I register.
LR00 to LR08—Location register. Contains the eight least significant bits of the program location, which specifies the location of a word within a page.
LSHL—Logical shift left.
LSHR—Logical shift right.
MDSA—Memory disable switch A.
MDSB—Memory disable switch B.
MROC—Memory reference operand cycle.
MR08 to MR13—M extension register. Upper six bits of memory address.
MSAX—Manual select A register. True in the step mode if A is selected for display.
MSCX—Memory start clock. Pulse that occurs every 8 microseconds when the computer is in the run mode.
MSIX—Manual select I register. True in the step mode if I is selected for display.
MSLX—Manual select L register. True in the step mode if L is selected for display.
MSPX—Manual select P register. True in the step mode if P is selected for display.
MSRX—Manual select R register. True in the step mode if R is selected for display.
MSTA—Manual set A register. Generates set pulses to A in the step mode when A is selected and a data switch is depressed.
MSTI—Manual set I register. Generates set pulses to I in the step mode when I is selected and a data switch is depressed.
MSTL—Manual set L register. Generates set pulses to L in the step mode when L is selected and a data switch is depressed.

MSTP—Manual set P register. Generates set pulses to P in the step mode when P is selected and a data switch is depressed.
MSTR—Manual set R register. Generates set pulses to R in the step mode when R is selected and a data switch is depressed.
MSTW—Manual set W register. Set pulses to the W register generated when MSTI or MSTR is generated.
OCY1—Operand cycle 1. Signal that is true when an operand is being read from or stored into the memory, or when the contents of the L register is being stored on a jump and save instruction.
OCY2—Operand cycle 2. Signal that is true when the contents of P is being stored in the memory during a jump and save instruction.
OCYE—Operand cycle enable. Signal that enables the OCY1 flip-flop indicating the next memory cycle is to be an operand cycle.
OSCX—Oscillator. 2-MHz pulse train derived from the basic oscillator in the processor.
OUTX—Output. Control signal on the I-O bus to indicate an output command is being executed. Two microseconds duration.
OVRE—Overflow reset enable. Signal generated during shifts that causes overflow to be reset.
OVSE—Overflow set enable. Signal generated during shifts that causes OV to be set.
OVXX—Overflow flip-flop. Set on arithmetic operations when the sign bit changes illegally, and on shifts or register change instructions.
PC00 to PC01—P counter (P register).
PH1X—Phase 1. 2-microsecond timing pulse that occurs each cycle.
PH2X—Phase 2. 2-microsecond timing pulse that occurs each cycle.
PH3X—Phase 3. 2-microsecond timing pulse that occurs each cycle.
PH4X—Phase 4. 2-microsecond timing pulse that occurs each cycle.
PH23—Phase 2 or 3.
PLSE—Pulse. Strobe signal (500 microseconds) on the I-O bus that is used by peripheral logic to form I-O command signals. True for input, output, and external control commands and during IARX.
PROT—Priority out. Signal from processor to I-O indicating that IL1X and IL2X are not active.
RC1X—Equal to (IR04)(IR05-). Used in register change logic

to indicate set or complement overflow.
RC3X—Register change phase 3. Signal that indicates phase 3 of a register change instruction.
RDXX—Read drive timing signal in memory.
REGS—Register selected. Signal generated in the step mode when any of the registers are selected for display.
RSXX—Read switch timing signal in the memory.
RSTX—Reset. Initializes control and peripheral logic. Caused by depressing the reset button on the console.
RUNX—Run. Signal is true when the controller is in the run mode; i.e., not stopped.
SB00 to SB07—S bus. Positive bus that routes information from A, P, L, M, and W registers to the adder.
SCMX—Sense condition met. Flip-flop that is set on a sense instruction if the sense response is obtained one microsecond after the beginning of the sense command.
SDBR—Select D bus receivers. Enables the contents of the D bus to be placed on the S bus.
SELA—Select A register. Signal that enables the contents of the A register to be placed on the S bus.
SELL—Select L register. Signal that enables the contents of the L register to be placed on the S bus.
SELP—Select P register. Signal enables the contents of the P register to be placed on the S bus.
SELR—Select R register. Enables the contents of the R register to be presented to the adder. If SELR and SLRN are both true simultaneously, zeros are presented to the adder on the U bus.
SELS—Select sum. Signal that enables the output of the adder to be placed on the A bus without shifting.
SETA—Set A register.
SETL—Set L register.
SETP—Set P register.
SETR—Set R register.
SETW—Set W register.
SFTX—Shift.
SHLI—Shift left input to least significant bit of A.
SHLX—Shift left.
SHR7—Shift right 7. Input to the most significant bit of A on a logical right shift.
SHRX—Shift right.
SKEX—Skip enable.
SKIP—Skip flip-flop. When true, indicates a skip is being performed and the L counter is being incremented twice. If L overflows, then P is incremented. Skip is true for 1.5 microseconds.

SLA1—Signal that is used to select the A register during the execution of an output A command or a masked input to A command.
SLAN—Select A Not. Signal that enables the 1s complement of the A register to be placed on the S bus.
SLL1—Signal that causes select L to be true while the skip flip-flop is set and L is being incremented twice. Also used to create two set L pulses.
SLL2—Signal that is used to cause select L during phase 1 of either ICY1 or ICY2 cycles for updating the L counter.
SLLM—Select lower M register. Signal that enables the M register contents to be placed on the S bus.
SLP1—Signal true during second half of phase 1 of each instruction cycle. Used to update the P register.
SLP2—Signal true during skip. Used to increment P if L overflows when incremented on a skip.
SLR1—Signal that is true during phase 4 of ICX2 during a memory reference instruction (except a direct jump). Used to form the address for the operand or address cycle.
SLUM—Select the upper M register signal that selects the contents of the M extension register on the X bus and thence onto the A bus.
SLRN-Select R Not. Enables the 1s complement of the R register to be presented to the adder.
SLW1—Signal true during phase 2 and 3 of the operand cycle of an increment and replace instruction. Allows W to be incremented during phase 2 and the results tested during phase 3.
SLW3—Signal true during ACX2 phase 3 of an indirect jump. Allows W to be transferred to P.
SLW4—Signal that is true during operand cycle phase 3 of an output A instruction. Allows W to be placed on the D bus.
S0XX to S7XX—Sum. Output of adder.
SSEX—Sense strobe enable. Generated during RDXX pulse.
STA2—Signal that is true if a sense condition is met during an I-O instruction that uses a sense test.
STA3—Signal that occurs during an input to A instruction. Used to create a set A pulse.
STA5—Signal that is true during the execution phase if an I-O instruction. (G1XX • ICY2 • PH3X)
STL1—Signal that is true during phase 4 of OCY2. This occurs only during the execution of a jump and save instruction where the contents of M plus 1 is being transferred to the L register.
STL2—Signal that is true during phase 3 of ICY2 during a direct jump. Used to cause the contents of the R register to be

transferred to the L register.

STL3—Signal that occurs during JMPX : ACY1 and phase 3 which is used to transfer the first word of an indirect address from the W register to the L register or an indirect jump.

STLM—Set lower M. Sets lower eight bits of the memory address.

STUM—Set upper M. Set the pulse to the M extension (ME) register.

STW1—Signal true during I-O operand cycle on an input to memory. (block input).

SUBX—Subtract. Signal true during operand cycle phase 3 of a subtract instruction.

T1XX—Timing pulse that occurs every two microseconds in the run mode.

T2XX—Timing pulse that occurs at the end of phase 2.

T3XX—Timing pulse that occurs at the end of phase 3.

T4DX—Delayed T4XX.

T4XX—Timing pulse that occurs at the end of phase 4.

T0XX—Timing pulse that occurs every microsecond in the run mode.

VXDX—Voltage for X drive. Analog voltage that supplies drivers in the X side of memory electronics.

VYDX—Voltage for Y drive. Analog voltage that supplies drivers in the Y side of memory electronics.

WDXX—Write drive timing signal in memory.

WEXX—Signal true when the memory cycle is to result in a store cycle. Enables the set W signal to be generated with T2XX.

WR00 to WR07—Word register. Word buffer register between the processor and memory.

WSXX—Write switch timing signal in memory.

XB01 to XB03—X bus. Used as an auxiliary input to the A bus. Pointer addresses and the interrupt addresses for IL1X and IL2X are transferred to L through the X bus.

XB00 to XB07—X bus. Auxiliary input to the A bus through the A bus driver. Allows information to be placed on the A bus without going through adder.

XIMX—Transfer I to M extension. The three bits of the pointer extension in a block I-O instruction are transferred to ME.

XPMX—Transfer P to M extension. P is normally transferred to ME at T4XX.

Chapter 16

System & Functional Components

The PDC 808, as with many small processors, is constructed on cards which plug into printed-circuit jacks wired on what is called a "back-plane." The pins on the printed-circuit jacks are numbered. Also, the connections (if any) to these pins are numbered and the numbers are shown in parentheses on the diagrams.

The logic diagrams that follow are the diagrams for the various registers. The upper left rectangle in Fig. 16-1 contains the designations PC01, 8, and 7475. The PC01 says that this latch is the bit 01 latch of the program counter register. The 8 is the IC number, again referencing the layout drawings not included in this book, and the 7475 is the type designator which can be referenced back to the diagrams shown in Chapter 15. The numbers on the input and output lines refer to the pin numbers on those same IC diagrams so that pin 2, referring back to Fig. 15-11 is the D or data input to that particular position.

For the logic gates, the number just outside and below each gate (upper left-hand corner for example) is the device number, in this case a Motorola Type 832 DTL device. The large rectangular block on the right-hand side is the adder for the two bits in Fig. 16-1 and the two bits in Fig. 16-2.

The DS01- signal mentioned earlier illustrates one of the problems in troubleshooting computers. This signal comes from some source but it does not indicate what that source is, so it becomes necessary to check the function index list.

PROCESSOR

The processor portion of the computer contains all the active registers, the adder unit, the control logic and the signal buses. There are eight registers in the processor (Figs. 16-1 through 16-4):

A register: The A register (AR) is the accumulator and the input-output buffer register. It is loaded through select gates. The contents of AR can be shifted, complemented,

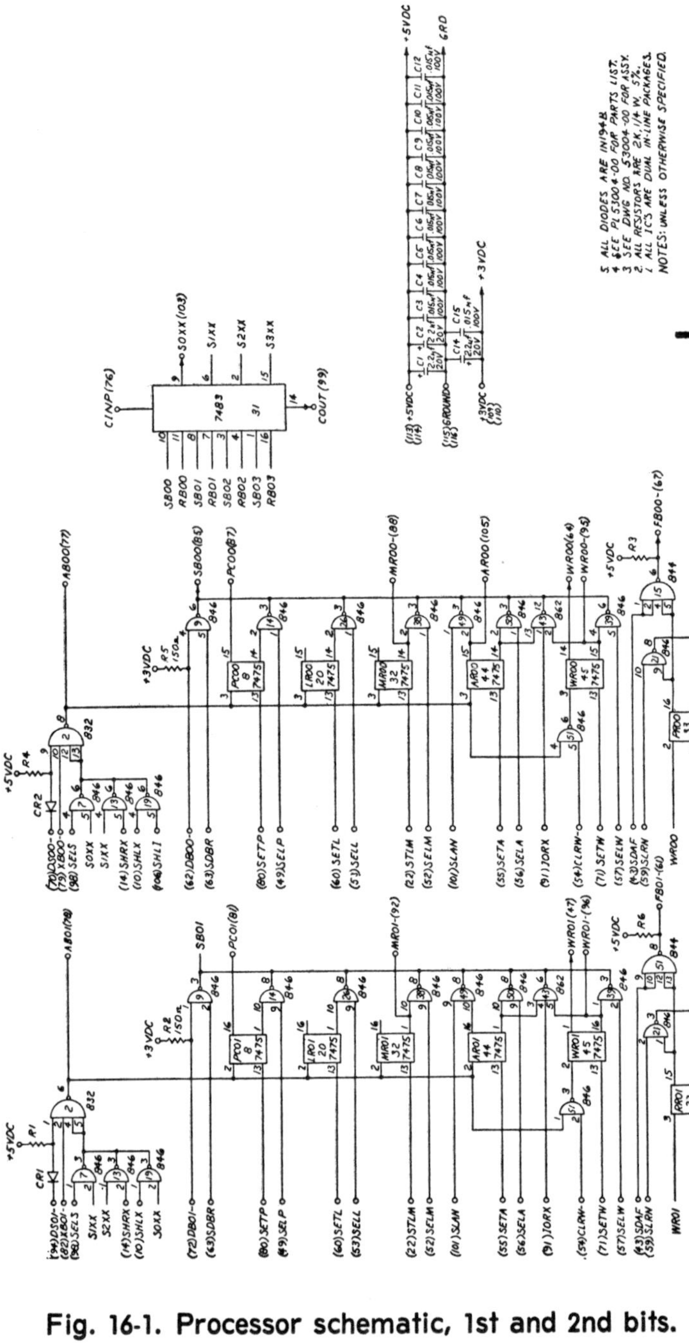

Fig. 16-1. Processor schematic, 1st and 2nd bits.

stored in memory, added, subtracted (memory subtracted from AR), cleared, outputed to the I-O bus, ORed with memory, ANDed with memory, and interchanged with memory. The register is eight bits long, constructed with "quad latch" integrated circuits and controlled by the following control signals: SELA, SLAN and SETA.

I register: The I register (IR) is the 8-bit instruction register that holds the single-word instructions being executed and holds the first word of double-word instructions. (The second word is held in the R register). The IR receives the instruction word from the W register, which is directly connected to IR and RR. The IR is loaded at T2 time during the instruction "fetch" cycle ICY1. The control signal associated with IR is: SETL.

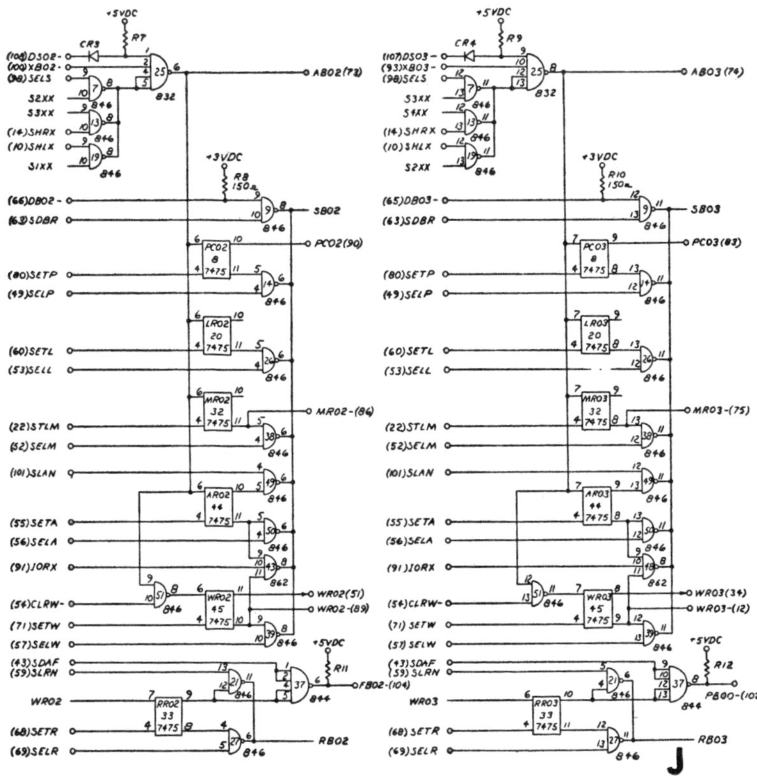

Fig. 16-2. Processor schematic, 3rd and 4th bits.

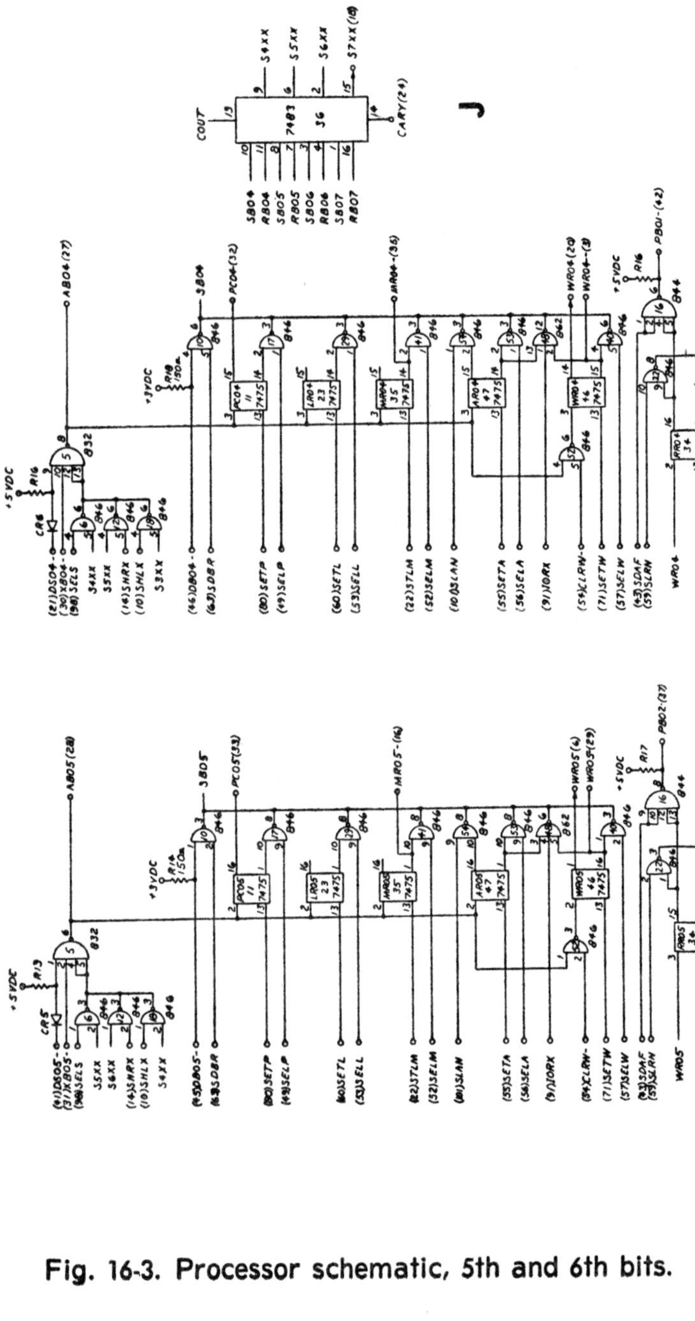

Fig. 16-3. Processor schematic, 5th and 6th bits.

R register: The R register (RR) is used as the operand address register for most memory reference instructions and also is used as an extension to the IR for double-word instructions. In that sense, it is a time-shared register. For instance, on a load A instruction, the second word of the instruction is held in RR until the operand from memory is obtained. The operand then replaces the instruction word in RR. For memory reference instructions, the contents of RR is the A field (the 8-bit operand address in the instructions) until the operand is obtained.

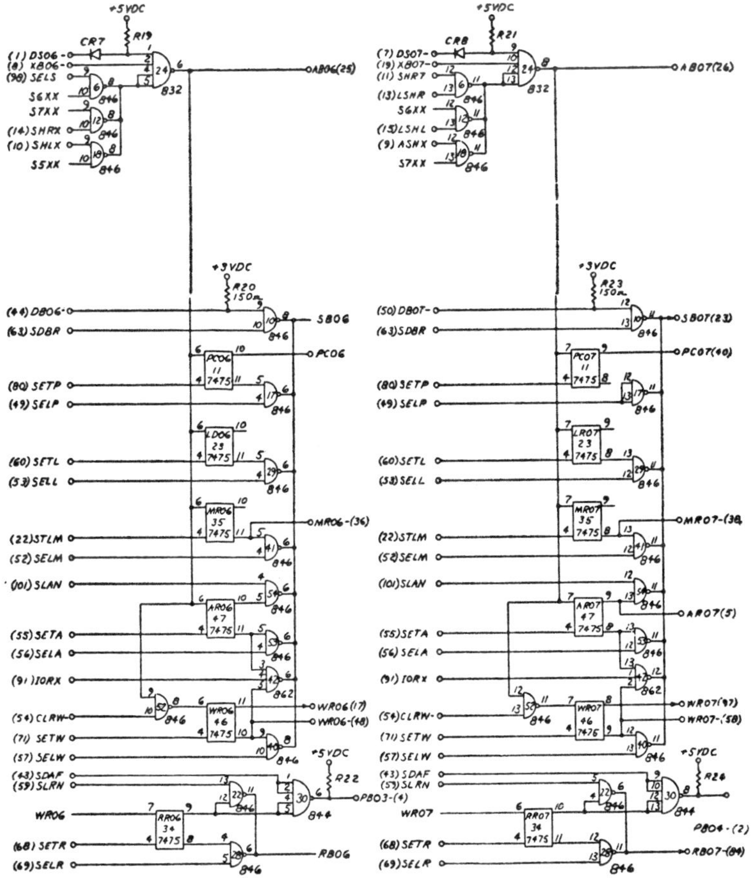

Fig. 16-4. Processor schematic, 7th and 8th bits.

For I-O instructions, RR contains the device address and function code portion of the instructions. The contents of RR is always seen on the P bus and the F bus in the I-O cable. The control signals associated with RR are: SELR, SLRN and SETR.

W register: The W register (WR) is the memory data word register that interfaces the processor to the memory. Any data to or from memory passes through the WR (except in the case of direct memory access). The WR is eight bits long (quad latch circuits) and is unconditionally cleared at the beginning of each memory cycle. The data from memory is read into the WR by "collector setting." That is, the reset side of the W flip-flop is pulled to ground by the sense amplifier if a 1 is detected in memory. This causes the set side of the flip-flop to go true, entering a 1 in the stage.

If data is to be stored into memory, it is transferred to W (replacing the data just read out of memory) just prior to the restore cycle. Thus the memory thinks it is always operating in a read-restore mode, but may be restoring completely new information. The WR is controlled by the following control signals: SELW, CLRW and SETW.

L register: The L register (LR) is the first half of the program sequencer. It holds the lower eight bits of the memory address where the next instruction word is to be obtained. Since LR is eight bits long and can specify 256 locations, it can be thought of as specifying the location within a 256-word page or sector of memory. For that reason it is sometimes referred to as the location counter.

The LR is incremented during the first phase of each instruction cycle, except for interrupts. The contents of LR is transferred to the M register just prior to starting an instruction cycle. LR is loaded from the A bus and the contents of LR is placed on the S bus through select gates. The signals associated with LR are: SELL and SETL.

P register: The P register (PR) is a 7-bit register that forms the upper half of the program sequencer. It is basically an extension to the LR. It holds the higher order portion of the memory address where the next instruction is obtained. Since LR specifies the word within a page of memory, the P register can be thought of as specifying which page. Thus it is sometimes referred to as the page counter.

The PR is incremented on an instruction cycle if the LR overflowed when it was incremented. Thus in very simplified form, the carry out of LR carries into PR. LR and PR constitute what is normally called the program counter in a computer. The contents of PR is normally transferred to the ME register just prior to an instruction cycle. There is a direct connection from the PR to the input gates to the ME register. The control signals associated with PR are: SELP, XPMX and SETP.

M register: The M register (MR) is an 8-bit register that holds the lower portion of the memory address while the memory cycle is in progress. It can thus be thought of as part of the memory address register. The MR is loaded from the A bus and the contents of MR can be selected onto the S bus through select gates.

The output of MR is wired directly to the memory modules. Only one side of each MR flip-flop is used since it is inverted in the memory addressing circuits to provide double-rail signals. The control signals associated with MR are: SELM and SETM.

M register extension: The M register extension (ME) is a 6-bit register that holds the upper portion of the memory address during a memory cycle. The ME and M registers together constitute a memory address register of 14-bits sufficient for 16,384 words of memory.

The ME receives information from PR, WR and IR, and is set to zero when addressing page 0. The output of each stage of ME is directly ORed to the memory similar to the M register. The control signals associated with ME are: STUM, XIMX, XPMX and RJIX.

Adder unit: The adder unit (AU) consists of two "quad adder" chips, each with four adder stages complete with serial carry and some associated gating. The two 8 bit words presented to the AU come from the S bus and the R bus. The R bus is the gated output of the R register.

An input carry allows adding 1 to the sum of R and S. The adder output is an 8-bit word which is the sum of R and S and a carry (if any). The output is gated through one level which allows shifting left or right if desired.

Since almost all instructions involve the AU, and not all instructions need additions, it is worthwhile to notice how data is handled for different cases.

Case 1. Normal addition of accumulator and operand: The contents of AR is selected onto the S bus and the contents of RR is selected onto the R bus. The carry into the adder is made zero. The sum is R and S which is selected onto the A bus through the SELS gate.

Case 2. Subtraction of R from A: AR is selected onto the S bus. The 1s complement of R is selected onto the R bus. By inputting a carry the 2s complement of R is created. The result is A - R.

Case 3. Transfer of A to W: A is selected onto the S bus. Nothing is selected onto the R bus, creating all 1s. Carry in is true. The result is A, which is strobed into WR.

Case 4. Increment A: The contents of A is placed on the S bus. Both R and $\bar{R}$ are selected to insure the R bus is all zeros. Carry in is true. The result is A +1.

Case 5. Decrement A: The contents of A is placed on the S bus. Neither R nor $\bar{R}$ is selected, leaving the R bus all 1s (-1). Carry in is false. The results is A-1.

Case 6. Shift A: The contents of A is placed on the S bus. Carry in is true. Neither R nor $\bar{R}$ is selected, leaving the R bus all 1s. SELS is false. SHR or SHL is true, depending on the desired direction of shift. Thus the contents of the A bus is equal to the S bus except shifted one place.

Transmission Buses

S bus: The S bus routes the output of the A, L, P, M, and W registers and the D bus to the adder unit. It is all ones when nothing is selected onto it. The A bus distributes the output of the adder unit (after the two levels of gating) to the A, L, P, M, and W registers and also to the D bus drivers and the console light drivers. It is ground when nothing is selected onto it.

R bus: The R bus routes the output of the R register to the adder unit. It is all 1s except when R or $\bar{R}$ is selected onto it.

The M and W buses are described in the memory section and the D bus is described in the I-O sections. (Fig. 16-5 shows the processor timing circuits.)

CONTROL

The control logic of the processor provides the timing, decoding, and sequencing required for the instructions. The basic timing element is the cycle, the time required for the memory to execute a full read-restore cycle. The cycle is broken into four equal phases of 2.0 microseconds. The subphase timing pulses are derived from the count-down timing chain driven by the 2.0-MHz crystal oscillator. Fig. 16-14 shows the primary timing signals in the processor and Figs. 16-6 and 16-7 the processor control circuits.

There are six types of cycles in three groups. The first we consider are the instruction cycles, ICY1 and ICY2. When the memory cycle is being used to retrieve an instruction, the cycle is an ICY1 or ICY2, depending on whether the first or second word of an instruction is being recalled, respectively.

ICY1 is set at the same time the memory cycle is started to retrieve the first instruction word. Halfway through the cycle, the instruction word is transferred from WR to IR (at T2). If the first word indicates that the instruction is a double-word, then ICY2 is set at the same time the next memory cycle is started. Halfway through ICY2, WR is transferred to RR, completing the instruction formation.

The second type of cycles are the operand cycles, OCY1 and OCY2. When the memory is referenced for data (data is stored into memory or retrieved from memory) the memory cycle is referred to as an operand cycle. For example, during the execution of an add instruction, the operand in memory must be obtained and added to the contents of the accumulator. When the memory cycle is started to recall the operand, the OCY1 flip-flop is set. Halfway through the cycle, the operand is available in the W register instructions during block I-O instructions. OCY2 occurs only during the jump and save instruction, when the contents of the P register is stored in memory.

The final type to be considered are the address cycles, ACY1 and ACY2. When the indirect addressing mode is used with memory reference instruction, the indirect address is obtained from two memory locations. ACY1 is set at the beginning of the first indirect cycle to indicate that the information being obtained is the first part of an address. ACY1 occurs during the block I-O instructions also. The input or output pointer is read from memory, incremented, and replaced during ACY1. ACY2 can occur only during memory reference instructions.

Instruction Addressing

In the 208 and 808 an instruction can make reference to two types of addresses: direct address and indirect address.

Direct Address: The direct address is the address specified by the second word of a double-word instruction. The A field specifies the location within a page and the page is

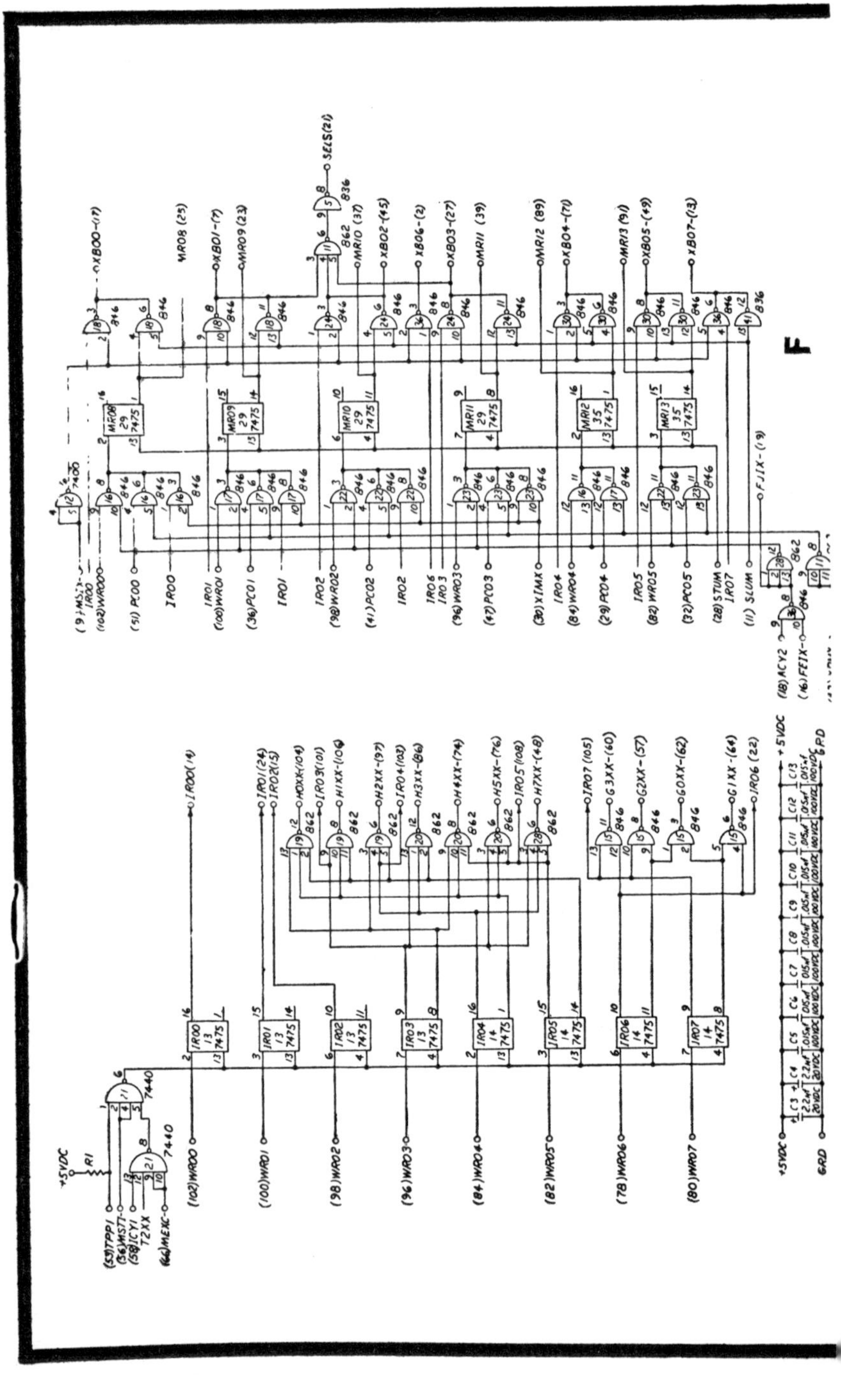

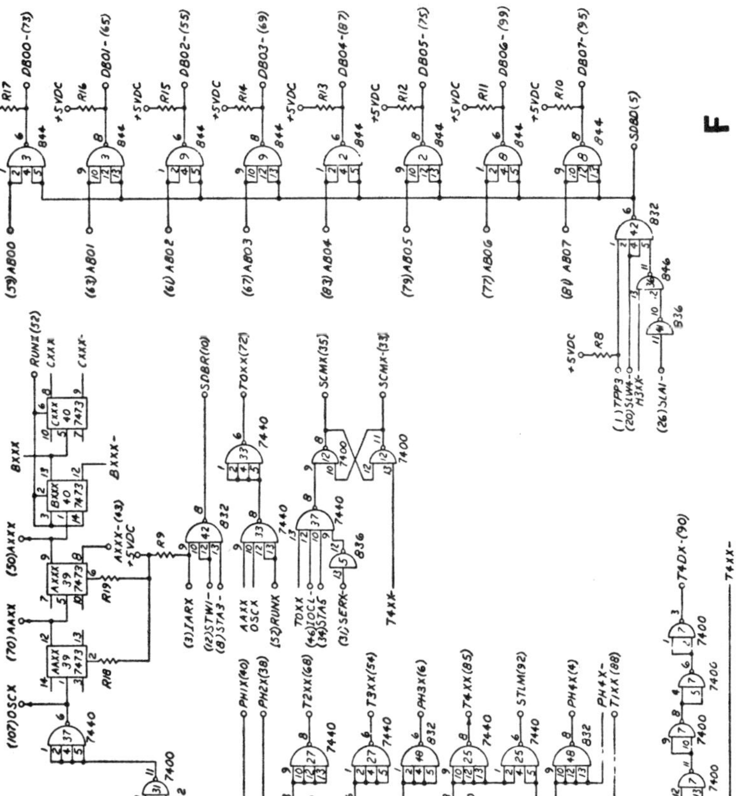

Fig. 16-5. Processor timing circuits.

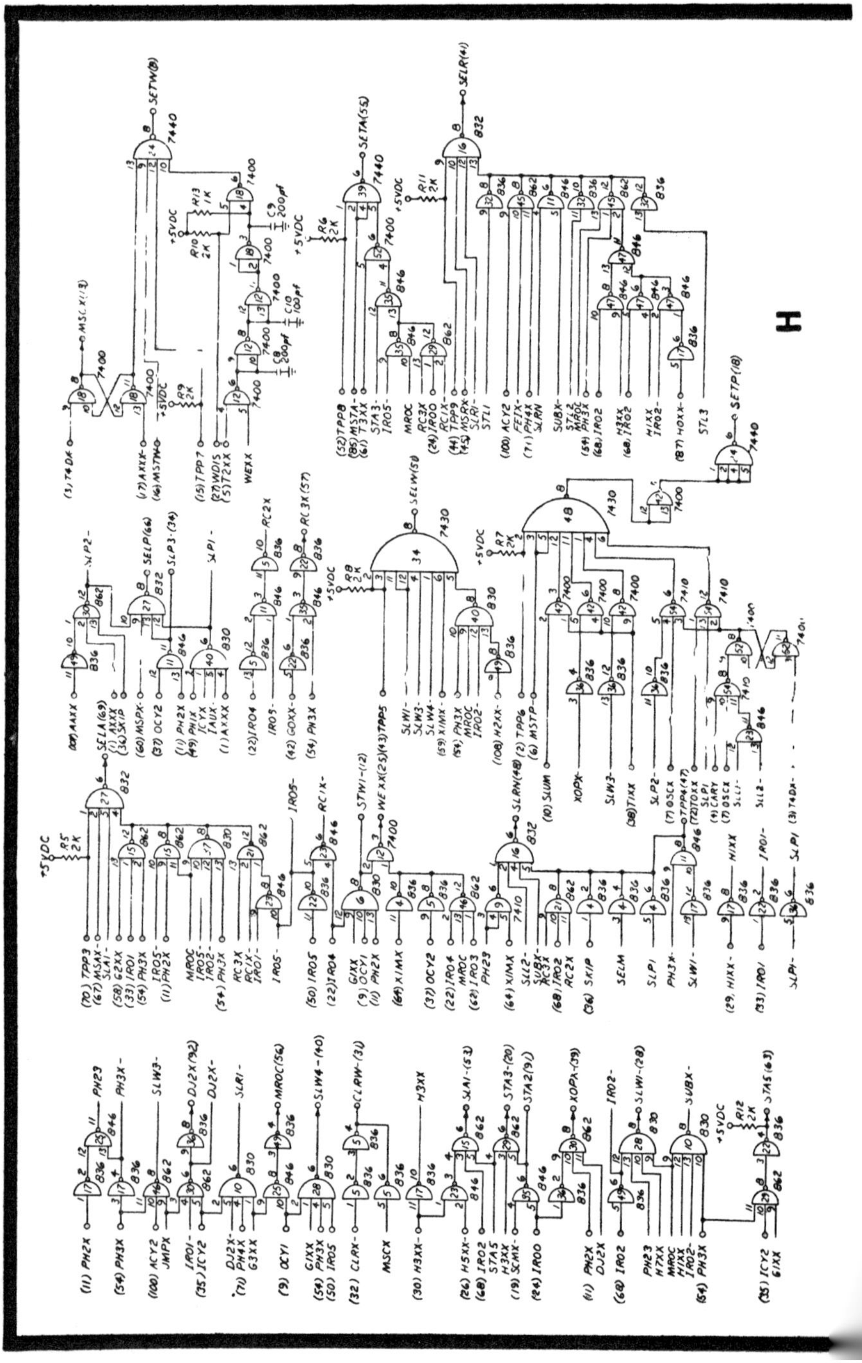
H

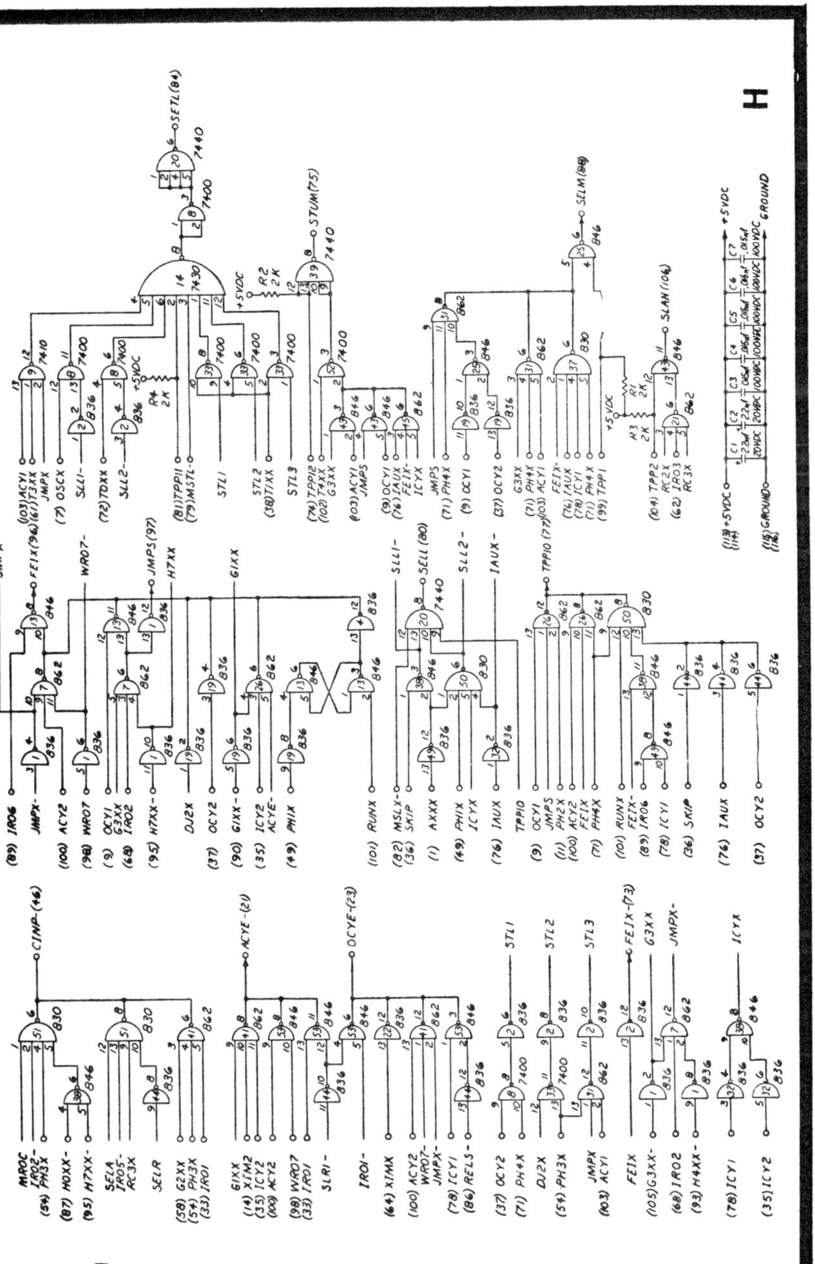

Fig. 16-6. Schematic of the processor control no. 1.

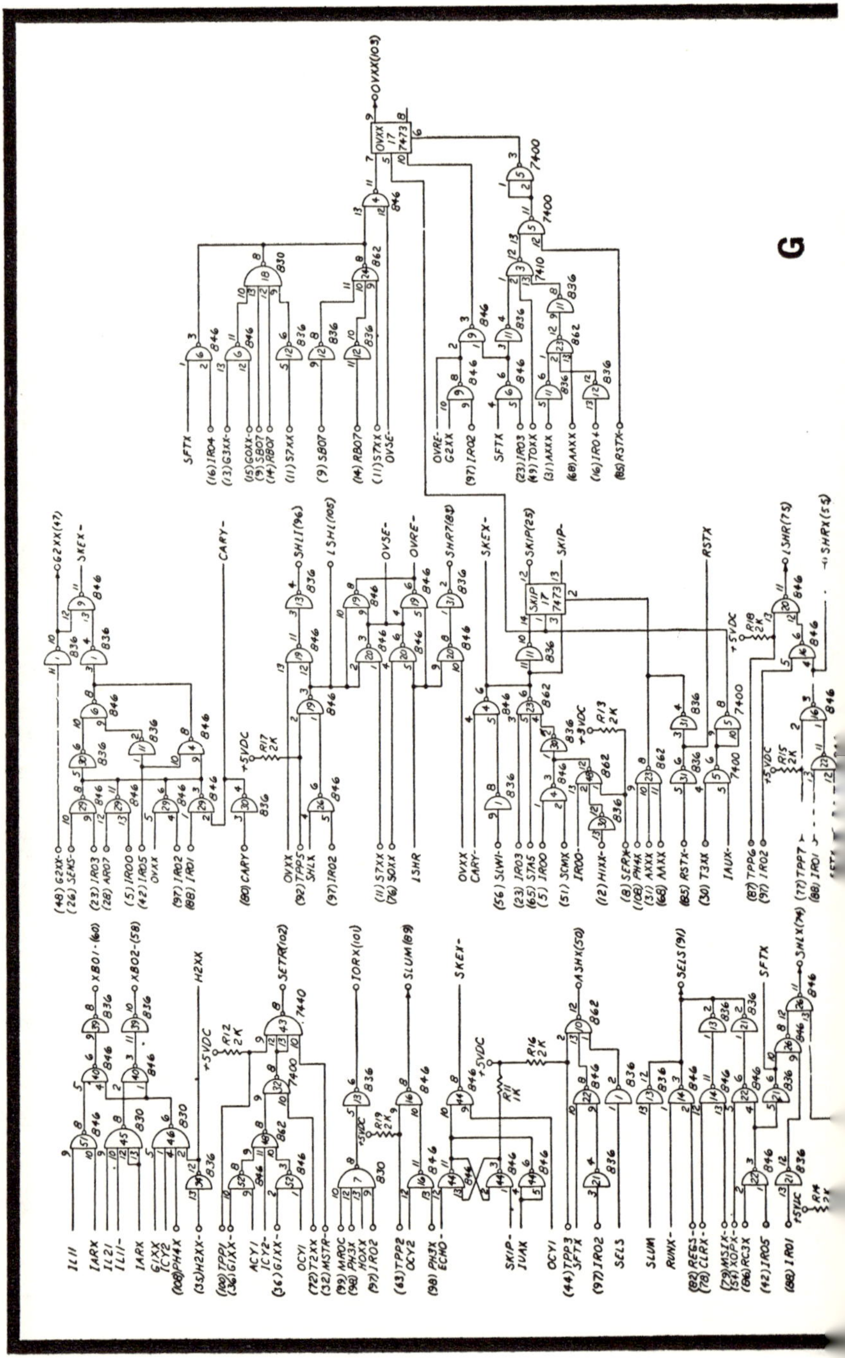
G

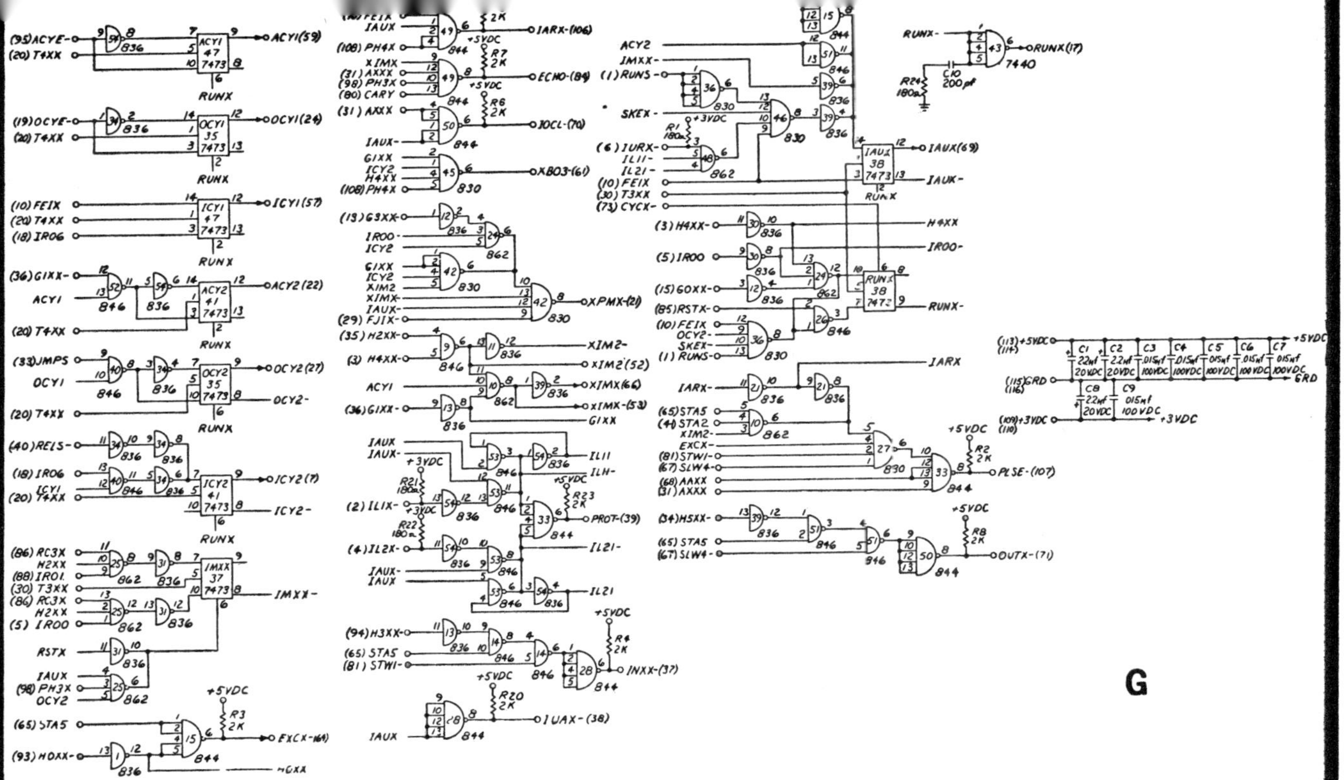

Fig. 16-7. Schematic of the processor control no. 2.

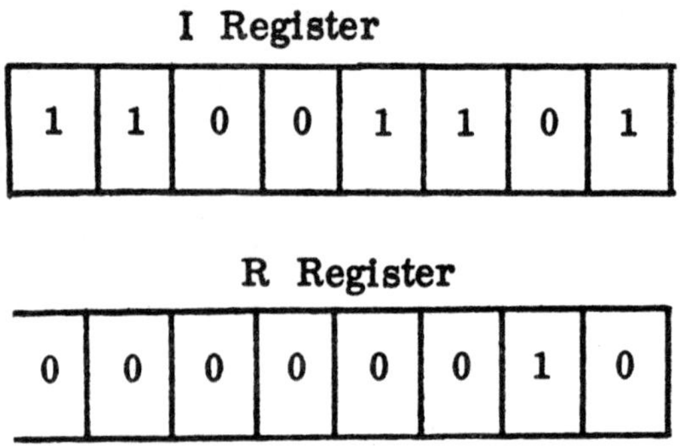

Fig. 16-8. Example of direct addressing.

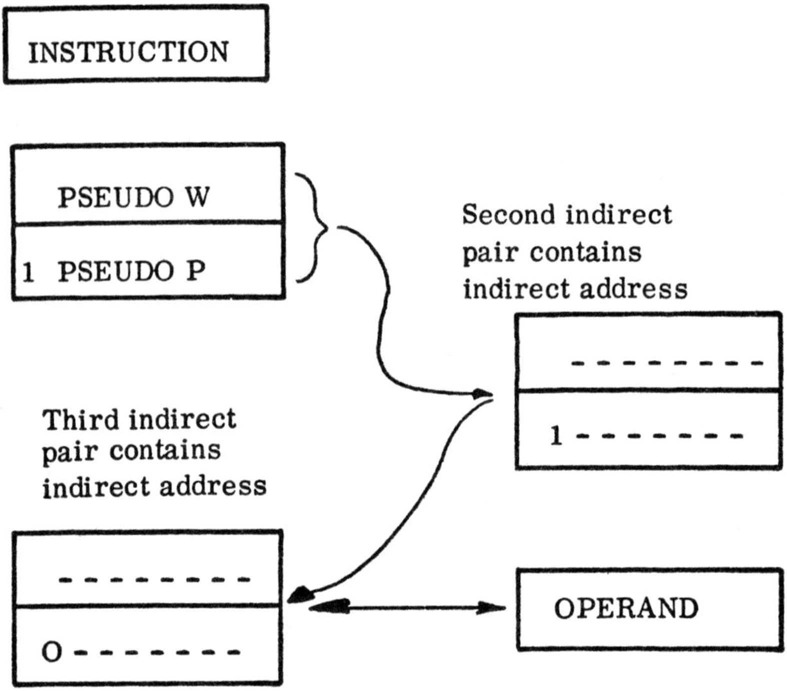

Fig. 16-9. Example of multi-level indirect addressing.

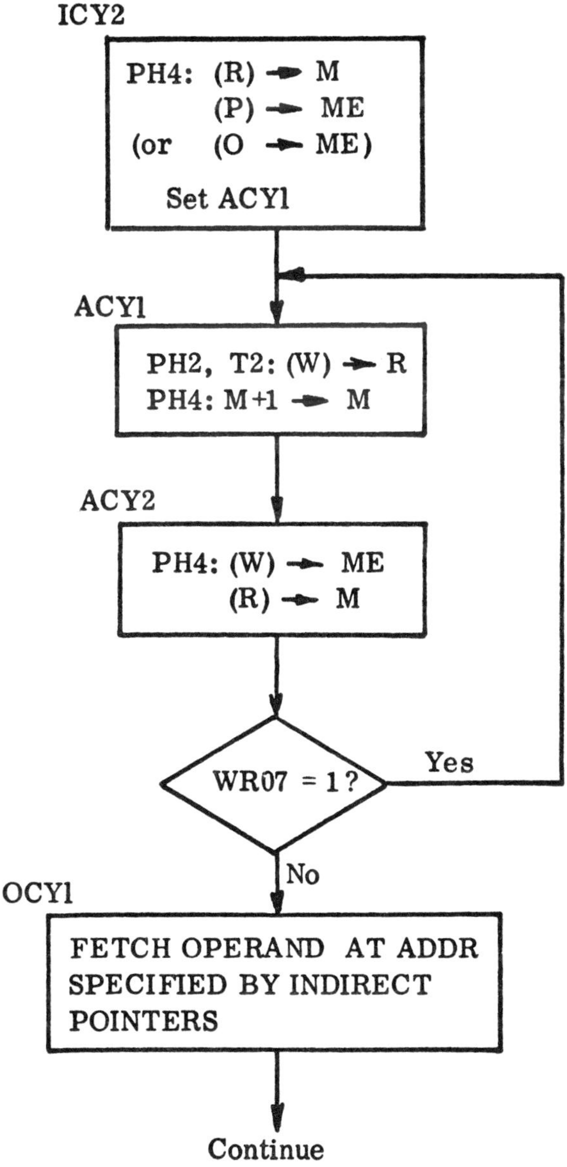

Fig. 16-10. Indirect addressing.

specified by a page tag. The page is either the zero page (P equals 0) or the current page (P equals 1). The address tag specifies either direct (A equals 0) or indirect (A equals 1) addressing. Direct addressing allows 512 memory locations to be reached directly. For example, the LDA instruction shown in Fig. 16-8 loads the contents of memory location 002 into the A register.

Indirect addressing (refer to Fig. 16-10). To reach locations outside this 512 word area, indirect addressing is used. This is accomplished by storing in two consecutive memory locations the location and page of the operand. The contents of the first word defines the location within a page and the contents of the second word defines which page. By setting the indirect bit in a memory reference instruction, the computer will access the location specified by the A field and page designator. The contents of that location is placed in the R register and the next memory location is accessed to obtain the page number. This is transferred to ME while R is transferred to M and the operand cycle started.

Multi-level indirect addressing: In some cases, it is not the operand address that is stored in the two memory words by the address of the operand address. To determine the difference, the computer examines the most significant bit of the second word (the page number). If that bit is a 1, then the contents of the two memory words is an address of an address rather than an address of an operand, and another level of indirect addressing is started in which another pair of memory locations is examined. See Fig. 16-9. The procedure for obtaining the indirect addresses is as follows:

1. During PH4 of ICY2, the contents of R (the A field) is transferred to M while ME is set to zero or is loaded with the contents of P. At T4, ACY1 is set and the memory cycles.

2. The first indirect word is transferred from W to R at T2 where it is held temporarily. The previous contents of R is lost.

3. During PH4 of ACY1, the contents of M is incremented to allow accessing memory for the next indirect pointer. M is not supposed to overflow since there is no provision for incrementing ME; thus the two indirect locations must always be in the same page. At the end of PH4, after M has been routed through the adder and incremented, ACY2 is set with PH4 and the memory cycled to get the second indirect pointer.

4. During PH4 of ACY2, the contents of R is transferred to M and the contents of W is transferred to ME. If WRO7 is true, indicating that another level of indirect addressing is required, then ACY1 is enabled. Otherwise, OCY1 is enabled. At T4, the memory is cycled again to retrieve operand or another indirect address.

MEMORY

Inhibit Driver: There are two inputs to the inhibit driver: Data input which is positive true and comes from the W register in the processor, and the WZSX strobe which comes from the inhibit strobe circuit. The data input acts as an enable to the driver to allow the driver to respond to the WZSX strobe signal. (See Fig. 16-11.)

Driver switch circuits: The driver-switch strobe circuits are used to strobe the switches and drivers in the XY drive electronics in the memory. The operation of the strobe circuit is identical to the inhibit strobe circuit except that +12v is used. There are four strobe circuits:

Read switch strobe, RSSX
Read driver strobe, RDSX
Write switch strobe, WSSX
Write driver strobe, WDSX

The strobe circuits pulse the X and Y drivers and switches during the read-restore memory cycle.

Fig. 16-12 shows the typical driver-switch circuit. It is identical for X and Y. The driver portion supplies current from a positive source (Y drive) and the switch sinks the current to -12v. The driver and switch in the same circuit are never turned on at the same time. Instead the driver on one side of the stack drives into a switch on the other side of the stack.

The operation of driving the stack is as follows: During read time, one driver-switch pair on each side of the stack is enabled. The driver on the left side is pulsed by RDSX and the switch on the right side is pulsed by RSSX. Thus current flows from the driver through the stack to the switch. During the write time, the circuits reverse functions to drive current back through the same stack line in the opposite direction. The driver is pulsed by WDSX and the switch is pulsed by WSSX. The outputs of the timing circuitry go to the following places:

A. RDXX-, WDXX-, RSXX-, WSXX-, go to the data board (Fig. 16-24) where they are amplified, inverted and routed to the driver-switch board.

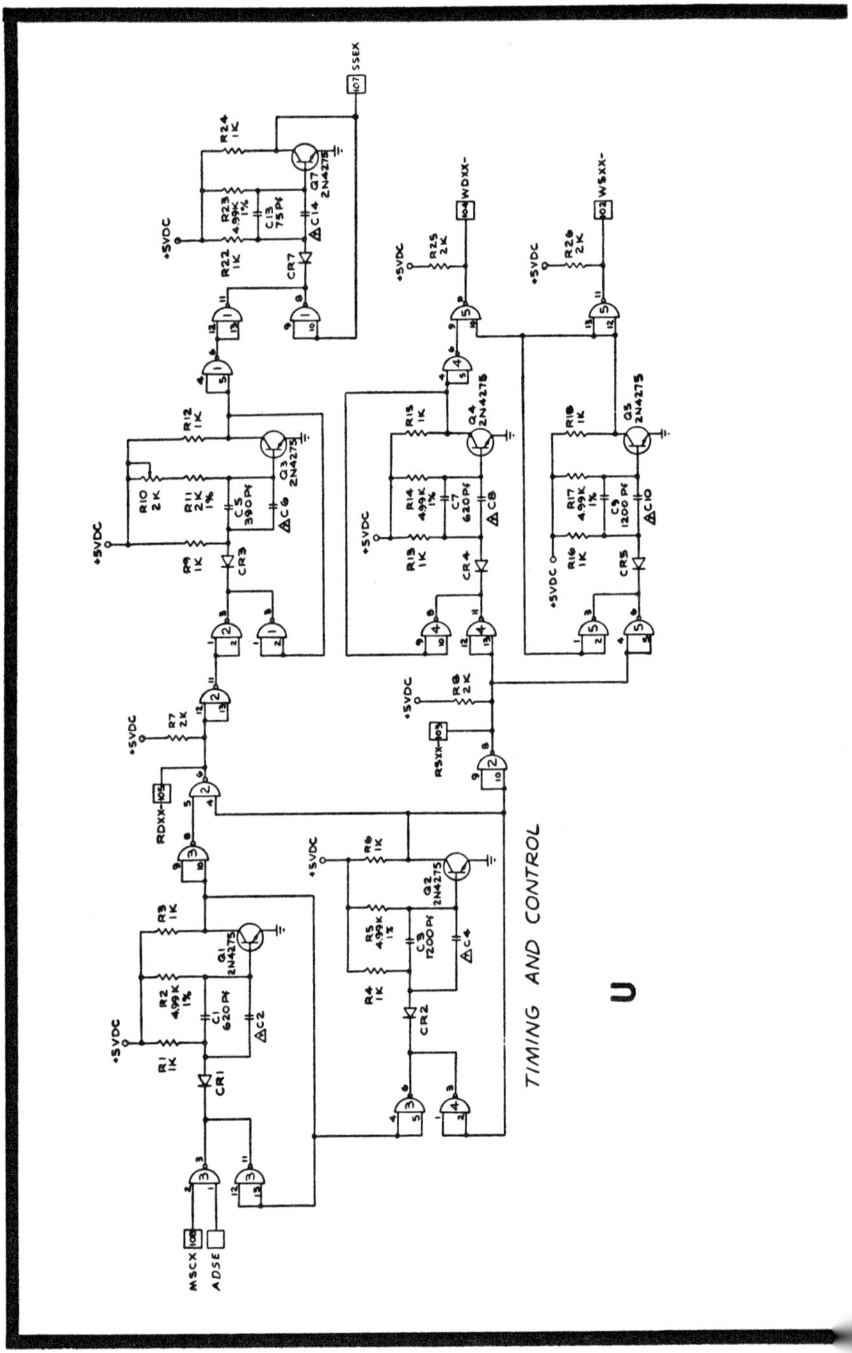
SSEX
107
R24 1K
Q7 2N4275
+5VDC
R23 4.99K 1%
C13 75Pf
C14
R22 1K
CR7
WDXX-
104
R25 2K
WSXX-
102
R26 2K
R12 1K
Q3 2N4275
R10 2K
R11 2K 1%
C5 390Pf
C6
R9 1K
CR3
R15 1K
Q4 2N4275
R14 4.99K 1%
C7 620Pf
C8
R13 1K
CR4
R18 1K
Q5 2N4275
R17 4.99K 1%
C9 1200 Pf
C10
R16 1K
CR5
R7 2K
R8 2K
RSXX-103
RDXX-105
R6 1K
Q2 2N4275
R5 4.99K 1%
C3 1200Pf
C4
R4 1K
CR2
R3 1K
Q1 2N4275
R2 4.99K 1%
C1 620Pf
C2
R1 1K
CR1
MSCX
100
ADSE
TIMING AND CONTROL
U

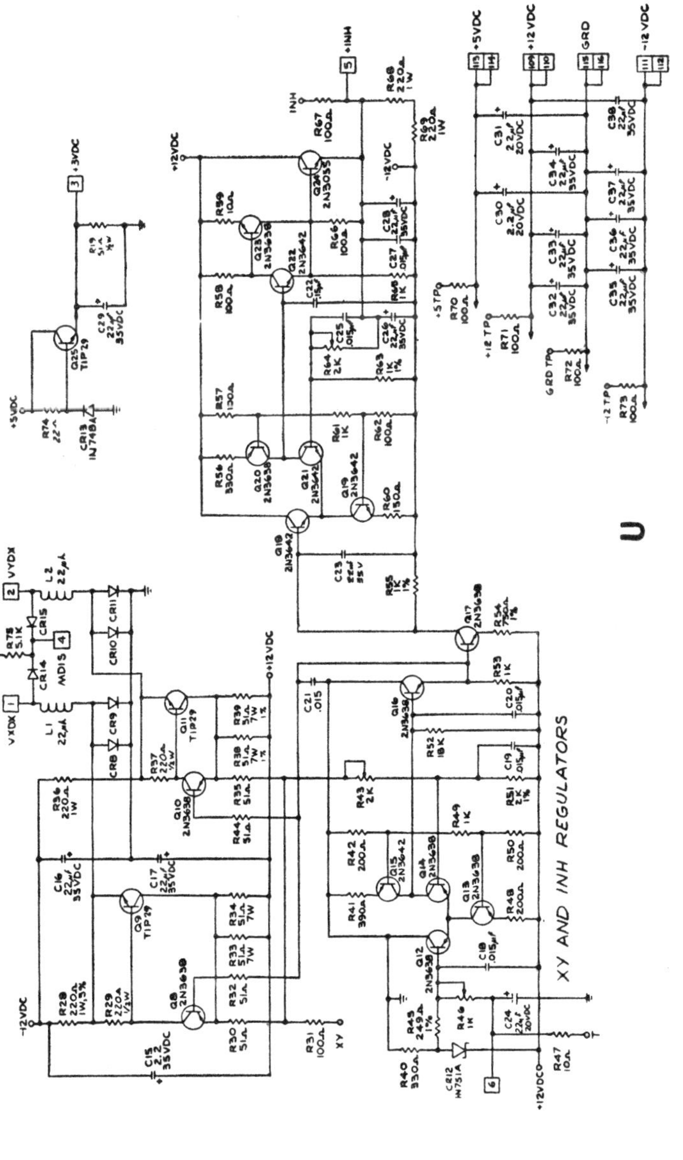

Fig. 16-11. Memory regulator schematic.

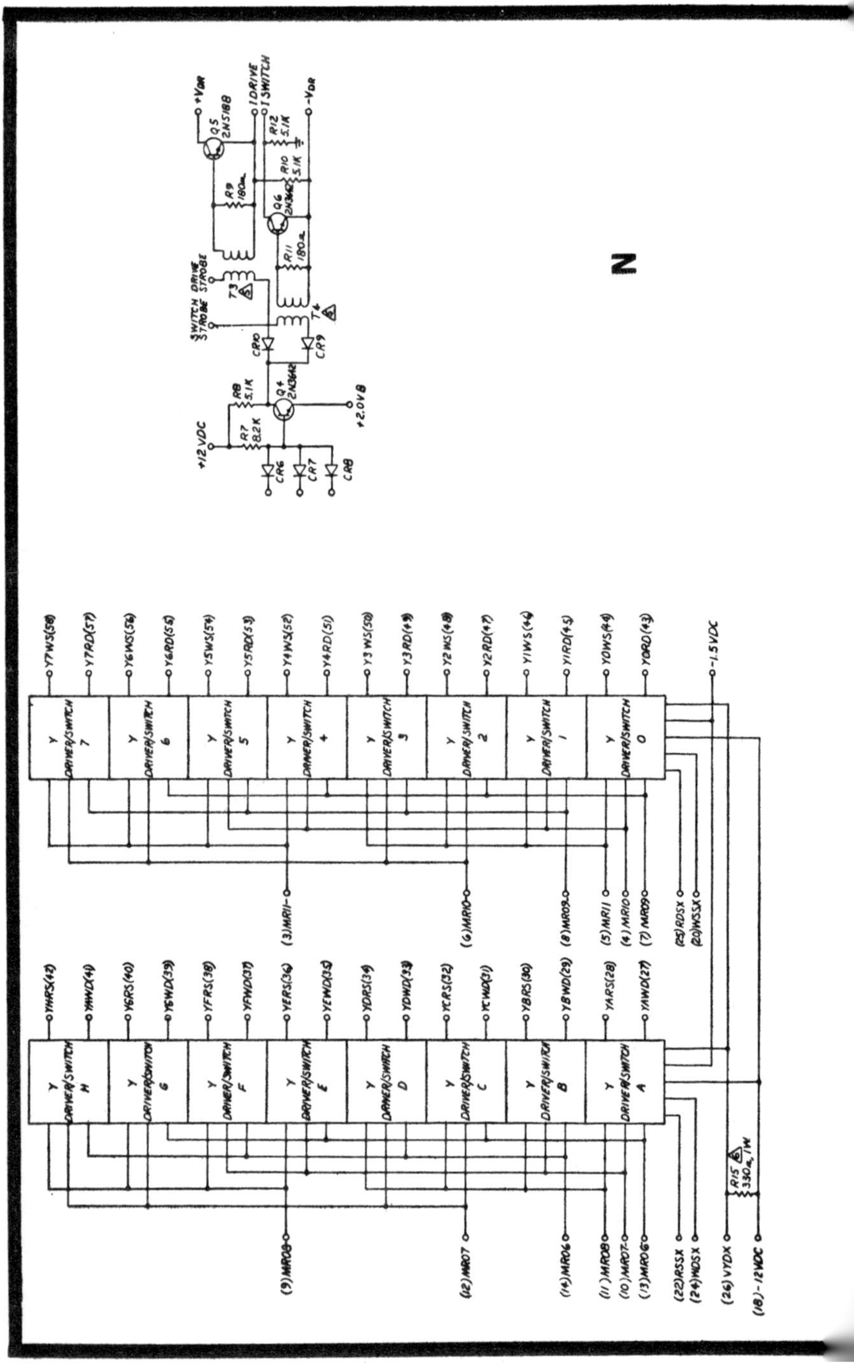

+VDR
Q5 2N5188
I DRIVE
I SWITCH
R12 5.1K
-VDR
R9 180Ω
R10 5.1K
Q6 2N3642
R11 180Ω
SWITCH DRIVE STROBE
SWITCH STROBE
T3
T4
CR10
CR9
R8 5.1K
R7 8.2K
Q4 2N3642
+2.0VB
+12VDC
CR6
CR7
CR8
N
Y DRIVER/SWITCH 7
Y DRIVER/SWITCH 6
Y DRIVER/SWITCH 5
Y DRIVER/SWITCH 4
Y DRIVER/SWITCH 3
Y DRIVER/SWITCH 2
Y DRIVER/SWITCH 1
Y DRIVER/SWITCH 0
Y7WS(58)
Y7RD(57)
Y6WS(56)
Y6RD(55)
Y5WS(54)
Y5RD(53)
Y4WS(52)
Y4RD(51)
Y3WS(50)
Y3RD(49)
Y2WS(48)
Y2RD(47)
Y1WS(46)
Y1RD(45)
Y0WS(44)
Y0RD(43)
-1.5VDC
(3)MR11
(6)MR10
(8)MR09
(5)MR11
(4)MR10
(7)MR09
(25)RDSX
(20)WSSX
Y DRIVER/SWITCH H
Y DRIVER/SWITCH G
Y DRIVER/SWITCH F
Y DRIVER/SWITCH E
Y DRIVER/SWITCH D
Y DRIVER/SWITCH C
Y DRIVER/SWITCH B
Y DRIVER/SWITCH A
YHRS(42)
YHWD(41)
YGRS(40)
YGWD(39)
YFRS(38)
YFWD(37)
YERS(36)
YEWD(35)
YDRS(34)
YDWD(33)
YCRS(32)
YCWD(31)
YBRS(30)
YBWD(29)
YARS(28)
YAWD(27)
(9)MR08
(12)MR07
(14)MR06
(11)MR08
(10)MR07
(13)MR06
(22)RSSX
(24)WDSX
(26)VYDX
(18)-12VDC
R15 330Ω 1W

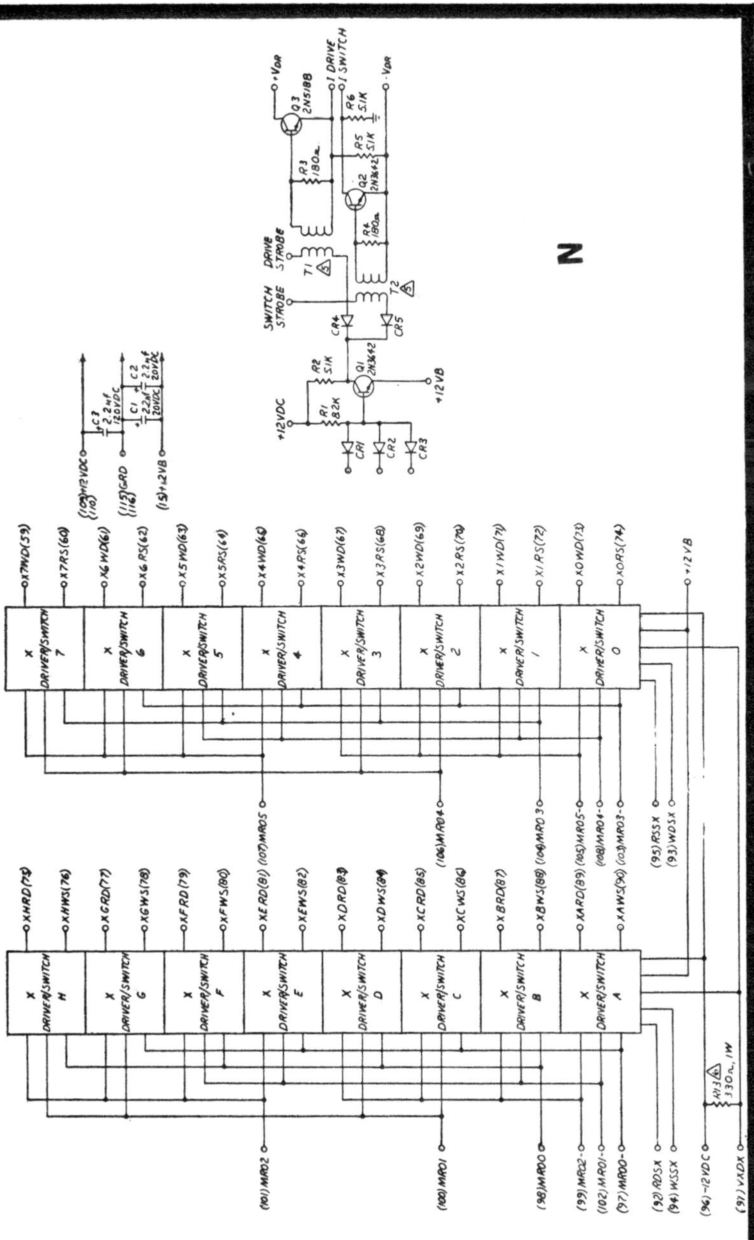

Fig. 16-12. Schematic of the driver-switch circuits.

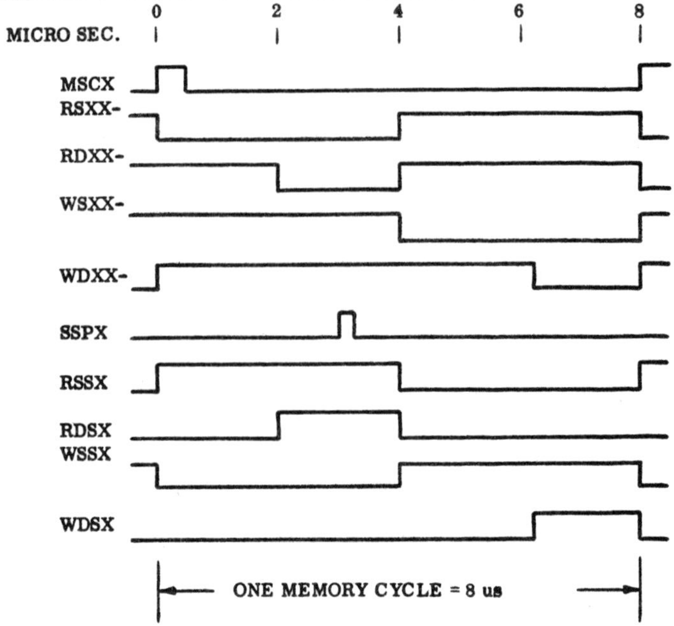

Fig. 16-13. Memory timing diagram.

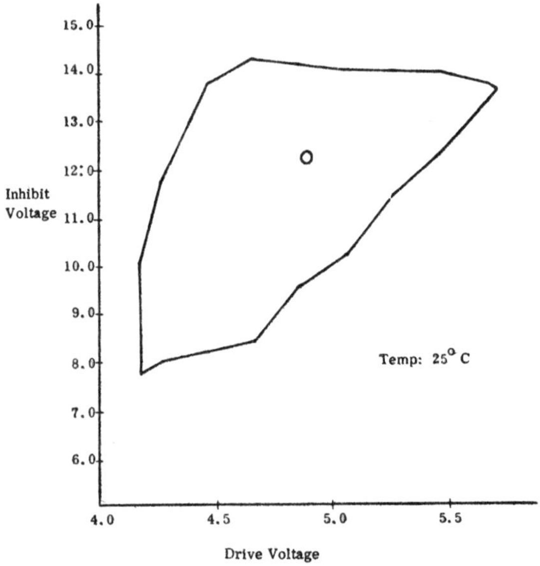

Fig. 16-14. Typical "shmoo" diagram.

Fig. 16-15. RSXX pulse viewed with a 1 microsec per div. sweep, 2v per div. Top pulse is the master clock start (MSCX).

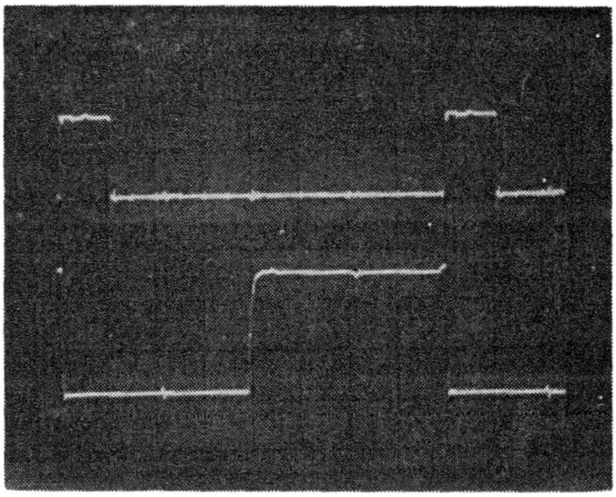

Fig. 16-16. RDXX pulse (bottom) and MSCX. 1 microsec per div. and 2v.

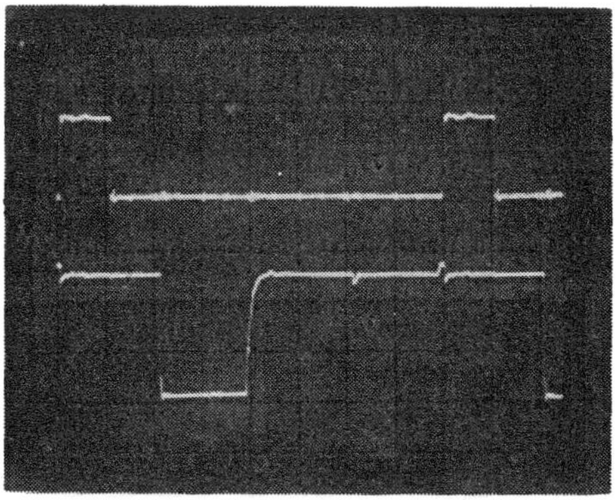

Fig. 16-17. WDXX pulse (bottom) and MSCX. 1 microsec per div. and 2v.

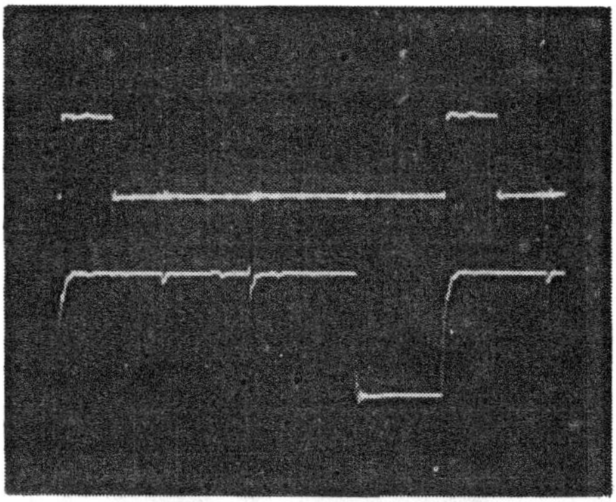

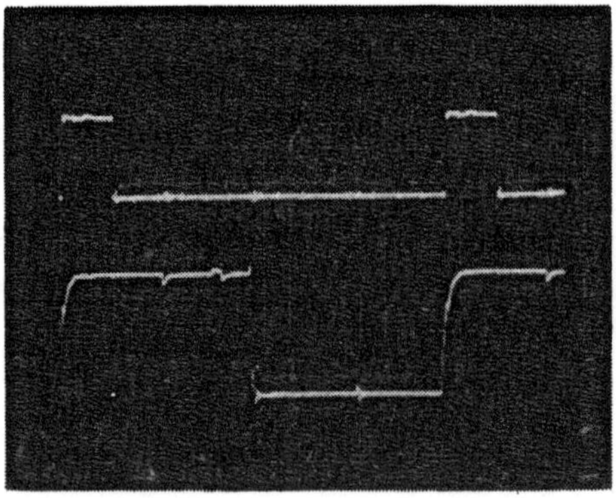

Fig. 16-18. WSXX pulse (bottom) and MSCX. 1 microsec per div. and 2v.

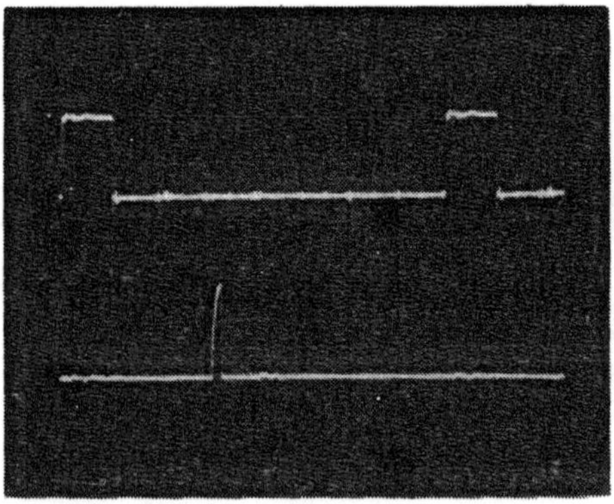

Fig. 16-19. SSPX pulse (bottom) and MSCX. 1 microsec per div. and 2v.

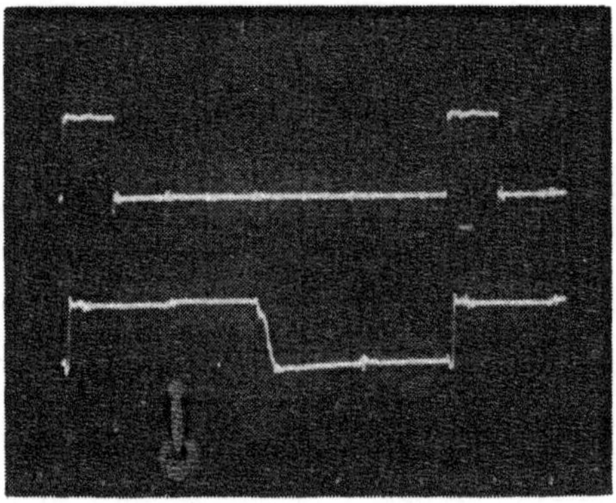

Fig. 16-20. RSSX pulse (bottom) and MSCX. 1 microsec div. and 2v.

Fig. 16-21. RDSX pulse (bottom) and MSCX. 1 microsec per div. and 2v.

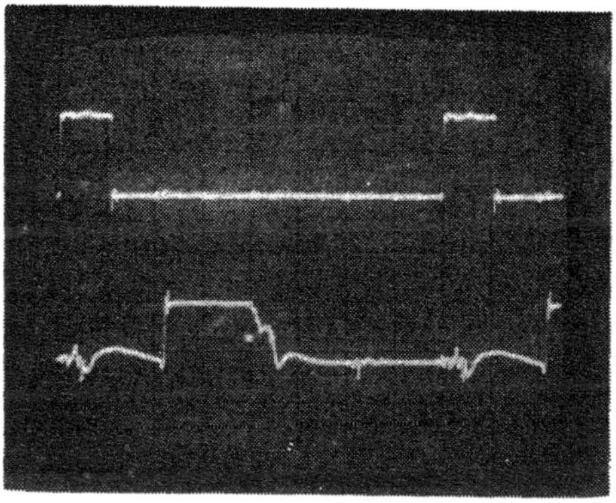

Fig. 16-22. WSSX pulse (bottom) and MSCX. 1 microsec per div. and 2v.

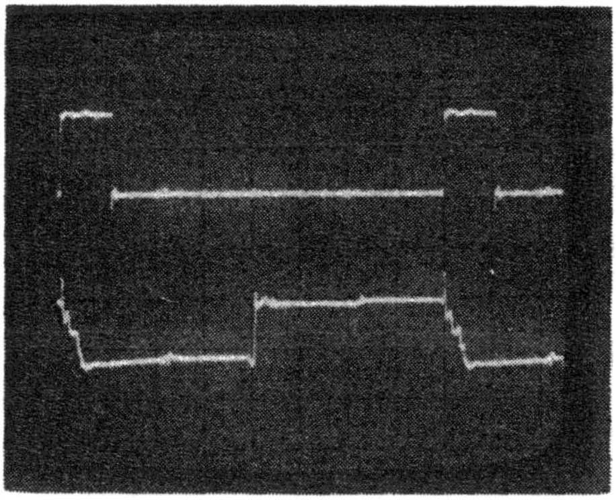

Fig. 16-23. WDSX pulse (bottom) and MSCX. 1 microsec per div. and 2v.

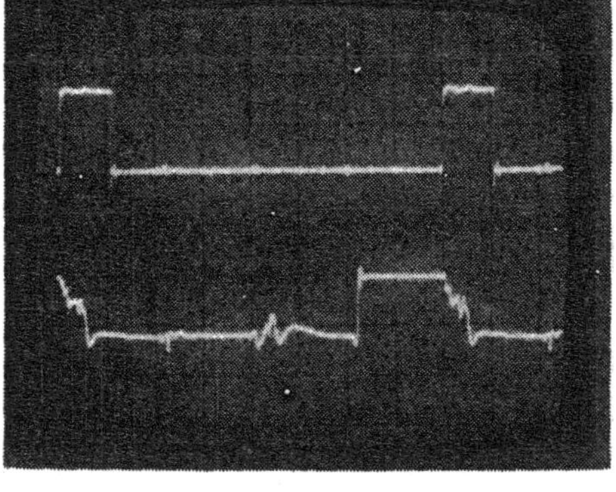

B. SSEX is the sense amplifier strobe and is routed to the data board.

C. ISSX is not used.

The 3-volt clamp voltage for the I-O cable is also generated on the regulator board by a zener diode and transistor. The timing chain for the memory is a series of one-shots formed by delay networks with feedback. The timing sequence is shown in Fig. 16-13. A typical shmoo curve is shown in Fig. 16-14. Figs. 16-15 through 16-23 show the various timing signals (bottom waveforms) and the master clock start (top waveform). All waveforms were taken on a Hewlett-Packard Model 180 oscilloscope.

The D-S circuits are enabled by address lines coming from the processor. The 3-diode AND gate enables Q1 which when conducting provides a path for current through the pulse transformers T1 and T2 (Fig. 16-12).

There are 64 X drive lines and 64 Y drive lines in a 4096-bit memory plane. The decoding diodes on the stack connect these 64 lines to eight drivers and eight switches on each side of the place. Thus an 8x8 matrix is created. Each driver can drive into eight switches, and each switch can service eight drivers.

Memory regulator board: The regulator board (Fig. 16-11) contains circuitry to regulate the XY drive and inhibit current to the memory, and contains the timing circuitry to control the current pulses, sense amplifier strobe, and inhibit strobes. The current regulator circuits are a controlled differential amplifier whose output can be adjusted by R46 and can also be changed by the resistance of thermistor RT1. The thermistor resistance decreases with temperature, causing the output currents to the memory to decrease. The rate of decrease of current per unit decrease of RT1's resistance is controlled by R46. The larger the value of R46, the less effect RT1 has. The output current level for the X and Y drive currents is determined by R43. The current range is 170 to 220 ma under normal operating conditions. The inhibit current regulator is slaved to the XY regulator. The offset is determined by R64. After the ratio of XY to inhibit currents has been set by R64, the inhibit current will track XY as the temperature changes.

Input-output devices

The following I-O devices are available on the 808 and 208:

1. 33 teletype option
2. High-speed reader option
3. High-speed punch option

Teletype interface: The teletype interface performs parallel-to-serial conversion when outputting to the TTY and serial-to-parallel conversion when inputting from the TTY. All data transmission between the computer and the TTY interface is parallel. The interface consists of the following major portions (Fig. 16-25):

A. **Buffer-shift register:** This register is loaded in parallel by the computer and the contents can be transferred in parallel to the computer. After data is loaded into the register by the computer, it is serially shifted out to the TTY. When the TTY is transmitting data, it is serially shifted into the register. Notice that the register is used for both input and output.

B. **Divide by 11 counter:** This counter is a 4-stage ripple counter with feedback to cause divide-by-11. It is used to measure the 100 ms period required for each character transmitted to or from the TTY. The counter stages are labeled BC01 through BC04 (Fig. 16-26). The input to the counter is from a flip-flop which divides the oscillator output by 2.

C. **Oscillator:** A gated multivibrator is used to synchronize the shifting operations. The oscillator is turned on by the write flip-flop, which is automatically set by an output command and by the read flip-flop, which is set by a space from the TTY if the read select flip-flop (RSEL) is on. The oscillator is turned off at the end of the 100 millisecond period by BC04, resetting either write or read (depending upon which is on). The positive-going edges of the oscillator output (Q2) are used to form narrow pulses which trigger flip-flop 24. The first pulse is not allowed to trigger 24-1. The flip-flop 24-5 disables 24-1 until the first pulse has occurred. This is required since the output of the oscillator goes high as soon as the oscillator is enabled.

D. **Shift pulse generator:** When outputting data to the TTY, shift pulses are required at the beginning of each bit time. When inputting from the TTY, shift pulses are required in the middle of each bit time. The phase shift is accomplished by using the set output of flip-flop 24-1 to form the read shift and the reset output to form the write shift. In both cases the positive-going edge of the flip-flop output is used to form a narrow (200 ns) pulse, which is gated with write or RSEL.

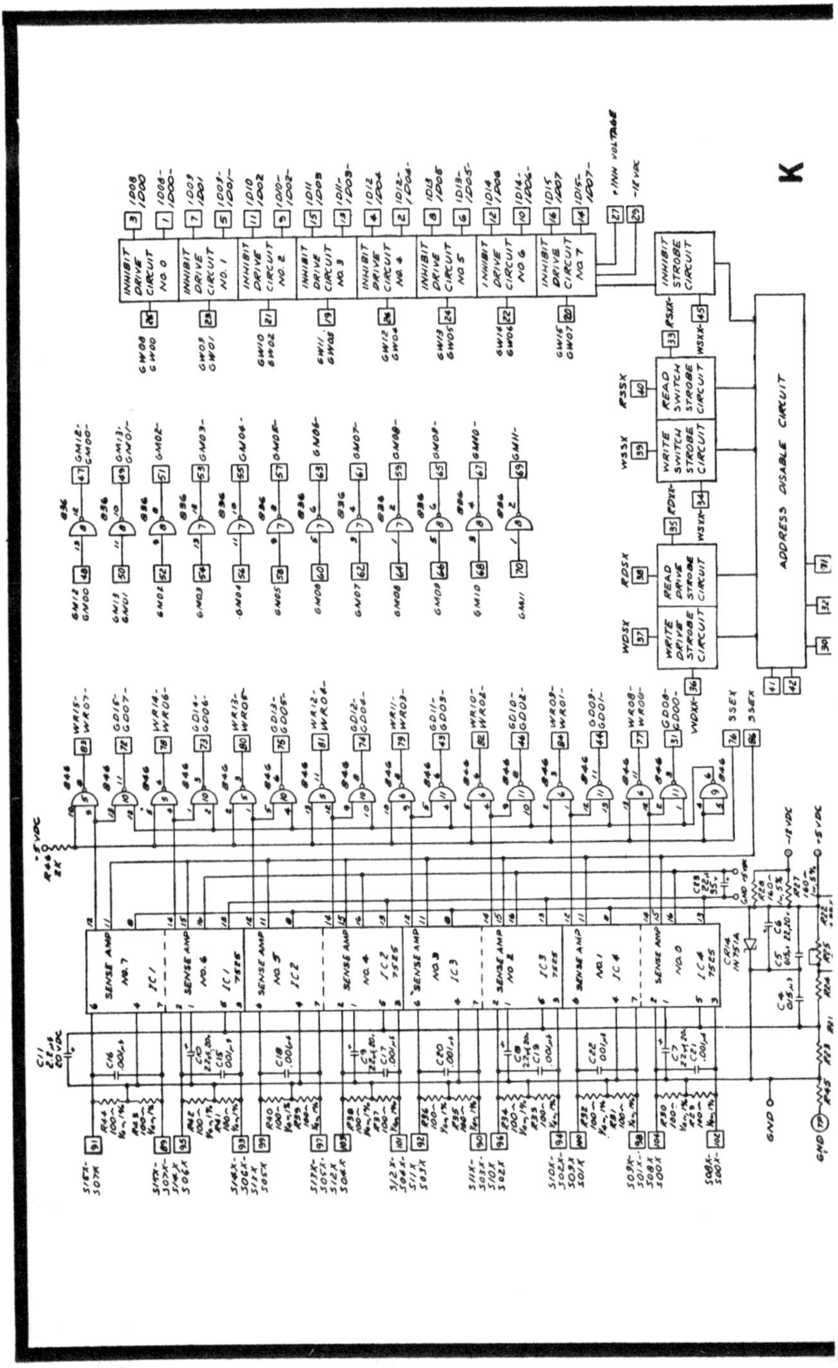
K
INHIBIT DRIVE CIRCUIT NO. 0
INHIBIT DRIVE CIRCUIT NO. 1
INHIBIT DRIVE CIRCUIT NO. 2
INHIBIT DRIVE CIRCUIT NO. 3
INHIBIT DRIVE CIRCUIT NO. 4
INHIBIT DRIVE CIRCUIT NO. 5
INHIBIT DRIVE CIRCUIT NO. 6
INHIBIT DRIVE CIRCUIT NO. 7
INHIBIT STROBE CIRCUIT
WRITE DRIVE STROBE CIRCUIT
READ DRIVE STROBE CIRCUIT
WRITE SWITCH STROBE CIRCUIT
READ SWITCH STROBE CIRCUIT
ADDRESS DISABLE CIRCUIT
+INH VOLTAGE
-12 VDC
+5 VDC
GND

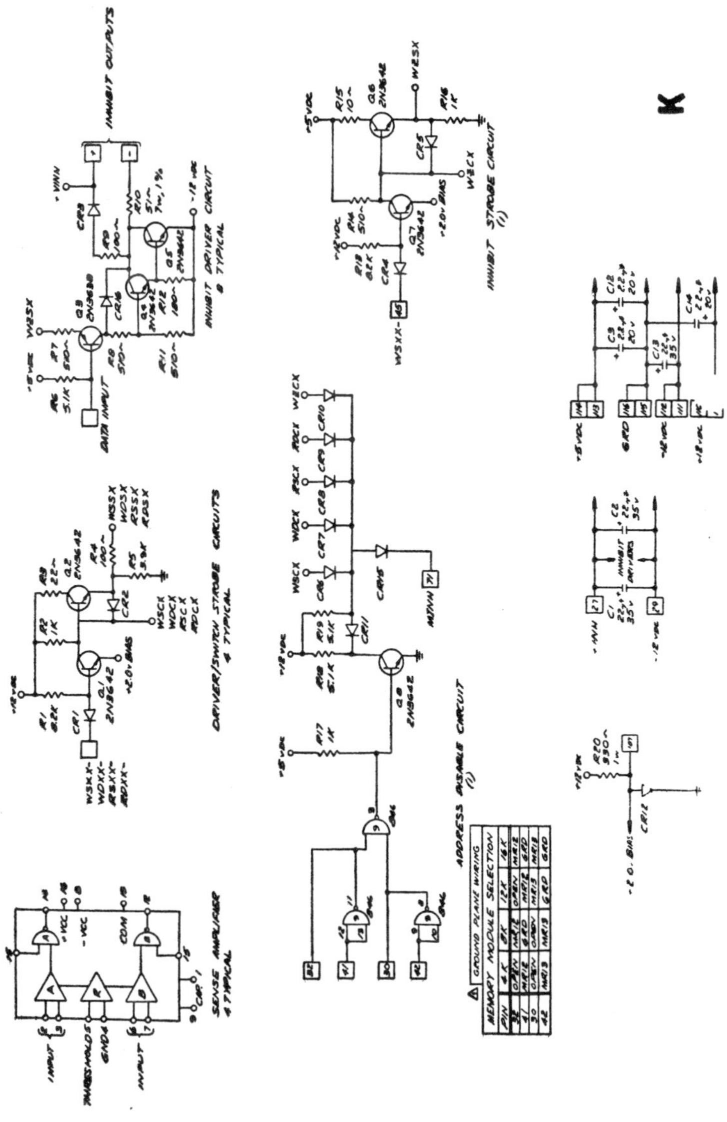

Fig. 16-24. Schematic memory data board.

Fig. 16-25. Teletype controller circuit board.

E. Control flip-flops: There are six flip-flops used for control and status:

Buffer ready (BUFR) is used to indicate when the interface is ready to receive or transmit data to the computer. It is reset by an input or output command and by external control commands 71, 72, and 73. It is set by the external control command 74 (initialize) and by BC04.

Read Select (RSEL) is set when the computer selects keyboard, step read on continuous read. When set, RSEL allows data to be shifted from the TTY into the shift register. It is reset by the initialize commande (74) and by an output to the interface (which implies write).

Write (WRTE) is set on an output command and is reset by BC04 at the end of the 100 ms period. When set, it enables the oscillator and gates the oscillator to the proper path for generation of write shift pulses. It is also reset by the initialize command.

Read is set by a space received from the TTY (if RSEL is on). (The first bit of the TTY is always a space which is used as a synchronizing bit.) When set it enables the oscillator. It is reset by BC04 at the end of the 100 ms period.

Step is set by the EXC 72 command and is reset about 20 ms later by feedback from a delay network. When set, it causes relay K3 to close, completing the current loop in the reader solenoid circuit, causing the TTY reader to read the character under the read station and advance the tape one position. (The switch on the TTY reader must be in the run position for this sequence, since K3 and the switch are in series with the solenoid.

Continuous (CONT) is a flip-flop that is set to cause the TTY reader to run continuously. It is set by EXC 73 and reset by EXC 77 and the initialize command.

F. Sense logic: Three functions in the TTY interface may be sensed by the computer: buffer ready, word transfer mask on, and oscillator enable off.

G. Interrupt logic: The TTY interface is equipped with drivers and masks for interrupt lines 1 and 2. Interrupt 1 is created by BUFR if the word transfer mask (WXMX) is set. Interrupt 2 is created by WXMX being off and the block transfer mask (BXM) being on. Both WXMX and BXM are reset by initialize and by EXC 77. In addition, WXMX is reset by the end-of-block echo when block I-O transfers are used.

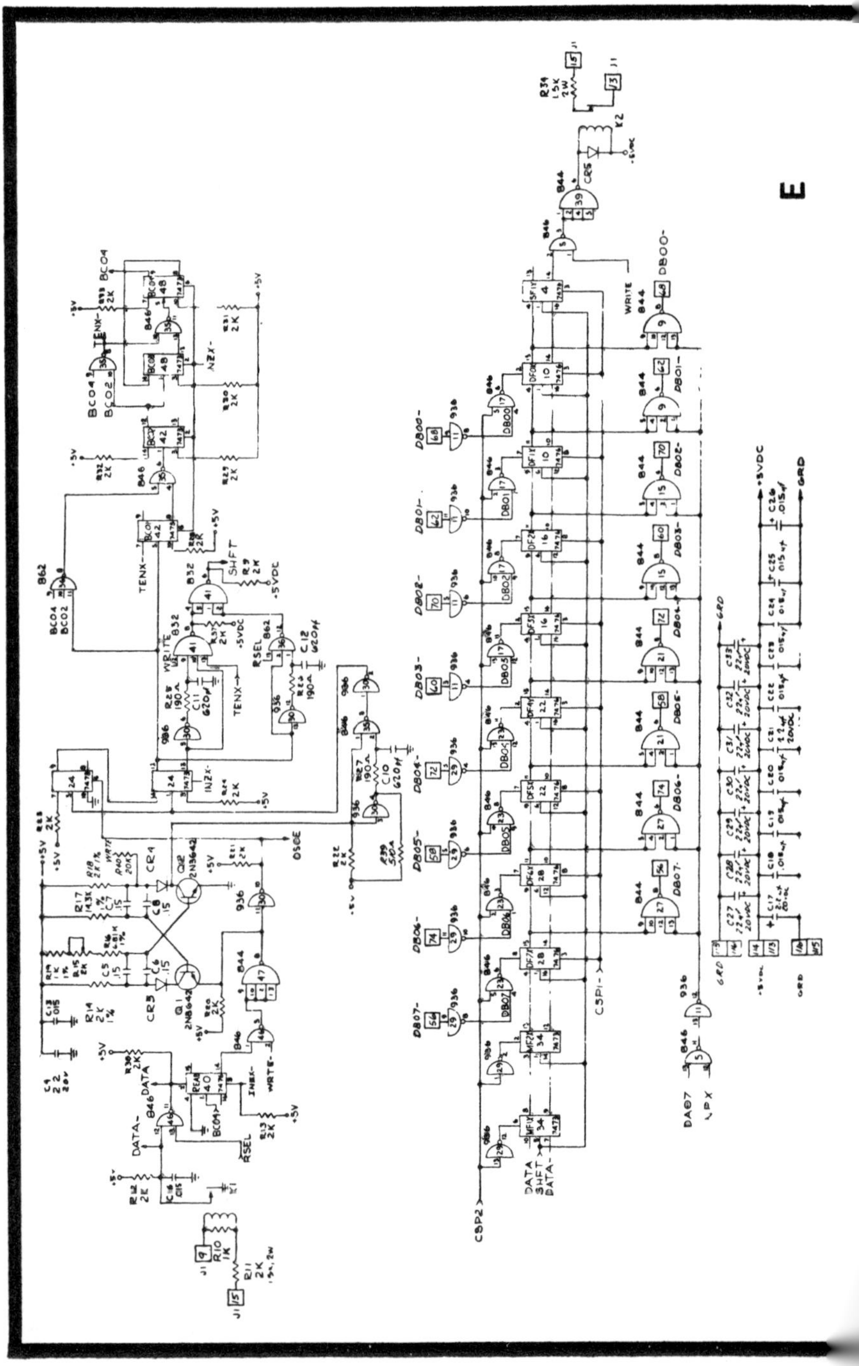
E
DB00-
DB01-
DB02-
DB03-
DB04-
DB05-
DB06-
DB07-
WRITE
TENX-
SHFT
RSEL
OSGE
CSP2
CSP1-
+5VDC
GRD

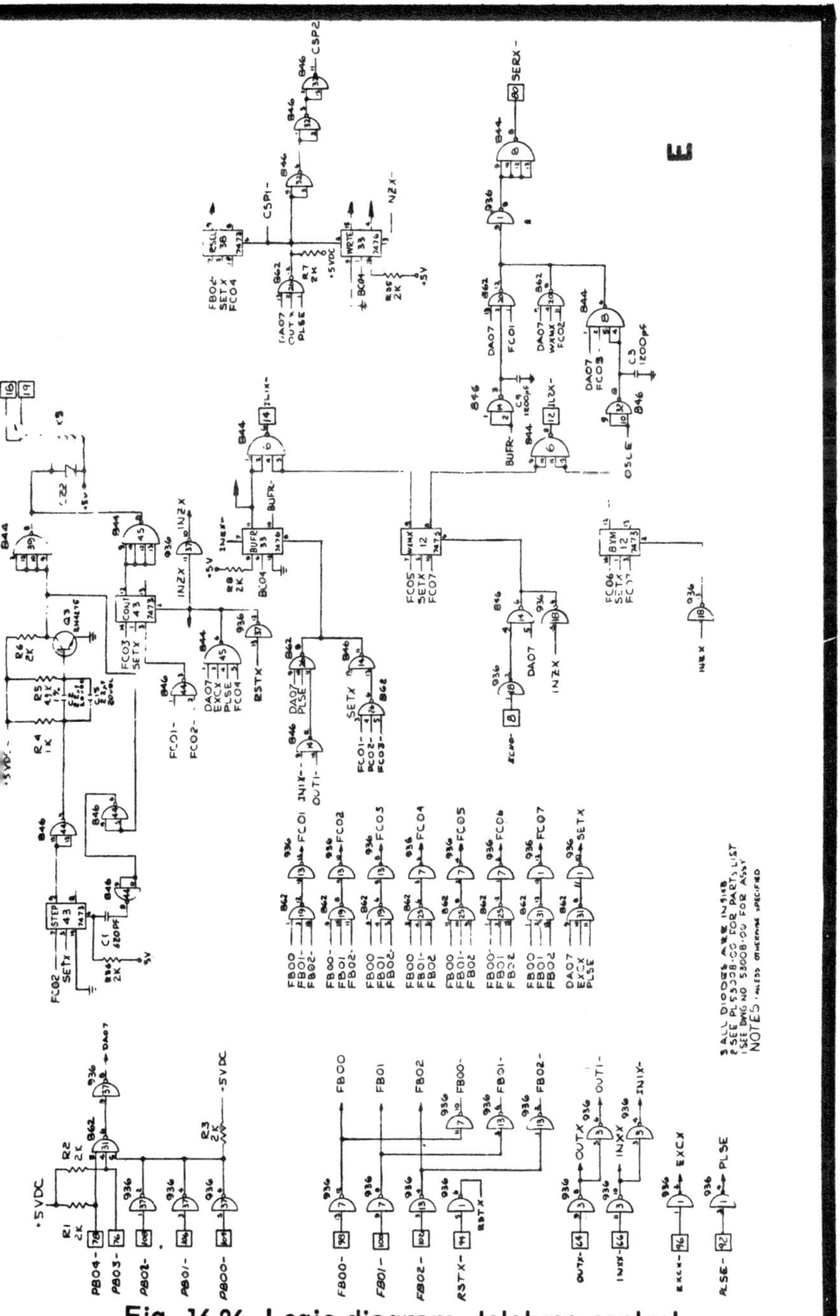

Fig. 16-26. Logic diagram, teletype control.

Fig. 16-27. Digital buffered input module 1.

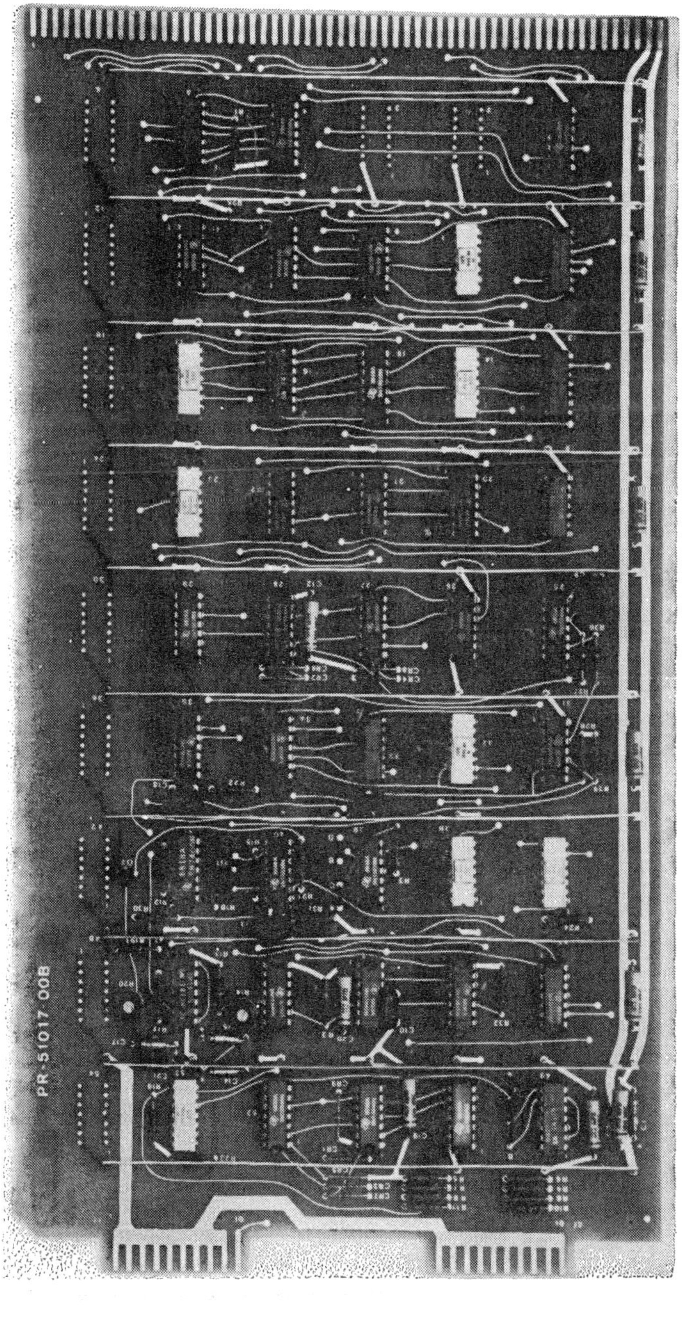

Fig. 16-28. Paper tape reader—paper tape punch module.

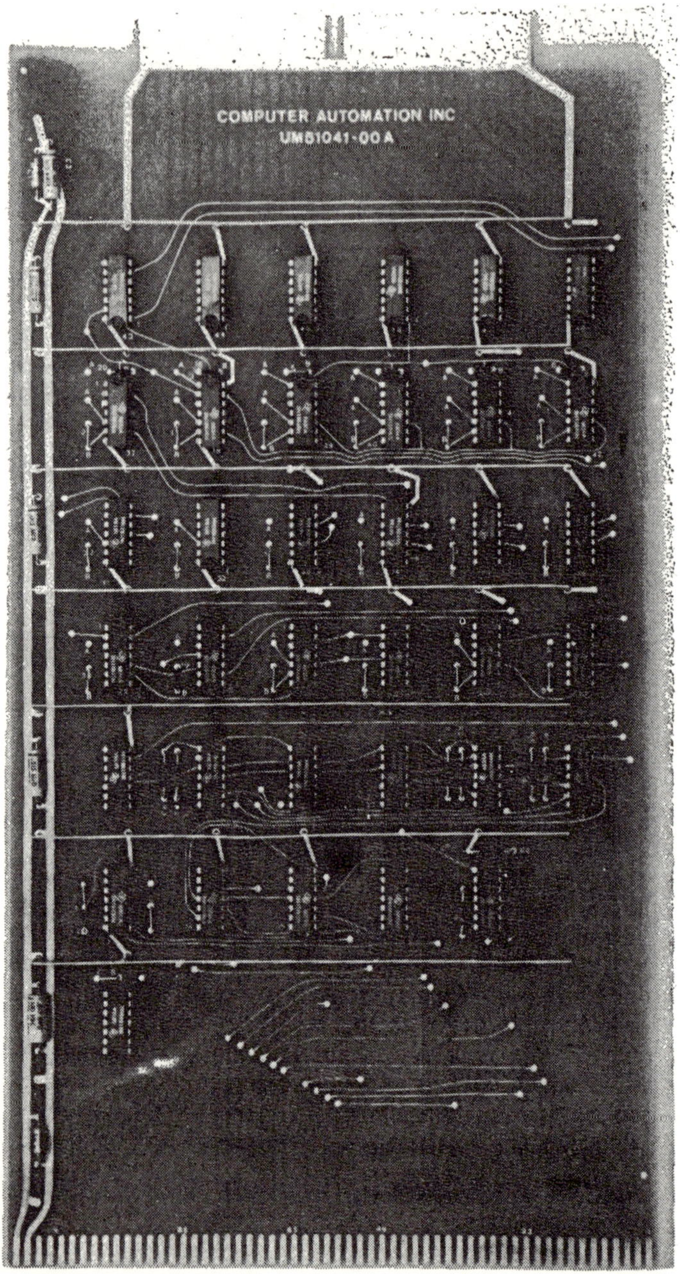

Fig. 16-29. Digital buffered input module 3.

H. I-O bus interface logic. The I-O interface circuits consist of line receives for data, device address, function code and control lines; and drivers for data and sense response.

J. TTY relay interface: Three reed relays are used to connect the interface logic to the TTY. K1 is in the TTY transmit loop. The relay contacts are closed while the loop has the 20 ma DC current flowing. K2 is in the TTY receive loop. It is kept closed in the idle (marking) state to maintain the 20 ma current in the loop. The open circuit voltage in these two loops is approximately 50v DC obtained from a power supply in the TTY. K3 completes a 120v AC circuit to the reader trip solenoid. It is normally open and is closed briefly for step read or closed continuously for continuous read.

Oscillator adjustment procedure

A. Set up the scope with internal sync, and observe BC04. (Connect scope to logic ground and not to chassis ground. Use an AC line adapter to plug into a 3-pronged 115v AC outlet.)

B. Temporarily ground OSC enable (OSCE-) at pac 47 pin 8. This causes the oscillator to run continuously.

C. Adjust pot R15 until the BC04 repetition rate is 99 ms.

D. Remove the ground from 47 pin 8.

E. Put the TTY in continuous read by executing EXC 73 command with a tape loop in the reader.

F. Observe OSCE- on the scope. Sync should be on the positive-going edge. A pulse of approximately 1 to 2 ms should occur every 100 ms.

G. Adjust R15 until the observed pulse is 500 microseconds, within 100 microseconds.

H. Seal the pot and remove the scope.

The high-speed reader and punch specifications are described in Chapter 14. Figs. 16-27 through 16-29 show several of the modules used in the interface.

SPECIAL CIRCUITS

Overflow Logic

The overflow flip-flop (OV) is used as an indication of an illegal arithmetic operation and as a link flip-flop for rotate shifts. For arithmetic operations, OV is set if two positive numbers result in a negative result or if two negative numbers result in a positive result. For instance, incrementing the number 01111111 will cause it to go negative: 10000000. This will cause OV to set.

For shift operations, OV is used to link the two ends of the A register on the rotate instructions. Rotate left causes AR07 to shift into OV and OV to shift into AROO. Nine shifts cause the OV and A register to return to the original condition. Rotate right is similar except the direction is reversed. OV can be set and reset under program control for use as a flag or indicator in a program. It is also reset by the reset switch on the console.

Interrupt Logic

The 808 and 208 interrupt logic consists of several major sections:

Three interrupt input lines: IL1X, IL2X and IURX.

Interrupt acknowledge flip-flop, IUAX, and associated gating.

Priority generator, the output of which is the priority out signal, PROT.

Interrupt address generator for IL1X and IL2X which generates the address associated with these two interrupt lines.

Interrupt mask flip-flop, IMXX, and associated gating. IMXX when set enables the 808 and 208 to respond to interrupts. Otherwise, interrupt requests are ignored.

Interrupt address request generator, IARX, which requests the interrupt address to be accessed for the interrupt instruction.

Interrupt clock generator, IOCL, which provides a clock signal to external interrupt logic.

The interrupt logic provides the capability of responding automatically to external stimuli, making the computer a powerful and flexible component in real time control applications. The operation of a typical interrupt sequence is as follows:

A. The interrupt system is assumed to be enabled; i.e., IMXX is true. A request for interrupt is generated by external logic driving one of the interrupt lines in the I-O bus to ground.

B. At the end of the current instruction, IUAX is set (if a skip is not to be accomplished, and the instruction is not a jump and save). Notice that the end of the current instruction is T3 of the last cycle in the instruction.

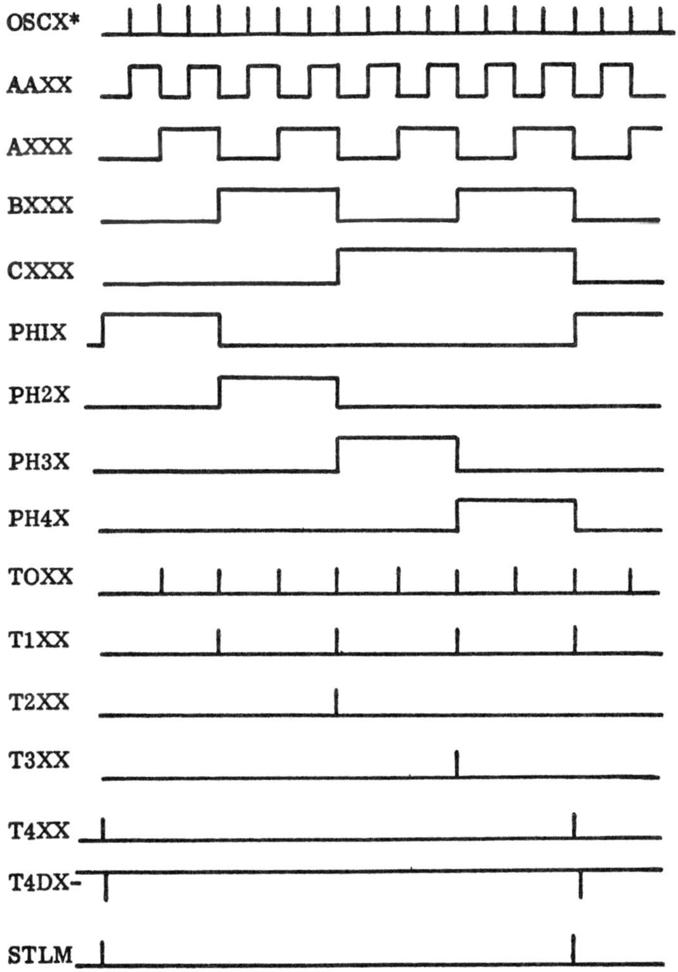

* One oscillator pulse should be 40–60 ns wide at the 1 volt point.

Fig. 16-30. Processor timing waveform.

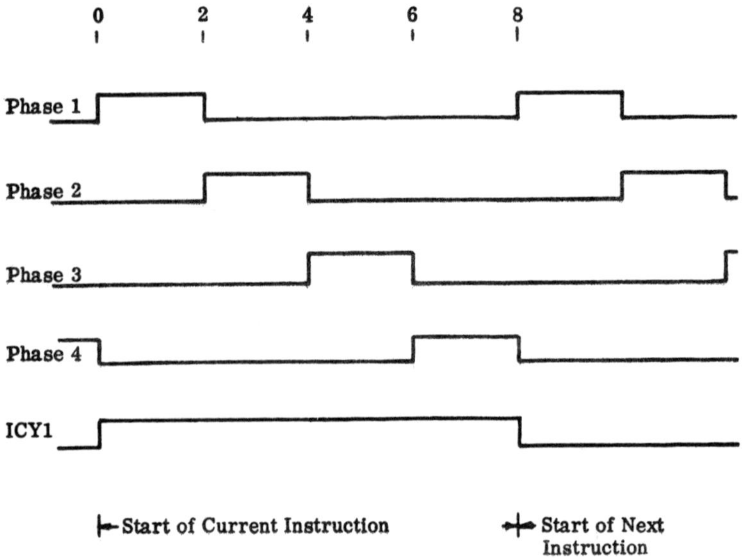

Fig. 16-31. Typical single-word instruction timing diagram.

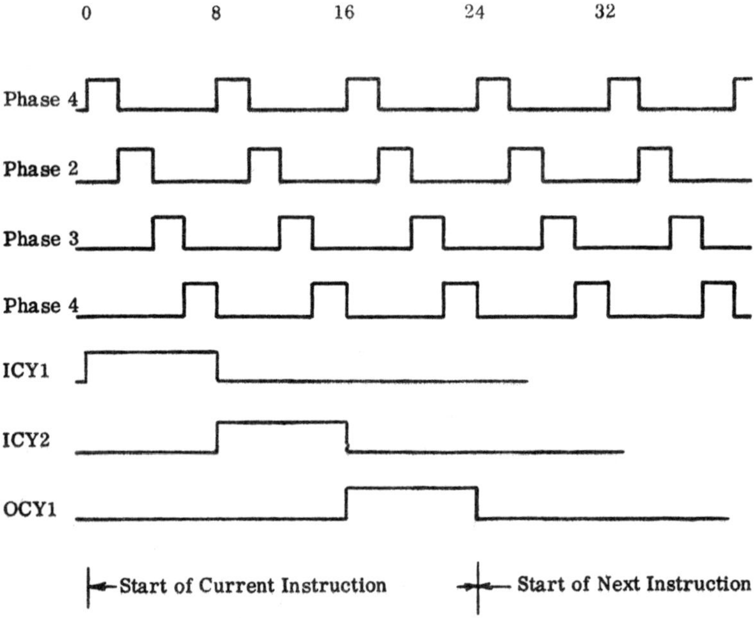

Fig. 16-32. Typical double-word instruction timing diagram.

C. Normally, PH4 of the last cycle of an instruction is used to generate the address to accept the next instruction; i.e., L →M and P→ME or 0 →ME. When IUAX comes on at the beginning of PH4, the interrupt address is sent to M and zero is sent to ME. This is accomplished by gating the interrupt address onto the X bus if IL1 or IL2 is requesting an interrupt. If IURX is the line causing the interrupt, then the interrupt address is obtained from the data bus and gated to the M register during PH4.

D. The instruction located at the interrupt address is established. If it is a double-word instruction, M is incremented to accept the second word. Notice that L and P are not used to establish the instruction nor are L and P incremented during ICY1 and ICY2 when IUAX is on.

E. The interrupt instruction is executed. It may be a single-word instruction or may be a double-word instruction four or five cycles long. In any case, IUAX remains on during the entire instruction and is not turned off until the end of the instruction, and at T3.

F. The next instruction in the program as specified by L and P is executed. This means that even with a continuous interrupt request, every other instruction executed will be from the program. This prevents interrupts from "hanging up" the processor.

If the interrupt instruction is a jump and save, the mask flip-flop IMXX is automatically reset. This allows the programmer to enter a subroutine and disable the device, creating the interrupt before allowing more interrupts to be acknowledged. If this were not done, the sequence would be jump and save, next instruction in interrupt subroutine, and another jump and save. This causes the save locations to point back to the interrupt subroutine instead of the main program and the program hangs up in the interrupt subroutine.

Priority among interrupts is established by the PROT line. IL1X has the highest priority and IL2X is next. If neither IL1X or IL2X are requesting, then priority is passed out to the "down stream" devices, allowing them to request an interrupt. By serially wiring PROT to the down stream devices, relative priorities may be established.

TIMING

The processor timing essentially consists of a crystal oscillator, a timing chain, and decoding logic. The crystal oscillator inputs timing pulses to the timing chain which is tapped at several points to generate various square waves. These are used to generate the four phases from which the timing pulses occur. Refer to Fig. 16-30 for the basic processor timing wave form. The oscillator schematic is in Fig. 16-5. OSCX is a 2-MHz pulse train derived from the basic oscillator. The pulse is actually 450 nanoseconds wide and taken from the timing chain. Also generated on the timing are:

AAXX, a 500 nanosecond square wave

AXXX, a 1 microsecond square wave

BXXX, a 2 microsecond square wave

CXXX, a 4 microsecond square wave

Timing resulting from the above square waves is under control of RUNX, meaning when the signal is true the computer is in the run mode; i.e., not stopped.

One processor cycle is 8 microseconds in duration. Each processor cycle is divided into four phases which are a result of square waves generated on the timing chain. The four phases are each 2 microseconds in duration. A single-word instruction takes 8 microseconds; i.e., four phases.

Phase 1 is used to increment the program sequencer, which consists of the L and P registers. During phase 2 different events occur, depending on the instruction being executed. Each instruction is described in detail by events that occur in each phase. In general, phase 3 is an execution cycle. Any variation in the instructions are described. Phase 4 is generally used as the address phase during which the address of the operand or the next instruction is transferred to M and ME.

Timing pulses, designated TXXX, are generated either continuously (TOXX, T1XX) or at the end of phase 2, 3, and 4. The timing pulses allow events within the computer to occur. TOXX is a 45 nanosecond wide timing pulse that occurs every microsecond in the run mode. T1XX is a 45 nanosecond wide timing pulse that occurs every 2 microseconds in the run mode. T2XX is a timing pulse that occurs at the end of phase 2. T3XX is a timing pulse that occurs at the end of phase 3. T4XX is a timing pulse that occurs at the end of phase 4. T4DX is a timing pulse delayed approximately 25 nanoseconds after T4XX. Single-word instructions require only one word in memory and the cycle sequence consists only of ICY1. Fig. 16-31 shows the timing diagram of a typical single-word instruction.

Double-word instructions such as I-O and block transfer instructions use two words in memory and require two memory cycles to assemble the complete instruction. A typical timing diagram of a double word address is shown in Fig. 16-32. ICY1 is true when the first word of the instruction is being read from memory to be placed in the I register. Instruction cycle 2 (ICY2) is true when the second word of the double-word instruction is being read from memory to be placed in the R register. Operand type instructions require an additional memory cycle, during which Operand cycle 1 (OCY1) is true. This is true when an operand is being read from or stored into memory, or when the contents of the L register are being stored on a jump and save instruction. Operand cycle 2 (OCY2) is true when the contents of the P register is being stored in memory during a jump and save instruction. Figs. 16-33 through 16-45 show various timing signals observed with a Hewlett-Packard Model 180 oscilloscope. The oscillator or clock waveform appears at the top in each case.

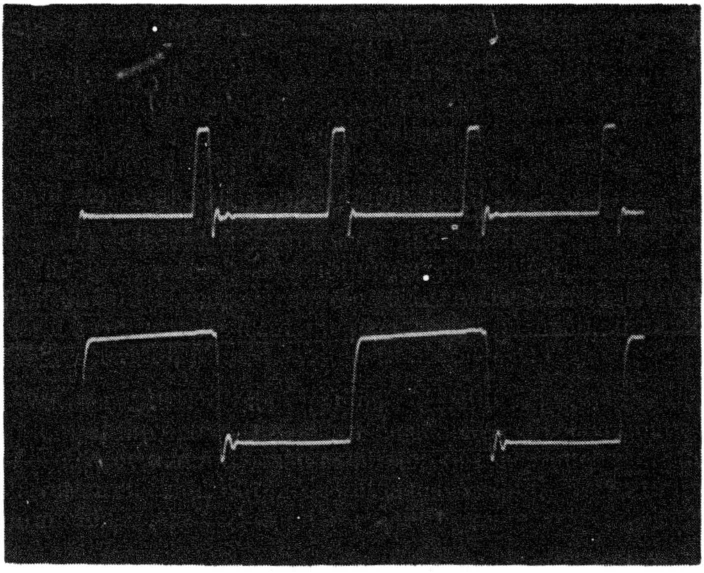

Fig. 16-33. AAXX waveform (bottom) and OSCX (top). 0.2 microseconds per div. and 2v.

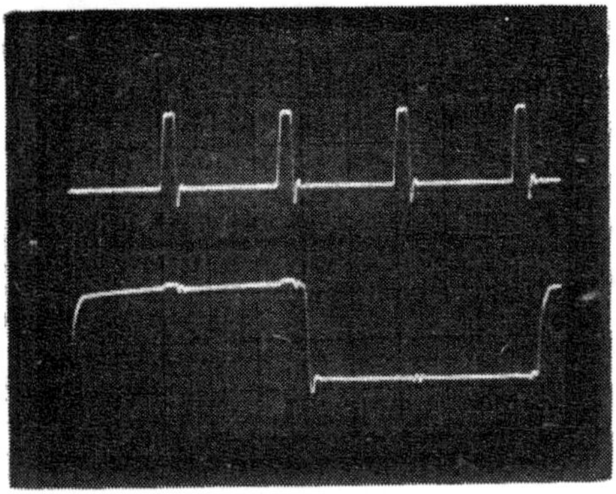

Fig. 16-34. AXXX waveform (bottom) and OSCX. 0.2 microseconds per div. and 2v.

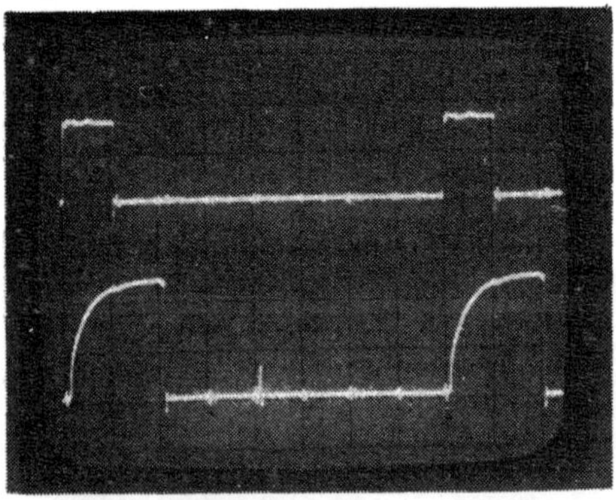

Fig. 16-35. PH1X waveform (bottom) and MSCX. 1 microsecond per div. and 2v.

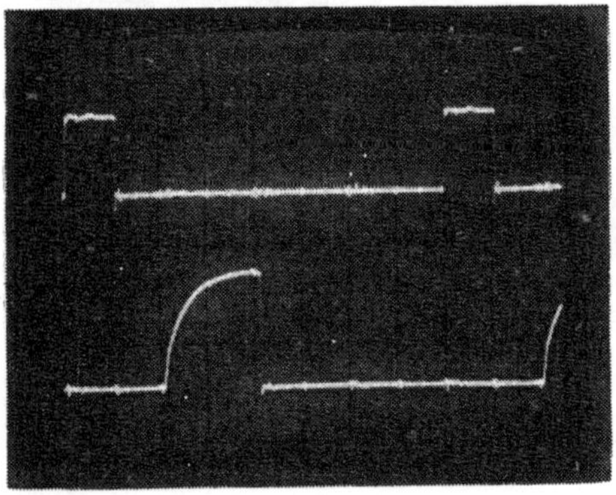

Fig. 16-36. PH2X waveform (bottom) and MSCX. 1 microsecond per div. and 2v.

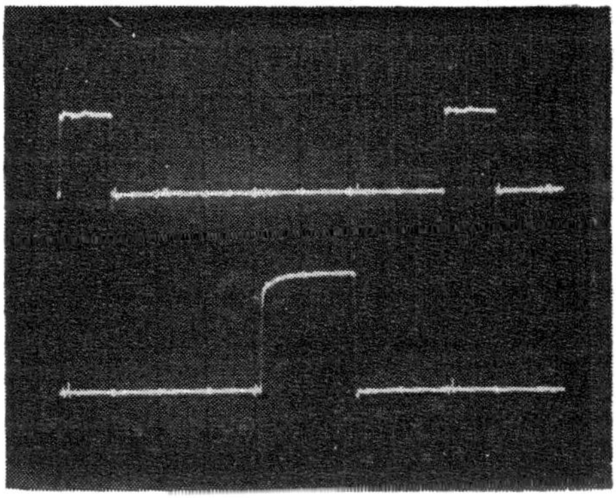

Fig. 16-37. PH3X waveform (bottom) and MSCX. 1 microsecond per div. and 2v.

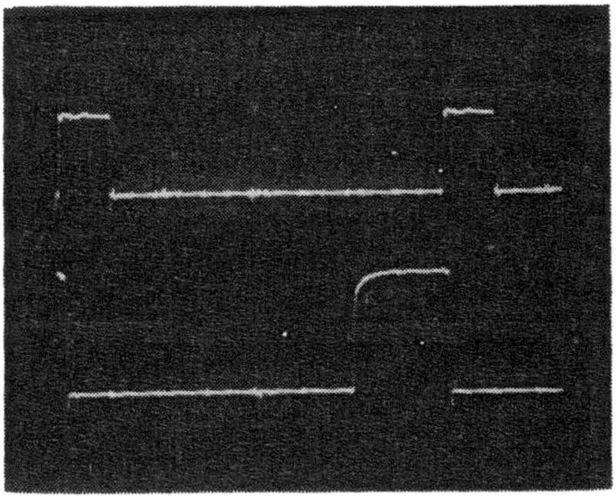

Fig. 16-38. PH4X waveform (bottom) and MSCX. 1 microsecond per div. and 2v.

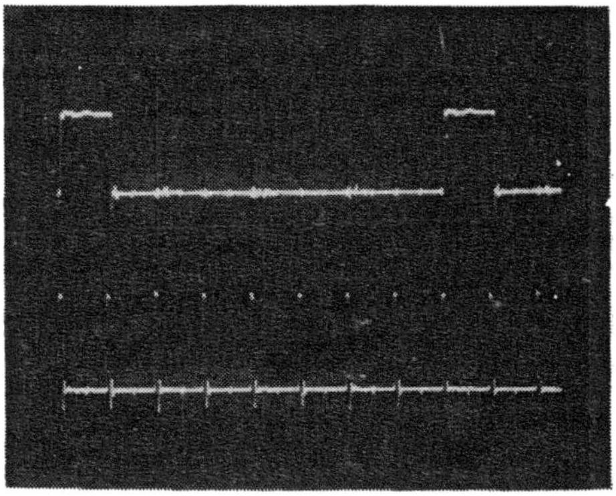

Fig. 16-39. T0XX waveform (bottom) and MSCX. 1 microsecond per div. and 2v.

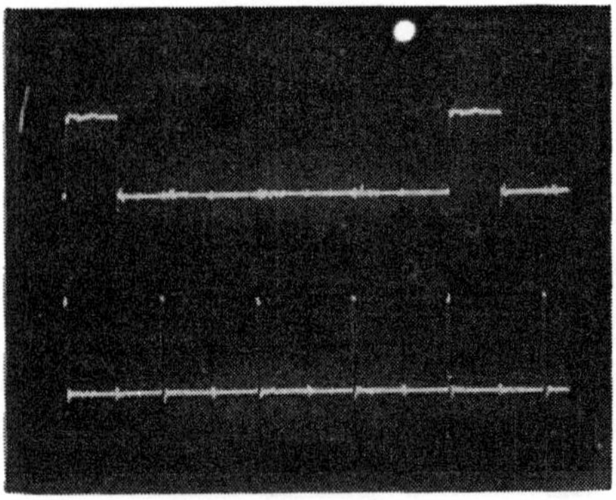

Fig. 16-40. T1XX waveform (bottom) and MSCX. 1 microsecond per div. and 2v.

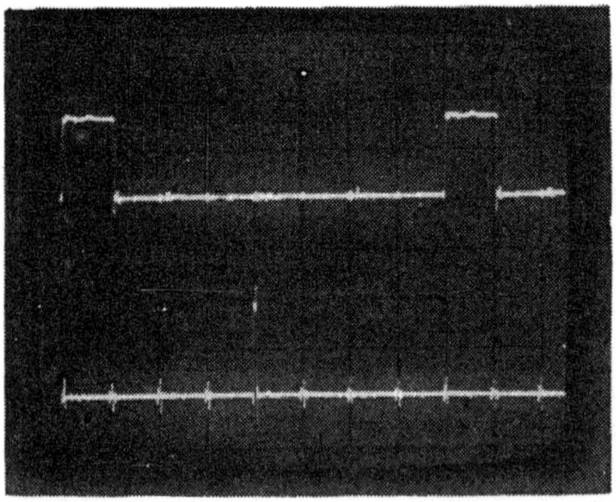

Fig. 16-41. T2XX waveform (bottom) and MSCX. 1 microsecond per div. and 2v.

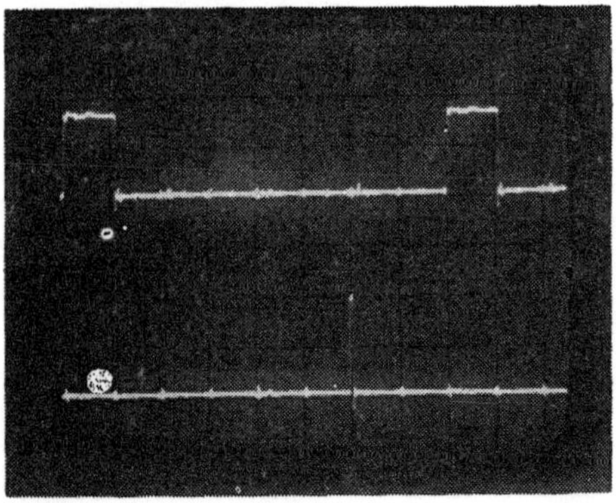

Fig. 16-42. T3XX waveform (bottom) and MSCX. 1 microsecond per div. and 2v.

Fig. 16-43. T4XX waveform (bottom) and MSCX.

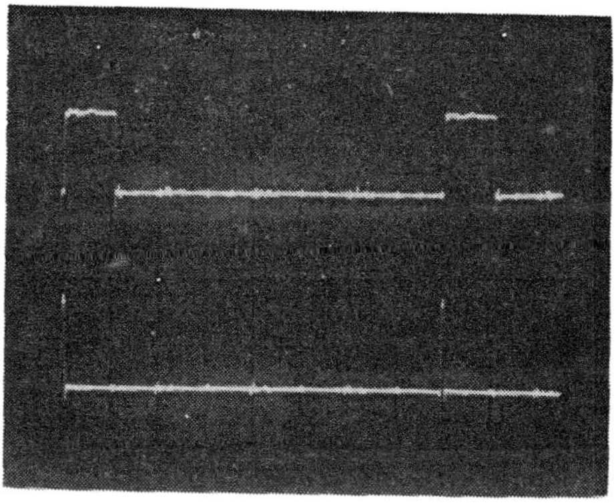

Fig. 16-44. T4DX-waveform (bottom) and MSCX. 1 microsecond per div. and 2v.

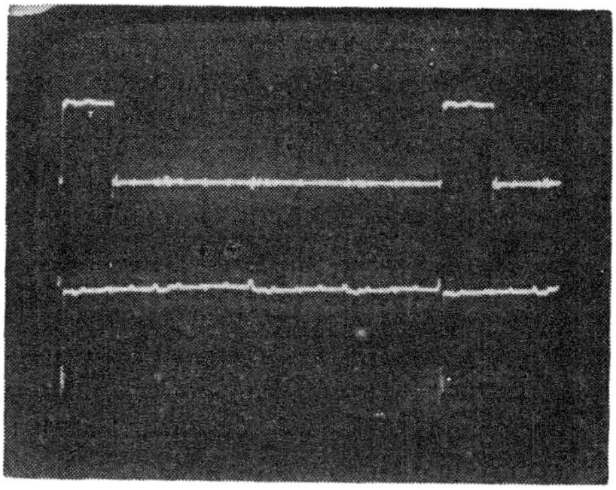

Fig. 16-45. STLM waveform (bottom) and MSCX. 1 microsecond per div. and 2v.

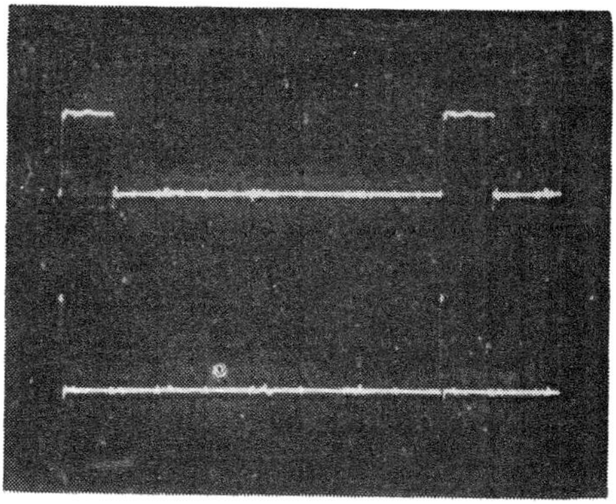

Chapter 17

Processor Operation

It is the purpose of this section to describe all the processor instructions in detail. There is a short introduction for each class, and in some cases, for each group of instructions within a class that differ in some respects. In addition, a flow-chart is included for each class, and in some instances, for each instruction where it is deemed necessary.

REGISTER CHANGE

The register change class contains the control, shift and register change instructions. All the instructions in this group are single-word.

CONTROL

NOP: No Operation

The execution of this instruction causes an 8-microsecond pause in the program currently being executed. See Figs. 17-1 and 17-2. The timing is 1.

Cycle Sequence: ICY1

Phase 1: W register cleared. L register incremented during the first half of Phase 1. SELL, SELR, SLRN, CINP, SELS, SET1, CLRW, SETW occur. If L overflowed, the P register is incremented during the second half of phase 1. SELP, SELR, SLRN, CINP, SELS and SETP occur.

Phase 2: Approximately halfway through phase 2, memory data is set into the W register. Contents of W is transferred to the I register at the end of the phase. SETI occurs.

Phase 3: No action.

Phase 4: Contents of the L register is transferred to the M register and the contents of the P register is transferred to the M extension register. SELL, CINP, SELS, STLM, XPMX, and STUM occur.

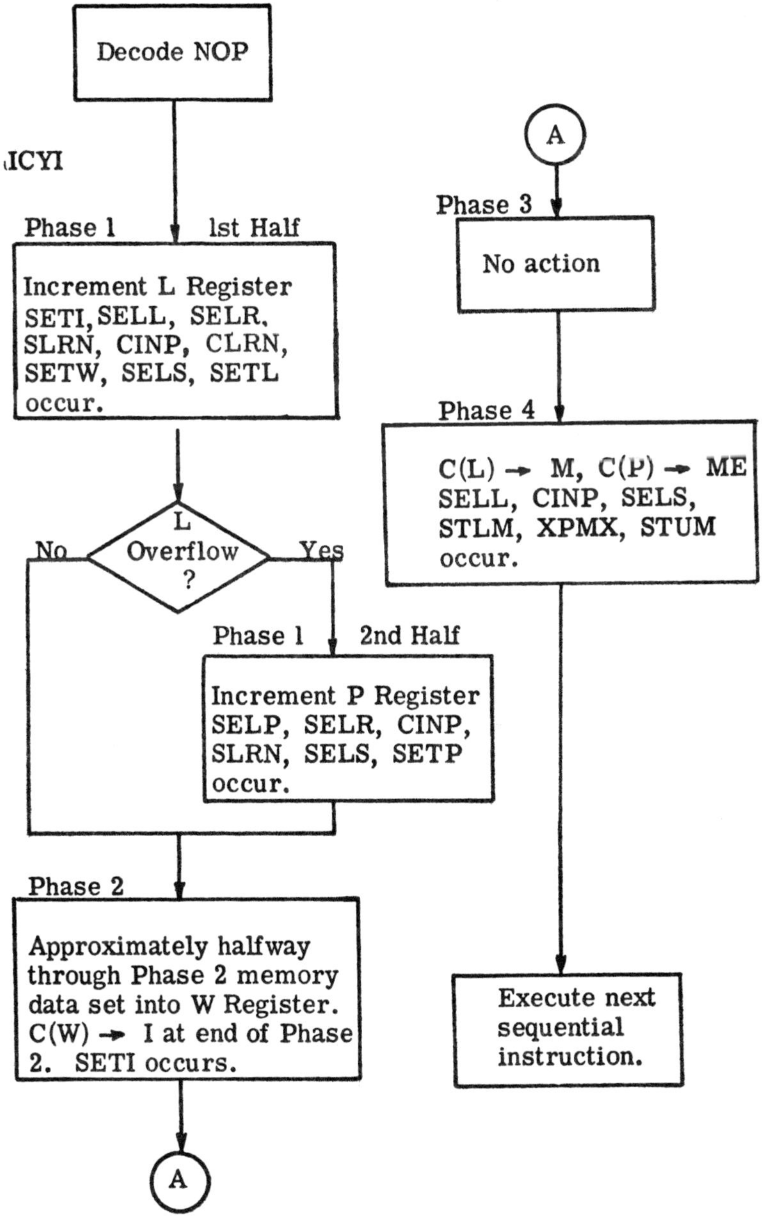

Fig. 17-1. NOP flow chart.

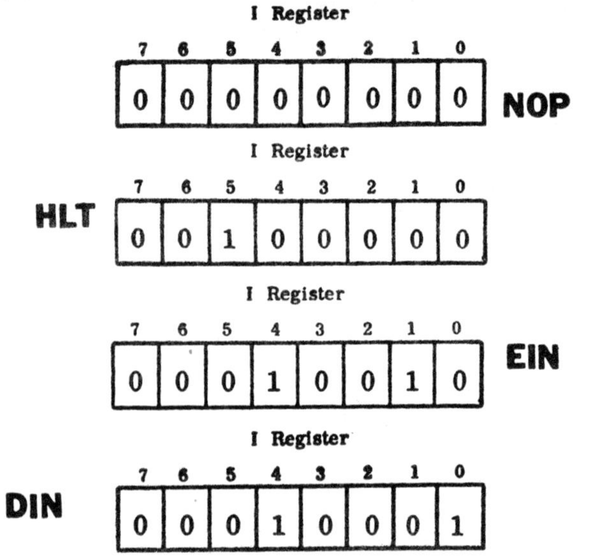

Fig. 17-2. Register change control instructions.

HLT: Halt

This instruction halts the computer. See Fig. 17-8. The timing is 1.

Cycle Sequence: ICY1

Phase 1: Same as NOP, phase 1.
Phase 2: Same as NOP, phase 2.
Phase 3: Processor halts at the end of phase 3 and does not enter phase 4. RUNX flip-flop turned off.
Phase 4: Same as NOP, phase 4.

EIN: Enable Interrupts

This instruction enables the computer to respond to a request for interrupt. The interrupt mask is affected. The timing is 1.

Cycle Sequence:

Phase 1: Same as NOP, phase 1.
Phase 2: Same as NOP, phase 2.

Phase 3: Set IMXX.
Phase 4: Same as NOP, phase 4.

DIN: Disable Interrupts

The instruction inhibits the computer from accepting a request for interrupt. The interrupt mask is affected. The timing is 1.

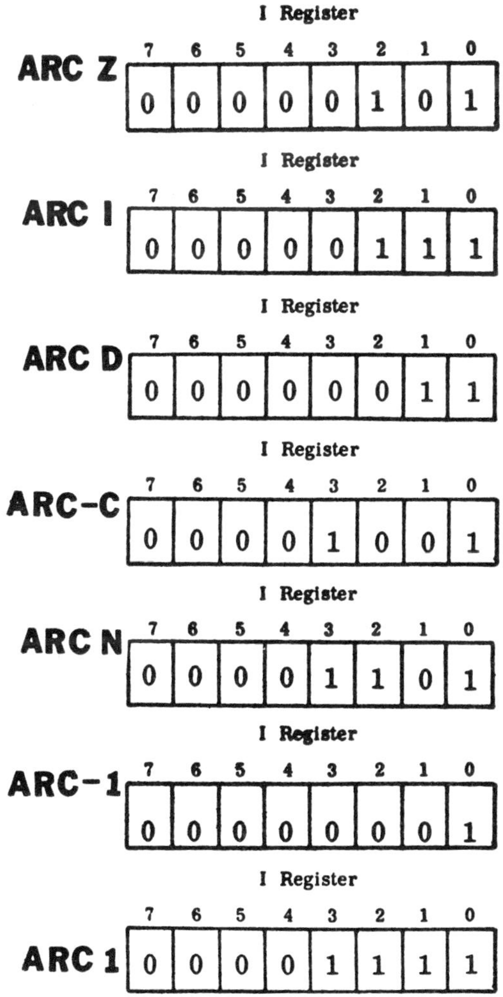

Fig. 17-3. A register change instructions.

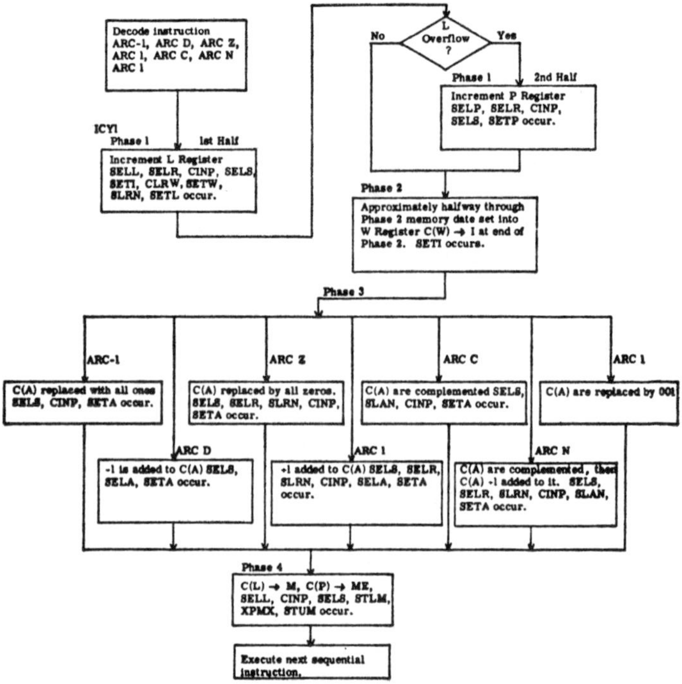

Fig. 17-4. A register change flow chart.

Cycle Sequence:

Phase 1: Same as NOP, phase 1.
Phase 2: Same as NOP, phase 2.
Phase 3:Reset IMXX.
Phase 4: Same as NOP, phase 4.

A Register Change

ARC Z: Clear A Register

ARC causes the C(A) to be replaced by zeros, affecting the A register. See Figs. 17-3 and 17-4. The timing is 1.

Cycle Sequence: ICY1

Phase 1: Same as NOP, phase 1.
Phase 2: Same as NOP, phase 2.

Phase 3: 000 entered into the A register. SELS, SELR, SLRN, CINP, and SETA occur.
Phase 4: Same as NOP, phase 4.

ARC I Increment A Register

The ARC I adds one (least significant bit) to the contents of A. OV is set if the contents goes from 0,1111111 to 1,0000000. The timing is 1.

Cycle Sequence: ICY1

Phase 1: Same as NOP, phase 1.
Phase 2: Same as NOP, phase 2.
Phase 3: +1 is added to the A register. SELS, SELR, SLRN, CINP, SELA and SETA occur.
Phase 4: Same as NOP, phase 4.

ARC D Decrement A Register

ARC D subtracts one (least significant bit) from the contents of A. OV is set if the contents goes from 1,0000000 to 0,1111111. The timing is 1.

Cycle Sequence: ICY1

Phase 1: Same as NOP, phase 1.
Phase 2: Same as NOP, phase 2.
Phase 3: -1 is added to the A register. SELS, SELA and SETA occur.
Phase 4: Same as NOP, phase 4.

ARC C 1s Complement A Register

ARC C performs the 1s complement (bit-by-bit inversion) of the contents of the A register. The timing is 1.

Cycle Sequence: ICY1

Phase 1: Same as NOP, phase 1.
Phase 2: Same as NOP, phase 2.
Phase 3: Contents of the A register is complemented. SELS, SLAN, CINP and SETA occur.
Phase 4: Same as NOP, phase 4.

ARC N 2s Complement A Register

ARC N performs the 2s complement of (negative) the contents of the A register. The timing is 1.

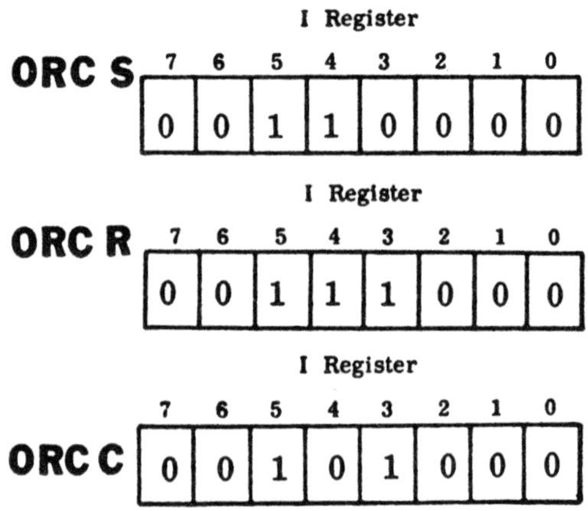

Fig. 17-5. Overflow register change instructions.

Cycle Sequence: ICY1

Phase 1: Same as NOP, phase 1.
Phase 2: Same as NOP, phase 2.
Phase 3: Contents of A register is complemented and A + 1 added to it. SELS, SELR, SLRN, CINP, SLAN and SETA occur.
Phase 4: Same as NOP, phase 4.

ARC-1 Transfer -1 to A

ARC-1 replaces the contents of the A register with 1,1111111. The timing is 1.

Cycle Sequence: ICY1

Phase 1: Same as NOP, phase 1.
Phase 2: Same as NOP, phase 2.
Phase 3: 377 set into the A register. SELS, CINP, and SETA occur.
Phase 4: Same as NOP, phase 4.

ARC 1 Transfer +1 to A

ARC 1 replaces the contents of the A register with 0,0000001. The timing is 1.

Cycle Sequence: ICY1

Phase 1: Same as NOP, phase 1.
Phase 2: Same as NOP, phase 2.
Phase 3: 001 is entered into the A register. SLAN, SELA, SLRN, SELR, CINP, SELS, and SETA occur.
Phase 4: Same as NOP, phase 4.

Overflow Register Change (ORC)

ORC S Set Overflow

ORC S sets the overflow flip-flop. If already set there is no change. The timing is 1. See Figs. 17-5 and 17-6.

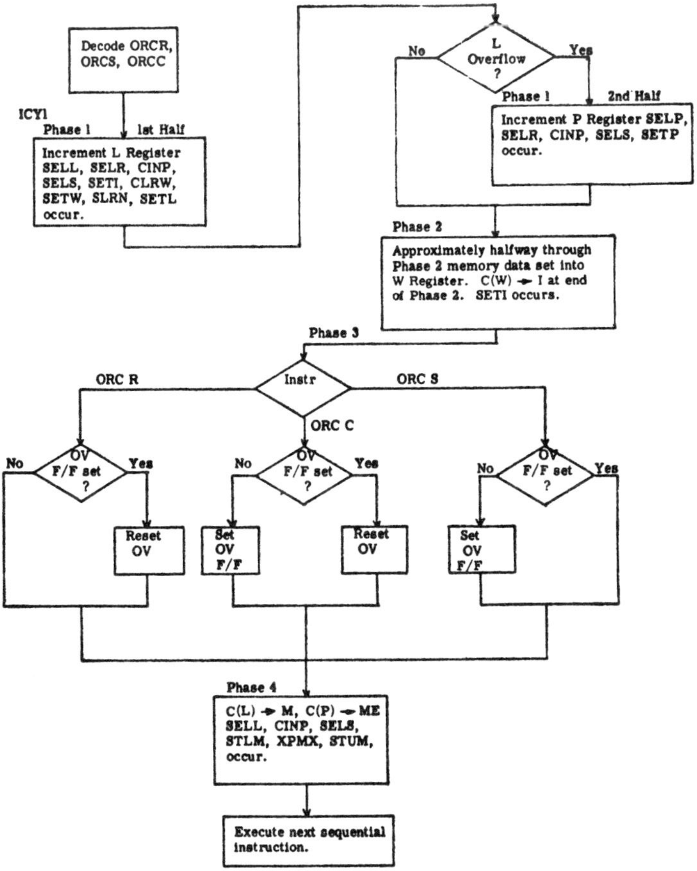

Fig. 17-6. Overflow register change flow chart.

Cycle Sequence: ICY1

Phase 1: Same as NOP, phase 1.
Phase 2: Same as NOP, phase 2.
Phase 3: Overflow flip-flop set at T3XX, the time OVSE occurs.
Phase 4: Same as NOP, phase 4.

ORC R Reset Overflow

ORC R resets the overflow flip-flop. The timing is 1.

Cycle Sequence: ICY1

Phase 1: Same as NOP, phase 1.
Phase 2: Same as NOP, phase 2.
Phase 3: Overflow flip-flop reset. OVRE occurs.
Phase 4: Same as NOP, phase 4.

ORC C Complement Overflow

ORC C complements the content of the overflow flip-flop. The timing is 1.

Cycle Sequence: ICY1

Phase 1: Same as NOP, phase 1.
Phase 2: Same as NOP, phase 2.
Phase 3: Complements the overflow flip-flop at T3XX.
Phase 4: Same as NOP, phase 4.

LOGICAL SHIFT

The logical shift instruction causes the contents of the A register to be shifted one place to the left or right. Zeros are shifted into one end of the register and the contents is shifted out and lost. Thus, if eight consecutive logical shift left instructions were executed, the A register would contain all zeros. Note: The overflow flip-flop is reset on a logical shift instruction at the beginning of the operation and may be set at the end of the instruction.

SHF R Logical Shift Right

SHF R resets OV, shifts the contents of the A register right one place. Zero is shifted into the sign bit and the LSB of A shifted into OV. The timing is 1. See Figs. 17-7 and 17-8.

Cycle Sequence: ICY1

Phase 1: Same as NOP, phase 1.
Phase 2: Same as NOP, phase 2.
Phase 3: Contents of the A register is shifted right one position. AROO shifts into the overflow flip-flop. Zero shifts into AR07. SELA, CINP, SETA, LSHR, SHRX occur.
Phase 4: Same as NOP, phase 4.

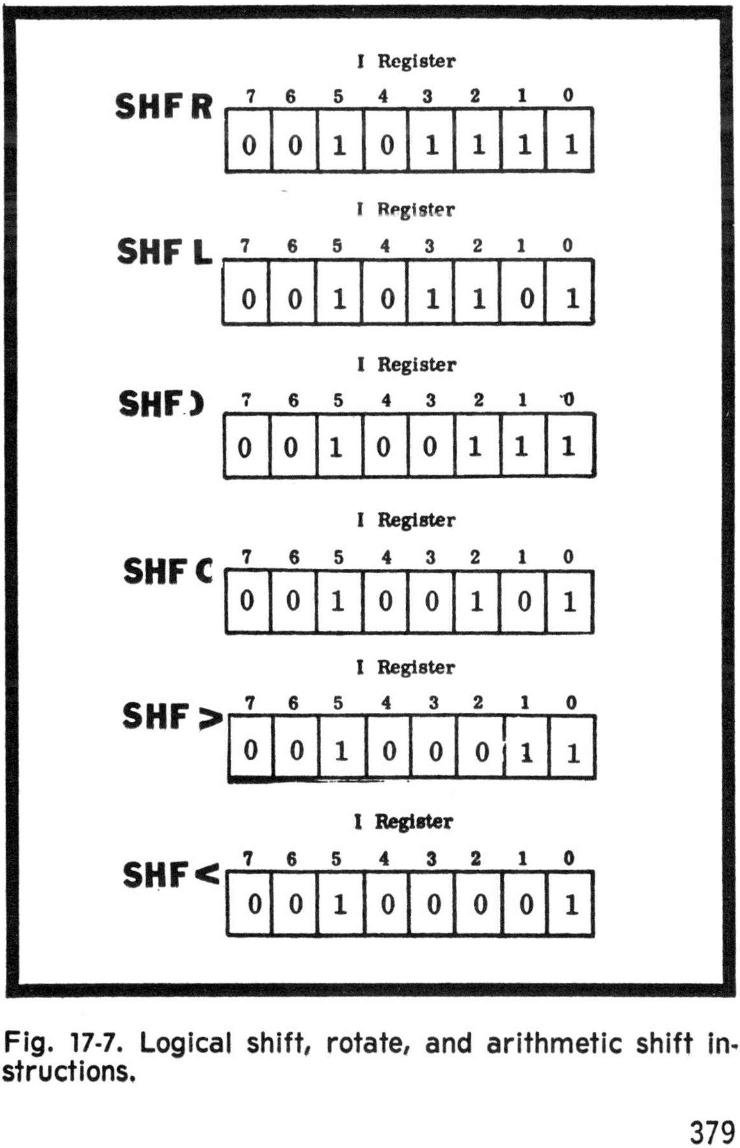

Fig. 17-7. Logical shift, rotate, and arithmetic shift instructions.

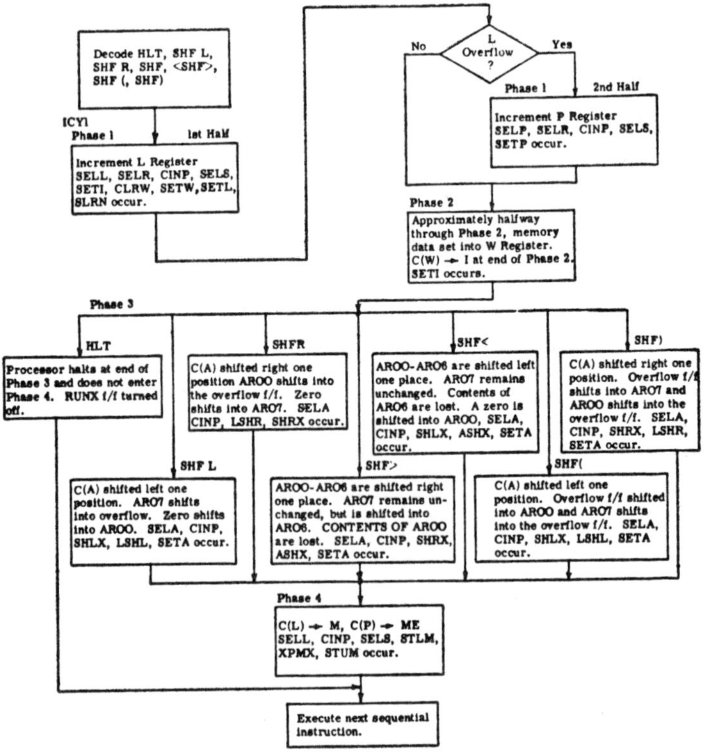

Fig. 17-8. Logical shift, rotate and arithmetic shift flow chart.

SHF L Logical Shift Left

SHF L resets OV, shifts the contents of the A register left one place. Zero is shifted into the LSB of A and the sign bit of A is shifted into OV. The timing is 1.

Cycle Sequence: ICY1

Phase 1: Same as NOP, phase 1.
Phase 2: Same as NOP, phase 2.
Phase 3: Contents of the A register is shifted left one position. AR07 shifts into overflow. Zero shifts into AR00. SELA, CINP, SHLX, LSHL, SETA occur.
Phase 4: Same as NOP, phase 4.

ROTATE

The rotate instruction, sometimes referred to as logical rotate, preserves the contents of the A register as it is shifted. For a rotate right (left), the content of the overflow flip-flop is shifted into bit 7 (bit 0) of the A register, and bit 0 (bit 7) of the A register is shifted into OV. This essentially creates a 9-bit register. Thus, nine consecutive rotate right (left) instructions leave the A register and the overflow flip-flop is unchanged. Shifting A through the overflow flip-flop facilitates testing bits of A. For instance, rotate right and then skip on overflow reset tests bit 0 of the A register. Rotate left restores A to its original state.

SHF) Rotate Right

SHF) shifts the contents of the A register right one place through OV. Previous contents of OV is shifted into A7. The timing is 1.

Cycle Sequence: ICY1

Phase 1: Same as NOP, phase 1.
Phase 2: Same as NOP, phase 2.
Phase 3: Contents of the A register is shifted right one position. AROO shifts into the overflow flip-flop. The previous contents of the overflow flip-flop is shifted into ARO7. SELA, CINP, SHRX, LSHR, SETA occur.
Phase 4: Same as NOP, phase 4.

SHF (Rotate Left

SHF (shifts the contents of the A register left one place through OV. Sign bit is shifted into OV. Previous contents of OV is shifted into the LSB of A. The timing is 1.

Cycle Sequence: ICY1

Phase 1: Same as NOP, phase 1.
Phase 2: Same as NOP, phase 2.
Phase 3: Contents of the A register is shifted left one position. ARO7 shifts into the overflow flip-flop and the previous contents of the overflow flip-flop is shifted into AROO. SELA, CINP, SHLX, LSHL, SETA occur.
Phase 4: Same as NOP, phase 4.

ARITHMETIC SHIFT

The arithmetic shift differs from the logical or rotate shifts in that the A register is assumed to contain a signed number. The sign bit is A7. Since shifting left multiples by 2 and shifting right divides by 2, the sign of a number must not change. Thus an arithmetic shift can affect only the magnitude position of the number and cannot change the sign bit. The PDC-808 uses 2s complement arithmetic. The arithmetic shift right causes the sign bit to be shifted while remaining unchanged. An arithmetic shift left performs a logical shift left, except the sign bit is unchanged.

SHF > Arithmetic Shift Right

SHF > shifts the lower seven bits of the A register right one place. Sign bit remains unchanged and is also shifted into A6. The LSB of A is lost. The timing is 1.

Cycle Sequence: ICY1

Phase 1: Same as NOP, phase 1.
Phase 2: Same as NOP, phase 2.
Phase 3: The lower seven bits of the A register are shifted right one place. ARO7, the sign bit, remains unchanged but is shifted into ARO6. The contents of bit position AROO is lost, since the contents of bit position O7 replaced it. SELA, CINP, SHRX, ASHX, SETA occur.
Phase 4: Same as NOP, phase 4.

SHF < Arithmetic Shift Left

SHF < shifts the lower seven bits of the A register left one place. Sign bit remains unchanged. A6 is lost and zero is shifted into the LSB of A. The timing is 1.

Cycle Sequence: ICY1

Phase 1: Same as NOP, phase 1.
Phase 2: Same as NOP, phase 2.
Phase 3: The lower seven bits of the A register are shifted left one place. ARO7 the sign bit, remains unchanged; position ARO6 is replaced by the contents of bit position ARO5. Bits ARO4-ARO2 are treated in a similar manner. A zero is shifted into AROO. SELA, CINP, SHLX, ASHX, SETA occur.

Phase 4: Same as NOP, phase 4.

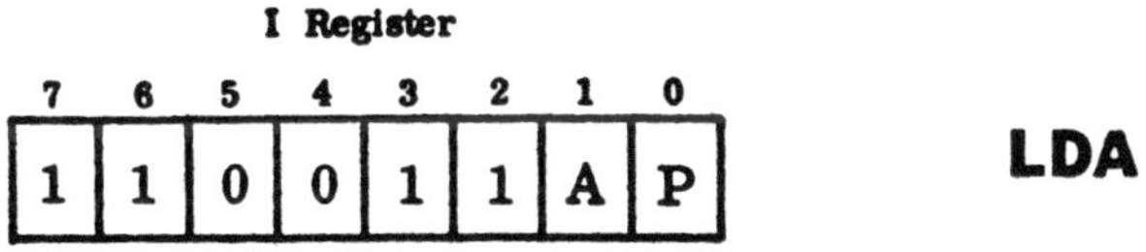

Fig. 17-9. Load A instruction.

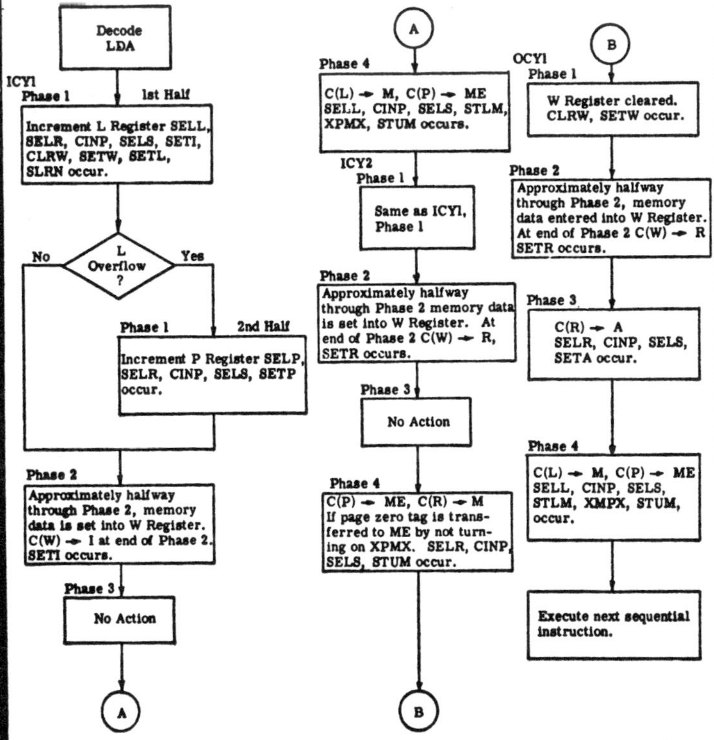

Fig. 17-10. LDA flow chart.

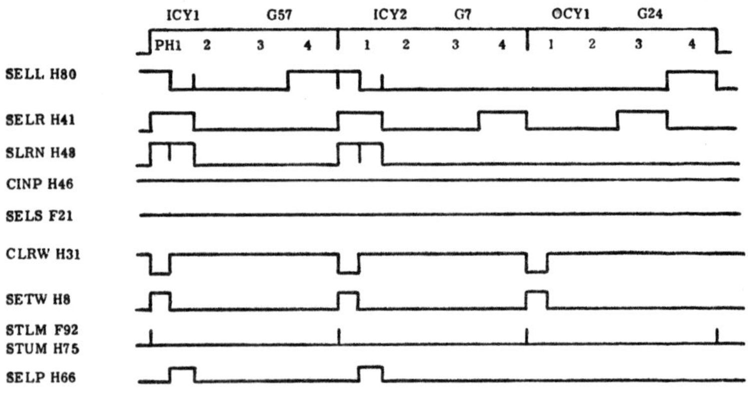

Fig. 17-11. LDA timing diagram.

STA

I Register								R Register
7	6	5	4	3	2	1	0	7 6 5 4 3 2 1 0
1	1	0	1	1	0	A	P	A Field

Fig. 17-12. Store A instruction.

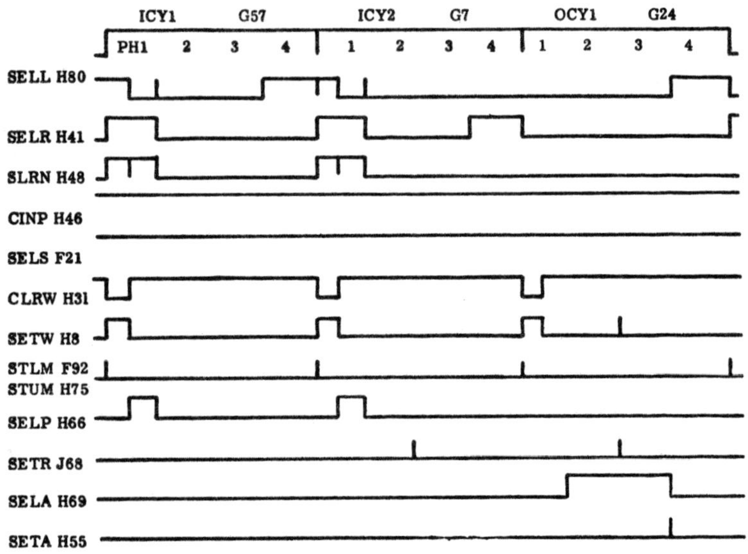

Fig. 17-13. STA timing diagram.

MEMORY REFERENCE

LDA LOAD A

LDA loads the contents of the effective memory location into the A register. The timing is 3 plus 2 for each indirect level. See Figs. 17-9, 17-10 and 17-11.

Cycle Sequence: ICY1, ICY2, OCY1

ICY1 cycle: Same as STA ICY1 cycle.
ICY2 cycle: Same as STA ICY2 cycle.
OCY1 cycle: Phase 1: Same as phase 1, OCY1 cycle, STA instruction. Phase 2: Approximately halfway through phase 2, memory data is entered into the W register. At the end of phase 2 the contents of the W register is transferred into the R register. SETR occurs. Phase 3: Contents of the R register is transferred to the A register. SELR, CINP, SELS and SETA occur. Phase 4: Same as NOP, phase 4.

STA Store A

STA stores the contents of the A register in the effective memory location. The timing is 3 plus 2 for each indirect level. See Figs. 17-11, 17-12, 17-13.

Cycle Sequence: ICY1, ICY2 OCY1

ICY1 cycle: Same as NOP.
ICY2 cycle: Phase 1: Same as NOP, phase 1. Phase 2: Approximately halfway through phase 2 the memory data is entered into the W register. At the end of phase 2 the contents of W is transferred to the R register. SETR occurs. Phase 3: No action. Phase 4: Contents of the P register is transferred to the M extension register and the contents of the R register is transferred to the M register. If page zero tag is used zero is transferred to the M extension register; by not turning on XPMX, SELR, CINP, SELS, STLM, and STUM occur.

OCY1 cycle: Phase 1: W register cleared. CLRW and SETW occur. Phase 2: Approximately halfway through phase 2 the memory data is entered into the W register. At the end of phase 2 the contents of the A register is transferred into the W register. SELA, CINP, SELS and SETW occur. Phase 3: No action. Phase 4: Same as NOP, phase 4.

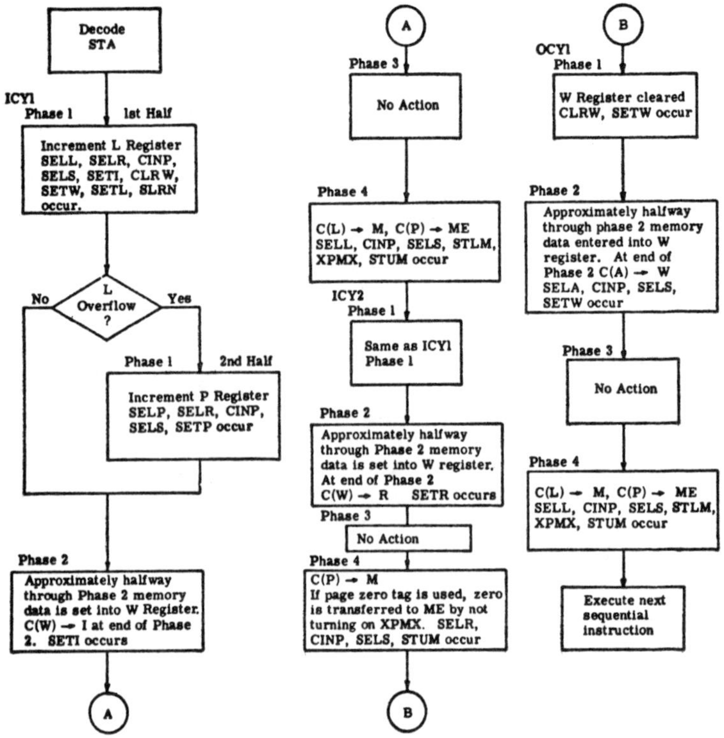

Fig. 17-14. STA flow chart.

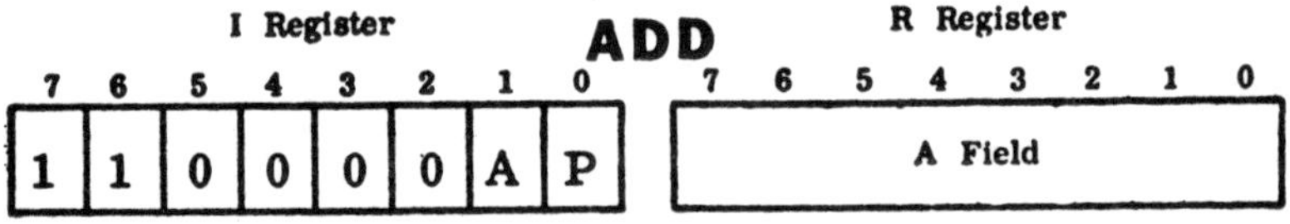

Fig. 17-15. ADD instruction.

ADD

ADD adds the contents of the effective memory location to the contents of the A register. The timing is 3 plus 2 each indirect level. See Fig. 17-15.

Cycle Sequence: ICY1, ICY2, OCY1

ICY1 cycle: Same as STA, 331.
ICY2 cycle: Same as STA, 331.
OCY1 cycle: Phase 1: Same as phase 1, OCY1 cycle STA instruction. Phase 2: Same as phase 2, OCY1 cycle, LDA in-

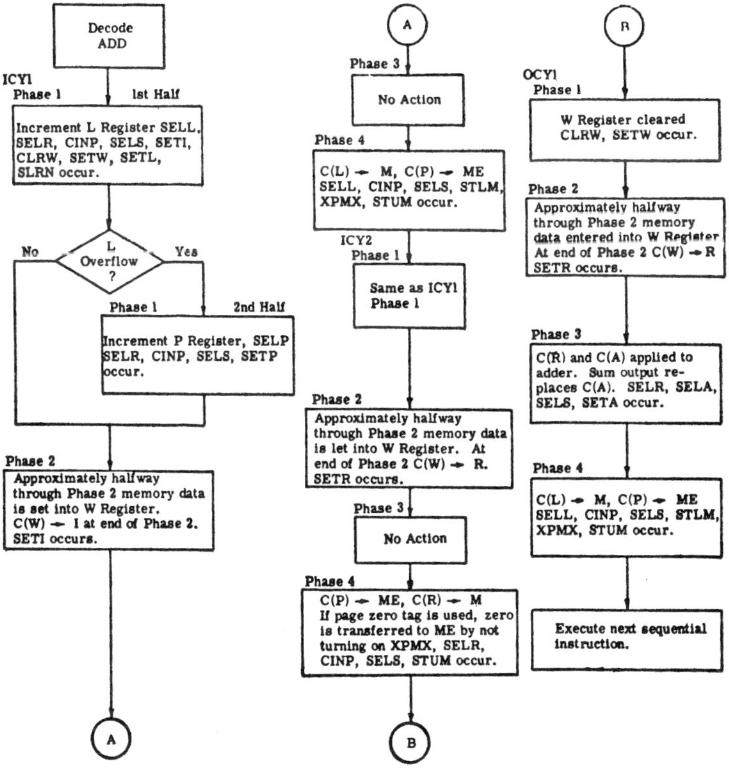

Fig. 17-16. ADD flow chart.

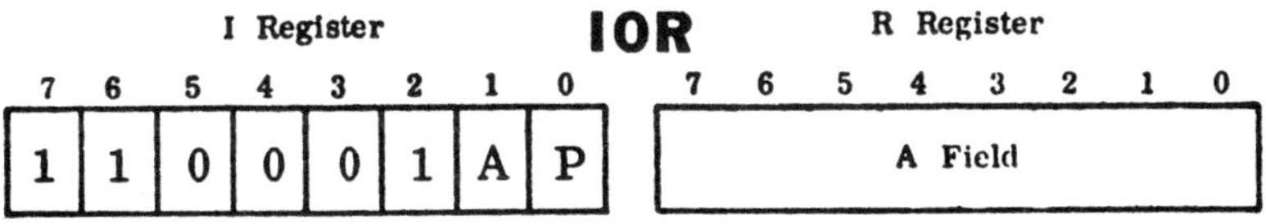

Fig. 17-17. IOR instruction.

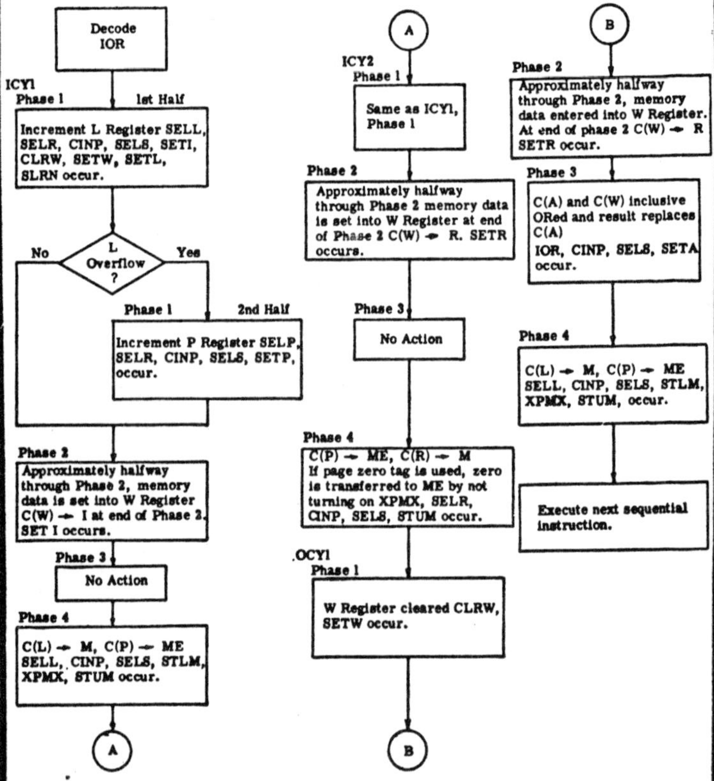

Fig. 17-18. IOR flow chart.

struction. Phase 3: Contents of the R and A registers are applied to the adder. Sum output entered into the A register. SELR, SELA, SELS and SETA occur. Phase 4: Same as phase 4, OCY1, STA instruction.

IOR Inclusive OR

IOR inclusively ORs the contents of the effective memory location to the contents of the A register. The timing is 3 plus 2 for each indirect level. See Figs. 17-17 and 17-18.

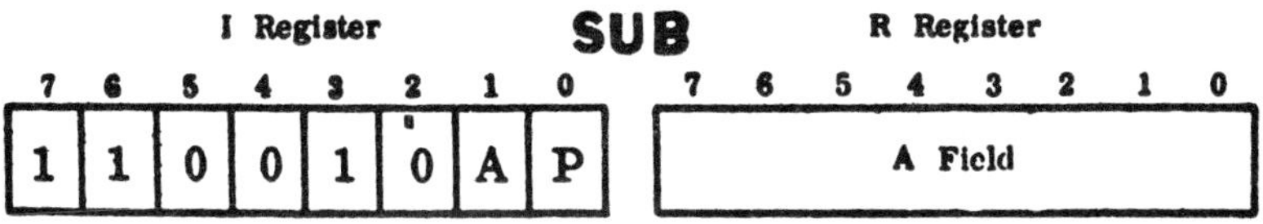

Fig. 17-19. SUB instruction.

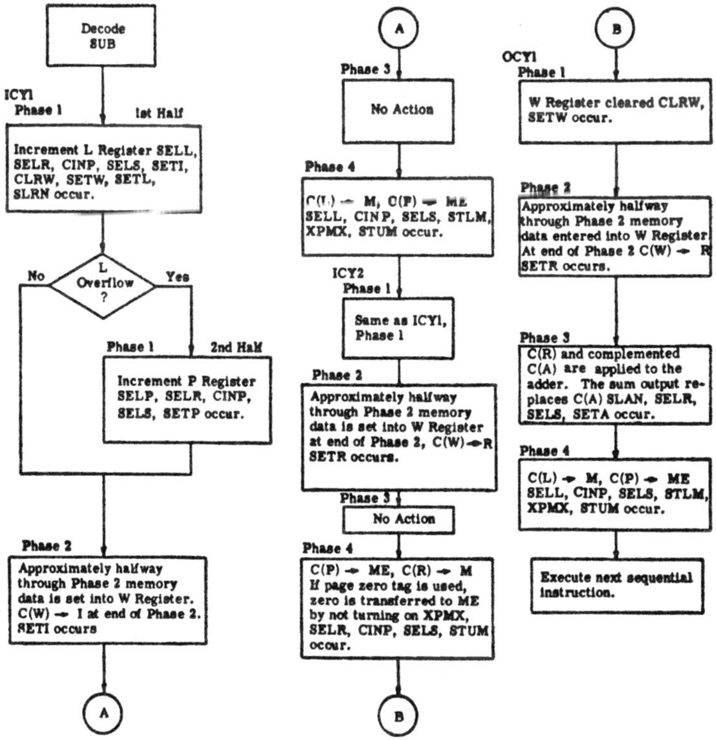

Fig. 17-20. SUB flow chart.

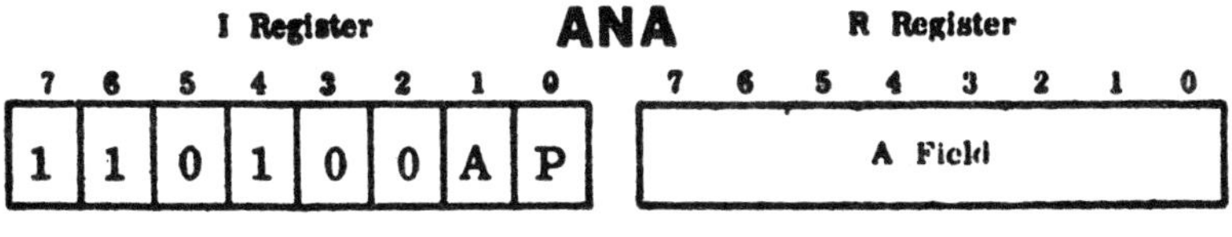

Fig. 17-21. ANA instruction.

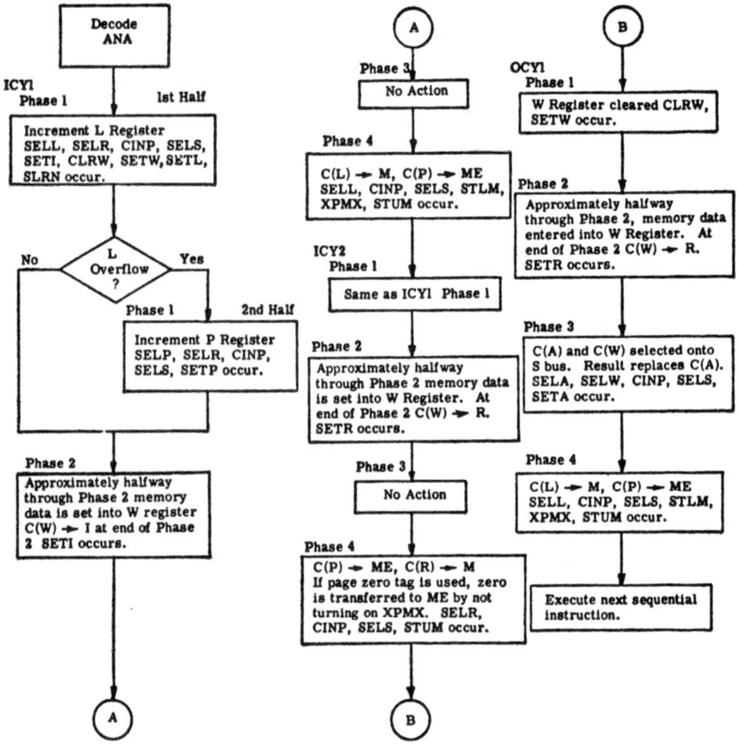

Fig. 17-22. ANA flow chart.

Cycle Sequence: ICY1, ICY2, OCY1

ICY1 cycle: Same as STA.

ICY2 cycle: Same as STA.

OCY1 cycle: Phase 1: Same as phase 1, OCY1, STA instruction. Phase 2: Same as phase 2, OCY1, LDA instruction. Phase 3: Contents of the A and W registers inclusive ORed result entered in the A register. IOR, CINP, SELS and SETA occur. Phase 4: Same as phase 4, OCY1 cycle, STA instruction.

SUB Subtract

SUB subtracts the contents of the effective memory location from the contents of the A register. The timing is 3 plus 2 for each indirect level. See Figs. 17-19 and 17-20.

Cycle Sequence: ICY1, ICY2, OCY1

ICY1 cycle: Same as STA.

ICY2 cycle: Same as STA.

OCY1 cycle: Phase 1: Same as phase 1, OCY1, STA instruction. Phase 2: Same as phase 2, OCY1 cycle, LDA instruction. Phase 3: Contents of the R register and the complemented contents of the A register are applied to the adder. The sum output is entered into the A register. SLAN, SELR, SELS and SETA occur. Phase 4: Same as phase 4, OCY1 cycle, STA instruction.

ANA AND to A

ANA ANDs the contents of the memory location specified by the A field and the C(A). Result is in A. The timing is 3 plus 2 for each indirect level. See Figs. 17-21 and 17-22.

Cycle Sequence: ICY1, ICY2, OCY1

ICY1 cycle: Same as STA.

ICY2 cycle: Same as STA.

OCY1 cycle: Phase 1: Same as phase 1, OCY1 cycle, STA instruction. Phase 2: Same as phase 2, OCY1 cycle, LDA instruction. Phase 3: Contents of the A and W registers are selected onto the S bus. Result is entered into the A register. SELA, SELW, CINP, SELS AND SETA occur. Phase 4: Same as phase 4, OCY1 cycle, STA instruction.

IMA Interchange A with Memory

IMA stores the contents of the A register in the effective memory location and loads the contents of the effective memory location into the A register. The timing is 3 plus 2 for each indirect level. See Figs. 17-23 and 17-24.

Cycle Sequence: ICY1, ICY2, OCY1

ICY1 cycle: Same as STA.

ICY2 cycle: Same as STA.

OCY1 cycle: Phase 1: Same as STA. Phase 2: Approximately halfway through phase 2 the memory data is entered in the W register. At the end of phase 2 the contents of the W register is transferred to the R register and the contents of the A register is transferred to the W register. SETW is delayed slightly from SETR to allow the transfer to take place. SELA, CINP, SELS, SETR and SETW occur. Phase 3: Contents of the R register is transferred to the A register. SELR, CINP, SELS and SETA occur. Phase 4: Same as phase 4, OCY1 cycle, STA instruction.

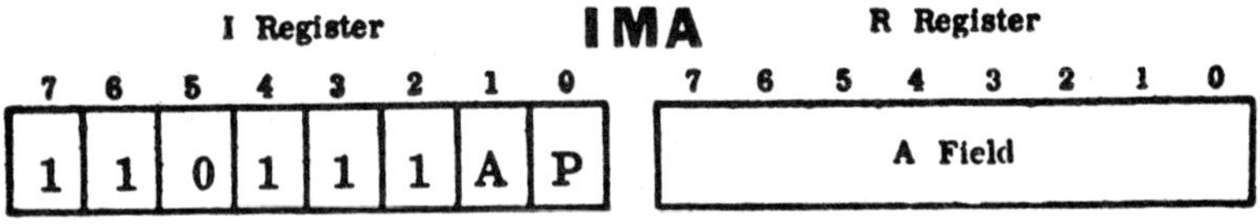

Fig. 17-23. IMA instruction.

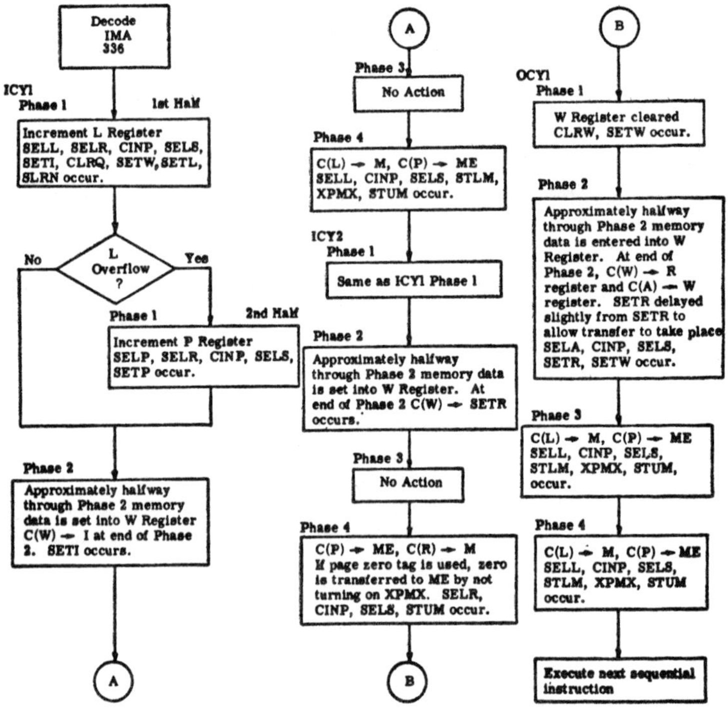

Fig. 17-24. IMA flow chart.

Fig. 17-25. JMP instruction.

JMP: Jump

The jump address is placed in the program counters for a direct jump to page zero; the P counter is reset and the A field transferred to L. A jump in the current page leaves P unchanged; an indirect jump causes the two indirect address words to be placed in the L and P counters. The timing is 2 plus 2 for each indirect level. See Figs. 17-25 and 17-26.

Cycle Sequence: ICY1, ICY2

ICY1 cycle: Same as STA.

ICY2 cycle: Phase 1. Same as phase 1, ICY2 cycle, STA

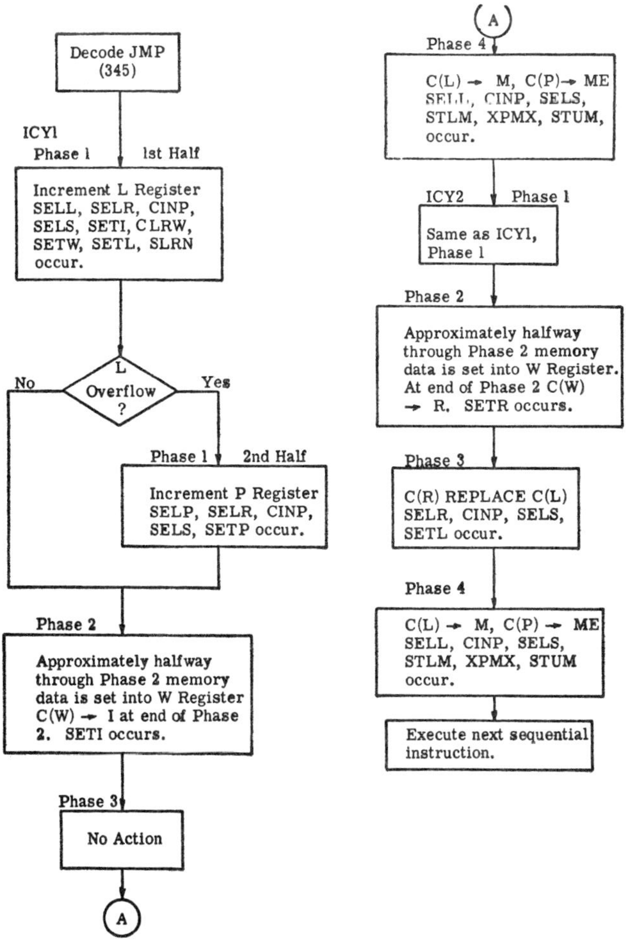

Fig. 17-26. JMP flow chart.

instruction. Phase 2. Same as phase 2, ICY2 cycle, STA instruction. Phase 3. Transfers the contents of the R register to the L register. SELR, CINP, SELS and SETL occur. Phase 4. Same as phase 4, ICY1 cycle, NOP instruction.

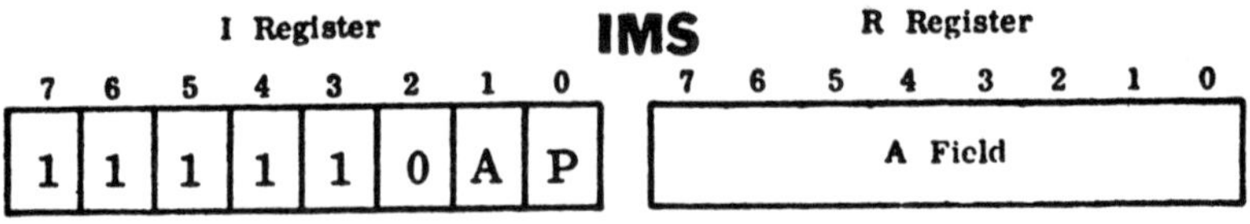

Fig. 17-27. IMS instruction.

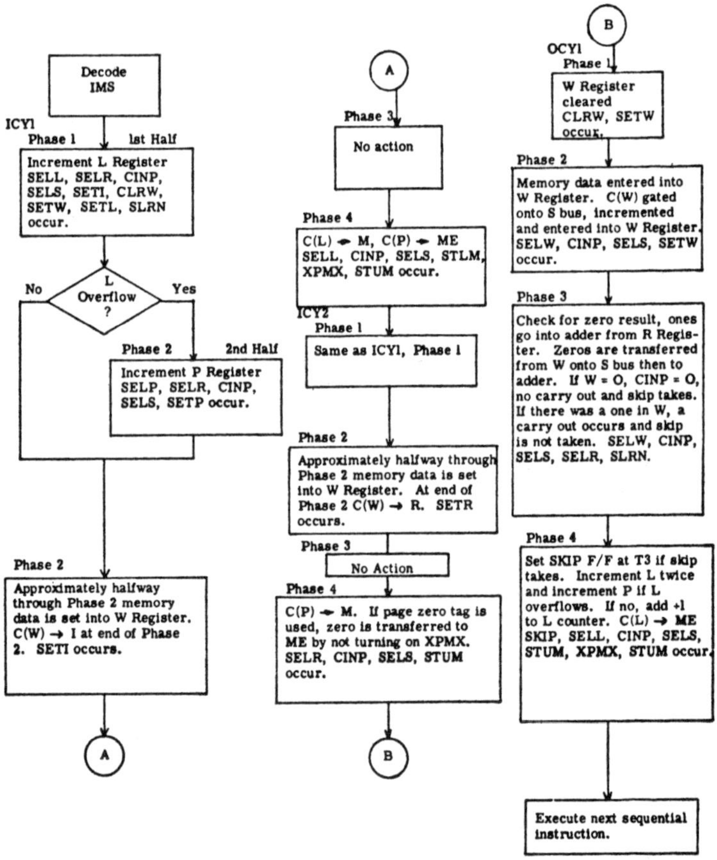

Fig. 17-28. IMS flow chart.

IMS: Increment Memory and Skip on Zero Result

The contents of the effective memory location is incremented by one count and replaced. If incrementing causes the result to become zero, a skip occurs. Overflow is set if the result of the incrementation is 200_8. Note: Neither skip nor OV occurs if IMS is executed as an interrupt instruction. The timing is 3 plus 2 per indirect level. See Figs. 17-27 and 17-28.

Cycle Sequence: ICY1, ICY2, OCY1

ICY1 cycle: Same as STA.
ICY2 cycle: Same as STA.
OCY2 cycle: Phase 1: Same as phase 1, OCY1 cycle, STA instruction. Phase 2. Memory data is entered into the W register. The W register's contents is gated onto the S bus, incremented and entered into the W register. SELW, CINP, SELS and SETW occur. Phase 3. Want to check for zero result, all 1s go into the adder from the R register. All zeros are transferred from W onto the S bus to the adder. If W was all zeros, CINP is 0 (no carry in) and there is no carry out. If there was a 1 in W, a carry out occurs and a skip is not taken. SELW, CINP-, SELS, SELR-, SLRN-, set skip F-F with T3. Phase 4: Same as skip, phase 54.

JST: Jump and Store L and P Counters

The contents of the L and P counters are stored in memory at the effective jump address and jump address plus one, and the counters are altered to contain jump address plus two. The timing is 4 plus 2 for each indirect level. See Figs. 17-29 and 17-30.

Cycle Sequence: ICY1, ICY2, OCY1, OCY2

ICY1 cycle: Same as STA.
ICY2 cycle: Same as STA.
OCY1 cycle: Phase 1: Same as Phase 1, OCY1, STA instruction. Phase 2. Approximately halfway through phase 2 the memory data is entered into the W register. At the end of Phase 2 the contents of W is transferred into the R register. After the transfer of W to R takes place the contents of L, which has been gated onto the A bus, is transferred into W. SELL, CINP, SELS, SETR and SETW occur. Phase 3: No Action. Phase 4: The contents of M is selected onto the S bus, incremented and placed back into the M register at T4 time. SELM, SELR, SLRN, CINP, SELS, SETM occur.

OCY2 cycle: Phase 1: Same as phase 1, OCY1 cycle, STA instruction. Phase 2: Approximately halfway through phase 2 the memory data is entered into the W register. At the end of Phase 2 the contents of the P register, which has been selected onto the A bus, is entered into the W register. SELP, CINP,

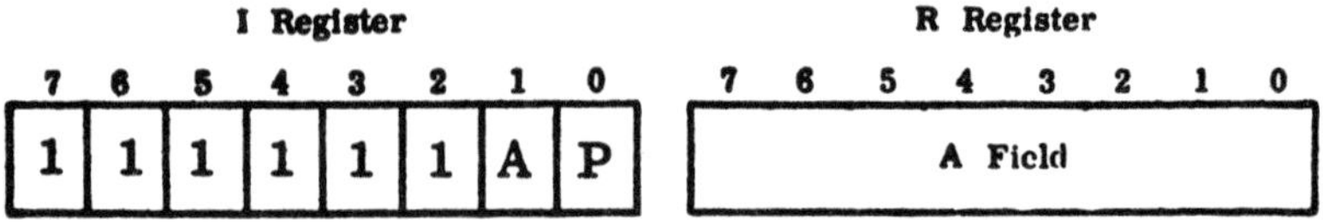

Fig. 17-29. JST instruction.

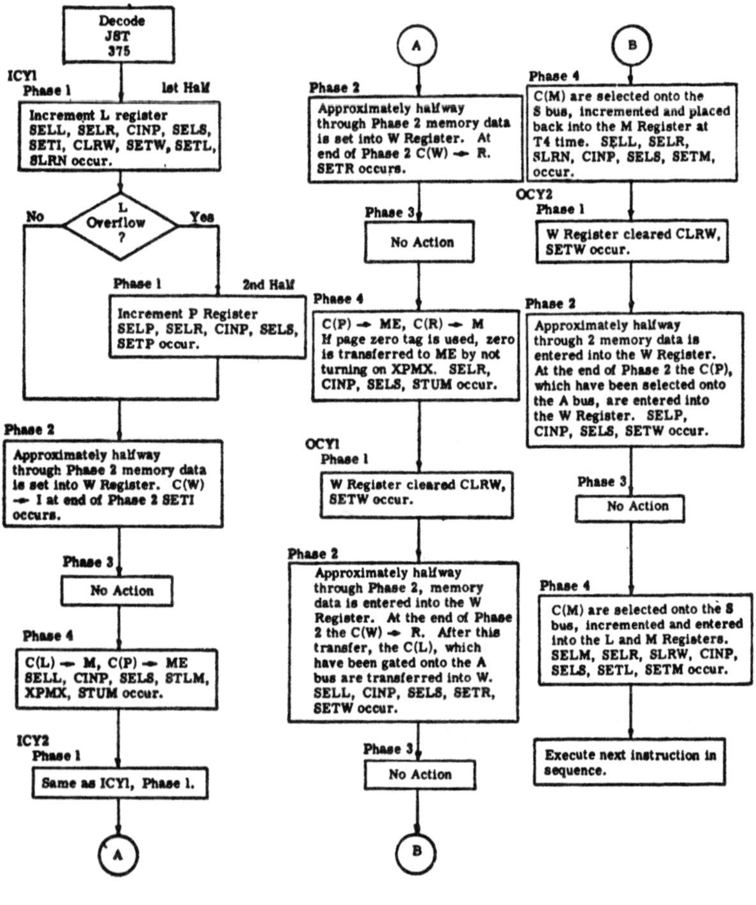

Fig. 17-30. JST flow chart.

SELS and SETW occur. Phase 3: No Action. Phase 4: Contents of the M register is selected onto the S bus, incremented and entered into the L and M registers. SELM, SELR, SLRN, CINP, SELS, SETL and SETM occur.

SKIP INSTRUCTIONS

The skip instructions allow the computer to make tests and take action based on the results of the tests. For this reason, they are referred to as IF TESTS, (IFT). "Skip if A equal to zero" tests the contents of the A Register and if the contents equals zero a skip occurs. Skips can also occur during the execution of instructions other than skips. Increment memory and skip on zero result, and I-O instructions involving sense can cause skips. When a skip occurs, the L register (counter) is incremented twice prior to accepting the next instruction. This causes two words to be skipped.

The sequence is as follows: During phase 3, the condition is tested. If the condition for a skip exists, the skip flip-flop is enabled and is set with T3 if IYAX is not on (a skip cannot be allowed during interrupts). Thus skip comes on during PH4X, the phase during which the address for the next memory cycle is usually formed, and stays on for 1.5 of the 2.0 microseconds of the phase. During this 1.5 microseconds, L is incremented twice, and P is incremented if L overflowed. During the last .5 microseconds of the phase, L and P are used to generate the memory address for the next instruction. NOTE: When manually stepping through a program, the computer normally stops when phase 4 comes on. If the instruction is a skip and the skip condition is met, the computer is not allowed to halt during phase 4, but instead made to continue and execute the next instruction.

Skip Logic

The skip flip-flop when set causes the L counter to be incremented twice, and if it overflows, the P counter is incremented. This causes two instruction locations to be skipped. A skip is not allowed if interrupt acknowledge is on since this would allow an interrupt to alter the L and P counters, causing havoc with the operating program.

Skip is set with T3 (if IUAX off) and is reset 1.5 microseconds later. Thus it is on for three-fourths of PH4. The L and P counters are modified during this time and the remaining 500 microseconds of PH4 are used to get the new address to the memory registers M and ME.

Normally the computer stops at the end of PH3 when going into the step mode. However, if a skip was about to be executed and the computer was allowed to stop at Te, skip would be set and when operation was resumed, even though L and P had been manually changed, the skip would cause L and P to be incremented. This is undesirable, hence the computer is not allowed to stop if skip is about to be set. This means that when manually stepping through a program containing skips, the computer will not stop at the end of a skip instruction if the skip condition is met, but will go ahead and make the skip, pick up the next instruction and execute it.

There are three ways the skip flip-flop can be set. By skip instructions, by increment memory and skip on zero result, and by block I-O executed under program control. In the first two cases, the skip condition is tested at the end of the instruction. In the case of block I-O, however, the skip condition is tested in the middle of the instruction (during ACY1) and the result of the test must be temporarily stored until the end of the instruction at which time skip is set. The storage device is a pair of gates cross coupled as a DC flip-flop and set by echo (if IUAX off). During OCY1, skip is enabled by this flip-flop if it has been set by echo. The format of the skip instruction appears in Chapter 12.

IFT-: Skip if A Negative

A skip will occur if the contents of the A register is less than zero. Otherwise, the next instruction in sequence is executed. The timing is 1.

Cycle Sequence: ICY1

Phase 1: W register cleared. L register incremented during the first half of phase 1. SELL, SELR, SLRN, CINP, SELS, SETI, CLRW, SETW occur. If L overflowed the P register is incremented during the second half of phase 1. SELP, SELR, SLRN, CINP, SELS and SETP occur.

Phase 2: No action.

Phase 3: Test condition. C (A) less than zero?

Phase 4: If yes, set the skip F-F at T3. Increment L twice and increment P if L overflows. If no, add +1 to the L counter and execute the next sequential instruction. Contents of the L register is transferred to the M register and the contents of the P register is transferred to the M extension register. SKIP, SELL, CINP, SELS, STLM, XPMX and STUM occur.

IFT Z: Skip if A Zero

A skip occurs if the contents of the A register is zero. Otherwise, the next instruction in sequence is executed. The timing is 1.

Cycle Sequence: ICY1

Phase 1: W register cleared. L register incremented during the first half of phase 1. SELL, SELR, SLRN, CINP, SELS, SETI, CLRW, SETW occur. If L overflowed the P register is incremented during the second half of phase 1. SELP, SELR, SLRN, CINP, SELA and SETP occur.

Phase 2: No action.

Phase 3: Test condition. C (A) equal 0?

Phase 4: If yes, set the skip F-F at T3. Increment L twice and increment P if L overflows. If no, add +1 to the L counter and execute the next instruction in sequence. Contents of the L register is transferred to the M register and the contents of the P register is transferred to the M extension register. SKIP, SELL, CINP, SELS, STLM, XPMX and STUM occur.

IFT-, Z: Skip if A Equal to or less than Zero

A skip occurs if the contents of A is zero or negative. Otherwise, the next instruction sequence is executed. The timing is 1.

Cycle Sequence: ICY1

Phase 1: W register cleared. L register incremented during the first half of phase 1. SELL, SELR, SLRN, CINP, SELS, SETI, CLRW, SETW occur. If L overflowed the P register is incremented during the second half of phase 1. SELP, SELR, SLRN, CINP, SELS and SETP occur.

Phase 2: No action.

Phase 3: Test condition. C (A) $\leq$ 0?

Phase 4: If yes, set the skip F-F at T3. Increment L twice and increment P if L overflows. If no, add +1 to the L counter and execute the next sequential instruction. Contents of the L register is transferred to the M register and the contents of the P register is transferred to the M extension register. SKIP, SELL, CINP, SELS, STLM, XPMX and STUM occur.

IFT S: Skip if OV Set

A skip occurs if the OV is set. Otherwise, execute the next sequential instruction. The timing is 1.

I Register

7	6	5	4	3	2	1	0
1	0	0	0	0	1	0	1

IFT–

I Register

7	6	5	4	3	2	1	0
1	0	0	0	0	0	1	0

IFT Z

I Register

7	6	5	4	3	2	1	0
1	0	0	0	0	0	1	1

IFT–,Z

I Register

7	6	5	4	3	2	1	0
1	0	0	0	0	1	0	0

IFT S

I Register

7	6	5	4	3	2	1	0
1	0	0	0	0	1	0	1

IFT S–

I Register

7	6	5	4	3	2	1	0
1	0	0	0	0	1	1	0

IFT S,Z

I Register

7	6	5	4	3	2	1	0
1	0	0	0	0	1	1	1

IFT S,Z,–

I Register

7	6	5	4	3	2	1	0
1	0	0	0	1	0	0	0

IFT O

I Register

7	6	5	4	3	2	1	0
1	0	0	0	1	0	0	1

IFT O-

I Register

7	6	5	4	3	2	1	0
1	0	0	0	1	0	1	0

IFT O,Z

I Register

7	6	5	4	3	2	1	0
1	0	0	0	1	0	1	1

IFT O,Z-

I Register

7	6	5	4	3	2	1	0
1	0	0	0	1	1	0	0

IFT O,S

I Register

7	6	5	4	3	2	1	0
1	0	0	0	1	1	0	1

IFT O,S-

I Register

7	6	5	4	3	2	1	0
1	0	0	0	1	1	1	0

IFT O,S,Z

I Register

7	6	5	4	3	2	1	0
1	0	0	0	1	1	1	1

IFT O,S,Z-

Fig. 17-31. Skip instructions for negative or zero.

Cycle Sequence: ICY1

Phase 1: W register cleared. L register incremented during the first half of phase 1. SELL, SELR, SLRN, CINP, SELS, SETI, CLRW, SETW occur. If L overflowed the P register is incremented during the second half of phase 1. SELP, SELR, SLRN, CINP, SELS and SETP occur.

Phase 2: No action.

Phase 3: Test condition. Is OV set?

Phase 4: If yes, set the skip F-F at T3. Increment L twice and increment P if L overflows. If no, add +1 to the L counter and execute the next sequential instruction. Contents of the L register is transferred to the M register and the contents of the P register is transferred to the M extension register. SKIP, SELL, CINP, SELS, STLM, XPMX and STUM occur.

IFT S-: Skip if OV Set Or A Negative

A skip occurs if the OV F-F is set or the C(A) is negative. Otherwise, execute the next sequential instruction. The timing is 1.

Cycle Sequence: ICY1

Phase 1: W register cleared. L register incremented during the first half of phase 1. SELL, SELR, SLRN, CINP, SELS, SETI, CLRW, SETW occur. If L overflowed the P register is incremented during the second half of phase 1. SELP, SELR, SLRN, CINP, SELS and SETP occur.

Phase 2: No action.

Phase 3: Test condition. Is the OV F-F set or are C(A) negative?

Phase 4: If either condition exists, set the skip F-F at T3. Increment L twice and increment P if L overflows. If neither condition exists, add +1 to the L counter and execute the next sequential instruction. Contents of the L register is transferred to the M register and the contents of the P register is transferred to the M extension register. SKIP, SELL, CINP, SELS, STLM, XPMX and STUM occur.

IFT S, Z: Skip if OV Set Or A Zero

A skip occurs if the OV F-F is set or C(A) are 0. Otherwise, execute the next sequential instruction. The timing is 1.

Cycle Sequence: ICY1

Phase 1: W register cleared. L register incremented during the first half of phase 1. SELL, SELR, SLRN, CINP, SELS, SETI, CLRW, SETW occur. If L overflowed the P register is incremented during the second half of phase 1. SELP, SELR, SLRN, CINP, SELS and SETP occur.

Phase 2: No action.

Phase 3: Test condition. Is OV F-F set or are C(A) equal to 0?

Phase 4: If either condition exists, set the skip F-F at T3. Increment L twice and increment P if L overflows. If neither condition exists, add +1 to the L counter and execute the next sequential instruction. Contents of the L register is transferred to the M register and the contents of the P register is transferred to the M extension register. SKIP, SELL, CINP, SELS, STLM, XPMX and STUM occur.

IFT S, Z,-: Skip if OV Set or A Zero

A skip occurs if either OV F-F is set or C(A) are 0. Otherwise, execute the next sequential instruction. The timing is 1.

Cycle Sequence: ICY1

Phase 1: W register cleared. L register incremented during the first half of phase 1. SELL, SELR, SLRN, CINP, SELS, SETI, CLRW, SETW occur. If L overflowed the P register is incremented during the second half of phase 1. SELP, SELR, SLRN, CINP, SELS and SETP occur.

Phase 2: No action.

Phase 3: Test condition. Is either OV F-F set or are C(A) equal to 0?

Phase 4: If either condition exists, set the skip F-F at T3. Increment L twice and increment P if L overflows. If neither condition exists, add +1 to the L counter and execute the next sequential instruction. Contents of the L register is transferred to the M register and the contents of the P register is transferred to the M extension register. SKIP, SELL, CINP, SELS, STLM, XPMX and STUM occur.

IFT 0: Skip if Sense Switch Off

A skip occurs if the console sense switch is off (not depressed). Otherwise, the next instruction in sequence is executed. The timing is 1.

I Register

7	6	5	4	3	2	1	0
1	0	1	0	0	0	0	1

IFT+

I Register

7	6	5	4	3	2	1	0
1	0	1	0	0	0	1	0

IFT N

I Register

7	6	5	4	3	2	1	0
1	0	1	0	0	0	1	1

IFT+.N

I Register

7	6	5	4	3	2	1	0
1	0	1	0	0	1	0	0

IFT R

I Register

7	6	5	4	3	2	1	0
1	0	1	0	0	1	0	1

IFT R.+

I Register

7	6	5	4	3	2	1	0
1	0	1	0	0	1	1	0

IFT R.N

I Register

7	6	5	4	3	2	1	0
1	0	1	0	0	1	1	1

IFT R.N.+

I Register

7	6	5	4	3	2	1	0
1	0	1	0	1	0	0	0

IFT 1

I Register

7	6	5	4	3	2	1	0
1	0	1	0	1	0	0	1

IFT 1.+

I Register

7	6	5	4	3	2	1	0
1	0	1	0	1	0	1	0

IFT 1. N.

I Register

7	6	5	4	3	2	1	0
1	0	1	0	1	0	1	1

IFT 1.N+

I Register

7	6	5	4	3	2	1	0
1	0	1	0	1	1	0	0

IFT 1.R

I Register

7	6	5	4	3	2	1	0
1	0	1	0	1	1	0	1

IFT 1. R.+

I Register

7	6	5	4	3	2	1	0
1	0	1	0	1	1	1	0

IFT 1.R.N.

I Register

7	6	5	4	3	2	1	0
1	0	1	0	1	1	1	1

IFT1.R.N.+

Fig. 17-32. Skip instructions for positive or non-zero.

Cycle Sequence: ICY1

Phase 1: W register cleared. L register incremented during the first half of phase 1. SELL, SELR, SLRN, CINP, SELS, SETI, CLRW, SETW occur. If L overflowed the P register is incremented during the second half of phase 1. SELP, SELR, SLRN, CINP, SELS and SETP occur.

Phase 2: No action.

Phase 3: Test condition. Is the sense switch off?

Phase 4: If yes, set the skip F-F at T3. Increment L twice and increment P if L overflows. If no, add +1 to the L counter and execute the next sequential instruction. Contents of the L register is transferred to the M register and the P register is transferred to the M extension register. SKIP, SELL, CINP, SELS, STLM, XPMX and STUM occur.

IFT O- Skip if Sense Switch Reset or A Negative

A skip occurs if either the console sense switch is reset or C(A) are negative. Otherwise, execute the next sequential instruction. The timing is 1.

Cycle Sequence: ICY1

Phase 1: W register cleared. L register incremented during the first half of phase 1. SELL, SELR, SLRN, CINP, SELS, SETI, CLRW, SETW occur. If L overflowed the P register is incremented during the second half of phase 1. SELP, SELR, SLRN, CINP, SELS and SETP occur.

Phase 2: No action.

Phase 3: Test condition. Is either console switch reset or are C(A) negative?

Phase 4: If either condition exists, set the skip F-F at T3. Increment L twice and increment P if L overflows. If neither condition exists, add +1 to the L counter and execute the next sequential instruction. Contents of the L register is transferred to the M register and the contents of the P register is transferred to the M extension register. SKIP, SELL, CINP, SELS, STLM, XPMX and STUM occur.

IFT O, Z: Skip if Sense Switch Reset or A Zero

A skip occurs if the console sense switch is reset or C(A) are zero. Otherwise, execute the next sequential instruction. The timing is 1.

Cycle Sequence: ICY1

Phase 1: W register cleared. L register incremented during the first half of phase 1. SELL, SELR, SLRN, CINP, SELS, SETI, CLRW, SETW occur. If L overflowed the P register is incremented during the second half of phase 1. SELP, SELR, SLRN, CINP, SELS and SETP occur.

Phase 2: No action.

Phase 3: Test condition. Is the sense switch off or are C(A) equal to 0?

....**Phase 4:** If either condition exists, set the skip F-F at T3. Increment L twice and increment P if L overflows. If neither condition exists, add +1 to the L counter and execute the next sequential instruction. Contents of the L register is transferred to the M register and the contents of the P register is transferred to the M extension register. SKIP, SELL, CINP, SELS, STLM, XPMX and STUM occur.

IFT O, Z- : Skip if Sense Switch Reset or A Zero or Negative

A skip occurs if the console sense switch is off or C(A) are 0 or C(A) are negative. Otherwise, execute the next instruction in sequence. The timing is 1.

Cycle Sequence: ICY1

Phase 1: W register cleared. L register incremented during the first half of phase 1. SELL, SELR, SLRN, CINP, SELS, SETI, CLRW, SETW occur. If L overflowed the P register is incremented during the second half of phase 1. SELP, SELR, SLRN, CINP, SELS and SETP occur.

Phase 2: No action.

Phase 3: Test condition. Is the sense switch reset or are C(A) equal to 0 or C(A) negative?

Phase 4: If any one of the conditions are met set the skip F-F at T3. Increment L twice and increment P if L overflows. If none of the conditions exist, add +1 to the L counter and execute the next sequential instruction. Contents of the L register is transferred to the M register and the contents of the P register is transferred to the M extension register. SKIP, SELL, CINP, SELS, STLM, XPMX and STUM occur.

IFT O, S: Skip if Sense Switch Reset or OV Set

A skip occurs if either the console sense switch is reset or the OV F-F is set. Otherwise, execute the next sequential instruction. The timing is 1.

Cycle Sequence: ICY1

Phase 1: W register cleared. L register incremented during the first half of phase 1. SELL, SELR, SLRN, CINP, SELS, SETI, CLRW, SETW occur. If L overflowed the P register is incremented during the second half of phase 1. SELP, SELR, SLRN, CINP, SELS and SETP occur.

Phase 2: No action.

Phase 3: Test condition. Is the sense switch off or the OV F-F set?

Phase 4: If either condition exists, set the skip F-F at T3. Increment L twice and increment P if L overflows. If neither condition exists, add +1 to the L counter and execute the next sequential instruction. Contents of the L register is transferred to the M register and the contents of the P register is transferred to the M extension register. SKIP, SELL, CINP, SELS, STLM, XPMX and STUM occur.

IFT O, S-,: Skip if Sense Switch Reset or OV Set

A skip occurs if either the console sense switch is reset or the OV F-F is set. Otherwise, execute the next sequential instruction. The timing is 1.

Cycle Sequence: ICY1

Phase 1: W register cleared. L register incremented during the first half of phase 1. SELL, SELR, SLRN, CINP, SELS, SETI, CLRW, SETW occur. If L overflowed the P register is incremented during the second half of Phase 1. SELP, SELR, SLRN, CINP, SELS and SETP occur.

Phase 2: No action.

Phase 3: Test condition. Is the sense switch off or the OV F-F set?

Phase 4: If either condition exists, set the skip F-F at T3. Increment L twice and increment P if L overflows. If neither condition exists, add +1 to the L counter and execute the next sequential instruction. Contents of the L register is transferred to the M register and the contents of the P register is transferred to the M extension register. SKIP, SELL, CINP, SELS, STLM, XPMX and STUM occur.

IFT O, S, Z: Skip if Sense Switch Reset or OV Set or A Zero

A skip occurs if any one of the three conditions is met. They are: 1. Sense switch off; 2. OV F-F set; 3. C(A) are 0. The timing is 1.

Cycle Sequence: ICY1

Phase 1: W register cleared. L register incremented during the first half of phase 1. SELL, SELR, SLRN, CINP, SELS, SETI, CLRW, SETW occur. If L overflowed the P register is incremented during the second half of phase 1. SELP, SELR, SLRN, CINP, SELS and SETP occur.

Phase 2: No action.

Phase 3: Test conditions. Sense switch off, or OV F-F set or C(A) equal to 0?

Phase 4: If any one of the conditions is met, set the skip F-F at T3. Increment L twice and increment P if L overflows. If none of the conditions exist, add +1 to the L counter and execute the next sequential instruction. Contents of the L register is transferred to the M register and the contents of the P register is transferred to the M extension register. SKIP, SELL, CINP, SELS, STLM, XPMX and STUM occur.

IFT O, S, Z-: Skip if Sense Switch Reset or OV Set or A Zero or Negative

A skip occurs if any one of the following four conditions is met: 1. Sense switch off; 2. OV F-F set; 3. C(A) equal 0; 4. C(A) are negative. The timing is 1.

Cycle Sequence: ICY1

Phase 1: W register cleared. L register incremented during the first half of phase 1. SELL, SELR, SLRN, CINP, SELS, SETI, CLRW, SETW occur. If L overflowed the P register is incremented during the second half of phase 1. SELP, SELR, SLRN, CINP, SELS and SETP occur.

Phase 2: No action.

Phase 3: Test conditions. Are any of the conditions listed above met?

Phase 4: If any one of the conditions is met, set the skip F-F at T3. Increment L twice and increment P if L overflows. If none of the conditions exist, add +1 to the L counter and execute the next sequential instruction. Contents of the L register is transferred to the M register and the contents of the P register is transferred to the M extension register. SKIP, SELL, CINP, SELS, STLM, XPMX and STUM occur.

AND SKIP GROUP

The 15 instructions in this group are a combination of the four conditions. If more than one condition is specified (by placing a 1 in the condition bit) the AND of all specified conditions must be met to cause a skip. For the skip instruction format, see Chapter 12.

IFT: Skip if A Positive

A skip occurs if the C(A) are positive. Otherwise, execute the next instruction in sequence. The timing is 1.

Cycle Sequence: ICY1

Phase 1: W register cleared. L register incremented during the first half of phase 1. SELL, SELR, SLRN, CINP, SELS, SETI, CLRW, SETW occur. If L overflowed the P register is incremented during the second half of phase 1. SELP, SELR, SLRN, CINP, SELS, and SETP occur.

Phase 2: No action.

Phase 3: Test condition. Are the C(A) positive?

Phase 4: If yes set skip F-F at T3. Increment L twice and increment P if L overflowed. If no, add +1 to the L counter and execute the next sequential instruction. Contents of the L register is transferred to the M register and the contents of the P register is transferred to the M extension register. SKIP, SELL, SINP, SELS, STLM, XPMX and STUM occur.

IFT N: Skip if A Non-Zero

A skip occurs if the contents of the A register is not zero. Otherwise, the next instruction in sequence is executed. The timing is 1.

Cycle Sequence: ICY1

Phase 1: W register cleared. L register incremented during the first half of phase 1. SELL, SELR, SLRN, CINP, SELS, SETI, CLRW, SETW occur. If L overflowed the P register is incremented during the second half of phase 1. SELP, SELR, SLRN, CINP, SELS and SETP occur.

Phase 2: No action.

Phase 3: Test condition. Does A contain any 1s?

Phase 4: If yes, set the skip F-F at T3. Increment L twice and increment P if L overflowed. If A contains all zeros, add +1 to the L counter and execute the next sequential instruction. Contents of the L register is transferred to the M register and the contents of the P register is transferred to the M extension register. SKIP, SELL, CINP, SELS, STLM, XPMX and STUM occur.

IFT +.N: Skip if A Greater than Zero

A skip occurs if C(A) are greater than zero. Otherwise, the next instruction in sequence is executed. The timing is 1.

Cycle Sequence: ICY1

Phase 1: W register cleared. L register incremented during the first half of phase 1. SELL, SELR, SLRN, CINP, SELS, SETI, CLRW, SETW occur. If L overflowed the P register is incremented during the second half of phase 1. SELP, SELR, SLRN, CINP, SELS and SETP occur.

Phase 2: No action.

Phase 3: Test condition. Is A positive and does it contain any 1s?

Phase 4: If yes, set the skip F-F at T3. Increment L twice and increment P if L overflowed. If no, add +1 to the L counter and execute the next sequential instruction. Contents of the L register is transferred to the M register and the contents of the P register is transferred to the M extension register. SKIP, SELL, CINP, SELS, STLM, XPMX and STUM occur.

IFT R: Skip if OV Reset

A skip occurs if OV is not on. Otherwise, the next instruction sequence is executed. The timing is 1.

Cycle Sequence: ICY1

Phase 1: W register cleared. L register incremented during the first half of phase 1. SELL, SELR, SLRN, CINP, SELS, SETI, CLRW, SETW occur. If L overflowed the P register is incremented during the second half of phase 1. SELP, SELR, SLRN, CINP, SELS and SETP occur.

Phase 2: No action.

Phase 3. Test condition. Is the OV F-F set?

Phase 4: If the OV F-F is not set then set the skip F-F at T3. Increment L twice and increment P if L overflowed. If OV F-F is set, add +1 to the L counter and execute the next sequential instruction. Contents of the L register is transferred to the M register and the contents of the P register is transferred to the M extension register. SKIP, SELL, CINP, SELS, STLM, XPMX and STUM occur.

IFT R.+: Skip if OV Reset and A Positive

A skip occurs if the OV F-F is reset and A is positive. Otherwise, execute the next instruction in sequence. The timing is 1.

Cycle Sequence: ICY1

Phase 1: W register cleared. L register incremented during the first half of phase 1. SELL, SELR, SLRN, CINP, SELS, SETI, CLRW, SETW occur. If L overflowed the P register is incremented during the second half of phase 1. SELP, SELR, SLRN, CINP, SELS and SETP occur.

Phase 2: No action.

Phase 3: Test condition. Are the C(A) greater than zero?

Phase 4: If yes, set the skip F-F at T3. Increment L twice and increment P if L overflowed. If no, add +1 to the L counter and execute the next sequential instruction. Contents of the L register is transferred to the M register and the contents of the P register is transferred to the M extension register. SKIP, SELL, CINP, SELS, STLM, XPMX and STUM occur.

IFT R.N: Skip if OV Reset and A Positive and Non-Zero

A skip occurs if the OV F-F is reset and C(A) are positive and greater than 1. Otherwise, execute the next sequential instruction. The timing is 1.

Cycle Sequence: ICY1

Phase 1: W register cleared. L register incremented during the first half of phase 1. SELL, SELR, SLRN, CINP, SELS, SETI, CLRW, SETW occur. If L overflowed the P register is incremented during the second half of phase 1. SELP, SELR, SLRN, CINP, SELS and SETP occur.

Phase 2: No action.

Phase 3: Test condition. Is the OV F-F reset and are C(A) positive and greater than 1?

Phase 4: If yes, set the skip F-F at T3. Increment L twice and increment P if L overflowed. If no, add +1 to the L counter and execute the next sequential instruction. Contents of the L register is transferred to the M register and the contents of the P register is transferred to the M extension register. SKIP, SELL, CINP, SELS, STLM, XPMX and STUM occur.

IFT R.N.+ Skip if OV Reset and A Positive and Non-Zero

A skip occurs if the OV F-F is reset and C(A) are positive and greater than zero. Otherwise, execute the next sequential instruction. The timing is 1.

Cycle Sequence: ICY1

Phase 1: W register cleared. L register incremented during the first half of phase 1. SELL, SELR, SLRN, CINP, SELS, SETI, CLRW, SETW occur. If L overflowed the P register is incremented during the second half of phase 1. SELP, SELR, SLRN, CINP, SELS and SETP occur.

Phase 2: No action.

Phase 3: Test condition. Is the OV F-F reset and are C(A) positive and greater than zero?

Phase 4: If yes, set the skip F-F at T3. Increment L twice and increment P if L overflows. If no, add +1 to the L counter and execute the next sequential instruction. Contents of the L register is transferred to the M extension register. SKIP, SELL, CINP, SELS, STLM, XPMX and STUM occur.

IFT 1: Skip if Sense Switch On

A skip occurs if the console sense switch is on. Otherwise. the next instruction in sequence is executed. The timing is 1.

Cycle Sequence: ICY1

Phase 1: W register cleared. L register incremented during the first half of phase 1. SELL, SELR, SLRN, CINP, SELS, SETI, CLRW, SETW occur. If L overflowed the P register is incremented during the second half of phase 1. SELP, SELR, SLRN, CINP, SELS, and SETP occur.

Phase 2: No action.

Phase 3: Test condition. Is the sense switch on?

Phase 4: If yes, set the skip F-F at T3. Increment L twice and increment P if L overflowed. If no, add +1 to the L counter and execute the next sequential instruction. Contents of the L register is transferred to the M register and the contents of the P register is transferred to the M extension register. SKIP, SELL, CINP, SELS, STLM, XPMX and STUM occur.

IFT 1. +: Skip if Sense Switch Set and A Positive

A skip occurs if the console sense switch is on and C(A) are positive. Otherwise, execute the next instruction in sequence. The timing is 1.

Cycle Sequence: ICY1

Phase 1: W register cleared. L register incremented during the first half of phase 1. SELL, SELR, SLRN, CINP, SELS, SETI, CLRW, SETW occur. If L overflowed the P register is incremented during the second half of phase 1. SELP, SELR, SLRN, CINP, SELS, and SETP occur.

Phase 2: No action.

Phase 3: Test condition. Is the sense switch on and are C(A) positive?

Phase 4: If yes, set the skip F-F at T3. Increment L twice and increment P if L overflows. If no, add +1 to the L counter and execute the next sequential instruction. Contents of the L register is transferred to the M register and the contents of the P register is transferred to the M extension register. SKIP, SELL, CINP, SELS, STLM, XPMX and STUM occur.

IFT 1.N: Skip if Sense Switch Set and A Non-Zero

A skip occurs if the console sense switch is on and the C(A) are greater than zero. Otherwise, execute the next sequential instruction. The timing is 1.

Cycle Sequence: ICY1

Phase 1: W register cleared. L register incremented during the first half of phase 1. SELL, SELR, SLRN, CINP, SELS, SETI, CLRW, SETW occur. If L overflowed the P register is incremented during the second half of phase 1. SELP, SELR, SLRN, CINP, SELS and SETP occur.

Phase 2: No action.

Phase 3: Test condition. Is the sense switch on and are C(A) more than zero?

Phase 4: If yes, set the skip F-F at T3. Increment L twice and increment P if L overflows. If no, add +1 to the L counter and execute the next sequential instruction. Contents of the L register is transferred to the M register and the contents of the P register is transferred to the M extension register. SKIP, SELL, CINP, SELS, STLM, XPMX and STUM occur.

IFT 1. N+: Skip if Sense Switch Set and A Positive and Non-Zero

A skip occurs if the console switch is set and C(A) are positive and non-zero. Otherwise, execute the next sequential instruction. The timing is 1.

Cycle Sequence: ICY1

Phase 1: W register cleared. L register incremented during the first half of phase 1. SELL, SELR, SLRN, CINP, SELS, SETI, CLRW, SETW occur. If L overflowed the P register is incremented during the second half of phase 1. SELP, SELR, SLRN, CINP, SELS and SETP occur.

Phase 2: No action.

Phase 3: Test condition. Is the sense switch set and are C(A) positive and greater than zero.

Phase 4: If yes, set the skip F-F at T3. Increment L twice and increment P if L overflows. If no, add +1 to the L counter and execute the next sequential instruction. Contents of the L register is transferred to the M register and the contents of the P register is transferred to the M extension register. SKIP, SELL, CINP, SELS, STLM, XPMX and STUM occur.

IFT 1. R: Skip if Sense Switch Set and OV Reset

A skip occurs if the console sense switch is set and the OV F-F is reset. Otherwise, execute the next instruction in sequence. The timing is 1.

Cycle Sequence: ICY1

Phase 1: W register cleared. L register incremented during the first half of phase 1. SELL, SELR, SLRN, CINP, SELS, SETI, CLRW, SETW occur. If L overflowed the P register is incremented during the second half of phase 1. SELP, SELR, SLRN, CINP, SELS and SETP occur.

Phase 2: No action.

Phase 3: Test condition. Is the sense switch on and the OV F-F reset?

Phase 4: If yes, set the skip F-F at T3. Increment L twice and increment P if L overflows. If no, add +1 to the L counter and execute the next sequential instruction. Contents of the L register is transferred to the M register and the contents of the P register is transferred to the M extension register. SKIP, SELL, CINP, SELS, STLM, XPMX and STUM occur.

IFT 1. R.+: Skip if Sense Switch Set and OV Reset and A Positive

A skip occurs if the console sense switch is set and the OV F-F is reset and the C(A) are positive. Otherwise, execute the next instruction in sequence. The timing is 1.

Cycle Sequence: ICY1

Phase 1: W register cleared. L register incremented during the first half of phase 1. SELL, SELR, SLRN, CINP, SELS, SETI, CLRW, SETW occur. If L overflowed the P register is incremented during the second half of phase 1. SELP, SELR, SLRN, CINP, SELS, and SETP occur.

Phase 2: No action.

Phase 3: Test condition. Is the sense switch on and the OV F-F reset and are C(A) positive?

Phase 4: If yes, set the skip F-F at T3. Increment L twice and increment P if L overflows. If no, add +1 to the L counter and execute the next sequential instruction. Contents of the L register is transferred to the M register and the contents of the P register is transferred to the M extension register. SKIP, SELL, CINP, SELS, STLM, XPMX and STUM occur.

IFT 1. R.N: Skip if Sense Switch Set and OV Reset and A Non-Zero

A skip occurs if the console sense switch is on and the OV F-F is reset and C(A) are non-zero. Otherwise, execute the next sequential instruction. The timing is 1.

Cycle Sequence: ICY1

Phase 1: W register cleared. L register incremented during the first half of phase 1. SELL, SELR, SLRN, CINP, SELS, SETI, CLRW, SETW occur. If L overflowed the P register is incremented during the second half of phase 1. SELP, SELR, SLRN, CINP, SELS, and SETP occur.

Phase 2: No action.

Phase 3: Test condition. Is the sense switch on and the OV F-F reset and are C(A) non-zero?

Phase 4: If yes, set the skip F-F at T3. Increment L twice and increment P if L overflows. If no, add +1 to the L counter and execute the next sequential instruction. Contents of the L register is transferred to the M register and the contents of the P register is transferred to the M extension register. SKIP, SELL, CINP, SELS, STLM, XPMX and STUM occur.

IFT 1. R.N.+: Skip if Sense Switch Set and OV reset and A Non-Zero And A Positive

A skip occurs if the sense switch is on, the OV F-F is reset and C(A) are non-zero and positive. Otherwise, execute the next instruction in sequence. The timing is 1.

Cycle Sequence: ICY1

Phase 1: W register cleared. L register incremented during the first half of phase 1. SELL, SELR, SLRN, CINP, SELS, SETI, CLRW, SETW occur. If L overflowed the P register is incremented during the second half of phase 1. SELP, SELR, SLRN, CINP, SELS and SETP occur.

Phase 2: No action.

Phase 3: Test condition. Is the sense switch on and the OV F-F reset and are C(A) non-zero and positive?

Phase 4: If yes, set the skip F-F at T3. Increment L twice and increment P if L overflowed. If no, add +1 to the L counter and execute the next sequential instruction. Contents of the L register is transferred to the M register and the contents of the P register is transferred to the M extension register. SKIP, SELL, CINP, SELS, STLM, XPMX and STUM occur.

Figs. 17-33 through 17-44 are waveforms of various processor instructions. In all cases the ICY1 waveform appears at the top.

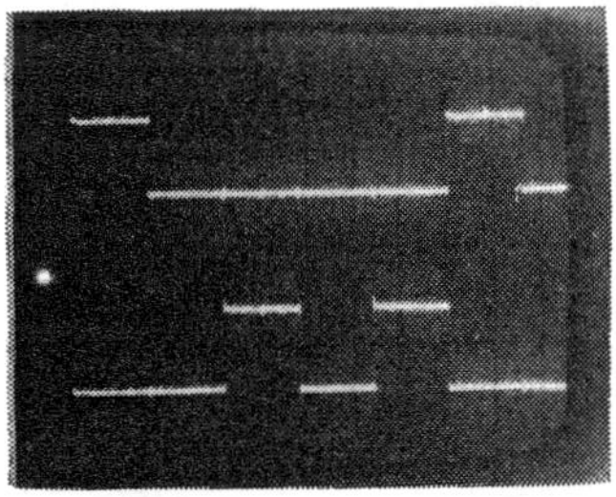

Fig. 17-33. ICY2 waveform (bottom) and ICY1. 5 microsecond sweep, 2v div.

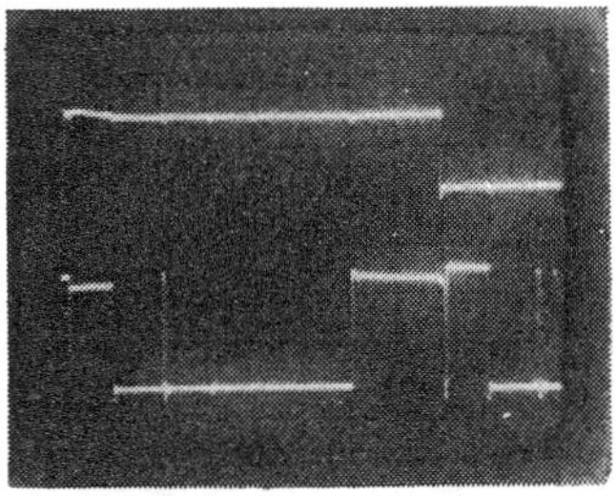

Fig. 17-34. SELL waveform (bottom) and ICY1. 1 microsecond sweep, 2v div.

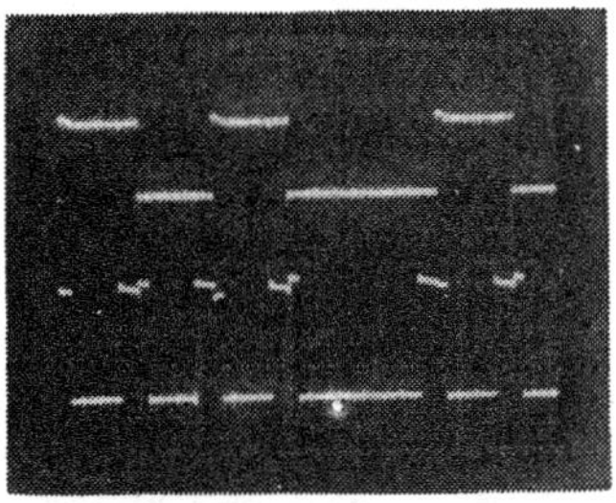

Fig. 17-35. SELL waveform (bottom) and ICY1. 5 microsecond sweep, 2v div.

Fig. 17-36. SLRN waveform (bottom) and ICY1. 5 microsecond sweep, 2v div.

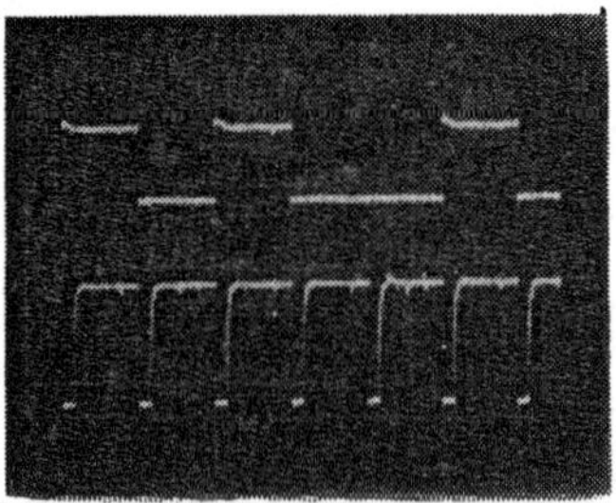

Fig. 17-37. CLRW waveform (bottom) and ICY1. 5 microsecond sweep, 2v div.

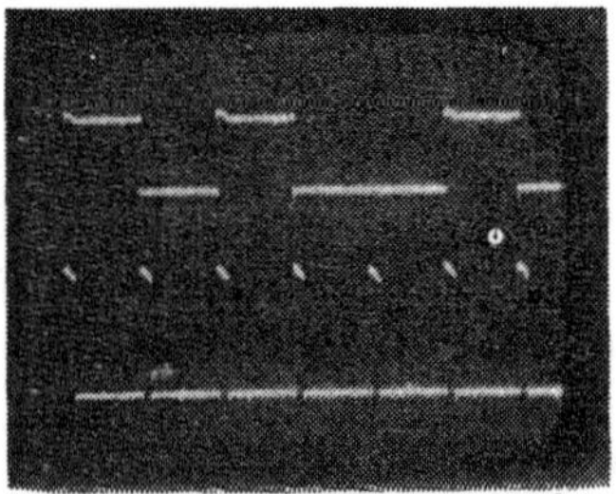

Fig. 17-38. SETW waveform (bottom) and ICY1. 5 microsecond sweep, 2v div.

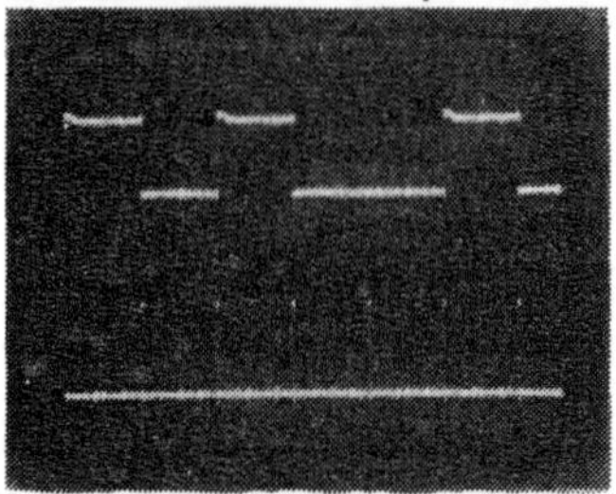

Fig. 17-39. STLM, STUM waveform (bottom) and ICY1.

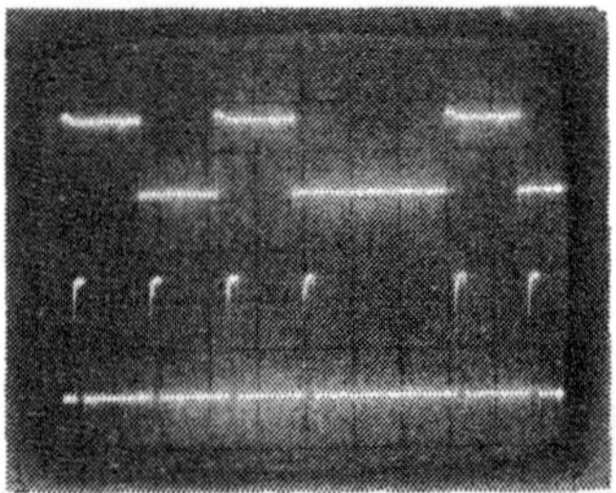

Fig. 17-40. SELP waveform (bottom) and ICY1. 5 microsecond sweep, 2v div.

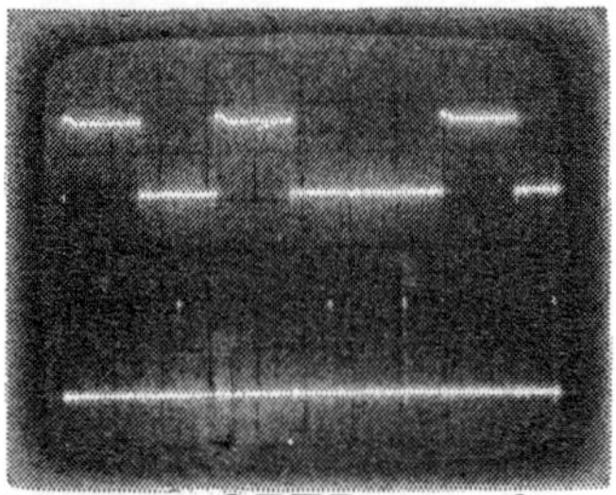

Fig. 17-41. SETR waveform (bottom) and ICY1. 5 microsecond sweep, 2v div.

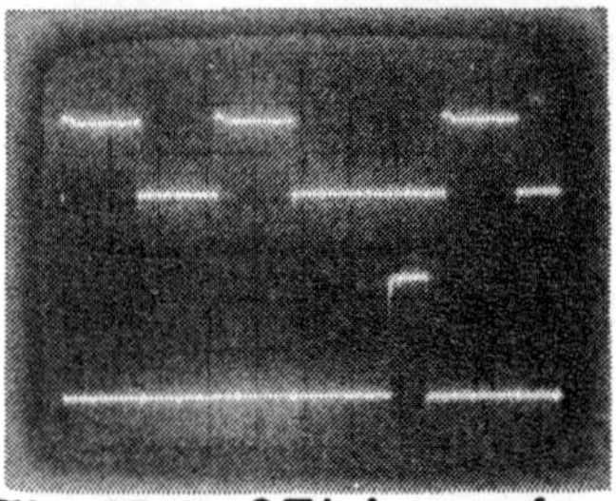

Fig. 17-42. SELA waveform (bottom) and ICY1. 5 microsecond sweep, 2v div.

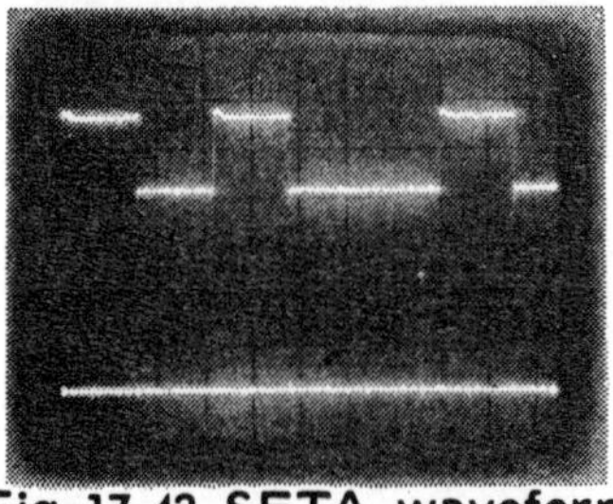

Fig. 17-43. SETA waveform (bottom) and ICY1. 5 microsecond sweep, 2v div.

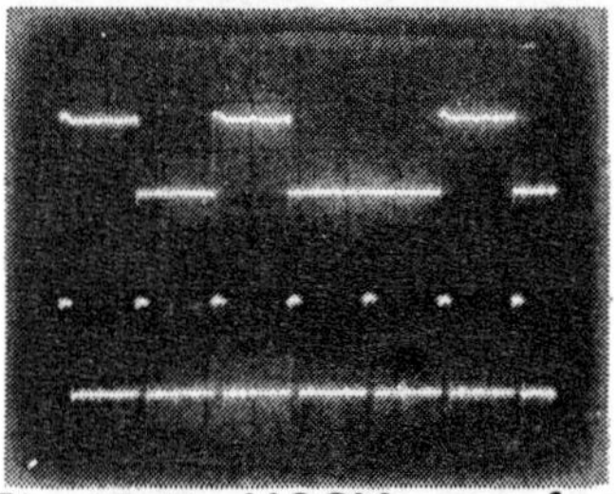

Fig. 17-44. MSCX waveform (bottom) and ICY1. 5 microsecond sweep, 2v div.

Chapter 18

Input-Output Operation

There are six types of I-O instructions: sense, external control, input to A, output from A, input block to memory, and output block from memory. By combining the sense and the input or output instructions two additional types are created: sense and input conditionally, and sense and output conditionally. Each I-O instruction may refer to one of 32 different device numbers or addresses. (The useful combination of I-O instructions in the 208 and 808 systems total over 1800 instructions.)

I-O instructions are double-word instructions as shown in Fig. 18-1. The first word specifies the class (I-O in this case), the operation code and special conditions available by micro-coding. The second word specifies the device address (5 bits) of the device with which communication is to take place, and a 3-bit function code. The 3-bit function code allows up to eight functions to be created within the same flip-flops and may be tested (sensed) by executing the "sense device 4" instruction eight times with the eight different function codes.

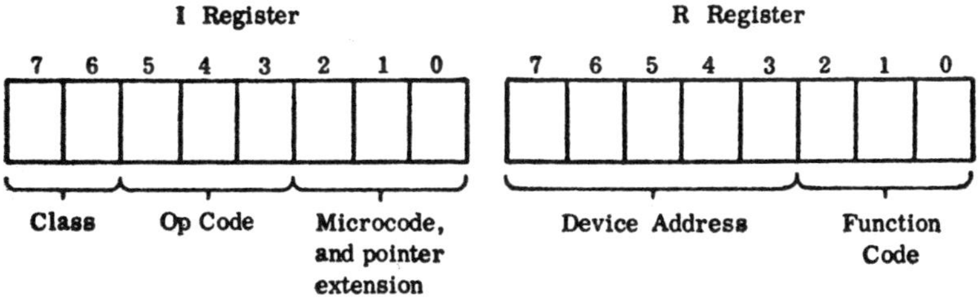

Fig. 18-1. Input-output instruction format.

DEVICE ADDRESSES

The following is a list of device address assignments for standard peripherals:

0		10	Real time clock
1	Computer automated tester	11	Magnetic tape
2		12	Magnetic tape
3		13	
4		14	
5	Card reader	15	
6	Paper tape reader-punch	16	
7	Teletype	17	Disc controller

20 to 27 This block is reserved for customer-designed interfaces and specials designed by CAI for customers.

30 to 37 These are reserved for utility modules.

Teletype Instructions

The teletype option uses 07 as the octal device address. The instructions associated with the teletype option are listed below.

100 071 — Select Keyboard: This instruction resets the buffer ready flip-flop and puts the teletype interface in the read mode.

100 072— Step Read: This command causes the character under the read station on the paper tape reader to be read and the tape advanced one character. The reader switch on the teletype must be in the run position. The buffer ready flip-flop is reset.

100 073— Select Continuous Read: This command causes the paper tape reader to continuously read at the rate of 10 characters per second until the reader is stopped or the tape runs out. The reader switch must be in the run position. The buffer ready flip-flop is reset.

100 074— Initialize the Teletype Interface: This command resets the control flip-flops, stops the oscillator and puts the interface in a static marking condition. The buffer ready flip-flop is reset.

100 075— Set Word Xfer Mask: This command sets a mask flip-flop in the interface to enable an interrupt to be generated by buffer ready flip-flop. (The interrupt line is wired according to system requirements.)

100 076 — Set Block Xfer Mask: This command sets a mask flip-flop in the interface to allow an interrupt to be generated when the word Xfer mask is in the off state. The interrupt can be used to indicate "end-of-block."

100 077 — Reset Masks: This instruction disables both interrupt lines in the teletype interface by resetting the mask flip-flops.

111 071 — Sense Buffer Ready: This instruction senses the on state of the buffer ready flip-flop; i.e., a true response will occur if the flip-flop is set.

111 072 — Sense Word Xfer Mask Off: This instruction senses the word Xfer mask flip-flop and generates a true response if the flip-flop is in the off state.

111 073 — Sense TTY Not Busy: This instruction senses the state of the TTY controller and generates a true response if the TTY is not printing or reading a character.

15X 070 — Output A Register to Teletype: This instruction transfers the contents of the A register (or all zeros) to the teletype interface and causes the character to be printed. If the punch is on, the character will also be punched.

14X 070 — Output Memory to Teletype: This is a block output instruction that causes one word of a block to be transferred from the memory location specified by X (in the instruction) and the output pointer (which the instruction automatically interrogates and updates). The character transferred is printed or punched on the teletype.

13X 070 — Input From Teletype to the A Register: The character in the teletype interface buffer is transferred to the A register. The word may be ANDed with the previous contents of A (masking) or A may be cleared prior to transfer.

12X 070 — Input From Teletype to Memory: This is a block input instruction that inputs the word from the teletype interface buffer to memory. The memory location is specified by X and the input pointer.

Paper Tape Reader Instructions

The paper tape uses 06 as the octal device address. The instructions associated with the paper tape reader are listed below.

100 064 — Initialize the Reader Interface: This instruction resets the control flip-flops in the interface and makes the "buffer not ready."

100 061 — Stop Reader: This instruction causes the reader to stop.

100 065 — Set Word Xfer Mask (WXM): This instruction causes the WXM flip-flop to be set, enabling interrupts to be generated with the buffer ready. (The actual use of interrupts is determined by system wiring.)

100 063 — Run: This instruction causes the reader to continuously slew tape at 30 inches per second.

100 062 — Step Read: This instruction causes the reader to read one character and stop.

100 066 — Set Block Xfer Mask (BXM): This instruction causes the BXM flip-flop to be set, enabling an interrupt to be generated when WXM is off; i.e., at end-of-block.

100 067 — Reset Masks: This instruction resets both the WXM and BXM flip-flops which disable interrupts for the buffer ready and end-of-block.

111 061 — Sense Buffer Ready: This instruction tests the state of the buffer ready flip-flop and generates a true response if the flip-flop is set.

111-062 — Sense Word Xfer Mask: This instruction tests the state of the WXM flip-flop and generates a true response if the flip-flop is off.

13X 060 — Input Buffer to A Register: This instruction transfers the contents of the buffer to the A register. Depending upon the value of X, the A register is either cleared first, or the contents of A is ANDed with the incoming data.

12X 060 — Input Buffer to Memory: This is a block input instruction that inputs the word from the buffer to memory. The memory location is specified by X and the contents of the input pointer.

Paper Tape Punch Instructions

The paper tape punch uses 06 as the octal device address. The instructions associated with the paper tape punch are listed below.

100 064— Initialize: This instruction resets all control flip-flops in the punch interface and makes the buffer "not ready."

100 060 — Punch Contents of Buffer: This instruction is used when copying an existing paper tape.

100 065 — Set Word Xfer Mask (WXM): This instruction causes the WXM flip-flop to be set, enabling an interrupt to be generated with the buffer ready. (The actual use of interrupts is determined by system wiring.)

100 066 — Set Block Xfer Mask (BXM): This instruction causes the BXM flip-flop to be set, enabling an interrupt to be generated when WXM is off; i.e., end-of-block.

100 067 — Reset Masks: This instruction resets both the WXM and BXM flip-flops which disable the interrupts for the buffer ready and end-of-block.

111 061 — Sense Buffer Ready: This instruction tests the state of the buffer ready flip-flop and generates a true response if the flip-flop is set.

111 062 — Sense Word Xfer Mask: This instruction tests the state of the WXM flip-flop and generates a true response if the flip-flop is off.

15X 060 — Punch Contents of A Register (or punch all zeros): This instruction causes the contents of the A register to be transferred to the punch interface and punched.

14X 060 — Output Memory and Punch: This instruction is a block output that outputs the word in memory specified by X and the output pointer. The word is transferred to the interface buffer and punched.

SENSE INSTRUCTIONS

To enable the controller to test the state of a device and take appropriate action, the sense skip instruction is used. The function code determines the condition to be tested. By decoding the three function code bits into the eight possible states, up to eight conditions may be tested in a particular device.

During PH3X of ICY2, the device being queried sends back a sense response if the condition being tested is met. If the condition is not met, no response is sent back to the controller. There is no sense control line. Instead, a sense occurs on every I-O command, but the processor ignores the response except for cases where it is applicable. There are two sense skip instructions: **Sense and Skip on Response** tests one of eight possible conditions within a device address. If a sense response is obtained at the processor within 1.0 microsecond after the beginning of PH3X during ICY2, the SCMX flip-flop is set and a skip occurs. **Sense and Skip on No Response** is identical except a skip occurs in the absence of a sense response.

SSR: Sense and Skip on Response

The function specified in Fig. 18-2 is tested in the device specified and a skip occurs if a response is obtained. If no response occurs, the next instruction in sequence is executed.

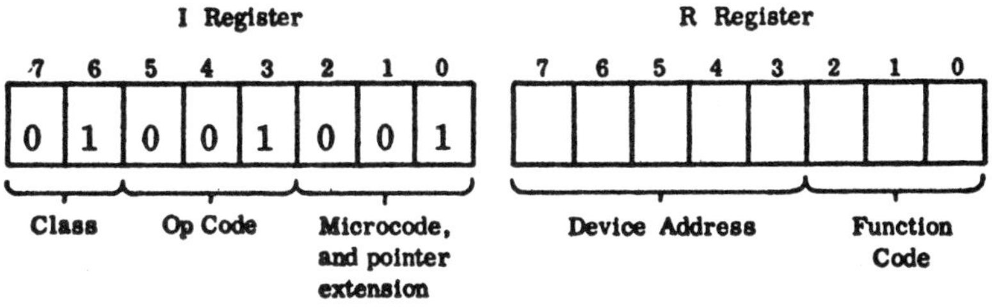

Fig. 18-2. Sense and skip on response instruction.

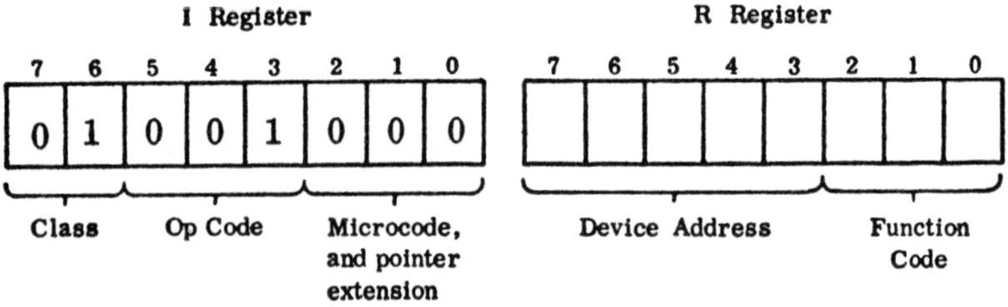

Fig. 18-3. Sense and skip on no response instruction.

Skip on response will occur if bit 0 of the I register is on. See Figs. 18-4 and 18-5. The timing is 2.

Cycle Sequence: ICY1, ICY2

ICY1 cycle: Phase 1: Same as NOP, phase 1. Phase 2: Same as NOP, phase 2. Phase 3: Same as NOP, phase 3. Phase 4: Same as NOP, phase 4.

ICY2 cycle: Phase 1: Same as NOP, phase 1. Phase 2: Same as NOP, phase 2. Phase 3: During ICY2, the device address (PB00-04) and the function code (FB00-02) are placed onto the peripheral address bus and function bus, respectively, for action in the I-O controller. Whether or not the

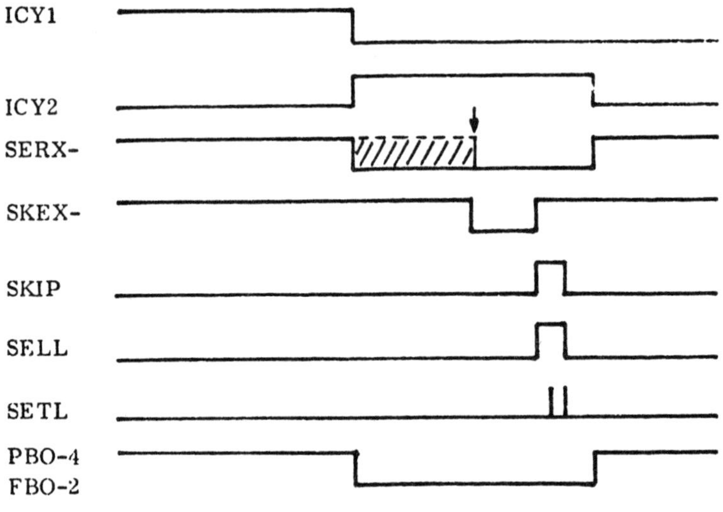

* Response must be at ground.

Fig. 18-4. SSR and SSN timing diagram.

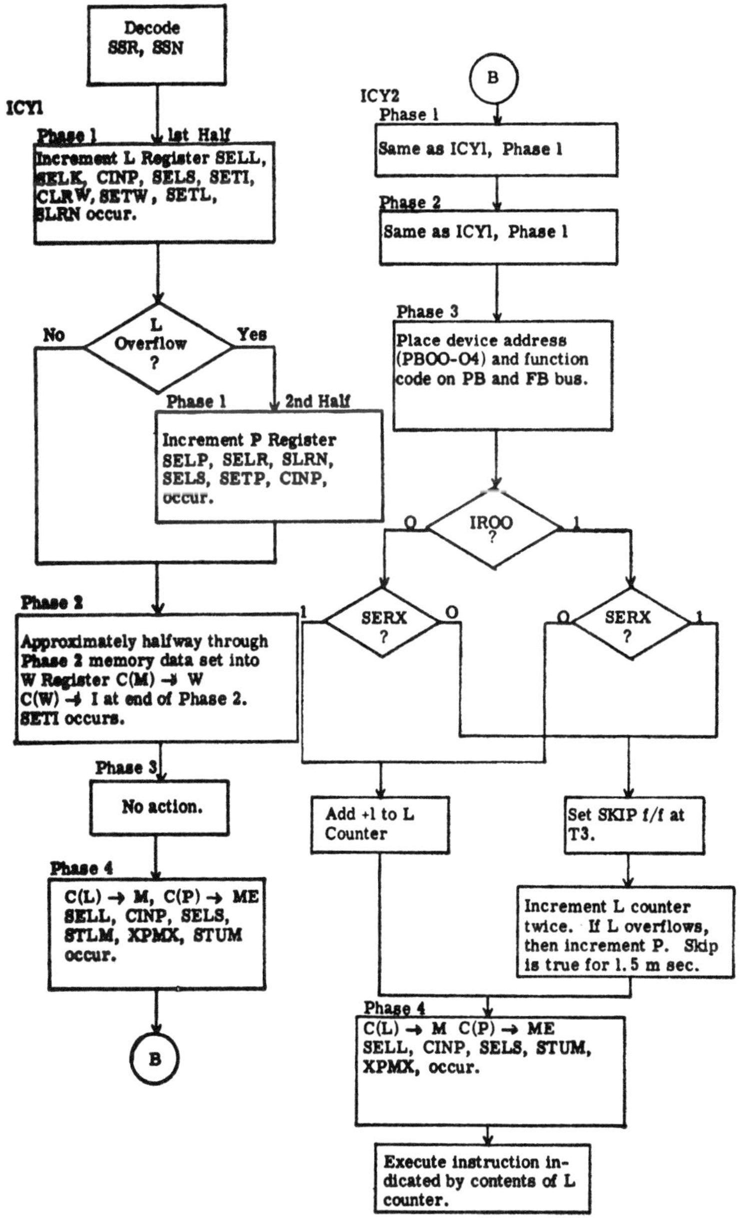

Fig. 18-5. SSR and SSN flow chart.

processor skips the next two words in the memory depends on the condition of the instruction register, bit 0, and the I-O signal (SERX-) from the I-O device being tested. A skip is taken if IR00 is a 1; i.e., SERX- is at ground (true). If the response is true the skip flip-flop is set at T3. PB0-4, FB0-2, SERX-, SKEX-, SKIP, SELL, SETL occur. Phase 4: Same as NOP, phase 4.

SSN: Sense and Skip on No Response

The function specified in Fig. 18-3 is tested in the device specified and a skip occurs if a response is not obtained. If a response occurs, the next instruction in sequence is executed. See Fig. 18-4. The timing is 2.

Cycle Sequence: ICY1, ICY2

ICY1 cycle: Phase 1: Same as NOP, phase 1. Phase 2: Same as NOP, phase 2. Phase 3: Same as NOP, phase 3. Phase 4: Same as NOP, phase 4.

ICY2 cycle: Phase 1: Same as NOP, phase 1. Phase 2: Same as NOP, phase 2. Phase 3: During ICY2, the device address (PB00-04) and the function code (FB00-02) are placed onto the peripheral address bus and function bus, respectively, for action in the I-O controller. In this case, the skip is taken; i.e., the L counter is incremented twice if IR00 is a 0 and there is no response. This is indicated by the signal SERX- being at 3v. If the skip flip-flop is not set, the next instruction in sequence is executed. SKEX-, SELL, SETL, SERX- occur. Phase 4: Same as NOP, phase 4.

EXTERNAL CONTROL INSTRUCTION

To enable the computer to control peripheral logic the external control (EXC) command is used. The EXC steers a pulse to one of eight destinations within a device address. The pulse may be used to set flip-flops, increment a counter, latch a relay, etc. The EXCX control line goes true for 2.0 microseconds (PH3X) during ICY2. The function code is decoded into eight codes to allow steering of the pulse signal, PLSE. Thus up to eight EXC functions may be implemented within a device address.

EXC: External Control

The control function specified by the function code in Fig. 18-6 is executed. The timing is 2. See Figs. 18-7 and 18-8.

Cycle Sequence: ICY1, ICY2

ICY1 cycle: Phase 1: Same as NOP, phase 1. Phase 2: Same as NOP, phase 2. Phase 3: Same as NOP, phase 3. Phase 4: Same as NOP, phase 4.

ICY2 cycle: Phase 1: W register cleared. L register incremented during the first half of phase 1. SELL, SELR, CINP, SELS, SETI, CLRW, SETW occur. If L overflowed the P register is incremented during the second half of phase 1. SELP, SELR, SLRN, CINP, SELS, SETB occur. Phase 2: Approximately halfway through phase 2 the memory data is set into the W register. C(W) are transferred to the I register at the end of the phase. SETI occurs. Phase 3: The device address (PB00-04) and the function code (FB00-02) are placed onto the peripheral address bus and function bus, respectively, for action in the I-O controller. During phase 3, two control signals are on the I-O control bus. They are the EXCX- and PLSE- signals. Phase 4: Same as NOP, phase 4.

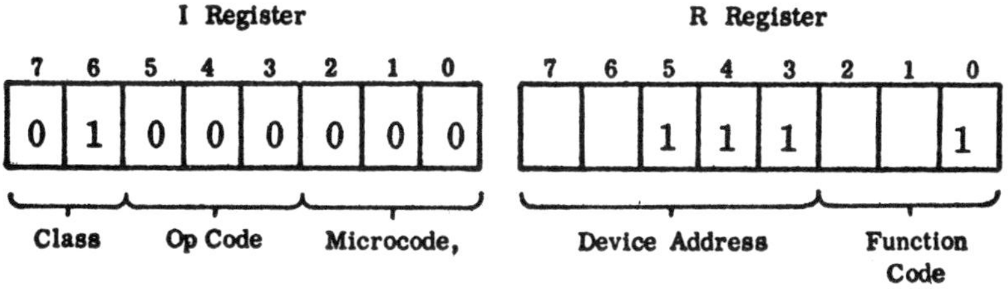

Fig. 18-6. External control instruction.

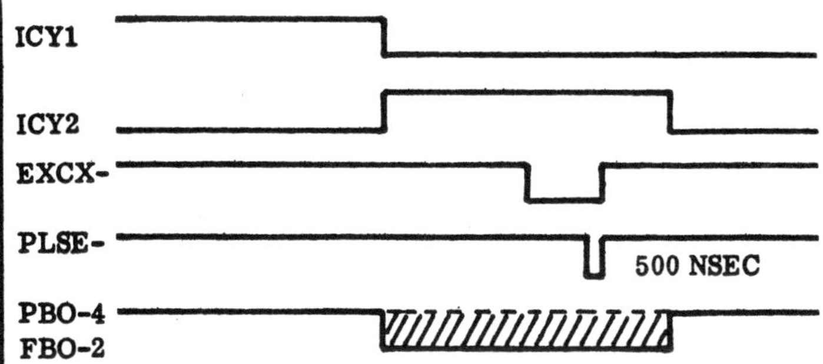

Fig. 18-7. Timing diagram for the EXC instruction.

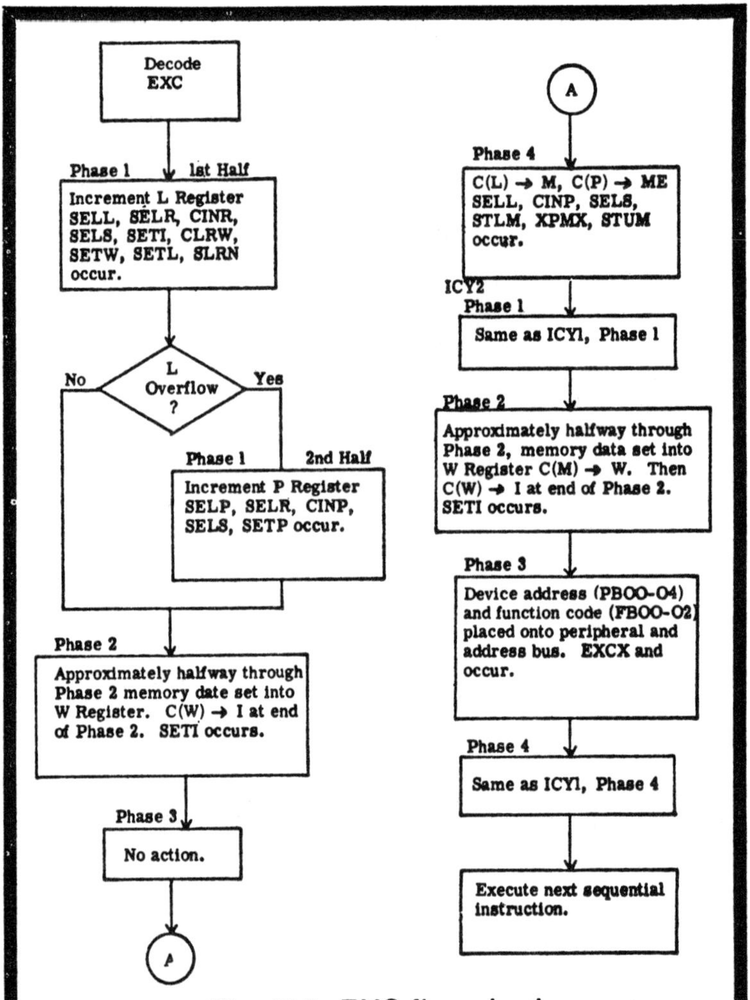

Fig. 18-8. EXC flow chart.

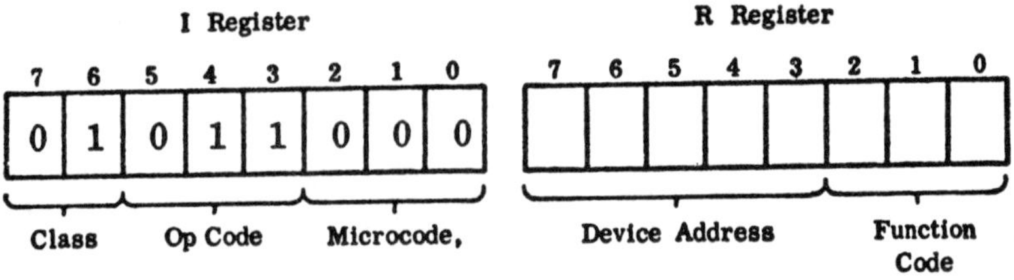

Fig. 18-9. Input to A register (unconditionally) instruction.

INPUT TO A REGISTER INSTRUCTIONS

There are four variations to the input to A instructions:

1. Input to A unconditionally causes the contents of the D bus to be transferred to the S bus, from the S bus to the adder (SELR and SLRN both off, CINP true) and from the adder to the A bus where it is strobed into A. PLSE occurs at the end of PH3 of ICY2 as in the case of output A unconditionally.

2. Input to A on sense response is identical to the unconditional input, except PLSE and SETA are gated by SCMX. If the sense response is not obtained halfway through PH3X, then PLSE and SETA are inhibited and a skip does not occur.

3. Masked input to A unconditionally is identical to the unconditional input except the contents of A is selected onto the S bus along with the contents of the D bus. Selecting A and D bus contents simultaneously causes the AND of the two, which is routed around to the A bus where it is strobed into A.

4. Masked input to A on sense response is identical to the unconditional masked input except PLSE and SETA are inhibited if the sense response is not received within 1.0 microsecond after the beginning of HH3X. If the response is received PLSE and SETA occur and a skip occurs.

The input to A instructions are used to transfer data from an output device to the processor A register. This is accomplished by generating the required signals which allows the device to place information on the data bus, DB00-07. This is accomplished by INXX, which indicates that an input instruction is being executed and the device addressed. The generation of these signals causes data to be placed on the D bus. The processor then selects data onto the S bus with SDBR, which enables the contents of the D bus to be placed on the S bus. This selected data is routed to the A bus and a SETA pulse causes the data to be entered into the A register. The SETA and PLSE- are generated under control of the sense response (SERX-) when executing an IAS or MIS instruction. SETA and PLSE- always occur on INA and MIA.

When conditions in the I-O device must be met, the signal PLSE- is an indication that they have been met. Instructions that are executed unconditionally also always generate PLSE-; i.e., the sense response is always true. After the conditions have been met, transfer of data occurs. The trailing edge of PLSE- is an indication that transfer has been completed. The conditions which give a sense response are: sense buffer ready, sense word transfer mask off, and sense device not busy.

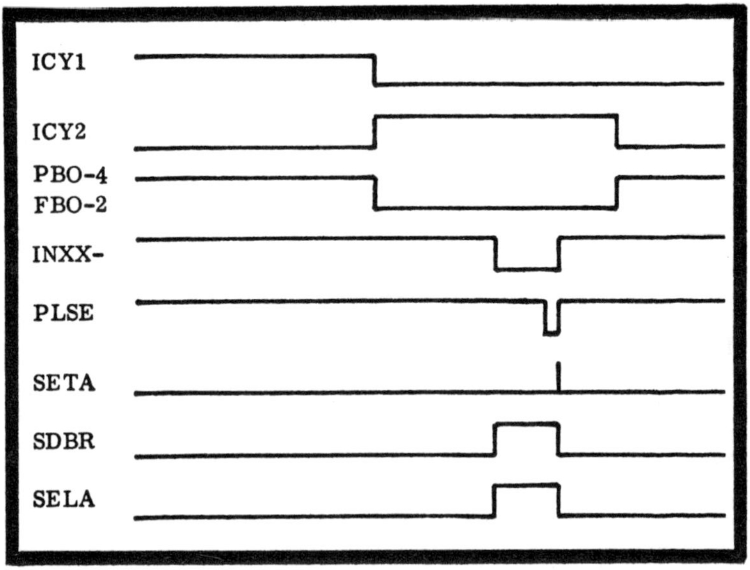

Fig. 18-10. Timing diagram of the INA, IAS, MIS, and MIA.

INA: Input to A Register (Unconditionally)

A data word will be transferred from the device specified to the A register. The function code can be used to designate the source of data within the device if multiple sources exist as in the case of a 16-bit converter output. Up to eight sources may be specified by the function code, allowing a 64-bit input data word to be handled in eight successive inputs, greatly simplifying the device logic. The timing is 2. See Figs. 18-10 and 18-11.

Cycle Sequence: ICY1, ICY2

ICY1 cycle: Phase 1: During the first half of phase 1, increment the L register. SELL, SELR, CINP, SELS, SETI, CLRW, SETW occur. If L overflows, increment the P register during the second half of phase 1. SELP, SELR, CINP, SELS, SETP occur. Phase 2: Approximately halfway through phase 2, memory data is set into the W register. C(W) go to the I register at the end of phase 2. SETI occurs. Phase 3: No action. Phase 4: C(L) go to M, C(P) to ME. SELL, CINP, SELS, STLM, XPMX, STUM occur.

ICY2 cycle: Phase 1: Same as ICY1, phase 1, except that the device address (DB00-05) and function code (FB00-02) are placed on the DB and FB bus, respectively. PB00-04, FB00-02 occur. Phase 2: Approximately halfway through phase 2, memory data is set into the W register. C(W) arrive at I at the end of phase 2. SETI occurs. Phase 3: The I-O device puts data on the I-O bus. Data then is loaded into A. INXX, PLSE, SDBR, SELA, SETA, occur! Phase 4: C(L) go to M and C(P) to ME. SELL, CINP, SELS, STLM, XPMX, STUM occur.

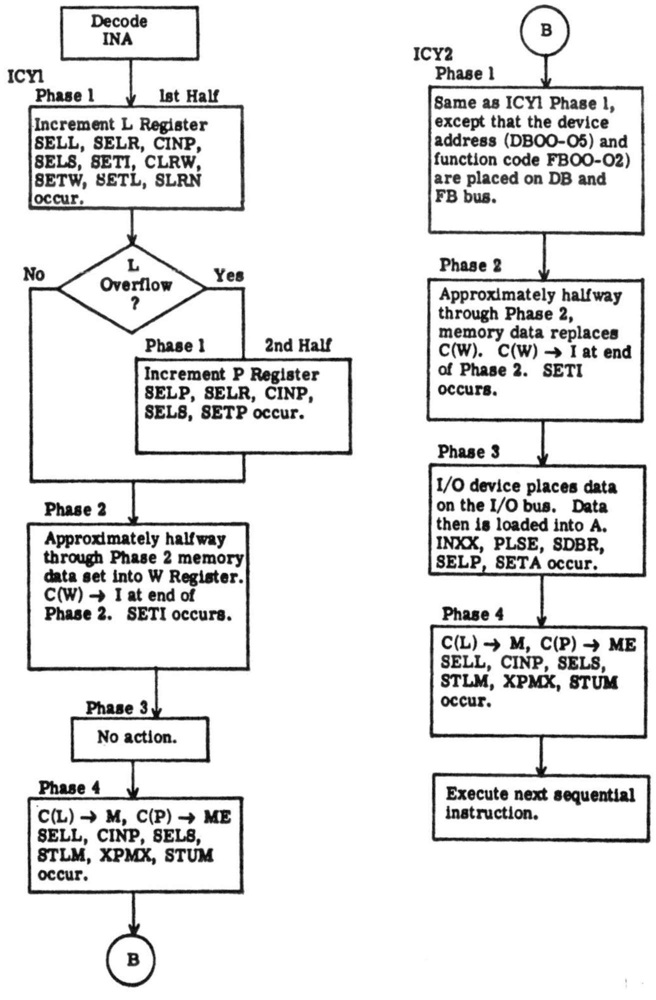

Fig. 18-11. INA flow chart.

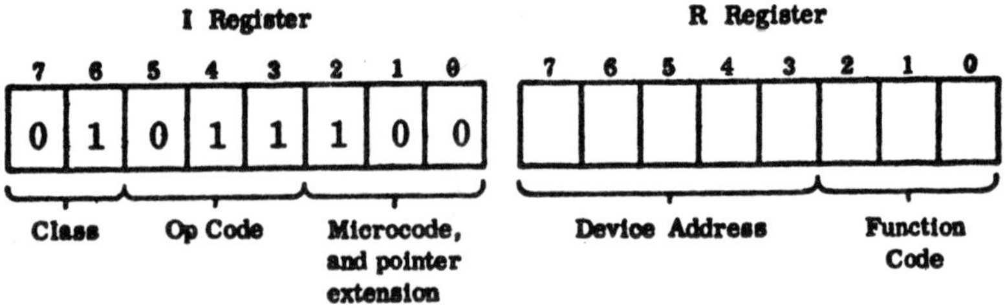

Fig. 18-12. Masked input to A register (unconditionally) instruction.

MIA: Masked Input to A Register (Uncondtionally)

The masked input instruction in Fig. 18-12 causes the input data word from the specified device to be ANDed with the previous contents of the A register and the results placed in the A register. The source of the data word within the device may be specified by the function code if multiple sources exist. The timing is 2. See Figs. 18-10 and 18-13.

Cycle Sequence: ICY1, ICY2

ICY1 cycle: Phase 1: During the first half of phase 1, increment the L register. SELL, SELR, CINP, SELS, SETI, CLRW, SETW occur. If L overflows, increment the P register during the second half of phase 1. SELP, SELR, CINP, SELS, SETP occur. Phase 2: Approximately halfway through phase 2, memory data is set into the W register. C(W) go to I at the end of phase 2. SETI occurs. Phase 3: No action. Phase 4: C(L) go to M, C(P) to ME. SELL, CINP, SELS, STLM, XPMX, STUM occur.

ICY2 cycle: Phase 1: Same as ICY1, phase 1, except that the device address (DB00-05) and function code (FB00-02) are placed on the DB and FB bus, respectively. PB00-04, FB00-02 occur. Phase 2: Approximately halfway through phase 2, memory data replaces C(W). C(W) go to I at the end of phase 2. SETI occurs. Phase 3: The I-O device places data on the I-O bus. Data is then ANDed with the previous contents of A. Results are placed back into A. SELA, SETA, STA3, INXX, PLSE, SDBR occur. Phase 4: C(L) go to M and C(P) to ME. SELL, CINP, SELS, STLM, XPMX, STUM occur.

IAS: Input to A and Skip on Response

The IAS instruction first senses the function specified by the function code within the device specified. If a response is obtained; i.e., device is ready, the data word is transferred to the A register and a skip occurs. If no response is obtained, the data word is not transferred, the A register is unchanged, and the next instruction in sequence is executed. The timing is 2. See Figs. 18-10 and 18-15.

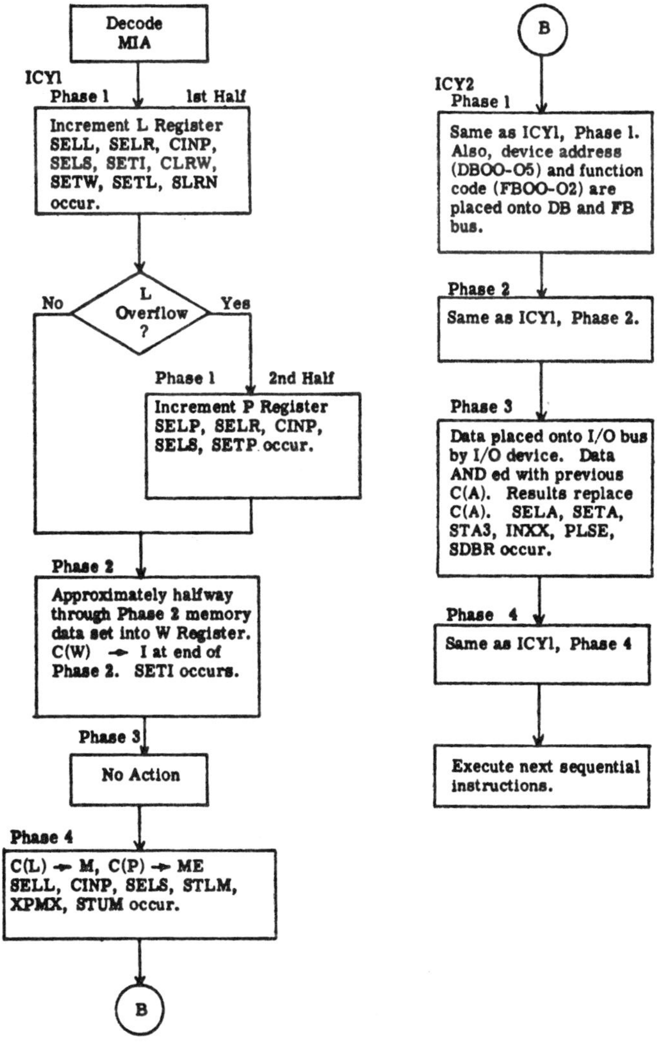

Fig. 18-13. MIA flow chart.

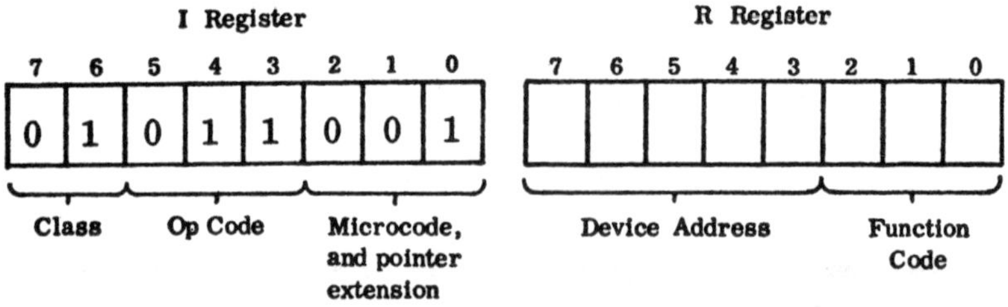

Fig. 18-14. Input to A and skip on response instruction.

Cycle Sequence: ICY1, ICY2

ICY1 cycle: Phase 1: During the first half of phase 1, increment the L register. SELL, SELR, CINP, SELS, SETI, CLRW, SETW occur. If L overflows, increment the P register during the second half of phase 1. SELP, SELR, CINP, SETP occur. Phase 2: Approximately halfway through phase 2, memory data is set into the W register. C(W) go to the I register at the end of phase 2. SETI occurs. Phase 3: No action. Phase 4: C(L) go to M, C(P) to ME. SELL, CINP, SELS, STLM, XPMX, STUM occur.

ICY2 cycle: Phase 1: Same as ICY1, phase 1, except that the device address (DB00-05) and function code (FB00-02) are placed on the DB and FB bus, respectively. PB00-04, FB00-02 occur. Phase 2: Approximately halfway through phase 2, memory data is set into the W register. C(W) go to I at the end of phase 2. SETI occurs. Phase 3: If the device addressed is ready, the condition tested is true; i.e., a response occurred. The data word is transferred to the A register. PLSE, SETA, SELA, SDBR, INXX occur. If the device addressed is not ready, no response occurs and the condition being tested is false. The data word is not transferred. INXX occurs. Phase 4: If the condition being tested is true the skip is taken; i.e., the L register is incremented twice prior to receiving the next instruction. Also, P is incremented if L overflowed. The skip F-F is set at T3XX if IYAX is not on. A skip is not allowed during interrupts. L and P are then used to generate the memory address for the next instruction. SKIP F-F is set at T3XX, SELL, SELP, SKIP, SETL, SETP occur. If the condition being tested is false a skip is not taken and the next instruction in sequence is executed.

MIS: Masked Input to A and Skip on Response

The instruction in Fig. 18-16 is a combination of the sense and the marked input to A. The instruction first senses the condition specified by the function code within the device specified. If a sense response is obtained, a masked input to the A register and a skip occur. If no sense response is obtained, the A register is left unaltered and the next instruction in sequence is executed. The timing is 2. See Figs. 18-10 and 18-17.

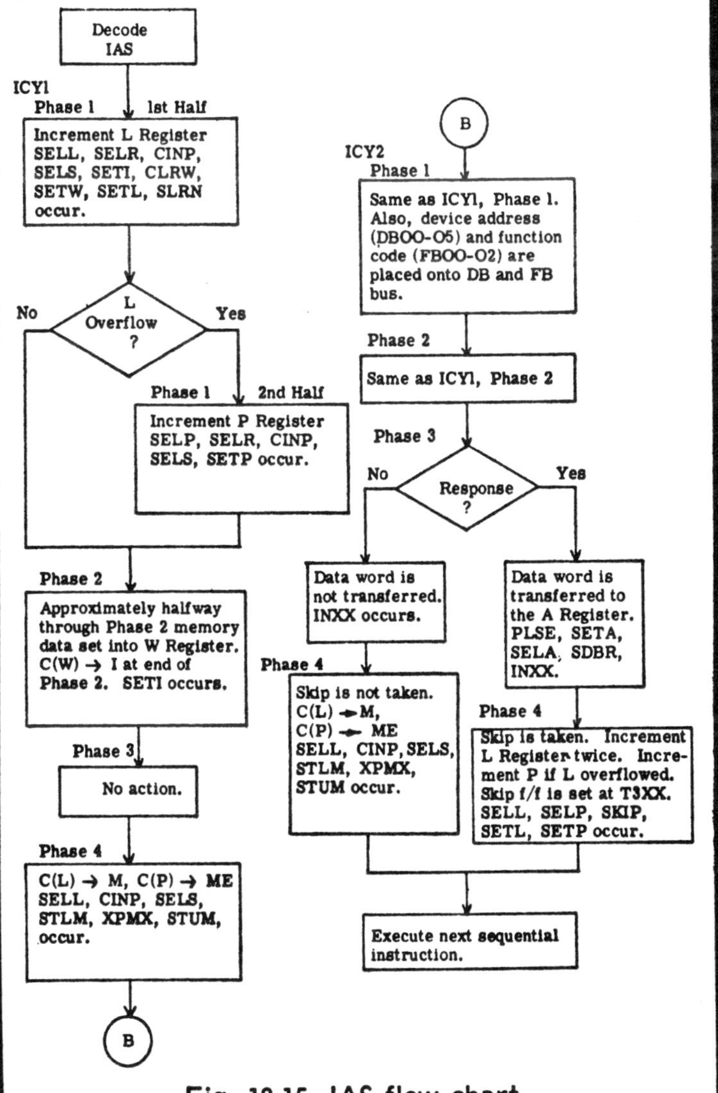

Fig. 18-15. IAS flow chart.

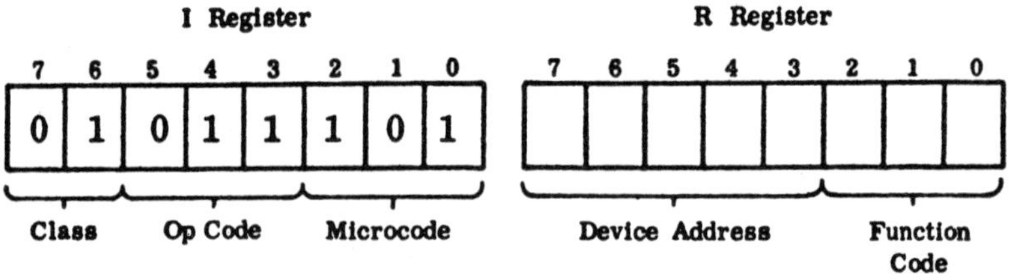

Fig. 18-16. Masked input to A and skip on response instruction.

Cycle Sequence: ICY1, ICY2

ICY1 cycle: Phase 1: During the first half of phase 1, increment the L register. SELL, SELR, CINP, SELS, SETI, CLRW, SETW occur. If L overflows, increment the P register during the second half of phase 1. SELP, SELR, CINP, SELS, SETP occur. Phase 2: Approximately halfway through phase 2, the memory data is set into the W register. C(W) go to the I register at the end of phase 2. SETI occurs. Phase 3: No action. Phase 4: C(L) go to M, C(P) to ME. SELL, CINP, SELS, STLM, XPMX, STUM occur.

ICY2 cycle: Phase 1: Same as ICY1, phase 1, except that the device address (DB00-05) and function code (FB00-02) are placed on the DB and FB bus respectively. Phase 2: Approximately halfway through phase 2, memory data is set into the W register. C(W) go to I at the end of phase 2. SETI occurs. Phase 3: If a response is obtained; i.e., if a device is ready to transmit data, the condition is true. The input data word from a specified device is ANDed with the previous contents of the A register and the results placed back into A. PLSE, SDBR, SELA, SETA, INXX occur. If no response is obtained; i.e., the device is not ready to transmit data, the A register is not changed. INXX occurs. Phase 4: If the condition being tested is true the skip is taken; i.e., the L register is incremented twice prior to introducing the next instruction. Also, P is incremented if L overflowed. The skip F-F is set at T3XX if IYAX is not on. A skip is not allowed during interrupts. L and P are then used to generate the memory address for the next instruction. Skip F-F is set at T3XX. SELP, SELL, SKIP, SETL, SETP occur. If the condition being tested is false, a skip is not taken and the next instruction in sequence is executed.

OUTPUT FROM A REGISTER INSTRUCTIONS

There are four variations of the output A instructions: Output A unconditionally causes the contents of A to be selected onto the S bus, through the adder (SELR and SCRN both off, CINP true), onto the A bus and onto the D bus. This happens during PH3 of ICY2. At the same time, the control line OUTX in the I-O cable goes true (2.0 microseconds). The strobe signal PLSE (500 ns) occurs during the last portion to OUTX, completing the instruction. Output A on sense response

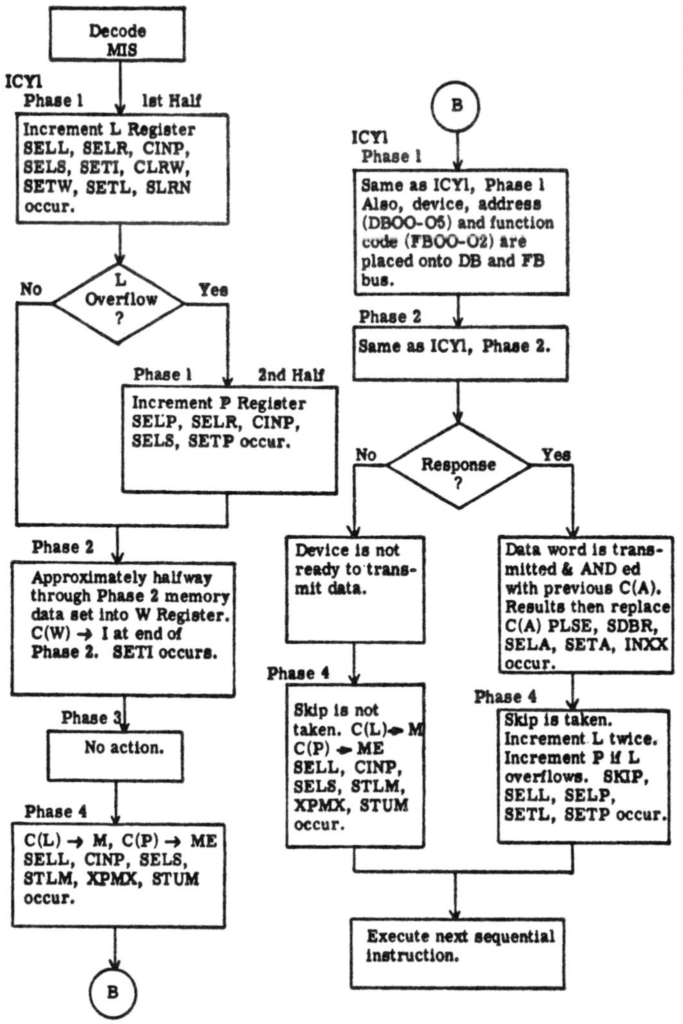

Fig. 18-17. MIS flow chart.

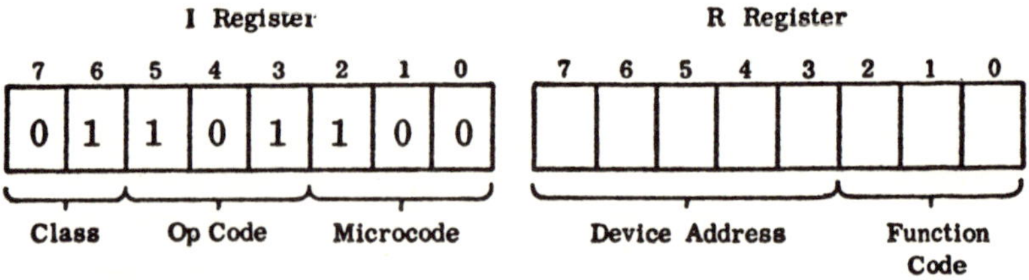

Fig. 18-18. Output A unconditional instruction.

is similar to the unconditional output except PLSE is gated with the sense condition met flip-flop, SCMX. If the sense response from the condition tested is not received within 1.0 microsecond after the beginning of PH3X, PLSE is inhibited and a skip does not occur. If the response is received in time, SCMX, is set, PLSE is allowed to occur and after the transfer, a skip occurs. Output zero unconditionally is identical with output A unconditionally, except the adder is not allowed to be gated onto the A bus.

The processor transfers the data from the A register to the S bus, through the adder to the A bus. The signal SLAI gates the data onto the D bus. The control signals OUTX- and PLSE- are also generated in the processor. These signals, when ANDed with the device address are normally used by the controller to set data into the A register.

OTA: Output A Unconditionally

The OTA instruction in Fig. 18-18 transfers the contents of the A register to the device specified. The A register is not altered. The function code can be used to steer the data into multiple registers if required. For instance, if a 32-bit register is to be loaded by OTAs the register can have four segments and each segment can be specified by the function code. The timing is 2. See Figs. 18-19 and 18-20.

Cycle Sequence: ICY1, ICY2

ICY1 cycle: Phase 1: W register is cleared. L register is incremented during the first half of phase 1. SELL, SELR, SLRN, CINP, SELS, SETI, CLRW, SETW occur. If L overflowed the P register is incremented during the second half of phase 1. SELP, SELR, SLRN, CINP, SELS and SETI occur. Phase 2: Approximately halfway through phase 2 memory data is set into the W register. The contents of W is transferred to the I register at the end of the phase. SETI occurs. Phase 3: No action. Phase 4: The contents of the L register is transferred to the M register and the contents of the P register is transferred to the M extension register. SELL, CINP, SELS, STLM, XPMX and STUM occur.

ICY2 cycle: Phase 1: Same as ICY1, phase 1 except that the device address (DB00-05) and function code (FB00-02) are placed on the DB and FB bus, respectively. Phase 2: Ap-

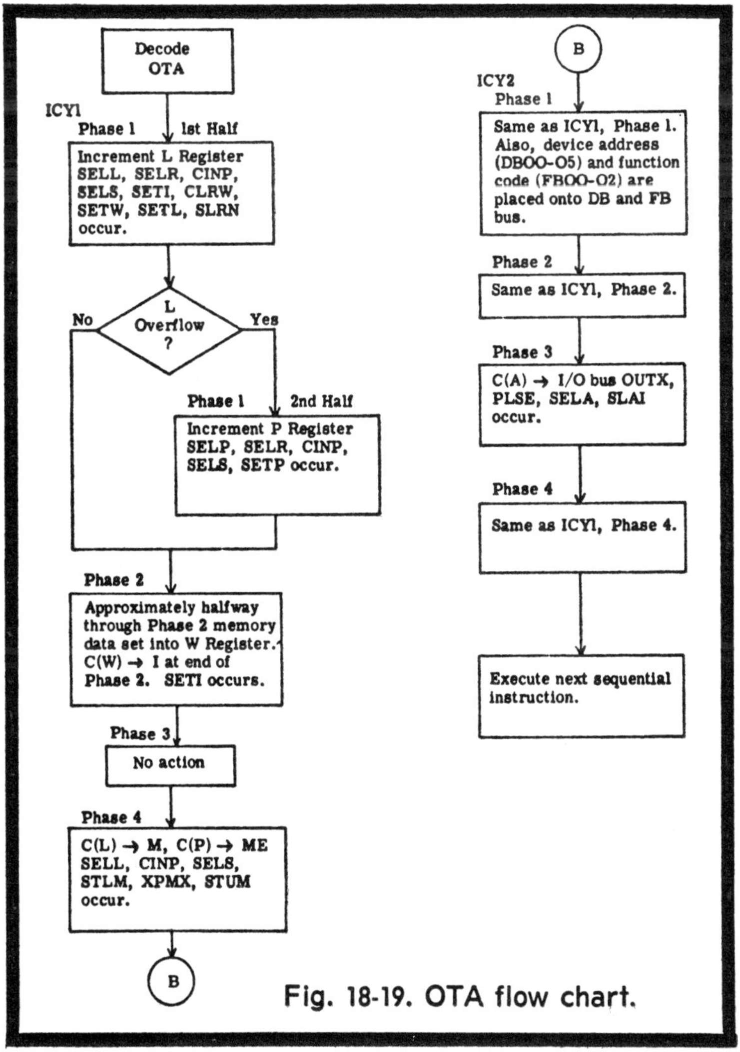

Fig. 18-19. OTA flow chart.

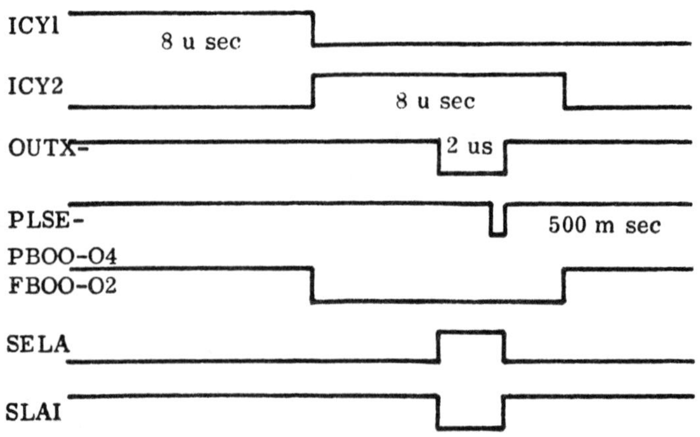

Fig. 18-20. Timing diagram of the output instructions.

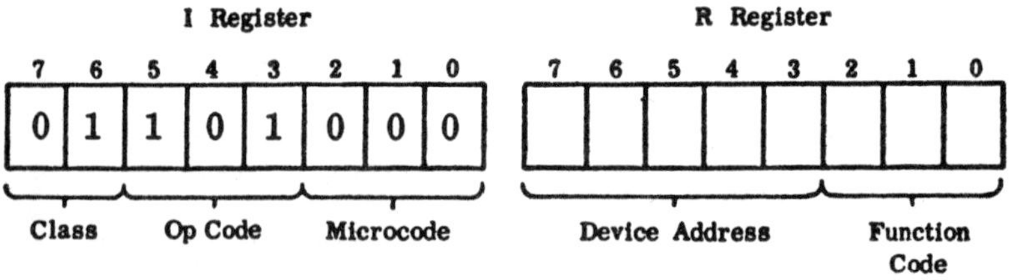

Fig. 18-21. Output zero (unconditionally) instruction.

proximately halfway through phase 2, memory data is set into the W register. C(W) go to I at the end of phase 2. SETI occurs. Phase 3: The signal OUTX, which is 2 microseconds in duration, occurs. This indicates that an output command is being executed. The data word in the A register is placed onto the S bus and routed through the adder. The A bus drivers place the word onto the A bus and the D bus drivers place the data word onto the D bus. The data word is then transmitted to the I-O device via the I-O cable. The signal PLSE- occurs unconditionally since the OTA instruction occurs unconditionally. OUTX-, SELA, SLAI, PLSE- occur. Phase 4: C(L) go to M, C(P) to ME. SELL, CINP, SELS, STLM, XPMX, STUM occur.

OTZ: Output Zero (Uncondtionally)

The OTZ instruction in Fig 18-21 is similar to the OTA, except the contents of the A register is not selected onto the I-O bus, resulting in a transfer of all zeros in the data word. The contents of A is not altered. The timing is 2. See Figs. 18-20 and 18-22.

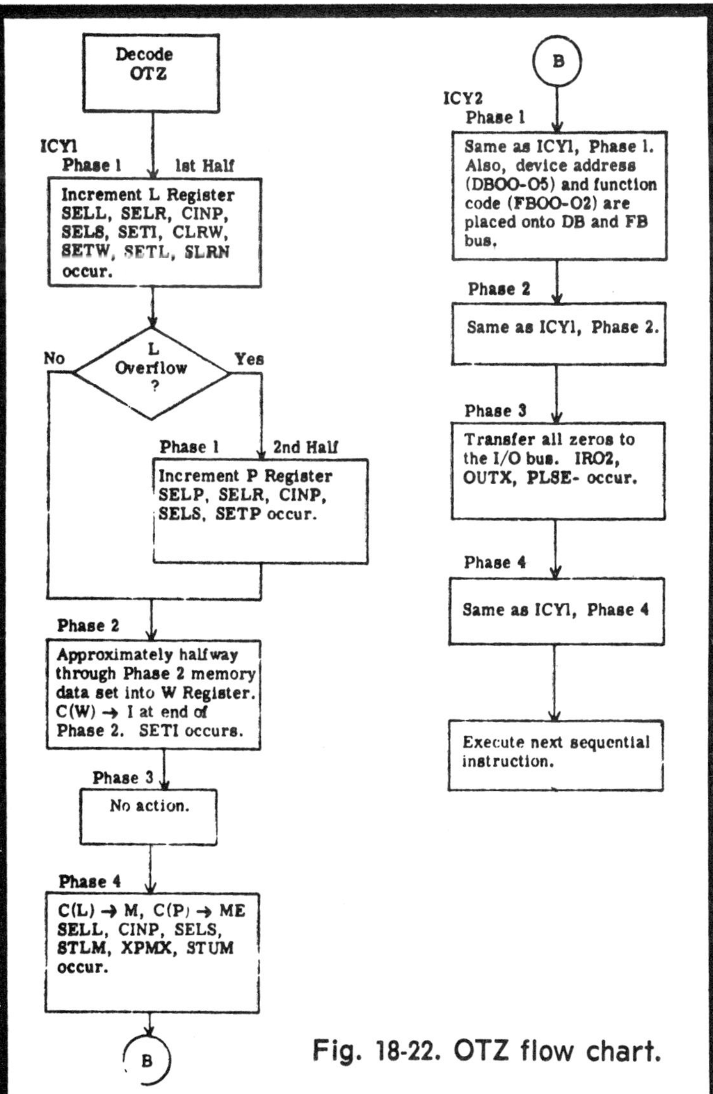

Fig. 18-22. OTZ flow chart.

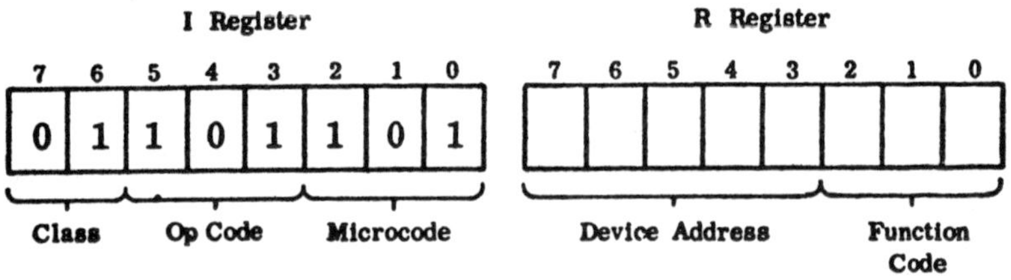

Fig. 18-23. Output A and skip on response instruction.

Cycle Sequence: ICY1, ICY2

ICY1 cycle: Phase 1: W register is cleared. L register is incremented during the first half of phase 1. SELL, SELR, SLRN, CINP, SELS, SETI, CLRW, SETW occur. If L overflowed the P register is incremented during the second half of phase 1. SELP, SELR, SLRN, CINP, SELS and SETP occur. Phase 2: Approximately halfway through Phase 2 memory data is set into the W register. Contents of W is transferred to the I register at the end of the phase. SETI occurs. Phase 3: No action. Phase 4: Contents of the L register is transferred to the M register and the contents of the P register is transferred to the M extension register. SELL, CINP, SELS, STLM, XPMX and STUM occur.

ICY2 cycle: Phase 1: Same as ICY1, phase 1, except that the device address (DB00-05) and function code (FB00-02) are placed on the DB and FB bus, respectively. PB00-04, FB00-02 occur. Phase 2: Approximately halfway through phase 2, memory data is set into the W register. C(W) go to I at the end of phase 2. SETI occurs. Phase 3: The C(A) are not selected onto the I-O bus, resulting in a transfer of all zeros in the data word. This is accomplished by IR02 being at ground and SELA not being generated. OUTX-, PLSE-, IR02 occur. Phase 4: C(L) go to M, C(P) to ME. SELL, CINP, SELS, STLM, XPMX, STUM occur.

OAS: Output A and Skip on Response

The OAS instruction in Fig. 18-23 is a combination of the OTA and the sense and skip instructions. The condition specified by the function code is first sensed and if a response is obtained, the contents of A is transferred to the I-O device and a skip occurs. If no sense response occurs, the transfer is not made and the next instruction in sequence is executed. The timing is 2. See Figs. 18-20 and 18-24.

Cycle Sequence: ICY1, ICY2

ICY1 cycle: Phase 1: W register cleared. L register incremented during the first half of phase 1. SELL, SELR, SLRN, CINP, SELS, SETI, CLRW, SETW occur. If L overflowed the P register is incremented during the second half of phase 1. SELP, SELR, SLRN, CINP, SELS and SETP occur.

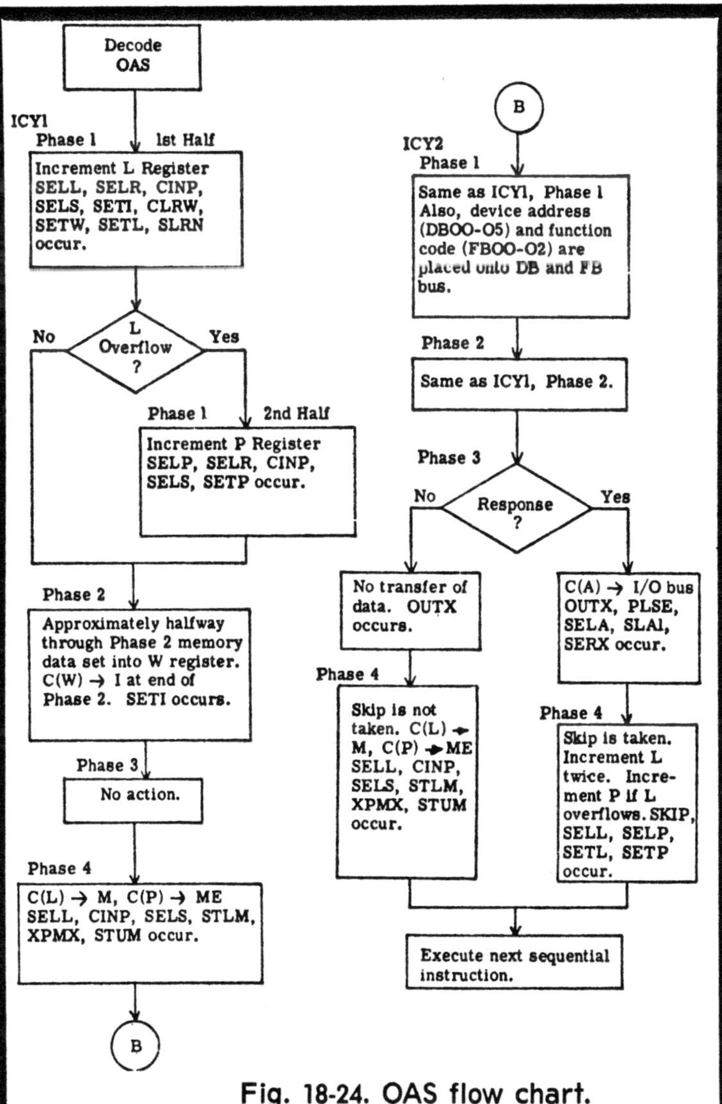

Fig. 18-24. OAS flow chart.

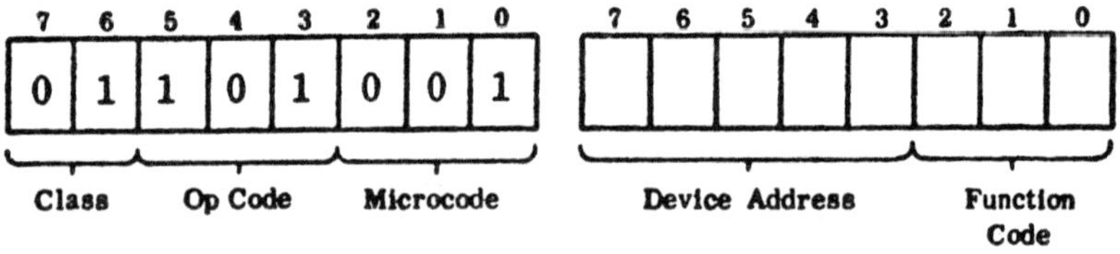

Fig. 18-25. Output zero and skip on response instruction.

Phase 2: Approximately halfway through phase 2 memory data is set into the W register. Contents of W is transferred to the I register at the end of the phase. SETI occurs. Phase 3: No action. Phase 4: Contents of the L register is transferred to the M register and the contents of the P register is transferred to the M extension register. SELL, CINP, SELS, STLM, XPMX and STUM occur.

ICY2 cycle: Phase 1: Same as ICY1, phase 1, except that the device address (DB00-05) and function code (FB00-02) are placed on the DB and FB bus, respectively. PB00-04, FB00-02 occur. Phase 2: Approximately halfway through phase 2, memory data is set into the W register. C(W) go to I at the end of phase 2. SETI occurs. Phase 3: If the condition being tested is true; i.e., a response occurred, the device is ready to receive data from A. Then SERX- is at ground. Transfer from the A to the I-O bus occurs in the following sequence: OUTX-, PLSE-, SELA, SLAI- and SERX-. If the condition being tested is false; i.e., no response occurred, the device is not ready to receive data, and SERX- is at +3v. The signal PLSE- is inhibited by STA2 being at ground. OUTX- occurs. Phase 4: If the condition being tested is true the skip is taken: i.e., the L register is incremented twice prior to receiving the next instruction. Also, P is incremented if L overflowed. The skip F-F is set at T3XX if IYAX is not on. A skip is not allowed during interrupts. L and P are then used to generate the memory address for the next instruction. Skip F-F is set at T3XX. SELL, SELP, SKIP, SETL, SETP occur. If the condition being tested is false a skip is not taken and the next instruction in sequence is executed.

OZS: Output Zero and Skip on Response

The OZS instruction in Fig. 18-24 is a combination of the OTZ and the sense and skip instructions. The function code specifies the condition to be sensed. If no sense response is obtained, the A register is unaffected and the next instruction in sequence is executed. The timing is 2. See Figs. 10-20 and 18-26.

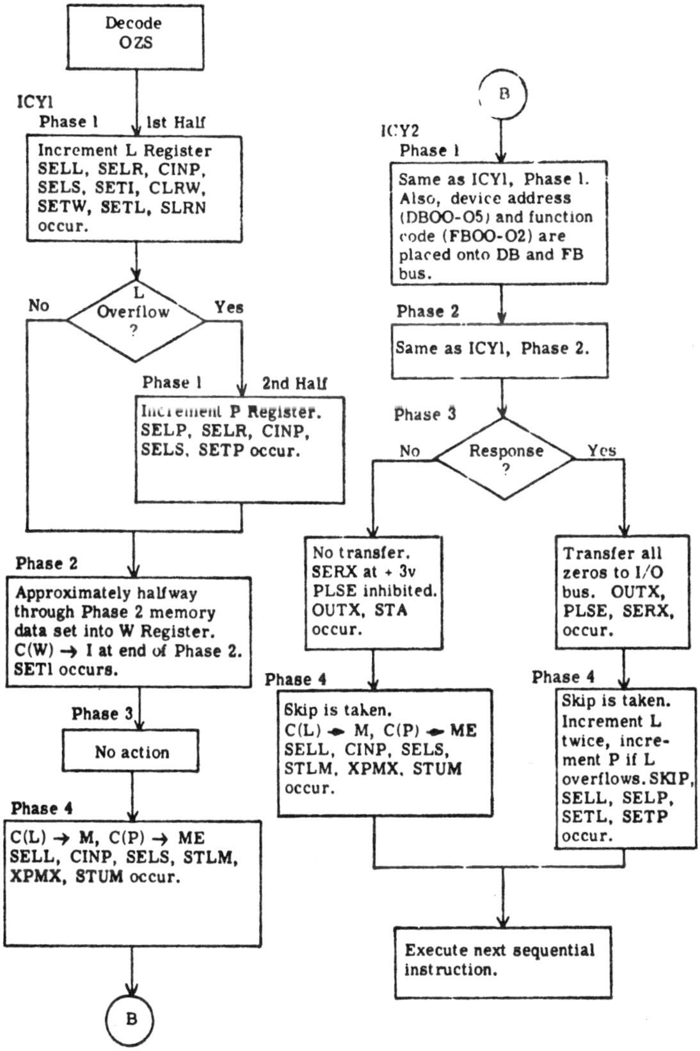

Fig. 18-26. OZS flow chart.

Cycle Sequence: ICY1, ICY2

ICY1 cycle: Phase 1: W register is cleared. L register is incremented during the first half of phase 1. SELL, SELR, SLRN, CINP, SELS, SETI, CLRW, SETW occur. If L overflowed the P register is incremented during the second half of phase 1. SELP, SELR, SLRN, CINP, SELS and SETP occur. Phase 2: Approximately halfway through phase 2 memory data is set into the W register. Contents of W is transferred to the I register at the end of the phase. SETI occurs. Phase 3: No action. Phase 4: Contents of the L register is transferred to the M register and the contents of the P register is transferred to the M extension register. SELL, CINP, SELS, STLM, XPMX and STUM occur.

ICY2 cycle: Phase 1: Same as ICY1, phase 1, except that the device address (DB00-05) and function code (FB00-02) are placed on the DB and FB bus, respectively. PB00-04, FB00-02 occur. Phase 2: Approximately halfway through phase 2, memory data is set into the W register. C(W) go to I at the end of phase 2. SETI occurs. Phase 3: If the condition being sensed is true (SERX- is at ground), a transfer of all zeros is accomplished by IROZ being at ground and SELA not generated. OUTX-, PLSE-, SERX- occur. If the condition being tested is false (SERX is at +3v) and the signal PLSE is inhibited by STA2 being at ground. OUTX, STA- occur. Phase 4: If the condition being tested is true the skip is taken; i.e., the L register is incremented twice prior to receiving the next instruction. Also, P is incremented if L overflowed. The skip F-F is set at T3XX if IYAX is not on. A skip is not allowed during interrupts. L and P are then used to generate the memory address for the next instruction. Skip F-F is set at T3XX, SELL, SELP, SKIP, SETL, SETP occur. If the condition being tested is false a skip is not taken and the next instruction in sequence is executed.

BLOCK TRANSFER INSTRUCTIONS

The block input-output instructions allow data transfers to and from memory without disturbing the A register and, when used with interrupts, without disturbing the L and P counters. Each time the instruction is executed, one word is transferred. When the last word of the block is transferred, notification is made either by a skip or an echo pulse to the transferring peripheral.

INB: Input Block to Memory

The instruction in Fig. 18-27 transfers a word from the specified device to memory at the location specified by the input pointers +1 and the pointer extension. If INB is executed as an interrupt instruction, an echo pulse is generated when the end-of-block occurs which can be used to create an end-of-block interrupt. (No skip can occur during an interrupt instruction execution). If INB is executed in a program (i.e., not as an interrupt instruction), a skip will occur at end-of-block. The timing is 4. See Fig. 18-28.

Cycle Sequence: ICY1, ICY2, ACY1, OCY1

ICY1 cycle: Phase 1: W register is cleared. L register is incremented during the first half of phase 1. SELL, SELR, SLRN, CINP, SELS, SETI, CLRW, SETW occur. If L overflowed the P register is incremented during the second half of phase 1. SELP, SELR, SLRN, CINP, SELS and SETP occur. Phase 2: Approximately halfway through phase 2 memory data is set into the W register. Contents of W is transferred to the I register at the end of the phase. SETI occurs. Phase 3: No action. Phase 4: Contents of the L register is transferred to the M register and the contents of the P register is transferred to the M extension register. SELL, CINP, SELS, STLM, XPMX and STUM occur.

ICY2 cycle: Phase 1: W register is cleared. L register is incremented during the first half of phase 1. SELL, SELR, SLRN, CINP, SELS, SETI, CLRW, SETW occur. If L overflowed the P register is incremented during the second half of phase 1. SELP, SELR, SLRN, CINP, SELS and SETP occur. Phase 2: Approximately halfway through phase 2 memory data is set into the W register. Contents of W is transferred to the I register at the end of the phase. SETI occurs. Phase 3: No action. Phase 4: Form an address to receive the pointer; for the input pointer, location 6, page 0. Turn off the SELS gate;

I Register

7	6	5	4	3	2	1	0
0	1	0	1	0	X	X	X
Class		Op Code			Pointer extension		

R Register

7	6	5	4	3	2	1	0
Device Address					Function Code		

Fig. 18-27. Input block to memory instruction.

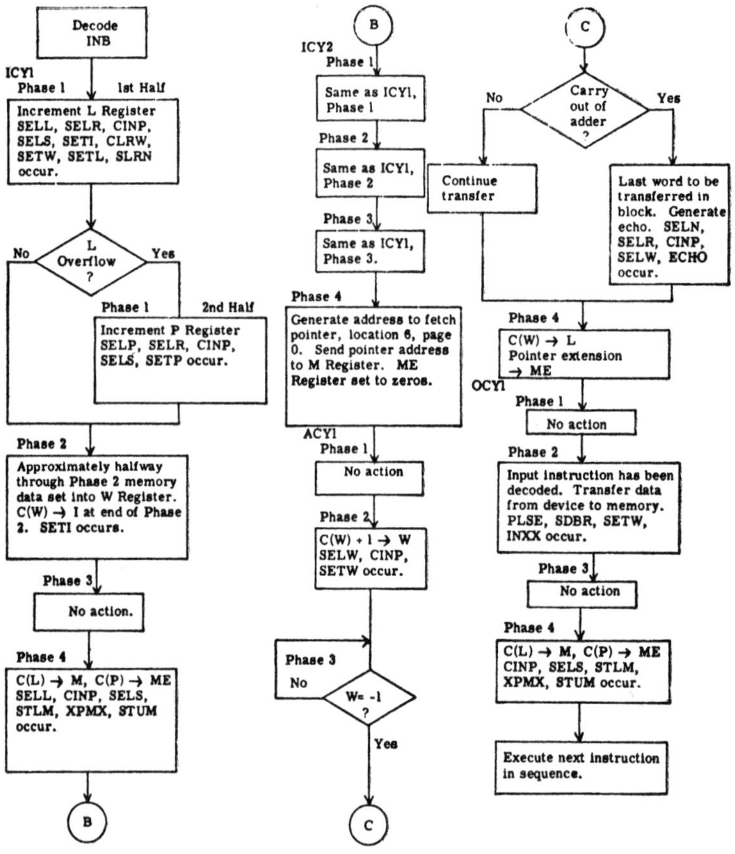

Fig. 18-28. INB flow chart.

send the pointer address to the M register. ME register is set to zero.

ACY1 cycle: Phase 1: No action. Phase 2: C(W) +1 go to W, index pointer. SELW, CINP, SETW occur. Phase 3: Check for W -1. No carry out indicates there still are words to be transferred. A carryout indicates that this is the last word to be transferred in the block. In this case, generate an ECHO. SELR, SELN, CINP, SELW, ECHO occur. Phase 4: C(W) go to L and the pointer extension to ME.

OCY1 cycle: Phase 1: No action. Phase 2: INXX signal indicates that an input instruction has been decoded. PLSE, SDBR, SETW occur. Phase 3: No action. Phase 4: C(L) go to M, C(P) to ME. SELL, CINP, SELS, STLM, XPMX, STUM occur.

OTB: Output Block from Memory

The instruction in Fig. 18-29 transfers a word from memory at the address specified by the output pointer +1 and the pointer extension to the specified device. If OTB is executed as an interrupt instruction, an echo pulse is generated when the end-of-block occurs, which can be used to create an end-of-block interrupt. (No skip can occur during an interrupt instruction execution). If OTB is executed in a program (i.e., not as an interrupt instruction), a skip will occur at end-of-block. The timing is 4. See Fig. 18-30.

Cycle Sequence: ICY1, ICY2, ACY1, OCY1

ICY1 cycle: Phase 1: W register is cleared. L register is incremented during the first half of phase 1. SELL, SELR, SLRN, CINP, SELS, SETI, CLRW, SETW occur. If L overflowed the P register is incremented during the second half of phase 1. SELP, SELR, SLRN, CINP, SELS and SETP occur. Phase 2: Approximately halfway through phase 2 memory data is set into the W register. Contents of W is transferred to the I register at the end of the phase. SETI occurs. Phase 3: No action. Phase 4: Contents of the L register is transferred to the M register and the contents of the P register is transferred to the M extension register. SELL, CINP, SELS, STLM, XPMX and STUM occur.

ICY2 cycle: Phase 1: W register is cleared. L register is incremented during the first half of phase 1. SELL, SELR, SLRN, CINP, SELS, SETI, CLRW, SETW occur. If L overflowed the P register is incremented during the second half of phase 1. SELP, SELR, SLRN, CINP, SELS and SETP occur. Phase 2: Approximately halfway through phase 2 memory data is set into the W register. Contents of the W is transferred to the I register at the end of the phase. SETI occurs. Phase 3:

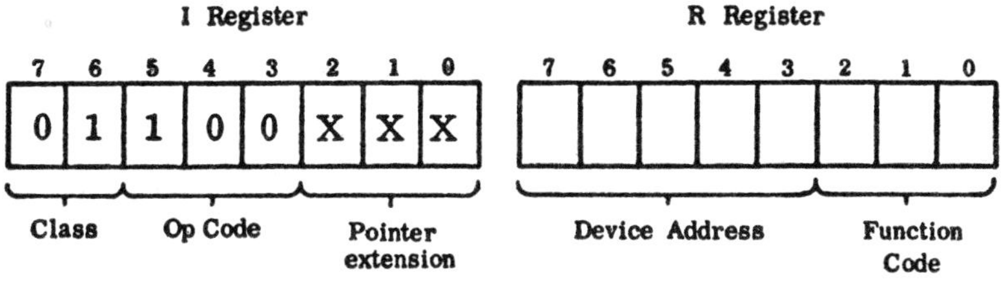

Fig. 18-29. Output block from memory instruction.

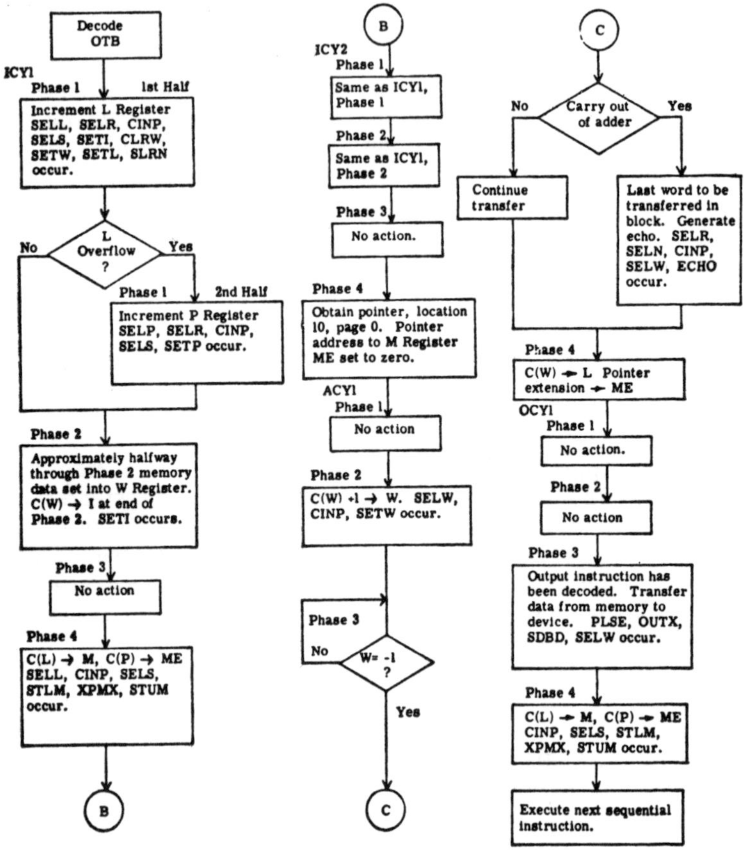

Fig. 18-30. OTB flow chart.

No action. Phase 4: Form the address to obtain the pointer. For the output pointer go to location 10, page 0. Turn off SELS gate. The pointer address goes to the M register. ME is set to zeros.

ACY1 cycle: Phase 1: No action. Phase 2: W +1 goes to W, index pointer. SELW, CINP, SETW occur. Phase 3: Check for

W equal to -1. No carry out indicates there are still words to be transferred. A carry out indicates that this is the last word to be transferred in the block. This causes an echo to be generated. SELR, SELN, CINP, SELW, ECHO occur. Phase 4: C(W) go to L and the pointer extension to ME.

OCY1 cycle: Phase 1: No action. Phase 2: No action. Phase 3: The signal OUTX indicates that an output instruction has been decoded. Phase 4: C(L) go to M, C(P) to ME. SELL, CINP, SELS, STLM, XMPX, STUM occur.

Chapter 19

Diagnostic Information

PROCESSOR MEMORY DIAGNOSTIC (PMD)

PMD tests every core of the memory to ensure that no bits are "picked up" or "dropped." Address logic is checked by storing every word address in itself. Words are read twice to check the read-restore memory cycle. Error diagnostics are typed on the teletype.

Memory Tests

The following three tests are run once for each cycle. Test 1 fills the memory with 0s then reads them back to check for "picked up" bits. Tests 2 fills the memory with all 1s then reads them back to check for "dropped" bits. Test 3 stores the address of each word of the memory in itself then reads them back to verify the memory address circuits.

Each of the three tests is run first for upper memory (page 10 and above) and then for lower memory (pages 0-7). Since this diagnostic destroys all of the memory a binary loader is stored at 350_8 to facilitate reloading the system's software.

Diagnostic Printouts

Error printouts appear in the following format, where all outputs are printed as four octal numbers; **ID, Location, Page** and Error bits.

Setup Procedures

1. Load the PMD in the memory using the object loader.
2. Place the step-run switch in the step mode.
3. Depress the A register select switch (A), depress the clear switch, and enter on the data switches one of the following numbers to indicate the size of the memory.
4. Set the sense switch to run the test continuously.
5. Place the step-run switch in the run mode.
6. Depress the cycle switch.
7. PMD will test the memory module indicated by the sense switch. To exercise the alternate memory module merely change the sense switch, the program will relocate itself and test the alternate memory bank.

```
000 000                 *
000 000                 *  7/30/68
000 000                 *
000 000                 *
000 000                 ***  PMD  PROCESSOR MEMORY DIAGNOSTIC
000 000                 *
000 000                 *    PMD TESTS MEMORY FOR 'PICKING'
000 000                 *    AND 'DROPPING' OF BITS BY FILLING
000 000                 *    CORE WITH ZEROES AND ONES AND
000 000                 *    THEN READING MEMORY BACK FOR
000 000                 *    VERIFICATION.  ADDRESS LOGIC IS
000 000                 *    CHECKED BY STORING THE ADDRESS OF
000 000                 *    EACH WORD IN ITSELF.  WORDS ARE
000 000                 *    READ TWICE TO CHECK THE READ/RESTORE
000 000                 *    MEMORY CYCLE.  EACH OF THE 3 TESTS
000 000                 *    IS RUN FIRST FOR UPPER MEMORY AND
000 000                 *    THEN FOR LOWER MEMORY (PAGES 0-10).
000 000                 *    SINCE THIS DIAGNOSTIC DESTROYS ALL
000 000                 *    OF MEMORY A BINARY LOADER IS STORED
000 000                 *    AT 0350 TO FACILITATE RE-LOADING
000 000                 *    THE SYSTEM SOFTWARE.
000 000                 *
000 000                 *    TO OPERATE
000 000                 *
000 000                 *    1) LOAD DIAGNOSTIC AT PAGE 0
000 000                 *
000 000                 *    2) SET SENSE SWITCH
000 000                 *       ON = TEST CONTINUOUSLY
000 000                 *       OFF= HALT AT END OF TEST
000 000                 *
000 000                 *    3) SET A REG TO CORE SIZE AND RUN
000 000                 *
000 000                 *        4K = 020
000 000                 *        8K = 040
000 000                 *       12K = 060
000 000                 *       16K = 100
000 000                 *
000 000                 *    ERROR DIAGNOSTIC MESSAGESARE
000 000                 *    PRINTED AS 4 OCTAL NUMBERS; ID,
000 000                 *    LOC, PAGE AND ERROR BITS.
000 000                 *
000 000                 *    ID = 0AB  WHERE
000 000                 *    WHERE A = 0  ERROR AT READ TIME
000 000                 *          A = 1  ERROR AT STORE TIME
000 000                 *          B = 0  ZERO TEST
000 000                 *          B = 1  ONES TEST
000 000                 *          B = 2  ADDR TEST
000 000                 *
000 000                 ***  ITEMS AND POINTERS **
000 000                 *
000 000   000 000            ORG  0
000 000   000                DEC  0       ZERO TEST WORD
001 000   377                DEC  -1      ONES TEST WORD
002 000   000           LOC  PTR  **      ADDR TEST WORD AND
003 000   000           PAG  PTR  **      STORAGE PTR
004 000   020           MEM  PTR  @20     CORE SIZE (4K STANDARD)
005 000   000           SAV  PTR  **      TEMP FOR TYP
006 000   000 000       CHK  DPT  **      TEST WORD PTR
010 000                 *
010 000                 ***  MAIN PROGRAM  ***
010 000                 *
010 000   315 004       PMD  LDA  MEM     GET CORE SIZE
012 000   040           040  HLT          OPERATOR MAY CHANGE IT
013 000   331 004            STA  MEM     SET CORE SIZE
015 000   005           PM1  ARC  Z       TEST UPPER MEMORY
016 000   331 007            STA  CHK+1   CHECK WORD IN PAGE 0
020 000   017 000       07   EQU  *-1     (ADDR = 07)
020 000   315 047            LDA  010
022 000   331 323            STA  BOM     BEGIN TEST AT PAGE 10
024 000   315 004            LDA  MEM
```

```
026 000   331 322         STA   EOM     END TEST AT END OF MEMORY
030 000   375 063   M3    JST   TST     TEST UPPER MEMORY
032 000   331 323         STA   BOM     BEGIN TEST AT PAGE 0
034 000   315 047         LDA   010
036 000   331 322         STA   EOM     END TEST AT PAGE 10
040 000   331 007         STA   CHK+1   CHECK WORD IN PAGE 10
042 000   375 230   CTR   JST   MOV     MOVE PGM TO PAGE 10
044 000   347 046        *JMP   *+1     GO TO PAGE 10
046 000   050             PTR   PM2     PTR TO PAGE 10
047 000   010       010   OCT   10
050 000   375 063   PM2   JST   TST     TEST LOWER MEMORY
052 000   375 230         JST   MOV     MOVE PGM TO PAGE 0
054 000   344 056         JMP   /PM3    GO TO PAGE 0
056 000   250       PM3   IFT   1       REPEAT TEST?
057 000   345 010         JMP   PMD     NO, GO HALT FOR OPERATOR
061 000   345 015         JMP   PM1     YES REPEAT
063 000   062 000   015   EQU   *-1     (ADDR = 015)
063 000             *
063 000             ***   TST   TEST SUBROUTINE
063 000             *
063 000   000 000   TST   DPT   **
065 000   005             ARC   Z       INITIALIZE
066 000   331 002         STA   LOC     MEMORY WORD PTR
070 000   331 006         STA   CHK     TEST WORD PTR
072 000   001       TS1   ARC   -1
073 000   331 231         STA   FLG     RESET STORE FLAG
075 000   315 323   TS2   LDA   BOM     INITIALIZE
077 000   331 003         STA   PAG     MEMORY WORD PTR
101 000   315 231   TS3   LDA   FLG
103 000   045             SHF   (       OV = STORE FLAG
104 000   317 006        *LDA   CHK     GET TEST WORD
106 000   244             IFT   R       STORING?
107 000   333 002        *STA   LOC     YES, STORE TEST WORD
111 000   317 002        *LDA   LOC     READ MEMORY
113 000   331 230         STA   TMP     DEVELOP EXCLUSIVE OR
115 000   307 006        *IOR   CHK     OF MEMORY AND TEST WORD
117 000   335 230         IMA   TMP
121 000   323 006        *ANA   CHK
123 000   011             ARC   C
124 000   321 230         ANA   TMP
126 000   242             IFT   N       MEMORY = TEST WORD?
127 000   345 170         JMP   TS4     YES, INCR MEM PTR
131 000   331 230         STA   TMP     NO, SAVE ERROR BITS
133 000   315 231         LDA   FLG     GET STORE/TEST FLAG
135 000   202             IFT   Z       TESTING?
136 000   315 047         LDA   010     NO, SET STORE IND
140 000   301 006         ADD   CHK     ADD TEST NO.
142 000   375 254   CNT   JST   TYP     TYPE TEST ID
144 000   315 002         LDA   LOC
146 000   375 254         JST   TYP     TYPE LOC
150 000   315 003         LDA   PAG
152 000   375 254         JST   TYP     TYPE PAGE
154 000   315 230         LDA   TMP
156 000   375 254         JST   TYP     TYPE ERROR BITS
160 000   315 062         LDA   015
162 000   375 312         JST   OTY     CR
164 000   301 030         ADD   M3
166 000   375 312         JST   OTY     LF
170 000   371 002   TS4   IMS   LOC     BUMP PTR
172 000   345 101         JMP   TS3
174 000   371 003         IMS   PAG     BUMP PAGE
176 000   315 003         LDA   PAG
200 000   311 322         SUB   EOM
202 000   202             IFT   Z       END OF MEMORY?
203 000   345 101         JMP   TS3     NO, CONTINUE
205 000   371 231         IMS   FLG     END OF TEST
207 000   345 213         JMP   *+3
211 000   345 075         JMP   TS2     NO, GO TEST
213 000   371 006         IMS   CHK     YES, BUMP CHK WORD PTR
215 000   371 042         IMS   CTR     3RD TEST?
```

```
217 000  345 072        JMP  TS1    NO, NEXT TEST
221 000  315 030        LDA  M3     YES RESET CTR
223 000  331 042        STA  CTR
225 000  005            ARC  Z
226 000  347 063       *JMP  TST    RETURN
230 000          *
230 000          ***    MOV  MOVE PGM TO ANOTHER PAGE  ***
230 000          *
230 000  000 000 MOV    DPT  **
232 000  331 003        STA  PAG    SET DESTINATION PAGE
234 000  001            ARC  -1
235 000  331 243        STA  PTR    SET PTR
237 000  005            ARC  Z
240 000  371 243 MO1    IMS  PTR    BUMP PTR
242 000  315 000        LDA  **     GET PGM WORD
244 000  243 000 PTR    EQU  *-1
244 000  333 002       *STA  LOC    MOVE TO OTHER PAGE
246 000  371 002        IMS  LOC    END OF PAGE?
250 000  345 240        JMP  MO1    NO LOOP
252 000  347 230       *JMP  MOV    YES, RETURN
254 000          *
254 000          ***    TELETYPE OUTPUT SUBROUTINES  ***
254 000          *
254 000          *      TYP  TYPE OCTAL WORD AND SPACE
254 000          *
254 000  000 000 TYP    DPT  **
256 000  050            ORC  R      BIT 8 = 0
257 000  045     TY1    SHF  (      NEXT 3 BITS
260 000  045            SHF  (
261 000  045            SHF  (
262 000  331 005        STA  SAV    SAVE BITS
264 000  321 017        ANA  07     KEEP LO 3 BITS
266 000  301 324        ADD  060    MAKE ASCII
270 000  375 312        JST  OTY    TYPE DIGIT
272 000  315 005        LDA  SAV    GET BITS
274 000  371 142        IMS  CNT    3RD DIGIT
276 000  345 257        JMP  TY1    NO, LOOP
300 000  315 030        LDA  M3     YES, RESET CTR
302 000  331 142        STA  CNT
304 000  315 012        LDA  040
306 000  375 312        JST  OTY    TYPE SPACE
310 000  347 254       *JMP  TYP
312 000          *
312 000          *      OTY  OUTPUT TO TELETYPE
312 000          *
312 000  000 000 OTY    DPT  **
314 000  155 073        OAS  @73    OUTPUT IF BFR RDY
316 000  345 314        JMP  *-3    BFR NOT RDY
320 000  347 312       *JMP  OTY
322 000          *
322 000          *      ITEMS
322 000          *
322 000  230 000 TMP    EQU  MOV    USE ENTRY AS TEMP STORE
322 000  231 000 FLG    EQU  MOV+1  AND FLAG
322 000  000     EOM    PTR  **     END PAGE OF TEST
323 000  000     BOM    PTR  **     BEGINNING PAGE OF TEST
324 000  060     060    OCT  60
325 000          *
325 000          *      BINARY LOADER
325 000          *
350 000  350 000        ORG  @350
350 000  331 002 PBL    STA  LOC    SAVE LOC PART OF ADR
352 000  331 003        STA  PAG    SAVE PAGE PART OF ADR
354 000  100 072 BL1    EXC  @72    SEL STEP READ PAPER TAPE
356 000  131 071        IAS  @71
360 000  345 356        JMP  *-3    TTY NOT READY
362 000  333 002       *STA  LOC    PUT CHAR IN NEXT PROG WD
364 000  371 002        IMS  LOC    GET ADR OF NEXT PROG WD
```

```
366 000   345 354     JMP  BL1    GO GET NEXT CHAR
370 000   371 003     IMS  PAG    END OF PAGE. INC PAGE NO.
372 000   210         IFT  0      IS LOADING TO BE HALTED
373 000   040         HLT         YES HALT
374 000   000         NOP
375 000   345 354     JMP  BL1    GO LOAD NEXT PAGE
377 000   010 000     END  PMD    (LOAD & EXECUTE FOR 4K CO
```

WORST PATTERN DIAGNOSTIC(WPD)

WPD occupies the first 85 words in page 0 and fills the remainder of the memory with a worst-case pattern of 0s and 1s. This causes most of the cores in the memory to be magnetized in the same direction. This pattern is then read out and verified under the worst-case noise level for memory. Since all of the memory is destroyed this should either be the first or last diagnostic exercised, since all loaders and bootstraps must be reloaded.

Setup Procedures

1. Load the WPD in the memory using the object loader.
2. Place the step-run switch in the step mode.
3. Depress the A register select switch (A), depress the clear switch, and enter on the data switches one of the numbers below to indicate the size of the memory. If running a 4k test, leave the A register as set (2).

$$40_8 = 8k$$

$$60_8 = 12k$$

$$100_8 = 16k$$

4. Set the sense switch to run the test continuously.
5. Place the step-run switch in the run mode.
6. Depress the cycle switch.
7. The memory will be filled with the worst pattern and verified. Errors cause a halt at 125-0 with OV equal to 1. The A register contains a 1 in the bit that failed. The address of the bad word is stored at location 10 of page 0. Press the cycle switch to continue the test.

```
000 000      *
000 000      ***  WPD  WORST PATTERN MEMORY DIAGNOSTIC
000 000      *
000 000      *    WPD RESIDES IN PAGE 0 AND FILLS THE
000 000      *    REMAINDER OF MEMORY WITH THE WORST
000 000      *    CASE PATTERN OF ZEROES AND ONES
000 000      *    TESTING MEMORY UNDER THE HIGHEST
000 000      *    NOSE LEVEL.
000 000      *
000 000      *    TO OPERATE
```

```
000 000                    *
000 000                    *     1) LOAD DIAGNOSTIC AT PAGE 0
000 000                    *     2) SET SENSE SWITCH
000 000                    *        ON = TEST CONTINUOUSLY
000 000                    *        OFF= HALT AT END OF TEST
000 000                    *
000 000                    *     3) SET A REG TO CORE SIZE AND RUN
000 000                    *
000 000                    *         4K = 020
000 000                    *         8K = 040
000 000                    *        12K = 060
000 000                    *        16K = 100
000 000                    *
000 000                    *     SYSTEM HALTS
000 000                    *
000 000                    *        OV OFF = NORMAL END OF TEST
000 000                    *        OV ON =  ERROR HALT, WHERE
000 000                    *           A REG CONTAINS ERROR BITS
000 000                    *           LOC 10-0 = ADDR OF ERROR WD
000 000                    *           (PRESS RUN TO CONTINUE TEST)
000 000                    *
000 000   000 000                ORG  0
000 000   377                    DEC  -1      WORST PATTERN TABLE
001 000   000                    DEC  0
002 000   000                    DEC  0
003 000   377                    DEC  -1
004 000   000                    DEC  0
005 000   377                    DEC  -1
006 000   377                    DEC  -1
007 000   000                    DEC  0
010 000                    *
010 000                    *     ITEMS AND POINTERS
010 000                    *
010 000   130          LOC   PTR  FLG     MEMORY ADDR PTR (LOC)
011 000   000          PAG   PTR  0
012 000   020          CSZ   OCT  20      CORE SIZE (4K STANDARD)
013 000                    *
013 000                    *     ENTRY TO DIAGNOSTIC
013 000                    *
013 000   315 012      WPD   LDA  CSZ     GET CORE SIZE
015 000   050                ORC  R       SET END OF TEST FLAG
016 000   040                HLT          LET OPERATOR CHANGE SIZE
017 000   331 012            STA  CSZ     SET MEMORY SIZE
021 000   005          WP1   ARC  Z
022 000   331 130            STA  FLG     SET STORE FLAG
024 000   331 011      WP2   STA  PAG     SET PAG PTR TO 0
026 000   315 023            LDA  SLC
030 000   331 010            STA  LOC     SET LOC PTR TO END OF PGM
032 000   371 010      WP3   IMS  LOC     BUMP LOC PTR
034 000   345 063            JMP  WP4
036 000   371 011            IMS  PAG     BUMP PAGE PTR
040 000   315 011            LDA  PAG
042 000   311 012            SUB  CSZ
044 000   202                IFT  Z       END OF CORE?
045 000   345 063            JMP  WP4     NO, GO STORE/TEST
047 000   315 130            LDA  FLG     GET STORE FLAG
051 000   371 130            IMS  FLG     BUMP STORE FLAG
053 000   242                IFT  N       END OF TEST?
054 000   345 024            JMP  WP2     NO, GO TEST
056 000   250                IFT  1       REPEAT REST?
057 000   345 013            JMP  WPD     NO, GO HALT
061 000   345 021            JMP  WP1     YES, REPEAT
063 000   315 010      WP4   LDA  LOC     USE LOC TO GET TBL ADDR
065 000   055                SHF  L       7 6543210Z
066 000   055                SHF  L       6 543210ZZ
067 000   041                SHF  <       6 53210ZZZ
070 000   041                SHF  <       6 5210ZZZZ
071 000   041                SHF  <       6 510ZZZZZ
072 000   045                SHF  (       5 10ZZZZZ6
073 000   045                SHF  (       1 0ZZZZZ65
```

```
0081  074 000   045             SHF  (       0 ZZZZZ651
0082  075 000   331 100         STA  *+2     SET TBLE ADDR IN LOAD INS
0083  077 000   315 000         LDA  **      GET WORST PATTERN
0084  101 000   202             IFT  Z
0085  102 000   070             ORC  C
0086  103 000   000             NOP
0087  104 000   315 130         LDA  FLG     GET CYCLE FLAG
0088  106 000   202             IFT  Z       STORING?
0089  107 000   345 116         JMP  WP5     NO, GO CHECK
0090  111 000   244             IFT  R       STORE ZEROES?
0091  112 000   001             ARC  -1      NO, SET ALL ONES
0092  113 000   060             ORC  S       SET ONE'S FLAG
0093  114 000   333 010        *STA  LOC     STORE PATTERN
0094  116 000   317 010   WP5  *LDA  LOC     GET MEM WORD
0095  120 000   244             IFT  R       SHOULD PATTERN BE ZEROES?
0096  121 000   011             ARC  C       NO, COMPLEMENT MEM WORD
0097  122 000   000             NOP
0098  123 000   202             IFT  Z       MEM WORD OK?
0099  124 000   060             ORC  S       NO, SET ERROR IND
0100  125 000   040             HLT          ERROR HALT
0101  126 000   345 032         JMP  WP3     YES, GO CHECK END OF TEST
0102  130 000   000       FLG   OCT  0       STORE/CHECK CYCLE FLAG
0103  131 000   023 000   SLC   EQU  WP2-1   (END OF PGM)
0104  131 000   013 000         END  WPD
```

PROCESSOR TELETYPE DIAGNOSTIC (PTD)

PTD tests all teletype I-O logic and checks the reader, punch, and printer for every character code ($0\text{-}377_8$). Also, the keyboard input is checked for any character the user may desire to test.

Sequence of Testing

First the initialize teletype command (EXC @ 74) is checked along with the different TTY sense instructions. Then if the sense switch is depressed, the diagnostic will output the leader and the CR-LF (carriage return and line feed). Leader and CR-LF will be punched out following each set of characters output. There are 64 characters output in each set.

The first set of characters output will be $0\text{-}77_8$. This will be followed by an input sequence which reads the characters ($0\text{-}77_8$) just output. Then these characters input are compared against those that were output. The comparison starts on the first character after the carriage return input. If any discrepancies exist, the processor will halt. At this point the A register will contain the input character which failed the test. (After any halt if the cycle switch is depressed twice, the diagnostic should proceed.) The sequence of output characters, output leader and input is repeated four times per pass with this diagnostic.

The following I-O instructions are used on these sequences:

Set	Character Codes	Output	Input
1	0-77 or 200-277	Output A reg.	Block-input
2	0-77 or 200-277	Block-output	Input-A reg. on sense
3	100-77 or 300-377	Output-A reg. on sense	Block-input (interrupt)
4	100-77 or 300-377	Block-output (interrupt)	Masked input

(Note: On every other pass the character codes are offset by 200_8.)

These sequences are run over and over until the sense switch is depressed. When the sense switch is depressed the diagnostic will not start another pass, but instead will "hang" in a loop waiting for an input from the keyboard. The keyboard test will just output each character that is input, timing out each input so that no garbage should be printed out.

Setup Procedures

1. Load PTD in the memory using the object loader.
2. Place the step-run switch in the step mode.
3. Make sure the relative and manual execute switches are released.
4. Depress the reset switch.
5. Depress the page register select switch (P), depress the clear switch, and enter on the data switches the page number in the memory where the teletype diagnostic starts (5).
6. Depress the location register select switch (L), depress the clear switch.
7. Depress the instruction register select switch (I), depress the clear switch.
8. Depress the A register select switch (A), depress the clear switch.
9. Punch the leader with the teletype on local and enter the tape (which is hanging from the punch) in the paper tape reader so that there is nothing but the leader between the reader and the punch. If the keyboard is to be tested, proceed to the next step. If the diagnostic is to be run continuously (I-O instruction diagnostic plus punch and reader diagnostic) depress the sense switch.
10. Place the TTY power on switch on the teletype in the line position.

11. Make sure the paper tape punch is on and the tape reader is on.

12. Place the step-run switch in the run mode.

13. Depress the cycle switch.

14. If the diagnostic halts, the A register will tell what input character failed. To determine what test failed and how, look at the attached listing. If it is desired to have the test run repeatedly, store a jump instruction (to the beginning of the test) in place of the two halts.

15. When the sense switch is depressed, the diagnostic will "hang," looking for an input from the keyboard.

16. If it is desired to continue after any halt, depress the cycle switch twice.

```
000 000                *
000 000                *  07/20/68
000 000                *
000 000                *
000 000                *     PROCESSOR TELETYPE DIAGNOSTIC (PTD)
000 000                *
000 000                *
000 005  000 005           ORG   0-5
000 005  100 074     SAR   EXC   @74
002 005  150 070           OTZ   @70       OUTPUT ZERO
004 005  100 074           EXC   @74
006 005  111 071           SSR   @71
010 005  040               HLT             READY FAILED
011 005  040               HLT
012 005  110 073           SSN   @73       NOT BUSY FAILED
014 005  345 020           JMP   *+3
016 005  040               HLT
017 005  040               HLT
020 005  111 072           SSR   @72       INT #1 OFF FAILED
022 005  345 026           JMP   *+3
024 005  040               HLT
025 005  040               HLT
026 005  374 216           JST   /SUP
030 005  005               ARC   Z
031 005  330 176           STA   /INT
033 005  331 234           STA   OCH
035 005  374 140           JST   /LDR
037 005  315 074     SPT   LDA   BIN       SET UP INPUT BLOCK
041 005  330 002           STA   /2        INST FOR INTRPT #1
043 005  250               IFT   1         IS KEYBOARD TO BE TESTED
044 005  344 100           JMP   /KBD      YES
046 005  315 234           LDA   OCH       SET UP OUTPUT WORD
050 005  111 073     OT1   SSR   @73
052 005  345 050           JMP   *-3       TEST OUTPUT
054 005  154 070           OTA   @70       INSTRUCTION
056 005  375 237           JST   INC
060 005  345 050           JMP   OT1
062 005  374 140           JST   /LDR      OUTPUT LEADER
064 005  374 177           JST   /CKC
066 005  100 073           EXC   @73
070 005  111 071     RD1   SSR   @71
072 005  345 070           JMP   RD1
074 005  120 070     BIN   INB   @70-10    TEST BLOCK INPUT
076 005  345 070           JMP   RD1
100 005  100 074           EXC   @74       SHUT OFF CONTINUOUS READ
102 005  375 264           JST   CAR       GO CHECK INPUT
104 005  111 073     OT2   SSR   @73
106 005  345 104           JMP   *-3
110 005  140 070     BOT   OTB   @70-10    TEST BLOCK OUTPUT
112 005  345 104           JMP   OT2
```

```
114 005   375 355         JST  RSB
116 005   100 072   RD2   EXC  @72      TEST STEP READER AND
120 005   131 071         IAS  @71      INPUT AND SENSE INST'S
122 005   345 120         JMP  *-3
124 005   375 323         JST  RCK      CHECK INPUT
126 005   345 116         JMP  RD2
130 005   315 234         LDA  OCH
132 005   155 073   OT3   OAS  @73      TEST OUTPUT AND SENSE
134 005   345 132         JMP  *-3      INSTRUCTION
136 005   375 237         JST  INC      INC OUTPUT WD
140 005   345 132         JMP  OT3
142 005   374 140         JST  /LDR     OUTPUT LEADER
144 005   374 177         JST  /CKC
146 005   100 075         EXC  @75      ENABLE MASK INT #1
150 005   111 072         SSR  @72      TEST OKAY?
152 005   040             HLT           YES
153 005   040             HLT
154 005   100 076         EXC  @76      ENABLE MASK INT #2
156 005   022             EIN           ENABLE INTRPT'S
157 005   100 073         EXC  @73      SEL CONT RD FOR INTRPT
161 005   314 176         LDA  /INT     IS BLOCK INPUT FINISHED
163 005   242             IFT  N
164 005   345 161         JMP  *-4      NO
166 005   315 110         LDA  BOT      YES, SET UP BLOCK OUTPUT
170 005   330 002         STA  /2       INST
172 005   375 264         JST  CAR      CHECK INPUT
174 005   100 074         EXC  @74      TEST BLOCK OUTPUT INIT
176 005   100 075         EXC  @75      TTY FOR INTRPT ENABLE
200 005   100 076         EXC  @76      INT MASKS #1 & #2
202 005   022             EIN
203 005   314 176         LDA  /INT     IS BLOCK OUTPUT FINISHED
205 005   242             IFT  N
206 005   345 203         JMP  *-4      NO
210 005   375 355         JST  RSB
212 005   100 072   RD4   EXC  @72      TEST MASKED INPUT
214 005   315 236         LDA  T77      CLEAR BIT 6
216 005   111 071         SSR  @71
220 005   345 216         JMP  *-3
222 005   134 070         MIA  @70
224 005   301 212         ADD  RD4      ADD BACK BIT 6
226 005   375 323         JST  RCK      CHECK INPUT
230 005   345 212         JMP  RD4
232 005   345 037         JMP  SPT      START OVER
234 005             *
234 005             *     LITERALS AND POINTERS
234 005             *
234 005   000       OCH   PTR  **
235 005   200       02H   OCT  200
236 005   277       T77   OCT  277
237 005             *
237 005             *     INCREMENT OUTPUT WORD SUB
237 005             *
237 005   000 000   INC   DPT  **
241 005   315 234         LDA  OCH
243 005   007             ARC  I        INC I/O WORD
244 005   331 234         STA  OCH
246 005   321 263         ANA  077
250 005   202             IFT  Z        IS THAT ALL FOR THIS TEST
251 005   345 257         JMP  *+5      NO
253 005   371 237         IMS  INC      YES
255 005   371 237         IMS  INC
257 005   315 234         LDA  OCH
261 005   347 237        *JMP  INC
263 005   077       077   OCT  77
264 005             *     COMPARE READ
264 005             *
264 005   000 000   CAR   DPT  **
266 005   374 216         JST  /SUP
270 005   331 321         STA  BFP
272 005   315 234         LDA  OCH
```

```
274 005   311 212         SUB  RD4     RESET I/O WORD
276 005   331 234         STA  OCH
300 005   371 321   CR1   IMS  BFP
302 005   313 321        *SUB  BFP     IS THIS CORRECT CHAR
304 005   242             IFT  N
305 005   345 313         JMP  *+5
307 005   317 321        *LDA  BFP
311 005   040             HLT          NO
312 005   040             HLT
313 005   375 237         JST  INC     YES, INC I/O WORD
315 005   345 300         JMP  CR1
317 005   347 264        *JMP  CAR     EXIT SUB
321 005   277 010   BFP   DPT  @277-10
323 005             *
323 005             *     READ CHECK SUB
323 005             *
323 005   000 000   RCK   DPT  **
325 005   331 354         STA  CHR     SAVE CHAR
327 005   315 234         LDA  OCH     NO, RESET I/O WORD
331 005   311 354         SUB  CHR     IS THIS CORRECT CHAR
333 005   242             IFT  N
334 005   345 342         JMP  *+5     YES
336 005   315 354         LDA  CHR     NO
340 005   040             HLT
341 005   040             HLT
342 005   375 237         JST  INC     INC I/O WD
344 005   347 323        *JMP  RCK     IMMED EXIT
346 005   371 323         IMS  RCK
350 005   371 323         IMS  RCK
352 005   347 323        *JMP  RCK
354 005   000       CHR   PTR  **
355 005   000 000   RSB   DPT  **
357 005   374 140         JST  /LDR
361 005   374 177         JST  /CKC
363 005   315 234         LDA  OCH
365 005   311 212         SUB  RD4
367 005   331 234         STA  OCH
371 005   347 355        *JMP  RSB
373 005             *
373 005             *     KEYBOARD TEST
373 005             *
100 000   100 000         ORG  @100
100 000   100 071   KBD   EXC  @71     SELECT KEYBOARD
102 000   131 071         IAS  @71
104 000   345 102         JMP  *-3
106 000   210             IFT  0
107 000   347 121        *JMP  STP
111 000   154 070         OTA  @70     OUTPUT CHARACTER JST INPU
113 000   111 071         SSR  @71
115 000   345 113         JMP  *-3
117 000   345 100         JMP  KBD     GO CHECK IF THAT'S ALL
121 000   037 005   STP   DPT  SPT
123 000             *
123 000             *     END OF BLOCK INTERRUPT SUB
123 000             *
123 000   000 000   EOB   DPT  **
125 000   021             DIN
126 000   111 073         SSR  @73
130 000   345 126         JMP  *-3
132 000   371 176         IMS  INT     IND EOB INTERRUPT
134 000   100 074         EXC  @74     INIT TTY
136 000   347 123        *JMP  EOB
140 000             *
140 000             *     OUTPUT LEADER SUB
140 000             *
140 000   000 000   LDR   DPT  **
142 000   315 142         LDA  *-1
144 000   151 073   LDI   OZS  @73
146 000   345 144         JMP  *-3
150 000   007             ARC  I
```

```
151 000   202                IFT  Z
152 000   345 144            JMP  LDI
154 000   314 235            LDA /012
156 000   155 073            OAS  '73
160 000   345 156            JMP  *-3
162 000   315 234            LDA  015
164 000   155 073            OAS  '73
166 000   345 164            JMP  *-3
170 000   111 071            SSR  '71
172 000   345 170     LD2    JMP  *-3
174 000   347 140           *JMP  LDR
176 000   000         INT    PTR  **
177 000               *
177 000   000 000     CKC    DPT  **
201 000   100 072            EXC  '72
203 000   131 071            IAS  '71
205 000   345 203            JMP  *-3
207 000   311 234            SUB  015
211 000   202                IFT  Z
212 000   345 201            JMP  *-10
214 000   347 177           *JMP  CKC
216 000               *
216 000               *
216 000   000 000     SUP    DPT  **
220 000   005                ARC  Z
221 000   330 176            STA /INT
223 000   315 233            LDA  N65
225 000   330 006            STA /6
227 000   330 010            STA /8
231 000   347 216           *JMP  SUP
233 000   277         N65    OCT  277
234 000               *
234 000               *
234 000   015         015    OCT  15
235 000   012         012    OCT  12
236 000               *
236 000               *
002 000   002 000            ORG  2
002 000   120 070            INB  '70-10
004 000   375 123            JST  EOB
006 000   277 000            DPT  '277-0
010 000   277 000            DPT  '277-0
012 000   000 000            END
```

PROCESSOR INSTRUCTION DIAGNOSTIC (PID)

PID tests all memory reference and register change instructions for all possible results and tests enough skip instructions to check all the skip logic. If any test on any instruction fails, the processor will halt.

General Processing

First of all, the jump (JMP) is tested to make sure a transfer takes place. Secondly, since the A register is set to zero upon starting the program, the IFT Z (skip if the A register is equal to zero) instruction is tested. Then the IFT N (skip if the A register is not equal to zero) and the IFT + (skip if the A register is positive) are tested respectively. Next the instructions tested to this point are used to test the LDA (load the A register from memory instruction). This sort of procedure (i.e., use of any of the previously checked instructions used to check the next instruction) is used to check all the remaining instructions.

The skip on the setting of the sense switch is the last instruction tested in each pass through the diagnostic. This test assumes that the sense switch is depressed. Therefore, if the sense switch is not depressed, the diagnostic should halt at the end of one pass, and if depressed, the diagnostic should go through another pass.

Operating Procedures

When a test fails the processor halts. At each halt two locations are reserved. These locations are reserved so that the maintenance engineer can store a jump instruction (to the beginning of the test that failed) in these locations. This gives the engineer the opportunity to run continuously a test that fails, so that he may look at associated signals with a scope.

Setup Procedures

1. Load the PID in the memory using the object loader.
2. Place the step-run switch in the step mode.
3. Make sure the relative and manual execute switches are released.
4. Depress the reset switch.
5. Depress the page register select switch (P), depress the clear switch, and enter on the data switches the page number in the memory where the instruction diagnostic starts (1).
6. Depress the location register select switch (L), depress the clear switch.
7. Depress the instruction register select switch (I), depress the clear switch.
8. Depress the A register select switch (A), depress the clear switch.
9. If the diagnostic is to be run continuously depress the sense switch.
10. Place the step-run switch in the run mode.
11. Depress the cycle switch.
12. If the diagnostic halts other than on location 324_8 of page 0, an instruction failed a test. To determine what test failed and how, look at the attached listing. If it is desired to have the test run repeatedly, store a jump instruction (to the beginning of the test) in place of the two halts.
13. When the sense switch is depressed, the diagnostic will halt at location 324_8, page 0.
14. If it is desired to continue after any halt, depress the cycle switch twice.

```
000 000                *
000 000                *    INSTRUCTION DIAGNOSTIC
000 000                *
000 000                *    THIS PROGRAM TESTS ALL INSTRUCTIONS
000 000                *    WITH EXCEPTION OF THE I/O INSTRUCTIONS.
000 000                *    IT TESTS EACH INSTRUCTION FOR ALL
000 000                *    POSSIBLE EFFECTS.
000 000                *
000 000                *    IF AN INSTRUCTION FAILS ON A TEST,
000 000                *    THE PROCESSOR WILL HALT. AT EACH HALT
000 000                *    THE HALT IS REPEATED. THE REASON FOR
000 000                *    THIS IS TO ALLOW THE ENGINEER TO
000 000                *    REPLACE THE TWO HALTS WITH A JUMP
000 000                *    INSTRUCTION TO THE BEGINNING OF THE
000 000                *    TEST THAT FAILED.  THE ENGINEER CAN
000 000                *    THEN HOOK-UP A SCOPE AND CHECK SIGNALS.
000 000                *
000 000                *
000 000                *    TO OPERATE
000 000                *
000 000                *    1) SET SENSE SWITCH
000 000                *       OFF = HALT AT END OF TEST PASS
000 000                *       ON  = TEST CONTINUOUSLY
000 000                *
000 000                *    2) IF PROGRAM HALTS OTHER THAN AT THE
000 000                *       NORMAL HALT, LOOK AT INSTRUCTIONS
000 000                *       WHICH PRECEDE THE HALT ON THIS
000 000                *       LISTING TO DETERMINE INSTRUCTION
000 000                *       THAT FAILED.
000 000                *
000 001   000 001          ORG  0-1
000 001   345 003   BGN    JMP  *+2     TEST JMP INST
002 001   040              HLT          FAILED
003 001   000              NOP
004 001   345 010          JMP  *+3
006 001   040              HLT          JMP FAILED
007 001   040              HLT          JMP FAILED
010 001   345 015          JMP  *+4
012 001   040              HLT          JMP FAILED
013 001   040              HLT          JMP FAILED
014 001   040              HLT          JMP FAILED
015 001   202              IFT  Z       TEST IFT ZERO INST, A = 0
016 001   040              HLT          IFT ZERO FAILED
017 001   040              HLT
020 001   242              IFT  N       TEST IFT NON-ZERO, A = 0
021 001   345 025          JMP  *+3
023 001   040              HLT
024 001   201              IFT  -       TEST IFT MINUS, A = 0
025 001   345 031          JMP  *+3
027 001   040              HLT          IFT - FAILED
030 001   040              HLT
031 001   315 030          LDA  *-2     TEST LDA INST & IFT Z
033 001   202              IFT  Z       WITH NON-ZERO VALUE
034 001   345 040          JMP  *+3
036 001   040              HLT          LDA FAILED OR IFT Z
037 001   040              HLT
040 001   242              IFT  N       TEST IFT NON-ZERO, A=NZ
041 001   040              HLT          IFT N FAILED
042 001   040              HLT
043 001   201              IFT  -       TEST IFT MINUS, A=;
044 001   345 050          JMP  *+3
046 001   040              HLT          IFT - FAILED
047 001   040              HLT
050 001   315 373          LDA  N1      MINUS ONE TO A
052 001   201              IFT  -       TEST IFT MINUS, A= -
053 001   040              HLT          IFT - FAILED
054 001   040              HLT
055 001   202              IFT  Z       TEST IFT ZERO, A= -
056 001   345 062          JMP  *+3
060 001   040              HLT          IFT Z FAILED
```

```
061 001   040              HLT
062 001   242              IFT  N      TEST IFT NON-ZERO, A= -
063 001   040              HLT         IFT N FAILED
064 001   040              HLT
065 001   005              ARC  Z      TEST ARC Z  INST
066 001   202              IFT  Z      WITH A NON-ZERO
067 001   040              HLT         ARC Z FAILED
070 001   040              HLT
071 001   315 364          LDA  ZER    TEST LDA INST
073 001   242              IFT  N      WITH ZERO
074 001   345 100          JMP  *+3
076 001   040              HLT         LDA  FAILED
077 001   040              HLT
100 001   202              IFT  Z
101 001   040              HLT         LDA FAILED
102 001   040              HLT
103 001   005              ARC  Z      TEST ARC Z INST
104 001   202              IFT  Z      WITH A ALREADY ZERO
105 001   040              HLT         ARC Z FAILED
106 001   040              HLT
107 001   315 365          LDA  C1     TEST SUB INST, A = 1
111 001   311 365          SUB  C1
113 001   202              IFT  Z
114 001   040              HLT         SUB FAILED
115 001   040              HLT
116 001   315 366          LDA  EVN    TEST SUB INST, WITH A
120 001   311 366          SUB  EVN    EVEN AND NEG
122 001   202              IFT  Z
123 001   040              HLT         SUB FAILED
124 001   040              HLT
125 001   315 367          LDA  ODD    TEST SUB WITH A =
127 001   311 367          SUB  ODD    TO HIGH ODD NUM
131 001   202              IFT  Z
132 001   040              HLT         SUB FAILED
133 001   040              HLT
134 001   315 366          LDA  EVN    TEST STA INST WITH A
136 001   331 370          STA  TMP    EVEN AND NEG
140 001   311 366          SUB  EVN
142 001   202              IFT  Z
143 001   040              HLT         STA DESTROYED CONTENTS
144 001   040              HLT         OF A-REG
145 001   315 367          LDA  ODD    TEST STA INST WITH A ODD
147 001   331 370          STA  TMP
151 001   005              ARC  Z      CLEAR A
152 001   315 370          LDA  TMP
154 001   311 367          SUB  ODD
156 001   202              IFT  Z
157 001   040              HLT         STA DID STORE INTO MEMORY
160 001   040              HLT
161 001   005              ARC  Z      CLEAR A
162 001   335 370          IMA  TMP    TEST IMA INST, A = 0
164 001   311 367          SUB  ODD    AND M = ODD NUM
166 001   202              IFT  Z
167 001   040              HLT         IMA FAILED TO LOAD WITH
170 001   040              HLT         CONTENTS OF MEMORY
171 001   335 370          IMA  TMP
173 001   202              IFT  Z
174 001   040              HLT         IMA FAILED TO STORE ZERO
175 001   040              HLT         INTO MEMORY
176 001   315 366          LDA  EVN    TEST IMA INST WITH A = 0
200 001   331 370          STA  TMP    AND M = EVEN AND NEG
202 001   005              ARC  Z      CLEAR A
203 001   335 370          IMA  TMP
205 001   311 366          SUB  EVN
207 001   202              IFT  Z
210 001   040              HLT         IMA FAILED TO LOAD A WITH
211 001   040              HLT         CONTENTS OF MEMORY
212 001   335 370          IMA  TMP
214 001   202              IFT  Z
215 001   040              HLT         IMA FAILED TO STORE ZERO
```

```
216 001   040                HLT          INTO MEMORY
217 001   315 365            LDA    C1    TEST ADD INST, A = 1
221 001   301 365            ADD    C1    ADDING POSITIVE NUM
223 001   311 371            SUB    C2
225 001   202                IFT    Z
226 001   040                HLT          ADD FAILED
227 001   040                HLT
230 001   315 365            LDA    C1    TEST ADD INST, A = 1
232 001   301 372            ADD    N2    ADDING NEG NUM, THEN POS
234 001   301 365            ADD    C1    NUM
236 001   202                IFT    Z
237 001   040                HLT          ADD FAILED
240 001   040                HLT
241 001   315 373            LDA    N1    TEST ADD INST, A = -1
243 001   301 371            ADD    C2    ADDING POS. NUM
245 001   311 365            SUB    C1
247 001   202                IFT    Z
250 001   040                HLT          ADD FAILED
251 001   040                HLT
252 001   315 373            LDA    N1    TEST ADD INST, A = -1
254 001   301 373            ADD    N1    ADDING NEG NUM, THEN
256 001   301 371            ADD    C2    ADD POS NUM
260 001   202                IFT    Z
261 001   040                HLT          ADD FAILED
262 001   040                HLT
263 001   315 373            LDA    N1    TEST SUB & ADD SEQUENCE
265 001   311 365            SUB    C1    SUB POS NUM, ADD POS NUM
267 001   301 371            ADD    C2
271 001   202                IFT    Z
272 001   040                HLT          SUB & ADD SEQ FAILED
273 001   040                HLT
274 001   315 373            LDA    N1    TEST SUB -1 FROM -1
276 001   311 373            SUB    N1
300 001   202                IFT    Z
301 001   040                HLT          SUB -1 FROM -1 FAILED
302 001   040                HLT
303 001   315 365            LDA    C1    TEST SUB & ADD SEQUENCE
305 001   311 373            SUB    N1    SUB NEG NUM, ADD NEG NUM
307 001   301 372            ADD    N2
311 001   202                IFT    Z
312 001   040                HLT          SUB & ADD SEQ FAILED
313 001   040                HLT
314 001   315 366            LDA    EVN   TEST ANA INST, A-REG EVEN
316 001   321 366            ANA    EVN   MASK EVEN
320 001   311 366            SUB    EVN
322 001   202                IFT    Z
323 001   040                HLT          ANA FAILED
324 001   040                HLT
325 001   315 367            LDA    ODD   TEST ANA INST, A-REG ODD
327 001   321 367            ANA    ODD   MASK ODD
331 001   311 367            SUB    ODD
333 001   202                IFT    Z
334 001   040                HLT          ANA FAILED
335 001   040                HLT
336 001   315 366            LDA    EVN   TEST ANA INST, A-REG EVEN
340 001   321 367            ANA    ODD   MASK ODD
342 001   202                IFT    Z
343 001   040                HLT          ANA FAILED
344 001   040                HLT
345 001   317 374           *LDA    ODP   TEST INDIRECT
347 001   311 367            SUB    ODD
351 001   202                IFT    Z
352 001   040                HLT          INDIRECT DID NOT WORK
353 001   040                HLT
354 001   347 360           *JMP    P2N   GO TO NEXT PAGE
356 001   040                HLT          INDIRECT JUMP
357 001   040                HLT          DID NOT WORK
360 001   000 002   P2N      DPT    NP2
```

```
362 001   040                HLT          IND JUMP WAS
363 001   040                HLT          DIRECT - FAILED
364 001              *
364 001              *   LITERALS AND STORAGE WORDS
364 001              *
364 001   000        ZER OCT  0
365 001   001        C1  OCT  1
366 001   252        EVN OCT  252
367 001   125        ODD OCT  125
370 001   000        TMP PTR  **
371 001   002        C2  OCT  2
372 001   376        N2  DEC  -2
373 001   377        N1  DEC  -1
374 001   363 002    ODP DPT  OD1
000 002   000 002        ORG  @0-2
000 002   315 363    NP2 LDA  OD1
002 002   305 363        IOR  OD1     TEST IOR INST, A-REG ODD
004 002   311 363        SUB  OD1     AND OR CONSTANT ODD
006 002   202            IFT  Z
007 002   040            HLT          IOR FAILED
010 002   040            HLT
011 002   315 364        LDA  EV1     TEST IOR INST, A-REG EVEN
013 002   305 364        IOR  EV1     AND OR CONSTANT EVEN
015 002   311 364        SUB  EV1
017 002   202            IFT  Z
020 002   040            HLT          IOR FAILED
021 002   040            HLT
022 002   315 364        LDA  EV1     TEST IOR INST, A-REG EVEN
024 002   305 363        IOR  OD1     AND OR CONSTANT ODD
026 002   301 365        ADD  01
030 002   202            IFT  Z
031 002   040            HLT          IOR FAILED
032 002   040            HLT
033 002   315 363        LDA  OD1     TEST IOR INST, A-REG ODD
035 002   305 364        IOR  EV1     AND OR CONSTANT EVEN
037 002   301 365        ADD  01
041 002   202            IFT  Z
042 002   040            HLT          IOR FAILED
043 002   040            HLT
044 002   005            ARC  Z       TEST IMS INST, A = 0
045 002   331 366        STA  TST     AND M = 0
047 002   371 366        IMS  TST
051 002   202            IFT  Z
052 002   040            HLT          IMS INST HAD EFFECT ON
053 002   040            HLT          A-REG
054 002   315 366        LDA  TST
056 002   311 365        SUB  01
060 002   202            IFT  Z
061 002   040            HLT          IMS INST FAILED TO INC
062 002   040            HLT
063 002   315 367        LDA  C77     TEST IMS INST FOR SKIP
065 002   331 366        STA  TST     ON ZERO RESULT, J = 177
067 002   371 366        IMS  TST
071 002   345 075        JMP  *+3
073 002   040            HLT          IMS SKIPPED WHEN GOING
074 002   040            HLT          FROM MAX POS TO MAX NEG
075 002   315 366        LDA  TST
077 002   201            IFT  -
100 002   040            HLT          IMS DID NOT INC FROM MAX
101 002   040            HLT          POS TO NEG
102 002   321 367        ANA  C77
104 002   202            IFT  Z
105 002   040            HLT          IMS DID NOT INC FROM MAX
106 002   040            HLT          POS TO MAX NEG
107 002   315 370        LDA  M1      TEST IMS INST FOR SKIP
111 002   331 366        STA  TST     ON ZERO RESULT, J = -1
113 002   371 366        IMS  TST     A = -1
115 002   040            HLT          IMS DID NOT SKIP ON
116 002   040            HLT          ZERO RESULT
```

```
117 002   242             IFT  N
120 002   040             HLT        IMS INST HAD EFFECT ON
121 002   040             HLT        A-REG
122 002   315 366         LDA  TST
124 002   202             IFT  Z
125 002   040             HLT        IMS INST DID NOT INC
126 002   040             HLT        MEMORY TO ZERO
127 002   050             ORC  R     RESET OV
130 002   244             IFT  R     IS OV RESET
131 002   040             HLT        ORC OV OR IFT R
132 002   040             HLT        FAILED
133 002   204             IFT  S     IS OV SET
134 002   345 140         JMP  *+3
136 002   040             HLT        IFT S INST FAILED
137 002   040             HLT
140 002   070             ORC  C     COMPLEMENT OV   0 TO 1
141 002   244             IFT  R     IS OV RESET
142 002   345 146         JMP  *+3   NO;
144 002   040             HLT        ORC C INST FAILED
145 002   040             HLT
146 002   070             ORC  C
147 002   204             IFT  S     IS OV SET
150 002   040             HLT        ORC C INST FAILED
151 002   040             HLT
152 002   060             ORC  S     TEST SET OV INST
153 002   204             IFT  S
154 002   040             HLT        ORC S FAILED
155 002   040             HLT
156 002   244             IFT  R     TEST ORC S FOR RESET OV
157 002   040             HLT        ORC S DID NOT RESET OV
160 002   040             HLT
161 002   060             ORC  S     SET OV
162 002   070             ORC  C     COMPLEMENT OV  1 TO 0
163 002   244             IFT  R     IS OV RESET
164 002   040             HLT        NO, ORC INST FAILED
165 002   040             HLT
166 002   315 367         LDA  C77   TEST SETTING OV WHEN
170 002   301 365         ADD  01    GOING FROM MAX POS TO
172 002   204             IFT  S     MAX NEG
173 002   040             HLT        OV WAS NOT SET - FAILED.
174 002   040             HLT
175 002   050             ORC  R     RESET OV
176 002   315 370         LDA  M1    TEST SETTING OF OV WHEN
200 002   301 365         ADD  01    GOING FROM MIN NEG
202 002   244             IFT  R     TO ZERO
203 002   040             HLT        OV WAS SET WHEN GOING
204 002   040             HLT        FROM -1 TO ZERO - FAILED
205 002   315 374         LDA  T25   TEST SETTING OF OV WHEN
207 002   311 367         SUB  C77   GOING FROM NEG
211 002   204             IFT  S     TO POS NUM
212 002   040             HLT        FAILED - OV SET
213 002   040             HLT
214 002   050             ORC  R     RESET OV
215 002   315 370         LDA  M1    TEST SETTING OF OV WHEN
217 002   301 370         ADD  M1    GOING FROM MIN NEG THRU
221 002   244             IFT  R     ZERO TO NEG
222 002   040             HLT
223 002   040             HLT
224 002   315 364         LDA  EV1   TEST LOGICAL LEFT SHIFT
226 002   055             SHF  L     A IS EVEN
227 008   204             IFT  S
230 002   040             HLT        FAILED BIT DID NOT GET
231 002   040             HLT        SHIFTED INTO OV
232 002   311 371         SUB  C24
234 002   202             IFT  Z
235 002   040             HLT        FAILED, WORD DID NOT GET
236 002   040             HLT        SHIFTED CORRECTLY
237 002   315 363         LDA  OD1   TEST LOGICAL LEFT SHIFT
241 002   055             SHF  L     A IS ODD
242 002   244             IFT  R
```

```
243 002   040                 HLT          FAILED - BIT WAS SHIFTED
244 002   040                 HLT          INTO OV
245 002   311 364             SUB   EV1
247 002   202                 IFT   Z
250 002   040                 HLT          FAILED, WORD DID NOT
251 002   040                 HLT          GET SHIFTED CORRECTLY
252 002   315 364             LDA   EV1    TEST LOGICAL RIGHT SHIFT
254 002   057                 SHF   R      A IS EVEN
255 002   244                 IFT   R
256 002   040                 HLT          FAILED, OV WAS SET
257 002   040                 HLT
260 002   311 363             SUB   OD1
262 002   202                 IFT   Z
263 002   040                 HLT          FAILED, WORD DID NOT
264 002   040                 HLT          GET SHIFTED CORRECTLY
265 002   315 363             LDA   OD1    TEST LOGIVAL RIGHT SHIFT
267 002   057                 SHF   R      A IS ODD
270 002   204                 IFT   S
271 002   040                 HLT          FAILED, OV DID NOT GET
272 002   040                 HLT          SET
273 002   311 372             SUB   O52
275 002   202                 IFT   Z
276 002   040                 HLT          FAILED, WORD DID NOT GET
277 002   040                 HLT          SHIFTED CORRECT;Y
300 002   005                 ARC   Z      CLEAR A
301 002   315 363             LDA   OD1    TEST ANA INST WITH A SET
303 002   321 364             ANA   EV1    ODD AND MASK EVEN
305 002   202                 IFT   Z
306 002   040                 HLT          ANA INST FAILED
307 002   040                 HLT
310 002   060                 ORC   S      SET OV
311 002   315 364             LDA   EV1    TEST ROTATE RIGHT SHIFT
313 002   047                 SHF   )      A IS EVEN
314 002   244                 IFT   R
315 002   040                 HLT          FAILED, OV WAS SET
316 002   040                 HLT
317 002   047                 SHF   )      TEST ROTATE RIGHT AGAIN
320 002   204                 IFT   S
321 002   040                 HLT          FAILED, OV WAS NOT SET
322 002   040                 HLT
323 002   311 373             SUB   C52
325 002   202                 IFT   Z
326 002   040                 HLT          SHIFT ) FAILED, WORD NOT
327 002   040                 HLT          SHIFTED CORRECTLY
330 002   050                 ORC   R      RESET OV
331 002   315 363             LDA   OD1    TEST ROTATE RIGHT SHIFT
333 002   047                 SHF   )      A IS ODD
334 002   047                 SHF   )
335 002   311 374             SUB   T25
337 002   202                 IFT   Z
340 002   040                 HLT          FAILED, WORD NOT SHIFTED
341 002   040                 HLT          CORRECTLY
342 002   060                 ORC   S      SET OV
343 002   315 363             LDA   OD1    TEST ROTATE LEFT SHIFT
345 002   045                 SHF   (      A IS ODD
346 002   244                 IFT   R
347 002   040                 HLT          FAILED, OV SET
350 002   040                 HLT
351 002   045                 SHF   (      SHIFT AGAIN
352 002   311 375             SUB   C26
354 002   202                 IFT   Z
355 002   040                 HLT          FAILED, WORD NOT SHIFTED
356 002   040                 HLT          CORRECTLY
357 002   347 361            *JMP   P3N    GO TO NEXT PAGE
361 002               *
361 002               *     LITERALS AND STORAGE WORDS
361 002               *
361 002   000 003     P3N     DPT   NP3
363 002   125         OD1     OCT   125
```

```
364 002    252         EV1   OCT   252
365 002    001         01    OCT   1
366 002    000         TST   OCT   0
367 002    177         C77   OCT   177
370 002    377         M1    OCT   377
371 002    124         C24   OCT   124
372 002    052         052   OCT   52
373 002    152         C52   OCT   152
374 002    225         T25   OCT   225
375 002    126         C26   OCT   126
000 003    000 003           ORG   @0-3
000 003    050         NP3   ORC   R       RESET OV
001 003    315 322           LDA   VEN     TEST ROTATE LEFT SHIFT
003 003    045               SHF   (       A= EVEN
004 003    045               SHF   (
005 003    311 324           SUB   T51
007 003    202               IFT   Z
010 003    040               HLT           SHF ( FAILED
011 003    040               HLT
012 003    315 326           LDA   DDO
014 003    041               SHF   <       TEST ARITH SHIFT LEFT
015 003    311 327           SUB   E52     A= ODD
017 003    202               IFT   Z
020 003    040               HLT           SHF < FAILED
021 003    040               HLT
022 003    315 322           LDA   VEN     TEST ARITH SHIFT LEFT
024 003    041               SHF   <       A= EVEN
025 003    311 330           SUB   TT
027 003    202               IFT   Z
030 003    040               HLT           SHF < FAILED
031 003    040               HLT
032 003    315 326           LDA   DDO
034 003    043               SHF   >       TEST ARITH SHIFT RIGHT
035 003    311 327           SUB   E52     A= ODD
037 003    202               IFT   Z
040 003    040               HLT           SHIFT > FAILED
041 003    040               HLT
042 003    244               IFT   R
043 003    040               HLT           SHF > FAILED, OV WAS SET
044 003    040               HLT
045 003    315 322           LDA   VEN     TEST ARITH SHIFT RIGHT
047 003    043               SHF   >       A= EVEN
050 003    311 331           SUB   TT5
052 003    202               IFT   Z
053 003    040               HLT           SHF> FAILED
054 003    040               HLT
055 003    315 326           LDA   DDO     TEST ONES COMPLEMENT A
057 003    011               ARC   C       A= EVEN
060 003    311 322           SUB   VEN
062 003    202               IFT   Z
063 003    040               HLT           ARC C FAILED
064 003    040               HLT
065 003    315 322           LDA   VEN     TEST ONES COMPLEMENT A
067 003    011               ARC   C       A= ODD
070 003    311 326           SUB   DDO
072 003    202               IFT   Z
073 003    040               HLT           ARC C FAILED
074 003    040               HLT
075 003    315 335           LDA   L1      TEST ONES COMPLEMENT A
077 003    011               ARC   C       A= -1
100 003    202               IFT   Z
101 003    040               HLT           ARC C FAILED
102 003    040               HLT
103 003    005               ARC   Z       CLEAR
104 003    331 114           STA   HLD     JST RETURN ADR STORE
106 003    331 115           STA   HLD+1   LOCATIONS
110 003    375 114           JST   HLD     TEST JUMP & SAVE
112 003    040         PTT   HLT           JST INST DID NOT TRANSFER
113 003    040               HLT
```

```
114 003   000 000  HLD  DPT   **
116 003   315 114       LDA   HLD
120 003   311 336       SUB   PPT
122 003   202           IFT   Z
123 003   040           HLT         LOC OF RETURN ADR
124 003   040           HLT         IS INCORRECT
125 003   315 115       LDA   HLD+1
127 003   311 337       SUB   PPT+1
131 003   202           IFT   Z
132 003   040           HLT         PAGE OF RETURN ADR
133 003   040           HLT         IS INCORRECT
134 003   315 322       LDA   VEN   TEST NEGATE A, A= EVEN
136 003   015           ARC   N
137 003   301 322       ADD   VEN
141 003   202           IFT   Z
142 003   040           HLT         ARC N FAILED
143 003   040           HLT
144 003   315 326       LDA   DDO   TEST NEGATE A, A = ODD
146 003   015           ARC   N
147 003   301 326       ADD   DDO
151 003   202           IFT   Z
152 003   040           HLT         ARC N FAILED
153 003   040           HLT
154 003   315 322       LDA   VEN   TEST INCREMENT A
156 003   007           ARC   I     A= EVEN
157 003   311 323       SUB   VEN+1
161 003   202           IFT   Z
162 003   040           HLT         ARC I FAILED
163 003   040           HLT
164 003   315 335       LDA   L1    TEST INCREMENT A
166 003   007           ARC   I     A= -1
167 003   202           IFT   Z
170 003   040           HLT         ARC I FAILED
171 003   040           HLT
172 003   315 332       LDA   K77   TEST ARC I
174 003   007           ARC   I     FOR OV
175 003   204           IFT   S
176 003   040           HLT         ARC I FAILED
177 003   040           HLT
200 003   001           ARC   -1    TEST INCREMENT A
201 003   007           ARC   I     A=-1
202 003   202           IFT   Z
203 003   040           HLT         ARC I FAILED
204 003   040           HLT
205 003   007           ARC   I     INC A & TEST DEC A
206 003   003           ARC   D     A = 1
207 003   202           IFT   Z
210 003   040           HLT         ARC D FAILED
211 003   040           HLT
212 003   315 334       LDA   TOO   TEST ARC D
214 003   003           ARC   D     FOR OV
215 003   204           IFT   S
216 003   040           HLT         ARC D FAILED
217 003   040           HLT
220 003   315 326       LDA   DDO   TEST DECREMENT A
222 003   003           ARC   D     A= ODD
223 003   311 325       SUB   DDO-1
225 003   202           IFT   Z
226 003   040           HLT         ARC D FAILED
227 003   040           HLT
230 003   017           ARC   1     TEST TRANS ONE TO A
231 003   003           ARC   D     A=1
232 003   202           IFT   Z
233 003   040           HLT         ARC 1 FAILED
234 003   040           HLT
235 003   050           ORC   R
236 003   315 332       LDA   K77   TEST IMS
240 003   331 333       STA   TLY   FOR OV
242 003   371 333       IMS   TLY
244 003   204           IFT   S
```

```
245 003   040              HLT          IMS FAILED
246 003   040              HLT
247 003   314 341          LDA /C31     TEST MR OF PAGE ZERO
251 003   311 340          SUB  K31
253 003   202              IFT  Z
254 003   040              HLT          MEMORY REFERENCE OF
255 003   040              HLT          PAGE ZERO FAILED
256 003   377 341         *JST  PJT     TEST INDIRECT JUMP & SAVE
260 003   040         ISB  HLT          JST INDIRECT FAILED
261 003   040              HLT
262 003   317 343         *LDA  IPE     TEST MULTI-LEVEL INDIRECT
264 003   311 322          SUB  VEN     MEMORY REFERENCE
266 003   202              IFT  Z
267 003   040              HLT          MULTI-LEVEL FAILED
270 003   040              HLT
271 003   017              ARC  1
272 003   377 345         *JST  IPS     TEST MULTI-LEVEL IND JST
274 003   040         BIS  HLT          TRANSFER FAILED
275 003   040              HLT
276 003   347 347         *JMP  IPJ     TEST MULTI-LEVEL IND JUMP
300 003   040              HLT
301 003   040              HLT          TRANSFER FAILED
302 003   374 342     BIJ  JST /PZS     TEST JST TO PAGE ZERO
304 003   040         ONW  HLT          TRANSFER FAILED
305 003   040              HLT
306 003   001              ARC  -1
307 003   376 337         *JST /IPZ     TEST IND JST TO PAGE 0
311 003   040         ONZ  HLT          TRANSFER FAILED
312 003   040              HLT
313 003   344 320          JMP /@320    TEST JUMP TO PAGE ZERO
315 003   040              HLT          TRANSFER FAILED
316 003   040              HLT
320 003   320 003          ORG  @320-3
320 003   040              HLT          TRANSFER TO PAGE ZERO
321 003   040              HLT          FAILED
322 003               *
322 003               *  LITERALS AND STORAGE WORDS
322 003               *
322 003   252         VEN  OCT  252
323 003   253              OCT  253
324 003   251         T51  OCT  251
325 003   124              OCT  124
326 003   125         DDO  OCT  125
327 003   052         E52  OCT  52
330 003   324         TT   OCT  324
331 003   325         TT5  OCT  325
332 003   177         K77  OCT  177
333 003   000         TLY  OCT  0
334 003   200         TOO  OCT  200
335 003   377         L1   DEC  -1
336 003   112 003     PPT  DPT  PTT
340 003   131         K31  OCT  131
341 003   000 004     PJT  DPT  SBR
343 003   102 004     IPE  DPT  NEV
345 003   341 203     IPS *DPT  PJT
347 003   351 203     IPJ *DPT  JIP
351 003   103 004     JIP  DPT  PIJ
000 004   000 004          ORG  0-4
000 004   000 000     SBR  DPT  **      SUB FOR TEST IND JST'S
002 004   242              IFT  N
003 004   345 034          JMP  SB1
005 004   241              IFT  +
006 004   345 054          JMP  SB3
010 004   315 000          LDA  SBR
012 004   311 100          SUB  SIB
014 004   202              IFT  Z
015 004   040              HLT          MULTI-LEVEL IND JST DID
016 004   040              HLT          NOT STORE COR LOC RET ADR
017 004   315 001          LDA  SBR+1
```

```
021 004   311 101        SUB  SIB+1
023 004   202            IFT  Z
024 004   040            HLT            MULTI-LEVEL IND JST DID
025 004   040            HLT            NOT SAVE COR PAGE RET ADR
026 004   371 000   SB2  IMS  SBR
030 004   371 000        IMS  SBR
032 004   347 000       *JMP  SBR
034 004   315 000   SB1  LDA  SBR
036 004   311 076        SUB  BSI
040 004   202            IFT  Z
041 004   040            HLT
042 004   040            HLT
043 004   315 001        LDA  SBR+1
045 004   311 077        SUB  BSI+1
047 004   242            IFT  N
050 004   345 026        JMP  SB2
052 004   040            HLT
053 004   040            HLT
054 004   315 000   SB3  LDA  SBR
056 004   311 074        SUB  SIX
060 004   202            IFT  Z
061 004   040            HLT
062 004   040            HLT
063 004   315 001        LDA  SBR+1
065 004   311 075        SUB  SIX+1
067 004   242            IFT  N
070 004   345 026        JMP  SB2
072 004   040            HLT
073 004   040            HLT
074 004   311 003   SIX  DPT  ONZ
076 004   260 003   BSI  DPT  ISB
100 004   274 003   SIB  DPT  BIS
102 004   252       NEV  OCT  252
103 004   347 107   PIJ *JMP  JIB      RETURN FROM MULTI IND JMP
105 004   040            HLT
106 004   040            HLT
107 004   302 003   JIB  DPT  BIJ
320 000   320 000        ORG  @320-0
320 000   210            IFT  0        TEST SENSE SWITCH OFF
321 000   345 325        JMP  *+3
323 000   040            HLT           IFT 0 FAILED OR SS
324 000   040            HLT           HAS BEEN RELEASED
325 000   250            IFT  1        TEST SENSE SWITCH ON
326 000   040            HLT           IFT  1 FAILED
327 000   040            HLT
330 000   005            ARC  Z        CLEAR A AND
331 000   347 335       *JMP  BNG      START OVER
333 000   040            HLT
334 000   040            HLT
335 000   000 001   BNG  DPT  BGN
337 000   000 004   IPZ  DPT  SBR
341 000   131       C31  OCT  131
342 000   000 000   PZS  DPT  **      SUB TO TEST JST TO PAGE 0
344 000   315 342        LDA  PZS
346 000   311 370        SUB  SIZ
350 000   202            IFT  Z
351 000   040            HLT          JST TO PAGE ZERO DID NOT
352 000   040            HLT          STORE LOC RET ADR
353 000   315 343        LDA  PZS+1
355 000   311 371        SUB  SIZ+1
357 000   202            IFT  Z
360 000   040            HLT          JST TO PAGE ZERO DID NOT
361 000   040            HLT          STORE PAGE RET ADR
362 000   371 342        IMS  PZS
```

```
  0689   364 000   371 342          IMS  PZS
  0690   366 000   347 342         *JMP  PZS
  0691   370 000   304 003   SIZ    DPT  ONW
A 0692   372 000   000 000          END
```

Index

T

U

V

W